TORT LAW

in principle

....

Thomson Reuters (Professional) Australia Limited

Head Office	100 Harris Street Pyrmont NSW 2009
Telephone	(02) 8587 7000
Fax	(02) 8587 7100
	www.thomsonreuters.com.au

For all customer inquiries please ring 1300 304 195 (for calls within Australia only)

INTERNATIONAL AGENTS & DISTRIBUTORS

NORTH AMERICA
Thomson Reuters North America
Eagan
United States of America

ASIA PACIFIC
Thomson Reuters Asia Pacific
Sydney
Australia

LATIN AMERICA
Thomson Reuters Latin America
São Paulo
Brazil

EUROPE
Thomson Reuters Europe
London
United Kingdom

TORT LAW
in principle

. . . .

FIFTH EDITION

Bernadette Richards

BA Dip Ed LLB (Hons)

Senior Lecturer in Law
The University of Adelaide

Karinne Ludlow

BSc LLB (Hons) PhD

Senior Lecturer in Law
Monash University

Andy Gibson

LLB Bjuris MA Dip Ed

LLB Course Coordinator
Southern Cross University

LAWBOOK CO. 2009

PUBLISHED IN SYDNEY BY
Thomson Reuters
        100 Harris Street, Pyrmont, NSW

First edition 1985
Second edition 1996
Third edition 2002
Revised third edition 2002
Fourth edition 2005
Fifth edition 2009

National Library of Australia
    Cataloguing-in-Publication entry

Gibson, Andrew, 1947–
    Tort law : in principle / Andy Gibson, Bernadette Richards and Karinne Ludlow.

    5th ed.
    9780455225746 (pbk.)

    In principle
    Includes index.
    Torts – Australia. Liability (Law) – Australia.
    Richards, Bernadette.
    Ludlow, Karinne, 1973-

346.9403

This edition is up to date as of 30 September 2008.

Editors: Wendy Fitzhardinge, Merilyn Shields
Product Developer: Sarah Hullah
Publisher: Robert Wilson

Typesetting: Midland Typesetters, Australia

Printing: Ligare Pty Ltd, Riverwood, NSW

Preface

This new edition of *Tort Law in Principle* continues the evolution of a valuable learning tool from David Baker's original *Introduction to Tort*, which has, for many years played an important role in introducing students of all levels to the concepts of the tort law. The previous edition was a direct response to the major review of the law of negligence and provided an overview of the, at that time, new civil liability legislation in each jurisdiction. This edition continues to track the development of the law under the civil liability regime and, where possible, includes judicial commentary on the impact of the legislation. Just prior to the previous edition there was significant progress made towards the implementation of a uniform defamation regime, but we were unable to include any insight into it as the process was continuing with no certainty in respect of what the uniform law would bring. Since that time, each jurisdiction has introduced a *Defamation Act* and Chapter 18 has undergone a substantial rewrite to reflect this significant development in the law. All other chapters have been carefully revised and additional insights into the law are provided through the inclusion of the most recent case law in every area.

The previous editions saw the introduction of a new format with a presentation of the material to the reader in a more user-friendly style. This latest edition continues the tradition of making the law of torts more accessible to students. The text aims to meet the practical needs of new law students by introducing them to the area of tort through the provision of thorough and yet succinct coverage of the area, along with assistance in preparation for examinations through practical exercises. This text may also provide some assistance to those in the business world seeking to develop risk-averse policies in relation to torts.

Each chapter contains:
- A chapter index.
- Further readings: Sappideen, Vines, Grant and Watson, *Torts: Commentary and Materials* (9th ed, Lawbook Co., 2006).
- A set of objectives to direct the reader's thoughts when reading.
- Principles that contain the body of the text, including figures which endeavour to summarise the main points.
- Practice questions and suggested answers, and other tutorial questions that are intended to guide the thoughts of teachers and students in discussing and considering the material in the chapter.

Some of the chapters also include a problem-solving guide to aid the readers in attempting the practice questions. These guides provide suggested key steps that can be used to solve set problems.

It is recognised by those who have prepared the additional materials that the reader ultimately must be responsible for his or her own learning. To this end the presentation of the material plays an important part in setting the scene for readers to take this responsibility and become self-directed learners. We hope that the new format achieves this aim.

BERNADETTE RICHARDS
KARINNE LUDLOW
ANDY GIBSON

November 2008

Acknowledgments

The following extracts attributed herein have been reproduced with kind permission of:

CCH Australia: www.cch.com.au
- Australian Torts Reporter (Aust Torts Reports).

Council of Law Reporting for the State of Victoria
- Victorian Reports (VR).

Council of Law Reporting for the State of Queensland
- Queensland Reports (Qd R).

HMSO: www.hmso.gov.uk
- Law Reforms.

Incorporated Council of Law Reporting for England & Wales: www.lawreports.co.uk
- Appeal Cases (AC).
- King's Bench (KB).
- Weekly News Reports (WLR).

New Zealand Council of Law Reporting
- New Zealand Law Reports (NZLR).

Reed International Books Australia Pty Limited t/a LexisNexis Butterworths, Sydney: www.lexisnexis.com.au
- Australian Law Reports (ALR).

Reed Elsevier (UK) Limited t/a LexisNexis Butterworths: www.lexisnexis.co.uk
- All England Reports (All ER).

Solicitors Journal (by Waterlow Professional Publishing): www.solicitorsjournal.com
- Solicitors Journal Reports (SJ).

Supreme Court of Canada: www.scc-csc.gc.ca
- Supreme Court Reports (SCR).

Sweet & Maxwell, UK: www.sweetandmaxwell.co.uk
- English Reports (ER).

Thomson Reuters and the authors are grateful to the publishers, agents and authors who have allowed us to use extracts of their work in this book. While every care has been taken to establish and acknowledge copyright, Thomson Reuters tenders its apology for any accidental infringement. The publisher would be pleased to come to a suitable agreement with the rightful owners in each case.

Table of Contents

Table of
Cases

[References are to paragraph numbers]

CASES

CASES

CASES

CASES

Jag Shakti, The [1986] AC 337 . . . .[5.205]

James v Commonwealth (1939) 62 CLR 339 . . . . [19.70], [19.95], [19.110]-[19.120]

James v Faddoul [2007] NSWSC 821 . . . .[19.55]

James v Wellington City [1972] NZLR 970 . . . . [17.10]

Janvier v Sweeney [1919] 2 KB 316 . . . .[4.105]

Jarvis v Williams [1955] 1 WLR 71 . . . .[5.110]

Jazairy v Najjar [1998] Aust Torts Reports 81-478 . . . .[13.30]

Jeffries v Fisher [1985] WAR 250 . . . .[12.130]

Jeffries v Great Western Railway (1856) SKI & B1 802; 119 ER 680 . . . .[5.115]

Jenner v Harbison (1879) 5 VLR (L) 111 . . . .[20.25]

Jenyns v Jenyns [1927] St R Qd 313 . . . .[19.160]

Jervois Sulphates (NT) Ltd v Petrocarb Explorations NL (1974) 5 ALR 1 . . . .[20.40]

Jobling v Associated Dairies [1982] AC 794 . . . . [11.60]

John James Memorial Hospital Ltd v Keys [1999] FCA 678 . . . .[15.65]

John Lewis Ltd v Tims [1952] AC 676 . . . . [7.115]

John Pfeiffer Pty Ltd v Canny (1981) 148 CLR 218 . . . .[14.20]

John Summers v Frost [1955] AC 740 . . . .[14.25]

John Walker & Sons v Herny List & Co Ltd [1970] RPC 489 . . . .[19.150]

Johns v Minister of Education (1981) 28 SASR 206 . . . .[10.95]

Johns Period Furniture Pty Ltd v Commonwealth Savings Bank (1980)
    24 SASR 224 . . . .[8.160]

Johnson v Emerson & Sparrow (1871) LR 6 Exch 329 . . . .[20.40]

Johnson Tiles Pty Ltd v Esso Australia Pty Ltd [2003] Aust Torts
    Reports 81-692; [2003] VSC 27 . . . . [8.153], [8.160]

Johnston v Fraser [1990] Aust Torts Reports 81-056 . . . .[10.140]

Johnstone v Stewart [1968] SASR 142 . . . .[22.25]

Jolley v Sutton London Borough Council [2000] 3 All ER 409 . . . .[9.60], [11.85]

Jones v Bartlett (2000) 205 CLR 166 . . . .[9.80]

Jones v Boyce (1816) 171 ER 540 . . . .[12.50]

Jones v Brown (1794) 1 Esp 216; 170 ER 334 . . . .[21.90]

Jones v Department of Employment [1989] QB 1 . . . .[8.240]

Jones v Dumbrell [1981] VR 199 . . . .[19.15]

Jones v Homeister (1976) 14 SASR 328 . . . .[10.95]

Jones v Linnett [1984] 1 Qd R 570 . . . .[17.20]-[17.25]

Jones v Livox Quarries [1952] 2 QB 608 . . . .[12.70]

Jones v Pritchard [1908] 1 Ch 630 . . . .[16.90]

Jones v Shire of Perth [1971] WAR 56 . . . .[22.135]

Jones v Skelton (1963) 63 SR (NSW) 644; [1963] 1 WLR 1362 . . . .[18.90]

Jones v Sutton (2004) 61 NSWLR 614 . . . .[18.280]

Jones v Swansea CC [1990] 1 WLR 54 . . . .[20.65]

Jones v Williams (1843) 11 M & W 176; 152 ER 764 . . . . [7.95]

Jones v Williams [1895] AC 1 . . . .[22.175]

CASES

Table of
Statutes

[References are to paragraph numbers]

STATUTES

SECTION

1

Introduction

This section considers the concept of tort, examines the availability of compensation outside the tort system and looks at the historical origins of the law of tort in the former writs of trespass and action on the case.

Chapter 1 examines the meaning of tort and compares it with other civil wrongs (particularly breach of contract), gives a brief account of the way in which torts are proved, and considers the way in which a tort claim may be lost through the expiry of a statutory limitation period.

Chapter 2 looks at compensation that is available outside the common law tort system for persons who have suffered injury or damage, and at the effect of insurance on the enforcement of rights of action in tort.

Chapter 3 considers the historical origins of the law of tort in the former writs of trespass and action on the case, and shows how these origins still have some importance in explaining the shape of contemporary tort law jurisprudence.

Significance of torts

Welcome to the law of torts. Torts is one of the most fascinating and enjoyable subjects in law. It is also one of the most significant branches of civil law. Along with the law of contract, the law of torts underpins most issues in civil litigation. A very thorough understanding of torts is therefore essential in the study, and indeed the practice, of law. In the study of law, the law of torts and contract law are invariably introduced at the early stages. This is because they provide the essential foundations for the study of other branches of the law. The time invested in the study and thorough appraisal of the law of torts will very certainly yield excellent returns in your future dealings with clients in civil law.

Torts, whilst having an ancient history, is a constantly evolving field of law, making it even more relevant for today's lawyers. Torts is being used to address many problems facing modern society – from human rights abuses to the invasion of a farmer's field by genetically modified pollen. For example, one of the most ancient of torts, trespass to the person, has been used in proceedings brought by non-Australian citizens in respect of alleged illegal detention (*Ruddock v Taylor* (2005) 222 CLR 612), by environmental activists in relation to their civil protests (*McFadzean v CFMEU* [2007] VSCA 289) and for "Stolen Generation" reparation (*Trevorrow v South Australia (No 5)* (2007) 98 SASR 136; [2007] SASC 285). The law of negligence is called on every day to respond to new problems, whether they be injuries caused by prenatal diagnosis (*Harriton v Stephens* (2006) 226 CLR 52) to injuries caused by new consumer products.

THEMATIC ESSENCE OF TORTS

The law of torts is designed to protect a set of interrelated interests of the person in the community. It consists of principles, doctrines, concepts and rules which the courts have developed over some hundreds of years to define the circumstances which will entitle a plaintiff to sue for damages for compensation, or for some other remedy, where a specified interest is breached or interfered with by the defendant's conduct. The particular tort or cause of action that may be invoked at any time, and the relevant remedy, will depend on the specific interest breached. The first step in the study of torts is therefore to understand the range of interests protected. Chapter 1 of this book sets out the interests protected in torts: see [1.40].

A range of torts has developed over the years to reflect the types of interests protected. Since all these torts have been fashioned from particular court decisions, it is necessary to study a good many cases in order to understand the nature and scope of the liability they represent. This book has been set out with this partly in mind. It is intended to state and clarify the various components of each tort discussed, by using cases wherever possible to demonstrate the relevant principles. But while the law may have evolved through traditional institutions of the common law, contemporary tort law is also very much a product of legislation and reflects modern social and economic realities. In this regard the law of torts provides an excellent tool for social engineering. However, while the judiciary and the legislature make the law, they are not the sole agents of change. As one author argues:

> [M]ost changes to operative legal rules (that is the law in action) are not produced by official bodies such as Law Reform Commissions or by specialised state institutions and offices such as legislatures and courts. The vast bulk of law reform operates at the level of individual and group conduct through normative beliefs, practices and verbalisations.[1]

Community groups, local councils, insurance companies and professional organisations are all examples of stakeholders who compete to shape and influence the development of tort law. While such stakeholders may not have actual authority to change tort law, they very much influence its development through constant interaction with the legislature entrusted with the authority to make law.

CASES

The substantial part of the law of torts is based on "common law" (court developed). It is thus "judge-made" law. As common law, the law of torts has evolved from the decisions of the courts in England from the period of the Norman Conquest, through the colonial period, and to the present day. As was noted by Brennan J in *Mabo v Queensland* (1992) 175 CLR 1 at 29: "Australian law is not only the historical successor

---

[1]   MacDonald, "Recommissioning Law Reform" (1997) 35 Alta L Rev 847 at 857.

of, but is an organic development from, the law of England." It will thus be evident in your study of the cases in tort that the authorities that underpin some of the basic principles in Australian tort law include centuries-old English cases such as *Weaver v Ward* (1616) Hob 134; 80 ER 284 and *Cole v Turner* (1704) 6 Mod 172; 87 ER 928. However, as was further noted by Brennan J, although Australian law:

> is the prisoner of its history, it is not now bound by decisions of courts in the hierarchy of an Empire then concerned with the development of its colonies ... [S]ince the Australia Act 1986 (Cth) came into operation, the law of this country is entirely free of Imperial control. The law which governs Australia is Australian law.

While Australian law is "binding authority" before Australian courts, the development of the common law of torts in Australia has also been influenced by decisions of courts from other members of the common law family such as the United States, Canada and New Zealand. Such decisions have persuasive authority in Australia.

As part of the common law process, the *law* in torts is to be found in the reasoning and the decisions in the cases. Many of the cases in torts discussed in this book are simply illustrations of rules and other features of the relevant tort, and can often be summed up in short paragraphs, or even one sentence. Other cases are more involved, because the ideas and doctrines they deal with are more complex or technical. Some cases appear difficult because their point is not obvious and requires interpretation, or because their impact on the pre-existing law is unclear or disputed. While the simpler cases will usually require some study of the relevant extracts in casebooks such as Sappideen et al's *Torts: Commentary and Materials*, the more complex cases will require reading the original judgments, as well as reference to the opinions and analysis provided in the textbooks.

A central feature of the common law as a source of the law of torts is the concept of stare decisis (to stand by things decided) and the related doctrine of precedent. As Brennan J noted in *Mabo* (at 29) and again in *Dietrich v The Queen* (1992) 177 CLR 292, this feature is "the skeleton of principle which gives the body of our law its shape and internal consistency". As a source of law in torts, the common law is both an advantage and a disadvantage. In dealing with disputes, courts of first instance and intermediate courts of appeal are usually constrained by binding precedents. While superior courts in Australia, including the High Court, can and occasionally do decline to follow their own previous decisions, the courts are nonetheless still constrained by the need for what has been described as "internal consistency". On the other hand, precedent offers the advantage of tradition and predictability.

Where no previous case clearly covers the present, judges must appeal to more general rules and principles to justify their particular decisions. They will try to ensure these standards are as consistent as possible with the large body of pre-existing law relied on by their predecessors (the doctrine of precedent). Both tasks will involve some scope for argument and conjecture, especially where a decision or rule appears to depart from the previous law.

Although the large bulk of modern tort law is relatively well settled, and can often be exemplified by citing definitive or leading cases, brief perusal of any textbook will show that in many areas there is still uncertainty, and that this may extend even to basic principles. Because courts have a duty to decide the merits of litigated cases where the law is in contest, it is natural for professional commentators and teachers to anticipate their answers to important questions of principle and doctrine by their own analysis of the relevant case law. In addition, torts is still very much a "live" subject in that superior courts find it necessary from time to time to review and restate even well established doctrines. Although courts tend towards a conservative approach, they may give innovative decisions where the past law is clearly unsatisfactory.

In spite of the ancient roots of the common law, it is of interest to note that the law of negligence, which is undoubtedly one of the most significant branches of the law of torts, only emerged in the 1930s with the decision in *Donoghue v Stevenson* [1932] AC 562. More significantly, the common law of negligence is still developing with the principles underpinning concepts such as duty and mental harm being redefined. The evolutionary character of tort law reflects changes in community attitudes, expectations and indeed values. It also reflects changes in socio-economic relations in the community. As one author notes, "the greater part of the law of torts is still being developed in and by the courts" with all the constant changes that we see in the community.[2]

> *It is this which gives the law of torts its fascination, as well as its difficulties. The fact that this area of the law has been and still is a fertile field for the operation of the judicial mind provides it with a flavour and excitement that is almost unique in the modern common law.*[3]

While the evolutionary character of the common law of torts certainly allows considerable scope for "judicial activism" or judicial "law-making", it is not the case that new law is made in torts every time the judiciary finds it desirable to do so. The Australian legal system is based on the doctrine of the separation of powers. Law making as such is the function of the legislature, not the judiciary. The strict role of the judiciary in the legal system is to interpret the law. In interpreting the law, judges can and do adopt new principles and expand on existing doctrines to reflect prevailing community standards and values. It is this process of interpretation that creates the foundations for common law as "judge-made" law. One must therefore distinguish carefully between the development of new tort principles through the common law process and the creation of new rules on torts through the positive action of the legislature. The common law process tends to develop new rules, but only through a logical appraisal and reinterpretation of existing law. For instance, in *Overseas Tankship (UK) Ltd v Morts Dock & Engineering Co Ltd (Wagon Mound (No 1))* [1961] 1 All ER 404 the Privy Council adopted a new rule on causation based on "reasonable foreseeability". Before the case, the rule on causation had been based on the principle of "directness" set out in *Re Polemis* [1921] 3 KB 560. In adopting the new rule, the Privy Council did not actually state "as of today we wish to change the law on causation". Viscount Simonds LJ (at 413-416) explained the *need* for departure from the old rule in these terms:

> *[Re Polemis] should no longer be regarded as good law. It is not probable that many cases will for that reason have a different result, though it is hoped that the law will be thereby simplified, and that, in some cases at least, palpable injustice will be avoided. For it does not seem consonant with current justice or morality that, for an act of negligence, however slight or venial, which results in some trivial foreseeable damage the actor should be liable for all consequences, however unforeseeable and however*

---

2   Fridman, *Introduction to the Law of Torts* (Butterworths, Toronto, 1978) p 14.

3   Fridman, above, n 2.

grave, so long as they can be said to be "direct". It is a principle of civil liability ... that a man must be considered to be responsible for the probable consequences of his act. To demand more of him is too harsh a rule, to demand less is to ignore that civilized order requires the observance of a minimum standard of behaviour ... For, if it is asked why a man should be liable for the natural or necessary or probable consequences of his act ... the answer is that it is not because they are natural or necessary or probable, but because, since they have this quality, it is judged, by the standard of the reasonable man, that he ought to have foreseen them ... Thus foreseeability becomes the effective test. In asserting this principle, their Lordships conceive that they do not depart from, but follow and develop, the law of negligence ...

However one may choose to characterise the development of the law of torts through judicial law making, it is a slow process. First, the process depends on issues and cases coming for litigation before the courts. The courts cannot on their own choose to identify areas of reform, however necessary, to develop new rules. Tort law reform and, indeed, adopting new *laws* and principles on torts as distinct from interpreting and expanding or modifying existing rules and principles, are functions of the Parliament as law maker. Second, even where a matter is presented to a court and a change is considered desirable, it may not be possible for the judiciary to justify a sudden departure from existing law. The judiciary, and for that matter the tort law making process in common law, can thus be constrained in several ways that do not affect how Parliament operates.

LEGISLATION

Legislation is also important in tort law. It may be enacted for a variety of purposes in tort law. For instance legislation may be adopted to clarify ambiguous elements of the common law. It can also be used to rectify anomalies in the common law. More significantly Parliament, unfettered by the constraints associated with the common law, can use legislation to reform tort law. In this process Parliament can, and occasionally does, enact legislation to modify or introduce new rules in tort law in the light of specific current social and economic developments. Where legislation modifies a common law rule, or introduces a new rule to replace the common law rule, the legislation provides the authoritative source of law on the issue. It thus follows that whenever there is "conflict" between a common law rule and a rule of legislation on a given issue, the legislation prevails. This is not of course to say that the common law cannot have an impact on legislation. Courts frequently interpret statutes. The decisions of courts in interpreting legislation provide a good source of law on the meaning and scope of the legislation as interpreted. In the process, a body of case law can be developed regarding a particular statute. This is easily demonstrated in the High Court's decisions on the *Australian Constitution* and in the many decisions on the *Trade Practices Act 1974* (Cth).

Legislation as a source of law can be thematic or general. For instance, the motor accidents compensation legislation adopted in most Australian jurisdictions is thematic to the extent that it deals specially with motor accidents compensation. On the other hand, the civil liability legislation enacted in most jurisdictions in Australia are general. In each instance such legislation deals with general principles that underpin tort liability generally or negligence liability in particular. In some cases, statutes with direct application in other branches of the law may "indirectly" provide important sources of the state of the law in tort law. For instance in dealing with the scope of the tort of defamation, the *Broadcasting Services Act 1992* (Cth), ss 6 and 206, provides an important source of law on defamation on the internet. Similarly the *Trade Practices Act 1974* (Cth) and fair trading legislation found in many Australian jurisdictions provide important sources of law concerning business practices and product liability, just as the *Foreign States Immunities Act 1985* (Cth) provides an important source of law on the tort liability of diplomatic and consular officials in Australia.

In the late 1990s Australia witnessed considerable increases in public liability insurance premiums. There is some dispute as to the exact triggers of these increases, but whatever the causes may have been initially, a number of external factors seemed to impact on the Australian insurance industry to compound the escalating cost of the premiums. Such factors included the rising costs of reinsurance as a result of world events, such as September 11, coupled with the sudden corporate failure of HIH Insurance Ltd, one of the major insurance companies in Australia. The Insurance Council of Australia also identified other factors such as increases in litigation and associated legal costs and exacerbating factors such as "no win/no pay" advertising by lawyers.[4]

There was also a general perception that the common law of negligence had become the last bastion of the welfare society, that it made it too easy for plaintiffs to establish liability for negligence on the part of defendants, and that the awards for damages were frequently too high. To the public this situation seemed well exemplified by the case of a Bondi man, who was awarded $3.75 million in damages for injuries sustained when he dived onto a sand bar at Bondi Beach in 1997. Another example was the case of a teenager awarded $50,000 for being injured while trying to break into a Sydney pub after being refused admission.

There were calls for reform to rebuild the common law from politicians, the media and sections of the community, particularly adventure tourism operators, sporting groups, community organisations and professional organisations, members of which were experiencing difficulties with insurance premiums. As Lozusic notes:

> *The response to the calls for reform included: two national ministerial meetings on the issue; the establishment of a Senate Inquiry; ACCC monitoring; a benchmarking study of Australian insurers' claims management practices; the introduction of legislation to remove tax barriers to structured settlements; the introduction of legislation to amend the operation of the Trade Practices Act 1974 (Cth); and the establishment of a Negligence Review Panel to investigate reforming negligence so as to limit claims.[5]*

The conventional view, rarely challenged, is that there was a litigation explosion in Australia, particularly in the area of negligence law, with concomitant increases in the number and size of insurance claims. In support of the increases in the insurance claims arguments, the Insurance Council of Australia (ICA) argued that data released by the Australian Prudential Regulation Authority (APRA) indicated that between "1998 and 2000 the number of public liability claims jumped by 33,000, from 55,000 to 88,000" with public liability claims rising by about 14% and the overall cost of claims increasing by 52%.[6]

---

4   See the excellent account by Roza Lozusic, *Public Liability: Briefing Paper No 7/2002* (NSW Parliamentary Library Research Service, 2002).

5   Lozusic, above, n 4, p 3.

6   Mason, ICA Executive Director, noted that the increase did not "necessarily reflect an increase in the number of claims made, rather an increase in the average cost of each claim ... In other words, court awards are becoming more generous": ICA, "Insurers Lose on Public Liability and Professional Indemnity Claims" (Media

The ICA's reliance on the APRA data is interesting because by APRA's own admission there were "a number of factors making interpretation of the claims data difficult, and considerable caution [was] required"[7] in relying on the data. The Australian Plaintiff Lawyers Association argued:

> The data on claims does not identify clear parameters about how a claim should be defined. As such, some insurers classify as claims the mere knowledge of circumstances that may result in a claim, for example, notification to the insurer that an injury has been sustained even though a damages claim may never be brought by the injured person.[8]

Related to the increase in the number and size of insurance claims, is the fact that Australians seem to have become more aware of their rights and are now more likely to pursue tort actions for any breaches. This, coupled with the availability of "no win/ no pay" legal service arrangements with solicitors in some jurisdictions, seems to have contributed to the increase in the level of civil litigation.

In response to the calls for reform, since 2002 all Australian States and Territories have adopted new legislation with important implications for tort liability, particularly in the area of negligence. The details of the civil liability statutes are set out in the Comparative Table. While the statutes vary in details, the general elements are similar. The Comparative Table provides an overview of the statutes and their main provisions. These reforms will be discussed further in the text but this table provides a good reference point for the ambit of the legislation in, and differences between, the jurisdictions. It should be remembered however, that in some instances a jurisdiction may have legislative provisions on a particular issue in a statute other than its civil liability statute and this is not shown in the table.

---

release, 2 August 2001).

[7] Quoted in Australian Plaintiff Lawyers Association (APLA), *National Ministerial Summit into Public Liability Insurance* (APLA Submission, 15 March 2002).

[8] APLA, above, n 7.

COMPARATIVE TABLE

	ACT	NT	NSW	Qld	SA	Tas	Vic	WA
	Civil Law (Wrongs) Act 2002	Personal Injuries (Liabilities and Damages) Act 2003	Civil Liability Act 2002	Civil Liability Act 2003	Civil Liability Act 1936	Civil Liability Act 2002	Wrongs Act 1958	Civil Liability Act 2002; Occupiers' Liability Act 1985
Negligence	Ch 4		Pt 1A	Ch 2	Pt 6	Pt 6	Pt X	Pt 1A
Duty of care	Pt 4.2		Div 2	Div 1	Div 1	Div 2	Div 2	Div 2
Causation	Pt 4.3		Div 3	Div 2	Div 2	Div 3	Div 3	Div 3
Assumption of risk			Div 4	Div 3	Div 3	Div 4	Div 4	Div 6
Recreational activities			Div 5	Div 4		Div 5		Div 4
Professional negligence	Sch 4 Professional standards		Div 6	Div 5	Div 4	Div 6	Div 5	Div 7
Non-delegable duties and vicarious liability			Div 7				Div 6	
Contributory negligence	Pts 7.1, 7.3	s 17	Div 8	Div 6	Pt 7	Div 7	Div 7	Div 5
Damages	Ch 7	Pt 4	Pt 2	Ch 3	Pt 8	Pt 7	Pts VB, VBA	Pt 2
Economic loss	s 98	Div 3	Div 2	Pt 3				Div 3
Non-economic loss (general damages)	s 99	Div 4	Div 3	Pt 3				Div 2
Interest on damages		Div 5	Div 4	Pt 3				
Third party contributions			Div 5					
Exemplary damages			Div 6	Pt 2				
Structured settlements	Pt 7.4	Div 6	Div 7	Ch 3 Pt 4		Pt 5	Pt VC	Div 4
Offenders in custody			Pt 2A					
Mental harm	Pt 3.2		Pt 3			Pt 8	Pt XI	Pt 1B
Proportionate liability	Ch 7A		Pt 4	Pt 2			Pt IVAA	Pt 1F
Liability of public and other authorities	Ch 8		Pt 5	Pt 3 Div 1		Pt 9	Pt XII	Pt 1C
Intoxication	ss 95, 96	ss 14, 15	Pt 6	Pt 4 Div 2		Pt 2	Pt IIB	
Self-defence and recovery by criminals	s 94	s 10	Pt 7	Pt 4 Div 1		Pt 3	Pt IIB	
Good samaritans	Pt 2.1	s 8	Pt 8		Pt 9 Div 11		Pt VIA	Pt 1D
Volunteers	Pt 2.2	s 7	Pt 9	Pt 3 Div 2		Pt 10	Pt IX	
Apologies	Pt 2.3	Pt 2 Div 2	Pt 10	Ch 4 Pt 1	Pt 9 Div 12	Pt 4	Pt IIC	Pt 1E
Damages for the birth of child			Pt 11					
Occupier's liability	Pt 12.1	s 9	Pt 1A Div 2		Pt 4		Pt IIA	1985 Act
Advertising/ touting legal services							Pt 3	
Defamatory words and libel	Ch 9				Pt 2		Pt I	
Misrepresentation	Ch 13							
Publishers							Pt 1A	
Seduction	s 210				Pt 9 Div 7		Pt II	
Wrongful act or neglect causing death	Ch 3				Pt 5		Pt III	

COMPARATIVE TABLE – *continued*

	ACT	NT	NSW	Qld	SA	Tas	Vic	WA
	Civil Law (Wrongs) Act 2002	Personal Injuries (Liabilities and Damages) Act 2003	Civil Liability Act 2002	Civil Liability Act 2003	Civil Liability Act 1936	Civil Liability Act 2002	Wrongs Act 1958	Civil Liability Act 2002; Occupiers' Liability Act 1985
Contribution							Pt IV	
Abolition of doctrine of common employment	s 216				Pt 9 Div 4		Pt IVA	
Contributory negligence	Ch 7.3						Pt V	
Assessment of damages							Pt VA	
Food donor protection							Pt VIB	
Abolition of liability in maintenance or champerty	s 221						Pt VII	
Animals straying to highway							Pt VIII	
Accommodation provider	Pt 11.1, Sch 1					Pt 10A		
Liability for animals	Pt 12.2				Pt 3			
Fires accidentally begun	Pt 12.3							
Shipowners					Pt 9 Div 2			
Common carriers	Pt 11.2, Sch 2							
Damage by aircraft					Pt 9 Div 3			
Rights as between spouses, employer/ employee					Pt 9 Divs 1, 5			
Costs raising child			Pt 11		Pt 9 Div 6			
Perjury on civil actions					Pt 9 Div 9			
Unreasonable delay in resolution in claim					Pt 9 Div 8			
Racial victimisation					Pt 9 Div 10			
Failed sterilisation procedure				Pt 5				
Terrorism associated risks	Pt 3.3							
Personal injuries claims: pre-court procedures	Ch 5							
Survival of actions on death	Pt 2.4							
Proceedings against wrongdoers	Pt 2.5							
Expert medical evidence	Ch 6							
Limitations on legal costs	Ch 14							
Various abolition of common laws	Pt 15.4							

CHAPTER 1

Meaning of a Tort

Reading

Sappideen, Vines, Grant and Watson, *Torts: Commentary and Materials*, Chapter 1.

Objectives

This chapter will explain:

* the meaning of a tort;
* the difference between an action in tort and other areas of law;
* the interests protected by torts; and
* some matters of procedure and proof.

Principles

Meaning of a tort

[1.05] A tort[1] may be defined as an act or omission by the defendant, constituting an infringement of a legally recognised interest of the plaintiff giving rise to a right of civil action for unliquidated damages.

The following points should be noted:

- The definition is not particularly informative. It does not tell us what sort of acts or omissions create torts nor what interests actually receive protection. Unfortunately, no definition of tort can provide a short cut to this information. To understand the wide variety of conduct that may be tortious, it is necessary to understand the law of tort itself. Two points should be appreciated at this early stage. First, the act or omission generally needs to be wrongful, in the sense that the defendant acted or omitted to act intentionally or negligently. However, in some cases a tort may be one of strict liability, that is it may be committed without fault on the part of the defendant. Second, certain interests receive protection against more than one tort (often several different torts), so that there may be considerable overlapping of torts arising from the same facts. For example the interests in security of person and property are heavily protected by the law of tort. The interest in not being brought unnecessarily to court in order to defend legal proceedings is, by comparison, protected by only one tort, malicious prosecution.

- The infringement of the plaintiff's interest required by the definition is not to be equated with causing the plaintiff actual damage. Some torts require that the plaintiff prove damage in order to establish a cause of action. In others, the plaintiff may be able to succeed in tort despite having suffered no actual damage at all. The latter type of tort is said to be actionable "per se".

- All torts give rise to a right to claim unliquidated damages, that is damages that are not fixed in amount in advance (by contrast, the term "liquidated damages" refers to fixed sum damages as, for example, in a claim on an insurance policy). Unliquidated damages are measured according to the loss suffered by the plaintiff so are not necessarily substantial. For example, a court may vindicate a plaintiff's right in a case where the plaintiff has suffered no loss by awarding nominal damages (that is, of no real money value) or even contemptuous damages (damages so small that they indicate disapproval of the action having been brought at all). Sometimes the court may award damages in excess of any actual damage the plaintiff has suffered by awarding aggravated damages to reflect matters such as the conduct of the defendant, the circumstances under which the tort was committed, and the effect of the tort on the plaintiff. In rare cases the court will award exemplary or punitive damages (damages which are not related to loss suffered by the plaintiff or the effect of the tort upon the plaintiff, but are intended to make an example of or punish the defendant). The same facts may justify an award of aggravated or exemplary damages or both.

---

[1]   See generally Winfield, *Province of the Law of Tort* (1931); Williams and Hepple, *Foundations of the Law of Tort* (2nd ed, 1984).

Tort and crime

[1.10] The requirement that a civil action must be taken in order to remedy a tort distinguishes torts from crimes, although much tortious conduct is also criminal. The essential difference between the tortious action and the criminal prosecution is one of purpose. Civil actions are brought in order to resolve private disputes between individuals by the award of some appropriate remedy such as the award of damages, an order for the return of property, or an injunction. On the other hand, a criminal prosecutor acts as a representative of the public interest in the redress and repression of crime. The outcome of criminal proceedings is the determination of whether the defendant is guilty or not guilty of the crime alleged, whereas the outcome of a civil action in tort is the recovery of damages by the plaintiff.

Tort and restitution

[1.15] The purpose of the law of tort may be expressed as the provision of a civil remedy for injury or damage to, or other infringement of, a recognised interest. This purpose serves to distinguish torts from other civil wrongs such as quasi-contract (or restitution as it is now generally called) or breach of trust. The function of the law of restitution is to protect the plaintiff's right to money or property which the defendant has and which the defendant has no right to keep as against the plaintiff.

Tort and trust

[1.20] Breach of trust is essentially a proprietary claim against the trustee to make good depletion of the trust property that has occurred as a result of the breach. Unliquidated damages, which are a common law remedy, are not awarded in relation to a breach of trust, which falls within the equitable jurisdiction. The appropriate remedies for breach of trust are to be sought from a court of equity.

Tort and contract

[1.25] Breach of contract, like tort, recognises a claim for unliquidated damages by way of compensation for loss arising from a contractual breach. In cases in which an action for unliquidated damages is available in an action for breach of contract, the definition of tort we started with does not adequately distinguish breach of contract. There is, in fact, no compelling analytical reason why breach of contract should not be regarded as a tort. In cases of concurrent liability (where liability arises in both tort and contract in relation to the same conduct of the defendant), the liability in tort is indistinguishable in substance from the failure to perform the contractual duty. This does not mean, however, that even in this case the mere breach of contract is by itself a tort. A breach of contract and facts that give rise to an action in tort are discrete causes of action, despite their factual coincidence. Concurrent liability has so far been found to exist only where the tort in question is negligence, and the contractual duty is one of reasonable care. In order that the breach of contract should amount to a tort, it must comply with the further requirements of the tort of negligence that a duty of care should exist and that actual damage to the plaintiff has resulted from the breach.

Figure 1.1:

	Tort	Contract
To whom is the duty owed?	Owed generally	Other contracting parties
What is the basis of the duty owed?	Duty is imposed by law	Duty arises as a result of undertakings made by the parties
What interests are protected?	Personal and mental security, property interests, fame and reputation, financial and economic interests	Expectation of a future benefit arising from the undertakings

Despite situations of overlap, tort duties and contractual duties are frequently quite dissimilar.[2] A number of typical differences exist between the two which explain and justify their separate treatment by past and present legal systems. However, these typical differences prove on examination to be incapable of establishing any absolute theoretical difference between the two. They will now be considered.

[1.30] The jurist Winfield thought that the main differences between tort and contract were that tort duties were imposed by law whereas contractual duties were imposed by agreement of the parties. Further, he argued that tort duties were owed to persons generally whereas contractual duties were owed only to the other party, or parties, to the contract.[3] There are two facets to the first distinction. First, it may be said that contractual duties arise by choice of the parties, whereas one has no choice about being subject to duties in tort. This is only partially true. Although it would be very difficult to altogether avoid tortious duties of care to other persons, quite a large number of duties of care arise from acts of conscious choice, for example to drive a motor car, to occupy land or to manufacture goods. Conversely, the "choice" element in a contractual obligation is in practice to some extent illusory, since it would be impossible to live life without entering into contracts. Second, the duty to perform the contract once entered into is imposed by law, not by the parties to the contract. Thus Winfield's point relates to the content of the obligation rather than the existence of it. Even so this does not adequately distinguish between the two because many contractual obligations are imposed by law rather than through agreement of the parties, one obvious example being terms implied under trade practices legislation as to the fitness and quality of goods, imposed upon the seller of goods in a contract of sale. Tort law also is capable of enforcing contractual obligations arising from a genuine agreement (express or implied) as, for example, in the case of concurrent liability or the tort of interference with contract.

Winfield's second distinguishing feature (that tort duties are owed to persons generally but contractual duties only to the other party to the contract) runs into the objection that at the level of abstraction not concerned with actual situations, the general duty to perform contracts is no different from the general duty to abstain from

---

[2]   Coote, "The Essence of Contract" (1988) IJ Contract L 91; Swanton, "Convergence of Tort and Contract" (1989) 12 Syd LR 40; Markesinis, "An Expanding Tort Law" (1987) 103 LQR 354.

[3]   *Winfield and Jolowicz On Tort* (14th ed, 1994) p 4.

committing torts. Neither duty is in any real sense "owed". Persons are merely subject to them in the same way as they are to other laws of the land. Once a contract has been entered into, the contractual duty becomes fixed in a way that may not be true of tort duties. In the case of negligence (which rests upon the concept of reasonable foreseeability where the class of persons to whom duties are owed is fluctuating and not fixed), the actual person to whom a duty is owed is only identified by a court once a negligence action is brought. The practical reality is that tort duties arise between particular persons at particular times and places.

Winfield's suggested distinctions therefore fail to establish any absolute categorical difference between tort and contract. The same is true of another difference between the two, which is typical rather than absolute. The law of contract can protect against both actual loss and loss of expectation, most commonly of an economic nature, deriving from the due performance of the contract. Tort law is more concerned with protecting against the loss of existing rights, such as the right to bodily inviolability, personal and real property and reputation. The law of tort sometimes gives protection to an expectation of future benefit by characterising loss as damage for the purpose of establishing a cause of action in negligence (see especially the numerous cases in which persons appointed beneficiaries under wills have succeeded in negligence against the solicitors through whose negligence the gift has failed). The tortious right, being in general one which protects us in the enjoyment or possession of what we already have, is generally concerned with imposing liability for misfeasance (that is, positive acts causing damage or other wrongful interference) as well as non-feasance (that is, omissions). The contractual right, on the other hand, is essentially applied in cases of non-feasance, for a failure to perform the contractual promise.

Elements of torts

Mental element

[1.35] It was pointed out at [1.05] that a tort requires an act or omission by the defendant, generally speaking accompanied by a mental element constituting "fault" and infringing a "protected" interest of the plaintiff. Fault has become increasingly important in tort law with the decline of the torts of strict liability. It is constituted by intentional, reckless or negligent conduct on the part of the defendant. "Intentional" here relates to the consequences of the defendant's conduct rather than the mental state necessary to perform the conduct itself, the latter normally being designated in relation to an act by the term "voluntariness". In order to be found to have committed an intentional wrong, the defendant must have intended the particular infringement of the plaintiff's interest that is required by the tort in question. Recklessness is defined as a subjective state of mind under which the defendant is taken to have had in mind as likely the consequences of his or her action, and to have acted in wilful disregard of them. It is equated by the law of tort with intention but up to now has had very little part to play in it, though recent decisions have indicated its relevance to the assessment of damages. The subjective test of the defendant's state of mind necessary to establish intention or recklessness is contrasted with the objective standard applied to determine what is negligence. Here the defendant is judged by the standard of what a reasonable person in the defendant's position should have foreseen and what action such person should have taken or refrained from taking as a result.

Torts of strict liability are the clearest example of a tortious principle, formerly of importance, falling into decline. The leading tort of strict liability, set out in *Rylands v Fletcher* (1868) LR 3 HL 330, has now been removed altogether from Australian law by the High Court of Australia: *Burnie Port Authority v General Jones Pty Ltd* (1994) 179 CLR 520. Nuisance, once thought of as a tort of strict liability, is now generally accepted as a tort requiring fault except in a few isolated cases: see Chapter 16. Strict liability for dangerous animals has to some extent disappeared in Australia, having been replaced by a liability for negligence: see Chapter 17. Breach of statutory duty as a tort is largely limited to statutes imposing industrial safety requirements in places of work. Even here strict liability is unusual, since the statutory standard is known in advance and the actual failure to comply with it is likely to be at least negligent: see Chapter 14. Some torts requiring intentional conduct on the part of the defendant (for example, trespass, conversion and the generic tort of defamation) may impose strict liability where the defendant intentionally infringed the plaintiff's interest but acted under a reasonable belief that he or she was entitled to carry out the act in question.

Interests protected by torts

[1.40] The interests protected by the law of torts are diverse. Figure 1.2 lists the more important interests (but does not purport to be comprehensive).

Figure 1.2

Interest protected	Tort
Interest in bodily and mental security	Battery, assault and negligence, action on the case for indirect intentional injury
Freedom of movement	False imprisonment
Interest in the security and enjoyment of property including intellectual property	Trespass to land, trespass to goods, conversion, detinue, negligence, nuisance, passing off
Fame and reputation	Defamation
Financial and economic interests	Negligence

Creation of new torts

[1.45] The contemporary law of tort is still largely a creature of the common law, which is interpreted and applied by the courts. Statute though is intervening more commonly, for example in establishing rules about the amount of damages payable, contributory negligence, contribution between tortfeasors or limitation of actions (though in Australia the effect of the combination of ss 52(1) and 82(1) of the *Trade Practices Act 1974* (Cth) has been to create a new tort whereby misleading or deceptive conduct in trade or commerce is actionable). The last general addition to the judge-made list of torts was, however, *Rylands v Fletcher* in 1868. As noted at [1.35] this tort has been removed from Australian law. Contemporary judges seem to prefer to take an incremental approach to the expansion, where appropriate, of existing causes of action to cover novel situations rather than creating a new tort altogether. An

English first instance decision (*Thomas v National Union of Mineworkers (South Wales)* [1986] Ch 20) which suggested that there was a tort of unreasonable harassment in the exercise of rights such as highway user has received no later confirmation, and the Court of Appeal's extension of the tort of private nuisance to cover certain cases of harassment has been overturned by the House of Lords.[4] In 1993, New Zealand appears to have recognised a tort of infringement of privacy: *Bradley v Wingnut Films Ltd* [1993] 1 NZLR 415. In more recent times, a number of Australian decisions have also paved the way for the acceptance of the tort of privacy. In 2001, the High Court held in *ABC v Lenah Game Meats Pty Ltd* (2001) 208 CLR 199 that there was no authority preventing the development of a tort of invasion of privacy in Australia. In 2003, the District Court in Queensland used the case as authority and awarded $178,000 damages to the plaintiff, following eight years of harassment and stalking by the defendant: *Grosse v Purvis* [2003] QDC 151.

Tort or torts

[1.50] The definition of tort with which this chapter began is of such generality that it is impossible to derive from it any genuine guidance as to the circumstances in which tortious liability will arise. In this, tort seems to contrast starkly with contract, where without exception it may be predicted that where a contract exists and a breach of it has been committed, liability arises. Difficulties may arise in deciding whether a contract exists and whether a breach has been committed, but the fundamental principle remains clear. The law of tort, on the other hand, yields only a series of particular statements as to the circumstances in which liability arises. Because of this there is still division of opinion as to whether we should speak of a law of "torts" rather than of "tort". The latter is chosen by this book, not merely because of the considerable convenience of being able to refer to, for example, an action in tort rather than torts, but also because there is sufficient in the definition of tort, to mark out torts as a category of civil wrong separate from other categories, apart from breach of contract. The definition has a set of conditions with which all torts must conform. Breach of contract, which also complies with the definition, must be separated from tort for reasons of history and convenience.

In general the law of tort does not provide any general principle of liability based on malice. So, it was found by the House of Lords not to be a tort to abstract water percolating in undefined channels beneath the defendant's land, thereby depriving other landowners of its flow, and it made no difference whether or not the defendant's conduct was malicious: *Bradford Corp v Pickles* [1895] AC 587; *Stephens v Anglian Water Authority* [1987] 1 WLR 1381; cf *Elston v Dore* (1982) 149 CLR 480. It was also found not to be a tort that a defendant had maliciously made lawful threats to an employer to induce the employer to lawfully terminate the plaintiff's employment, which the employer did: *Allen v Flood* [1898] AC 1. The latter decision in particular gave rise to acute controversy at the time and divided a specially convened House of Lords.[5] Another example is the decision of the High Court in *Cabassi v Vila* (1940) 64 CLR 130 that it is not a tort to conspire to give false evidence in court against the plaintiff. The need to protect witnesses

---

[4]   *Khorasandjian v Bush* [1993] 3 WLR 476 has been overruled by *Hunter v Canary Wharf* [1997] 2 WLR 684. England now has the *Protection Against Harassment Act 1997* (UK).

[5]   See further Gutteridge, "Abuse of Rights" (1935) 5 CLJ 22; Ames in *Selected Essays on the Law of Torts* (Harvard Law Review Assoc, 1924) pp 150-161.

in court from possible liability in tort was held to be the paramount consideration, even where the plaintiff could show a predominant intention on the part of the witness to injure the plaintiff. There is, however, a limited number of torts that require malice as a determinant of liability. An example of such a tort is malicious prosecution. Malice may also be an issue in some instances of nuisance. Malice may further be relevant to the quantum of damages. But the principle established by the above cases is that, in general, malice cannot convert to a tort that which is in itself not a tort.

Matters of procedure and proof

Procedure

[1.55] Torts must be proved in civil process, that is, by the plaintiff taking a civil action against the defendant. Two matters about the way in which the plaintiff establishes his or her case are particularly important. First, in accordance with the normal requirement of proof, both in civil actions and criminal trials, corresponding to the maxim, "He who alleges must prove", the legal burden of proof rests on the plaintiff. The necessary "amount" of proof in a civil action and in a criminal trial is, however, different. In a civil action, the plaintiff need only make out its case on the so-called balance of probabilities; in a criminal trial, the guilt of the accused must be proved beyond reasonable doubt. The explanation of this difference is clear enough; the deleterious consequences of a criminal conviction are generally much greater than those attending a civil liability to pay damages.

The second feature of the civil action is that it is quite common for the trial to be held before a judge sitting alone without a jury. Conversely, a defendant is entitled to a trial by jury in criminal cases concerned with indictable offences. In New South Wales and Victoria, jury trial in civil actions is still relatively common, but in other States it is unusual.[6] The consequences of this are a little hard to gauge. Criticism against jury verdicts is sometimes levelled on the ground that they are based on an imperfect understanding of the law or are emotive, but since it is impossible to conduct empirical research into the way juries reach their verdicts, this sort of criticism is unsustained. A major difference between a jury verdict and that of a judge sitting alone is concerned with the powers of an appellate court. Juries will be instructed on the relevant law by the trial judge, but will then be asked to decide questions of a broad general nature such as "was the defendant negligent?" or "did the defendant's negligence cause damage to the plaintiff?" A jury verdict will not indicate the primary findings of fact upon which the jury has reached its conclusion, and this means that an appellate court will be unable to interfere with those conclusions unless they are wholly unreasonable and against the

---

6   See *Juries Act 1927* (SA), s 5 and the *Supreme Court Act 1933* (ACT), s 22: no civil trial is to be held before a jury; *Juries Act 1963* (NT), s 7: court has discretion to order jury trial but seldom does so; *Civil Liability Act 2003* (Qld), s 73: a claim for personal injury damages must be decided by the court sitting without a jury, while in other cases the judge may with the consent of the parties decide questions of fact; *Supreme Court Act 1995* (Qld), s 51: court has discretion to order jury trial but seldom does so. The same is true in the following States though both parties by agreement may require a jury trial: *Supreme Court Civil Procedure Act 1932* (Tas), ss 27, 29; *Supreme Court Act 1935* (WA), s 42. Under the *Supreme Court Act 1970* (NSW), s 85, trial is to be without jury unless the court orders otherwise. In Victoria, O 47.02 of the *Supreme Court (General Civil Procedure) Rules 2005* allows either party to require the trial to be by jury, subject to that party's payment of the prescribed fee. New South Wales and Victoria make more extensive use of juries in civil trials than the other States and Territories. Pursuant to the Defamation Acts in NSW, NT, Qld, Tas, Vic and WA, a party may elect to have a trial by jury.

weight of the evidence. A judge sitting without a jury will, on the other hand, normally state the findings of primary fact before stating what the conclusions from them are (so-called "inferential" findings of fact). An appellate court will always accept the trial judge's findings of primary fact, but may overturn inferences from those facts if it disagrees with them, on the basis that the appellate court is in just as good a position as the trial judge to draw those inferences. The result of this is that the appellate court has greater power of interference with the decision of a trial judge than with that of a jury. Matters of proof, and especially proof of negligence, are considered in Chapter 13.

Limitation of actions

[1.60] The effect of the expiration of a limitation period on a cause of action in tort is in general procedural rather than substantive. The cause of action is not extinguished but merely rendered incapable of being sued on by the plaintiff. As such it must be specifically pleaded as a defence by the defendant, and is also capable of being waived.

Any detailed account of limitation as it affects actions in tort is beyond the scope of this book. However, since limitation issues arise very frequently in tort actions, a brief account of the fundamentals of the subject is desirable. Limitation periods in Australia are entirely statutory,[7] although in the case of actions in tort against the Commonwealth of Australia it is necessary to use s 64 of the *Judiciary Act 1903* (Cth) to "pick up" State limitation periods in order to provide a limitation period on the action. There is considerable uniformity among Australian States as to present-day limitation periods on actions in tort. They are in general barred by the expiration of six years from the date of accrual of the cause of action, except in the Northern Territory where a three year period applies. Western Australia also has a limitation period of three years for trespass to the person whether or not harm was caused and the limitation period for defamation proceedings is one year from the date of publication of the matter complained of in all States except Tasmania. All States have reduced the limitation period on causes of action for personal injuries to three years from the date of the injury. All States except South Australia have provided to the effect that in the case of successive causes of action in conversion or detinue of chattels the six-year limitation period begins to run from the first in time of these.

It is important to know what is meant by the date of accrual of the cause of action. In the case of torts that are actionable per se (without proof of damage) this is the date of the act committing the tort. In the case of torts such as negligence, which require proof of damage as part of the cause of action, this is the date when that damage occurs. The difference is illustrated by *Wilson v Horne* [1999] Aust Torts Reports 81-504. The plaintiff had been subjected while a child to sexual assaults by the defendant. Many years later she had developed a stress disorder when memories of the assaults became revived. Her cause of action for trespass had long since been barred by the passing of time, but her cause of action for negligence was brought within time, since the cause of action did not accrue until the stress disorder developed.

[1.65] Cases of latent injury or damage cause difficulty. In *Cartledge v Jopling* [1963] AC 758, a case concerning the contracting of pneumoconiosis through exposure to silica

---

[7]   *Limitation Act 1985* (ACT); *Limitation Act 1969* (NSW); *Limitation Act 1981* (NT); *Limitation of Actions Act 1974* (Qld); *Limitation of Actions Act 1936* (SA); *Limitation Act 1974* (Tas); *Limitation of Actions Act 1958* (Vic); *Limitation Act 2005* (WA).

dust, the House of Lords held that the cause of action for negligence accrued when the disease established itself, not when the plaintiff became aware of it. This could cause manifest injustice, since a cause of action could become unenforceable through limitation before the plaintiff had had time to pursue it. This has caused universal statutory provision in Australia to allow courts a discretionary power to extend the limitation period in the case of personal injury and disease. Victoria has gone further by providing that a cause of action in respect of disease does not accrue until the plaintiff knows of it and knows that it was caused by the act or omission of another person: *Limitation of Actions Act 1958* (Vic), s 5(1A) (but now see Pt IIA).

Where houses or buildings have been negligently constructed, the defects in the buildings may not become apparent for a lengthy period of time, thus creating a similar problem to that caused by latent injury. In this case, however, the problem has been addressed judicially rather than by legislative intervention. In *Bryan v Maloney* (1995) 182 CLR 609 the High Court held that where the defendant builder had negligently constructed a dwelling-house on defective footings, the damage sustained by a later purchaser of the house was pure economic loss rather than damage to property (since the house was always defective rather than damaged). That damage did not occur until the defect became manifest (that is, when cracking occurred in the walls of the house). "Becoming manifest" was interpreted in a later decision to mean being discoverable by the exercise of due diligence on the plaintiff's part: *Bailey v Redebi* [1999] Aust Torts Reports 81-523. The effect of *Bryan* was to create the possibility of negligence actions being litigated many years after the relevant facts occurred, and the provision by the ACT of a discretionary power to extend the limitation period in cases of this sort, but only until 10 years after the act of negligence occurred, has been overtaken by the operation of the ordinary limitation period as estimated under the ruling in *Bryan*: *Building Act 2004* (ACT), s 142(1).

Where there is a genuine case of damage to property arising from a tort, the cause of action accrues when the damage occurs, not when it is discoverable by due diligence. This is subject to the usual provision in the Limitation Acts under which the limitation period does not run in favour of a defendant who is fraudulent or has fraudulently concealed the cause of action. *Hawkins v Clayton* (1988) 164 CLR 539 may suggest the possibility of a more generous measure where the plaintiff is justifiably unaware of the damage the property has suffered. In that case, where damage to property belonging to a deceased's estate had occurred through the defendant's negligent failure to inform the plaintiff executor of his appointment, Brennan and Deane JJ held that the limitation period did not commence until the executor took up his appointment. But *Hawkins* may be of no significance to cases of damage to property in general, since the plaintiff not only did not know of his appointment but was also not in a position to take action relating to the damage before his becoming executor.

Practice Questions

Revision Questions

1.1 Why would a victim prefer to initiate a tort action in preference to the perpetrator being charged criminally? Do you see any particular advantage in pursuing a tort claim?

1.2 Does the limitation period for torts run from the date of injury?

Answers to Practice Questions

Revision Questions

1.1 There are many instances where a person's wrongful act could be a crime as well as a tort. An obvious example is sexual assault. The victim in these circumstances needs to determine whether he or she wishes to see the perpetrator punished or whether to obtain compensation. The criminal law has as its purpose a desire to pre-empt criminal behaviour by threatening punishment and so protect society as a whole. The law of tort has the wronged person as its focus and endeavours to compensate him or her in such a way as to place that person back in the position he or she would have been in before the accident. The wronged person in most criminal matters receives no compensation at all, apart from the satisfaction of seeing the perpetrator penalised in some way. Another advantage with pursuing a claim in torts is that the plaintiff has the advantage of proving his or her case on the balance of probabilities as opposed to proving it beyond reasonable doubt in a criminal action. It is, of course, open to the aggrieved party to pursue a civil claim in tort as well as the complaint in criminal law.

1.2 If there is a latent injury or damage, then the date from which the limitation period runs becomes more complicated. In cases of personal injury and disease the cause of action does not accrue until there is knowledge of the disease. In relation to defective buildings, the determinant is when the defect becomes manifest.

Tutorial Questions

Discussion Questions

1.1 Can you think of situations where it may be difficult to determine which interests or rights should be protected?

1.2 Even though the common law is slow to recognise new torts as such, there are good indications that it can change with the times as seen in recent cases that seem to recognise the tort of breach of privacy. Should the common law also recognise a tort of "harassment"?

1.3 In both tort law and criminal law, the plaintiff bears the burden of proof generally. However, in criminal law the Crown is required to prove its case beyond reasonable doubt, while in tort law the plaintiff is required to prove his or her case on the balance of probabilities. What is the basis for such a fundamental difference between criminal law and tort law?

CHAPTER 2

Statutory Compensation Schemes for Torts Claims

Reading

Sappideen, Vines, Grant and Watson, *Torts: Commentary and Materials*, pp 684-686.

Objectives

This chapter will explain:

* the significance of remedies in tort law;
* the range of remedies available in tort law;
* compensation as an essential element in tort law;
* the structure of compensation schemes outside the traditional domain of tort law; and
* insurance schemes:
  — motor accidents compensation schemes;
  — workers' compensation schemes;
  — criminal injuries compensation schemes; and
  — total no-fault compensation schemes.

Principles

Remedies in tort law

No action without an infringement

[2.05] In Chapter 1 we defined a tort as an *act or omission* of the defendant that constitutes *an infringement* of an interest of the plaintiff *recognised by law*. Where the defendant's act or omission does not interfere with the plaintiff's interest, there is no basis for an action. Even where there is an "infringement" in the sense of an interference with an *interest* of the plaintiff, he or she can only bring an action if such interest is of a type protected by law. Where the plaintiff chooses to bring an action, the aim is to seek a *remedy* for the infringement or the *breach* of his or her interest. If the defendant is found to be at fault, and for that matter liable, the plaintiff is then entitled to the award of a remedy (against the defendant). The pursuit of remedies, then, is the very essence of tort law. This is illustrated in Figure 2.1.

Figure 2.1

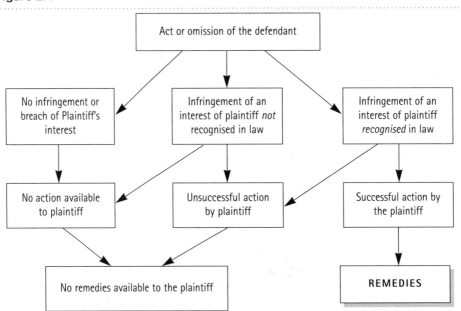

Range of remedies in the law of torts

[2.10] In the law of torts there is a wide range of remedies available to the plaintiff depending on the interests to be protected and the infringement by the defendant. A remedy in torts may be coercive or substitutionary. A good example of a coercive remedy is an injunction (a court order) directed at a noisy neighbour directing him or her to stop causing a nuisance. An example of a substitutionary remedy is *compensation* in the form of damages. Damages can be purely compensatory, nominal or punitive in character. Compensatory damages are awarded to make good the damage caused by the defendant. Nominal damages are awarded as tacit recognition of the harm caused to the plaintiff by the defendant's conduct where the plaintiff has not suffered any real or significant harm. Punitive (more commonly called exemplary) damages, rarely awarded in Australia, are designed to deter future conduct of the kind in issue and to punish (as the term "punitive" suggests) the defendant. Punitive damages are criticised on the grounds that they represent a blurring between the civil and criminal jurisdictions.

As noted in Chapter 1, liability in tort law is based on fault. Liability attracts the payment of compensation. In some cases, however, parties may protect themselves by insuring against their liability. Such insurance is not restricted to damage to others or their property. People may also choose to protect themselves from the cost of injury or damage to themselves, generally irrespective of whether such damage occurs accidentally or through the fault of others.

Statutory compensation

[2.15] Self-protection against personal injury or property damage by means of insurance is part of the law of contract. Liability insurance, which is extremely important in tort law, depends upon proof that a tort has been committed. Other forms of compensation provide alternatives to suing in tort and do not depend upon proof that a tort has been committed. Limited accident compensation schemes for personal injury exist in the shape of workers' compensation legislation (universal throughout Australia), the motor accident compensation schemes present in the Northern Territory, Tasmania and Victoria, and the criminal injuries compensation schemes (also present throughout Australia). The social security system is not related to accident compensation as such, but may be of assistance to a tort claimant. In Australia there is no general accident compensation scheme replacing the tort action, such as exists in New Zealand. The New Zealand Parliament has abolished the common law of negligence and replaced it with a no-fault statutory scheme, though compensation can also be acquired. In 1974 the Woodhouse Committee on Compensation and Rehabilitation recommended such a scheme that was even more extensive than that in force at the time. Legislation introducing the scheme into Australia lapsed with the dissolution of Parliament in 1975, and for a number of reasons (among which might be cited the difficulties of imposing such a scheme on the States, the absence of popular demand for such a scheme, and the influential opposition of lawyers), similar legislation has not been reintroduced.

Deficiencies in the torts system

[2.20] The existence of these schemes of protection for the victims of accidents points to deficiencies in the torts system. Four main problems may be identified:

- The first problem is litigation cost:[1] the cost of obtaining compensation. As this involves litigation or prospective litigation, lawyers' fees, court costs and witnesses' expenses must be paid, leading to final costs that may be a high proportion of the compensation amount awarded (and which can often exceed it). If obtaining compensation did not involve litigation, these costs

---

[1] See also Australian Law Reform Commission Report, *The Cost of Federal Civil Litigation* (ALRC IP 20, 1999) for a general discourse on costs.

would be markedly reduced, although it should be noted that some Australian jurisdictions, as part of their civil liability reforms, have attempted to reign in litigation costs.[2]

- The second problem is the difficulty with proof. A considerable number of persons injured in accidents go uncompensated through not being able to prove a tort. Proof of a tort generally requires proof of fault on the part of another person. Even if a tort is proved, the defendant may be insolvent or uninsured, or the plaintiff's damages may be substantially reduced for contributory negligence.

- The third problem is the delay that is usually involved in obtaining tort compensation. This would cause extreme hardship in the case of an injured person no longer capable of earning money through employment, were it not for the existence of the alternative schemes of accident compensation mentioned in [2.15]. Notwithstanding this, the delay involved places pressure on the tort victim to settle the action, thereby creating the risk of under-compensation.

- The final problem is the problem with lump sum payments. The general practice of courts, in tort cases, is to award damages in the form of a lump sum in final satisfaction of the claim against the tortfeasor (although there are alternatives to this in some States).[3] The lump sum can never be an accurate estimate of the plaintiff's actual loss because of matters such as the possible worsening of the injury in future or of inflation leading, for example, to a rise in medical expenses. The court may take such matters into account in fixing the lump sum, but this can never be more than imprecise. In recent times the law reform process has attempted to address the problems of lump sum payments with the introduction of structured settlements. A structured settlement usually takes the form of an agreement between the parties to a personal injury case, in which the parties accept that part of the settlement funds will be paid to the plaintiff in the form of periodic payments. Such periodic payments are usually funded by the purchase of an annuity from a life insurance company. Under such an agreement, a successful plaintiff usually receives a smaller up-front lump sum, which is then followed with an "income" stream of periodic payments which may be tailored to meet future medical and living expenses. While the concept of structured settlements is not new, legislation in most Australian jurisdictions now makes it mandatory for practitioners to advise their clients of the availability of these arrangements. For example, s 25 of the *Civil Liability Act 2002* (NSW) requires a legal practitioner to advise a plaintiff wishing to settle a personal injury claim as to:

  - the availability of structured settlements; and

  - the desirability of the plaintiff obtaining independent financial advice about structured settlements and lump sum settlements of the claim.

---

[2]   *Civil Liability Act 2002* (NSW) (restricted to structured settlements); *Legal Profession Act 1987* (NSW); *Personal Injuries Proceedings Act 2002* (Qld); *Civil Law (Wrongs) Act 2002* (ACT).

[3]   Damages in the form of periodic payments may be awarded in South Australia under the *Supreme Court Act 1935* (SA), s 30B, and in Western Australia under the *Motor Vehicle (Third Party Insurance) Act 1943* (WA), s 16(4).

This is no doubt a very welcome development in the Australian torts system. It is important to note that, while the legislation makes it mandatory for the practitioner to provide advice on the availability of such arrangements, it is not mandatory for plaintiffs to accept it. Structured settlements have clearly not been introduced in order to replace the traditional lump sum arrangements for damages.

Benefits of statutory compensation schemes

[2.25] Compensation schemes on the other hand are better able to meet the difficulties generally associated with the common law system of compensation in torts. For instance, under a compensation scheme, loss of earnings may be compensated for by periodical payments adjusted in accordance with inflation. Similarly, a victim's medical expenses may be met through the scheme as and when they become due. The Pearson Commission, which reported on accident compensation in England in 1978,[4] found that the torts system operated to overcompensate the plaintiff where the injury was minor (no doubt because of generous awards for non-economic loss in the form of pain and suffering), but under-compensated in the case of serious, permanent injury. The capacity for courts to deal with problems of this sort is limited, although a court may reduce the discount rate applicable to lump sum damages awards for loss of earnings for personal injury, in part to counter the effects of inflation: see Chapter 22.

Compensation schemes are funded through pooled contributions from the community or potential beneficiaries. By nature they are similar to general insurance schemes. We will first examine the nature of general insurance as a form of compensation before we look at compensation schemes.

Compulsory insurance

[2.30] The law of insurance does not create rights additional to those existing under the common law. However the existence of compulsory liability insurance, in the case of motor accidents causing personal injury, enormously strengthens the enforceability of rights of action covered by that insurance. The fact that a plaintiff or defendant is insured cannot operate as a factor in the determination of a tort claim. And generally, even where a judgment obtained is enforceable against the defendant's insurance company (as with compulsory insurance), the insurer must not be named as a party. The plaintiff's possession of personal accident or property insurance is only relevant to the question of whether sums received under the policy are to be deducted from damages received for the tort. This matter is considered in detail in Chapter 22, but we may briefly state here that money received under a personal accident insurance policy is not deducted, whereas money received under a property damage policy is deducted. In the latter case, the insurance company is subrogated to the insured's rights against the defendant.

Statutory provision for compulsory insurance against tort liability for injury caused by motor vehicles exists throughout Australia. The provisions, though not entirely uniform, show considerable similarity.[5]

---

[4]   Cmnd 7054 (1978).

[5]   *Motor Accidents Compensation Act 1999* (NSW); *Motor Accident Insurance Act 1994* (Qld); *Motor Vehicles Act 1959* (SA); *Motor Accidents (Liabilities and Compensation) Act 1973* (Tas); *Motor Vehicle (Third Party Insurance) Act 1943* (WA); *Road Transport (General) Act 1999* (ACT). In Victoria and the Northern Territory, the matter is regulated as part of the provision for no-fault compensation for motor accidents.

For example, there is a uniform provision that the relevant death or injury should be caused by, or arise out of, the use of a motor vehicle. "Use" is given a broad interpretation. In *Dawson v Stevens Bros Pty Ltd* (1983) 34 SASR 338,[6] the court held that where a wheeled compressor (which was a motor vehicle for the purposes of the Act) was being unloaded from a truck, an injury caused to the plaintiff employee through its sudden movement arose out of its use within the meaning of the Act. There is also uniform provision that the insurance should cover liability where the vehicle is uninsured, the driver is unauthorised or unidentified, or an insured driver has committed a breach of the insurance policy. In cases of this sort, however, provision is often made for the compulsory insurer to recover an indemnity from the driver of the vehicle.

Under the principle of subrogation, an insurer that has paid out on an insurance policy to a tort victim becomes entitled to rely on the victim's causes of action in tort against the tortfeasor.

[2.35] Subrogation is allowed only in the case of indemnity insurance. It is available in the case of insurance against property damage or loss, but not personal accident insurance where only a specific sum of money is promised by the policy. Subrogation is also available in the case of compulsory motor vehicle insurance, since the insurer indemnifies the defendant against tort damages, thus enabling the insurer to seek a contribution or an indemnity from persons who are jointly liable in tort, along with the insured driver, to the victim. Since these persons are likely to be joined by the insured driver as joint defendants to the victim's action (thus allowing the court to apportion liability among them), subrogation is not particularly important here.

In relation to property insurance, subrogation has been the subject of criticism, particularly in the case of collisions between motor vehicles,[7] on the ground that it creates litigation costs in transferring liabilities between insurance companies. Since most insurance companies operate as both liability and property insurers, there seems to be little overall advantage to be gained by pursuing tort liability. "Knock-for-knock" agreements, which some insurance companies operate in relation to damage to motor vehicles, have the desirable effect of eliminating these costs.

Compulsory liability insurance ran into extreme difficulties in Australia in the 1980s,[8] caused partly by an increase in the size of damages awards made to accident victims, and partly by an unwillingness by governments to offset this by charging anything other than increasingly inadequate flat-rate premiums for motor vehicle insurance. The eventual consequence has been statutory reductions in the damages in tort that may be awarded for non-economic loss (that is, for pain and suffering or loss of amenity) in motor accident cases.

In New South Wales and South Australia, restrictions have been placed on damages for non-economic loss in motor accident cases without affecting the right to bring the action in tort (and the latter State has placed a limit on the amount recoverable for lost earning capacity). In Victoria serious restrictions are placed on the latter right, and even in cases where it exists, restrictions are placed on the total amounts that may be recovered for both economic and non-economic loss.

The different forms of non-tortious no-fault schemes of compensation are now examined in turn. In all of these, there is no reduction in the plaintiff's

---

6   See also *Dickinson v Motor Vehicle Insurance Trust (WA)* (1987) 163 CLR 500 fn 7.
7   Fleming, *Law of Torts* (9th ed), p 440.
8   Keeler, "The Crises of Liability Insurance" (1988) 1 Insurance LJ 182.

entitlement because of the plaintiff's contributory negligence, although there may be reductions of entitlement, as under the *Transport Accidents Act 1986* (Vic), for drunken driving.

No-fault schemes of compensation

Motor accident compensation

[2.40] No-fault accident compensation for injury caused in motor accidents exists in the Northern Territory, Tasmania and Victoria and very limited recovery is available in New South Wales for those catastrophically injured and children.[9] The rationale behind schemes of this sort is mainly to remove the perceived inequity between those injured in accidents who can prove fault, and those who cannot. A second basis, that of reducing the legal costs involved in establishing fault, may be accepted for the Northern Territory (which has abolished the tort action altogether for Territory residents), is altogether absent from Tasmania (where the scheme retains the tort action in full) and is only dubiously present in Victoria (where the tort action is to some extent retained, and where the compensation provisions are so complex that the legal costs of administering the scheme must be high).

Eligibility for compensation differs between the three schemes. All three favour the resident of the State over the non-resident. Victoria has the most favourable scheme for the non-resident. It is available to non-residents of Victoria in relation to accidents occurring outside Victoria, but within Australia, to the driver of or passenger in a Victorian registered vehicle. Further, the Victorian scheme extends to accidents caused by trains and trams. All three States have certain exclusions in common, in particular where the claimant has been guilty of some serious criminal offence in connection with the driving of the vehicle (though in Victoria this does not deprive the claimant of medical benefits). The compensation provisions of the schemes are too complex and various for consideration here. Tasmania, which has retained the common law tort action, provides limited medical benefits and altogether excludes a claim for non-economic loss (that is for pain and suffering and loss of amenity). Victoria, which seriously restricts the common law claim, and the Northern Territory, which abolishes it in favour of its residents, are more generous in providing medical benefits and compensation for non-economic loss.

The compensation provided under all the schemes is of course much less than that obtainable at common law as damages. In the Northern Territory, the common law action for tort is not available to residents of the Territory in respect of injury suffered in a motor accident, and non-residents are precluded from suing for non-economic loss over and above a prescribed amount. Victoria allows the tort action only where the claimant proves a more than 30% impairment of bodily function or the Transport Commission deems it to be a serious injury. Tasmania retains the common law tort in

---

9   *Motor Accidents Compensation Act 1979* (NT); *Motor Accidents (Liability and Compensation) Act 1973* (Tas); *Transport Accidents Act 1986* (Vic); *Motor Accident (Lifetime Care and Support) Act 2006* (NSW); *Motor Accidents Compensation Act 1999* (NSW). As to the width of the usual requirement that the death or injury be one caused by or arising out of the use of a motor vehicle, see *Dickinson v Motor Vehicle Insurance Trust* (1987) 163 CLR 500 — two children who were burned while playing with matches in a car while left inside it when their father went shopping were held to be entitled to claim on the ground that their injuries arose out of the use of a motor vehicle.

its full force. States such as New South Wales and South Australia, which have no or a very limited motor accident scheme, have nevertheless placed considerable restrictions on the recovery of common law damages.

Workers' compensation

[2.45] Statutory compensation for injury suffered at work is universally provided throughout Australia.[10] The usual requirement for eligibility is that the injury should have arisen out of, or in the course of, the employee's employment. Tasmania retains the former need for it to have arisen both out of and in the course of employment. New South Wales, Queensland and the Australian Capital Territory require that the employment should have been a significant factor in causing the injury as well. All the schemes, except possibly Tasmania's, compensate for mental injury. However, New South Wales, Queensland, South Australia and the Australian Capital Territory exclude the case of psychological injury caused by reasonable management action such as that taken in relation to promotion, dismissal or transfer of the employee. Compensation covers wage loss and property damage, together with a sum designed to compensate for so-called non-economic loss where the worker has sustained a permanent injury. The effect of the provision of statutory workers' compensation on the common law action of the employee against the employer varies as between the different jurisdictions. In the Australian Capital Territory and Tasmania the common law survives in full. In the Northern Territory and South Australia it has been altogether abolished, apart from in the latter State in the case of injury caused by the employer's vehicles. Other States have placed considerable restrictions on the availability of the common law right to claim damages.

Social security

[2.50] Typical social security benefits that may be payable to tort victims under the *Social Security Act 1991* (Cth) are disability support benefit, sickness benefit, unemployment benefit and mobility allowance. Payment of the benefit is discretionary and generally is made periodically. Some social security benefits have been held to be deductible from damages awarded for an injury at common law, so that their payment operates to the benefit of the tortfeasor. However, the Act of 1991 provides that these benefits are not generally payable to a person who has received common law damages. If they have been paid, they are recoverable by the Commonwealth from the recipient. This provision largely solves the courts' problem whether to deduct the benefit from common law damages: in the case of the benefits covered by the provision no deduction will be made. The Act also makes provision for the Commonwealth to recover paid benefits from the compensation payer, but since this will only apply where the benefit has gone in reduction of common law damages, the provision previously mentioned will ensure that this is a rare situation.

---

[10]   *Workers Compensation Act 1951* (ACT); *Safety, Rehabilitation and Compensation Act 1988* (Cth); *Workplace Injury Management and Workers Compensation Act 1998* (NSW); *Workers' Compensation and Rehabilitation Act 2003* (Qld); *Workers' Rehabilitation and Compensation Act 1986* (SA); *Workers Rehabilitation and Compensation Act 1988* (Tas); *Accident Compensation Act 1985* (Vic); *Workers' Compensation and Injury Management Act 1981* (WA); *Work Health Act 1986* (NT).

Criminal injuries compensation schemes

[2.55] All States and Territories have legislative provisions enacted for the purpose of compensating victims of crime.[11] One of the main reasons behind the existence of these schemes is the inability of offenders, if they can be found in the first place, to satisfy any judgments made against them in tort. It is misleading to talk of "compensation" in relation to the legislation, since awards are always subject to prescribed maxima and will never cover the victim's losses in the same way as damages in tort. Recovery under an award is no bar to the later bringing of a tort action against the offender, nor is the victim of a crime in Australia now likely to be inconvenienced by the former rule that in cases of felony the criminal proceedings must precede the civil: *Smith v Selwyn* [1914] 3 KB 98.[12]

The various schemes differ in their details but closely resemble each other in their general features. By and large the schemes protect only against injury, which is defined to include death or bodily injury, mental or nervous shock and pregnancy. All criminal offences causing such injury are generally included, although New South Wales requires an "act of violence". The test for eligibility of the injury for compensation has been held to be a purely causal one, not importing tort rules as to remoteness of damage. So in *Fagan v Crimes Compensation Tribunal* (1982) 150 CLR 666, a child's nervous shock on being told of the murder of its mother was held to be compensable, because it occurred "by or as a result of the criminal act" — it did not need to be foreseeable. Payment of the award is discretionary up to a prescribed maximum. Itemisation of the compensable heads of damage is unusual, though present in Victoria. There is generally provision for recovery of the amount awarded from the offender, or from the victim where the latter has obtained damages from the offender. The claim is available to dependants, or in some cases close relatives.

Total no-fault accident compensation

[2.60] Mixed accident compensation schemes, such as Victoria's workers' compensation and motor accidents schemes, encounter the objection that they are undesirable halfway houses, in that not all accident victims receive compensation. The partial retention of the torts system, and hence the need to incur litigation costs, prevents the freeing of resources which would enable a broader based compensation scheme to be established. The logic of this has been accepted in New Zealand, which first established a general accident compensation scheme in 1972 and has maintained it in force subject to amendments, the present position being governed by the *Injury Prevention, Rehabilitation and Compensation Act 2001* (NZ). The benefits of the scheme in terms of cost savings have proved to be considerable, however, more important has been the benefit in terms of social equity, since the vast majority of accident victims receive some form of compensation without the need to prove fault. A necessary concomitant of the scheme is the abolition of the tort action for personal injury that falls within

---

[11] *Victims Support and Rehabilitation Act 1996* (NSW); *Criminal Offence Victims Act 1995* (Qld), s 663; *Victims of Crime Act 2001* (SA); *Victims of Crime Assistance Act 1976* (Tas); *Victims of Crime Assistance Act 1996* (Vic); *Criminal Injuries Compensation Act 2003* (WA); *Victims of Crime (Financial Assistance) Act 1983* (ACT); *Crimes (Victims Assistance) Rules 2002* (NT).

[12] Even in those States which retain the felony/misdemeanour distinction, the courts may allow civil proceedings to precede the determination of the criminal: *Ceasar v Sommer* [1980] 2 NSWLR 929; *Westpac Bank v Halabi* (1988) ACLD 184; but cf *Gypsy Fire v Truth Newspapers Pty Ltd* (1987) 9 NSWLR 382.

the compensation provisions of the scheme, and s 317(1) of the 2001 Act provides for this. The basic purpose of the scheme is to ensure rehabilitation of the victim. This extends to individual, social and vocational rehabilitation under Pt 4 of the Act. During that rehabilitation period, the victim is able to recover fair compensation for personal loss from injury (ss 3, 67) covering medical treatment, rehabilitation costs and loss of earnings. Under the 2001 Act, where the victim is an employee, it is the employer's duty to pay up to 80% of the first week's salary of an injured employee (s 97(2)) and there is also a right to a weekly sum by way of an independence allowance (s 100). Under s 20(2) of the Act there is cover for personal injury (which includes the death of or nervous shock to the victim) caused:

- by accident to the victim (though not to someone other than the victim);
- by gradual process, disease or infection arising out of, and in the course of, the victim's employment;
- by medical misadventure; or
- as a consequence of treatment for personal injury.

With April 2009 marking the 35th anniversary of the scheme's operation, there is, it seems, little support in New Zealand for a return to common law liability for accidents, even on the part of the New Zealand Law Society.

Practice Questions

Revision Questions

2.1 List the possible avenues whereby a person who is injured may recover compensation.

2.2 Identify the possible inadequacies of the torts system.

2.3 How does the role of insurance affect the torts system?

2.4 Could you describe the criminal injuries compensation schemes as no-fault schemes? Why or why not?

Answers to Practice Questions

Revision Questions

2.1 An injured plaintiff may have an action in tort, for example negligence or breach of statutory duty. Depending on where the accident happened the injured person might be able to access a no-fault statutory scheme, for example a workers' compensation or motor accident compensation system. A disabled person who is not a worker and who cannot show fault, can still claim social security. If a faulty product has caused the person's injuries, Pt VA of the *Trade Practices Act 1974* (Cth) may provide a claim. A person injured as a result of criminal activity may apply as a victim of a criminal offence under the legislation of their State.

2.2 The text identifies four main problems:

- Tort law is costly, particularly because of its adversarial nature.
- Tort law benefits only a few people. Many people are not eligible to claim in tort because there is no-one to blame, and even if they are able to identify such a person, the question arises "do they have the ability to pay?"
- The delays cause trauma and additional costs.
- The lump sum can be problematic. It is very difficult to accurately assess a plaintiff's loss.

  Note: In this respect read Patrick Atiyah's two essays, "An Unjust and Inefficient Compensation System" and "What Can We Do About It?", Chs 6 and 8 of *The Damages Lottery* (Hart, 1997), pp 138-158 and 174-193.

2.3 The court is not allowed to acknowledge the presence of the insurance company when determining compensation. However, on reflection it can be seen that tort would not be a suitable avenue for those injured if insurance were not available to pay the claims.

2.4 These schemes provide a very important supplement to the tort system as, typically, perpetrators of violent crimes do not have the funds to pay the award. The funds are financed by taxation. However, they should not be described as no-fault schemes, since an injured person must first establish that they have been the victim of a violent crime before they become entitled to claim.

Tutorial Questions

Discussion Questions

2.1 What are the aims of tort law? Are these aims best achieved through no-fault accident schemes?

2.2 Can the law of negligence be justified as a system of compensation for personal injuries?

2.3 What are the merits of a no-fault accident scheme? Do you see such schemes or the use of first party insurance schemes as preferable regimes of compensation?

2.4 What is a structured settlement? Explain the merits of a structured settlement arrangement. What difficulties, if any, do you see with structured settlement arrangements?

CHAPTER 3

Trespass and Case

Reading

Sappideen, Vines, Grant and Watson, Torts: Commentary and Materials, Chapter 2.

Objectives

This chapter will explain:

- the historical development of trespass and case;
- the English and Australian positions; and
- the distinguishing features of trespass and case.

Principles

Historical development

[3.05] It is desirable to say something about the distinction between trespass and case, not only because it explains the present day shape of the law of torts, but also because, in Australia at least, it still may have effects of substance. In its early development, the common law was very much dependent on the "writ system". A typical litigation involved first the issuing of an appropriate "writ". A writ is a document issued in the Queen's name and under the seal of the Crown. In the early years of the common law an "original writ" provided the basis for commencing every action. The writ set out the cause of action available to a plaintiff in a particular standard form. To be successful in an action, the plaintiff had to ensure that the facts of his or her case were covered by, or fitted into, a standard writ. Where the facts of a case were not covered by a writ, the plaintiff was bound to fail in his or her action as there was no remedy. There were two principal forms of writ in the early days of the common law: trespass and (action on the) case.

Trespass evolved during the 13th century in England as a quasi-criminal proceeding. It covered cases of forcible *direct injury* to the person, or direct interference with land or chattels. Trespass at this early period was both a crime and a tort, both aspects being disposed of by the court in one proceeding. Case, or to give its full title, the action on the case of trespass (that is, in effect by analogy to trespass), evolved later. It was a civil action for damages in respect of injury or damage which was *the indirect or consequential* result of the defendant's act.[1]

Distinction between trespass and case

[3.10] The stock example of the distinction between the two is, nevertheless, the most informative. It was a trespass if the defendant threw a log on to the highway and hit the plaintiff. If, however, the log lay on the highway and the plaintiff drove his horse into it and was injured, it was case.[2] Trespass contained an allegation of forcible or violent conduct directly causing the interference complained of (vi et armis et contra pacem regis). The pleading in case required merely a statement of the facts on which the plaintiff relied. An incorrect choice of pleading led to the plaintiff being non-suited. The action would have to be started again, using the correct pleading. In *Scott v Shepherd* (1773) 2 Black W 892; 96 ER 525, the defendant threw a lit firework into a crowded marketplace. It was thrown on by two other persons, acting in self-preservation, and finally exploded, putting out the plaintiff's eye. The court held that the plaintiff's action in trespass was correctly brought since his injury was a sufficiently direct and immediate result of the defendant's act. Blackstone J dissented, however, on the ground that the injury was indirect because the two intervening persons were free agents and case should have been brought instead. He also observed that if eminent judges could differ on the issue of directness, it hardly seemed just that by making an incorrect decision on

---

[1]   For the historical development, see Milsom, "Not Doing is No Trespass" [1954] CLJ 105; "Trespass from Henry III to Edward III" (1958) 74 LQR 195, 407, 561; Pritchard, "Trespass, Case and the Rule in Williams v Holland" [1964] CLJ 234.

[2]   For this example see the judgment of Fortescue J in *Reynolds v Clarke* (1726) 92 ER 410.

this question the plaintiff should be put to the inconvenience and expense of having to come back to court at a later date.

Figure 3.1

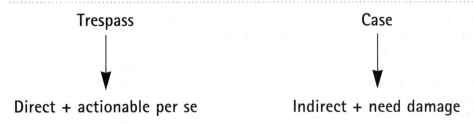

One further characteristic difference between the two forms of action must be mentioned. Since the typical case for which trespass lay was the intentional and direct application of physical force, either to the plaintiff's person, or constituting an invasion of the plaintiff's land or chattels, the plaintiff was not required to show that he or she had suffered any actual physical injury or damage as a result. Trespass was, therefore, actionable per se (although, of course, the plaintiff could claim damages in trespass for any actual injury or damage suffered). Case, however, being associated more with negligent rather than intentional wrongs, and with injury or damage arising indirectly rather than directly, required the plaintiff to prove injury or damage as part of the cause of action.

The following developments then took place. The civil aspects of trespass came to be dealt with exclusively by the civil courts. Trespass retained its criminal function but this was determined on prosecution before the criminal courts. Trespass was applied to all direct physical contacts, even if not forcible, and, as a result of the running-down cases,[3] was also applied to negligent, direct intrusions upon the plaintiff's person or property. In the 19th century, however, the courts decided to allow the plaintiff to sue in the alternative in case for negligently caused injury or damage arising directly. So, here, trespass and case were both available and the plaintiff's difficulty over choice of the correct pleading disappeared: *Williams v Holland* (1833) 10 Bing 112; 131 ER 848.

Finally, and most importantly, the English legislature in the 19th century abolished the forms of action, including trespass and case (*Common Law Procedure Act 1852*), and later provided that all the plaintiff need do was to state the facts upon which he or she relied to establish the cause of action: *Supreme Court of Judicature Act 1873*. If these facts would have amounted to trespass or case prior to the abolition, the plaintiff was entitled to succeed. No longer could the plaintiff lose the action by an incorrect choice of the relevant procedure. Legislation to the same effect has been enacted in all the Australian States.[4]

---

[3] *Leame v Bray* (1803) 3 East 593; 102 ER 724; *Hopper v Reeve* (1817) Taunt 698; 129 ER 278; *Williams v Holland* (1833) 10 Bing 112; 131 ER 848.

[4] *Federal Court Rules 1979*, O 11 r 2; *Court Procedures Rules 2006* (ACT), r 406; *Uniform Civil Procedure Rules 2005* (NSW), r 14.7; *Supreme Court Rules 1987* (NT), O 13 r 13.02; *Uniform Civil Procedure Rules 1999* (Qld), r 149(1); *Supreme Court Civil Rules 2006* (SA), r 98(2); *Supreme Court Rules 2000* (Tas), Div 17 r 227(1); *Supreme Court (General Civil Procedure) Rules 1996* (Vic), O 13 r 13.02; *Rules of the Supreme Court 1971* (WA), O 20 r 8(1).

Later developments

[3.15] The disappearance of trespass and case as forms of action did not mean their disappearance as causes of action. If we define a cause of action as a state of facts which gives rise to a legal remedy before a court, the cause of action in trespass may be defined as intentional or negligent direct interference with the plaintiff's person or property. The cause of action in case may be defined as the intentional or negligent act of the defendant indirectly causing actual injury or damage to the plaintiff. It should be noted that while there was no possibility of overlap between the two causes of action where the injury or damage arose intentionally but indirectly or intentionally but directly, both causes of action were available where it was caused directly by the defendant's negligence. Nothing that happened in the years immediately following the abolition of the forms of action suggested that these causes of action no longer existed. However, a new development took place. Since the plaintiff no longer needed to identify the cause of action as trespass or case, it tended to be called negligence when negligence was the gist of the action, whether the resulting damage arose directly or indirectly, and trespass, where the action was based on an intentional invasion of person or property. At this point negligence came to be regarded as a separate tort, though one having the characteristics of the former action on the case; that is, the burden of proof on all relevant issues including fault resting on the plaintiff and the plaintiff having to prove actual injury or damage as part of the cause of action. As pointed out earlier in this chapter, the tort of trespass could be committed negligently, but doubt arose whether, in the light of the development of negligence itself, negligent trespass had any continuing importance. As regards trespass to the person, the Court of Appeal in England concluded that not only was negligent trespass no longer of importance but that it no longer even existed. Where negligence was the gist of the plaintiff's claim, the tort of negligence was the only available cause of action. Trespass to the person was therefore limited to the case of intentional, direct interference with the plaintiff's person: *Letang v Cooper* [1965] 1 QB 232; confirmed by the House of Lords in *Stubbings v Webb* [1993] 1 All ER 322.

Figure 3.2: Position in England

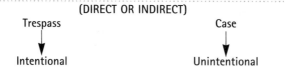

This result, though a rational one, could only have been reached by a process of judicial legislation, and in an earlier case the High Court of Australia had reached a different conclusion. The High Court in *Williams v Milotin* (1957) 97 CLR 465 made the following rulings:

- Where a negligent, direct injury to the person was complained of, the two causes of action were still available and the plaintiff was entitled to choose between them.

- The two causes of action, although they might coexist on the same facts, had distinguishing characteristics that enabled the Court to determine which was relied on (for example, case needed an allegation of want of due care by the defendant and of consequent actual injury, but trespass needed neither).

Figure 3.3: Position in Australia

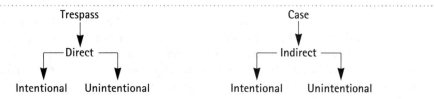

How important is it to resolve this difference of opinion between the Court of Appeal in England and the High Court? Is there any advantage to be gained by framing the cause of action in trespass rather than negligence?

Certain cases decided soon after the removal of the differences in pleading between trespass and case arose out of attempts to succeed in trespass to the person without any need for fault on the defendant's part. In the light of an early decision in *Weaver v Ward* (1616) 80 ER 284 which established the non-liability in trespass of one who was "utterly without fault", these actions were unlikely to succeed. It became established that trespass, whether it occurred on or off the highway, was not a tort of strict liability but required fault on the defendant's part, whether in the form of intentional or negligent wrongdoing: *Holmes v Mather* (1875) LR 10 Ex 261; *Stanley v Powell* [1891] 1 QB 86; *Blacker v Waters* (1928) 28 SR (NSW) 406; *McHale v Watson* (1964) 111 CLR 384.

Onus of proof of fault

[3.20] Fault is therefore necessary in all forms of trespass. The case law just considered concerned trespass to the person, but the same rule undoubtedly applies to trespass to chattels and to land by analogy. There is, however, a difference between trespass and negligence in relation to the burden of proving such fault. In trespass, the former rule seems to have been that the plaintiff need prove only the direct interference arising from the defendant's act. The burden of proof was then on the defendant to show either that the act was involuntary or that the defendant acted neither intentionally nor negligently in relation to that interference (the so-called defence of inevitable accident).[5] In the action on the case, however, there was no doubt that the burden of proof of fault lay on the plaintiff. Australian authority supports the view that the defendant in trespass still must prove inevitable accident. In *McHale v Watson* (1964) 111 CLR 384 the defendant had thrown a sharp piece of metal at a wooden post. The metal had either missed or glanced off the post and struck the plaintiff in the eye. Windeyer J, sitting as a single judge of the High Court acting in its original jurisdiction, held that the burden of proof in an action of trespass lay on the defendant to show that he or she was not at fault (that is, neither intentional, reckless nor negligent). On appeal, the case was decided in the same way, but no objection to the statement of law by the trial judge was made by the judges of the High Court. It should be noted that the case was one of trespass occurring off the highway, but Windeyer J appeared to be laying down a rule for all cases of trespass to the person. In *Venning v Chin* (1974) 10 SASR 299, however, the Supreme Court of South Australia held that in the case of a highway trespass the burden of proof of fault, whether in the form of intentional or negligent conduct, lay

---

5   The clearest evidence for this being the law is *Weaver v Ward* (1616) 80 ER 284.

CHAPTER 3

on the plaintiff, despite the fact that in non-highway trespass the defendant had the burden of proof.

Venning v Chin is a binding authority only in South Australia, although the High Court on appeal decided the case in the same way without disapproving the distinction drawn by the State Supreme Court. But the decision has never been questioned since then and it follows that a distinction must be drawn between highway and non-highway trespasses in the matter of the burden of proof, an unacceptable result for reasons considered below.

Figure 3.4

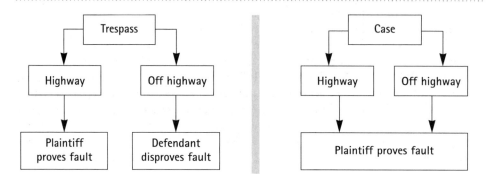

Distinguishing highway and non-highway trespass

[3.25] There are difficulties with drawing the line between highway and non-highway trespasses. Bray CJ recognised the difficulty in *Venning v Chin* (1974) 10 SASR 299. He thought highway trespasses at least included:

- collisions between vehicles on the highway or between vehicle and pedestrians;
- damage to property adjoining the highway caused by a vehicle running off the highway (see *Nickels v City of Melbourne* (1938) 59 CLR 219 in which the defendants' horse and cart backed into the plaintiff's shop window); and
- contacts between things lowered or carried out of such property and people using the highway.

It is arguable, however, that the concept should be limited to highway traffic, vehicular and pedestrian. It would not extend, for example, to the case where one person on the highway throws a stone and hits another person on the highway. Difficulty in drawing the distinction arises where the wrongful act takes place on the highway but the direct contact occurs some way off the highway on private property, for example where part of a motor vehicle is flung into a field and hits the plaintiff, or in the converse case where contact takes place on the highway but as a result of an act occurring off the highway. Whether such cases fall within highway trespass is at the moment not clear.

The distinction drawn by the Australian cases between highway and non-highway trespass as far as the burden of proof of fault is concerned is illogical. If the argument is that one who ventures onto the highway assumes the risk of accidental bodily contacts occurring there and, therefore, must prove fault on the defendant's part, the argument falls down because that person also has the risk of accidental contacts occurring off the highway. If the argument is that direct contact provides presumptive evidence of fault, then highway cases are more likely than non-highway to provide examples of such direct contacts. And if direct highway contact does not provide such presumptive evidence, then it seems that the same should apply to direct contacts wherever they occur. This leads to the more general question of where the burden of proof on the fault issue should lie in trespass generally.

The submission here is that the burden should be on the plaintiff to establish fault on the part of the defendant, whether in the form of intention or negligence. Difficulties commonly associated with the burden of establishing negligence in general are countered by the ability of the plaintiff to rely on circumstantial evidence (such as the position on the road and condition of motor cars after a road accident), and by the evidentiary principle, res ipsa loquitur (the facts speak for themselves). That principle, which in the appropriate case allows the mere facts of the case to afford presumptive evidence of negligence, does not depend on directness of contact between the defendant's act and the plaintiff's person. Rather, it implies that the accident to the plaintiff is one which in the nature of things would not have occurred without negligence on the part of the person controlling the activity in question.

The anomaly of placing the burden of proof of fault on the defendant was pointed out by Kirby P in his dissenting judgment in *Platt v Nutt* (1988) 12 NSWLR 231. He argued that fault being an essential part of the plaintiff's cause of action, the burden of establishing it should be on the plaintiff. It is, perhaps, significant that in no reported Australian decision has the burden of proof rule for non-highway trespass made any difference to the result of the case. In *McHale v Watson* (1964) 111 CLR 384 the High Court found on the facts that negligence had not been established against the defendant without reference to the burden of proof. In *Platt*, in which the slamming of a glass door by the defendant in the plaintiff's direction had caused injury to the plaintiff's hand, the majority in the New South Wales Court of Appeal found it unnecessary to examine the fault issue since the plaintiff had caused her own injury by voluntarily putting her hand towards the door as it was closing.[6] Most revealing of all is *Hackshaw v Shaw* (1984) 155 CLR 614. In that case the defendant had fired a shot in the direction of a motor car containing two trespassers who had been stealing petrol from a bowser on his land, and had injured one of them (the plaintiff in the action). The case thus was a clear example of trespassory contact occurring off the highway. However, this was simply ignored by the High Court, which treated the matter as one requiring application of the rules of the tort of negligence (including the burden of establishing that the defendant was negligent being with the plaintiff). Further, this required the plaintiff to establish that the defendant owed her a duty of care as a trespasser, even though by relying on trespass she in theory ought to have been able to succeed without needing to establish a duty of care on the part of the defendant. The case suggests that trespass has become altogether redundant in the negligence area, though that conclusion has yet to be explicitly drawn.[7]

Granted that the burden of proof rule for trespass confers only a nugatory advantage to plaintiffs, the advantages of that tort over negligence for plaintiffs is now limited to the case of intentional or reckless trespass. Trespass, unlike negligence, is actionable per se (without proof of damage). When the plaintiff has suffered an

---

[6]   The majority did express the view that the present rule as to burden of proof of fault was not unsatisfactory. Kirby P found for the plaintiff on the ground that her act of raising her hand towards the door was inadvertent and not truly voluntary and that she had proved the defendant's fault.

[7]   In favour of placing the burden of proof on the fault issue in all forms of trespass: *Fowler v Lanning* [1968] 1 QB 232; *Beals v Hayward* [1960] NZLR 131; *Walmesley v Humenick* [1954] 2 DLR 232; but another Canadian decision is in line with the Australian position: *Larin v Goshen* (1975) 56 DLR (2d) 719.

intentional or reckless trespass without suffering any injury or damage, there may be an entitlement to substantial damages in the form of aggravated or exemplary damages. Also, an intentional trespass may operate as a tort of strict liability, since at common law reasonable mistake is no defence. Again, one who intentionally trespasses on the plaintiff's property, claiming a right to do so, may be sued in trespass to determine the issue of title. These points emerge more fully in the chapters on trespass in Section 2 of this book. An incidental advantage relevant to the choice of cause of action as between trespass and case (or negligence) pertained to the limitation period. Some Limitation Acts created different limitation periods for trespass and case (or negligence), and it was the effect of the High Court's decision in *Williams v Milotin* (1957) 97 CLR 465 that the plaintiff could choose the more favourable limitation period by selecting the appropriate cause of action. In *Williams* itself, the advantage to the plaintiff lay with the action on the case rather than with trespass, but the reasoning of the High Court did not treat this as material. However, this advantage now seems to have largely, if not totally, disappeared, since modern Limitation Acts do not differentiate between limitation periods according to the cause of action. For example, actions in tort for personal injury must be brought within the same limitation period no matter what the cause of action.[8] Other possible advantages for trespass over negligence seem now to be non-existent or of merely theoretical interest. For example, trespass does not allow the plaintiff to sidestep the duty of care requirement in negligence, as *Hackshaw* demonstrates. Negligent trespass in the form of false imprisonment enables a person who has been detained temporarily without suffering injury or other loss to establish a cause of action, but the claim is unlikely to attract anything beyond nominal damages.

Trespass and case in modern tort law

[3.30] Trespass is now generally only of importance in those cases where the defendant has intentionally infringed the plaintiff's interest. As well as trespass to the person (comprising assault, battery and false imprisonment), there are the torts of trespass to chattels and trespass to land.

Case is the ancestor of the modern tort of negligence. The essential characteristics of negligence are those of case (as the High Court pointed out in *Williams v Milotin* (1957) 97 CLR 465) as are those of other torts such as conversion, nuisance, defamation and the various "economic torts". It is, in fact, the ancestor of every common law tort not deriving from trespass.

Practice Questions

Revision Questions

3.1   Can you identify instances when bringing an action in trespass may be more attractive to a plaintiff?

---

[8]   Including that in South Australia, whose original limitation provision gave rise to the decision in *Williams v Milotin* (1957) 97 CLR 465: *Limitation of Actions Act 1936* (SA), s 36.

Answers to Practice Questions

Revision Questions

3.1 Since courts in Australia allow a plaintiff to take an action in negligent trespass as well as negligence (when the act of the defendant has been unintentional), this question requires students to consider the requirements of these actions that might be particularly beneficial to a plaintiff in certain circumstances.

- *No need to prove damage in trespass* — Trespass is useful, as there is no need to prove damage. Circumstances where a plaintiff has suffered humiliating or insulting remarks may be an instance when trespass alone can help, for example distress and mere grief are "real" problems but they do not produce "actual" injuries as required by negligence. In trespass a plaintiff can claim aggravated damages. However, if the plaintiff has not suffered damage, an action in negligence is not possible anyway because, being derived from case harm is necessary for such an action.

- *No need to show a duty of care* — Trespass does not require a plaintiff to prove a duty of care.

- *Onus of proof shifts* — In an off-highway situation, once the plaintiff proves direct injury in a trespass claim, it is up to the defendant to show that he or she was not negligent.

- *Contributory negligence* — The High Court in *Horkin v North Melbourne Football Club* [1983] 1 VR 153 and *Fontin v Katapodis* (1962) 108 CLR 177 found that contributory negligence does not apply in a trespass action concerning off-highway matters. However in relation to highway cases it could very well be available: see the judges' comments in *Venning v Chin* (1974) 10 SASR 299 and in *Horkin*.

Tutorial Questions

Discussion Questions

3.1 Do you agree that an anomaly has arisen in the treatment of trespass in Australia?

3.2 Should Australia follow the English example and make the distinction between trespass and case turn on whether the act was intentional or unintentional? Is that in fact the only distinguishing feature of the torts in England?

CHAPTER 3

SECTION

2

Intentional Interference with Person or Property

Intentional interference with the person or property of the plaintiff will either be trespassory or non-trespassory.

Trespassory interference takes three forms:

- trespass to the person;
- trespass to chattels; and
- trespass to land.

Trespass to the person may comprise assault, battery or false imprisonment. All forms of trespass require a direct invasion of the plaintiff's interest and fault on the part of the defendant in producing that invasion. Trespass is actionable per se (that is, without proof of injury or damage) because the interests protected by it are considered so important that protection is given whether or not damage has been suffered.

Property and/or possession of chattels are mainly protected by three torts: trespass, conversion and detinue.

Possession of land is protected by trespass to land. Recovery of land from one wrongfully in possession of it is achieved by means of the action of ejectment.

An action on the case lies for intentional, indirect (non-trespassory) interference with person or property causing actual injury or damage. There is also a remedy in tort for personal injury or mental harm where this arises from a wilful act of the defendant calculated to cause such injury or harm.

Proving an intentional wrong may entitle the plaintiff to a greater measure of damages than that representing the actual injury or damage suffered. For example, aggravated damages may be awarded based on the humiliating or insulting nature of the defendant's conduct (though justified by the courts as being within the compensatory function of damages, since it compensates for injury to feelings). The court may also award exemplary (or punitive) damages, which are intended as a punishment of the defendant rather than as compensation of the plaintiff.

CHAPTER 4

Trespass to the Person

Reading

Sappideen, Vines, Grant and Watson, *Torts: Commentary and Materials*, Chapter 3.

Objectives

This chapter will explain:

* the concept of intentional direct interference with the person;
* the nature of trespass generally;
* battery as a form of trespass;
* assault as a form of trespass;
* false imprisonment;
* remedies for trespass to the person; and
* intentional indirect interference with the person.

Principles

Introduction

[4.05] As indicated in Chapter 1, fault in torts is mainly based on either intention or negligence. In this chapter we consider those torts that protect the plaintiff against intentional interference with his or her person.

Trespass generally

What is trespass?

[4.10] Trespass is defined as the intentional or negligent act of the defendant that directly interferes with or causes an injury to the plaintiff or the plaintiff's property without the plaintiff's consent or lawful justification. Trespass is a generic tort, of which there are three forms:

- trespass to the person;
- trespass to land; and
- trespass to chattels.

Figure 4.1: What is trespass?

- Intentional or negligent act of the defendant which directly interferes with or causes an injury to the plaintiff or the plaintiff's property without lawful justification.
- Common elements of trespass:
  - positive and voluntary act by defendant;
  - interference must be direct;
  - injury may be with the plaintiff or the plaintiff's property;
  - no lawful justification;
  - actionable per se;
  - fault: intentional or negligent act.

What is trespass?

- Intentional or negligent act of the defendant which directly interferes with or causes an injury to the plaintiff or the plaintiff's property without lawful justification.
- Common elements of trespass:
  - positive and voluntary act by defendant;

— interference must be direct;

— interference may be with the plaintiff or the plaintiff's property;

— no lawful justification;

— actionable per se;

— fault: intentional or negligent act.

All forms of civil trespass have the following features in common:

- The defendant must commit a voluntary act. Trespass can therefore not be brought where the act in question had been brought about by an epileptic fit (*Public Transport Commission (NSW) v Perry* (1977) 137 CLR 107) or by the force of a third party (*Smith v Stone* (1647) 82 ER 533 — defendant thrown on to land by third party did not commit trespass). Nor can it be committed by an omission to act: "not doing is no trespass".[1]

- The interference with the plaintiff must follow directly upon the defendant's act. Directness raises an issue of fact. Immediacy is one means of establishing directness, as the log on the highway example illustrates: see *Reynolds v Clarke* (1726) 92 ER 410 where it is said that the throwing of a log on the highway and hitting someone in the process is a trespass but where the log lands on the road and later trips a passerby, it is an indirect interference and therefore not trespass. *Scott v Shepherd* (1773) 2 Black W 892; 96 ER 525 (throwing on of a lighted firecracker by two individuals before exploding in the plaintiff's face) shows that the presence of intervening causes does not rule out directness where, for example (and as in that case), they are human acts of self-preservation committed in the agony of the moment. However, cases concerning trespass to land (discussed in Chapter 6) show that immediacy is not always necessary where there are no intervening causes between the act and its consequences.

- The defendant's trespassory act must be accompanied by either an intentional, reckless or negligent mental state. Trespass is no longer (if it ever was) a tort of strict liability. Which party must prove this is discussed in Chapter 1.

Fault: the intentional act in trespass

[4.15] A central element in trespass is that the act of the defendant must be "intentional". The concept of intention needs consideration at this point. The defendant's intention is judged in relation to the consequences of the act, not the act itself (to which a test of "voluntariness" rather than intention is applied). This means that the defendant must have intended the relevant interference with the plaintiff's person required by the tort in question. It is not necessary though for the defendant to intend to trespass. So a man who embraces a woman thinking her to be his wife commits battery, no matter how reasonable his belief, since mistake is not a defence to trespass. So, also, one who walks on another's land thinking wrongly that he or she owns it commits trespass to the land. A person who seized goods thinking he had a right to their possession was found to have committed trespass, without reference to the question whether the belief was

---

[1]   *Innes v Wylie* (1844) 174 ER 800, in which a police officer "stood like a wall" in front of the plaintiff such as to obstruct the plaintiff's path.

reasonable. The defendant acted "at his peril": *Colwill v Reeves* (1811) 170 ER 1257. Intention is distinguished from recklessness as to consequences but both are sufficient to satisfy fault for the purposes of trespass. Recklessness arises where the consequences of the defendant's act are so likely that they are taken to have been foreseen by the defendant, but not so substantially certain that they are taken to have been intended by the defendant. Recklessness, therefore, means an indifference to consequences on the part of the defendant (rather than a desire to bring them about) or a knowledge that they will occur. Recklessness as a concept has, up to now, played very little part in the law of tort possibly on the ground that, unlike the case of criminal law where it is of importance, a trespass action can be maintained on the basis of negligence. But case law allowing an award of increased damages for reckless conduct on the defendant's part may well increase the importance of establishing recklessness: *Midalco Pty Ltd v Rabenalt* [1989] VR 461; *Coloca v BP Australia Ltd* [1992] 2 VR 441. Intention and recklessness are subjective states of mind. In this they are distinguishable from negligence, which requires to be determined objectively; that is, by the standard of a reasonable person in the defendant's position.

Forms of trespass to the person

[4.20] There are three forms of trespass to the person. These are:

- battery;
- assault; and
- false imprisonment.

Assault, battery and false imprisonment are all common law misdemeanours. Apart from the fact that their mens rea is limited to intention, these crimes are, in most respects, identical to their civil counterparts, so that many of the relevant authorities are criminal cases.[2]

Figure 4.2: Specific forms of trespass

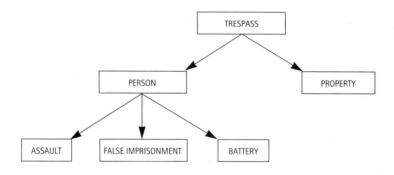

---

[2] Where an intentional assault, battery or false imprisonment is alleged to have been committed, the civil standard of proof on the balance of probabilities (rather than the criminal standard of proof beyond a reasonable doubt) applies, but the proof required must reflect the gravity of the allegation: *Rejfek v McElroy* (1965) 112 CLR 517; *Lemmer v Bertram* (1971) 2 SASR 397; *Brown v G J Coles & Co Ltd* (1985) 8 FCR 304.

Battery

[4.25] Battery is the intentional or negligent act of the defendant which directly causes a physical interference with the body of the plaintiff without the plaintiff's consent or lawful justification. As a form of trespass, it has the general elements of the tort common to all forms of trespass, that is:

- fault;
- directness;
- absence of lawful justification; and
- interference with the rights of the plaintiff.

Battery is distinct from other forms of trespass by reason of the form of interference involved, namely physical interference with the person of the plaintiff. The interests protected by battery include physical integrity and personal dignity: *Stingel v Clark* (2006) 226 CLR 442 at [57] per Gummow J.

A typical example of a battery is where one person hits or pushes another without lawful justification. Battery need not be forcible, nor need the plaintiff know of its being committed. It may, therefore, be battery to move a sleeping person. It may be committed through the use of a weapon, such as a missile or a gun. It is battery to throw water over clothes being worn by the plaintiff, seemingly without the need for any contact with the actual body of the plaintiff, though trespass to chattels would serve equally well here: *Pursell v Horn* (1838) 112 ER 966. It is battery to push over the chair in which the plaintiff is sitting or to snatch a book from the plaintiff's hand.[3] In *Kaye v Robertson* [1991] FSR 62 the Court of Appeal accepted the possibility that shining the flashlight of a camera in the eyes of a hospital patient, thereby causing him injury, could be battery. To cut the rope on which the plaintiff is climbing is arguably battery, since the defendant has made use of the force of gravity to affect the plaintiff's person, and there is no difference in principle between that and using the force necessary to propel a bullet from a gun. This principle is further supported by an American case in which it was held that battery was committed when a chair was removed from beneath the plaintiff as she was about to sit down, thereby causing her to fall and injure herself: *Garratt v Dailey* (1955) 279 P 2d 1091.

Figure 4.3: Battery – summary

- An intentional or negligent act of the defendant which directly causes a physical interference with the body of the plaintiff without lawful justification.
- Distinguishing element: physical interference with plaintiff's body.
- Essence of the tort is protection of the person of plaintiff. An act short of physical contact is therefore not a battery.

---

[3] See also *Hopper v Reeve* (1871) 129 ER 278 (collision with coach containing plaintiff, throwing plaintiff out of coach); *Fisher v Carrousel Motor Hotel Inc* (1967) 424 SW 2d 627 (snatching plate from plaintiff's hand).

Is hostility an element?

[4.30] As indicated earlier, a typical form of battery is where one hits or pushes another without lawful justification. Indeed "the least touching of another in anger is battery": *Cole v Turner* (1704) 87 ER 907 per Holt CJ. However, it is important to note that "hostility" is not an element in the tort despite *Wilson v Pringle* [1987] QB 237. *Wilson* held that the pulling of the plaintiff's satchel from his shoulder in the course of a schoolboy prank, thereby causing him to fall and suffer injury, was not battery in the absence of hostility on the defendant's part. It proceeded on the basis of an unwarranted extrapolation from cases in which there is no battery because the contact with the plaintiff's person is of an everyday variety to which the plaintiff is deemed to consent, for example jostling in a football crowd or congratulatory back-slapping. Whilst those cases are correct, they do not permit a general conclusion that hostility is necessary for battery as *Collins v Wilcock* [1984] 3 All ER 374 (which *Wilson* purported to follow) highlights. In *Collins* it was found to be a battery for a police officer to lay a restraining hand on the accused's arm otherwise than in the course of lawful arrest.

In holding that a surgical operation was a battery in the absence of the plaintiff's consent, a later case refused to follow *Wilson* on the grounds that it was inconsistent with *Collins*: *T v T* [1988] 1 All ER 613. The hostility requirement is also inconsistent with a decision of the High Court of Australia in a criminal case: *Boughey v The Queen* (1986) 161 CLR 10.

Hostility on the part of the defendant would, of course, take a contact normally within the category of the everyday permitted variety outside that category, although that would be true of any other form of wrongful intention or even negligence.[4]

Acts and omissions in trespass

[4.35] Trespass cannot in general be committed by an omission to act. But in *Fagan v Metropolitan Police Commissioner* [1969] 1 QB 439 the accused had accidentally driven his car onto the foot of a police constable. The accused, becoming aware of this, deliberately delayed in reversing his car for a reasonable period of time. He was convicted, by the majority of the court, of a criminal assault. There is logical force in the dissenting judgment of Bridge J who argued that, at the time the accused did the act of driving he had no mens rea, and after he had formed the mens rea, he did not act. There is also, however, practical force in the majority decision that the defendant committed trespass, not on the basis supported by the majority, but on the basis that there was a continuing act by the accused (rather than treating the consequences of the act as continuing at the time the accused formed his wrongful intent).

In the criminal case of *R v Latimer* (1886) 17 QBD 359 the accused, A, was convicted of unlawfully wounding B although the intention behind his action was to strike C. In the United States, a doctrine of "transferred intent" has arisen under which C could succeed against A in a civil action for battery. This doctrine seems to serve no purpose in Australia, although there is a dictum of a High Court judge in its support: per Latham CJ in *Bunyan v Jordan* (1936) 57 CLR 1 at 12. C would in any case be entitled to succeed in actions of trespass or negligence against A, based on A's negligent or even reckless intent towards C. Where an element of recklessness could be shown,

---

[4]   See, eg, the award of £1000 damages for assault (that is battery) arising from a "vice-like handshake and a friendly flick to the stomach" in *Leach v Findon, Daily Telegraph*, 24 March 1994.

C would have a claim for aggravated and/or exemplary damages. An inability to establish intent towards C on A's part is no real disadvantage to the plaintiff here.

Consent of plaintiff in battery

[4.40] As a form of trespass, battery always involves the absence of lawful justification. Consent is lawful justification. The absence of consent may be a good indication of the absence of lawful justification. However, it is important to stress that the absence of consent does not necessarily mean that there is no lawful justification. For example, where a police officer makes an arrest, the person being arrested may not consent to the physical contact, but this does not make the contact necessarily unlawful.

Battery is defined to exclude a requirement that the plaintiff should have to prove his or her absence of consent to the contact, though there is some authority that absence of consent must be established by the plaintiff.[5] Consent to battery is dealt with in Chapter 7.

Assault

[4.45] Assault is the intentional or negligent act or threat of the defendant that directly places the plaintiff in reasonable apprehension of an imminent physical interference with his or her person, or the person of someone under his or her control. Like battery, assault protects physical integrity and personal dignity.

Figure 4.4: Assault – summary

- There must be a direct threat.
- In general, mere words are not actionable.
- In general, conditional threats are not actionable.
- The apprehension must be reasonable: the test is objective.
- The interference must be imminent.

The tort requires the plaintiff to apprehend physical interference to be committed against him or herself, or someone under their control, by the defendant. So a defendant saying insulting words at a plaintiff is unlikely to be an assault because there is no threatened physical interference. Words spoken by the defendant may be relevant in interpreting physical gestures that would otherwise be threatening or ambiguous. In *Tuberville v Savage* (1669) 86 ER 684 the defendant's laying his hand on the handle of his sword in front of the plaintiff was found to be no assault on the ground that it was accompanied by the words: "If it were not assize-time, I would not take such language from you." On the other hand, in *Fogden v Wade* [1945] NZLR 724 the accused's following the female complainant at a short distance away from her, back to her lodgings, was an assault because it was accompanied by the making of an immoral suggestion. Assault

---

5   *Christopherson v Bare* (1848) 11 QB 473 at 477; 116 ER 554; contra *Sibley v Milutinovic* [1990] Aust Torts Reports 81-013; also McHugh J in *Department of Health & Community Services v B* (1992) 175 CLR 218 at 310-311.

requires proof of an intention (or recklessness or negligence) by the defendant to create in the plaintiff an apprehension of imminent physical interference. It does not require an intention to actually do the physical interference: *Rixon v Star City Casino Pty Ltd* (2001) 53 NSWLR 98.

Reasonable apprehension

[4.50] "Apprehension" in the context of assault means to anticipate physical interference in the knowledge and expectation that it will take place. Fear is not necessary although its existence helps to show apprehension. Some writers take the view that the plaintiff's apprehension must be reasonable.[6] It may be agreed that in the case of negligent assault, apprehension in order to be foreseeable should be reasonable, but negligent assault is of no practical importance. If, in contrast, the defendant intends to raise apprehension in the plaintiff and the plaintiff actually experiences that apprehension, there seems to be no reason why that apprehension should have to be reasonable. This draws support from the obiter dicta of Bray CJ in *Macpherson v Beath* (1975) 12 SASR 174 at 177: "if the defendant intentionally puts in fear of immediate violence an exceptionally timid person known to him to be so then the unreasonableness of the fear may not prevent conviction".

Words alone as assault

[4.55] It now appears to be recognised that assault may be committed by words alone, provided that they directly raise in the plaintiff's mind the apprehension of a physical interference by the defendant. There seems no reason to doubt that in certain circumstances words alone are just as potent as acts as a means of arousing the necessary apprehension in the plaintiff. An early case, *Read v Coker* (1853) 13 CB 850; 138 ER 1437,[7] accepted in principle that words spoken between parties in each other's presence may constitute assault, though in that case there were also threatening actions. However, Jervis CJ merely observed: "there was a threat of violence, exhibiting an intention to assault, and a present ability to carry the threat into execution".

In accordance with the above, a conditional threat of violence is assault, provided there is the necessary apprehension of imminent violence if the threat is not complied with. The cases have concerned a combination of verbal threat and threatening physical gestures, but the latter seems unnecessary as a matter of law. In *Police v Greaves* [1964] NZLR 295 the threat of a knife attack upon police if they approached further or did not leave the premises immediately, made by a person brandishing a carving-knife, was held to be assault. But a conditional threat of force, which the defendant is entitled to use, is not assault. So, an occupier of land may legitimately threaten a trespasser on the land with the use of reasonable force in order to induce the trespasser's departure, since the occupier is entitled to use that force: see [7.60]. However, the force threatened must not exceed the privilege the occasion gives rise to. A taxi driver who produced a knife when threatened with a minor physical assault by another taxi driver committed assault. Although an occasion for self-defence existed, the use of a knife exceeded what the law allowed as self-defence in those circumstances: *Rozsa v Samuels* [1969] SASR 205.

---

[6]   Trindade and Cane, *The Law of Torts in Australia* (4th ed, OUP, 2007), p 53.

[7]   See further Williams, "Assault and Words" (1957) Crim LR 219; Handford, "Tort Liability for Threatening or Insulting Words" (1976) 54 Can Bar Rev 563.

Imminent interference

[4.57] There must be at least a possibility of physical contact for there to be a reasonable apprehension of imminent physical contact. If there is no means of carrying the threat into effect, there can be no assault (eg, *Thomas v National Union of Mineworkers (South Wales)* [1986] Ch 20). However, it is not necessary that the parties be in close proximity or that the threat be carried out by the defendant in person. Where the parties are not in each other's presence there would be no difficulty in finding an assault; for example, where the defendant telephones the plaintiff informing him that he has placed a bomb in the plaintiff's room, which is about to go off presently. However, a verbal threat of future violence made, for example over the telephone or by letter or email, creates a greater problem. In *Barton v Armstrong* [1969] 2 NSWR 451 Taylor J refused to strike out a cause of action in assault based on a telephoned threat of future violence, but gave no clear indication as to the circumstances in which assault could be established. In particular, his proposed test of "how immediate does the fear of physical violence have to be" has received criticism. In *Zanker v Vartzokas* (1988) 34 A Crim R 11 White J held that the correct question should be: "How immediate must the threatened violence be after the utterance of the threat which creates the fear?"

In *Zanker's* case, White J found an assault proved on the following facts: a young woman voluntarily entered the accused's van but asked to be let out when he offered her money for sexual favours. The accused accelerated and refused to let her out, saying: "I am going to take you to my mate's house. He will really fix you up." Although the threat made here was one of future violence the accused was convicted of assault since the violence threatened would occur at the end of a period of imprisonment imposed by the accused and with a high degree of certainty. There was, therefore, the necessary relationship of immediacy between the feared violence and the threat. As a matter of principle, there seems to be no good reason why a person should in any situation escape liability for threatening future violence. Arguably the test of immediacy should be satisfied where the defendant has created an immediate fear of future violence at least where that violence cannot be avoided by the plaintiff. Where the plaintiff has acted on a threat of future violence to his or her loss, the defendant commits the tort of intimidation: see [19.70].

False imprisonment

[4.60] False imprisonment is the intentional or negligent act of the defendant that directly causes the total restraint on the liberty of the plaintiff and thereby confines the plaintiff to a delimited area without lawful justification. The tort reflects the common law's interest in protecting individual liberty and freedom of movement.

The act involved

[4.65] False imprisonment is distinguishable from battery in that the defendant's act need have no physical effect upon the plaintiff's person. A wrongful arrest, for example, may be committed without any laying on of hands. In *Symes v Mahon* [1922] SASR 447 the defendant, mistakenly thinking the plaintiff to be a person for whom the defendant held a warrant for arrest, ordered the plaintiff to accompany him to Adelaide by train the following day. This the plaintiff did, travelling in a separate compartment from the defendant. On arrival in Adelaide, the plaintiff and defendant separated, while the plaintiff was allowed to book in at a hotel before travelling to court, at which point the mistake was discovered and the plaintiff allowed to leave. This was held to be a wrongful arrest from the time the train journey commenced until the time the plaintiff was allowed to leave the court, since during that period the plaintiff had submitted to the defendant's control. Another example of this is *Myer Stores Ltd Ltd v Soo* [1991] 2 VR 597 in which the plaintiff was confronted by an employee of Myer and two policemen, and required to go to the store's office where he was interviewed for an hour and then charged with theft. This was held to be imprisonment by all three, since the plaintiff was under direct restraint, even though there had been no physical invasion of his person. False imprisonment is distinguishable from assault in that it does not require the plaintiff to apprehend physical interference by the defendant. In *Innes v Wylie* (1844) 1 Car & K 257; 174 ER 800 the court observed that where a constable stood outside the door of a meeting room in order to deter entry into the room, this could not have been, without more, an assault against those who were deterred from entering. If we alter the facts and assume the presence of the constable inside the room to deter exit, this again would not have been assault of those in the room but would have amounted to false imprisonment.

Since false imprisonment is a form of trespass, the imprisonment must follow directly upon the defendant's act. Where it follows indirectly, the imprisonment must cause actual damage in order to support an action for negligence or an action on the case for intentional, indirect infliction of damage. In *Sayers v Harlow UDC* [1958] 1 WLR 623 the plaintiff became locked inside the cubicle of the defendant's lavatory. The imprisonment arose because of the defective and negligent maintenance of the lock of the cubicle door by the defendants. The plaintiff climbed to the top of the cubicle wall in order to attempt an escape but then slipped and injured herself. She recovered damages in negligence from the defendants, since her act of climbing the wall was not in the circumstances unreasonable and did not operate to interrupt causation. In the absence of injury to herself, however, the plaintiff would have had no cause of action since her imprisonment arose indirectly and false imprisonment would not have been available. This rests on the assumption that the imprisonment itself would not have amounted to actual damage for the purpose of suing in negligence. However, in *De Freville v Dill* (1927) 96 LJKB 1056 the court held that an action for negligence lay against a medical practitioner who had negligently certified the plaintiff to be insane, so causing an order to be made by a third party for her detention in an asylum for two days (after which she was released on being found to be sane). The defendant did not directly imprison the plaintiff, so that he could not have been liable for false imprisonment. Further, the only damage capable of sustaining the negligence action was the imprisonment itself; nevertheless, UK£50 damages was awarded. The question at issue here was not discussed by the court, but it may be that courts will distinguish between indirect imprisonment (which causes mere temporary inconvenience) and imprisonment such as that in *De Freville* (which is capable of causing damage to the plaintiff's reputation or good standing), recognising the latter as actual damage. An earlier Australian case, *Smith v Iffla* (1881) 7 VLR (L) 435 is to the same effect as *De Freville*. Australia, of course, continues to allow an action for negligent false imprisonment where the imprisonment arises directly. But in the absence of any damaging effects consequent on the imprisonment, the plaintiff could expect to receive no more than nominal damages in such a case.

False imprisonment by omission

[4.70] Like other forms of trespass, false imprisonment cannot, in general, be committed by omission to act. There seems to be good reason, however, for applying the reasoning in *Fagan v Metropolitan Police Commissioner* [1969] 1 QB 439 to false imprisonment. If the defendant has without fault directly imprisoned the plaintiff, the defendant would then be liable if he or she fails to take reasonable steps to release the plaintiff once the plaintiff's predicament is discovered. Fagan also supports liability in the situation where the defendant, with the plaintiff's consent, imprisons the plaintiff, but subject to an agreement that the defendant will release the plaintiff at an agreed time. The defendant should be liable in false imprisonment for failure to release the plaintiff at that time. Directness is satisfied by the original act of locking up the plaintiff, even though this is lawful by reason of the plaintiff's consent. This result is supported in principle by the decision of the House of Lords in *Herd v Weardale Steel, Coal & Coke Co* [1915] AC 67, although the decision in that case created a different problem, that of the withdrawal of consent before the agreed time for release. In that case, the defendants' employees were taken down to their work as miners by means of a lift that was controlled and operated by the defendants' servants. The plaintiffs had been taken down in the lift to begin work on their shift but they refused to complete the shift and demanded to be taken back to the surface, arguing that the work was dangerous. The defendants' manager refused for some time to allow the lift to be used for this purpose, even when the lift was lying vacant at the bottom of the shaft for 20 minutes. Their action for false imprisonment failed because the defendants had no duty to take positive action to release the plaintiffs beyond the contractual obligation that arose at the termination of the shift.

A number of points may be made regarding this decision of the House of Lords. The case was not one of pure omission since the plaintiffs were initially imprisoned by the act of the defendants. The House of Lords' reasoning was largely based on consent, but although the plaintiffs clearly consented to the initial imprisonment, and although they were contractually bound to work the shift, this does not seem to amount to consent to being imprisoned to complete the shift. The House of Lords did not determine whether the plaintiffs were in breach of contract, but even if they were, this should not affect the issue as there is no privilege to detain people in order to enforce performance of their contract. Again, the fact that the defendants were not in breach of their contractual obligation to the plaintiffs was irrelevant, since a duty to act could arise independently of contract. The decision seems, therefore, to rest on no very firm basis.[8] There seems, in fact, to be no clear reason why even a person who has given a clear consent to being detained by the defendant for a certain period of time should not be able to revoke consent before the expiry of the period and demand release, as long as that demand is capable of being satisfied without the making of unreasonable demands on the defendant.

Liberty is an interest highly valued by the law. In general, however, false imprisonment cannot be committed by omission to act, but it is not clear how absolute the rule concerning omission is. For example, is an occupier of land entitled to take no steps to release a person who, without any act on the part of the occupier, becomes imprisoned on the land? In the absence of a direct act of imprisonment, false imprisonment appears

---

[8] For the view that *Herd* is wrongly decided, see Glanville Williams, "Two Cases on False Imprisonment" in *Essays on Law, Justice and Equity*.

not to lie. In the present state of the law, the imprisoned person must, it seems, prove injury in order to prove a cause of action in negligence.

What is imprisonment?

[4.75] In the first place, it is clear that imprisonment does not require the use of a prison. Any form of deprivation of liberty is sufficient, even for a short period of time (for example, imprisonment inside a moving car) and that restraint may be through physical restraint or mental coercion. Coercion may be comprised of a threat againt the plaintiff, another person or it seems, property.

But there must be a wrongful imprisonment. The House of Lords has held that the detention of a prisoner in gaol under allegedly intolerable conditions cannot constitute false imprisonment, although it may amount to other torts: *R v Deputy Governor of Parkhurst Prison* [1992] 1 AC 58.

The better opinion appears to be that a person may be falsely imprisoned although that person does not know of the detention until after it is over. This is generally supported on the basis that the imprisonment may affect interests other than freedom of movement protected by the tort, for example reputation or economic interests. This was the basis of the judgment of Atkin LJ in *Meering v Graham-White Aviation* (1919) 122 LT 44, in which a majority of the English Court of Appeal held that the plaintiff had been falsely imprisoned by the stationing of two police outside a room in which he was being questioned about certain thefts from the defendants, his employers. The police would have prevented his leaving had he wished to, but the plaintiff did not discover their presence until after he left the room. *Meering* was contrary to the case of *Herring v Boyle* (1834) 149 ER 1126, in which it was held that a schoolmaster who refused to release the plaintiff schoolboy from school until fees were paid did not commit false imprisonment, since no act was committed against the boy (the refusal being made to the boy's mother) and the boy did not know of his detention. *Herring v Boyle* received the disapproval of the House of Lords in *Murray v Minister of Defence* [1988] 1 WLR 692, which stated the law to be in conformity with *Meering* (although this was obiter since the conclusion of fact in the case was that the plaintiff there probably knew she was under detention even though she hadn't actually been informed of this). The problem in *Herring v Boyle* of there being no act aimed at the boy, seems to disappear, granted that a clear intention to detain was expressed to the mother, and that there is no need for a physical act for false imprisonment to occur.

In support of Atkin LJ's reasoning in *Meering*, it is clear that damages for injury to reputation may be awarded in the tort of false imprisonment. In *Walter v Alltools Ltd* (1944) 61 TLR 39 the plaintiff had been wrongfully detained by the defendants on suspicion of a theft. The defendants' behaviour subsequent to the plaintiff's release, and their expressions of opinion before the trial, indicated that they continued to maintain that their actions had been justified. The trial judge's award of UK£100 damages was upheld on appeal. Lawrence LJ observed:

> *In my opinion any evidence which shows or tends to show that the defendant is persevering in the charge ... is evidence which may be given for the purpose of aggravating the damages. In the same way, the defendant would be entitled to give any evidence which tended to show that he had withdrawn or had apologised for having made the charge [that is, for the purpose of limiting the award of damages].*

In *Myer Stores Ltd v Soo* [1991] 2 VR 597 an award of $5,000 damages for false imprisonment by the trial judge was increased to $10,000 by the Appeal Court, on the basis that Myer had persisted in its expressed suspicion of the plaintiff's guilt, and no apology was forthcoming.

Authority is lacking on the converse case, where there is no imprisonment but the defendant has induced in the plaintiff's mind the belief that he or she is imprisoned, for example by telling the plaintiff falsely that the plaintiff's house is patrolled by armed guards: *Harnett v Bond* [1925] AC 669. There seems no reason why this should not constitute imprisonment; the plaintiff need not put his or her rights to the test. The case is not too far different from that where a person is arrested or detained by mere show of a non-existent authority to arrest or detain, which constitutes false imprisonment as *Symes v Mahon* [1922] SASR 447 indicates.

Where the plaintiff is aware of the potential for total restraint by the defendant but chooses not to exercise their right to freedom of movement for their own reasons, uninfluenced by the defendant's actions, it seems there is no false imprisonment: *McFadzean v Construction Forestry Mining & Energy Union* [2007] VSCA 289. In that case environmental protestors totally surrounded by loggers chose not to ask for police assistance in leaving a blockaded campsite because they wanted to delay logging work at that place and because of collegiate spirit.

Restraint must be total

[4.80] In *Bird v Jones* (1845) 115 ER 668 the defendant blocked the public footpath over one side of Hammersmith Bridge. The plaintiff wishing to use the footpath was prevented from doing so by the defendant. This was found not to be false imprisonment because the plaintiff could have used the footpath on the other side of the bridge, and the restraint was therefore not total (the plaintiff could have sued by an action in public nuisance for any special damage arising from the obstruction of the highway). Also there is no imprisonment if a reasonable escape route exists. The question of reasonableness is a question of fact. It should be noted, however, that it is not identical with the question of whether the plaintiff acted reasonably in attempting to escape. The plaintiff in *Sayers v Harlow UDC* [1958] 1 WLR 623, for example, was found to have acted reasonably in attempting to climb out of the toilet, but the climb would hardly have been classified as a reasonable escape route. It may generally be suggested that no escape route is reasonable if it involves danger to life or limb, even if it is probable that the plaintiff could have coped with the danger. Threat or danger to property (including the property of others), distance and time and legality are all also relevant to the reasonableness of a potential means of escape: *McFadzean v Construction Forestry Mining & Energy Union* [2007] VSCA 289.

The partial restraint rule lies at the base of the decision in *Robinson v Balmain New Ferry* [1910] AC 295. The defendants operated a ferry service from Sydney to Balmain. Entrance to the wharf on the Sydney side was through a turnstile. The charge was a penny and this was payable on entrance from the Sydney side or on exit at that side having travelled from Balmain. The plaintiff had entered at the Sydney side, paid his penny, but then, having missed the boat, demanded his release through the entrance turnstile. He was prevented by the defendants' servant from leaving through the turnstile unless he paid a further penny. The next boat was due to leave in 20 minutes' time. The plaintiff sued the company for false imprisonment but his action failed both in the

High Court and the Privy Council. In delivering the judgment of the Privy Council, Lord Loreburn LC said: "there is no law requiring the defendants to make the exit to their premises gratuitous to people who come upon a definite contract which involves their leaving by another way".

The partial restraint rule clearly explains the decision. The plaintiff's contract was relevant, not towards showing a consent to imprisonment, but to showing the reasonableness of the alternative escape route from the premises. In additional remarks Lord Loreburn LC said that the defendants were entitled to impose a reasonable condition on exit back past the turnstile and that the payment of a penny was a reasonable condition.

Glanville Williams supports the view taken in the text that the *Robinson* decision is based on the partial restraint of the plaintiff. However he disagrees with the decision that there was a sufficiently reasonable means of escape so the restraint on the plaintiff's liberty did not amount to false imprisonment.[9] However it could be argued that since the use of a turnstile at the Sydney side alone was in general beneficial to users of the ferry, being calculated to reduce overall costs, and since it would have defeated that system if the defendants had had to investigate the bona fides of persons who claimed not to have taken the trip from Balmain, the condition imposed by the defendants was reasonable. The case seems, therefore, to be limited to its own facts and to be of small general importance. It says nothing about hypothetical alternatives such as the boat trip being of an extensive nature, or the plaintiff not being in possession of a penny. Nor does it run contrary to the well known principle that it is not lawful to imprison someone in order to enforce payment of a civil debt (for example, a restaurant bill): *Sunbolf v Alford* (1838) 150 ER 1135. The basis of the decision in *Robinson* was that there was no imprisonment.

False imprisonment for non-payment of debt

[4.85] It is false imprisonment to imprison someone in order to enforce payment of a debt. In *Sunbolf v Alford* (1838) 150 ER 1135 the defendant innkeeper forcibly removed his guests retaining the plaintiff's coat as security against payment for the plaintiff's stay at the inn. Innkeepers are entitled at common law to a lien over guests' property against non-payment of their bill, but this does not extend to clothes being worn by the guest. It was held that the defendant committed battery. Detention of the guest for the same purpose would clearly have been false imprisonment. The case of *Vignoli v Sydney Harbour Casino* [2000] Aust Torts Reports 81-541 is modern authority for the rule. The plaintiff in that case had been playing at the defendant's casino when he was informed by the defendant that he had received an over-payment. He requested to see a video replay of the incident but this was refused. He therefore refused to repay the amount demanded. At this point he was detained in the casino by the defendants for several hours and subjected to certain indignities at the hands of their staff. Some time after his release it was established that there had in fact been an over-payment. The plaintiff's action for false imprisonment against the defendants succeeded: see [4.100] for the award of damages in the case.

---

9   Williams, above, n 8.

Figure 4.5: False imprisonment – summary

....

> - Basic elements of trespass:
>   – intention/negligent act;
>   – directness;
>   – absence of lawful justification/consent.
> - Total restraint:
>   – implies the absence of a reasonable means of escape.
> - In general, there is no false imprisonment where one voluntarily submits to a form of restraint.

Fault in false imprisonment

[4.90] In accordance with the general rule for trespass, false imprisonment requires fault, so that the defendant must have intended the imprisonment or have been negligent in bringing it about. An intentional act of imprisonment may, however, give rise to strict liability where the defendant is acting under a reasonable though mistaken belief in the defendant's right to imprison the plaintiff. An example of this is *Cowell v Corrective Services Commission* (1988) 13 NSWLR 714[10] in which the plaintiff was detained as a prisoner beyond the due date for his release. His action for false imprisonment against the Commission succeeded even though it was accepted there had been no negligence on the part of the defendant (on the ground that it had been acting in accordance with the law relating to remission of sentence, which was subsequently reversed by the High Court).

Distinguished from malicious prosecution

[4.95] Where a legal process involves the plaintiff's arrest, there is sometimes difficulty in distinguishing false imprisonment from the tort of malicious prosecution. False imprisonment, as a form of trespass, requires that the defendant should directly bring about the arrest. Malicious prosecution (which includes the tort of malicious arrest) arises where the defendant has indirectly procured the plaintiff's arrest. The distinction assumes importance in view of the difficulty of proving malicious prosecution. Malice on the defendant's part, absence of reasonable cause for the prosecution and actual damage are necessary. False imprisonment requires none of these. Most of the problems over directness in false imprisonment have concerned police arrests on information supplied by the defendant. It is not false imprisonment merely to give information to the police in consequence of which a police arrest follows: *Grinham v Willey* (1859) 4 H&N 496; 157 ER 934; *Davidson v Chief Constable* [1994] 2 All ER 597. Nor is the mere signing of the charge sheet at the police station enough to render the defendant liable in false imprisonment for the ensuing arrest, though it may identify the defendant as the prosecutor for the purpose of the action of malicious prosecution: *Sewell v National Telephone* [1907] 1 KB 567; cf *Chubb v Wimpey & Co* [1936] 1 All ER 69. Where the facts make it clear that the police officer exercised no independent

---

[10]   See to like effect *R v Governor of Brickhill Prison; Ex parte Evans (No 2)* [2000] 3 WLR 843 (HL).

discretion in making the arrest (for example, where the police indicate that an arrest will not be made unless the defendant signs the charge sheet) and the defendant has done so and the arrest is made, the defendant is liable for false imprisonment: *Dickenson v Waters* (1931) SR(NSW) 593. In *Myer Stores Ltd v Soo* [1991] 2 VR 597 the defendants' employee had indicated to two policemen that a person suspected of theft was in the defendants' store, and the three indicated to that person, the plaintiff, that he should go to the store office for questioning, which he did. The court held that the plaintiff was under detention from the moment he went to the office and that the employee was sufficiently directly involved in the arrest to be liable for false imprisonment.

Where the plaintiff has been wrongfully arrested or detained by the defendant, the interposition of an independent discretion, judicial or otherwise, continuing the detention operates as a new cause so that the defendant is not liable for the subsequent imprisonment. Hence, where a wrongfully arrested person is brought before a magistrate who then remands them in custody, the remedy for the initial arrest is false imprisonment. However, there is no liability for any confinement after the remand unless it is for malicious prosecution: *Davidson*.

Remedies for trespass to the person

[4.100] The damages that may be awarded for trespass to the person are nominal damages (equivalent in law to no damages but expressed in terms of a nominal amount), compensatory damages, aggravated damages and exemplary damages. Where there is no conscious misconduct on the part of the defendant in committing the trespass, damages will be limited to either of the first two. But it was accepted in *Vignoli v Sydney Harbour Casino* [2000] Aust Torts Reports 81-541 and *Thompson v Commissioner of Police* [1997] 3 WLR 403 that substantial compensatory damages for the mental distress and humiliation inflicted by the tort may be awarded in such a case, even if the plaintiff has suffered no actual injury. Where there is conscious misconduct on the defendant's part, there is the possibility of aggravated and/or exemplary damages being awarded in addition to compensatory damages. Aggravated damages are awarded for the added insult to the plaintiff's feelings caused by the outrageous or humiliating nature of the defendant's conduct; exemplary damages to mark the court's disapproval of the defendant's conduct. In *Vignoli*, in which the plaintiff was falsely imprisoned for several hours by the defendants without suffering any injury, the court awarded a substantial amount of compensatory damages ($30,000) for the distress and humiliation caused to the plaintiff, a smaller amount ($10,000) by way of aggravated damages for the fact that the defendants contested liability and put the plaintiff through the ordeal of a trial when liability was obvious, and a large sum ($35,000) by way of exemplary damages. A similar approach was taken by the English Court of Appeal in *Thompson* in an action brought against the police for false imprisonment and malicious prosecution. Compensatory damages were awarded for the distress caused to the plaintiff arising from the tort, but an additional equal amount of aggravated damages was awarded to represent the humiliating nature of the police's conduct in the case. There was also a substantial award of exemplary damages. Lord Woolf MR gave frank recognition to the fact that the aggravated damages award itself contained a "penal" element.

An injunction may be obtained against a future apprehended assault and battery. The injunction will be of the quia timet variety,[11] since previous assaults will be completed at

---

[11] That is, for an apprehended tort rather than a presently continuing one.

the time of the proceedings. The evidence necessary to prove reasonable apprehension of a future assault will often be based on the infliction of previous assaults on the plaintiff by the defendant, but this is not necessary as a matter of law. The case law is concerned with cases of domestic violence,[12] but there is no limitation on the right to obtain an injunction to cases of this sort: *O'Kane v Fogarty* [1985] 2 NSWLR 649. The basis of the court's intervention in these cases is that the criminal sanction against the defendant's conduct is, for whatever reason, an insufficient deterrent.

Intentional, indirect infliction of personal injury

[4.105] Trespass involves the intentional infliction of a direct injury on the plaintiff. However, it is possible to intentionally inflict an injury on the plaintiff *indirectly*. The element of directness is central to the tort of trespass. Where the injury is direct and intentional there is a basis for trespass. Where the injury is intentional but indirect, there is no trespass. The plaintiff cannot sue in negligence because the injury is intentional but can however sue in an action on the case. A defendant causes a direct injury to the plaintiff where for instance he or she hits the plaintiff. The injury would be indirect if the defendant intentionally sets a trap that causes an injury to the plaintiff when the plaintiff triggers the trap.

An early example of such an indirectly caused injury is the case of *Bird v Holbrook* (1828) 130 ER 911. The plaintiff, a trespasser, discharged a spring-loaded gun which had been set as a booby trap by the defendant to protect his allotment from theft. He recovered damages because the use of a gun could not be regarded as being within the landowner's privilege to take reasonable measures to eject or deter trespassers. An extension of the liability for intentional infliction of injury was provided by *Wilkinson v Downton* [1897] 2 QB 57.[13] The defendant, by way of a practical joke, told the plaintiff falsely that the plaintiff's husband had been seriously injured in an accident. Because of her emotional distress, the plaintiff suffered a prolonged nervous illness (that is, nervous shock which is regarded as actual damage). For this the defendant was held liable in damages. According to Wright J (at 58-59):

> the defendant has wilfully done an act calculated to cause harm to the plaintiff ... and has in fact thereby caused harm to her ... the wilful injuria is in law malicious, although no malicious purpose to cause the harm which was caused nor any motive of spite was imputed to the defendant.

These remarks give rise to some difficulties. It is clear that the words "calculated to cause" do not require intentional, or even reckless, causation but do require conduct which is substantially more certain than merely foreseeably likely to bring about the harm suffered. That is apparent from the words quoted, and also from the judgments of the High Court of Australia in *Bunyan v Jordan* (1936) 57 CLR 1 (discussed below). See also *Nationwide News Pty Ltd v Naidu* [2007] NSWCA 377. This raises the question of where the element of malice referred to by the judge resides. It is submitted that malice must be found in the pointless raising of feelings of alarm, distress or fright in the plaintiff which are foreseeably likely to produce actual nervous shock or mental harm. On this view of the principle, there is no need for the plaintiff to prove the high

---

[12] *Parry v Crooks* (1981) 27 SASR 1; *Daley v Martin (No 1)* [1982] Qd R 23; *Zimitat v Douglas* [1979] Qd R 454; *Corvisy v Corvisy* [1982] 2 NSWLR 557.

[13] See generally Mullany and Handford, *Tort Liability for Psychiatric Damage* (1993), Ch 14.

likelihood of shock which would establish recklessness as to that consequence on the defendant's part, though no doubt that would be possible in some cases. The assessment of intention in such cases is therefore an objective one: *Carrier v Bonham* [2002] 1 Qd R 474. The utility of the *Wilkinson v Downton* principle seems to be limited to the case of words causing shock, though it is stated widely enough to cover acts causing shock and words causing physical injury. The likelihood is that these latter situations will be covered by the tort of negligence,[14] whereas there is considerable doubt whether a duty of care can be established in relation to words causing shock.[15]

Figure 4.6: Action on the case for indirect intentional harm

- Defendant is liable in an action on the case for damages for intentional acts which are calculated to cause damage to the plaintiff and which in fact cause damage to the plaintiff.
- Elements:
  - the act must be intentional;
  - it must be one calculated to cause harm/damage;
  - it must in fact cause harm/actual damage.
- Where the defendant intends no harm from the act, but the harm caused is reasonably foreseeable, the defendant's intention to cause the resulting harm can be imputed/implied.

The High Court of Australia has accepted the *Wilkinson v Downton* principle, despite finding that on the facts the defendant was not liable: *Bunyan v Jordan* (1937) 57 CLR 1; *Northern Territory v Mengel* (1995) 185 CLR 307 at 347. In *Bunyan* the defendant had, in the hearing of the plaintiff, who was no relation to him, and apparently for the purpose of putting emotional pressure on his sons, threatened suicide. The plaintiff knew he had a revolver and soon afterwards she heard a shot.

In consequence she suffered mental harm. The defendant had no intention of committing suicide and had only fired the revolver to create a scare. The High Court held that in the circumstances the behaviour was not calculated or likely to cause harm to a person in the plaintiff's circumstances because harm was not foreseeable here. Thus, liability could not exist under the *Wilkinson v Downton* principle. The cases in which the principle has been applied are few. *Janvier v Sweeney* [1919] 2 KB 316 held actionable a threat to expose the plaintiff as a person having contact with a German spy; *Stevenson v Basham* [1922] NZLR 225 a threat by a landlord to burn his tenant, the plaintiff, out of the tenanted property. In both cases, the mental harm suffered by the plaintiff was found to be within the principle established in *Wilkinson v Downton*. In

---

[14]   See, eg, *Magill v Magill* (2006) 226 CLR 551; [2006] HCA 51. But in *Purdy v Woznesensky* [1937] 2 WWR 11 the plaintiff recovered damages under *Wilkinson v Downton* [1897] 2 QB 57 for shock suffered when the defendant assaulted her husband in her presence.

[15]   In *Barnes v Commonwealth* (1937) 37 SR(NSW) 511 an action for negligence was allowed where a pensioner suffered mental harm through negligently being informed by the defendant's servant that her husband had been confined to a lunatic asylum. Negligent words causing shock were also found to be actionable in *Furniss v Fitchett* [1958] NZLR 396, although in *Guay v Sun Publishing Co* (1953) 4 DLR 577, a negligent newspaper report of the deaths of the plaintiff's estranged husband and their three children which caused the plaintiff mental harm, was found to be not actionable.

Khorasandjian v Bush [1993] QB 727 the principle was applied to enable an injunction to be awarded against the making of abusive phone calls to the plaintiff by her former fiancé, on the ground that these were calculated to cause her shock: see also *R v Ireland* [1997] 1 All ER 865. In *Nationwide News Pty Ltd v Naidu* [2007] NSWCA 377 it was applied to the psychiatric injury suffered by a security guard because of humiliating and harassing treatment by an employee of the premises the plaintiff patrolled.

Uncertainty over the precise status of the *Wilkinson v Downton* principle lies behind an extension of it in the United States under which the principle applies to what may be described as outrageous conduct causing injury to feelings. The case law embodying this development was recognised by the Restatement of the Law (Second) of Torts in 1965, which provides that there is liability if a person, by extreme or outrageous conduct, intentionally or recklessly causes severe emotional distress to another person. This recognition of distress as sufficient damage to maintain a cause of action has not been followed in Australia or other common law countries.

Practice Questions

Problem Questions

Battery

4.1 For the purposes of battery, what is the act that must be intended?

4.2 To what extent is the element of hostility relevant in an action for battery?

4.3 The following fact situation is taken from *Australian Practice Management* magazine. "A man was admitted for abdominal surgery for which he duly consented. While the patient was under general anaesthetic, his surgeon noticed a sebaceous cyst on the top of his head. The patient was bald and the surgeon decided to do him a favour and get rid of it. He removed it without incident. In the recovery ward, the patient was incensed when he discovered what had happened. His cyst had apparently been the source of many a free pint of ale. He habitually wore a bowler hat and it had been his habit to place a second, tiny bowler hat on top of the sebaceous cyst itself. When he removed his hat at the local hostelry to expose the tiny bowler underneath, sitting on the cyst, this invariably caused general amusement and free shouts of beer. The patient was upset at the loss of the cyst, his one major social asset."

The patient has been advised that since he did not suffer any "real damage" he can hardly expect to succeed in a tort action against the surgeon. Explain why you agree or disagree with this advice.

Assault

4.4 How does the tort of assault differ from battery?

4.5 Why is the knowledge of the plaintiff in a case of assault essential?

4.6 Critically examine the view that "words on their own" do not constitute assault.

False imprisonment

4.7   Moses is a self-proclaimed reformed alcoholic. In February he and a group of friends formed an association which they call the Community Salvation Unit. The principal objective of the Unit is to help alcoholics to overcome their drinking problems by providing a "safe house" in which the Unit keeps the members away from alcohol. The safe house is an isolated cottage at Clear Waters, 45 km outside metropolitan Sydney. It is run on a hostel system where members take turns in the daily chores.

   The practice of the Unit is to patrol public parks in the Sydney area in search of drunken homeless people taking refuge in such parks. Upon finding them, the Unit would then take them (usually) in a van owned and driven by Moses to the safe house to help them "dry out". According to Moses, the people taken to the safe house usually come willingly because of the good it would do to them; in some cases however force is used to take them to the safe house rather than leave them drunk in the park without any shelter.

   Parkes and Norman are both unemployed and known around Kings Cross pubs as "drunks". On one evening in July both men took shelter in Hyde Park after a heavy drinking session. That evening Moses and one of the Unit's executive members came across Parkes and Norman apparently asleep in the southern end of the park. Moses woke both men up, still in their intoxicated state, and tried to persuade them to come in his van to the safe house. Being drunk at the time, the recollection of the events of the evening by the two men is not very clear. However it appears only Parkes agreed to go to the safe house voluntarily. According to Moses, Norman declined the invitation saying he was "extremely happy sleeping under the stars in the park". With the aid of his accomplice, Moses then proceeded to use what he describes as "gentle force" to get Norman to come with them. They forced Norman into the van, to join Parkes. In the process, Norman kicked and punched Moses and his accomplice, cutting Moses in the face. As Norman was forced into the van, Norman's struggles caused him to bang his head on the side of the van.

   (a)   What cause(s) of action may be open to Norman on the facts? Would you recommend the same cause of action for Parkes?

   (b)   Norman cannot claim any damages for injuries sustained by banging his head on the sides of the van because he caused them himself. Do you agree?

   (c)   The action of Moses is socially commendable; and since both Norman and Parkes have benefited from the events of that night and even appear to have enjoyed their stay, they can obviously not claim a right to sue. Do you agree?

   (d)   Norman would not be liable for any injuries sustained by Moses that evening. Is this correct?

Intentionally inflicted indirect injuries (Wilkinson v Downton)

4.8   Arthur is a Senior Superintendent in the New South Wales Police Force, and a childhood friend of Simon Mead, a merchant banker. The two attended high school together, and have kept in close contact over the years. Last April, Arthur decided to play an April Fool's joke on Simon who lives on a two-acre property in Belrose with his wife Marian and their only son Ben. He subsequently telephoned the Mead household intending to talk to Simon, whose birthday was 1 April. The call was answered by Marian, who indicated that Simon was not home and that he had left only a few minutes earlier to take Ben to a sports camp. Marian also told Arthur that "Simon shouldn't be very long since the camp is only 20 minutes away".

In the absence of Simon, Arthur decided to go ahead with his April Fool's joke in any case. He asked Marian if she had been watching the news on television or listening to the radio. Marian said "no"; and that she had been doing the usual Saturday chores and had not been listening to the news. Arthur then proceeded to tell Marian that a "tribal war" had broken out between two bikie groups, the Bandicoots and the Blistering Barnacles and that the main "battle front" was on Morgan Road, less than a kilometre from the Mead property and the principal access from the property to the main road. He also said that the fighting was quite fierce and that "some innocent people have been caught in the cross fire and have been badly wounded". He then said "if I were you, I would lock all doors and stay indoors until Simon gets home".

After the conversation Marian immediately hung up the phone and locked all doors, as suggested by Arthur. She then remembered that Simon and Ben were using the Morgan Road access to go to the sports camp; she therefore became extremely concerned that they may be caught up in the bikie war. She grew more anxious when Simon failed to return by noon, two hours after leaving the house.

Simon, who had gone to his office in North Sydney to pick up some documents after dropping Ben off at the sports camp, eventually returned home at 12.45 pm. When Simon telephoned Arthur to confirm the story about the bikie war, Arthur explained that it had all been a joke and that he did not think Marian would take it seriously. In spite of this, Marian developed an acute psychiatric condition due to her early anxiety over the fate of Simon and Ben, and required medication for several weeks afterwards.

The Meads wish to know if they have a cause of action against Arthur. Advise them accordingly.

Answers to Practice Questions

Problem Questions

Battery

4.1   For the purpose of battery, what is the act that must be intended?

The act that causes the application of force to the body of the plaintiff is the relevant intentional act: *Wilson v Pringle* [1987] QB 237. It may be added that "intention" in this context presumes that the act was voluntary, that is an act of conscious volition: *National Coal Board v Evans* [1951] 2 KB 861. Further, the defendant need not have intended to harm the plaintiff, as intention relates only to the intention to commit the act causative of the application of force rather than an intention to cause harm as a consequence of that act: *Wilson*. Reckless acts are considered intentional if a reasonable person similarly situated to the defendant would have foreseen that the application of force was a substantially certain consequence of their conduct: *R v Parker* (1977) CA (UK).

4.2   To what extent is hostility relevant to an action in battery?

Hostility is not relevant to an action in battery given that there is no mental element contained in the definition of the tort. Battery is merely the direct and unlawful application of force. Unlawfulness in this context generally relates to the absence of consent or other lawful justification. This is illustrated where an act underpinned by a good intent, but in direct opposition to the will of the plaintiff, is still a battery: for example *Mallette v Schulman* (1990) 67 DLR 321 (Jehovah's Witness blood transfusion). Nevertheless, proof of hostility may serve as prima facie evidence of lack of consent and associated unlawfulness. Equally, proof of lack of consent is suggestive of a hostile motive. In this second context, the presence of hostility is merely incidental to the battery, not a requirement of the action.

4.3   Explain why you agree or disagree with this advice.

This advice is disagreed with on the basis that a battery is actionable per se, that is without proof of damage. Whether the plaintiff has suffered any "real damage" is therefore irrelevant to the success of the action. It is only necessary for the plaintiff to demonstrate that the defendant intentionally and unlawfully applied force to him or her. Unlawfulness is established by lack of consent. On the facts, the plaintiff consented only to abdominal surgery. Notwithstanding the doctor's benevolent intent and skilful conduct, the act is unlawful because the plaintiff did not consent to the removal of the cyst.

Assault

4.4   How does the tort of assault differ from battery?

A tortious assault is defined as the intentional or reckless threat or act by the defendant placing the plaintiff in reasonable apprehension of imminent physical contact. Battery is the direct and unlawful application of force. The actions may occur independently of each other. An assault may take place where there is a threat of physical contact but no subsequent contact. Equally, there may be a battery with or without apprehension of the contact as the action simply requires contact in fact.

4.5   Why is the plaintiff's knowledge of the threat essential in an action for assault?

Unless the plaintiff has knowledge of the threat, there can be no apprehension of imminent physical contact as the formation of apprehension arises from knowledge.

4.6   Critically examine the view that words alone do not constitute an assault.

Words alone cannot constitute an assault as the tort requires the reasonable apprehension of physical contact. One cannot be battered by words. However, where words are accompanied by present ability to effect the purpose of the verbal threat, the words may constitute an assault in that they raise reasonable apprehension of harm in the mind of the plaintiff: *Barton v Armstrong* [1969] 2

NSWR 451. Similarly, a conditional verbal threat in the form of an ultimatum is an assault if it represents an intention and a means with which to batter the plaintiff unless he or she succumbs to the demand: *Barton*. Therefore, while words alone cannot raise apprehension of contact, when accompanied by the capacity to carry out the threat, an assault can be established.

False imprisonment

4.7(a) What cause(s) of action may be open to Norman on the facts? Would you recommend the same action for Parkes?

An action in false imprisonment is open to Norman, although not for Parkes. False imprisonment can be established where the defendant causes the unlawful restraint of the plaintiff so as to deprive the plaintiff of liberty. Unlawfulness, as for battery, encompasses the absence of consent. On the facts, Norman was gently "forced" into the van by the defendant after he stated that he would prefer to remain in the park. Absence of consent is further evidenced by Norman's struggle against Moses and his accomplice. For the purpose of an action in false imprisonment, restraint must be total. As Norman was being pushed into a van from which he could not reasonably escape once it was moving, restraint is adequate for the purpose of the action: *Burton v Davies* (1963) St R Qd 26 (not reasonable to attempt to escape from a moving vehicle).

Second, the safe house to which the men were taken was located 45 km outside metropolitan Sydney. Whether being taken to Clear Waters amounts to imprisonment is arguable. Inconvenience does not amount to imprisonment because the person is not totally deprived of their liberty: *Bird v Jones* (1845) 115 ER 668. In this case, Norman would have been able to leave the cottage, notwithstanding the fact that it was isolated and difficult for Norman to return to Kings Cross. Only in cases where the escape is unreasonably dangerous is it possible to construct imprisonment: *Burton*. Therefore, Norman has a cause of action in false imprisonment related to being forced into the van but not in respect of being at the house.

Parkes consented to accompany the defendant thus it could not be said that his enclosure in the van was unlawful.

4.7(b) Norman cannot claim damages for any injury sustained by banging his head on the side of the van because he caused it himself. Do you agree?

Norman can claim damage for these injuries by bringing an action on the case. An action on the case may be brought where the plaintiff has sustained an injury as a result of the intentional act of the defendant but where the means of contact was indirect or consequential. The indirectness of the act renders an action in trespass to person inappropriate. The defendant intentionally forced Norman into the van, causing him to bump his head on the way because he was struggling. The issue of causation asks whether the injury would not have been sustained but for the defendant's act (*March v E & MH Stramare Pty Ltd* (1991) 171 CLR 506). It is possible to argue that but for the defendant's act of forcing Norman into the van, Norman would not have resisted and struggled to break free. The extent to which damages would be awarded for this damage would be calculated with reference to the extent to which Norman contributed to the damage.

CHAPTER 4

4.7(c) The action of Moses is socially commendable and since both Norman and Parkes have benefited from the events of that night and even appear to have enjoyed their stay they cannot claim the right to sue. Do you agree?

This is incorrect. Trespass is actionable provided that the elements of the tort can be established on the facts. Whether the plaintiffs derived any later benefit is irrelevant to the possibility of establishing a case.

4.7(d) Norman would not be liable for any injuries sustained by Moses that evening. Is this correct?

The success of a cross-claim by Moses against Norman for the damage would depend on whether Norman can prove that his actions were justified by self-defence, thus not unlawful. Norman is entitled to exercise a reasonable and proportionate degree of force in self-defence: *Bird v Holbrook* (1828) 130 ER 911. Norman kicked and punched Moses causing a cut to Moses' face. While the actual damage to Moses' face is not material to an action (since trespass is actionable per se), it provides evidence as to the extent of force adopted by Norman. On the other hand, Moses used "gentle force" to coerce Norman into the van. It would seem unreasonable to use violent force in response to gentle coercion. For this reason, Norman would be liable for the injury caused although the damages awarded may be reduced in view of Moses' contribution to the harm by way of provocation.

Intentionally inflicted indirect injuries (Wilkinson v Downton)

4.8 The Meads wish to know if they have a cause of action against Arthur. Advise them accordingly.

The Meads can bring an action on the case against Arthur for causing Marian's mental harm following the principles of *Wilkinson v Downton* [1897] 2 QB 57. This action requires proof of intent and proof of damage, that is, proof that the defendant subjectively intended to shock the plaintiff and that the damage was objectively likely to result. Statements made to the plaintiff that are intended to cause harm are actionable if they cause mental harm.

On the facts, the defendant subjectively intended to play a practical joke on the plaintiff, suggestive of the possibility that her family were endangered by a bikie gang war. Although Arthur did not possess a spiteful motive, such action would be regarded as malicious at law because it is objectively likely that a person, told of the possible danger in which her family may be placed, would suffer from mental harm. This is supported by the fact that Arthur is a senior member of the police service, meaning that his story would be believed by Marian and taken seriously.

Clearly Marian sustained damage in the form of mental harm, which required medication for several weeks. The facts of the case clearly indicate that the injury was caused by the practical joke.

CHAPTER 5

Torts to Chattels

Reading

Sappideen, Vines, Grant and Watson, *Torts: Commentary and Materials*, Chapter 5.

Objectives

This chapter will explain:

- concepts necessary for all torts to chattels: the meaning of chattel and standing to sue;
- the concept of intentional interference with chattels;
- trespass, conversion and detinue as torts relevant to chattels;
- the difference between, and relationship of, these forms of tort;
- the difference between possession and ownership;
- the fault element required for an intentional tort against chattels;
- bailment in the context of torts to goods;
- the defences to torts against chattels;
- remedies for torts to chattels; and
- action on the case for damage to a reversionary interest in a chattel.

Principles

Causes of action

[5.05] Property and possession in chattels are protected by tortious actions. The normal remedy is the action for damages, which are obtainable as of right. Alternatively, restitution (return) of a chattel lies in the discretion of the court and only for certain tortious wrongs.

The three torts to chattels that are important today are trespass, conversion and detinue. Replevin survives almost exclusively as a means of contesting a wrongful distress of a chattel (for example, seizure for non-payment of rent), but its function in Australia is now largely served by interlocutory orders, which a court may make for the preservation of the property pending an action. An action on the case for causing damage to a chattel is available where none of the three main torts is available.

Trespass, conversion and detinue formerly served quite distinct purposes, but as the law developed considerable overlap occurred between trespass and conversion, on the one hand, and detinue and conversion on the other. Trespass to chattels continues to serve a distinct purpose where conversion is not available. However, the substantive area of operation of detinue outside conversion seems mainly to be covered by the action on the bailment. The measure of damages in conversion and detinue now appears to be the same, although only in the case of detinue may the plaintiff seek restitution of the chattel. Detinue has been abolished in England, its substantive and remedial characteristics being transferred to conversion.[1]

Figure 5.1:

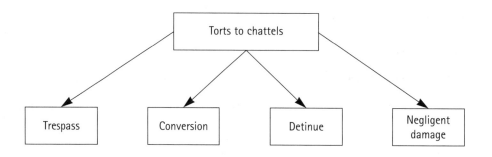

---

[1]   *Torts (Interference with Goods) Act 1977* (UK) s 2.

Preliminary matters

Definition of chattel

[5.10] A chattel (or good) may be defined as any tangible property that is not land or attached to land. It includes cheques (since these are regarded as tangible), living goods such as animals and substances such as gases.

Plaintiff's interest: standing to sue

[5.12] Where there has been a wrongful interference with a person, it is usually obvious who can bring tort proceedings because of it. But in the case of a wrongful interference with a chattel (or land, considered in the next chapter) it is not always obvious. Even living goods, such as pets, do not have legal rights to start proceedings against a wrongdoer. Each of the torts to chattels (and land) have particular standing requirements that must be met before any particular person can successfully bring proceedings against a wrongdoer. To put it another way, the person bringing proceedings must have a particular right to or interest in the chattel concerned.

Chattels may be owned or possessed but other rights to or interests in chattels can also exist. Ownership is a proprietary interest and may be regarded as the ultimate or residual right in the chattel, arising through some legitimate title. The owner of a chattel may be in possession of it, but it is quite possible for ownership to be in one person and possession in another. Unlike ownership, possession describes the factual, rather than legal, status of the chattel.

Possession is established where a person intends to hold the chattel for that person's own purposes (animus possidendi), and has sufficient control over it (corpus possessionis). Provided there is the requisite animus, suffcient control necessary to establish possession is easily satisfied. Thus a person who leaves a car parked on the public highway with the door unlocked and the keys in the ignition continues to possess the car and its contents. To distinguish that the person is not physically with the car, they can be said to be in constructive possession rather than actual possession, but both are considered possession for these purposes. The requirement that the holding be for the holder's own purposes means that where a person has factual control, but the holding is entirely for another's purposes, this does not amount to possession. Employees, therefore, do not possess their employers' property: the computer on which a bank teller enters your withdrawal of funds is therefore not in the possession of the teller, although it is in the teller's control – it remains in the possession of the teller's employer, the bank. Such holdings by the teller are sometimes called custody, sometimes possessio naturalis, and sometimes detentio.

A further relationship with chattels can arise pursuant to a bailment. A bailment is a transfer of possession of a chattel from one person to another for a limited period of time. The transferor is called the "bailor", the receiver the "bailee". All bailees have possession but not ownership. The bailment may be made in pursuance of a contract which may or may not alter the common law rules of bailment, but this is not necessary. It may be made on the understanding that it may be terminated at any time on demand of the bailor, in which case it is said to be "at will"; or it may be for a specific period of time, in which case it is said to be "for a term". The term need not be an exact period of time. For instance, if a car is bailed to a garage for repairs, the term lasts until the repairs are complete and paid for, at which point the repairer's lien of the garage is terminated, and the owner has the right to immediate possession.[2]

The common law imposes a number of duties on bailees including a duty to return the goods at the end of the bailment as directed by the bailor; a duty to take reasonable care of the goods and a duty not to convert the goods. A breach of one of these terms gives rise to a cause of action for breach of duty as a bailee. It may also be one of the torts to chattels discussed below.

Trespass to chattels

[5.15] The definition of trespass to chattels is simply an application of the general features of trespass to the special case of chattels. It is committed by an act of the defendant which, whether intentionally[3] or negligently, directly interferes with the *possession* of a chattel which the plaintiff enjoys at the time of the act. Like other forms of trespass, it is actionable per se.

Plaintiff's interest: possession

[5.20] Trespass exists to protect possessors against acts interfering with their possession. The plaintiff need only establish actual or constructive possession as the title to sue. For example, a plaintiff in constructive possession of a chattel that is interfered with can sue in trespass such as where an employee holds their employer's goods in their custody: *Wilson v Lombank Ltd* [1963] 1 WLR 1294. Ownership is not necessary although an action in trespass may resolve a dispute as to the proprietary rights in a chattel.

It is generally assumed that the possession need not be lawful, although authority is hard to find. A thief might sue in trespass to protect a possession gained by the theft,[4] though an act of lawful recapture of the chattel by the owner, or anyone else with a right to possession superior to that of the thief, would be a defence to the action. In some circumstances, even the owner may commit trespass against a mere possessor of the chattel.

In *Rose v Matt* [1951] 1 KB 810, the purchaser of some goods pledged his clock, with the seller of the goods, as security for the loan of the purchase price. Later, he returned and took away the clock secretly. This was found to be theft, showing that the removal of the clock was a trespass (since larceny requires a trespassory taking).

Figure 5.2: Trespass to goods/chattels

- The *intentional/negligent* act of the defendant which directly interferes with the plaintiff's *possession of a chattel* without lawful justification.
- The plaintiff must have possession at the time of the interference.
- It is actionable per se.

---

[2]   Although the repairer's lien may be waived, eg, by allowing the bailor an account with the garage, in which case the bailment is at will (as in *Wilson v Lombank* [1963] 1 WLR 1294).

[3]   Intention includes recklessness.

[4]   *Bird v Fort Francis Municipality* [1949] 2 DLR 791 is authority that a thief may bring conversion.

Exceptions to the requirement for possession

Bailment

[5.25] The need for possession to have standing to sue in trespass generally means bailors cannot bring trespass proceedings. However, it is established that a bailor at will can sue for trespasses to the bailee's possession, even though the bailor is not in actual possession: *Lotan v Cross* (1810) 2 Camp 464; 170 ER 1219; *Wilson v Lombank Ltd* [1963] 1 WLR 1294. It is also clear that the bailor for a term cannot so sue: *Gordon v Harper* (1796) 7 TR 9; 101 ER 828. The reason for the difference appears to be that the bailor at will, through his or her right to demand the return of the chattel immediately from the bailee, is in a position tantamount to actual possession – they have an immediate right to possession. Therefore both the bailor and bailee could sue the third party in trespass in *some* circumstances.

Actual and constructive possession

[5.30] The need for a trespassory act against the bailee before a bailor at will is entitled to bring trespass was emphasised by *Penfolds Wines Pty Ltd v Elliott* (1946) 74 CLR 204. In that case Penfolds had sold wine in bottles which were marked with an indication that the bottles remained the property of Penfolds. The plaintiff's customers, having bought and consumed wine sold in the plaintiff's bottles, were in the position of bailees at will of the bottles. They took these bottles to the defendant hotelier to be filled with wine that the defendant had sold to them. Whilst the movement of bottles and use of them as receptacles were considered interferences sufficient to allow an action in trespass by Dixon J, the plaintiff did not have standing to sue and therefore could not succeed in trespass.[5] The plaintiff was not in possession, and therefore could not claim its possession had been interefered with. Further, although a plaintiff with an immediate right to possession has standing to sue if the possession of the person with actual possession is interfered with, in this case because the customers had consented to the defendant refilling the bottles, it could hardly be claimed that their possession had been interefered with. The bailor could also not sue the bailee in trespass in this case because as the majority view of trespass in *Penfolds* suggests, trespass cannot be committed by the bailee itself since the bailee can hardly invade its own possession. Therefore a bailor at will cannot sue a bailee in trespass where that bailee for example, gives away the chattel.

The exception to this is where the bailee has committed an act repugnant to the bailment. Generally even in that scenario, although the bailor gains an immediate right to possession because the bailment (whether at will or for a term) ends, that is still not sufficient "possession" for standing to sue in trespass although it may be for conversion and detinue. But where the subject of the bailment is destroyed in such a case, the bailor gains an immediate right to possession such that they will have standing to sue in trespass. Dixon J in *Penfolds* suggested in obiter (at 227-228) that a bailee who "broke bulk" and so altered the thing in law that it is no longer the same thing which was bailed would have destroyed the chattel and could be sued in trespass. In *Burnard v Haggis* (1863) 14 CB (NS) 4-5 the court held an infant bailee liable in trespass for allowing a mare, which he had hired out only for riding, to be jumped. The case does not distinguish according to whether the bailment is at will or for a term. Even if it is

---

5   Latham CJ thought that this could be a trespass on the strength of decided cases, though logic was against this: at 217.

of the latter variety, it may be that the trespassory act is so repugnant to the bailment in these cases that it terminates it and allows trespass to be brought in relation to the act itself.

The general proposition is that in a simple bailment, if the bailee repudiates the bailment by doing an act entirely inconsistent with the bailment terms, then the bailment comes to an end causing the right to possession to revert to the bailor and gives standing in conversion and detinue: *Anderson Group Pty Ltd v Tynan Motors Pty Ltd* (2006) 65 NSWLR 400; [2006] NSWCA 22 at [63] per Young J in Eq; *Penfolds Wines Pty Ltd v Elliott* (1946) 74 CLR 204 at 227. However, if the bailment is created by contract, the contractual terms may override the common law principles and provide that other steps are necessary before this will happen: *Hill v Reglon Pty Ltd* [2007] NSWCA 295 at [46]-[47].

Other cases

[5.35] Certain cases of no general significance for the law of torts exist in which persons out of possession are allowed to sue in trespass. Executors and administrators of an estate can sue for trespassory acts to the chattels belonging to the estate between the death of the testator and the moment they take possession of the estate: *Burnard v Haggis* (1863) 14 CB (NS) 4-5. The owner of a franchise in a wreck may sue one who has seized chattels from the wreck: *Kirk v Gregory* (1876) 1 Ex D 55. And trustees may sue for trespass to chattels possessed by a beneficiary: *Dunwich Corp v Sterry* (1831) 109 ER 995.

Jus tertii and trespass

[5.40] Given the plaintiff need only establish possession rather than a right to possession because of, for example, ownership, at the time of the defendant's act as the title to sue, a plea by the defendant that a third party has a better right to the chattel (such a plea being called jus tertii) than the plaintiff is no defence. Instead, while recognising the plaintiff's title, it sets up a superior title in a third party, thereby defeating the plaintiff.

In certain cases it may operate as a defence, the law on this point not differentiating between the torts of trespass and conversion. The operation of jus tertii is dealt with at [5.115].

Acts constituting trespass

[5.45] Any form of direct interference with possession is sufficient. Thus, destroying, damaging, use, dispossession and a mere asportation of a chattel are forms of trespass: *White v Morris* (1852) 11 CB 1015; 138 ER 778. This is one of the chief differences between trespass and conversion since an asportation and other minor interferences as such will not constitute the latter tort.

Opinions appear to differ on the question of whether a mere touching of a chattel without damaging it is trespass. There seems no reason to deny the possessor of a chattel a remedy by way of injunction against one who repeatedly touches a chattel without permission. There is authority that a mere negligent touching of a chattel without damaging it is not actionable as trespass: *Everitt v Martin* [1953] NZLR 298. This is plausible in the case of a negligent trespass, the situation with which *Everitt* was dealing. That case purported to lay down a rule for trespass generally. The rule in the case is debatable, however, since trespass is generally actionable per se.

In *Wilson v Marshall* [1982] Tas SR 287, where the driver of a car refused to open its door when requested to by a police officer, the latter committed no trespass by using a piece of wire to turn the lock. This case is hard to accept on any grounds other than policy. Arguably, the act in question went beyond mere touching. In any case, would the same decision have been reached if the actions were that of a thief caught in the act of picking the lock? There seems to be no sufficient reason for excluding intentional trespass to chattels from the general principle that trespass is actionable per se.

Where there is no directness, there is no trespass but the defendant's act will be actionable if there is fault and it causes actual damage. That action will be as an action on the case or as negligence.[6]

Fault element

[5.50] All that was said in relation to the mental state of the defendant in trespass to the person, applies to trespass to chattels. Thus, it is not a tort of strict liability but requires proof of fault in the form of intention or negligence: *National Coal Board v Evans* [1951] 2 KB 861. But liability for an intentional trespass may be strict, in that reasonable mistake is no defence: *Colwill v Reeves* (1811) 170 ER 1257; *Wilson v New Brighton Panel Beaters* [1989] 1 NZLR 74. The same rules as to the burden of proof will also, no doubt, apply.

Remoteness of damage

[5.55] This has not yet been authoritatively settled for trespass to chattels. A remoteness rule based on culpability would hold the defendant liable only for those consequences of the trespass which the defendant intended or should have foreseen. A more extensive liability could be imposed by also holding the defendant liable for the direct consequences of the trespass, even where these were not reasonably foreseeable.

It was pointed out that Canadian law holds the defendant liable for the direct physical consequences of an intentional trespass to the person: *Wilson v New Brighton Panel Beaters* [1989] 1 NZLR 74. In *Wilson*, a New Zealand decision, the defendant was held liable for the loss of the plaintiff's car, which followed directly from the defendants' intentional trespass to it, even though the defendants acted in good faith and were not found negligent. The defendants had removed the car from the plaintiff's premises and delivered it to a rogue who claimed to have bought it. In the case of trespass, it is necessary to consider the question of remoteness of damage in relation to the loss of the chattel. In conversion this is not necessary. Once a conversion is proved, the plaintiff is entitled to the whole value of the chattel as damages.

Remedy: measure of damages

[5.60] The measure of damages for trespass to chattels is considered in Chapter 22 at [22.120]ff.

---

[6]   Cf *Hutchins v Maughan* [1947] VLR 131 — putting down poisonous baits that were taken and eaten by the plaintiff's dogs was too indirect to be a trespass. Also, negligence was negatived, so there was no liability for the dogs' death.

Conversion

[5.65] Conversion (originally known as trover) may be defined as an intentional act of dealing with a chattel in a manner that is inconsistent with the plaintiff's right to possession of the chattel so as to amount to a denial of it.

Difference between trespass and conversion

[5.70] Certain differences between trespass and conversion follow from this definition. As conversion is available where the plaintiff is out of possession at the time of the defendant's act, it can be committed in a wider variety of methods than trespass. Trespass, with its requirement of possession, is pre-eminently the tort protecting possessors of chattels. Conversion, with its emphasis on right to possession, is pre-eminently the tort protecting owners (although it shares this proprietary function with detinue). This difference, although typical, is not absolute. As pointed out at [5.25] trespass will often protect an owner as a bailee at will, and it is equally true that conversion may protect mere possessors.

Most questions in an action of conversion will revolve around two essential points:

- Did the plaintiff have the requisite interest in the chattel at the time of the defendant's act?
- Was the nature of the defendant's act such that it ought to be regarded as a conversion of the chattel?

Figure 5.3: Conversion

> - The act of the defendant in relation to the plaintiff's chattel which constitutes an unjustifiable denial of the plaintiff's title.

Plaintiff's interest: possession or immediate right to possession

[5.75] It is essential that the plaintiff be in possession or have an immediate right to possession at the time of the defendant's act. One effect of this is that the bailor for an unexpired term cannot bring an action in conversion: *Gordon v Harper* (1796) 7 TR 9; 101 ER 828. The bailor's right in that case is to future, not immediate, possession. Where a car has been left at a garage for repairs, conversion cannot be brought for any act done to the car during the period of repair, since the garage owner has a lien over the car during the period of repair, which enables it to retain possession until the repairs are paid for. A bailor at will can, of course, sue in conversion because they have an immediate right to possession.

Figure 5.4: Conversion – who can sue?

- Those in possession or entitled to immediate possession:
  — bailees;
  — bailors;
  — mortgagors and mortgagees;
  — finders.

Problem of hire-purchase contracts

[5.80] The doctrine set out at [5.75] has caused a practical problem in hire-purchase contracts. If the hire-purchaser (that is, the bailee) wrongfully disposes of the chattel during the term of the bailment, conversion cannot, in theory, be brought because the bailment is for a term that has not expired. The courts overcame this difficulty by holding that if the act of the bailee is wholly repugnant to the bailment, the act terminates the bailment, and the owner of the chattel can sue in conversion a third party who has received the chattel from the hire-purchaser, or even the hire-purchaser: *North Central Wagon v Graham* [1950] 2 KB 7.

It was not clear whether this doctrine applied where the hire-purchase contract made express provision as to its method of termination, for example by requiring either party to give notice to the other. However, the Court of Appeal in New South Wales held that a mere contractual right to terminate was not intended to exclude the independent ipso jure (that is, by the operation of the law itself) termination of the bailment by act of the bailee. Although that doctrine could be expressly excluded by the contract, it would require the clearest possible language for it to do so: *Hill v Reglon Pty Ltd* [2007] NSWCA 295.

Immediacy of possession

[5.85] An immediate right to possession of a chattel is conferred by actual ownership. This includes a statutory property, as in *Butler v Egg Marketing Board* (1966) 114 CLR 185 (the property in the eggs became the statutory property of the Board when they were hatched). Equitable title to property may also be enough (*International Factors Ltd v Rodriguez* [1979] 1 QB 351), as is the special property held by persons having commercial interests in chattels such as pledges and liens: *Standard Electronic Apparatus Pty Ltd v Stenner* [1960] NSWR 447 (lienee). It seems clear that any bailee who has acquired possession for a term under an agreement with the true owner is entitled to bring conversion, on the basis of what is termed a "special property" in the chattel.[7] Thus a mere hirer of the chattel could sue.

---

[7]   That phrase was used in *Standard Electronic Apparatus Pty Ltd v Stenner* [1960] NSWR 447 to describe the holding by a lienee, a person with a recognised possessory interest in the chattel binding the lienor. But there does not seem to be any reason for excluding other persons who enjoy possession under a contract with the owner, even though the holding does not confer a recognised possessory interest such as a lien. The result in *Lord v Price* (1847) LR 8 Ex 54 may possibly be defended on the ground that the plaintiff had not paid for the cotton, and in the absence of delivery by the auctioneer, was not liable for the price of the cotton.

The owner is not entitled to bring conversion where he or she has surrendered the right to immediate possession of the chattel, for example by bailing it for a term. This applies both as against the bailee and third parties: *Gordon v Harper* (1796) 7 TR 9; 101 ER 828. Rules of commercial law may deny the owner the right to immediate possession of the chattel. In *Lord v Price* (1847) LR 8 Ex 54 the plaintiff bought two lots of cotton at an auction, thereby under the law relating to sale of goods becoming their owner. The terms of the sale required immediate payment, but only a deposit had been paid. When the owner came to collect the last lot, he found that it had been taken in mistake by the defendant, whom he then sued in conversion. The action failed on the ground that until the full price of the cotton was paid he was not entitled to immediate possession. For the action to succeed the plaintiff must have been either in actual possession, or entitled to immediate possession of the goods when they were converted.

Possession once enjoyed confers a right to retain the chattel, or reacquire it from other persons, provided that those persons do not have a superior right to that of the possessor. The clearest recognition of this state of the law is the following statement contained in the joint judgment of Isaacs and Rich JJ in *Russell v Wilson* (1923) 33 CLR 538 at 546: "Possession is not merely evidence of absolute title; it confers a title of its own, which is sometimes called possessory title. This possessory title is as good as the absolute title as against, it is usually said, every person except the absolute owner." (Note that this qualification is too narrowly stated.)

It should be noted that possessory title is stated here in general terms, rather than in terms of special cases such as finders' possessory title, although the latter is a clear example of the general principle.

Russell concerned the right of a stakeholder of illegal betting money to recover it from the police by whom it had been seized prior to a successful prosecution. Holding the stakeholder entitled to maintain detinue against the police for their refusal to return the money, the two judges in question found this established on the basis of the stakeholder's previous possession of the money rather than his title to it, since no title had passed to him under the illegal transaction. The joint judgment is an example of possession being protected for its own sake, rather than as providing evidence of title. An example of recognition of a possessory title is also provided by the case of *Perpetual Trustee v Perkins* [1989] Aust Torts Reports 80-295. In this case, it was held that the previous custodians of certain family paintings were entitled to succeed in conversion against the executors of another family member to whom they had been lent, even though the plaintiffs could not show actual title.

Illegally obtained possession

[5.90] The fact that possession has been illegally acquired does not prevent a possessory title being successfully asserted against third parties against whom the illegality was not perpetrated. In *Bird v Fort Francis Municipality* [1949] 2 DLR 791 the finder of banknotes was allowed to succeed in conversion against the Municipality, which had acquired the money from the police who had seized it from the plaintiff's possession. The court refused to entertain the question whether the plaintiff committed larceny by finding, holding this to be irrelevant to whether the plaintiff had a valid possessory title.

Finders' possessory title

[5.95] The original recognition of finders' possessory title was in *Armory v Delamirie* (1722) 1 Strange 505; 93 ER 664. A chimney-sweep's boy found a jewel in a chimney and took it to the defendant jeweller for valuation. The boy refused the defendant's offer for the jewel, and then successfully sued him in conversion for refusing to return it. The court stated that the finder "has such property as will enable him to keep it against all but the rightful owner". This statement is too wide in two respects.

First, it is clear that persons other than the owner may have superior rights to the finder, even arguably those with a previous possessory title that has not been voluntarily surrendered. Second, in some situations the occupier of the land on which the finding takes place has a superior possessory title to that of the finder. In *Armory* itself, the action was not brought against the owner of the house. However, in *Bridges v Hawkesworth* (1851) 21 QB 75, it was held that the plaintiff finder acquired a title superior to that of the defendant owner of a shop on the floor of which he had found some money.

Later cases have established the superior title of the occupier to that of the finder in the case of things found attached to land (*South Staffordshire Water Company v Sharman* [1896] 2 QB 44; *City of London v Appleyard* [1963] 1 WLR 982) or buried underneath it: *Ewles v Brigg Gas Co* (1886) 33 Ch D 562; *Ranger v Griffin* (1968) 87 WN (NSW) 531. These cases were based on the legal principle that the occupiers in these cases had possession of the chattel before it was found, even without their knowing of its existence. They seem also to provide tacit recognition of a policy element based on the fact that the landowner is in a much better position than the finder to restore the finding to its true owner. The force of this reasoning led to some questioning of the decision in *Bridges* concerning goods found on the surface of private land and the suggestion that it should be limited to its own facts, that is, to goods found in the public part of the shop.

Parker v British Airways Board [1982] QB 1004[8] recognised the relevance of the policy issue to the question of who gets possessory title on a finding. The case more or less successfully resolves the issue where title should go in the case of a finding on the surface of private land. It also, less successfully, attempts to provide a "quasi-legislative" code for finding cases in general. The case concerned a finding of a bracelet on the floor of the executive lounge of the defendants' airway by the plaintiff, a first-class passenger. Entry to the lounge was limited to first-class passengers and staff. After handing in the bracelet to the lost property office, the plaintiff later found that the defendants had sold it. The plaintiff successfully sued the defendants for conversion of the bracelet. The question at issue between plaintiff and defendants was who had possessory title, the owner of the bracelet never being discovered. Donaldson LJ, giving the leading judgment in the Court of Appeal, laid weight upon the policy element favouring possessory title in the

---

[8]   See also *Flack v National Crime Authority* [1998] Aust Torts Reports 81-459 – inducement to report the find in the form of finders' title. The finder was likely to disappear with the find. Here, therefore, the finder should be awarded the title. The test of "privacy" was whether the occupier of the building "has manifested an intention to exercise control over the building and the things which may be upon it or in it". Application of this test produced a spectrum of possible results, according to the degree of public access to which the land was subject. At one extreme was the public park; at the other, the bank vault containing safe deposits. In between were forecourts of petrol filling situations, unfenced front gardens and the public parts of shops and supermarkets. The lounge of the airport was in the middle band, and there was no sufficient manifestation of an intention to exercise control over it by the occupier to justify a holding that it had a possessory title to things found there.

occupier in the case of a finding on private land, but found that policy to be much weaker where the finding was on private land to which the public had access.[9]

Donaldson LJ expressed the principles about findings on the surface of land in terms of buildings alone, but the examples quoted above from his judgment cover finding on land appurtenant to buildings, and even in a public park. Perhaps some reservation would apply with respect to a finding on a vast tract of private land, even though the occupier has the necessary intention to exclude the public. Findings in chattels capable of occupation, such as ships or airplanes, are equated in *Parker* with findings in buildings.

[5.100] Under the "quasi-legislative" code, the finder acquires very limited rights over the chattel if he or she takes it with dishonest intent or in the course of trespassing; but how limited? (Compare *Bird v Fort Francis Municipality* [1949] 2 DLR 791, where the plaintiff, who seems to have been trespassing and who may also have committed larceny by finding, was accorded title to sue in conversion.)

The finder "has an obligation to take such measures as are reasonable to acquaint the true owner of the finding". It is not clear what is the legal basis of this obligation, assuming it adds anything to the normal rule that in certain circumstances a finder commits larceny if he or she fails to take steps to inform the owner of the find. Finally, Donaldson LJ confirms the generally understood position that an "employee or agent who finds in the course of his or her employment or agency and not wholly collaterally thereto finds on behalf of his employer or principal".

There is some Australian authority in support of this, but it is weak,[10] and is contradicted by a majority decision in *Byrne v Hoare* [1965] Qd R 135. It is not clear why a finding in the course of employment should go to the employer; and it is by no means clear what is the course of employment, but not "wholly collateral thereto".

Treasure trove

[5.105] Finders' title does not apply in cases of so-called treasure trove: *R v Hancock* [1990] 2 WLR 640. Under the rules of treasure trove, the Crown has a prerogative right to gold or silver in the form of coin, plate or bullion found in such circumstances that its ownership is unknown but the circumstances of the finding indicate that the property was not lost or abandoned (for example, it is hidden in the earth or other private place).

The relevant Australian Crown for these purposes is the State Crown where the finding is in State land, and the Commonwealth Crown where it is found in land belonging to the Commonwealth.

Proprietary rights

[5.110] The plaintiff's right to sue in conversion must be based on a right of property

---

[9] *Flack v National Crime Authority* [1998] Aust Torts Reports 81-459 – occupier of premises entitled as against the police to money found on premises during a police search and which the police believed to represent the proceeds of crime. The Court of Appeal in *Waverley RC v Fletcher* [1995] 4 All ER 756 resolved a conflict between the "public access land" principle and the attachment principle in favour of the latter – the finding of a brooch by use of a metal detector in a public park went to the Council, not to the finder.

[10] *Ranger v Griffin* (1968) 87 WN (NSW) 531; *Willey v Synan* (1937) 57 CLR 200 (no clear ruling on the point).

or possession in the chattel. A mere contractual right to immediate possession is not enough. In *Jarvis v Williams* [1955] 1 WLR 71,[11] A had a contractual right to immediate delivery of some bathroom fittings from B. The fittings were in the possession of C, who refused A's demand for the fittings. This was held not to be detinue (which is no different from conversion on the title to sue), because A's only right was a contractual one against B. The result is logical. C also may have had contractual rights regarding the fittings against B and there is no reason why A's contractual rights should receive priority over these. Property in the chattel would, on the other hand, have given A a claim in rem (available against persons generally) and would have been superior to whatever contractual rights C possessed against B.

Some doubt was cast upon *Jarvis* by *International Factors Ltd v Rodriguez* [1979] 1 QB 351. In that case, Sir David Cairns (with whom Bridge LJ agreed) held that the defendant was liable for the conversion of cheques to which the plaintiffs had a mere contractual right to immediate possession of, on the ground that the plaintiffs on the facts had an equitable proprietary interest in the cheques. Buckley LJ came to the same conclusion on the differing ground that the plaintiffs' contractual right to immediate possession was sufficient to entitle them to bring conversion. In *MCC v Lehmann Bros* [1997] EWCA 4421,[12] the Court of Appeal limited the majority ratio in *International Factors* to the situation in that case, that is, that the plaintiffs had both an equitable proprietary right and a right to immediate possession. A holder of an equitable interest is in general not allowed to bring conversion, since that right rests in the trustee who has the right to immediate possession.

Jus tertii and conversion

[5.115] The principles stated here apply to the torts of trespass to chattels and to conversion. Jus tertii may be translated as the right of a third party: *Eastern Construction v National Trust* [1914] AC 197; *Edwards v Amos* (1945) 62 WN (NSW) 204. The problem to be faced is whether, and in what circumstances, the plaintiff with a superior title to the defendant may be defeated, if the defendant shows that a third party has a superior title to that of the plaintiff. The problem largely arises because of the courts' recognition of possessory titles, which permits the possible existence of two titles to one chattel: one arising from a "paper title" and one from possessory title. In particular, a plaintiff with possessory title may sometimes be defeated by showing that paper title to the chattel exists in a third party. Generally, jus tertii is clearly available as a defence to the plaintiff's action in three circumstances:

- Where the defendant has throughout acted on the instructions of the third party.
- Where the defendant has been evicted from the chattel by title paramount, that is, of the third party; though not, according to the unsatisfactory decision in *Wilson v Lombank Ltd* [1963] 1 WLR 1294, where the defendant has voluntarily made satisfaction to the third party.
- Where the defendant is defending the action under the authority of the third party: *Biddle v Bond* (1865) 6 B&S 225; 122 ER 1179.

---

[11]   Cf *Hunter BNZ Finance Ltd v Mahoney* [1990] VR 41: where a contractual party had exercised a right to rescind a contract for fraud, the property revested in the rescinding party enabling it to bring conversion.

[12]   See in general Atiyah (1955) 18 MLR 97; Jolly (1955) 18 MLR at 371; Baker (1990) 16 UQLJ 46.

All three cases in which the defence has been allowed may be explained on the basis that the third party has intervened in the dispute. In effect, the contest is between the plaintiff and the third party. What is the position where this is not so? First, it is established that where the defendant has invaded an existing possession, an action of trespass or conversion cannot be defeated by a plea of jus tertii: *Wilson v Lombank* (trespass); *Jeffries v Great Western Railway* (1856) SKI & B1 802; 119 ER 680 (conversion). Where, on the other hand, the plaintiff is relying on the right to possession of the chattel at the time of the defendant's act, the text writers generally say that the right to possession must be affirmatively established, and is defeated by the defence showing a better title in a third party.[13]

The leading case[14] on which this view is based was one where the plaintiff had no title to sue in conversion whatsoever.[15] In *Leake v Loveday* (1842) 4 Man & G 972; 134 ER 399, the plaintiff's title to certain furniture under a bill of sale became overridden by the superior title of the assignees in bankruptcy when the hirer of the furniture became bankrupt. The plaintiff was, therefore, unable to succeed in an action of conversion against the sheriff who had seized and sold the furniture under a writ of execution and had handed the proceeds of sale to the assignees. The sheriff successfully relied on the title of the assignees to defeat the plaintiff's action for conversion.

This was not a case of jus tertii. The plaintiff was shown by proof of the assignees' title to have no actual title to the furniture, and was unable to establish a possessory title, never having been in possession of the furniture. As a matter of principle, there seems to be no good reason for allowing a possessory title to be defeated by a defence of jus tertii, unless the third party has intervened in the matter by asserting its title. This applies whether the plaintiff is complaining of an invasion of possession or is asserting a right to possession based on previous possession.[16]

A bailor who is suing the bailee in conversion is relying on a right to possession rather than actual possession at the time of the bailee's act. Nevertheless, in this situation it is clear that jus tertii cannot be pleaded by the bailee except in the three exceptional cases detailed above. The bailor's title to sue is sometimes said to arise from estoppel against the bailee, arising from the latter's acceptance of the chattel. If the bailor has actual title, there is no need for estoppel. If not, the bailor is able to rely on the rule concerning possessory title. That being so, the case supports the general proposition that jus tertii should not be allowed to defeat possessory titles except in the three exceptional cases.

A bailee who is faced with inconsistent demands for the chattel by the bailor and a third party is faced with a dilemma: if the bailee were to comply with the demand of the person who proves not to be entitled to the chattel, that would be a conversion against the other, and it may be impossible or very difficult for the bailee to determine who has the superior title. The bailee's solution is to institute interpleader proceedings, joining the bailor and the third party. The court then determines the issue of title as between them, and the bailee is protected against liability by surrendering this chattel in accordance with the order of the court.

---

[13] *Salmond's Law of Torts* (13th ed, 1961) p 280; Rogers, *Winfield and Jolowicz on Tort* (14th ed, 1994) p 501.

[14] *Leake v Loveday* (1842) 4 Man & G 972; 134 ER 399. There is also some weak obiter authority in Australia in support of the text book position: *Wood v Mason Bros Ltd* (1892) 13 LR (NSW) 66; *Henry Berry & Co Pty Ltd v Rushton* [1937] St R Qd I 09.

[15] See Atiyah (1955) 18 MLR 97.

[16] See the argument in support of this in Baker (1990) 16 UQLJ 46.

Nature of defendant's act

[5.120] Certain fundamentals apply to all acts regarded as conversion. First, there must be an intentional act of dealing with the chattel. Conversion, unlike trespass, requires an intentional act; mere negligence is not enough. It does not follow that there must be an intention to convert the chattel; an intention to deal with it is enough, provided the dealing amounts to a conversion. Many innocent, although intentional, dealings with chattels are conversion, so that the tort may operate as one of strict liability.

The strict liability involved in conversion may operate more harshly than that involved in trespass to chattels. In the latter case, the defendant almost invariably knows that he or she is committing an invasion of another person's possession, although the defendant may have reason to think it to be justified. In conversion there may be nothing to indicate to the defendant the plaintiff's connection with the chattel. Strict liability in conversion is partly to be explained by reference to the proprietary function of the tort. It may be brought to resolve a dispute over title, and fault is irrelevant to the question of title.

The Law Reform Committee in England found there to be support for strict liability in conversion among commercial dealers in chattels on the ground of the certainty in the law that this brought about, together with the avoidance of expensive litigation over fault. Such dealers will no doubt occupy the position of plaintiff in the action in as many cases as they are defendants. And in the latter case they will possess insurance. But hard cases undoubtedly arise out of liability on the part of honest, uninsured persons.

The second fundamental is that, subject to what is said below, there must be a physical dealing with the chattel. So, it is not conversion to sell the chattel without effecting delivery of it (*Lancashire Waggon Co Ltd v Fitzhugh* (1861) 6 H & N 502; 158 ER 206); nor is it conversion to assert a title to a chattel that one does not have: *Short v City Bank of Sydney* (1912) 15 CLR 148.

Although conversion may be established without showing that the defendant either knew or ought to have known of the plaintiff's rights in the chattel, proof of knowledge is clearly relevant to showing that a conversion has been committed. Almost any dealing with a chattel, even the retention of possession of it, committed after knowledge that it is inconsistent with the plaintiff's right to possession of the chattel, will rank as conversion.

Finally, it must be emphasised that the test of whether a conversion has been committed is a general one. Certain typical cases of conversion exist and are covered in this chapter, but they are not exhaustive of the tort. The test laid down in the definition put forward at [5.65] is that the defendant's act must be so seriously inconsistent with the plaintiff's right to possession of his or her chattel as to amount to a denial of it. Examination of the case law shows that the cases in which a conversion has been found to have been committed tend to divide into two kinds. The first is where the *exercise* of the right to possession is denied, in that the defendant's act either deprives the plaintiff of possession or renders it more difficult to obtain it. The second is where the defendant, by purporting to deal with the title to the chattel, has denied the plaintiff's title and thereby the right to possession.

This division is not an absolute one. Some cases of conversion fall into both categories; others are difficult to fit within either.[17] We start with cases where the essence of the conversion is the threat to the plaintiff's possession.

---

17   Conversion by innocent user is difficult to fit within either category, but it may not be conversion.

Conversion by acts threatening plaintiff's possession

Dispossession

[5.125] In general, it is conversion to dispossess the plaintiff, at least where the defendant intends to hold the chattel for him or herself. This qualification led to a finding of no conversion in *Fouldes v Willoughby* (1841) 8 M&W 540; 151 ER 1153. In this case the defendant, wishing to evict the plaintiff from his ferry boat, put the plaintiff's horses off the boat. The plaintiff remained on board and took the crossing. The plaintiff's action for conversion failed. The case does not turn on the fact that the plaintiff dispossessed himself, since he was entitled to remain on the boat unless he was guilty of conduct justifying his removal, and this was not determined. The ground for the decision was that the defendant had set up no claim of his own to the horses: "the simple removal of the horses by the defendant, for a purpose wholly unconnected with the least denial of the right of the plaintiff to the possession of them, is no conversion of the horses". The defendant's action clearly constituted trespass, but at the time of the case the forms of action system still prevailed, and the plaintiff chose to sue in conversion. A thief clearly commits conversion, as does a joyrider, even if the joyrider takes the vehicle intending to return it: *Aitken Agencies Ltd v Richardson* [1967] NZLR 65.

The qualification in *Schemmel v Pomeroys* (1989) 50 SASR 45 (doubted by Young J in *Flowfill Packaging Machines Pty Ltd v Fytore Pty Ltd* [1993] Aust Torts Reports 81-244) that joyriding is only conversion if the defendant intended to drive the car recklessly or destructively at the time of taking, or the car is actually destroyed, seems inconsistent with principle. The New Zealand decision in *Wilson v New Brighton Panelbeaters Ltd* [1989] 1 NZLR 74 raised a doubt whether dispossession amounts to conversion where it is done in good faith, even if it is for the defendant's own purposes. This doubt runs contrary to the Victorian case of *Rendell v Associated Finance Pty Ltd* [1957] VR 604, which emphasised the strict liability element in conversion. *Rendell* also shows that dispossession of the plaintiff's bailee amounts to conversion against the plaintiff.

Destruction

[5.130] It is conversion to intentionally destroy the plaintiff's chattel or to change its form. The crushing of grapes in order to produce wine is a conversion, as is the grinding of another's corn, but not the bottling of wine in order to preserve it.[18] Partial damage to the chattel is actionable under other torts such as trespass or negligence.

Misdelivery

[5.135] It is conversion for a carrier or bailee to deliver a chattel, which is the subject-matter of the contract of carriage or bailment, to the wrong person. It is no defence that the defendant acted under a reasonable mistake, since conversion here imposes strict liability, although there is no liability for delivery in accordance with the instructions received from the consignor: *McKean v McIvor* (1870) LR 6 Ex 36.

---

[18] *Hollins v Fowler* (1875) LR 7 HL 757 at 764, 768; *Philpott v Kelly* (1853) 3 Ad & E 106; 111 ER 353; *Youl v Harbottle* (1791) Peake 68; 170 ER 81; *Tozer Kennsley & Millbourn (A'Asia) Pty Ltd v Colliers Interstate Transport Service Ltd* (1956) 94 CLR 384. The defendant must be in possession: *Ashby v Tolhurst* [1937] 2 KB 242 (where a car was parked in a car park under licence, the car park owner did not have possession and the attendant did not convert the car by giving it to a rogue).

Misdelivery by an involuntary bailee is treated differently. An involuntary bailment arises where a person comes into possession of goods against that person's wishes, the paradigm case being that of mail delivered to the wrong address. If the bailee takes reasonable steps to redeliver the chattel to the person entitled to it, even though, in fact, redelivery is made to a rogue, there is no liability.

Conversion here depends on negligence: *Elvin & Powell Ltd v Plummer Roddis Ltd* (1933) 50 TLR 158. In order to take advantage of this alleviation, the defendant must be in the position of an involuntary bailee. Conversion occurred where the defendant, not being in possession of goods, endorsed a delivery note, under which the goods were deliverable by the railway company which had possession of them to the order of the plaintiff or defendant, in favour of a rogue who was then able to get possession of the goods from the railway company and disappear with them: *Elvin*. The defendant was not an involuntary bailee, so there was no reason for him to have acted as he did, the goods being obtainable by the plaintiff on demand from the railway company.

Demand and refusal

[5.140] It is conversion for a person in possession of a chattel to refuse to return it on demand made by the person entitled to its immediate possession: *Howard E Perry & Co Ltd v British Railways Board* [1980] 1 WLR 1375; *Upton v TVW Enterprises* [1985] ATPR 40-611. Refusal of the demand must be unreasonable. Where the demand is made by the plaintiff's agent, it is not unreasonable to ask for evidence of the agent's authority to make the demand (*Clayton v LeRoy* [1911] KB 1031); nor is it unreasonable to refuse to return the chattel where inconsistent demands are made on the defendant and the defendant is instituting interpleader proceedings: *EE McCurdy v Postmaster General* [1959] NZLR 553.

Conversion is only available in the case of a demand and refusal where the defendant has possession at the time of the demand. Where a bailee has lost goods, conversion based on demand and refusal therefore does not lie (although other bases for conversion may exist), but detinue may be available: see [5.175].

Conversion by negligence

[5.145] Although conversion requires an intentional rather than a negligent dealing with the chattel, it seems that where an intentional dealing is foreseeably likely to lead to the ultimate loss or destruction of the chattel the defendant is liable if that loss or destruction occurs.

An old case held that a mere asportation of a chattel was a conversion where the chattel was placed at a location likely to lead to its loss and that loss occurred: *Forsdickz v Collins* (1816) 1 Stark 173. Furthermore, in *Moorgate Mercantile Co v Finch* [1963] 3 WLR 110, the Court of Appeal held there was liability in conversion where the defendant drove the plaintiff's car with a quantity of uncustomed Swiss watches inside, in consequence of which the car was seized by the authorities and permanently forfeited. The court endeavoured to explain this on the basis of an intentional conversion, either on the now outmoded concept of intention (that one is taken to intend the natural and probable consequences of one's acts), or on the high degree of likelihood of seizure and forfeiture of the car, which seems open to question.

The case seems explicable as one in which conversion was based on negligence. The defendant intended the act of driving the car with the watches inside and ought to have foreseen the risk of its loss. If negligence is the essential ingredient of this type of conversion, it might seem to possess no advantage over an ordinary action for negligence, though on the facts of *Moorgate Mercantile* it is possible that a duty of care might have been difficult to establish. Under statutory provisions it is necessary to prove negligence in an action against a bank for conversion of a cheque.

Conversion by purported dealing in title

[5.150] The cases on dealing in title have as their central characteristic that the defendant, having acquired possession of the chattel in good faith, purports to deal with the title to it, for example by selling it. These cases do not depend upon any threat to the plaintiff's possession as a result of the dealing. The chattel's possession is already effectively lost and the defendant's act of innocent dealing with the chattel does not have any further detrimental effect upon the plaintiff's ability to regain possession. The essence of conversion is that the purported dealing in title to the chattel is in derogation of and denies the plaintiff's own title. The main question is: what sort of dealings have this effect?

In *Hollins v Fowler* (1875) LR 7 HL 757, the defendant, Hollins, a cotton broker, bought the plaintiff's cotton from a rogue who had no power to sell it to him, and then purported to sell it to his usual principal, Micholls (although on these facts Hollins was found to have acted as a principal rather than as agent). Hollins was in entire good faith throughout, but his sale and delivery of the cotton was held to be conversion. The question was thought to be important enough for a specially convened House of Lords of ten judges to hear it, and there is considerable disparity among the majority of eight who thought it to be conversion. Some members of the House of Lords thought that it was important that Hollins acted as principal rather than agent. The judgment of Blackburn J, which is now taken as a correct statement of the relevant principles, found this distinction to be unimportant, but thought the relevant matter to be whether the defendant's dealing with the chattel was of a mere ministerial nature, or whether it purported to affect title to the chattel. On this basis, Hollins clearly committed conversion since his act of sale was intended to transfer title to the buyer.

The question then arises as to what dealings fall within the non-ministerial variety so as to attract liability in conversion. Sale is the prime and obvious example of the non-ministerial dealing. Indeed it is almost the exclusive example as far as the case law is concerned, although other transactions under which a transfer of title is intended are clearly included, such as gift, or mortgage. It soon became established that persons such as auctioneers who sell as agents rather than principals commit conversion: *Consolidated Co v Curtis* [1892] 1 QB 495. Employees also, even if merely acting under their employer's instructions, may be liable: *Stephens v Ewall* (1815) 4 M&S 259. It is now clear that the buyer under the sale also commits conversion.[19] There can be no good ground for differentiating the buyer from the seller. No case yet decides whether hire-purchasing a chattel is a conversion of it. The doubt arises because hire-purchase operates initially as a bailment of the chattel with final transfer of title delayed until payment of the hire-purchase is complete. A mere bailment of a chattel is not conversion since, even though it may purport to create rights that are inconsistent with those of the true owner, it is nevertheless a mere temporary transfer of possession with no intention to transfer title.

---

[19] A modern example is *Hillesden Securities Ltd v Ryjack* [1983] 1 WLR 959.

Hire-purchases and pledges

[5.155] Hire-purchase is something of a halfway house. So too is pledge, in which possession of goods is transferred as security for a loan subject to retransfer upon repayment of the loan, with the proviso that in the event of non-payment the pledgee may sell the goods, thus purporting to transfer title from pledgor to pledgee and then to buyer. Pledge is like hire-purchase, but contemplates a later transfer of title. The case law on whether the initial act of pledging is conversion is unclear. There is authority to the effect that receipt by a pledgee is not conversion (*Spackman v Foster* (1883) 11 QBD 99; *Miller v Dell* [1891] 1 QB 468), but that conversion is committed by the pledgor in pledging the goods: *Parker v Godin* (1728) 2 Strange 813; 93 ER 866 (where the pledge was probably committed innocently). This is unsatisfactory because, as in the case of sale, both parties to the transaction should convert or neither. The authority in favour of the pledgor is slight and unsatisfactory compared with the clear decision that the pledgee does not. It is suggested that the latter represents the more satisfactory state of the law.

Difficulties have arisen where the defendant has not negotiated but merely facilitated the transaction transferring title to the goods. Blackburn J in *Hollins v Fowler* (1875) LR 7 HL 757 thought that the defendant would be liable here if he or she could be fixed with knowledge that the transaction was one affecting title to the goods. He indicated the possibility of this applying to carriers of goods, although noting the unlikelihood of their possessing the relevant knowledge, and pointing to the early case of *Stephens v Elwall* (1815) 4 M&S 259 in which an employee who bought goods on behalf of his employer and transferred them to his master who was overseas was held liable in conversion even though he had acted on behalf of his employer. Blackburn J recognised the extreme hardship of this case, and some later authority went against it. In *National Mercantile Bank v Rymill* (1881) 44 LT 767, an auctioneer who merely delivered goods in his possession, knowing this to be in furtherance of a private sale conducted by his client, did not commit conversion.[20] In some strong obiter dicta, the Court of Appeal found this case to be inconsistent with the principles laid down in *Hollins*: *RH Willis v British Car Auctions* [1978] 2 All ER 392. Further, delivery to a rogue under a supposed sale was held to be a conversion, even though no such sale existed: *Wilson v New Brighton Panel Beaters* [1989] 1 NZLR 74.

Actual and constructive delivery of goods

[5.160] A question arises as to what is the position where the defendant is not in possession at the time of the dealing. A mere sale unaccompanied by delivery of the goods is not conversion. It is different where the sale effects a constructive delivery, or where it changes the character of possession held by a person, thus appearing to release that person from their obligations in relation to the goods.

---

[20] See also *Greenway v Fisher* (1827) 7 B&C 436; 108 ER 786; *Re Samuels* [1945] Ch 408. In neither case was there an intended dealing with title.

Figure 5.5: Acts of conversion

....

> • Mere asportation is no conversion.
> • The defendant's conduct must constitute an unjustifiable denial
>   of the plaintiff's right to the chattel, such as:
>   – destruction of the chattel;
>   – taking possession;
>   – withholding possession;
>   – misdelivery;
>   – unauthorised dispositions.

In *Motor Dealers Ltd v Overland* (1931) 31 SR(NSW) 516 the defendants had bought the plaintiffs' car from a rogue, and without taking delivery, had resold it to a third party. The rogue delivered the car to the third party acting on the defendants' instructions. This was held to be a conversion by the defendants, since there had been a constructive delivery of the car by them through the rogue. An example of the latter type of case is *Van Oppen v Tredegars Ltd* (1921) 37 TLR 504. The plaintiffs had delivered certain goods to the premises of a firm, which was then in the position of an involuntary bailee for the plaintiffs. The defendants' managing director purported to sell the goods to the firm, which disposed of them in the course of business. The sale by the managing director was held to be a conversion by the defendants, since it changed the character of the possession held by the firm. Initially the firm was an involuntary bailee, but through the purchase acquired the belief it was owner of the goods.

Public Trustee v Jones (1925) 25 SR(NSW) 526 is distinguishable from *Van Oppen* in that the sale in this case was commissioned by a third party through the defendant as an auctioneer. The defendant's mere sale of furniture did not change the character of possession held by the third party; nor was it the effective cause of delivery being made, since the sale had been held on the third party's instructions. In order to amount to a conversion under the category of a dealing without physical transfer of possession by the defendant, the dealing must purport to affect the right to possession of the chattel in question. It was not conversion for the Commonwealth wrongfully to give one of certain joint owner/possessors a customs clearance relating to a ship, thereby enabling that person to sail the ship away, since the clearance did not affect the right to possession of the ship: *Kitano v Commonwealth* (1974) 129 CLR 151.

Problematic cases of conversion

....

Absolute denial of plaintiff's title

[5.165] It is not conversion merely to assert a title to the plaintiff's chattel, although it may constitute other torts such as slander of title to goods or defamation. In *England v Cowley* (1873) LR 8 Ex 126, Kelly CB thought that an act that constituted an absolute denial and repudiation of the plaintiff's title was a conversion. In *England* the defendant prevented the plaintiff from removing certain furniture from the premises at night which the plaintiff was in possession of under a bill of sale, the defendant's motive being that she would thereby be able to levy a distress on the furniture during daylight hours. This was held to not be a conversion since the plaintiff was always left in possession of the furniture and, therefore, his right to possession was unaffected.

Kelly CB said that there could be no conversion here unless the act of the defendant amounted to an absolute denial and repudiation of the plaintiff's title. Would it therefore have made a difference in *England* if the defendant had also denied the plaintiff's title to possession of the furniture? It is hard to see why, since the essence of the plaintiff's complaint was the interference with the exercise of his possessory rights over the chattel. It is easy to see the force of the dissenting judge's view in *England* that there was a conversion, since although the plaintiff was left in possession, the only incident of that possession which he was interested in exercising (the removal of the furniture), was denied by the defendant's act.

The utility of Kelly CB's concept seems to be open to doubt but it was applied as the ratio decidendi of Scrutton LJ in *Oakley v Lyster* [1931] 1 KB 148. The plaintiff had taken a lease of land in order to store on it a quantity of hard core which he owned. The plaintiff was therefore in possession of the land and of the hard core. The defendant, having acquired ownership of the land, without any justification claimed ownership of the hard core, and used some of it. He also by letter to the plaintiff refused him permission to remove the hard core, adding that he would be treated as a trespasser if he did so.

Scrutton LJ found the defendant liable in conversion of the whole of the hard core, even though he had not taken possession of the part of it he had not used. The defendant's conduct amounted to an absolute denial and repudiation of the plaintiff's title, since the defendant had claimed ownership and supported this by acts, that is by using part of the material and by his letter denying the plaintiff access to it: *Oakley* at 153-154.

Greer LJ agreed with this ratio, but also supplied an alternative: that the defendant, by combination of acts and statements, had actually taken possession of the whole of the material and, therefore, dispossessed the plaintiff of it: *Oakley* at 155. This interpretation of the facts certainly seems to have been open to the court, thereby rendering the "absolute denial" ratio unnecessary. The same is true of *Motor Dealers v Overland* [1931] 1 KB 148, in which the "absolute denial" reasoning was used as a second ratio. At the moment the need for Kelly CB's concept is not established.

A related problem arises out of the rule that it is not conversion or detinue for an occupier of land to refuse to return a chattel that has arrived on to the land without any act of the occupier, or to allow the plaintiff entry in order to recover it: *British Economical Lamp Co v Empire Theatre Mile End Ltd* (1913) 29 TLR 386. The problem is exacerbated by reason of the fact that no right of recaption of the chattel exists unless the chattel has arrived on the land "accidentally" or by the felonious act of a third party. If the occupier has taken possession of the chattel, a refusal to return it on demand will constitute conversion, so that the difficulty exists only where the occupier has simply left the chattel in position and refused to return it.

What if the occupier has without taking possession claimed ownership or other entitlement to it? It is hard to see that this should make a difference. It is possible that under the reasoning based on absolute denial and repudiation it may do so.

Wrongful user

[5.170] The question whether wrongful user is a conversion effectively arises only where the defendant has come into possession of the chattel without any prior trespass or conversion on his or her part. It is necessary here to distinguish user in bad faith (that is, in the knowledge that it is contrary to the plaintiff's right to possession of the chattel) from innocent user. The former should be conversion on the basis that almost any dealing with a chattel in the knowledge that it is inconsistent with the plaintiff's right to possession is conversion, even possibly mere retention of the chattel. Despite the denial by Dixon J in *Penfolds Wines Pty Ltd v Elliott* (1946) 74 CLR 204 that user could in any circumstances amount to conversion, there is considerable Australian authority that user in bad faith constitutes conversion: *Model Dairy Pty Ltd v White* (1935) 41 ALR 432; *Craig v Marsh* (1935) 35 SR(NSW) 323; *Cook v Saroulos* (1989) 97 FLR 33.

The problem centres on innocent user. At first sight it seems difficult to bring innocent user within either of the two categories of conversion considered above. User by one who has acquired possession in good faith and without dispossessing the plaintiff does not deny the plaintiff possession, nor, even though it is done under a belief in a right to use, does the user deny title since there is no attempt to deal in title. The latter point has been regarded as a reason for finding innocent bailees not liable in conversion by their receipt of goods; but this would seem pointless if they commit conversion by subsequently using the goods. Authority on the question of innocent user is divided.

In *Penfolds*, two members of the High Court, Latham CJ and McTiernan J, thought it to be conversion on the ground that in that case it was done under a claim of right that denied the plaintiff's title. But the majority of the High Court judges did not support the point: Dixon J ruling out altogether conversion by wrongful user, William J finding the user in that case to be in bad faith and Starke J merely assuming there to be a conversion without giving reasons. However, the views of Latham CJ and McTiernan J drew the support of Young J in *Flowfill Packaging Machines Pty Ltd v Fytore Pty Ltd* [1993] Aust Torts Reports 81-244, although this was obiter dictum.

Wrongful use by a bailee is governed by the same principles, but has the added complication that where the bailment is for a term the bailor has no right to immediate possession and cannot bring conversion. However, an act of the bailee that is totally inconsistent with the bailment and repugnant to it enables the bailor to bring conversion in relation to the act itself. Whether the wrongful user is so totally inconsistent with the bailment depends upon the facts of the case.[21]

Detinue

[5.175] The essence of detinue is demand and refusal. We saw in relation to conversion that an unreasonable refusal to return the plaintiff's chattel by a person in possession of it amounted to conversion. Detinue is identical to conversion in this situation as regards its substantive characteristics, although there are differences as to remedy.

However, detinue is wider than conversion in that it lies against one who no longer has possession at the time of the demand. Three leading examples of this form of detinue

---

[21]   *McKenna & Armistead Pty Ltd v Excavations Pty Ltd* [1956] 57 SR(NSW) 515 proceeded on the basis that even mala fide use by a bailee did not constitute conversion, although this was based on Dixon J's views in *Penfolds Wines Pty Ltd v Elliott* (1946) 74 CLR 204. The court limited the bailor's rights to recovering for damage caused by the use, including depreciation. The defendant is under an obligation to the plaintiff to retain possession. This will normally arise under a bailment, although it is not limited to bailments. It could arise, eg, where the defendant has seized goods acting under authority of law and then is in some way responsible for their loss or destruction.

need consideration. The examples are stated in terms of bailment, although they could apply to non-bailees. First, the bailee may have lost possession of the chattel by a prior conversion of it. Here the only difference between the two causes of action relates to the limitation period, the cause of action in detinue not accruing until the date of demand and refusal: *JF Goulding v Victorian Railways* (1932) 48 CLR 157. All States, except South Australia and Western Australia, have legislated to make the limitation period on the first cause of action the only relevant one where there are successive causes of action for conversion and/or detinue.[22]

The second case is where the bailee has deviated from the terms of the bailment and in the course of the deviation the goods have been lost or destroyed. In *Lilley v Doubleday* (1881) 7 QBD 510, the defendant bailee had stored goods in a warehouse other than the one in which it was required by the terms of the bailment to store them, and the goods were destroyed by fire. The bailee was held liable in detinue. The liability imposed here was strict since there was no question of the bailee's being liable for the fire. Nor could the bailee have been sued for conversion: the destruction through fire of the goods was not conversion, nor was storing them in the wrong warehouse.

The third case is where the goods have been lost or destroyed through negligence on the bailee's part: *Houghland v RR Low (Luxury Coaches)* [1962] 1 QB 694. Again conversion is not available, since it does not lie for negligence. The case law establishes that the legal burden of disproof of negligence lies on the bailee. The bailee must show a cause of the loss inconsistent with negligence on its part, or that it took all reasonable care, so that the court may infer the loss had another cause: per Willmer J at 700. A recent Australian example is *Westpac Banking Corp v Royal Tongan Airlines* [1996] Aust Torts Reports 81-403. In this case Qantas as bailee of some parcels of foreign currency for Westpac was held liable for their loss, since it was unable to establish that it maintained careful supervision of the mail parcels after they passed into its possession.

Figure 5.6: Detinue

- The wrongful refusal to tender goods upon demand by the plaintiff who is entitled to possession. It requires a demand coupled with subsequent refusal.
  - Plaintiff must specifically make demand for the return of the goods on the person with possession of them.
  - Plaintiff must have immediate right to possession at time of demand.
  - Plaintiff's demand must be refused by defendant.
  - Where goods are in the actual possession of the defendant, refusal to return the goods to the plaintiff must be unreasonable.

The law relating to what is demand and refusal seems to be identical to the respective law for conversion. Detinue cases have indicated that there is no sufficient demand where the plaintiff requires delivery from the defendant but does not indicate at what

22   *Limitation Act 1985* (ACT), s 18; *Limitation Act 1981* (NT), s 19; *Limitation Act 1969* (NSW), s 21; *Limitation of Actions Act 1974* (Qld), s 12; *Limitation Act 1974* (Tas), s 6; *Limitation of Actions Act 1958* (Vic), s 6; *Limitation Act 2005* (WA), s 60.

place, or indicates places of delivery which put an undue burden on the defendant: *Lloyd v Osborne* (1899) LR(NSW) 603; *Capital Finance Co Ltd v Bray* [1964] All ER 603.

As regards refusal, it was held in *Nelson v Nelson* [1923] St R Qd 37 that a mere failure to reply to a letter making a demand for goods did not constitute refusal. This may be based, however, upon the fact that the defendant's inaction was not sufficiently unequivocal as to amount to refusal. Bollen J in *Crowther v Australian Guarantee Corp Ltd* [1985] Aust Torts Reports 80-709 even thought that demand itself was unnecessary where the defendant had demonstrated "that he intends not to deliver the goods come what may". And formal demand and refusal may seem inappropriate where it is quite clear to both parties that the goods have been lost or destroyed.

As in the case of conversion, the defendant's refusal to return the chattel must be unreasonable. Title to sue in detinue is governed by the same principles as conversion. That title must continue until delivery up of the goods or judgment, as the case may be: *General & Finance Facilities v Cooks Cars (Romford)* [1963] 1 WLR 644 at 648 per Diplock LJ; *Au v Keelty* (2007) 94 ALD 132.

In all the cases considered above of loss or destruction of goods, which are the subject of a bailment, the action on the bailment is an alternative cause of action to that in detinue. Further, it has the same advantage as detinue that where the loss is proved the bailee has the legal burden of disproving fault on his or her part. The action on the bailment lies also for damage caused to the goods in the course of the bailment, whereas detinue requires their total loss or destruction. Detinue may, of course, lie against non-bailees, and there is also some doubt as to whether the action on the bailment is limited to commercial bailments. There is conflicting authority on this matter, whereas it is clear that detinue has no such limitation.[23] Whatever the cause of action, the standard of care of a gratuitous bailee will be lower than that applying in the case of a bailment for reward.[24]

Relationship between trespass, conversion and detinue

[5.180] Whereas trespass covered wrongful taking or asportation of chattels, detinue essentially dealt with wrongful detention. The law did not deal with situations in which the defendant had wrongfully taken the plaintiff's goods and subsequently converted them as such and was therefore unable to restore possession to the owner. The remedy of trover was developed to cover this situation. Indeed, the word "conversion" was coined from the fact of the defendant taking the plaintiff's property and subsequently converting it to his or her own use. These forms of action overlap with each other as much as they differ. It has been said before that whenever trespass for taking goods will lie (that is, where they are taken wrongfully), trover (conversion) will lie. This is not always the case. For instance, conversion will lie for a wrongful detention of goods which have not been

---

[23] *Lieberopolous v Jetner* (1987) 140 LSJS 25 and *Cowper v Goldner Pty Ltd* (1986) 40 SASR 457 contain suggestions that the action on the bailment is limited to commercial bailments. *Coggs v Barnard* (1703) 2 Ld Raym 909; 92 ER 107 allows it in the case of gratuitous bailment.

[24] *Coughlin v Cillinson* (1899) 1 QB 145; *Andrews v Home Flats* [1946] 2 All ER 698. There is inconclusive authority as to whether an involuntary bailee owes any duty of care as regards the safekeeping of the goods: *Howard v Harris* (1884) Cababe & Ellis 253 (no duty of care); *Newman v Bourne & Hollingsworth* (1915) 31 TLR 209 (liability only for gross negligence).

wrongfully taken, but trespass will not lie. Where the taking and subsequent detention of the chattel are both wrongful, conversion and trespass will lie.

A much more important difference between trespass and conversion can be discerned in their theoretical basis. The theory of trespass is that the plaintiff remained the rightful possessor of the chattel despite having his or her possession temporarily interfered with or interrupted by the defendant's trespassory act. The plaintiff is required to accept the chattel when it is returned and also to accept any damages awarded for the interference or loss of possession. The damages would invariably be lower than the full value of the chattel. On the other hand, the theory of conversion is that the defendant, by depriving the plaintiff of his or her property, has appropriated (or converted) such chattel to the defendant's own use or the use of another, and must therefore pay for it. The plaintiff is consequently not required to accept the chattel when the defendant returns it. The plaintiff is entitled to the value of the chattel as to the time when it was appropriated. In effect, the defendant is compelled to buy the chattel. Many interferences with goods, involving the withholding of such goods from the person entitled to immediate possession, provide bases for action in both conversion and detinue. To this extent, the two torts overlap. However, a plaintiff may want to sue in detinue because it allows the court, in appropriate circumstances, to order the defendant (detaining the goods) to return such chattels to the plaintiff and to pay for any losses sustained by the plaintiff as a result of the detention of the goods.

A much more significant difference between conversion and detinue is that, whereas demand and refusal constitute the gist of the action in detinue, demand and refusal constitute only one of many possible forms of conversion. For instance, no demand is necessary if conversion can be established some other way, for example, when the defendant had wrongfully disposed of the plaintiff's chattels. Here the plaintiff will maintain the action for conversion on the basis of a wrongful disposal and not a demand and a subsequent refusal. There are situations in which a demand and a subsequent failure to tender the goods to the plaintiff will not necessarily be actionable in conversion, because a bailee does not become a convertor on demand when the goods are no longer in his possession. Furthermore, if a bailee damages or loses goods through negligence the bailee cannot be sued in conversion because in this tort liability is predicated solely on intentional acts of misfeasance. On the other hand, if the bailee has wilfully disposed of the goods by delivering them to the wrong person the bailee is liable in conversion for the act, but not for his or her subsequent failure to tender the goods on demand. In contrast, in detinue it is immaterial whether the bailee's inability to re-deliver is due to a prior intentional act of wrongful disposition or to mere negligence resulting in the loss or destruction of the goods.

The relationship between the forms of action are represented in Figure 5.7. In the shaded areas the plaintiff would have a choice of remedy. If a bailee failed on lawful demand to return goods to the bailor, the situation would generally fall within the shaded area of the left-hand circle, so that both detinue and conversion would be available to the bailor. However, if the goods had been lost owing to the negligence of the bailee, then the situation would fall within the unshaded area of that circle and the bailor would have to sue in detinue. Similarly, if the defendant took goods out of the possession of the plaintiff, the facts would usually fall within the shaded area of the right-hand circle, so as to give rise to alternative remedies in trespass or conversion. However, if the defendant did not manifest an intention to exercise a right inconsistent with the plaintiff's rights, then the situation would fall within the unshaded area of that circle and trespass alone would lie.

Figure 5.7: Conversion, trespass and detinue

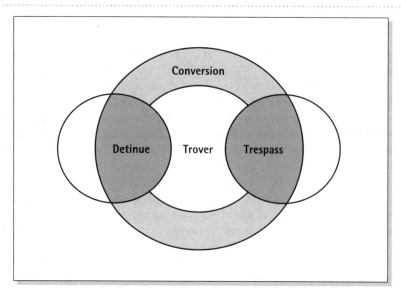

Defences to conversion and detinue

[5.185] There are certain statutory defences to actions for conversion or detinue available to bailees and involuntary bailees. These are dealt with in Chapter 7.

Satisfaction of judgment in conversion

[5.190] Where the defendant has satisfied a judgment in conversion by paying the whole value of the chattel to the plaintiff, the effect is to transfer the plaintiff's title to the defendant: *Ellis v Stenning* [1932] 2 Ch 81. This is not peculiar to conversion. Trespass and detinue also have this characteristic where the defendant is compelled to pay the whole value of the chattel as damages. In the case of conversion, the defendant may be denied the option of returning the chattel to the plaintiff, which is available in the case of the other torts, and therefore have to pay the whole value as damages. This "compulsory sale" aspect of conversion is discussed at [5.195]ff.

Where the defendant has satisfied a judgment obtained against him or her by the true owner by paying the value of the chattel, the defendant becomes the owner and is then immune to subsequent actions in tort brought by holders of possessory titles in the chattel. Where the holder of a possessory title has sued first and obtained a satisfied judgment for the value for the chattel, the defendant is still liable to be sued by the true owner, thereby being exposed to double liability: *Attenborough v London & St Katherines Docks* (1878) LR 3 CPD 450.

The same is not true where the first satisfied judgment is obtained by a bailee, since this bars a subsequent action against the defendant by the bailor.[25] This rule has its basis in the fact that the bailee has to account to the bailor for the amount of damages recovered that exceed the bailee's limited interest in the chattel, but has been criticised by Fleming on the ground that it exposes the bailor to various mishaps such as the

---

[25]   *The Winkfield* [1902] P 42 at 61; *Nicholls v Bastard* (1835) 2 Cr M&R 659. Satisfaction made to the bailor also
        bars an action by the bailee: *O'Sullivan v Williams* [1992] 1 All ER 385.

mishandling of the litigation by the bailee or the latter's insolvency or absconding with the proceeds.[26]

However, any solution to the problem presents difficulties. The bailee must be allowed to sue, since bailors for a term generally have no right to sue; nor should a defendant who has paid in full be prejudiced by the state of affairs between bailor and bailee. Fleming suggests that the bailee should recover only the amount of his or her limited interest from the defendant unless the bailor agrees otherwise. This, however, exposes the defendant to two sets of litigation. An alternative is to change the rule under which bailors for a term are denied the right to sue for trespass, conversion or detinue.[27] Only one action should then be possible, and it would be a matter for decision between bailor and bailee who should bring it.

Remedies for conversion and detinue

Damages

[5.195] An action for damages is the primary remedy for conversion and is also a remedy for detinue. In detinue, which is based on an unsatisfied demand for the return of the chattel, the defendant may comply with this demand and leave the plaintiff to continue the action for damages for any further loss resulting from the tort. In conversion the plaintiff may refuse the chattel's return and continue to claim damages based, among other things, on the value of the chattel.

The court has a discretion to stay an action in conversion where the defendant is willing to return the chattel and pay the plaintiff's costs up to that point, and the court is of the opinion that the plaintiff could have no further claim for compensation once having received the chattel's return: *Fisher v Prince* (1762) 3 Burr 1363; 97 ER 876. Further, a plaintiff who unreasonably refuses to accept a return of the chattel may be penalised in costs, even if the action is successful.

Valuation of the chattel

[5.200] The valuation of the chattel for the purposes of assessing damages presents two main problems: determining the date of valuation of the chattel and the nature of the plaintiff's interest in it. As regards the date of valuation, the differing natures of the causes of action in conversion and detinue was at one time thought to produce a difference in the measure of damages. Conversion, since it was complete at the moment of conversion, required the chattel to be valued at the date of conversion; detinue, being a wrong continuing until the date of judgment, required the chattel to be valued at that date.

Conversion was therefore more advantageous on a falling market, detinue on a rising market. There is considerable authority to support the view that the plaintiff in conversion is allowed increments in the value of the chattel at the date of the judgment, provided there has been no delay in bringing the action in order to take advantage of a rising market: *Sachs v Miklos* [1948] 2 KB 23; *Ley v Lewis* [1952] VLR 119; *Egan v State Transport Authority* (1982) 31 SASR 481. Nor does it seem that the limitation in

---

[26]   Fleming, *Law of Torts* (9th ed, 1998) p 79.

[27]   As advocated by Warren, "Qualifying as Plaintiff for an Action in Conversion" (1935-1936) 49 Harv L Rev 1084.

Sachs, that the plaintiff is only allowed this concession where conversion and detinue are alternative actions on the same facts, any longer applies. Recognition of the absence of any difference between the two actions in this respect was provided by *Egan*.

In *Egan* conversion of the plaintiff's machinery took place in 1966. Judgment was not given until 1982, but the machinery was valued for both torts as at the date of the judgment. The delays in bringing the action were not the plaintiff's fault and in any case the increased amount awarded was due to an inflationary fall in money value, not to an actual increase in the machinery's value.

Authority supports valuation at the date of conversion where the defendant has sold and thereby converted goods on a falling market. In *Solloway v McLaughlin* [1938] AC 247,[28] the defendant had certain shares belonging to the plaintiff deposited with him. He sold them, and when the market fell bought in an equivalent as replacement. He was held liable in conversion for the value of the shares at the date of conversion, less the value of the replacements. The basis of the award seems here to be restitutionary rather than compensatory. The plaintiff had suffered no loss from the defendant's wrongful dealing, but if the defendant had been allowed to keep the profit he would have benefited from his own fraud. The same result would not necessarily have been ordered against a bona fide converter. Detinue would have been available on the same facts as these, although under the original rule the chattel would have been valued at the date of the judgment. But no case actually supports this application of the measure of damages in detinue in the case of a falling market.

The general conclusion concerning date of valuation is that it should not be subject to fixed rules distinguishing between conversion and detinue, but should be designed to afford just and equitable compensation according to the circumstances of the case. There is further recognition of the need for flexibility in matters of compensation in decisions concerning the value to be placed on the chattel. The former tendency was to award the successful plaintiff the whole value of the chattel in all circumstances. Thus a bona fide possessor of a car has been held to be entitled to its whole value, even though at the time of the action, the car had been redelivered to its true owner: *Wilson v Lombank Ltd* [1963] 1 WLR 1294.

[5.205] It is also settled law that a bailee may recover the whole value of the chattel from a tortfeasor, although this is clearly justified on the ground of the bailee's duty to account for the amount exceeding the bailor's interest in the chattel to the bailor: *The Winkfield* [1902] P 42; *The Jag Shakti* [1986] AC 337. Recovery of the full value of the chattel was pushed to an extreme in *Healing (Sales) Pty Ltd v Inglis Electrix Pty Ltd* (1968) 121 CLR 584. In that case, the High Court held that unpaid sellers of goods, who had converted the goods by repossessing them from the buyer, must pay the whole value of the goods to the buyer, even though the latter remained liable for the price, which would then need to be recovered by separate action.

The case seems contrary to a later decision of the High Court, *Butler v Egg Marketing Board* (1966) 114 CLR 185. In this case the Board, which became by statute the owner of the eggs on their being laid, was held to be entitled in an action for conversion against the producer of the eggs only to the difference between the amount the Board would have obtained on sale of the eggs and the amount it would have had to pay to the producer. A similar approach is seen in hire-purchase cases. The finance company

---

[28]   *BBMB Finance Ltd v EDA Holdings* [1990] 1 WLR 409.

is entitled, by way of damages for conversion, to the amount of unpaid instalments or the actual value of the goods, whichever is the less: *Western Credits Pty Ltd v Dragon Motors Pty Ltd* [1973] WAR 184; *Chubb Cash v John Crilley & Son* [1983] 1 WLR 599; *Pacific Acceptance Corp Ltd v Mirror Motors Pty Ltd* (1961) SR(NSW) 548. A hirer suing the hire-purchase company for wrongful repossession of the goods is limited by way of damages, to the value of the goods less the amount of unpaid instalments: *Roberts v Roberts* [1957] Tas SR 84; *Harris v Lombard New Zealand Ltd* [1974] 2 NZLR 161.[29]

These limitations only operate where the action is being brought between the original parties to the hire-purchase agreement or persons deriving title through one of them. There is no reason to place a limit on recovery of the whole value of the chattel where, for example, the hire-purchaser is suing an unconnected third party, as *Millar v Candy* (1981) 38 ALR 299 shows. Here, the rule allowing the bailee to recover the full value of the chattel applies.

Figure 5.8: Damages in conversion and detinue

- In conversion, damages *usually* take the form of pecuniary compensation.
- In detinue, the court may in appropriate circumstances order the return of the chattel.
- Damages in conversion are calculated as at the time of conversion; in detinue it is at the time of judgment.

Consequential loss

[5.210] The plaintiff is entitled in both conversion and detinue to compensation for consequential loss arising from the tort. The old case of *Bodley v Reynolds* (1846) 8 QB 779; 115 ER 1066 continues to provide a convenient example. In that case it was held that a carpenter was entitled to damages for loss of trade arising from the conversion of his tools. The normal duty to mitigate damages on the part of the plaintiff applies in this situation, so that the consequential loss will only be allowed until the time at which it was reasonable for the plaintiff to purchase a replacement.

Liesbosch Dredger v SS Edison [1933] AC 449 held that this limit on the recovery of consequential loss must be applied even though the plaintiff's lack of means rendered it impossible for him to purchase a replacement; impecuniosity operated as a new cause. *Liesbosch* has proved to be an unpopular decision in England and Australia and is frequently distinguished. So in *Egan v State Transport Authority* (1982) 31 SASR 481 the court held that where the impecuniosity was the foreseeable result of the defendant's tort, the *Liesbosch* rule had no operation. Compensation is allowed for loss of the chance of future profit, even though there is no probability that the profit will be made, the amount being reduced to reflect the contingency. In *Electricity Trust v O'Leary* (1986) 42 SASR 26, damages were only allowed in relation to the death of a racehorse for the loss of the chance of making a future profit from racing the horse; in *Cowper v*

[29] Also an action by a lienee: *Standard Electronic Corp v Stenner* [1960] NSWR 447.

Goldner Pty Ltd (1986) 40 SASR 457 they were allowed for the loss of the chance of a mare, which had been killed through the defendant's negligence, producing a foal the following year.

Market value of chattel

[5.215] The plaintiff is entitled to the market value of the chattel, not the price at which the plaintiff has sold it to a third party, although the latter measure was allowed in a case where there was no market available to the plaintiff in time to satisfy the contract: *France v Gaudet* (1871) LR 6 QB 199. That case was interpreted by the majority in *The Arpad* [1934] P 189 to mean only that the contract price was admitted as evidence of the value of the goods.[30]

Where the plaintiff has received payments that are clearly intended to discharge the defendant's liability in conversion, the plaintiff must give credit for those payments that will be taken into account in fixing the award of damages. The plaintiff does not have to give credit for payments received where these relate to a collateral transaction (*Australia and New Zealand Banking Group Ltd v AAIEV Finance Ltd* [1989] Aust Torts Reports 80-228); nor where there is no clear evidence as to the purpose of making the payments or their source; nor where the purpose of making the payments is to conceal a fraud practised on the plaintiff: *Hunter BNZ Finance Ltd v ANZ Banking Group Ltd* [1990] VR 41; [1991] 2 VR 407.

As an alternative to attempting to assess the loss arising from the tort, the plaintiff may be allowed as damages a hiring charge based on the benefit obtained by the defendant from using the goods. The requirements established by the case law are that the plaintiff must be a hirer out of the goods, and that the defendant should have both used the goods profitably and denied possession of them to the plaintiff: *Strand Electric & Engineering Co v Brisford Entertainments* [1952] 2 QB 246; *Gaba Formwork Constructors Pty Ltd v Turner Corp Ltd* [1991] Aust Torts Reports 81-138.

The claim on this basis in *McKenna & Armistead Pty Ltd v Excavations Pty Ltd* [1956] 57 SR(NSW) 515 failed on the latter ground, since the bailee's improper use of the goods had not denied the plaintiffs possession. The basis of the claim for a hiring charge is restitutionary rather than compensatory: the defendant is being made to pay for the benefit received. This means that the plaintiff need not show the likelihood that he or she would have been able to hire out all the goods in the defendant's possession. Where the plaintiff is not in the business of hiring out equipment, as in *Egan v State Transport Authority* (1982) 31 SASR 481, a similar claim to that based on *Strand Electric & Engineering Co v Brisford Entertainments* [1952] 2 QB 246 may be allowed to the plaintiff as an alternative to proving actual loss. The assessment is made on the basis of hiring in rather than hiring out similar equipment (although in general this seems unlikely to differ); however, a reduction is made from the cost of the notional hiring in respect of the notional cost of maintenance of the equipment.

Improvements to chattel

[5.220] The defendant prior to committing the tort may have improved the chattel. In *Munro v Wilmott* [1949] 295 1 KB the defendant spent £85 in making improvements to the plaintiff's car and then sold it. The court held that the defendant's cost of making the improvements must be deducted from the car's value at the time of the conversion,

---

[30] Followed in *Furness v Adrium Industries Pty Ltd* [1993] Aust Torts Reports 81-245 which held that anticipated retail sales could not be taken into account when estimating damages.

even though the defendant had acted in good faith in making the improvements and in selling the car. Something must have turned on the facts that the plaintiff had left the car in the defendant's yard (which the defendant wished to convert into a garage), with permission and that the defendant was unable to communicate with the plaintiff before acting. The case establishes no absolute right to be compensated for improving the chattel.

Another possibility is that the court will refuse to order specific restitution of a chattel unless the plaintiff pays the defendant for improving it. The basis of this is restitutionary: the plaintiff must not be unjustly enriched at the defendant's expense. It follows that the rules of restitution apply. In *McKeown v Cavalier Yachts* (1988) 13 NSWLR 303, the plaintiff had acquired ownership of a completed yacht by accession. The defendant had provided valuable parts and labour. The plaintiff was not required to compensate the defendant as a condition for obtaining restitution of the yacht since there was no sufficiently free acceptance of the benefit provided; nor was there an incontrovertible benefit to the plaintiff in view of the fact that the plaintiff had incurred a detriment to a third party as part of the transaction.

Damages for deprivation of non-profitable use

[5.225] There is some difficulty with the question whether damages may be awarded for conversion where the plaintiff has been deprived of the use of the chattel without causing any actual loss.

In *The Medianal* [1900] AC 113 Lord Halsbury stated that more than nominal damages may be awarded in such cases. This statement was referred to with approval in two High Court decisions but interpreted in different ways. In *Baume v Commonwealth* (1906) 4 CLR 97 the High Court held that more than nominal damages could be awarded for depriving the plaintiff of certain documents, but only if the plaintiff had suffered actual pecuniary loss.

In *Turner v Mont de Piete Deposit & Investment Co Ltd* (1910) 10 CLR 539 the High Court on similar facts approved an award of substantial damages, even though no actual loss had been proved. Lord Halsbury's principle has been accepted and applied in certain English decisions, the measure of damages being assessed by awarding interest on the capital value of the property at the time of the wrong: *The Marpessa* [1900] AC 241; *Admiralty Commissioners v SS Susquchanna* [1926] AC 636; *The Hebridean Coast* [1961] AC 545 (although this is not invariable); *Birmingham Corp v Sowsberry* (1969) 113 SJ 577.

By contrast, in *Brandeis Goldschmidt & Co Ltd v Western Transport Ltd* [1981] QB 864,[31] the court awarded only nominal damages where the defendant wrongfully detained the plaintiffs' copper during a period when the market was falling, on the grounds that the plaintiffs did not intend to sell the copper or use it in their business. *Graham v Voigt* (1989) 89 ACTR 11 provides a possible alternative basis for compensation in a case where the plaintiff can prove no actual loss. In that case the plaintiff, whose collection of stamps had been converted by the defendant, was allowed damages for loss of his hobby. The stamps here had considerable value, but that was not a necessary part of the decision.

---

31   This case is difficult to reconcile in principle with *Solloway v Maclaughlin* [1938] AC 247 at 5-30, though it concerned a claim for wrongful detention rather than sale.

Specific restitution in detinue

[5.230] The chief reason for suing in detinue in the present day is to enable the plaintiff a claim for specific restitution of the chattel, a claim that is not possible in conversion. The remedy of restitution is discretionary. The court may make one of three orders:[32]

- for the value of the chattel and damages for its detention;
- for return of the chattel or recovery of its value and damages for its detention; or
- for return of the chattel and damages for its detention.

A judgment in the first form deprives the defendant of the common law option of returning the chattel, and once liability has been established, the plaintiff is entitled to this form of judgment as of right if the chattel has not been returned by the date of judgment. Under the first form of judgment, return of the chattel is not available to either party. Under the second, it is available to both: to the defendant as an option, to the plaintiff only by application to the court. The third form of judgment requiring return of the chattel was observed to be "unusual" by Lord Diplock in *General and Finance Facilities v Cooks Cars (Romford)* [1963] 1 WLR 644.

Action on the case for damage to reversionary interest

[5.235] In *Mears v London and South Western Railway Co* (1862) 11 CB (NS) 850; 142 ER 1029 it was held that an owner without the immediate right to possession of a chattel, but with a right to future possession, could sue by means of action on the case a third party who had destroyed or permanently damaged the chattel. The owner's interest is described as a reversionary interest in the chattel. The plaintiff here needs to establish intentional or negligent conduct causing damage to or destruction of the chattel. "Permanent" damage merely means damage that will last unless it is repaired. Negligence may even be available to an owner who has no reversionary interest in a chattel. In *Lee Cooper v Jeakins & Sons Ltd* [1967] 2 QB 1 the plaintiff, who had sold and caused delivery to be made of a chattel through the defendant firm of carriers, but who retained ownership until delivery, was allowed to succeed in negligence when the chattel was lost though the defendant's carelessness.[33]

---

[32] *General and Finance Facilities v Cooks Cars (Romford)* [1963] 1 WLR 644 per Diplock Ll at 650. There is an art in overlapping equitable jurisdiction to award specific restitution: *McKeown v Cavalier Yachts Pty Ltd* (1988) 13 NSWLR 303; *Doulton Potteries Ltd v Bronotte* [1971] 1 NSWLR 591.

[33] In *Leigh & Sillivan v Aliatmon Shipping Co* [1986] QB 350 the House of Lords accepted that the seller of goods that had been dispatched for delivery by sea and had been damaged in the course of loading on board by the negligence of the defendant stevedores, could recover damages for the amount of the damage from the defendants, even though the risk in the goods had passed to the buyers on the conclusion of the contract.

Practice Questions

Problem Questions

5.1 In August, Jones, driving taxi No TX009X arrived at Hadley's Hotel at 11:45 to take Louise on her requested service. Upon entering the taxi, Louise found a diamond ring on the front passenger seat. She showed the ring to Jones who admitted he had not seen the ring before and did not know who it belonged to. Both parties agreed it may have been left behind by a passenger on an earlier service.

In line with the policy of Southern Taxis Incorporated, on lost and found properties, Jones indicated to Louise that he would submit the ring to the police and subsequently took the ring to the Kingston Police Station. At the Station, Constable Tolbert took the names and addresses of both parties and informed them that the ring would be returned to the finder, if it was not claimed by the true owner in two months.

In October Jones telephoned Constable Tolbert to inquire about the ring, and was told that since the true owner had not claimed it within the two-month period, the ring had been returned to Louise as the finder. Louise has since confirmed that she has the ring and intends to keep it.

Jones seeks legal advice from Messrs Martin and Martin Associates of which you are an Articled Clerk. You are asked to *write an opinion to indicate the legal position* of Jones.

5.2 In April 2008 Chris bought a crate of "Magna" beer. He was given the following notice together with his receipt:

PUBLIC NOTICE
COLLINS BREWERY AND BOTTLING LTD
156 Collins St, Hobart Tasmania

TAKE NOTICE that all bottles branded with the "Magna" logo and or a statement that the bottles are the property of the Collins Brewery and Bottling Ltd remain the property of this company at all times.

TAKE NOTICE ALSO that all plastic crates marked "The Property of the Collins Bottle Co" remain the property of this company at all times and shall not be used for any purpose other than re-delivery to the company for re-use. The contents of all such bottles and crates are sold upon the express condition that the bottles and crates remain the property of this company and must be returned to the company or delivered up to the company upon demand after consumption of those contents.

Upon no account may any bottles or crates be damaged destroyed or detained nor shall they be used for any purposes other than re-delivery to the company after consumption of the contents.

DATED this 25th day of January, 2008.
COLLINS BREWERY AND BOTTLING LTD
Howarth XU McKay
Solicitors of the company

Chris wishes to use the empty "Magna" bottles and crate for his homebrew beer. He seeks your advice.

Answers to Practice Questions

Problem Questions

5.1 Jones is unable to establish an action in either conversion or detinue because of a lack of standing to sue. In order to sue either the police or Louise, Jones would have to be able to demonstrate a right to immediate possession of the ring. Where an item is found, the finder may retain the item unless the real owner claims possession: *Armory v Delamirie* (1722) 1 Strange 505; (1722) 93 ER 664. On the facts, Louise is the finder of the ring and able to assert the right of possession until the true owner appears. This is because if an item is found on the land of another party, the occupier of the land must show an intention to exercise control over the area such as to indicate that all things found on it were in their possession before the finder actually discovered the relevant item in order to be considered in possession of chattels on the land: *Parker v British Airways Board* [1982] QB 1004. Whilst the taxi is private property in the same way as land, Jones stated that he had never seen the ring before; nor is there any evidence to suggest that all property found inside the car is controlled by the driver.

As Louise had possession of the ring before its surrender to Jones only for the purpose of passing it on to the police, the police were correct to release it into her possession. Her refusal to give the ring to Jones is not an issue in view of the fact that she is the owner of the ring until such time as the true owner claims possession. Jones could not rely on the defence of jus tertii to claim the ring (that is, that the true owner of the ring has better title than Louise): *Wilson v Lombank Ltd* [1963] 1 WLR 1294.

5.2 Chris should not use the bottles for the purpose of storing his home brew. The terms of the notice (and it seems the statement on the bottles) expressly provide that the bottles and crate remain the property of the brewery at all times. This means that whilst Chris has possession of the chattels, he is not the owner of them. More importantly, the condition that the bottles and crate must be delivered back to the company whenever the brewery may demand, means the brewery has an immediate right to possession. Chris therefore holds the empty bottles and crate as bailee under a revocable bailment (bailment at will). If Chris should act contrary to the expressed condition that the bottles and crate are not to be used for *any purpose other than redelivery to the company for re-use* he would be liable to the brewery in conversion. Chris would not be liable in trespass because although the use of the bottles as receptacles would be sufficient invasions for trespass according to Dixon J in *Penfolds*, the brewery would not have title to sue Chris in respect of that trespass because it would not be in possession at the time of such use. Detinue is irrelevant because there has been no demand for the bottles return by the brewery. Nevertheless, the majority in *Penfolds* found that filling the bottles in that case with wine from another company when the defendant knew the terms of bailment that were inconsistent with this behaviour was sufficiently serious to constitute conversion, although Dixon J dissented on this point. This dealing with the goods combined with the brewery's standing to sue (namely an immediate right to possession) means that conversion would probably be successfully brought against Chris.

CHAPTER 6

Trespass to Land

Reading

Sappideen, Vines, Grant and Watson, *Torts: Commentary and Materials*, Chapter 4.

Objectives

The chapter will explain:

- the concept of land in law;
- the nature of trespass to land;
- possession as the primary interest protected in trespass to land;
- the nature of the act of trespass; and
- remedies for trespass to land.

Principles

Defining trespass to land

[6.05] Trespass to land is the last link in the discussion of the generic tort of trespass. As Figure 6.1 indicates, it is a form of infringement on property rights and is, therefore, best discussed and understood in that context.

Figure 6.1: Specific forms of trespass

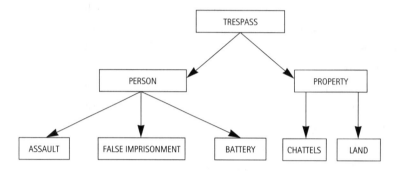

As in the case of trespass to chattels, defining trespass to land is merely a matter of applying the general features of trespass to the case of land. Trespass to land is thus defined as the intentional or negligent act of the defendant, which directly interferes with the plaintiff's exclusive possession of land.[1] Like other forms of trespass, it is actionable per se. Like other forms of trespass, the tort also has the essential elements of:

- intention/negligence;
- directness; and
- absence of lawful justification.

The distinguishing feature is the element of interference with the plaintiff's rights, which consists of interference with the plaintiff's exclusive possession of land.

Figure 6.2: Trespass to land

> • The *intentional* or *negligent act* of the defendant which *directly interferes* with the plaintiff's exclusive possession of the land.

---

[1]   Intention includes recklessness.

What is land?

[6.10] Land is a wide term, meaning:

- the actual land or soil;
- the air space above it; and
- the area beneath it.

The actual land includes buildings on the land, rooms in those buildings, plants and vegetables on the land, and articles permanently attached to the land ("fixtures") as opposed to items or chattels that are capable of being separately possessed.

Traditionally in common law, the view was that land included what was fixed to the land, the air space above the land up to the sky and the soil content beneath the land down to the depths. This notion was usually summed up in the Latin maxim, *usque ad coelum usque ad inferos* (he who owns the land, his also is the sky and the depths beneath it). This is now an overstatement. The modern law allows a landowner to possess, and maintain an action in trespass in relation to, the airspace above the land or the subsurface beneath to the extent that is reasonably necessary for the enjoyment of the land or the extent to which control can be exercised.

In relation to air space, *Kelsen v Imperial Tobacco Co* [1957] 2 All ER 343 held that an advertising sign placed by the defendants 24 cm over the boundary to the plaintiff's property constituted trespass. On the other hand, in *Bernstein v Skyviews & General Ltd* [1978] QB 479 the court held that an airplane flight by the defendants over the plaintiff's land for the purpose of photographing it did not constitute trespass. The flight did not come within the airspace that the plaintiff would expect to use as a "natural incident of his use of the land". Griffiths J thought that repeated flights of this nature might amount to the tort of nuisance. *Bernstein* held also that the defendant in the case was entitled to rely on the defence provided by the *Civil Aviation Act 1949* (UK). The Act provides that no action shall lie in respect of trespass or nuisance by reason only of the flight of an aircraft over any property at a height above the ground which, having regard to wind, weather and all the circumstances of the case, is reasonable. This Act has its counterpart in several Australian States.[2]

There has been frequent litigation in recent years over the question whether an invasion of the plaintiff's airspace in the course of building operations constitutes trespass. The usual view is that, where the plaintiff has no present or future intention of using the airspace at that level, under the *Bernstein* test the action would fail. On the other hand, the right to resist entry by building contractors may be one of considerable commercial value. An English court in *Woollerton & Wilson v Richard Costain* [1970] 1 WLR 411 arrived at a solution of a somewhat Delphic character in this situation. An injunction was granted against the builder, but its operation was suspended until the completion of the building operations. Australian decisions, on the other hand, have favoured the landowner's right to an immediate injunction: *Graham v K D Morris & Sons Pty Ltd* [1974] Qd R 1; also to a mandatory injunction to remove scaffolding and to damages for the trespass: *LJP Investments Pty Ltd v Howard Chia Investments Pty Ltd* [1989] Aust Torts Reports 80-269. In *Bendal Pty Ltd v Mirvac Project Pty Ltd* (1991) 23 NSWLR 464 the test of the landowner's capacity to exploit the airspace was stated in

2   *Civil Aviation Act 1949* (UK), s 40; *Damage by Aircraft Act 1952* (NSW), s 2; *Civil Liability Act 1936* (SA), s 62(2); *Damage by Aircraft Act 1963* (Tas), s 3; *Wrongs Act 1958* (Vic), s 30; *Damage by Aircraft Act 1964* (WA), s 4. For more limited protection for international flights see *Damage by Aircraft Act 1999* (Cth).

CHAPTER 6

terms of what that person *may* see fit to undertake, a test that seems more generous to the landowner than that in *Bernstein*.

The issue of how far beneath the soil one can make claim to land has been less litigated. Mining rights undoubtedly belong to the landowner at common law, though in Australia they vest in the Crown. In an interesting American decision, *Edwards v Sims* (1929) 24 SW 2d 619, the defendant owned the entrance to a cave below his land that he used as a tourist attraction. The cave passed, at one point, some 120m below the land of the plaintiff. The court found the defendant was liable in trespass for causing the entry of persons at this level. In the absence of any present ability by the plaintiff to control the subsurface at this level for his or her own purposes, the decision seems questionable.

Figure 6.3: Land and the interest protected

- *Land* includes the actual soil, the structures on it and the airspace above it, and what is beneath it.
- The interest protected is the *exclusive possession* of the plaintiff.

Plaintiff's interest: possession

[6.15] The primary requirement of trespass to land is that the plaintiff should be in actual possession of the land at the time of the defendant's act. It is not available to an owner out of possession, although the owner has a remedy in the action of ejectment (see [6.70]) which may enable the owner to regain possession. It was confirmed in *Newington v Windeyer* (1985) 3 NSWLR 555 that de facto possession is sufficient title to maintain trespass. There is, therefore, no need to prove any legal or equitable title to the land.

Nevertheless, title to land may be of considerable importance in cases of trespass to land. The owner of land is favoured by the fact that title to land is considered to be relevant towards establishing possession of it. In *Ocean Estates v Pinder* [1969] 2 AC 19 the plaintiffs, who had freehold title to land but whose possessory acts in relation to it had been exiguous, succeeded in trespass against the defendant who had been growing vegetables on part of the land.[3] The case also illustrates the operation of the action of trespass to determine a dispute over title to the land. Had the defendant been found to be in possession, he would have established a sufficient period for adverse possession to defeat the plaintiff's title.

A second reason for considering title important is that an owner of land who takes steps to evict its present possessor and regain possession does not commit trespass to land. This is so even though in these circumstances the owner may commit the crime of forcible entry on land. In *Delaney v TP Smith & Co* [1946] 1 KB 393 the plaintiff and defendant had concluded an oral agreement under which the plaintiff was to become

---

3   See also *Fowley Marine v Gafford* [1968] 2 QB 618.

the tenant of the defendant's premises. The plaintiff entered the premises secretly before the lease was signed and was forcibly evicted by the defendant. The plaintiff's action for trespass to land failed. In the absence of a written agreement he had no right to possession of the premises and his actual possession of them was of no avail against the owner. Of course, a different result would have been reached had a proper lease been in existence.[4]

Figure 6.4: The nature of the plaintiff's interest in the land

- The plaintiff must have *exclusive possession* of the land at the time of the interference.
- Exclusive possession refers to the right to use or hold the land to *the exclusion of all others*.

Position of licensees

[6.20] There is still some doubt over the question whether a licensee can sue in trespass to land. A licensee does not have possession. However, given that de facto possession of land is protected by the tort, it would not seem unreasonable to extend this to a licensee with sufficiently exclusive occupation of the land. The holder of a grazing licence was allowed in an early case to sue for trespass where the defendant had filled a quarry hole with night soil, thus endangering cattle: *Vaughan v Shire of Benalla* (1891) 17 VLR 129.[5] A later case, however, required the plaintiff's occupation to be established under a proprietary or possessory interest in the land: *Moreland Timber Co v Reid* [1946] VLR 237. There is no doubt that a licence coupled with a proprietary interest such as an easement or profit à prendre entitles its holder to bring trespass.[6]

Trespass to the highway

[6.25] A landowner/possessor may, it seems, complain by way of an action of trespass of a use by a member of the public of the highway adjacent to the plaintiff's land where that use goes beyond the normal exercise of the right of passage and re-passage. The highway is essentially a public right of way over private land. In some cases, the right to possession of the surface of the highway is vested in the highway authority, while in other cases it remains in the possession of the adjacent landowners, subject to the easement of way. In either case, however, it appears that trespass lies against one who misuses the highway. Examples of such misuse are use of the highway for the purpose of interfering with grouse-shooting on adjacent land: *Harrison v Duke of Rutland* [1883] 1 QB 142. Or for the purpose of watching horse-racing trials on

---

[4]   See also *Haniotis v Dimitriou* [1983] 1 VR 498.

[5]   *Burwood Land Co v Tuttle* (1895) 21 VLR 129 allowed a licensee to bring a joint action for trespass with a mortgagor in possession.

[6]   *Nicholls v Ely Beet Sugar Factory* [1931] 2 Ch 84 (right of fishery); *Mason v Clarke* [1955] AC 778 (profit à prendre); *Moreland Timber Co v Reid* [1946] VLR 237 (right to cut timber).

such land: *Hickman v Maisey* [1900] 1 QB 752. However, it does not include parking a car on a highway and thereafter trespassing on the adjacent land: *Randall v Tarrant* [1955] 1 WLR 255.

Jus tertii

[6.30] As in trespass to chattels and conversion, jus tertii is no defence to one who has disturbed the plaintiff's actual possession of the land: *Davison v Gent* (1897) 1 H & N 744; 156 ER 1400; *Nicholls v Ely Beet Sugar Factory* [1931] 2 Ch 84. The exceptions to this rule considered in relation to torts to chattels (that is, that the defendant has the authority of the true owner for the trespass, or is acting on the true owner's behalf in defending the action, or has been compelled to surrender possession to the true owner) will no doubt apply to trespass to land.

Act of defendant

[6.35] The defendant's voluntary act must directly cause the intrusion upon possession that the plaintiff has suffered. In *Southport Corp v Esso Petroleum Co Ltd* [1954] QB 182; [1956] AC 218 the defendants' ship had become stranded in the Ribble Estuary. The master caused the discharging of some 400 tons of fuel oil from the ship in order to refloat her. This oil was carried by the force of the tide onto the plaintiff's foreshore, causing damage. Lord Denning in the Court of Appeal, supported by Lords Radcliffe and Tucker in the House of Lords, thought that this was too indirect to be trespass. This seems the correct view, but Morris LJ in the Court of Appeal said that if the defendant had made use of the forces of wind and water to produce the invasion this would be trespass. This confuses the issue of directness with that of fault. If the defendant had done what Morris LJ said and this had produced damage, an action would lie for intentional, indirect infliction of damage or for negligence. In two similar cases, in which piled-up rubbish and bulldozed earth moved gradually and settled on the plaintiffs' land, the courts largely concentrated on the issue of whether the invasion was a natural and probable consequence of the defendant's act, rather than whether it was a direct consequence, holding in both cases that a trespass was established: *Gregory v Piper* (1829) 9 B&C 591; 109 ER 220; *Watson v Cowen* [1959] Tas SR 194. Again the issue of natural and probable consequences seems relevant to culpability rather than directness. But in the later case of *Watson*, Green J thought the invasion to be "inevitable" rather than merely probable, and it may be that an inevitable though gradual invasion is sufficiently direct to be trespassory (although this is difficult to reconcile with *Lemmon v Webb* [1895] AC 1 in which the encroachment of boughs of trees onto neighbouring land was held to be nuisance, rather than trespass).

Trespass by unlawful entry

[6.40] This is the standard form of trespass to land. Entry by the defendant personally, or through the direct introduction of animate or inanimate objects on to the land, is sufficient (trespass by a person's animals is a separate tort, dealt with in Chapter 17). Where there is no entry on land, there can be no trespass. In *Perera v Vandiyar* [1953] 1 WLR 672 the defendant landlord had turned off the plaintiff tenants' electricity from outside their premises. This was actionable as a breach of the contract in the lease, but not as trespass to land. The taking of photographs of the land or its occupants from outside the land is not considered trespass: *Bathurst CC v Saban* (1985) 2 NSWLR 704.

Entry under licence: revocation of licence

[6.45] Entry under the terms of a licence express or implied is not trespass. The burden of showing the existence of a licence to enter rests on the entrant. It has been stated obiter that temporary and harmless entries on land such as stepping on the occupier's driveway from the highway to avoid a vehicle parked on the footpath, or to retrieve property or an errant child, are within the ambit of an implied licence: *Halliday v Nevill* (1984) 155 CLR 1 at 7 per the majority. So also, it is not trespass to proceed along the normal route to the front door of the house to discuss business with the occupier: *Halliday*; *Robson v Hallett* [1967] 2 QB 939. The implied licence here extends to entry by the police for the purpose of questioning or even, in some cases, arresting the occupier (majority in *Halliday*, Brennan J dissenting: cf *New South Wales v Ibbett* (2007) 231 ALR 485), but does not cover entry for the purpose of administering a breath test to the occupier: *Munnings v Barrett* (1987) 5 MVR 403.[7]

A person who enters the land for a purpose not covered by the licence is a trespasser, even though a licence to enter exists. In *Barker v The Queen* (1983) 153 CLR 338 a person who had the authority of the occupier of the house to keep an eye on it while the occupier was away, and who was told the whereabouts of the house key, was held to be a trespasser when he gained entry to the house for the purpose of theft, even though he clearly had an authority to enter the house for reasons connected with security. The High Court distinguished *Byrne v Kinematograph Renters Society* [1958] 1 WLR 762 in which cinema inspectors visited the plaintiff's cinema to investigate fraud. They bought tickets and watched a performance, but the purpose of their entry was to check the numbers on the tickets and the number of the audience. They were held not to be trespassers, since there was an invitation to persons generally to enter the cinema and that could not be limited to a particular purpose. *Byrne* seems to be a dubious decision, and is hard to reconcile with later Australian authority. In *Lincoln Hunt Aust Pty Ltd v Willesee* (1986) 4 NSWLR 457,[8] the plaintiff's business premises were visited by the defendant's television reporters and camera operators. A reporter asked questions that had nothing to do with the plaintiff's ordinary business and the camera operator took video pictures and opened interior doors on the premises. It was held that the defendants were trespassers from the moment of entry, since their entry had nothing to do with any purpose for which persons were permitted to be on the premises.

A bare licence, that is, one not conferring any interest in land, may be revoked at any time and the licensee required to leave the premises. Should the licensee fail to do so within a reasonable time, he or she becomes a trespasser. What is a reasonable time

---

[7] The implied licence was also exceeded where police forced their way to the back door of a house past trees, shrubs and a fence, in order to interview a child in the house about suspected offences: *M v A J* (1989) 44 ACR 373.

[8] An injunction against the use of videotaped material obtained in the course of the trespass was refused in this case, but allowed in *Emcorp Pty Ltd v ABC* [1988] 2 Qd R 169 in similar circumstances; also in *Rinsale Pty Ltd v ABC* [1993] Aust Torts Reports 81-231.

depends on the facts: *Kuru v New South Wales* (2008) 82 ALJR 1021; [2008] HCA 26. The fact that the revocation may constitute a breach of contract makes no difference in this situation: *Cowell v Rosehill Racecourse Co Ltd* (1937) 56 CLR 605.[9] The licensee's remedy here is an action for breach of contract.

Where one tenant in common of property grants the defendant permission to enter the property whilst another tenant in common purports to refuse or revoke that permission, it will be trespass for the defendant to enter or remain on the property unless the first tenant's permission was reasonable and incidental to that tenant's possession and use and enjoyment of the common property: *New South Wales v Koumdjiev* (2005) 63 NSWLR 353; [2005] NSWCA 247.

Trespass after lawful entry by licensee

[6.50] Trespassory acts may be committed by a licensee after lawful entry. For instance, in *Singh v Smithenbecker* (1923) 23 SR(NSW) 207, the defendant had lawfully entered the land of a person from whom he had bought sheep. He then, without permission, wrongfully removed the gate and drove away the sheep. These acts were held to be trespass, as was the act of the defendant in *Bond v Kelly* (1873) 4 AJR 153 in cutting more than the permitted amount of timber on land which he had been permitted to enter. It is not clear whether the act in question must relate to the land itself, or whether any act which falls outside the purpose for which permission is given to enter would be sufficient (both the above cases satisfied the first requirement). In *Healing (Sales) Pty Ltd v Inglis Electrix Pty Ltd* (1968) 121 CLR 584 the defendants entered land in the exercise of a contractual right to enter and take possession of certain goods. They seized not only those goods, but also other goods which they were not entitled to take, and it appeared they intended to do this at the time of entry. Among the members of the High Court who considered the issue of trespass to land, there was agreement that the original entry was not trespassory, since part of the purpose of entry was lawful. Kitto J, however, thought that the seizure of the wrong goods constituted trespass to land, thereby supporting the view that an interference with the land itself is not necessary in this type of case.

Trespass ab initio

[6.55] Under this ancient common law doctrine, one who entered land under authority of law might become a trespasser ab initio, that is from the moment of entering, because of actions committed subsequent to entry which were an abuse of the purpose of that entry. Three points about the doctrine should be noted:

- It applied only where the right to enter was conferred by law, not where it was by licence of the occupier. Originally it applied only to entry in order to levy a distress but eventually was generalised to all entries made under authority of law.
- It applied only to acts of misfeasance committed on the land, not to non-feasance. In the *Six Carpenters Case* (1610) 77 ER 695 it was held that a refusal

---

[9]   Not following the English decision in *Hurst v Picture Theatres* [1915] 1 KB 1. Where a tenant holds over on the expiration of a tenancy, the remedy of the landlord is ejectment, not trespass: *Hey v Moorhouse* (1839) 6 Bing NC 52; 133 ER 20; *Falkingham v Fregon* (1899) 25 VLR 211; *Commonwealth v Anderson* (1960) 105 CLR 303; although the landlord may legitimately resort to self-help: *Haniotis v Dimitriou* [1983] 1 VR 498.

to pay for wine after original lawful entry could not constitute trespass ab initio.

* Where some ground exists justifying an original lawful entry despite later acts of trespass committed on the premises, there is no trespass ab initio. In *Elias v Pasmore* [1934] 2 KB 164 the defendant policeman had lawfully entered the plaintiff's premises in order to arrest a person present there, and in addition had seized documents present on the premises, some unlawfully. Since the arrest was effected, and since some of the documents were lawfully taken, there was no trespass ab initio.

The rationalisation of the doctrine is uncertain. The view could be taken that the later act of misfeasance rendered the original entry unlawful because it showed an intent to enter for an unlawful purpose. Possibly this is true, but it hardly seems important if the later act is itself a trespass. This view would have greater significance if mere non-feasance constituting an abuse of entry called the doctrine into play.

It has also been suggested that the doctrine may justify the award of increased damages and thereby operate as a restraint on oppressive acts by public officials in the exercise of powers conferred on them to enter premises. The courts' ability to award exemplary damages against such officials seems, however, a sufficient safeguard here. Recent judicial authority has suggested that the doctrine serves no obvious purpose, whatever its original purpose was, and perhaps even no longer exists: *Chic Fashions v Jones* [1968] 2 QB 299.

Continuing trespass

[6.60] A continuing trespass arises where, after an initial trespassory entry or failure to leave land, the person or object constituting the trespass remains on the land. Where there is a continuing trespass, causes of action for the trespass arise de die in diem (from day to day) so that the limitation period runs from the last day. The doctrine also has importance in that action lies in relation to the trespass by a future transferee of the land.

There must be a continuing trespassory invasion, so the doctrine does not arise in relation to unrepaired damage to the land arising from the trespass. The leading case, *Konskier v Goodman Ltd* [1928] 1 KB 421, was an action against a contractor who in breach of contract had failed to remove rubbish left behind after completion of the work. At first sight this looks like trespass by omission to act, there being no original trespassory act, but it appears to fall within a similar principle to that recognised by the House of Lords in *Herd v Weardale Steel & Coke Co Ltd* [1915] AC 67. Since there was a direct and positive act of depositing the rubbish, although one rendered not actionable by reason of a contractual consent, this became trespassory on later failure to remove the rubbish in breach of contract.

State of mind of defendant

[6.65] The trespass must arise from the voluntary act of the defendant. So in *Smith v Stone* (1647) 82 ER 533 the defendant, who was thrown by third parties onto the land of the plaintiff, did not commit trespass.

In order to commit trespass the defendant must be at fault, that is, the doing of the act of trespass must have been intentional or negligent. Accordingly, falling onto a railway track because of an epileptic fit is not a trespass even though you are forbidden from going there: *Public Transport Commission (NSW) v Perry* (1977) 137 CLR 107. But as in the case of other forms of trespass, strict liability may attend an intentional trespass even though the defendant has no reason to believe a trespass is being committed. The rule as to burden of proof on the fault issue is no doubt the same as in the case of trespass to the person, distinguishing between highway and non-highway trespass to land. It should be noted that an English case has retained the concept of a negligent trespass to land even though the Court of Appeal had decided in an earlier decision that a cause of action no longer existed for negligent trespass to the person: *League Against Cruel Sports v Scott* [1985] 3 WLR 400.

Action of ejectment

[6.70] Trespass is a means of protecting the present possessor of land against invasions of that possession. The remedies that are available in trespass, namely damages for trespass and injunction against further trespasses, assume that the plaintiff remains in possession of the land. There is an obvious need for an additional remedy enabling the plaintiff to regain possession of the land to which the plaintiff is entitled. This remedy is the action of ejectment. The action is available against one in actual possession of land to one with an immediate right to its possession.

Mesne profits

[6.75] Ejectment lies only for recovery of the land. No damages may be awarded in the action itself, but under procedural reforms effected in England and the various Australian States, the action may be combined with an action for mesne profits.

Under this action the plaintiff is able to recover both for damage done by the defendant to the land during the period of occupancy and for profits taken from it during that time. It was originally a separate action and depended for its success upon proof that the plaintiff had succeeded in recovering possession of land. It was trespassory in nature and therefore proof of present possession was needed, even though the complaint related to actions of the defendant committed before that possession arose. The courts were eventually able to justify allowing it to be combined with ejectment by the doctrine of trespass by relation back – the possession regained through suing in ejectment related back to the date when it was originally lost.[10]

Jus tertii in ejectment

[6.80] The question of the rights of third parties in trespass to land is similar to the issue in trespass to chattels and conversion, although slightly different because of the special nature of land. It is clear that a person who has been evicted from actual possession of land by the defendant can base the action of ejectment upon the possession previously held. Equally, a person may legitimately retake possession without committing trespass to land. Should the dispossessed person choose to rely on the action of ejectment, jus tertii is no defence to that action unless the defendant had the authority of the true owner of the land for the dispossession of the plaintiff: see [6.30]. The estoppel

---

[10]   For the historical development of the law, see Holdsworth, *A History of English Law*, Vol 7, p 15.

principle also applies so that, for example, a tenant is not entitled to plead jus tertii against the landlord, should the latter sue in ejectment for recovery of the land, in the same way as a bailee is not allowed to dispute the title of the bailor: *Dalton v Fitzgerald* [1897] 2 Ch 86; *Smith v Smythe* (1890) 11 LR(NSW) 295. The question in dispute is whether, apart from the above two cases, the defendant may succeed by establishing jus tertii.

On this there are two broadly competing viewpoints. Holdsworth takes the view that present-day law requires the plaintiff to show an absolute rather than a relative title in ejectment, so that proof of jus tertii is a defence.[11] The defendant in effect succeeds merely by showing that the plaintiff has no title at all, for in that case a third party must have one. Hargreaves takes the view that a title based on mere possession (a relative title) is enough in ejectment, because this justifies an inference of seisin.[12] If, however, the defendant can show that a third party has actual title the inference cannot be drawn and the defendant will succeed. Australian authority supports Hargreaves, at least to the extent that it is not necessary to prove an absolute title to succeed in ejectment: *Allen v Roughley* (1955) 94 CLR 98. The jus tertii defence is nevertheless wider in ejectment than it is in its application to torts to chattels. No authority on the part of the true owner to defend the action on its behalf appears to be necessary.

Remoteness of damage

[6.85] Two Australian cases decided after *The Wagon Mound (No) 1* [1961] AC 388 held that an intentional trespasser was liable for the foreseeable consequences of the trespass. In *Hogan v Wright* [1963] Tas SR 44 the defendant had broken down the plaintiff's fence using a bulldozer, and the plaintiff's filly escaped through the damaged fence and suffered injury. The court held the defendant liable on the ground that the injury to the filly was a foreseeable consequence of the trespass. However, neither in this case nor in a South Australian decision to similar effect (*Svingos v Deacon Avenue Catage & Storage Pty Ltd* (1971) 2 SASR 126) was it determined that as a matter of law the consequence of the trespass must be, if not intended by the defendant, reasonably foreseeable. New Zealand cases have applied a test of direct rather than foreseeable consequences to intentional trespass to land (although no doubt recovery would also be available in relation to indirect, foreseeable consequences). In *Mayfair Ltd v Pears* [1987] 1 NZLR 459 the defendant had unlawfully parked his car on the plaintiff's premises. The car some time later inexplicably caught fire and damaged the plaintiff's building. Accepting that an intentional trespasser could be held liable for the direct unforeseeable consequences of the trespass, the majority nevertheless held the defendant not liable because the fire was not a direct consequence of parking the car.

Remedies

[6.90] The remedy by way of seeking damages is considered in Chapter 22 as part of the general consideration of the measure of damages for damage to property. Prohibitory injunction against the commission of the trespass will lie in most cases as of right (*Patel v W H Smith Ltd* [1987] 2 All ER 569; *LJP Investments v Howard Chia Investments Pty Ltd* [1989] Aust Torts Reports 80-269; *Bendal Pty Ltd v Mirvac Project Pty Ltd*

---

[11]   Holdsworth (1940) 56 LQR 479.
[12]   Holdsworth, above, n 11.

(1991) 23 NSWLR 464) – the plaintiff need not show any damage or inconvenience arising from the trespass. Mandatory injunctions, which would be necessary in a case where the defendant would be obliged to undertake expensive work in order to remove the trespass, are more difficult to obtain. This matter is also considered in Chapter 22.

Other cases of interference with rights

[6.95] As in the case of chattels, a reversioner (that is, a person with an eventual rather than an immediate right to possession of land) may sue a third party by way of an action based on the former action on the case in relation to acts of the third party that have permanently damaged the land, and the third party intended to cause the damage or was negligent in relation to it: *Baxter v Taylor* (1832) 4 B&Ad 72; 110 ER 382. "Permanent" merely requires that the damage be lasting unless it is repaired.

Practice Questions

Problem Questions

6.1   The plaintiff Edward Jones is the father-in-law of the defendant Giovanni Branchini. On 7 June, the defendant and his wife Mary Branchini separated after a series of marital problems. Mrs Branchini subsequently left the family home at 61 Grosvenor Street, and took up residence with her father, the plaintiff. The title on the property at 61 Grosvenor Street indicates that Mr and Mrs Branchini are joint tenants. Following the separation, the defendant was the sole occupant of the family home.

On 12 June Mrs Branchini requested the plaintiff to accompany her to 61 Grosvenor Street to enable her to collect some clothes she had left behind. They arrived at 61 Grosvenor Street at about 4.00 pm and discovered the defendant was not home. After waiting for about 30 minutes Mrs Branchini indicated that she could not wait any longer because she had an appointment with her hairdresser at 5.00 pm in the city. But before they could leave, the plaintiff decided to check the back door to see if it was open. He found it locked but with the help of a pair of tweezers from Mrs Branchini he was able to pick the lock to open the back door. The pair of them subsequently gained entry into the house.

Before they could get into the main bedroom where Mrs Branchini thought her clothes might be, they were confronted in the hallway by the defendant who had just arrived home and entered the house by the front door. After a heated verbal exchange between the parties, the defendant ordered Mrs Branchini and the plaintiff to leave the house. The defendant admits that he warned that if the plaintiff and his daughter did not leave he would break their necks.

The plaintiff and Mrs Branchini agreed to leave the house, but in the main doorway, the plaintiff turned around and yelled at the defendant "you are a bully and a thug; I don't blame you, I blame your stupid parents". The defendant immediately rushed to the door and tried to shut it but the plaintiff resisted by pushing the door back. The defendant was able to slam the door shut but with such force that the glass in the door shattered. A piece of glass cut the plaintiff's face. The plaintiff's left middle finger was also caught in the door as it shut, causing the finger to bruise.

At the trial, Solomon J held for the defendant on the basis of the relevant authorities that the plaintiff, along with his daughter, was a trespasser and that the defendant had the lawful excuse to use reasonable force to eject them from the property: *Shaw v Hackshaw* [1983] 2 VR 65.

(a)   Counsel for the plaintiff wishes to appeal the decision and seeks your advice. Advise her.

(b)   Explain the meaning of "exclusive possession". Did the defendant have exclusive possession?

6.2   John and Mary are squatters currently occupying a council property. They returned one evening to find that Nick and his girlfriend Tina had moved in and taken over the property. They had also thrown out clothes and books belonging to John and Mary.

John and Mary have approached you at the Community Legal Centre seeking legal advice as to whether they can sue Nick and Tina for trespass. Advise them.

Answers to Practice Questions

Problem Questions

6.1   (a) The judgment can be addressed on two grounds: whether the plaintiff was a trespasser and whether the force used by the defendant in defence of his property was reasonable.

Was the plaintiff a trespasser?
The plaintiff is the father of the wife of the defendant. He has no independent right of entry into the premises, however the title indicates that Mrs Branchini is a joint tenant with the defendant. In this case, she is able to invite her father onto the property, thus affording him a right of entry for the duration of the invitation. Mr Branchini is sole occupier of the house, but he does not have exclusive possession of it due to the status of the title and so cannot deprive his ex-wife of access. The plaintiff can therefore demonstrate that he had a right to enter the house in the first instance.

A trespass will be committed if the purpose of entry exceeds the scope of the invitation: *Coles-Smith v Smith* [1965] QD R 494. The plaintiff verbally abused the defendant by calling him a "bully and a thug". The invitation to enter was based on helping his daughter to retrieve some clothes. Thus the additional abuse overstepped the scope of the invitation and may be regarded as a trespass. In conclusion, the plaintiff cannot appeal the decision on the basis of being a lawful entrant.

Was the use of force reasonable?
A trespasser may be repelled by force in order to protect property rights but the level of violence must be justifiable: *Hackshaw v Shaw* (1984) 155 CLR 614. The plaintiff had agreed to leave the house and was in the process of leaving when the defendant slammed the door, shattering glass and bruising the plaintiff's finger.

Therefore, the use of force was totally unreasonable and disproportionate given that the plaintiff was otherwise obeying the wishes of the defendant. This forms a successful basis of appeal against the decision. (The defendant may also be liable to the defendant in assault and battery in any counterclaim by the defendant.)

(b) Exclusive possession means possession that is singular to the person claiming possession. The defendant did not have exclusive possession because the title to the property was shared with his ex-wife. The defendant was sole occupier, but not sole owner or possessor of the land.

6.2   John and Mary have an action in trespass to land because they can demonstrate actual possession of the land, thus establishing standing to sue. They can assert their rights over the other squatters in that only the owner of land, or a person with legal possession (such as a tenant), can exercise superior rights over them: *Haddrick v Lloyd* [1945] SASR 40.

The conduct with respect to the clothes and books is actionable in trespass to goods. John and Mary are able to prove that they had actual possession of the items and a right to immediate possession at the time that the goods were taken: *Penfolds Wines Pty Ltd v Elliott* (1946) 74 CLR 204. The act of throwing the clothes out directly infringes upon their right to possession and was intentionally done, thus establishing the action.

CHAPTER 7

Defences to the Intentional Torts to Person and Property

Reading

Sappideen, Vines, Grant and Watson, *Torts: Commentary and Materials*, Chapter 6.

Objectives

This chapter will:

* examine the defences available to defendants in relation to intentional torts to the person or property;
* recognise the importance of these defences, that is, their ability to excuse defendants from blame;
* determine whether consent is an element or a defence; and (in particular)
* note the circumstances in which self-defence, defence of others and defence of property may be used.

Principles

Introduction

[7.05] The defences dealt with in this chapter generally assume an intentional invasion of the plaintiff's interest by the defendant. Some of them (for example consent, contributory negligence and illegality) also have an extensive operation in the field of negligence. Once the plaintiff has established an intentional invasion of his or her interest by the defendant, the legal burden of proving the facts necessary to constitute a defence lies on the defendant. Only the main common law defences are dealt with here.

Mistake

[7.10] An innocent mistake is generally no defence to an action brought for an intentional tort, and the reasonableness of the mistake is irrelevant. Thus in *Basely v Clarkson* (1682) 3 Lev 37; 83 ER 565, the defendant entered the plaintiff's land and cut down some grass on it under the misapprehension that the land was his own. He was held liable in trespass. Similarly, in *Cowell v Corrective Services Commission* (1988) 13 NSWLR 714, a mistaken belief that a prisoner was not due for release was no defence to an action for false imprisonment. This was so even though the defendant acted reasonably on the assumption that a certain state of the law existed justifying the prisoner's detention, whereas in fact the law had been changed. Reasonable mistake may, however, sometimes operate as a defence, for example in the case of arrest: see [7.115].

Inevitable accident

[7.15] The existence of this defence and its effect are discussed at [3.20]. It is a plea that the defendant either committed no voluntary act or did not intentionally invade the plaintiff's interest and took all reasonable care to avoid doing so. The defence in trespass is now only necessary where the plaintiff is relying on a non-highway trespass.

Consent

Figure 7.1: Consent

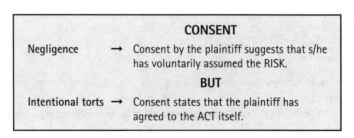

[7.20] Consent is a defence of considerable importance. An act of sexual intercourse without consent is a battery, as is a surgical operation committed without consent. The defence is usually referred to as consent where the intentional torts are concerned, and volenti non fit injuria where negligence is complained of.

In both situations, consent may be express or may be inferred from the plaintiff's conduct. In the latter case, however, there is still in general the need to establish the existence of a subjective consent on the part of the plaintiff. Where the defendant pleaded the display of an exclusionary notice on his land to justify the wheel-clamping of the plaintiff's car, the Court of Appeal held that, although it would normally be presumed that the car owner had read such notices and would have consented to the clamping, the plaintiff had established she was not aware of the notice and was entitled to succeed in trespass: *Vine v Waltham Forest London BC* [2000] 4 All ER 169.[1]

Figure 7.2

Consent →	Plaintiff to prove lack of consent as an element to the action?
	OR
Consent →	Defendant to claim and prove consent as a defence? → Better view in Australia.

There is some authority that in battery the plaintiff must prove his or her own absence of consent: *Christopherson v Bare* (1848) 11 QB 473 at 477; *Freeman v Home Office* [1984] QB 524. The better view, however, is that it is for the defendant to establish the plaintiff's consent: *Sibley v Milutinovic* [1990] Aust Torts Reports 81-013; McHugh J in *Secretary, Department of Health & Community Services v JWB* (1992) 175 CLR 218 at 310-311. Consent is, therefore, considered along with the other defences to the intentional torts to person and property.

The courts have established three general principles concerning this defence:

- the consent must be given to the act complained of;
- there must be no vitiating factors nullifying consent; and
- the consent must be genuine.

These three principles overlap and it may be hard to distinguish them in particular cases.

Figure 7.3: To be valid the consent must be given –

- in relation to the act complained of;
- voluntarily (duress and deceit will nullify);
- by a competent person; and
- with knowledge.

---

[1] *Arthur v Anker* [1996] 2 WLR 602 was explained by the Court of Appeal in *Vine* on the ground that in that case the plaintiff was aware of the notice.

Consent must be given to act complained of

[7.25] In some cases, the nature of the act is obvious. For example, an adult could hardly be heard to say that he or she did not know the nature of sexual intercourse. However in *R v Williams* [1923] 1 KB 340, an unusually naive teenage girl consented to sexual intercourse on the faith of the defendant's dishonest assertion that this was an operation that would clear her breathing passages for singing. The court held that she had not given a legal consent.

The rule that the consent must be shown to be given to the act complained of often has to be considered in the case of surgical operations. It is established law that the surgeon must not, in the course of the operation, exceed the terms of the plaintiff's consent. Thus in *Mulloy v Hop Sang* [1935] 1 WWR 714 (see also *Murray v McMurchy* [1949] 2 DLR 442), the plaintiff recovered substantial damages for the amputation of his hand when, after he had injured it, he came to the defendant for treatment but specifically instructed that he did not want the hand amputated. Where the surgeon discovers, during the course of an operation, a condition of danger necessitating an operation exceeding the plaintiff's consent (for example, as being necessary to save life or preserve health), the surgeon is not liable if that operation is performed with due care, whatever its consequences. But the defence there is one of necessity, rather than consent: see *Marshall v Curry* [1933] 3 DLR 260.

Another problem that arises in respect to surgical operations is the extent of the surgeon's duty to communicate information about the operation to the patient prior to the operation. The plaintiff is entitled to have the nature and effect of the operation explained to him or her. In the absence of a proper explanation, the plaintiff's consent cannot be given and the plaintiff may sue for battery: *Freeman v Home Office* [1984] QB 524. A further question arises as to how much information must be provided by the surgeon as to the risks of an operation conducted without negligence on the surgeon's part. It is now clear that a failure to provide the necessary information concerning risks cannot give rise to an action of battery where an uncommunicated risk has materialised, provided the patient has understood the nature of the operation to be performed. The patient's action in this situation would be for negligent failure to warn of the risks (to be considered in connection with the issue of breach of duty of care by medical practitioners in Chapter 9).

Vitiating factors

[7.30] The question of the effect of vitiating factors arises where the plaintiff understands the nature of the act to be performed and has consented to it, but this consent has been induced by a factor that vitiates consent. Duress, undue influence and fraud are possible vitiating factors. The issue of duress was examined in *Latter v Braddell* (1881) 50 LJKB 448. The plaintiff, the maidservant of the defendants, submitted reluctantly to an examination by a doctor, at the insistence of the defendant (her employer), in order to see whether she was pregnant. She was not. The Court of Appeal held that there was no duress here sufficient to nullify consent. The plaintiff had merely acted under a mistaken belief that the employer had the right to require her to undertake the examination. However, the case is a marginal one. The plaintiff was thereafter dismissed. Would not a threat of dismissal, if the examination was not undergone, constitute duress?

As to the effect of fraud, *Hegarty v Shine* (1878) 14 Cox CC 145 held that no battery was committed by one who had sexual intercourse with the plaintiff without revealing his syphilitic condition and who thereby infected her. The plaintiff understood the nature of the act to be performed, and the defendant's silence did not vitiate her consent. Some of the dicta in the case suggest that battery would have been committed had the defendant fraudulently misrepresented his condition. This seems acceptable in theory, but there is authority that fraud does not vitiate consent unless it misrepresents the nature of the act rather than its possible consequences. So, fraudulent misrepresentation by a bigamist that he and the plaintiff were lawfully married did not convert sexual intercourse into rape: *Papadimitropolous v The Queen* (1957) 98 CLR 249. The Court in *Smythe v Reardon* [1949] QSR 74 allowed an action for deceit in these circumstances. However, the tentative suggestion that the plaintiff might have had an action for assault (and battery) may be limited, in Queensland at least, by the provisions of the Queensland *Criminal Code*. The plaintiff in *Hegarty* could have succeeded in an action for negligence or for the intentional, non-trespassory infliction of disease upon her.

Capacity to consent

[7.35] In the case of a child, consent may be given on the child's behalf by the parent or guardian. Where the child has reached an age of sufficient understanding, the child may give a valid consent on his or her own behalf: *S v McC* [1972] AC 24; *Gillick v West Norfolk Health Authority* [1986] AC 112; *Secretary, Department of Health & Community Services v JWB* (*Marion's* case) (1992) 175 CLR 218. There is no fixed determinant of that age – the matter depends on the individual child. In *Gillick* the House of Lords held that a 15-year-old girl could validly consent to being administered a contraceptive pill. This was approved in principle by the High Court in *Marion's* case. There are limits to the validity of a consent given by parent or child. The parent's consent is not effective in the case of the sterilisation of an intellectually disabled girl or of other non-therapeutic procedures. In such a case, consent of the court under the *Family Law Act 1975* (Cth), s 63E, must be sought: see *P v P* (1994) 181 CLR 583 (in which State legislation derogating from the power of the Family Court was void for unconstitutionality). There is legislation throughout Australia providing for the overriding of parental consent where such consent to a blood transfusion on the child has been refused: for example *Medical Practitioners Act 1938* (NSW), s 49B. It has also been held in England that the court's power to act for the welfare of a child will allow it to overrule a child's refusal to accept treatment thought by the court to be in the best interests of the child, even though on the *Gillick* test the child has sufficient understanding of the matter: *Re W (A Minor)* [1993] Fam 64 (in which the court overruled the refusal of a 16-year-old to receive treatment for anorexia nervosa).

In the case of intellectually disabled adults the question of consent, particularly in relation to medical procedures, will generally depend on relevant State or Territory mental health legislation concerning the protection of such persons. In the absence of any specific provision covering the matter, the House of Lords held in *Re F* [1990] 2 AC 1 that the court could grant a declaration that the sterilisation of an intellectually disabled woman was legal, based on the principle of necessity, on the ground that she had formed a relationship with another intellectually disabled person.

Consent to illegal act

[7.40] First, in the criminal context, physical assault may be committed even though the victim has consented. Examples are assaults committed in the course of an unlawful prize fight (*R v Coney* (1882) 8 QBD 534),[2] sexual intercourse with a person under the age of 16 (*Madalena v Kuhn* (1989) 61 DLR (4th) 392), and sado-masochistic assaults causing actual bodily harm in the course of homosexual activity: *R v Brown* [1993] 2 WLR 556. However, the criminal nature of the activity does not automatically prevent the defence of consent being available in a civil action brought by one of the participants in the activity against another participant: *Madalena*. In *Bain v Altoft* [1967] Qd R 32 the court held that a person who engaged in a fight and suffered injury could be met by a defence of consent even though the fight may have involved criminal conduct, unless the defendant used unnecessary force by, for example, using a weapon. Since consent applied, the court did not find it necessary to consider the plea of illegality. The latter defence is also generally ignored where the defendant alone is the perpetrator of the crime. For example, the right of recovery of damages in actions by passengers against drunken drivers has turned entirely on the issue of consent or contributory negligence; the fact that the passenger may have been a participant in the activity leading to the illegal drunken driving being ignored: see [12.130]. Also, consent rather than illegality was considered to be the issue in an action brought by the plaintiff against a person who had committed the crime of having unlawful intercourse with her while she was under the age of 16 years: *Madalena*. But the defence failed for public policy reasons.

Consent and sporting activities

[7.45] Persons engaged in a sport involving some degree of physical contact impliedly consent to those contacts that arise incidentally to the playing of the game within its rules: *Giumelli v Johnston* [1991] Aust Torts Reports 81-085; *Canterbury Bankstown Rugby League Football Club Ltd v Rogers* [1993] Aust Torts Reports 81-246; *Re Lenfield* [1993] Aust Torts Reports 81-222; *Sibley v Milutinovic* [1990] Aust Torts Reports 81-013. They may also be held to consent to certain rule infringements such as tripping or pushing: *Giumelli*. There is no consent to deliberate acts of violence not directed towards the playing of the game: see *McNamara v Duncan* (1971) 26 ALR 584; *Canterbury Bankstown*. How far consent will be found to exist in cases where the rules are breached and there is likelihood of physical contact as a result will often be a matter of degree. Even though the plaintiff's implied consent may preclude an action for battery, there is still the possibility of an action for negligence. Here the risks incidental to the sport are relevant to fixing the standard of care of the defendant. The matter is dealt with under breach of duty of care in negligence.

Self-defence

[7.50] The existence of the privilege to act in self-defence is clearly established. It operates as a defence where:

(a) a genuine occasion for self-defence appears to exist; and

(b) the force used in self-defence is no more than reasonable.

---

[2]   As to what constitutes an unlawful prize fight, see *Pallante v Stadiums Pty Ltd* [1976] VR 331.

Figure 7.4: Self-defence
....

> - Whether it was reasonable for the defendant to defend him/herself.
> - Whether the force used was reasonable or proportionate.

As regards (a), the test is not whether an actual need for self-defence has arisen, but whether the defendant reasonably thought there to be such a need: *Zecevic v DPP* (1987) 162 CLR 645; *Beckford v The Queen* [1988] AC 130; but see *Criminal Code* (WA): *Hall v Fonceca* [1983] WAR 309. As regards (b), in *McLelland v Symons* [1951] VLR 157 the defendant, who was much bigger than the plaintiff, made threatening gestures with his fists at the plaintiff, who in response picked up and loaded a rifle and pointed it at the defendant. The defendant then struck the rifle aside with a crowbar, knocking the plaintiff to the ground and he possibly struck the plaintiff another blow with the crowbar while he was lying on the ground. The Victorian Court held that the burden of proving the assault lay on the plaintiff and the burden of proving the need to act in self-defence lay on the defendant. The defendant had discharged the evidential burden because the pointing of a loaded rifle at the defendant involved the use of excessive force in retaliation for the mere threat of blows. The burden of showing that the defendant had used excessive force lay on the plaintiff, and he failed on this issue since he could not establish that the defendant had made the second use of the crowbar (which would have been excessive). The case was later qualified in South Australia in *Pearce v Hallett* [1969] SASR 423. The plaintiff has the burden of proof on the issue of excessive force only if he or she is complaining of the number of blows that were struck. Each blow, as a separate battery, must be proved by the plaintiff. The defendant has the burden of showing that the amount of force used was not unreasonable. The test of excessive force is that the force used must not be disproportionate to the harm to be averted. It is now established that this does not require retreat to as far as possible before striking a blow, although this is clearly material to the question of reasonableness: *R v Bird* [1985] 1 WLR 816.

Mere provocative conduct on the plaintiff's part does not establish the privilege of self-defence, although it may be relevant to the issue of whether exemplary or aggravated damages should be awarded: *Fontin v Katapodis* (1962) 108 CLR 177. However, provocation is a defence under the Criminal Codes of Queensland and Western Australia: *Criminal Code Act 1899* (Qld), s 269; *Criminal Code* (WA), s 246; see *Wenn v Evans* (1985) 2 SR (WA) 263; see also *Criminal Code Act 1996* (NT), ss 33, 34.

Defence of others

[7.55] At common law, it is generally accepted that one member of a family or household may legitimately come to the defence of any other member, including a servant. In *Pearce v Hallett* [1969] SASR 423, Bray CJ put the matter on a wider basis: "Every man has the right of defending any man by reasonable force against unlawful force."

There is no obvious argument against this, although the actual case was of a son defending his father. The test of reasonable force appears to be the same as that for self-defence.

CHAPTER 7

Figure 7.5: Defence of others

> • Was it reasonable for the defendant to protect the other person
>   in this way?
> • Was the amount of force reasonable and proportionate?

Defence of property

[7.60] The paradigm case of this, in fact the only clearly established one, is that of the person in possession of land or premises who is entitled to use reasonable force to eject a trespasser on that property, or to deter entry by a trespasser. The privilege is limited to the possessor and the force used must be no more than reasonable: *Holmes v Bagge* (1853) El & Bl 782; 118 ER 629; *Stroud v Bradbury* [1952] 2 All ER 76 (reasonable to resist entry with clothes-prop and spade); *Haddrick v Lloyd* [1945] SASR 40. An owner of land who has a right to immediate possession, and who has entered the land for the purpose of asserting that right, is not a trespasser, even though the owner may commit the crime of forcible entry on to the land.[3] An owner out of possession has no privilege to eject trespassers from the land; but there seems no reason why such an owner should not be allowed to use force to prevent anticipated damage to the property. In the case of defence of property by non-owners, the defence of necessity may be available: see [7.65].

Where the defendant had set a spring-gun on his land and the mechanism was activated by the plaintiff trespasser, who was shot, it was found that this was not the use of reasonable force for the ejection of a trespasser. Thus in *Bird v Holbrook* (1828) 4 Bing 628; 130 ER 911, the plaintiff succeeded in an action on the case in circumstances where the defendant had given no notice of the spring-gun. In *Llott v Wilkes* (1820) 3 B & Ald 304; 106 ER 674, however, where a notice of the presence of spring-guns on the land had been displayed outside the land, and the plaintiff was aware of this notice, and subsequently entered and was injured, the defendant was held not liable. The court was divided upon the question of whether the basis of the defence was the plaintiff's consent to the risk of the spring-gun, or that the defendant was entitled to take reasonable steps to deter trespass to his land. Whatever its basis, the case would now be differently decided on its own facts, since shooting a trespasser in order to deter entry would not now be regarded as reasonable force: *Hackshaw v Shaw* (1984) 155 CLR 614 (the case necessarily implies this, although its ratio concerned negligence on the occupier's part in shooting the trespasser). The issue of whether the occupier is justified in shooting a trespasser *after* knowledge of the trespasser's entry is considered in Chapter 10. On the other hand, *Llott* appears to justify the use of broken glass or spikes at the top of walls to deter entry. It has been held by the Court of Appeal in England

---

[3]   Although under the Criminal Codes of Queensland, Tasmania, Western Australia, the ACT and the Northern Territory it is lawful for a person in peaceable possession under a claim of right to defend that interest even against a person who is entitled to possession of the land: *Criminal Code* (Qld), ss 275, 278; *Criminal Code* (Tas), ss 42, 44; *Criminal Code* (WA), ss 252, 255; *Criminal Code 2002* (ACT), s 410; *Criminal Code Act 1996* (NT), s 43.

(*Cummings v Grainger* [1979] QB 377) that the keeping of a guard dog in a scrap-yard is a reasonable measure for the protection of the property, provided a proper notice was displayed outside the yard. But in Australia, the question of liability for the acts of dogs is subject to statutory provision: see Chapter 17.

At common law, the defendant has a right to take reasonable measures of protection against marauding animals, by, for example, shooting them. In *Cresswell v Sirl* [1948] 1 KB 241, the defendant shot the plaintiff's dogs, who were harrying his sheep. The Court of Appeal held that the defendant had a defence if the property being protected was in real or imminent danger, and the trespassory act of shooting the dogs was the only feasible method of protection.

Necessity

[7.65] The defence of necessity has been found available in relation to the following acts:

- An act that damages property for the purpose of preserving life. In *Mouse's* case (1609) 12 Co Rep 63; 77 ER 1341, the plaintiff complained that some of his property had been thrown overboard from a ferry travelling up the Thames. The defendant's plea of necessity succeeded, since it was established that a need to lighten the ship had arisen because of a storm that threatened the lives of passengers. The paramount necessity of protecting human life is recognised by uniform statutory provisions throughout Australia giving fire brigades immunity from liability for destroying houses where this is necessary to prevent the spread of fire: for example *Fire Brigades Act 1997* (NSW), s 128.

- An act done solely to preserve the life or health of the plaintiff or the plaintiff's property. Thus in *Leigh v Gladstone* (1909) 26 TLR 139 the defence was available where the defendant had force-fed the plaintiff, a prisoner, who was on a hunger strike. The decision in this case is no longer conclusive following English and Canadian decisions to the effect that an adult person of sound mind may refuse consent to medical treatment, even where the consequence of being denied the treatment is likely to be that person's death: *Re T* [1992] All ER 649; *Home Secretary v Robb* [1995] 2 WLR 722; *Malette v Shulman* (1990) 67 DLR (4d) 321.[4] Providing treatment in the absence of consent would in these circumstances amount to battery. In *Proudman v Allen* [1954] SASR 336, the defendant saw the plaintiff's car running driverless down a slope in the direction of another car. He turned the steering wheel in order to avoid a collision and the effect of this was that the car rolled into the sea. The court held the defendant not liable; his action had been reasonably done in the belief that it would protect the plaintiff's property. The actual effect of the act was not relevant in the absence of negligence.

- A situation in which some minor discomfort or even temporary illness is inflicted on a person who constitutes a danger to the public. In *Rigby v Chief Constable of Northamptonshire* [1985] 1 WLR 1242 police were able to rely on the defence to use CS gas to flush out an armed psychopath from premises.

---

[4]   In *Airedale NHS Trust v Bland* [1993] AC 789 the House of Lords held that it was lawful to terminate the artificial feeding and treatment by antibiotics of an unconscious patient, where there was no possibility of recovery of consciousness, even though the inevitable result of this was the death of the patient.

Figure 7.6: Necessity

- The act must be reasonably necessary to protect the person or property.
- An urgent situation of imminent peril must be present.

[7.70] In no other case is the defence of necessity clearly available. No case has established that it is legitimate to take or endanger life in order to preserve life. It is also not clearly established that it is permissible to destroy property in order to preserve property. In *Cope v Sharpe (No 2)* [1912] 1 KB 496, the defendant had set fire to the plaintiff's heather in order to protect from a fire other land over which his employer held sporting rights and which harboured a number of game birds. The defendant was held not liable for this trespass. As an authority on the defence of necessity the case seems to be of limited significance, since the sporting rights were of considerable value, whereas the damage to the heather was nominal in amount. It is also possible to regard the case as turning on defence of property rather than necessity: the defendant as a gamekeeper had a real interest in protecting his employer's rights. The case shows that the necessity of the defendant's action must be judged at the time it is committed. If it appears to be reasonably necessary at that time, it makes no difference that, as in *Cope*, it proves to have been unnecessary (the fire burned itself out before reaching the heather).

The defendant is not liable for taking purely defensive measures against some threatened peril emanating from outside his or her land, such as floodwaters (*Nield v London & North Western Railway Co* (1874) LR 10 Ex 4) or a plague of locusts (*Greyvensteyn v Hattingh* [1911] AC 355), even though the inevitable or likely result is to divert the danger to the land of a neighbour. This is more a case of the defendant committing no tort, than an application of the defence of necessity. The activity in question is akin to those activities that a landowner is permitted to carry out on his or her land even though the inevitable result is damage to the land of a neighbour: for these situations see Chapter 16.

Necessity would also not seem to be a reason for excusing the acts of the persons who threw the stray firework in *Scott v Shepherd* (1773) 2 Black W 892; 96 ER 525. Necessity does not legitimate the exposure of other persons to danger in order to save oneself; still less would it excuse the act of the person who threw the firework on in order to save his goods. Another possibility is to regard both persons as not being negligent in these circumstances because they acted in the agony of the moment, having no time to think. The problem with this argument is that the agony of the moment principle has never as a matter of law been applied to defendants, other than altruistic rescuers, as in *Horsley v McLaren* [1972] SCR 441: see [8.235]. De Grey CJ stated obiter in *Scott* that there would have been no legal liability on the part of those responsible for the intervening acts on the facts of the case, although he did not justify this opinion.

Rigby v Chief Constable of Northamptonshire [1985] 1 WLR 1242 shows that necessity is not available to a negligent defendant. In that case, the police defendants fired a canister of CS gas into the plaintiff's premises in order to flush out an armed psychopath who was feared to present an imminent danger to the public. As a result the premises caught fire and were destroyed. Although necessity was found by the court to be available in principle as a defence in this situation, the police were liable for the destruction of the premises, since there was a foreseeable risk of fire and it was negligent to have fired the canister before summoning fire services which were readily available.

An early case suggested that one who escaped liability for damaging another person's property by pleading necessity should nevertheless have to compensate that person for the damage: *Vincent v Lake Erie Transportation Co* (1910) 109 Minn 456. The problem with this is that to require compensation would effectively nullify the defence.

Contributory negligence

[7.75] The possible applicability of this defence to the intentional torts is of relatively recent origin. When contributory negligence was a complete defence, it was never successfully applied against the plaintiff by an intentional tortfeasor. Furthermore, the various contributory negligence statutes in Australia define fault (for the purpose of recognising the defence of contributory negligence as a ground for reduction of damages) as: "omission which would, apart from this Act give rise to the defence of contributory negligence".

Australian decisions have refused the statutory defence where an intentional tort was committed on the ground that before the statutory reform, contributory negligence would not have been a defence: *Horkin v North Melbourne Football Club* [1983] 1 VR 153. This is so even where liability for conversion requires as a matter of law that the dealing be negligent, as in the case of conversion of a cheque by a bank: *Day v Bank of New South Wales* (1978) 18 SASR 163; *Hilton v Commonwealth Trading Bank* [1973] 2 NSWLR 644; *Grantham Homes Pty Ltd v ANZ Bank* (1979) 26 ACTR 1. On the other hand, a New Zealand and an English case have applied the apportionment provisions of the Act where the defendant's tort was committed negligently even though as a conversion it required an intentional dealing: *Helson v McKenzies* [1950] NZLR 878; *Lumsden v London Bank* (1971) 1 Ll R 114.[5] In trespass, which can be committed intentionally or negligently, contributory negligence operates as a defence where a negligent trespass is relied on: *Venning v Chin* (1975) 10 SASR 299.

Self-help

[7.80] In certain situations a person is entitled to resort to self-help, which provides a defence against an action in tort. In some of these cases self-help also provides a *remedy* in tort. The right to recapt a chattel may exist against a non-tortfeasor. The leading examples of self-help providing a defence are:

- recaption of chattels;
- entry on land for the purpose of repossessing it;
- abatement of nuisance; and
- distress damage feasant.

The availability of a defence of self-help is not limited to these cases. In *R v Chief Constable of Devon* [1982] QB 458, the applicants had entered land of another person in order to assess its suitability for the stationing of a nuclear power station. However,

---

[5] But the Australian position was followed in an action for deceit: *Alliance & Leicester Building Society v Edgestop Ltd* [1993] 1 WLR 1462.

they were hampered in their efforts by protesters who lay down in front of moving vehicles, chained themselves to equipment, and otherwise hindered the working effort. The Court of Appeal found that the applicants could have lawfully resorted to the use of reasonable force to remove the protesters, and this without reference to the question of whether torts had been committed by the protesters.

Recaption of chattels

[7.85] The term refers to the retaking, if necessary by reasonable force, of a chattel to which the defendant has the right to immediate possession and of which the plaintiff is in possession at the time of the taking. The most recent case is a 19th century one: *Blades v Higgs* (1861) 10 CB(NS) 713; 142 ER 634. Its effect is controversial. It appears to establish that the defendant has the defence in whatever circumstances the plaintiff came into possession of the chattel. The case is sometimes explained on the basis that the plaintiff had acquired possession by means of a wrongful taking, vis à vis the defendant.[6] However this question may now be resolved. A Canadian case exists (*Devoe v Long* [1951] 1 DLR 203) to the effect that there is no right of recaption against a bailee of a chattel who has come into possession lawfully and then refused, however wrongfully, to restore possession to the bailor.[7] The effect of the "right of recaption" where it exists is to establish a defence to the plaintiff's action of assault and/or battery.

Recaption of chattels may also operate as a defence to an action of trespass to land, that is where the defendant has entered the plaintiff's land in order to exercise a purported right of recaption of the chattel. The combination of two old cases (*Patrick v Colerick* and *Anthony v Haney*) suggests that this right exists where:

- the chattel came on the land by the act of the occupier of the land (*Patrick v Colerick* (1838) 3 M & W 483; 150 ER 1235);[8]

- the chattel came on the land by the felonious act of a third party;

- the chattel came on the land by accident, the example given being that of fruit falling from the boughs of trees on to the plaintiff's land, and thus seeming to exclude the case where the chattel arrived on the plaintiff's land by the defendant's negligence; or

- where the occupier refuses the owner's demand for the chattel, on the ground that this is evidence of a conversion by the occupier.[9]

The following points may be noted. First, no right of recaption exists where the defendant is responsible for the chattel's presence on the plaintiff's land. Second, the felony/misdemeanour distinction here appears to be archaic. It would be better to extend the rule to any criminal offence that has played a part in depriving the owner of the chattel. Third, the last case put by *Anthony v Haney* (1832) 8 Bing 186; 131 ER 372

---

6   The lower court's decision was affirmed by the House of Lords, which decided that the plaintiff had originally wrongfully taken the chattels. This, however, cannot disturb the original ratio of the Exchequer Chamber that the right of recaption existed however the plaintiff came into possession: contra, Fleming, *Law of Torts* (9th ed), pp 100-101.

7   The Queensland, Tasmanian, Western Australian, ACT and NT Criminal Codes give a right to retake possession of a chattel using only reasonable force from any person who does not hold it under a claim of right, thus not requiring an original wrongful taking by that person: *Criminal Code* (Qld), s 276, *Criminal Code* (Tas), s 45; *Criminal Code* (WA), s 253; *Criminal Code 2002* (ACT), s 38; *Criminal Code 1996* (NT), s 27(k).

8   Or where the chattel is placed on land with the occupier's consent: *Huet v Lawrence* [1948] St R Qd 168.

9   The last three examples are derived from obiter dicta in *Anthony v Haney* (1832) 8 Bing 186; 131 ER 372.

causes problems, since the probable ratio decidendi of *British Economical Lamp Co v Mile End Theatre* (1913) 29 TLR 383 does not distinguish according to the circumstances in which the chattel came onto the land: the defendant does not commit conversion or detinue unless he or she has taken possession of the chattel. Granted the presence of the chattel on the land, and the plaintiff's right to possession of it, it would not seem to be an undue extension of legal principle if the unreasonable refusal to allow the plaintiff access to the chattel were to be regarded as conversion.

Entering land for purpose of repossession

[7.90] A person entitled to immediate possession of land may enter the land for the purpose of retaking possession of it, and expel the occupier, using only reasonable force. The defence here is similar to that considered in relation to recaption of chattels: see [7.85]. An additional complication is the *Forcible Entry Act 1381* (5 Rich II, St 1, c 7) that was received into Australia, and has been confirmed by some later State legislation: *Crimes Act 1958* (Vic), s 207; *Criminal Law Consolidation Act 1935* (SA), s 243; *Criminal Code* (WA), s 69; *Criminal Code* (Tas), s 79(1); *Criminal Law Consolidation Act 1935* (NT), s 243; by reception: *R v Waugh* (1935) 53 WN(NSW) 20. The Act makes any kind of forcible entry, even by one entitled to possession of the land, a criminal offence. However, it appears to have no effect at all in relation to the rights of one who is entitled to retake possession under the civil law, according to *Hemmings v Stoke Poges Golf Club* [1920] 1 KB 720. In that case, the plaintiff and his wife were occupying the house of the plaintiff's employer as part of the plaintiff's contract. The contract ended and the defendant served upon the plaintiff notice to quit. This having expired, the plaintiff, his wife and his furniture were forcibly removed by the defendant's servants. The Court of Appeal held that this was not trespass to land, assault or battery, the notice to quit being valid and the force used being no more than reasonable for the purpose of eviction. The fact that it was criminal behaviour under the Act made no difference.[10]

Abatement of nuisance

[7.95] Undoubtedly, a privilege to abate a nuisance exists in certain circumstances. It is not often exercised in the present day. The case law is derived mainly from often nebulous decisions made before the end of the 19th century. Where the privilege exists, it operates by way of a defence to an action for trespass to land or chattels, whether arising from the original entry or trespassory acts committed after entry.

The following rules apply:

- The abater must not commit unnecessary damage. Even if damage is necessary to remove the nuisance, it appears that this must not be disproportionate to the nature of the right sought to be upheld. Thus in *Perry v Fitzhowe* (1846) 8 QB 757; 115 ER 1057, it was held that it was not reasonable to demolish a house that allegedly interfered with the plaintiff's easement of pasture.

- It is probable that abatement is not available at all where the court would only have awarded damages for the nuisance, rather than an injunction to remove

---

[10] But a person in peaceable possession who resists entry under a claim of right is given a defence in the Code States: *Criminal Code* (Qld), s 276; *Criminal Code* (Tas), s 45; *Criminal Code* (WA), s 253; *Criminal Code 2002* (ACT), s 410; *Criminal Code Act 1996* (NT), s 43.

it: *Burton v Winters* [1993] 3 All ER 847 (mandatory injunction refused, so plaintiff could not resort to self-help to remove trespassing building). This, however, presents the would-be abater with a seemingly insoluble dilemma.

- Notice of the intention to abate is not required where:
  — no entry on land is required to abate, as in the lopping-off of projecting branches of trees (*Lemmon v Webb* [1895] AC 1);
  — an emergency exists, creating an immediate danger to life or limb or of damage to property; or
  — the land is still occupied by the original creator of the nuisance (*Jones v Williams* (1843) 11 M & W 176; 152 ER 764).[11]

  In other cases, notice is seemingly required.

- The privilege is available only to one who can seek redress in the courts for the nuisance. So the technical rules of locus standi to sue in nuisance (Chapter 16) apply also in abatement.

An Australian decision, *Proprietors of Strata Plan No 14198 v Cowell* [1991] Aust Torts Reports 81-083, allowed the plaintiff in a nuisance action the costs of abatement as damages where these had been incurred in reasonable mitigation of damages, although the right to compensation was thought by the court to be limited to abatement carried out on the plaintiff's own land.

Distress damage feasant

[7.100] At common law, the occupier of land had a privilege to take and retain possession of an animal that had trespassed on his land and caused damage there. The defence did not exist, however, where the animal remained in possession of its owner. It was also available in the case of a chattel that had unlawfully entered land and caused damage thereon: *Ambergate, Nottingham & Boston & Eastern Junction Railway Co v Midland Railway Co* (1853) 2 El & Bl 793; 118 ER 964.

Distress damage feasant has been generally replaced by statutory provisions conferring a similar privilege: for example the *Impounding Act 1993* (NSW), s 27.[12]

Discipline

[7.105] At common law, certain disciplinary powers existed that excused the commission of what would otherwise be tortious acts. A husband could administer "reasonable" corporal punishment to his wife, a parent to its child and a school teacher to a pupil. The person in command of a ship could exercise disciplinary powers against its crew or passengers. The husband's power no longer exists, but the other three powers survive. The power of a school teacher to administer corporal punishment to a pupil arises not through implied delegation of authority from the parents of the child, but independently by virtue of the relationship between teacher and pupil and the need to maintain order and discipline in the school. It is limited to school hours and premises, and is invariably subject to statutory regulation. But it is questionable to what extent such regulations

---

[11] The purpose of this rule is not clear, hence the authority of this case must be in doubt.
[12] Distress damage feasant has been abolished in New South Wales: *Animals Act 1977* (NSW), s 5; ACT: *Civil Law (Wrongs) Act 2002*, s 213; Tas: *Police Offences Act 1935*, s 20AA; and Vic (in relation to motor vehicles): *Road Safety Act 1986*, s 90B.

deny the teacher the defence of lawful discipline. Force used in discipline by parent or teacher must be moderate and reasonable, and must be suitable to the circumstances of the case and the physical and mental characteristics of the child or pupil. The special needs of discipline at sea will dictate the legality of disciplinary action taken by the person in command of the ship to enforce it. It has been held to exceed the disciplinary privilege to put a passenger in irons for calling the captain "the landlord of a floating hotel" (*R v Franklin* (1858) I F & F 360; 175 ER 764) or to confine a passenger in his room for seven days for thumbing his nose at the captain: *Hook v Cunard Steamship Co* [1953] 1 WLR 682.

Military personnel are subject to military discipline, which may legitimise action that would otherwise be an incursion on their civil rights.

Illegality

[7.110] The question at issue is to what extent it is a defence that the plaintiff was a party to an illegal activity affecting the circumstances in which a cause of action arose. Illegality may constitute a defence both to intentional torts and to negligence, although special considerations apply to the latter (considered in Chapter 12). There is so little by way of general principle in relation to illegality as a defence to intentional torts that it is difficult to state general legal propositions. It is generally accepted that the plaintiff's property rights remain enforceable even though the plaintiff has been a party to an illegal transaction, provided it is not necessary for the plaintiff to refer to that transaction in order to establish the right.

In *Bowmakers Ltd v Barnet Instruments Ltd* [1945] KB 65, the plaintiffs, who had entered into illegal hire-purchase agreements concerning their goods with the defendants, were able to succeed in actions for conversion of the goods by the defendants, who had sold them. This was because both the plaintiff's property in the goods and the defendants' conversion of them could be established without reference to the illegal contracts. On the other hand, in *Thomas Brown Ltd v Fazal Deen* (1962) 108 CLR 391, the plaintiff was unable to establish a cause of action in detinue against the defendants. The defendants had acted as bailees of the plaintiff's gold bars and had converted them. However, in order to succeed in detinue the plaintiff had to establish a right to possession of the gold. He was unable to do so without referring to the terms of the contract of bailment, which was an illegal transaction because it breached exchange control regulations. The High Court found no difficulty in protecting the plaintiff's property right in money that represented the proceeds of illegal betting, in an action for detinue against the police, even though reference to the illegal betting was necessary in order to show the nature of the plaintiff's property right: *Russell v Wilson* (1923) 33 CLR 538. In *Gollan v Nugent* (1988) 166 CLR 18 the High Court upheld the plaintiffs' claim to the return of certain articles held by the police which they alleged were to be used to commit offences under the *Indecent Articles Act 1975* (NSW). (This was so even though the court gave the police leave to defend the action on the ground that the articles by their very nature were such that it might be contrary to public policy to return them.) The court in *Thackwell v Barclays Bank* [1986] 1 All ER 676 refused to hold the bank liable in conversion for not honouring the plaintiff customer's cheque, since the cheque was drawn on money representing the proceeds of a fraud to which the plaintiff was a party and allowing him to succeed would enable him to profit from his crime.

The court retains a measure of discretion as to how far to allow actions to succeed where the plaintiff has been guilty of illegal conduct. One approach to the problem, drawing support from the judgment of Windeyer J in *Smith v Jenkins* (1970) 119 CLR 397, is to distinguish between mere minor or technical breaches of the law and more serious breaches by the plaintiff. But this has commanded no general judicial support and an English judge has expressed his opposition to it.[13] Another approach, which is generally more favoured, is to examine the closeness of connection between the illegal conduct and cause of action. In dictum, Asquith LJ said in *National Coal Board v England* [1954] AC 403 that if two burglars were on the way to commit a burglary and while proceeding one burglar picked the other one's pocket, he had no doubt that an action would lie. This line of argument may constitute the best explanation of *Saunders v Edwards* [1987] 1 WLR 1116. The plaintiff had bought a house from the defendant but had unlawfully evaded the payment of stamp duty on the transaction. Nevertheless she was able to succeed against the defendant in respect of a fraudulent misrepresentation made to her prior to the purchase. The illegality committed by the plaintiff had no connection with the wrong committed by the defendant.

Legal process

Arrest

[7.115] The subject of arrest is a difficult one, the original common law having been subjected to a considerable and complex statutory overlay that differs from jurisdiction to jurisdiction. Only the basic rules can be outlined here. Where the arrest has taken place under a warrant granted by a Justice of the Peace or a magistrate, a police officer has no protection at common law against an action for wrongful arrest if the warrant turns out to be invalid. However, statutory provisions now generally provide a defence, although there is no protection where the terms of the warrant have been exceeded, however innocently. For details of this protection, the reader is referred to *The Laws of Australia* (Lawbook Co., subscription service) 33 Torts, [33.9.560].

Where the arrest takes place without a warrant, it is justified if:

- the arrest is reasonably thought to be necessary by the arresting person to prevent a breach of the peace or to stop the continuance of one that has already arisen (*Albert v Lavin* [1981] 3 WLR 955); or

- the arrest is for the commission of a treason or felony, or it is reasonably apprehended that one is likely to be committed in the near future.

Where the arrest is for the commission of a treason or felony, there is a difference between the power of arrest of the police officer and that of the private citizen. The police officer is allowed to arrest on reasonable suspicion, both as to the actual commission of the treason or felony and of its commission by the arrested person. The private citizen is allowed to arrest on reasonable suspicion only of the second fact, not the first, and must therefore show that the treason or felony has actually been committed: *Walters v W H Smith* [1914] 1 KB 595.[14] It has been held that in the case of

---

13   Dillon LJ in *Pitts v Hunt* [1989] 3 WLR 795 thought that a "graph of illegality" was unworkable (supported by Balcombe LJ; also by Lord Goff in *Tinsley v Milligan* [1993] 3 WLR 126).

14   The rule was confirmed in *R v Self* [1992] 1 WLR 687, but trenchantly criticised by Hopkins [1992] CLJ 405.

arrest by a police officer, the reasonable suspicion must exist in the mind of the officer. It is not sufficient to act on the instructions of a superior officer in effecting the arrest: *O'Hara v Chief Constable of Royal Ulster Constabulary* [1997] 1 All ER 129.

Where the offence is a misdemeanour, there was no power at common law to arrest at all. Statute has made very considerable incursions on this rule in all States. For details of the statutory provisions concerning arrest, the reader is referred to *The Laws of Australia* (Lawbook Co., subscription service) 33 Torts, [33.9].

The arrested person is entitled to know the reason for the arrest, and if the reason given is a false one, a tort is committed even though a reason did exist that would have justified the arrest: *Christie v Leachinsky* [1947] AC 573. The scope of this rule has been qualified in a number of recent English cases. In *Christie* the stated ground for arrest was invalid though a valid ground for arrest did exist. In *R v Chalkeley* [1998] 2 All ER 155 the stated ground for arrest was valid and the only ground for arrest that existed, but the motive for arresting the accused was the ulterior one of preventing him from committing more serious crimes. This was held not to invalidate the arrest. Another case held that a breach of the rule in *Christie* causes the arrest to be unlawful only until the breach is repaired: *Lewis v Chief Constable of South Wales* [1991] 1 All ER 206. It is not necessary to accurately define legally the offence for which the arrest was made. The phrase "unlawful possession" of a motor vehicle was therefore held to be sufficiently informative although it covered three different offences: *Abbassy v MPC* [1990] 1 WLR 385. Nor is it necessary to inform the person of the reason for the arrest if the circumstances are such that the person must know the general nature of the alleged offence.

There is no power to arrest for questioning and that type of arrest is unlawful even if the answers to the questions give rise to a reasonable suspicion that the arrested person had committed the offence. *Holgate-Mohammed v Duke* [1984] AC 437 does not conflict with this principle, since the ratio of that case was that where a reasonable suspicion already exists in the arrester's mind at the time of making the arrest, the arrest is not unlawful by reason of the fact that the motive for making the arrest was the belief that the arrested person would be more likely to respond truthfully to questioning under police custody. The arrested person must be brought before a magistrate as soon as reasonably possible, or in the case of arrest by a private person, handed over to the police: *John Lewis Ltd v Tims* [1952] AC 676. A reasonable delay for the purpose of deciding whether to prosecute or of formulating charges is justifiable, but there is no power to make further investigations by questioning the arrested person or taking him to his house to seek further confirmation of his guilt. On the latter point the High Court of Australia in *Williams v The Queen* (1986) 161 CLR 278 disapproved of the decision in *Dallison v Caffery* [1965] 1 QB 348, insofar as it was to the contrary. The ratio of *Holgate-Mohammed* is not in conflict with the High Court decision since in it the complaint was only as to the original arrest, not as to the time held in police custody.

A power exists at common law, incidental to arrest, of search of the arrested person and seizure of goods found in his or her possession. The seizure must be related to purposes such as ensuring the prisoner does not escape or assist others to do so, does not injure him or herself or others, does not destroy or dispose of evidence and does not commit further crimes.

Entry on land to effect legal process

[7.120] In the absence of a search warrant or of a statutory authority to enter, the right to enter must be found to exist under common law principles. At common law there is a right of entry under the following circumstances:

(a) by a police officer or a citizen to prevent murder;

(b) by a police officer or a citizen if a felony has, in fact, been committed and the felon has been followed to a house;

(c) by a police officer or citizen if a felony is about to be committed and will be committed unless prevented; and

(d) by a police officer following an offender running away from an affray: *Lippl v Haines* (1989) 18 NSWLR 620.

In *Lippl* it was held that the common law powers of entry under (b) (and by inference (c)) should be extended to the case of a statutory power of arrest by a police officer for a "crime". That case also held that there must be reasonable grounds for suspecting the presence of the person about to be arrested on the premises entered; and that, save in exigent circumstances, the occupier of the premises must be made aware that the police officer wishes to exercise an authority to enter and be given an opportunity to permit entry to be made without force.

Where no arrest is to be made on the premises, the right of entry to effect legal process is governed by the third rule in *Semayne's* case (1604) 5 Co Rep 91a at 91b; 77 ER 194, that "in all cases where the King is party, the sheriff may break into the house, whether to arrest, or do other execution of the King's process, if he cannot otherwise enter". In *Plenty v Dillon* (1991) 171 CLR 635 the defendant police officers had entered the plaintiff's land in order to serve a summons on the plaintiff's daughter to appear before the magistrates for the commission of an offence. The entry had been made in circumstances in which it was clear the plaintiff had negated any implied licence on the part of the police to enter. This was held to be a trespass to land on either of two grounds: (a) that even if the King was party to the summons, which was doubtful, the service of summons was not the execution of process since it was not coercive;[15] or (b) that the King was not a party, summary procedure being distinguishable from trial on indictment.[16]

Holder of unwanted goods

[7.125] A number of statutory defences are available to the holder of unwanted goods. The first case to consider is that of the involuntary bailee. It was pointed out in Chapter 5 that an involuntary bailee who takes reasonable steps to return the chattel to the person entitled to it is not liable if in some way the chattel goes astray. A further question arises as to the position of one who receives unsolicited goods through the mail as part of an attempt to persuade the recipient to pay for them. The Commonwealth of Australia has legislated against this pernicious practice in the *Trade Practices Act 1974* (ss 64, 65), and there is now uniform State provision of the same character. Section 73(1) of the *Fair Trading Act 1987* (SA) provides that the recipient:

---

15 This was the ground of the majority, Mason CJ and Brennan and Toohey JJ.
16 This was the ground of Gaudron and McHugh JJ.

- is under no liability to pay for the goods;
- becomes owner of them on the expiry of a notice period, where notice has been given to the sender in accordance with the Act; and
- is not liable for the loss of or damage to the goods during the notice period unless this has been caused by a wilful and unlawful act on his or her part.

The acquisition of ownership provision does not apply in certain circumstances, in particular where the recipient knew or might reasonably be expected to know that the goods were not intended for the recipient.

The second case to consider is that of the voluntary bailee who wishes to return goods to their owner but is unable to make contact with the latter to arrange for their return. Again this situation is subject to uniform provision throughout the Australian States. For example, under the *Uncollected Goods Act 1995* (NSW) the bailee is allowed to sell and dispose of the goods either under court order or at public auction after giving due notice under the Act. The proceeds of sale may then first be applied in satisfaction of the bailee's charges, and the balance may be claimed as unclaimed money under the *Unclaimed Money Act 1995* (NSW).

Incapacity

[7.130] Incapacity is not a defence to an action in tort as such. The defendant must establish the incapacity, but it is then for the plaintiff to establish that despite that incapacity the elements of the tort can be proved. The central question is whether the incapacity is such that the defendant is able to form the requisite mental element required for the tort in question. This section deals only with liability for intentional torts (incapacity in relation to negligence is dealt with in Chapter 10 on breach of duty).

In the case of the insane person, the now generally approved position is that, provided that person knows the nature of the act being committed, it is not necessary that he or she knows it to be wrongful. So in *Morris v Marsden* [1952] 1 All ER 925, an insane person was held liable for an assault and battery under this principle. This means that an earlier New South Wales decision (*White v Pile* (1951) 68 WN(NSW) 176) conferring a general immunity from liability on the insane person is seen as wrong. The fact that intentional trespass is actionable, even though the defendant has no reason to believe that he or she is acting wrongfully, seems to be important here. The same result would no doubt be reached in the case of other intentional torts that impose strict liability, such as conversion. A different result would, on this argument, follow in the case of a tort such as the intentional, non-trespassory infliction of injury or damage, where a wrongful intent is required (unless, despite the insanity, the wrongfulness of the act is known).

In the case of children there is clearly no immunity from liability in tort in the case of the older child, whether the conduct is intentional or negligent.[17] As in the case of the insane person, a very young child may fall within the strict liability of intentional torts such as trespass or conversion, where the child knows the nature of the act being committed. So, a five-year-old child was held liable for slashing a playmate with a razor: *Hart v A-G (Tas)* (unreported, Supreme Court, Tasmania, 1979). But a six-year-old child

---

17   In *Tsouvalla v Bini* [1966] SASR 157, an older boy was held liable for an intentional trespass, though in default of defence on his part. The general availability of tort liability against older children is assumed by the High Court in *McHale v Watson* (1966) 16 CLR 199.

CHAPTER 7

was not liable for firing a gun and wounding a companion, since the child did not appreciate that the gun could go off in these circumstances: *Hogan v Gill* [1992] Aust Torts Reports 81-182.

Practice Questions

Revision Questions

7.1 It has been established that a person's consent must be voluntary but does that consent need to be expressed?

7.2 The necessity of saving a human life has in the past justified a trespass. Does the current emphasis on people's rights alter the acceptance of this?

Problem Question

7.1 Bert suffered a serious injury to his left eye while walking in the forest. He was rushed to the hospital. Richard, the doctor in charge of the emergency room, took one look at him and advised that surgery was necessary. Bert was very concerned about this. He said to the doctor: "Do I need to have the surgery now? Who will perform it? Do you know what you are doing? I am a model and need to keep my looks for as long as possible; it is my career." The doctor replied: "I am a very good surgeon. If you do not have the operation you will lose your sight." Fading in and out of consciousness from the pain, Bert said: "Please be careful. I am a photographic model. I would have no career if my face were scarred." The surgery was performed without negligence but Bert experienced one of the likely complications. The nerves around the left eye were weakened and the left side of his face noticeably sagged. Bert now has no job.

If Bert sues the doctor for battery are there any defences that would justify the doctor's actions? (Please ignore the possible action of negligence for failure to warn of the ramifications of the surgery.)

Answers to Practice Questions

Revision Questions

7.1 A person can expressly consent by their words or deeds. A patient may verbally agree to treatment or signify consent by signing an authority for treatment. However consent may also be implied. For instance a patient who rolls up his sleeve at a vaccination point implies consent. As we walk up a busy street we impliedly give our consent to others bumping into us. We also impliedly consent to the rules of a sporting contest when we participate in that sport or fail to protest or resist when there is opportunity to do so.

7.2 The defence of necessity effectively justifies someone invading the interests of another (a plaintiff) in order to save that person. In the classic case of *Leigh v Gladstone* the defence of necessity justified the defendant who force-fed a suffragette who had gone on a hunger strike. However, it is questionable whether the courts would decide the case similarly today since cases have now established that the principle of the sanctity of life is not absolute and does not authorise the forcible feeding of prisoners on hunger strikes: see the English case *Home Secretary v Robb* [1995] 2 WLR 722. The Canadian case *Malette v Shulman* (1990) 67 DLR (4d) 321 also questions the earlier principle. There a doctor administered a blood transfusion to a known Jehovah's Witness and was held liable for battery. The defence requires the courts to balance the need for people to act out of good intentions against the need to recognise a person's autonomy.

Problem Question

7.1   Any surgery is prima facie a trespass to the person. However, if Bert has consented or the doctor can establish that the surgery was necessary then his actions will be justified. So, can Richard argue either that:

- consent *to the surgery* was obtained; or
- there was an emergency situation which necessitated the surgery?

The arguments for Richard are:

- Bert impliedly consented to the surgery by his words: "Please be careful … ." And he did this voluntarily.
- The surgery was necessary to save Bert's eye. Richard could probably argue that if he had not operated then Bert would have been in an equally disturbing predicament concerning his career since he may have lost his eye altogether.

The arguments for Bert are:

- The fact that Bert was "fading in and out of consciousness" weakens Richard's argument that Bert was competent at the time he had supposedly given consent to the surgery. A person lapsing into unconsciousness may not have the requisite knowledge of his situation to decide whether or not to have surgery. The facts suggest that Bert was asking a lot of questions, but they do not establish that he was completely aware of what was happening. In fact, his plea to Richard to take care because of his concern that his face (and consequently his career) would be detrimentally affected is arguably a denial of consent. This argument would certainly challenge the claim by Richard that Bert impliedly consented to the surgery.
- Bert was not in a life-threatening situation. He may say that he would rather have lost the sight in his eye than suffer damage to the nerves in his face. The loss of sight may not have affected his modelling career at all. In fact, it is established that a competent person who is in a life-threatening situation may refuse treatment and so he should have been able to refuse the treatment in his situation.

On balance, Bert's arguments are stronger in relation to both defences. Richard's claim that Bert consented will probably fail and it will be very difficult to establish necessity since the operation was not performed in response to a life-threatening situation. It should be noted that there will certainly be an element of sympathy with Richard, since it is recognised that doctors have a strong desire to do all they can to heal a person, and that desire would override any concerns that a patient would voice concerning an ability to continue modelling. This type of proactive behaviour, which the community expects of people such as doctors, is considered to be advantageous to the community.

Tutorial Questions

Discussion Questions

7.1   In relation to sporting injuries the courts appear to be grappling with the boundaries of consent. Do you think there should be different rules for contact sports and non-contact sports? Is there a difference between a friendly game and a competitive game?

7.2   Should the unequal strength of the parties, the culture or community background, or a person's gender be taken into account to determine whether the person used an appropriate level of force in defending him or herself?

SECTION

Negligence: The Tort

The tort of negligence underwent review and reform in 2005. There is now a significant legislative component that must be considered when addressing the question of whether or not a defendant has been negligent. As yet, there has been minimal judicial consideration of the legislation and we are left to speculate on what, if any, impact the legislation will have on the practical application of negligence. This section of the book will deal with the development of the tort of negligence and outline the review and subsequent reform, addressing the question of whether this has resulted in significant changes or simply served to give legislative voice to existing common law approaches.

Negligence is more than actionable carelessness. The tort divides into four parts. There must be a duty of care owed to the plaintiff by the defendant; the defendant must be in breach of that duty; the breach must cause the plaintiff damage of a legally recognised kind; and that damage must not be too remote. The four-fold division is conceptually valid, though judges often run together the separate parts of negligence in such a way as to confuse the student. Each step in the process of determining whether or not there is actionable negligence will be carefully considered and clearly explained.

ELEMENTS OF THE TORT OF NEGLIGENCE

Duty of care

The issue of whether a duty of care is owed divides into two questions. The first is a question of reasonable foreseeability and whether a duty is capable of arising as a matter of law; the second is whether a duty arises on the actual facts of the case. Duty on the facts is concerned with whether the defendant on those facts should have foreseen harm to the plaintiff. The notion of foreseeability, as established in court decisions, is quite comprehensive and fairly easy to satisfy. This means that establishing duty on the facts generally presents the plaintiff with few problems, but the requirement is useful in ruling out hopeless cases. Establishing a duty of care in law is generally simple where the defendant has, by positive conduct, caused harm of a physical nature to the plaintiff. In other, more complex, cases difficulties can arise because of the nature of the harm suffered. These situations will be considered in Chapter 8.

Breach

Breach of duty is concerned with whether the defendant has been careless. In law the question of breach is framed in terms of whether the defendant's response (in acting or failing to act) to a foreseeable risk is reasonable or otherwise. In determining whether or not the response of the defendant was appropriate in the circumstances, the court will balance the degree and seriousness of the foreseeable risk against the cost or difficulty of removing it, and the possible loss of public advantage or utility in requiring its removal (the "calculus of negligence" addressed in Chapter 10).

An important component of breach is the issue of standard of care and whether or not the defendant has met the requisite standard. This is determined by considering a number of factors including the relationship between the defendant and plaintiff, any special skills that the defendant may have and the level of knowledge of the plaintiff. The standard of care is a question of fact and may vary in different circumstances.

Causation

Causation of harm raises the question of whether, in the absence of the defendant's breach, the harm to the plaintiff would have occurred. Causation is a question of fact which the courts have generally addressed by applying common sense. While reference is made in judgments to the "but for" test, this is no longer considered the definitive test. The court must be able to identify a clear link between the breach and the loss or damage sustained. Mere coincidence of events will not be sufficent to establish causation.

Remoteness of damage

Remoteness of damage is concerned with whether the harm that the defendant caused was reasonably foreseeable. The test for determining duty on the facts and breach, on the one hand, and remoteness of damage on the other, is based on reasonable foreseeability. Given this, it is particularly easy for a court to conflate the two issues by asking whether the defendant was negligent in relation to the actual harm that has occurred. This approach is sufficient to dispose of a large number of cases. Cases can occur where a breach is readily established by showing a reasonable possibility of some harm to the plaintiff, whereas the actual harm the plaintiff suffers is much less likely to occur. The remoteness question in cases of this sort must be treated separately.

The phenomenon of multiple causation is now firmly established as a feature of modern tort law. As between defendant and plaintiff, an apportionment of the damage is possible according to the finding of the court that the plaintiff was partly to blame for that damage. This is called contributory negligence by the plaintiff. As between defendants who are jointly responsible for causing the same damage, the court has power to apportion responsibility between them (though each defendant is liable to the plaintiff for the whole of that damage).

Contributory negligence is the name of the partial defence that is applied against plaintiffs, where the damages awarded are reduced to reflect the plaintiff's fault. Two other significant defences to negligence are volenti non fit injuria (voluntary assumption of risk) and illegality.

Proof of negligence is determined in the same way as proof of other factors in civil litigation (see Chapter 13), but the plaintiff in a negligence action is assisted by the evidentiary principle known as res ipsa loquitur (the thing itself speaks).

TORT REFORM

Until recently the law of negligence was considered to be well established. There was, however, increasing public concern that the scope of negligence became too broad resulting in upwardly spiralling insurance costs. The broad public perception was that there was a crisis in negligence law that needed to be addressed with some urgency. This, combined with such factors as the collapse of HIH Insurance Ltd in 2001, resulted in negligence law becoming the subject of review.

The first report addressing the perceived crisis was the Trowbridge Report[1] which levelled criticism at the courts, arguing that they were changing the constitution of negligence. The report also argued that there had been a "[d]rift in definition of negligence": p 8. Public perception and the Trowbridge Report combined to galvanise the legislature into action and tort law reform was placed firmly on the political agenda. A panel of "eminent persons" (the Ipp Committee) was convened and directed to "examine a method for the reform of the common law with the objective of limiting liability and quantum of damages arising from personal injury and death".[2]

The panel conducted a wide ranging review of negligence over a short period of time. The report contained 42 recommendations, all aimed at legislative reform to meet the perceived crisis. The result has been widespread reform across all States and Territories.

It is important to note that the existence of a crisis in the tort of negligence was not universally accepted. There have been criticisms levelled at the swift "knee jerk" response by the legislature to public concerns which may have been fuelled by the popular media and amount to "unsubstantial assumptions and perceptions".[3] There have been further concerns that the "whirlwind of legislative action" has, instead of bringing clarity to the debate, resulted in greater confusion and uncertainty which will, in turn, lead to increasing litigation as courts strive to interpret the new provisions.[4]

On the other side of the argument there are those who argue that the future of medical services in Australia has been placed at risk and that the redefinition of the concept of negligence and capping of some heads of damage has not gone far enough.[5] This is reinforced by arguments that the "crisis" has gathered momentum and that it is

---

[1]   Trowbridge Consulting, *Public Liability Insurance: Analysis for Meeting of Ministers*, 27 March 2002 (Trowbridge Report).

[2]   *Review of the Law of Negligence: Final Report* (September 2002) (Ipp Report), "Terms of Reference".

[3]   Underwood P, "Is Ms Donoghue's Snail in Mortal Peril?" (2004) 12(1) *Torts Law Journal* 39.

[4]   R G Atkinson J, "Tort Law Reform in Australia" (Speech to the Australian Plaintiff Lawyers Association Queensland State Conference, 7 February 2003).

[5]   Sedgely M, Chair of the AMA Medical Professional Indemnity Task Force Committee, "Medical Indemnity – It's Crunch Time", 9 April 2003 (Speech to the Doctors' Rally, Sydney, 9 April 2003): http://www.ama.com.au?web.nsf/duty of care/WEEN-5LEVUH.

undoubtedly real.[6] Public perception was summarised by the Premier of New South Wales when he called for a move away from the concept of "total justice" towards a restoration of "personal responsibility accompanied by a diminishing of the culture of blame". The only way he could see such a shift being achieved was through a fundamental rethink of the law of negligence.[7]

Whether or not there was a crisis in negligence law, reform is now a reality. This section of the book will explore the common law development of the components of negligence. This will be followed by a brief summary of the appropriate Ipp recommendations and presentation of the relevant statutory reforms from each State and Territory.

---

[6] Senator the Hon Helen Coonan, "Liability Reform: It's Not a Waiting Game" (Speech at the Australian Insurance Law Association, 18 October 2002).

[7] Carr B, "A New Agenda for Government" (Address to the Sydney Institute, 9 July 2002) in (2002) 14(3) *The Sydney Papers* 98 at 107-108.

CHAPTER 8

Negligence: Duty of Care

Reading

Sappideen, Vines, Grant and Watson, *Torts: Commentary and Materials*, Chapters 7, 8 and 10.

Objectives

This chapter will explain:

- the role and meaning of the "duty of care" in negligence;
- the test for the duty of care and recognise that there are certain categories of relationships where the duty is established; and
- the application of the test for a duty of care in different circumstances, ie economic loss and mental harm.

Principles

Preliminary matters

[8.05] Negligence is a universal concept in legal systems. But as a ground of liability in itself for causing damage, rather than as a mode of incurring other types of liability, it is not so common. The sophisticated legal system represented by Roman law never had a generalised action for negligence. Nor until the 20th century did the common law. As we saw in Chapter 3, negligence was merely a means of incurring liability in trespass or case. The main step in the development of the modern tort of negligence was the abolition of the forms of action of trespass and case by the legislation of the English Parliament in the late 19th century (corresponding legislation now applies throughout Australia). From that point actions for negligently produced damage or injury, whether arising directly or indirectly, were described as actions for negligence rather than as actions for trespass or case. Thus action on the case provided the foundations for the recognition of a separate tort and it is from this foundation that the characteristics of the modern law of negligence emerged: the need for the plaintiff to prove lack of care on the defendant's part and to show damage or injury arising from that carelessness.

Complete recognition of the status of negligence as a separate tort did not, however, arrive until 1932 in the House of Lords' decision in *Donoghue v Stevenson* [1932] AC 562. That case is important in establishing, as a necessary requirement of the tort of negligence, that the plaintiff must demonstrate the existence of a duty of care owed by the defendant to the plaintiff, a requirement that was hinted at in earlier cases[1] but not completely settled until *Donoghue*.

Why a duty of care?

[8.10] The law will not call someone to account for loss or injury in which they have no involvement. To establish negligence there must be a firm basis of liability – that basis is found in the identification of a duty of care. Lord MacMillan in *Donoghue v Stevenson* [1932] AC 562 at 619 refers to the duty of care as a "cardinal principle" of negligence and (at 618) highlights the fact that: "The law takes no cognisance of negligence in the abstract. It concerns itself with carelessness only where there is a duty to take care and where failure in that duty has caused damage."

The starting point of any negligence inquiry is therefore to establish whether or not there is a duty of care. The other components (breach and causation) will be considered in the following chapters. The essence of negligence can therefore be summarised:

Figure 8.1: Negligence

- Ethos: protects our right to physical and emotional integrity against unintentional wrongful conduct.
- Developed from action on the case.
- Elements: duty of care; breach of duty of care (involving consideration of standard of care); damage; causation.

---

[1]   See, eg, Lord Brett MR, *Heaven v Pender* (1883) 11 QBD 503 at 509 where he foreshadows Lord Atkin's neighbourhood principle.

Donoghue v Stevenson

[8.15] In *Donoghue v Stevenson* [1932] AC 562 the House of Lords had to consider the appropriateness of the existence of a duty of care in the absence of a contractual relationship. Mrs Donoghue (the plaintiff) and a friend were in a café in Scotland and the friend purchased a drink for the plaintiff to consume. The drink was a bottle of ginger beer and was sealed by the manufacturer and served in an opaque bottle, making inspection of the contents impossible. The plaintiff drank a portion of the ginger beer and it was when she was pouring the remainder into a glass that she discovered a decomposed snail. As a result of this unpleasant surprise, Mrs Donoghue claimed to have suffered gastroenteritis and nervous shock (now referred to as mental harm) and brought an action in negligence against the defendants. In order to understand the significance of the case the various relationships must be understood; these are set out in Figure 8.2.

Figure 8.2

Donoghue v Stevenson involved the following scenarios:
- Manufacturer (Stevenson) —— sale ——▶ Shopkeeper (Wellmeadow Café in Paisley).
  (Contract: supply of ginger beer to shopkeeper by manufacturer for payment).
- Shopkeeper —— sale ——▶ Donoghue's friend
  (Contract: sale of ginger beer to Donoghue's friend).
- Friend of Donoghue —— gift ——▶ Donoghue
  (No contract between Donoghue and anyone else, so no action lies in contract).

The case before the House of Lords turned not on the question of Mrs Donoghue's loss but on the fundamental issue of whether she could bring an action in negligence against the defendants. The defendants disputed her claim on the ground that it disclosed no cause of action because the defendants were in a contractual relationship with the suppliers of the ginger beer, not the plaintiff. It was their contention that they did not owe her a duty of care.[2] The House of Lords, by a majority of 3:2, found that the defendants' objection, based on "privity of contract", was fallacious. There was no reason why parties to a contract should not be liable in negligence to persons outside the contract, since the action was not being brought in contract, but in tort for negligence. The House of Lords thus laid down the so-called "narrow rule" in *Donoghue v Stevenson*: the manufacturer of products owes a duty of care in the preparation of those products to the ultimate consumer of them. This case owes most of its importance, and certainly its fame, to the attempt by Lord Atkin to furnish a statement of general principle concerning liability in the tort of negligence:

> *The rule that you are to love your neighbour becomes in law, you must not injure your neighbour; and the lawyer's question, who is my neighbour? receives a restricted reply. You must take reasonable care to avoid acts or omissions which you can*

---

2   This argument derived from a 19th century decision, *Winterbottom v Wright* (1842) 152 ER 402, which held that an action for negligent performance of a contract could only be brought by a contracting party.

reasonably foresee would be likely to injure your neighbour. Who then, in law, is my neighbour? The answer seems to be — persons who are so closely and directly affected by my act that I ought reasonably to have them in contemplation as being so affected when I am directing my mind to the acts or omissions which are called into question.[3]

Thus my neighbour at law is the person whom I could reasonably identify as being at risk of harm by my careless actions.

Foreseeability of harm to the "neighbour" became, under Lord Atkin's formulation, the basis of a duty of care owed to that neighbour, and the neighbourhood principle a touchstone of negligence. The "universality" of negligence as a tort appeared to be established. There were, however, difficulties with Lord Atkin's statement that were recognisable and indeed recognised at the time of its making and have become more apparent since then. Even if the neighbour principle formed part of Lord Atkin's ratio decidendi in *Donoghue*, the other two members of the majority in the case said nothing as broad, Lord MacMillan merely observing (at 580) that "the categories of negligence are never closed". It was accepted at the time of the decision that there existed a number of cases in which no duty of care would arise despite the harm being foreseeable. Some of these cases of no duty of care continue to exist, although their extent has been curtailed; in other cases the gaps have been closed.[4] Lord Atkin himself lent credence to the view that he was not laying down a simple test of foreseeability for the existence of a duty of care. The neighbour must be a person "closely and directly affected". He also (at 581) spoke of the need for "proximity" between defendant and plaintiff. It was possible to explain these statements on the basis that foreseeability of harm must be reasonable rather than fantastic or far-fetched in order to found a duty of care. In Australia, the concept of proximity has been interpreted to mean a requirement other than foreseeability for establishing a duty of care, and has been used as a means of distinguishing those cases in which a duty of care exists from those in which it does not.[5]

There is no doubt that the establishing of a separate tort of negligence has been a powerful rationalising influence in the law. For example, several special situations with their own specific formulations of duty of care are now regarded as mere manifestations of the general principles of negligence. Examples are the duty of care owed by an occupier of land or premises towards lawful visitors and that owed by an employer towards his or her employees: see Chapter 9. It is even arguable that the specific formulation in *Donoghue* of the manufacturer's duty of care towards consumers of its products has become obsolete and is now covered by general negligence principles. In addition, the recognition of a general tort of negligence has led to the removal from the law of a number of anomalous "no duty of care" situations, for example the former rule

---

3   For a full statement, see *Donoghue v Stevenson* [1932] AC 562 at 599.

4   As examples of the closure of gaps: vendors or lessors of premises owe a duty of care as regards defective condition of the premises where this arises from building or other work done on the premises by the vendor or lessor prior to the sale or lease (see Chapter 9); occupiers of land and premises owe a duty of care to trespassers (see Chapter 9); and an occupier of land, except in Queensland, owes a duty of care to prevent the occupier's domestic, non-dangerous animals from straying on the highway: see Chapter 17.

5   The doctrine of proximity attained a pre-eminent position in the determination of the existence of duty of care and has since declined in popularity. The "rise and fall" of the doctrine as a central component of the duty question is outlined at [8.30]ff.

that the vendor/builder of a house owed no duty of care to persons injured through the defective condition of the house: see Chapter 9. Finally, the growth of negligence has influenced other torts. Negligent trespass has now ceded its place in the law more or less entirely to negligence. Negligence-based liability is generally now necessary for nuisance, once thought to be a tort of strict liability: see Chapter 16. And the prime example of a tort of strict liability, *Rylands v Fletcher* (1868) LR 3 HL 330, has been removed from Australian law by the High Court and replaced with a non-delegable duty of care.

The issue of duty of care is not straightforward in every situation. Where physical loss or injury is sustained, a duty of care is relatively easy to identify. Where the nature of the harm suffered is either more difficult to identify or quantify, then more than reasonable foreseeability is generally required. These more complex areas include: liability for statements or acts causing pure economic loss; liability for omission to act; liability in relation to the exercise of statutory powers; liability for nervous shock (now called mental harm); liability for harm caused by third parties; and liability in regard to the conduct of litigation before a court, particularly that of an advocate in relation to the handling of the case in court. Some of these cases run together; for example, the question of liability for the exercise of statutory powers or for acts of third parties is to some extent bound up with the issue of liability for omission to act. Although in all these areas it may be possible to establish a duty of care, in none of them is it possible to do so by a simple application of a test of foreseeability of harm. These cases will each be considered later in this chapter.

Duty of care and precedent

[8.20] There is strong precedent for a duty of care where physical injuries have been caused by direct physical contact. In such cases, a plaintiff need only demonstrate that the injuries are reasonably foreseeable: *Rylands v Fletcher* (1868) LR 3 HL 330. In situations where there is no precedent, the courts have attempted to identify a unifying principle to facilitate identification of actionable duty; and while some principles have emerged for brief moments of prominence as doctrines essential to the identification of duty, they have tended to decline to the status of guiding principles without the force of binding precedent.

Search for a unifying principle

Reasonable foreseeability

[8.25] The first step in determining liability in negligence is to address the question of reasonable foreseeability as enunciated in Lord Atkin's neighbourhood principle. The concept of reasonable foreseeability is addressed at the duty stage as a question of identity of the plaintiff: the plaintiff either being personally foreseeable or a member of a foreseeable class of those persons likely to be affected by the actions of the defendant.[6] It is not an onerous test and is not sufficient on its own to establish liability.

The limitations of reasonable foreseeability as a test for duty of care were identified in *Sullivan v Moody* (2001) 207 CLR 562 at [42]. The Full Bench of the High Court,

---

6   Reasonable foreseeability as a question of type and risk of injury or damage will be addressed in the breach and causation discussion in Chapters 10 and 11.

in recognising that the main argument of the appellant was based on the question of reasonable foreseeability, categorically stated that as a test, it is not sufficient to found liability on its own:

> [T]he fact that it is foreseeable, in the sense of being a real and not far-fetched possibility, that a careless act or omission on the part of one person may cause harm to another does not mean that the first person is subject to a legal liability to compensate the second by way of damages for negligence if there is such carelessness, and harm results.[7]

If the test for liability was so undemanding as to stop at reasonable foreseeability, then (the court argued at [42]), the burden of potential liability would be "intolerable" and result in a restraint on freedom of action. There will only be liability in negligence where the law imposes a duty to take such care. The question, therefore, is when will the law impose such a duty? It is in endeavouring to answer this question that the courts first acknowledged, developed and finally rejected the doctrine of proximity.

Proximity

[8.30] The doctrine of proximity achieved ascendancy in the High Court during the time of Deane J and its general acceptance and application is usually attributed to his efforts. Proximity was a constant thread throughout the judgments of Deane J wherever duty of care was in issue. He referred to it as "a touchstone for determining the existence and content of any common law duty of care": *Jaensch v Coffey* (1984) 155 CLR 549 at 583. Also as a "general overriding control of the test of reasonable foreseeability": *Stevens v Brodribb Sawmilling Co Pty Ltd* (1986) 160 CLR 16 at 52, and a "unifying theme explaining why a duty ... has been recognized": *Stevens* at 53. Proximity was not, however, left only to Deane J. In *Burnie Port Authority v General Jones Pty Ltd* (1994) 179 CLR 520 at 543, the joint judgment of Mason CJ and Deane, Dawson, Toohey and Gaudron JJ, considering the centrality of proximity to the duty question, explained:

> Without it, the tort of negligence would be reduced to a miscellany of disparate categories among which reasoning by the legal processes of induction and deduction would rest on questionable foundations since the validity of such reasoning essentially depends upon the assumption of underlying unity or consistency.

This of course opens the question: what exactly is proximity? It is the consideration to be addressed once the requirement of reasonable foreseeability has been met. In *Jaensch* (at 584-585), Deane J described it as a complex concept addressing the nature of the relationship between the parties. It involves:

> notions of nearness or closeness and embraces physical proximity (in the sense of space and time) between the person or property of the plaintiff and the person or property of the defendant, circumstantial proximity such as an overriding relationship of employer and employee or of a professional man and his client and causal proximity in the sense of the closeness or directness of the relationship between the particular act or cause of action and the injury sustained.

---

[7]   Note also *Jaensch v Coffey* (1984) 155 CLR 549 at 583 when Deane J stated: "it is not and never has been the common law that the reasonable foreseeability of risk of injury to another automatically means that there is a duty to take reasonable care with regard to that risk of injury."

A simpler description was offered by Hayne J when he explained proximity as addressing questions of "nearness, hearness or dearness": *Tame v New South Wales; Annetts v Australian Stations Pty Ltd* (2002) 211 CLR 317 at [25]-[26]. The key to finding that a duty of care existed was therefore to closely consider the nature of the relationship between the parties and, where relevant, the physical proximity to the negligent act.

Proximity did not, however, achieve universal acceptance among the members of the High Court, with Brennan J resisting the ascendancy of the doctrine and calling instead for a return to the development of novel categories of negligence "incrementally and by analogy to established categories": *Sutherland SC v Heyman* (1985) 157 CLR 424 at 481. With the departure of Deane J from the High Court in 1995, the view of proximity as a predominant test in the determination of a duty of care went into decline and was finally categorically rejected in *Sullivan v Moody* (2001) 207 CLR 562 (per Gleeson CJ, Gaudron, McHugh, Hayne and Callinan JJ at [48]). In this case it was accepted that, while proximity provides focus in the inquiry into the nature of the issue at hand, it has limited utility.

The notion of proximity has not been entirely rejected in all circumstances; it continues to be relevant in particular areas of negligence, such as economic loss and mental harm. This was reinforced by Ipp J in *Annetts v Australian Stations Pty Ltd* [2001] Aust Torts Reports 81-586, when he referred to the High Court's decision in *Perre v Apand Pty Ltd* (1999) 198 CLR 180 but expressed the view that the requirement of proximity was still relevant to claims for psychiatric injury, and this continues with legislation now incorporating proximity into the inquiry.

The search for a unifying principle continues with no satisfactory conclusion. Kirby J in *Pyrenees SC v Day* (1998) 192 CLR 330 at [241] recognised that the many tests tend to overlap and accepted that there is a suggestion that a "single concept exists, although it has so far proved impossible to define". It is clear, therefore, that while the High Court has expended a lot of time and energy seeking to identify the unifying principle underlying duty of care, it has proven elusive. All that can be said with certainty is that there are many factors to be considered; and perhaps the reality is, as Deane J suggested in *Jaensch v Coffey* (1984) 155 CLR 549 at 607, that liability in negligence simply rests on a "general public sentiment of moral wrongdoing".

Relevance of policy

[8.35] Despite the absence of a unifying principle underlying the imposition of a duty of care, recent High Court decisions reveal other factors which are relevant when inquiring whether or not a duty of care exists. These factors can be grouped under the general heading, policy considerations. Deane J's judgment in *Jaensch v Coffey* (1984) 155 CLR 549 made a number of references to policy considerations, suggesting that these may still have an independent operation. For instance, on the question of whether a person may recover damages for psychological injury caused by hearing news of the death of a close relative brought about by the defendant's negligence, Deane J (at 463) expressed doubt as to what policy consideration should preclude recovery in this case.[8] Policy seems to be intimately connected with the recognition of a duty of care in mental harm cases. For example, even Brennan J (who in *Jaensch* thought that the duty

CHAPTER 8

---

8   Psychological injury was previously referred to as "nervous shock" but this term has recently been rejected by the court as out of date and not in step with medical developments. The concept of psychological injury and the special duty considerations surrounding this form of injury are considered at [8.195]ff.

as regards "nervous shock" turned entirely on the foreseeability of the shock)
:d to recognise a limitation of policy in requiring the shock to be suffered by "sudden, sensory perception" of an accident: *Jaensch* at 430.[9] As discussed at [8.210], these policy considerations have altered under two recent decisions (*Tame v New South Wales; Annetts v Australian Stations Pty Ltd* (2002) 211 CLR 317 and *Gifford v Strang Park Stevedoring* (2003) 214 CLR 269), but the significance of policy is still recognised by the court.[10]

The need to restrict psychological injury claims on policy grounds is firmly recognised in the judgments of the House of Lords in *Alcock v Chief Constable of South Yorkshire* [1991] 3 WLR 1057. Policy arguments also influenced the non-recognition of duties of care in *Robertson v Swincer* (1989) 52 SASR 356 (no general duty of supervision owed by a parent to a child), *Hill v Chief Constable of Yorkshire Police* [1989] AC 53 (police owed no duty of care to apprehend criminal to later victim of that criminal), and *Giannarelli v Wraith* (1988) 165 CLR 543 (barrister owed no duty of care to client in relation to the conduct of the case in court). The nature of the policy will, of course, differ from case to case. The reception of policy arguments as to the need for a duty of care is to be welcomed, on the ground that although the policy arguments are often extremely difficult to resolve, they at least have a meaningful content, which is not so in the case of proximity. However, there is still judicial reluctance to admit evidence substantiating the various policy considerations that might apply in a given situation. For example, the availability and incidence of insurance is relevant to the determination of the question of a duty of care in relation to the causing of pure economic loss; but apart from an eloquent plea by a Canadian judge in a dissenting judgment, the issue has been decided without reference to the insurance factor: *Canadian National Railway v Norsk Pacific Steamship Co* [1992] 1 SCR 1021 per La Forest J.

There is still left the relevant question of what constitutes a "policy" consideration. At its simplest, it is a term which supports the lifting of judicial eyes from the facts of the case before them and the taking into account of broader considerations including the potential impact of a decision in favour (or not) of the plaintiff.

Duty of care in law and duty on the facts

[8.40] The distinction between duty of care in law and duty on the facts of the case is best exemplified by the case of the motorist. It is settled law that the motorist owes a duty of care while driving the car to persons who might be affected by a lack of care in driving. This is the duty of care in law. The foreseeability element involved is of a generalised nature − in general, motorists should foresee that carelessness on their part may injure other persons. Which persons actually come within the range of the motorist's duty is, however, a different question which can only be answered by examining the facts of the case. If the plaintiff falls within the class of persons foreseeably likely to be affected by the defendant's negligent driving, then a duty of care arises to the plaintiff on the facts of the case. The determination of duty on the facts is simply a question of fact and one which a court can only decide retrospectively by

---

9   Of note is that this restriction has now been removed by more recent cases, largely on the ground of rejection of relevant policy considerations.

10   For example, refer Gleeson CJ in *Gifford v Strang Park Stevedoring* (2003) 214 CLR 269 at [9]-[12] and the discussion of Hayne J in *Tame v New South Wales; Annetts v Australian Stations Pty Ltd* concerning the "floodgates" arguments and considerations which have been relevant in this context at [243]-[244].

looking at what actually occurred. The duty of care in law may, on the other hand, be stated in general terms and prospectively, and has the force of precedent.

Utility of the distinction

[8.45] The relevance of distinguishing between the two questions of duty in negligence is to clarify the process of determining whether or not a duty exists, and to assist in explaining why a duty may or may not exist in given circumstances. As stated, the duty of care in law may be put in prospective terms and with precedent force. To say that there is a duty of care binding motorists, is to inform that class of persons that if they drive negligently and injure others they will have to pay compensation. The duty of care in law in this case therefore prescribes conduct and this is the function it performs in a large number of situations ("duty situations"). Its limits must, however, be noted. Only where the particular duty is settled as a matter of law is it capable of prescribing conduct: no prescription is possible where no duty of care is known to apply in a particular situation. Further, if we say that no duty of care applies in a given situation, this is not a legal invitation to persons in that situation to be careless. The policy of the law must be to exhort care. But the second reason points to the second function of the duty of care in law. This is to act as a means of controlling the extent of the tort of negligence. We have seen already that a duty of care does not exist in every case of foreseeable harm. Now that this has become settled, the need for a concept to determine which cases of negligence are actionable becomes clear. The chosen concept is the duty of care.

As regards the duty of care on the facts, this had considerable importance when foreseeability appeared to be the exclusive determinant of duty of care and at a time in the early development of negligence when many duty situations had not been identified as a matter of law. Finding a duty of care on the facts would, in many cases, also establish a duty of care in law. This dual function is now of considerably reduced importance. A large number of duty situations are now settled and *the imposition of new duties of care will often raise issues of proximity and policy as well as foreseeability*. The consideration of foreseeability with respect to duty on the facts can be relevant to the question of breach of duty. This point was accepted by the High Court in *Nagle v Rottnest Island Authority* (1993) 177 CLR 423. The court considered the question whether the defendant occupier of Rottnest Island was liable to a person who suffered serious injury when diving into a rock pool in a coastal basin off the island's coast and hitting his head on a rock. The court first noted that it was unlikely that persons would take the risk of diving into the water in these circumstances, since some danger was foreseeable to them. However, the presence of rocks immediately below the surface was not visually detectable. Therefore there was a slight, though sufficient, risk of the occurrence of the event, which was therefore reasonably foreseeable. This the High Court treated as a matter of breach, it being established as a matter of law that the defendant as occupier owed a duty of care to lawful visitors to the island. The following passage from the judgment (at 429) shows, however, that the court continues to see a role for the duty on the facts as a determinant of duty of care in law:

> This is a case in which it is possible to ascertain the existence of a generalised duty of care to take reasonable steps to avoid the foreseeable risk of injury to members of the public who resort to the Basin without looking to foreseeability, a concept which in many other situations is the influential, if not decisive, determinant of the existence of a relationship of proximity. Here – foreseeability is of critical importance

> *in determining not whether there was a duty of care but whether there was a breach of duty. However, it is convenient to deal with it as a separate issue [from breach].*

Foreseeability on the facts of the case may therefore still be decisive in establishing the existence of a duty of care as a matter of law where there is no precedent establishing a legal duty and there are no determinants of proximity other than foreseeability. Such situations are today less common than the above extract suggests, but two examples may be given. In *O'Connor v South Australia* (1976) 14 SASR 187 it was held that a judge who opened a door with unnecessary force, and injured the plaintiff who was standing on the other side of the door, was liable in negligence. No previous case touched on the question of the duty of care of persons opening doors, and the duty of care issue was based solely on foreseeability. In another South Australian case, *Akers v P* (1986) 42 SASR 30, the defendant police had intervened in a domestic dispute between the plaintiff and another person. The plaintiff was obviously in a drunken state but the police ordered him to leave the scene with his motor bike. Soon afterwards he was seriously injured while driving the bike. The court held that the police were under a duty of care to the plaintiff based on normal principles of foreseeability, there being present no circumstances that would go towards denying the existence of such a duty. Again there was a clear breach of that duty by the police.

Duty in specific situations

[8.50] While it is difficult to find a single unifying principle for identifying a duty of care, there are some specific situations in which particular guidelines have been developed to assist in determining the question of duty. Each situation can be categorised by the nature of the loss or harm suffered by the plaintiff or a particular relationship between the plaintiff and defendant. The remainder of this chapter will consider these situations and explore the guidelines which move well beyond the concept of reasonable foreseeability. The following will be considered:

- liability for pure economic loss whether caused by a negligent statement (see [8.55]ff) or a negligent act (see [8.145]ff);
- liability of manufacturer to consumer (see [8.185]ff);
- liability for mental harm (see [8.195]ff);
- liability for omission to act (see [8.230]ff);
- liability for the negligent exercise of statutory powers (see [8.240]ff);
- liability for harm caused by third parties (see [8.285]ff);
- liability of the legal advocate or adviser in connection with the handling of litigation (see [8.295]ff); and
- child and parent at pre-natal stage (see [8.300]).

Negligence causing pure economic loss

[8.55] *Pure economic loss is economic loss suffered by the plaintiff which is not consequential upon injury to the plaintiff or damage to the plaintiff's property.* Pure economic loss, as opposed to physical loss or injury, can be difficult to determine. As a result, the courts have developed a specific approach where this kind of loss is suffered. Two distinct categories of action are identified by the courts:

- negligent acts leading to pure economic loss; and
- negligent statements leading to pure economic loss.

The law relating to these sources of injury is different and must be separately considered. Underlying the discussion of these is the issue of indeterminacy which has resulted in some initial reluctance by the courts to recognise actionable negligence where the loss was purely economic. In the words of an American case, the liability of the defendant may be for pure economic loss to an "indeterminate class, for an indeterminate time and in an indeterminate amount": *Ultramares Corp v Douche* (1931) 174 NE 441 at 444. This problem does not exist to the same extent in compensating personal injury or damage to property, although of course personal injury may be widespread and may take a long time to show itself, as in claims for asbestosis. In the case of liability for negligent statements, the law has allowed pure economic loss to be compensated in a significant number of cases by retaining proximity as a guiding principle: the test being a close consideration of the nature of the relationship between the plaintiff and defendant including such factors as reliance, occasion of the communication and reason for supply of information. Negligent acts and negligent statements will be dealt with separately.

Negligent statements causing pure economic loss

[8.60] While it is now clear that a duty of care may exist in relation to statements – whether causing pure economic loss, personal injury or damage to property – this was not always the case. At one time the law excluded liability for negligent statements causing pure economic loss. The reason for this exclusion was clearly set out by Lord Pearce in *Hedley Byrne & Co v Heller* [1964] AC 465 at 534:

> Words are more volatile than deeds. They travel fast and far afield. They are used without being expended and take effect in combination with innumerable facts and other words. Yet they are dangerous and can cause vast financial damage ... How far they are relied on unchecked must in many cases be a matter of doubt and difficulty ... Damage by negligent acts to persons or property on the other hand is more visible and obvious; its limits are more easily defined.

The decision in *Hedley Byrne* signalled a turnaround in the courts' approach to negligent statements causing pure economic loss. The approach of the courts continued to reflect the need for caution and, as will be seen in a series of cases, carefully set out a number of factors relevant to the determination of a duty of care in the situation of negligent statements leading to pure economic loss. These factors continue to operate to address the indeterminacy of liability and scope of the action. At a time when the doctrine of proximity has declined in respect to negligent acts leading to physical loss or damage, it continues to be a controlling factor in the establishment of a duty of care in the context of negligent statements leading to pure economic loss. This is an area of law which the High Court recognises is still developing and is approached not by the application of broad principle "but incrementally from established cases": *Perre v Apand* (1999) 198 CLR 180 at [93] per McHugh J.

CHAPTER 8

Hedley Byrne & Co v Heller

[8.65] The decision of the House of Lords in *Hedley Byrne & Co v Heller* [1964] AC 465 has been taken to establish conclusively that in certain circumstances a duty of care may arise in relation to a negligent misstatement causing pure economic loss. In this case the House of Lords held that a duty of care may exist when someone in the plaintiff's position approaches a bank for a reference as to the financial position of one of the bank's clients. The plaintiffs suffered financial loss through entering into a contract with the client in reliance on the bank's reference. On the actual facts, however, no duty of care arose because the defendants had expressly excluded responsibility for the reference. The judgments in the House of Lords all emphasised the need for a special relationship to exist between defendant and plaintiff for a duty of care to arise. It is important to note that there is a general exclusion of duty of care arising from the mere fact that the reliance was foreseeable. Lord Reid (at 486) thought that such a relationship arose where:

> the party seeking the information or advice was trusting the other to exercise such a degree of care as the circumstances required, where it was reasonable for him to do that, and where the other gave the advice when he knew or ought to know that the inquirer was relying on him.

Lord Morris's formulation (at 502-503) is broader and has a different basis:

> If someone possessed of a special skill undertakes, quite irrespective of contract, to apply that skill for the assistance of another person who relies upon the skill, a duty of care will arise. The fact that the service is to be given by means of words can make no difference. Furthermore, if in a sphere in which a person is so placed that others could reasonably rely on his judgment or his skill or his ability to make careful inquiry, a person takes it upon himself to give information or advice to … another person, who as he knows or ought to know, will place reliance upon it, then a duty of care arises.

To Lord Morris, therefore, liability for negligent statement was merely part of a general duty of care as regards the performance of voluntary services or undertakings. Lord Devlin would go no further than to say (at 529) that a relationship "equivalent to contract" must exist between defendant and plaintiff. The judgments in the House of Lords also make considerable reference to the need for a voluntary assumption of responsibility by the defendant in relation to the making of the statement. But it is by no means clear what this requirement adds to that of special relationship, apart from the fact that it allows the defendant to exclude a duty of care by express statement or provision. Barwick CJ in *Mutual Life & Citizens' Assurance v Evatt* [1971] AC 793 (see [8.70]) analysed the special relationship requirement of a duty of care in essentially the same terms as those of Lord Reid; that is:

- the plaintiff must be trusting or relying on the defendant;
- the defendant must know or have reason to know of that fact; and
- the circumstances of the case must make reliance reasonable.

Barwick CJ spoke in general terms, rather than as Lord Reid did, of the statement being made in response to the plaintiff's request, and added that the statement must be made in connection with some matter of business or serious consequence. Lord Pearce in *Hedley Byrne* spoke (at 539) in similar terms on the latter point:

> *If, for instance, they disclosed a casual social approach to the inquiry, no such special relationship would be assumed. To import such a duty, the representation must normally cover a business or professional transaction whose nature makes clear the gravity of the inquiry.*

Much of this discussion was recently reiterated in the Supreme Court of Victoria decision, *Derring Lane Pty Ltd v Fitzgibbon* (2007) 16 VR 563; [2007] VSCA 79 when the court was considering the duty of care owed by a valuer to the purchaser of land. Ashley JA emphasised that the action which resulted in a loss must be induced by faith in the reliability of the misstatement (at [15]) and that the person making the statement must know that his assertions would be relied upon (at [26]) and finally, the possibility of a disclaimer operating to negate a duty of care was also recognised (at [36]).

Mutual Life & Citizens' Assurance Co v Evatt

[8.70] In *Mutual Life & Citizens' Assurance Co v Evatt* [1971] AC 793 the Privy Council in an Australian appeal sought to whittle down the generality of the statements of the House of Lords in *Hedley Byrne & Co v Heller* [1964] AC 465. The Privy Council held that the officers of a life assurance company owed no duty of care to a policy holder in the company in relation to statements made to them about the financial affairs of another company, Palmer (both the companies being subsidiaries of a third company). In consequence of acting on the advice, the policy holder suffered economic loss. Lord Diplock, giving the judgment of the majority, held that the duty of care arose only where the advice was given in the exercise of business or professional skill possessed or claimed by the adviser, or possibly where the adviser had a financial interest in the advice being acted on. None of these applied in the case itself, since the officers neither had nor claimed to have any particular skill in evaluating the shares or assets of companies. The main ground for this limitation was that it was only possible to fix an appropriate standard of care by reference to the business or professional skill necessary to give the appropriate advice. Lords Reid and Morris dissented: they thought it possible to fix a standard of care in the matter even though that might be a lower standard of care than that expected of the skilled investment adviser.

Shaddock & Associates Pty Ltd v Parramatta CC

[8.75] The limitations imposed by *Mutual Life & Citizens' Assurance Co v Evatt* [1971] AC 793, while appearing reasonable in relation to the offering of advice on matters requiring skilled business or professional knowledge, seemed far less so as regards the mere provision of information, the giving of which required no such skill. The matter was put to the test in *Shaddock & Associates Pty Ltd v Parramatta CC* (1981) 150 CLR 225, with the majority of the High Court resorting to the full vigour of *Hedley Byrne & Co v Heller* [1964] AC 465. The defendant Council had, through its employee, informed the plaintiff over the telephone that there was no road-widening scheme affecting land that the plaintiff wished to purchase. Later a certificate was provided by the defendant to the plaintiff which failed to mention the existence of such a scheme. In fact, there was a road-widening scheme affecting the land, and knowledge of that fact was exclusive to the Council and its employees. The plaintiff purchased the land in the belief that no road-widening scheme existed and suffered loss when the scheme became public knowledge. The High Court held that a duty of care existed in relation to the provision of information of this sort. There was a breach of that duty in relation to the provision of the certificate without mention of the scheme, but not in relation to the telephone statement, which was made neither in relation to an identified person nor for an identified type of transaction. Gibbs CJ and Stephen J were able to decide the case without departing from the principles laid down in *Mutual Life*. The Council as an exclusive storer of the relevant information was tantamount to a person exercising business or professional skill: *Shaddock* at 234, 241. However, the majority of the court (Mason, Aikin and Murphy JJ) felt it necessary to depart from the principles of *Mutual Life* and return to the original breadth of the *Hedley Byrne* judgments, thereby supporting the dissent of Lords Reid and Morris in the former case: *Shaddock* at 251.

The *Shaddock* case concerned information rather than advice, and information requiring no particular skill to provide. However, the rejection of *Mutual Life* by the majority in *Shaddock* (particularly the judgment of Mason J) seems total, applying equally to information or advice requiring business or professional skill to provide. Liability on the part of the unskilled person for the provision of such information or advice is, however, generally unlikely. Reasonable foreseeability and reasonableness of reliance would not be easily established. Also, where the absence of skill was known to the plaintiff, the standard of care would be a reduced one; that is, what was reasonable given the defendant's own knowledge and experience. Even on this reduced standard, liability could arise, as in the case where a defendant claimed to have access to the knowledge of a skilled person. But the courts will not readily assume that an unskilled defendant was purporting to give advice on a matter requiring business or professional skill. In *Norris v Sibberas* [1990] VR 161, glowing statements made by an estate agent about the prospects of a motel business were found to be limited to matters within the agent's expertise (such as the desirability of the motel's position and the public demand for motels within the area). These could not be taken to refer to the financial condition of the business at the time it was purchased by the plaintiff. The significance of special or professed skill was highlighted in the judgment of Marks J (for the court at 172):

> *It would not be reasonable to rely upon advice or information given by another unless the person giving it either professed to have some special skill which he undertook to apply for the assistance of another or was so placed that others could reasonably rely upon his judgment or his skill or upon his ability to make careful inquiry.*

The case may be distinguished from *Roots v Oentory Pty Ltd* [1983] 2 Qd R 745.[11] In that case an estate agent's statements to a purchaser clearly related to the financial condition of the business being purchased, and the agent had no sufficient basis for making them, merely having relied on assurances by the vendors. Of significance in this case were the circumstances in which the information was imparted, as they were such as to imply a special skill or knowledge. The agent advertised a capsicum processing plant for sale and stated a specific weekly turnover. (In contrast, the statements in *Norris* were general in nature, referring to the potential earnings.) The figure was confirmed by the agent in the presence of the vendor and the purchaser proceeded in reliance on these statements. In these circumstances, there was actionable negligence as it was deemed reasonable to presume that the agent possessed special skill or knowledge on the basis of the specificity of the statements made.

---

[11] See also *Rawlinson & Brown Pty Ltd v Witham* [1995] Aust Torts Reports 81-341 – estate agent liable for misstating the capacity of a water bore in reliance on the vendor's statement – agent having no technical skills in this regard.

San Sebastian Pty Ltd v Minister

[8.80] In *San Sebastian Pty Ltd v Minister* (1986) 162 CLR 340 the plaintiff developers had purchased land in Woolloomooloo in reliance on a scheme which had been adopted by Sydney City Council in 1969. The redevelopment scheme was displayed publicly and operated until the Council abandoned it in 1972. Once the scheme was abandoned the developers suffered a financial loss and sought recompense from the Council. The decision provided the High Court with the opportunity to further consider the basis of liability for negligent statements. The majority in the High Court regarded such liability as capable of being brought within, and rationalised in terms of, the concept of proximity, which at that time was regarded as a unifying element in regard to the duty of care in general. Where pure economic loss resulted from a negligent statement, "the element of reliance plays a prominent part in the ascertainment of a relationship of proximity between the plaintiff and defendant and therefore in the ascertainment of a duty of care": at 169. Such a statement clearly leaves unresolved a number of important issues, including whether it is the plaintiff who must rely on the statement, and if the actual knowledge of the plaintiff by the defendant is needed or mere foreseeability is sufficient.

Formulations of the duty of care in relation to statements (such as that of Barwick CJ in *Mutual Life & Citizens' Assurance Co v Evatt* [1971] AC 793) were categorised as mere "attempts to give precise expression to those conditions" under which a duty of care will arise. However, Brennan J, as pointed out earlier, did not favour the concept of proximity as a determinant of duty of care: he specifically approved the Barwick formulation of duty of care for negligent statements on the ground that outside the areas of negligent acts causing physical injury or damage (where foreseeability ought to be the only criterion of duty), it was necessary to find appropriate limitations on the duty of care. However, although the formulations of Lord Reid in *Hedley Byrne & Co v Heller* [1964] AC 465 and Barwick CJ in *Mutual Life* are detailed, they are not entirely satisfactory. It is not clear how the various categories fit together, and there seems to be some duplication between them. In particular, what is the relationship between reasonableness of reliance and reasonable foreseeability of reliance? If reliance is reasonably foreseeable, it seems to follow that it is reasonable. It is possible that the factor of reasonable reliance relates to some legal rule which limits liability despite the reasonable foreseeability of the reliance. One possibility is the statement made on the casual social occasion: it might be thought unfair to hold the defendant responsible for such a statement, even though it is reasonably foreseeable that the plaintiff will act on it. Another suggestion in the judgment of Brennan J in *San Sebastian* is that reliance on a statement of intention by a public body is unreasonable, given that the body may generally resile from that intention if it thinks it in the public interest to do so. But the general practice of Australian courts has been to conflate the factors of foreseeability and reasonableness of reliance. The Reid and Barwick formulations also present too limited a picture of liability under the *Hedley Byrne* principle. They presuppose the position of A making a statement to B which B acts on to his or her loss. We shall see, however, that liability for statements may exist also in the case where A's statement is acted on by B to the loss of C (although it is disputed whether this is true *Hedley Byrne* liability or only a cognate form). Also, the Reid and Barwick formulations do not allow for the fact that liability under the principle may exist in relation to the negligent performance of services rather than the mere making of statements.

Some clarification of the approach can perhaps be gained by a more recent High Court consideration of the matter in *Butcher v Lachlan Elder Realty Pty Ltd* (2004) 218

CLR 592. In this instance the court had to consider a situation in which a glossy sales brochure contained a faulty survey diagram which the purchasers relied on to their financial detriment. Of relevance in finding that the estate agent did not owe a duty in these circumstances was the relationship between the parties, the clear indication that the survey was supplied by the vendor and the fact that the agent did not purport to do anything more than pass on information supplied by another or others (at [51]). Importantly, Gleeson CJ, Hayne and Heydon JJ noted that "the mere fact that a person had engaged in the conduct of supplying a document containing misleading information did not mean that that person had engaged in misleading conduct: it was crucial to examine the role of the person in question" (at [37]).

Tepko Pty Ltd v Water Board

[8.85] The facts of *Tepko Pty Ltd v Water Board* (2001) 206 CLR 1 involved a complex business and loan arrangement concerned with the purchase and development of land. Certain aspects of the arrangement collapsed. It was argued that the collapse of these arrangements and subsequent financial loss was due to a breach by the Water Board of a duty of care to accurately state the cost of the provision of water to a subdivision which was one of the features of the arrangement. The difficulty in establishing the duty in this instance lay in the fact that the landowners accessed a letter which the Water Board had written to a third party and the landowners showed the letter to the bank who acted in reliance on it. Clearly the Water Board was unaware of the existence of the landowners as a potential audience for its advice and did not offer any direct advice to them.

The judgments in *Tepko* re-stated the key issues identified in earlier cases. The significance of the relationship between the parties, combined with the concept of reasonable reliance in establishing a duty of care, was acknowledged.[12] Gaudron J (at [73]) highlighted the need for a specific kind of relationship to call a duty of care into existence and emphasised (at [76]) that reliance is not *actual* but *reasonable* reliance. All judgments highlighted the significance of the specific facts and circumstances of the case,[13] demonstrating that in the area of negligent statements the courts will address specific considerations while paying close attention to the actual context of the exchange of advice.

Figure 8.3: Factors relevant to inquiry

- Gravity of the inquiry.
- Nature of the relationship.
- Special skill (either actually possessed of a special skill or holding oneself out as possessing such a skill).
- Nature of the subject matter.
- Reliance – reasonable reliance indicates a duty of care, actual reliance establishes breach of that duty.

The court will also consider the context of the interchange:
- Professional environment?
- Social events?
- Request for information?

12 At [47] per Gleeson CJ, Gummow and Hayne JJ, referring with approval to comments by Barwick CJ in *San Sebastian Pty Ltd v Minister* (1968) 122 CLR 556 at 571.
13 At [78] per Gaudron J and [7], [8] per Gleeson CJ, Gummow and Hayne JJ.

Other considerations

[8.90] In addition to these broad general considerations, there are some specific fact situations which have given rise to the need to consider other factors impacting on both the existence and breach of a duty of care in the context of negligent statements. These include:

- gravity of the inquiry (see [8.95]);
- voluntary assumption of responsibility (see [8.100]);
- exclusion of responsibility (see [8.100]);
- relationships based on reliance (see [8.105]); and
- third party reliance (see [8.110]).

Each of these will be considered in turn.

Gravity of the inquiry

[8.95] The issue of the gravity of the inquiry has produced little in the way of legal debate in the decided cases. The only notable case that has turned on the issue produced a mixed response from the court. In *Howard Marine Co Ltd v A Ogden & Sons Ltd* [1978] QB 574 a misstatement concerning the carrying capacity of barges was made in the course of pre-contractual negotiations by the plaintiffs' marine manager to the defendants' representatives. The defendants needed barges of a certain capacity to fulfil a contract for which their tender had been accepted. The manager had travelled from London to the defendants' registered office in north-east England to discuss the matter, and when he made inquiries regarding the capacity of the barges the manager responded from memory, quoting a figure which he had seen in Lloyd's Maritime Register. Unfortunately this figure was incorrect, a fact which could have been easily ascertained by checking the true capacity as clearly listed in the ships documents which were in the owner's possession. Once the true capacity (which was below that required) was discovered, the defendants suffered a loss. The court was not uniform in its consideration of the gravity of the inquiry. Lord Denning MR found that the circumstances in which the conversation took place did not sufficiently emphasise the gravity of the inquiry and that the manager was not negligent in merely relying on his memory. Bridge LJ merely expressed doubt on the question. Shaw LJ thought that the circumstances sufficiently emphasised the gravity of the inquiry, since the capacity of the barges was vital to the defendants' ability to carry out its tender. He therefore found that an unqualified response by the manager, when he had the means of obtaining the accurate information at his disposal, was negligent. The view of Shaw LJ seems more convincing than that of Lord Denning, particularly when it is borne in mind that all that was necessary to discharge the duty of care was to indicate that the reply was not a considered one and perhaps to direct the defendant to a reliable source of information which was readily available.

There continues to be some doubt about the legal status of the gravity of the inquiry issue. The judges in *Howard Marine* appear to treat the matter as a separate rule of law, exonerating the defendant even where the other conditions of liability for misstatement are fulfilled. But it would be equally possible to treat the question as turning on the breach of duty of care – the defendant in general is not in breach in circumstances not emphasising the gravity of the inquiry, since reliance here is not reasonably foreseeable.

This formulation would merely require the defendant, in order to discharge the duty of care, to give an express warning that the statement is not a considered one; such a warning would render the reliance neither foreseeable nor reasonable.

Voluntary assumption of responsibility, exclusion of responsibility

[8.100] The emphasis placed upon the need for a voluntary assumption of responsibility in the judgments in *Hedley Byrne & Co v Heller* [1964] AC 465 was questioned by Lord Griffiths in *Smith v Eric S Bush* [1990] 1 AC 831.[14] In this case Lord Griffiths said (at 862) that he did not:

> think that the phrase was a helpful or realistic test of liability. The phrase could only have real meaning if it is understood as referring to the circumstances in which the law will deem the maker of the statement to have assumed responsibility to the person who acts on the advice.

In other words, the concept appears merely to rephrase that of special relationship. But it has, as Lord Griffiths accepted, another significance that may be its only justification. A voluntary assumption of responsibility may be negatived by express provision by the defendant, as happened in *Hedley Byrne* (and indeed in *Smith*). If the concept of voluntary assumption of responsibility (which has never been accepted by Australian courts) were to disappear, the basis of this unilateral exclusion of liability would be less easy to explain. Barwick CJ observed in obiter in *Mutual Life & Citizens Assurance Co Ltd v Evatt* [1971] AC 793 that the presence of a disclaimer of liability was merely one factor in determining whether a duty of care should exist. This was adopted as the basis of Allen J's judgment in *Burke v Forbes SC* [1987] Aust Torts Reports 80-122 in holding a disclaimer clause to be ineffective. However, the chief reason for this holding was that the Council had a statutory duty to issue the certificate in question: a situation in which, although liability for a negligent misstatement may exist, it is impossible to apply the concept of voluntary assumption of responsibility. Another possible justification for upholding disclaimers is the consent of the plaintiff. However this would only operate if the disclaimer were brought to the plaintiff's attention before acting on the statement. This then runs into the problem that disclaimer clauses have been found to be effective to exclude liability even in the three-party situation where A makes a statement to B which B relies on to C's loss (that is, where the plaintiff has no possibility of knowing of the exclusion clause): *BT Australia Ltd v Raine & Horne Pty Ltd* [1983] 3 NSWLR 221.

Disclaimers of responsibility must be distinguished from warnings that care has not been taken. The latter operates as a performance of the duty of care and acts as an indication of reasonable reliance. Disclaimers on the other hand function as an exclusion of duty of care.

Extent of relationships based on reliance

[8.105] Statements may be made in circumstances in which there is a foreseeable likelihood of reliance being placed on them by a substantial body of persons. Examples

---

[14]   This was a judgment concerning two separate valuations, for two separate clients, by two separate valuers. In both instances the valuer had stated that the valuation report was not a structural report and, on both occasions, recommended that an independent structural report be obtained.

are statements in company accounts prepared by auditors, or financial advice given in newspapers. The judgments in *Hedley Byrne & Co v Heller* [1964] AC 465 were not entirely conclusive on the issue of whether a duty of care could be owed to any person who had acted to his or her loss in reliance on such a statement, or whether some degree of knowledge of the plaintiff as an identifiable person likely to act on the advice was necessary (although the careful terms in which the special relationship was formulated suggest the latter). Even so, some cases have accepted reasonable foreseeability of reliance as the test of duty: *Scott Group Ltd v McFarlane* [1978] 1 NZLR 553 (majority decision, Richmond P dissenting); *JEB Fasteners Ltd v Marks & Bloom* [1981] 3 All ER 289. The matter has been settled in England in favour of a more restrictive test than mere foreseeability of reliance. In *Caparo Industries plc v Dickman* [1990] 2 AC 605, the House of Lords held that when preparing the annual accounts of a company, accountants did not owe a duty of care to any person who, in reliance on the accounts, purchased shares in the company and suffered loss because the accounts overstated the value of the assets. The basis of the decision was that the annual accounts are prepared with no particular person in mind but are produced for the benefit of the company and the body of shareholders as a whole. Approval was given to a dissenting judgment of Richmond P in a New Zealand case, *Scott Group Ltd v McFarlane* [1978] 1 NZLR 553, also concerning misstatements in the annual accounts of a company. In this case Richmond P stated that the special relationship did not come into existence unless:

> the maker of the statement, was, or ought to have been, aware that his advice or information would in fact be made available to and be relied on by a particular person or class of persons for the purposes of a particular transaction or type of transaction.

These principles have been subsequently applied in a number of English decisions: eg *Al-Nakib (Jersey) Ltd v Longcroft* [1990] 2 All ER 321; *Morgan Crucible v Hill Samuel* [1991] Ch 295; *Calou Ltd v Bright Grahame Murray* [1994] 1 WLR 1360.

The position of Australia is less certain, largely because of difficulties in interpreting the High Court's judgment in *San Sebastian Pty Ltd v Minister for Environment and Planning* (1986) 162 CLR 340. As outlined above ([8.80]), the court considered the question of reliance on the apparent statement by the Council that the plan was feasible. The action failed on the ground that no statement as to the feasibility of the plan had been made expressly or impliedly by the Council. The High Court did, however, consider the question of whether the plaintiff would have been a person entitled to succeed in an action for negligence had such a statement been made. The High Court saw no apparent problem with statements made in response to a prior request, assuming that proximity would exist here without reference to the question of whether the defendant knew of the purpose for which the plaintiff intends to use the advice. It was found that as regards statements that were volunteered without request, as in the instant case, a duty of care could arise in a number of circumstances. For example (at 170) the defendant being:

> known to possess or professing skill or competence in the relevant area, or warranting or assuming responsibility for the correctness of the advice; or by inviting the recipient of the advice to act on it, or by intending to induce the recipient to act in a particular way or through having an interest in the recipient so acting.

It is apparent that the first set of situations differ markedly from the second, in that in the first there is no requirement that the plaintiff be known to the defendant as a person likely to act on the advice. The High Court thought that the facts of *San Sebastian* had to be fitted within the category that the defendant intended to induce reliance by the plaintiff on the plan (a more stringent requirement than merely intending reliance by the plaintiff). However, because no misstatement was found to have been made, the question did not have to be resolved in the case itself.

This question again came before the High Court in *Tepko Pty Ltd v Water Board* (2001) 206 CLR 1 (for facts see [8.85]). In this instance, the High Court held that to attract a duty of care there must be known reliance on the advice, an assumption of responsibility by the adviser or a combination of the two. It is not essential that a person making the statement knows the precise use to which the information will be put; it is sufficient that they know that it is being used for a serious purpose. In this case the majority (four judges) found that there was no duty. The dissenting judgment (three judges) disagreed. The dissenting judges concluded that the Water Board would know of a developer's reliance on its advice; it had special knowledge and provided the advice for a serious matter. This case shows that a relationship must be established to determine that a duty of care exists, but establishing the requisite relationship is not a clear-cut process.

Another context in which this question has arisen is that of the preparation of the annual audited accounts of companies which is done without any prior request by the plaintiff. The *San Sebastian* judgment seems applicable to such accounts and it has been applied in two State court decisions. In *R Lowe Lippman Figdor & Frank v AGC (Advances) Ltd* [1992] 2 VR 671 liability for negligence on the part of accountants in preparing the company's annual accounts to a lender of money to the company, was denied. Although the loan appeared in the accounts and would therefore be known to the defendants, and although it was likely that the accounts would be relied on by the lender in deciding whether to call in the loan, there was no liability, since the accounts were not prepared for the purpose of inducing reliance by the lender. The same result was reached in *Esanda Finance Corp Ltd v Marwick Hungerfords* [1994] Aust Torts Reports 81-265 by the South Australian Full Court.[15] Here the plaintiff lent money to a company called Excel, relying on accounts of that company that had been audited by Peat Marwick Hungerfords. The company defaulted on the loan, primarily because the accounts were overstated. The High Court held unanimously that the defendant did not owe the plaintiff a duty of care because there had been no request for information or intention to induce the financier to act upon the accounts.

This seems to imply that the maker of a statement will seldom owe a duty of care to anyone other than the immediate recipient of the information unless they are aware of the existence of the final recipient *and* the use that they will make of the information provided. The question of course becomes more complicated in the scenarios considered at [8.110], where a third party becomes involved.

Three-party situation

[8.110] In the typical three-party situation, A makes a statement to B which B acts on to C's loss. Quite soon after *Hedley Byrne & Co v Heller* [1964] AC 465, a case that is relevant in this context was considered by the Court of Appeal in England: *Ministry of*

---

15   However, cf Rolfe J in *Columbia Coffee v Churchill* (1992) 29 NSWLR 141 at 164-165 (obiter to the contrary).

Housing v Sharp [1970] 2 QB 223. The Minister held a development charge over land. A prospective purchaser of the land applied to the defendant's department to discover whether there were any charges affecting the land. A clerk in the department issued the purchaser with a "clear" certificate which omitted to mention the Minister's charge. The effect of this was that on completion of the purchase, the Minister's charge was lost. The Court of Appeal unanimously held the defendant vicariously liable to the Minister for the clerk's negligence. There was disagreement as to the basis of the liability, Lord Denning MR thinking this to be a case of *Hedley Byrne* liability, Salmon LJ thinking another principle was involved. However, there was agreement that a duty of care was owed to the Minister as a person within the contemplation of the clerk as capable of being affected by negligence on his part. Salmon LJ's view was based on the fact that *Hedley Byrne* liability is limited to cases where the plaintiff acts in reliance on the statement to his or her own loss.

The matter was again put to the test in *Ross v Caunters* [1980] Ch 297 which considered the situation in which the plaintiff had been named as a beneficiary under the testator's will, but because of the negligence of the defendant solicitor the gift to the plaintiff failed. Megarry VC held that the solicitor was liable in negligence to the plaintiff. This liability arose not under the *Hedley Byrne* principle (since the plaintiff had in no way placed reliance on the solicitor), but on the ground that the justice of the case demanded that an exception be made to the general rule that a duty of care generally does not extend to the infliction of pure economic loss. The possible objections to the decision – based on the fact that allowing the tort action would override privity of contract, and that the plaintiff was being allowed to recover damages for loss of an expected benefit rather than (as in the normal torts claim) actual out-of-pocket loss – were found not to be of sufficient weight to rule out liability. The objection based on the fact that the plaintiff was suing in relation to pure economic loss was answered by reason of the closeness of proximity between the defendant and plaintiff. The plaintiff was identified to the solicitor even to the extent of being known by name. The justice of the case also supported a remedy, since if the solicitor was not liable to the beneficiary he would escape altogether from liability since the testator was dead and the estate suffered no loss.

Ross has been followed in a number of Australian jurisdictions,[16] although the Victorian Supreme Court in *Seale v Perry* [1982] VR 193 found the objections to liability raised in *Ross* sufficiently convincing to refuse to apply it. A similar principle to that in *Ross* was applied outside the area of wills in the New South Wales decision of *BT Australia v Raine & Horne* [1983] 3 NSWLR 221. In this case, a firm of valuers was held liable for a negligent valuation of property given to the trustees of a superannuation fund, in consequence of which units in the fund were purchased by the trustees at an overvalue and the beneficiaries of the funds suffered loss. This was the three-party situation, since the trustees had relied on the valuation to the detriment of the beneficiaries, but Wootten J thought that the case should be decided under *Hedley Byrne* principles of negligent misstatement. Nevertheless, he agreed with the approach that the determining factor was the close proximity between the defendant and the plaintiff trustees suing on behalf of their funds, since units of this sort were not on general sale to the public but were held only by a limited number of superannuation funds, and this was known to the defendants.

---

16 *Watts v Public Trustee for Western Australia* [1980] WAR 97; *Van Erp v Hill* [1995] Aust Torts Reports 81-317; see also *Cartside v Sheffield* [1983] NZLR 37.

Ross has been confirmed in England by the House of Lords decision in *White v Jones* [1995] 1 All ER 691, another case of negligence by a solicitor, this time in failing to draw up before the testator's death a replacement will which would have conferred benefits on the plaintiff. Among the majority of three judges, Lords Goff and Browne-Wilkinson thought the case to be one of extended *Hedley Byrne* liability, on the basis of an assumption of responsibility by the solicitor towards the proposed beneficiary, even though no reliance had been placed by the beneficiary on the solicitor. Lord Nolan was more disposed to place the duty on the general justice of the case. Emphasis was placed by Lords Goff and Browne-Wilkinson on the special features of this case that, unless a remedy were given to the defeated beneficiary the solicitor's negligence would go unpunished, and that with the testator's death there is no other way of putting the matter right. This led Lord Goff to distinguish the case where the solicitor's negligence related to an inter vivos gift and the mistake is discovered in time for the donor to remedy it.[17] Further, on the basis of an extended *Hedley Byrne* type liability, Lord Goff thought the difficulties mentioned in *Seale* were disposed of. In particular, there was no problem in imposing liability for an omission (because of the assumption of responsibility to act for the defendant); nor did a difficulty arise by reason of the fact that the loss was pure, economic and of an expectation of profit.

Liability in the three-party situation was also imposed by the House of Lords on an employer who negligently supplied a defamatory reference for the plaintiff, his employee, as a result of which the plaintiff became effectively unemployable: *Spring v Guardian Assurance plc* [1994] 3 All ER 129. Lord Goff again based liability on *Hedley Byrne* on the ground that the employer had voluntarily assumed responsibility for the provision of a careful reference and the plaintiff had relied on this.[18] The other members of the majority were less specific about the basis of the duty of care in the case, although again the degree of proximity is clear, the plaintiff being known as a named individual to the employer. An additional factor complicating the decision was the fact that qualified privilege attaches to references of this sort, so that no action for defamation is available in the absence of malice on the part of the defendant. The majority in the House of Lords dismissed the arguments that allowing an action for negligence would subvert the qualified privilege rule. The two causes of action in negligence and defamation were distinct and there was no juristic reason why a rule for defamation should apply to an action for negligence.[19] The House of Lords was also on the whole unimpressed by the policy argument that to allow the action would produce damaging effects such as total refusal by employers to provide references, or the provision of bland, uninformative references. Policy effects of this sort were capable of merely being guessed at in a court; in any case, the possibility of negligence liability should improve the quality of references that were provided, and the fearful employer was entitled to exclude liability for the reference.

In the *Ross* situation, the defendant is being held responsible for failing to properly perform his contract with a third party, although the liability is through the medium of an action in tort. There are, in fact, a number of situations in which the negligent performance of a contract will give rise to a liability in tort: see [8.115]. In *Ross* itself,

---

[17]   As was decided in *Hemmens v Wilson Browne* [1993] 4 All ER 826.

[18]   Although this was still the three-party situation, the reference would influence other employers to act to the plaintiff's loss.

[19]   The New Zealand Court of Appeal in *South Pacific Manufacturing Co Ltd v New Zealand Security Consultants Ltd* [1992] 2 NZLR 282 declined to follow on this point.

Megarry VC was careful to limit the obligations of the solicitor to properly discharging his contractual obligation to the testator. No independent obligation could arise towards a third party, as a later case shows. The High Court's decision in *Bryan v Maloney* (1995) 182 CLR 609 (see also [8.120]) may be interpreted as tacit approval of *Ross*, although the factual situations are different. In *Bryan* the court held that a builder who had built a house for a third party under contract with that party was liable to a subsequent purchaser for defects in the house caused by negligent construction of the footings by the builder. This affirmation that negligence in the performance of the contract may be the basis of a tortious action by a third party who has suffered pure economic loss as a result, serves also as a justification of *Ross*. Indeed the latter is a stronger case, since the degree of proximity between solicitor and defeated beneficiary is much closer than that between builder and later purchaser of the house.

Tort and contract

[8.115] In the first place, there is no doubt that liability in tort may arise for a negligent pre-contractual statement by the defendant inducing the making of a contract between the defendant and the plaintiff. This assertion is supported by *Esso Petroleum Co v Mardon* [1976] QB 801 and *Howard Marine Co Ltd v A Ogden & Sons Ltd* [1978] QB 574. In this situation the liability in tort is an alternative to liability for the making of a negligent misrepresentation in those States that have a Misrepresentation Act.[20] Second, there is no problem about imposing liability in tort and contract where the defendant has made a negligent misstatement to the plaintiff on which the plaintiff has acted to his or her loss, and the misstatement also constitutes the breach of a contractual warranty (as in *Esso* in which negligent statements as to the petrol sales of the defendants' service station were held to give rise to liability in both tort and contract).

A more fundamental question is whether a tort action for negligence is available in relation to a negligent failure to perform a contractual obligation that the law regards as necessary for the satisfactory discharge of the contract. Unlike *Esso*, the tort obligation does not arise in this case independently of the contract, but is entirely governed by what the contract requires. Yet in a large number of cases, concurrent liability of this sort has been established. Many of the cases concern the liability of persons in the professions, or closely allied occupations. Thus solicitors, accountants, architects, engineers and members of a Lloyd's underwriting syndicate have been found to be subject to concurrent liability.[21] The close association of concurrent liability with that of professional persons is due to the fact that very often, particularly in the case of the solicitor, there is an absence of contractual terms, and merely an implied obligation of reasonable care. If there are express terms, the basic obligation to perform the contract is defined in terms of requiring reasonable care in its discharge. Concurrent liability is therefore less likely to be found applicable to commercial, business contracts where the obligations of the parties are likely to be spelled out in great detail and there is no room for the implication of a further obligation to take care to carry out the object of

CHAPTER 8

---

20   *Misrepresentation Act 1972* (SA); *Civil Law (Wrongs) Act 2002* (ACT).

21   With respect to solicitors refer [8.117]. As to engineers, see *Brickhill v Cooke* [1984] 3 NSWLR 396; architects, see *Carborundum Realty Pty Ltd v RAIA Archicentre* [1993] Aust Torts Reports 81-228. Cf *Frederick W Nielsen (Canberra) Pty Ltd v PDC Construction (ACT) Pty Ltd* [1987] Aust Torts Reports 80-086 – building contract containing detailed terms – no possibility of imposing a duty of care in negligence as regards its perfor-mance.

the contract (although in *Junior Books Ltd v Veitchi* [1982] 3 WLR 477 a subcontractor's obligation to lay a proper floor in a factory was defined as being one of reasonable care, even though the likelihood was that the contract in question was of a commercial nature and probably containing detailed provisions).

The first case concerning concurrent liability of the sort now under consideration concerned a solicitor. The defendant in *Midland Bank v Hett, Stubbs & Kemps* [1979] Ch 384 was held liable in both contract and tort for negligently failing to register an option to purchase land, the result being that the holder of the option was unable to enforce it against a purchaser of the land. Oliver J held that earlier decisions rejecting the ability to sue in the alternative in tort in these circumstances must now be held to be overtaken by the decision of the House of Lords in *Hedley Byrne & Co v Heller* [1964] AC 465, the principles of which applied even though plaintiff and defendant were in a contractual relationship. This has more recently been confirmed by *Henderson v Merrett Syndicates Ltd* [1994] 3 All ER 506, a decision recognising concurrent liability in contract and tort on the part of a Lloyd's agent towards Lloyd's names with whom the agent was in contractual relationship. The concurrent liability in tort was based on the speeches of Lords Morris and Devlin in *Hedley Byrne*. In particular, Lord Morris's idea of the voluntary performance of a service was extended to contractual services. The House of Lords in *Henderson* differed from the judgment of Deane J in *Hawkins v Clayton* (1988) 164 CLR 539, in which Deane J took the view that the tort duty of care was a complete replacement for implied duties of care arising under the contract. According to *Henderson* the two duties are concurrent.

The next question to arise regarding concurrent liability is what difference it makes to the liability of the parties that an alternative cause of action in tort exists. The main differences at the moment affect the incidents of the remedy rather than its substance. Many of the cases, including *Midland Bank* and *Henderson*, concern the limitation period. The tort limitation period is more favourable to plaintiffs since it runs only from the moment damage occurs, not as in contract from the date of breach. *Henderson* confirmed the plaintiff's ability to choose the more favourable tort limitation period. Measure of damages would appear to be more favourable to the plaintiff in contract than tort, since the plaintiff is entitled to choose between an expectation measure and an indemnity measure, whereas in tort the plaintiff may be confined to the latter. But tort is more likely to favour the plaintiff as far as remoteness of damage is concerned, since it allows more extensive recovery than does contract.[22] But in cases of concurrent liability, these differences could well disappear. The plaintiff does not appear to be entitled to side-step the rules relating to contributory negligence by suing in contract rather than tort: *Forsikringsaktieselskapet Vesta v Butcher* [1986] 2 All ER 488.[23] The defendant is also favoured, although not as against the plaintiff, by being able to claim contribution from a fellow tortfeasor if the claim against him or her is one attracting concurrent liability in contract and tort (*Aluminium Products Pty Ltd (Qld) v Hill* [1981] Qd R 33; *Macpherson v Kevin G Prunty Associates* [1983] 1 VR 573), although this is generally not possible where the only liability on his or her part is contractual.

Whether there is any substantive difference between the tort obligation and the contractual obligation in cases of concurrent liability is a difficult and as yet unresolved

---

[22] The rule in *Hadley v Baxendale* (1854) 9 Ex 341; 156 ER 145 requires a greater likelihood of the loss being suffered than the tort rule.

[23] But the plaintiff may gain an advantage through suing in tort where, eg, the plaintiff's fault operated as a complete defence to an action in contract: *Sole v WJ Hallt* [1973] 1 QB 574.

question. The English courts have answered this question in the negative, but the Australian position seems more open. The Privy Council in *Tai Hing Cotton Mills Ltd v Liu Chong Hing Bank Ltd* [1986] AC 80 refused to hold that a bank customer's duty of care towards his bank went beyond those duties which were implied in the contractual relationship; that is, not to facilitate fraud by the method of writing cheques, and to inform the bank of any unauthorised drawings on the account which came to the customer's attention. There was therefore no duty of care to scrutinise bank statements for the purpose of discovering such unauthorised drawings, and it made no difference whether the customer's obligation was laid in tort. A similar refusal to extend the contractual duty by means of tort was made, where the contractual obligations were express rather than implied, in *Greater Nottingham Co-Operative Society Ltd v Cementation Piling Ltd* [1989] QB 71.

Australian decisions concerning solicitors have occasionally revealed a willingness to impose a tort obligation going considerably beyond that envisaged by the contractual retainer. The judgment of Deane J in *Hawkins v Clayton* (1988) 164 CLR 539 is an outstanding example. In *Hawkins*, Deane J held that a solicitor who had drawn up a will for a client, and had then retained the will for purposes of safekeeping, owed a duty of care to the executor under the will to take reasonable steps to inform him of his appointment, since this was necessary for the will to operate. The duty arose from the assumption of responsibility by the solicitor to give business efficacy to the transaction with the testator and reliance on that by the testatrix. The duty of care arose in tort alone, since, granted the existence of the tort duty, there was no need to imply a similar obligation in contract. The assumption of responsibility found here clearly exceeded the terms of the original retainer and Mason CJ and Wilson J dissented on this point. Brennan and Gaudron JJ, although agreeing in the result of the case with Deane J, based the defendant's obligation on grounds other than contractual relationship between the defendant and the testatrix. By placing the solicitor's duty in tort alone, Deane J may have been indicating a desire to extend the obligations of solicitors beyond the narrow terms of the retainer. Whether or not that is a correct interpretation of his judgment, it certainly seems true of the decision in *Waimond Pty Ltd v Byrne* [1988] Aust Torts Reports 80-152, which purported to follow Deane J's views in *Hawkins*. That case held that a solicitor, who was retained to act for third parties in connection with a mortgage of land, owed a duty of care to a previous client of theirs to warn him about the deleterious effect of the mortgage on his interest in the property. The firm had knowledge from previous dealings with the client of that interest. However, it is difficult to justify the obligation here in respect of the original retainer, and to the extent the decision imposes obligations on solicitors to discover the effect of later transactions on earlier ones in which they have acted, it seems to present them with an impossible task.

Another example of contract duties being extended through the medium of tort occurred in *BGJ Holdings Pty Ltd v Touche Ross & Co* (1989) 18 NSWLR 642, although the recognition was obiter. In that case, the court took the view that the contractual duty of care of an auditor to a company (basically one of ensuring that the balance sheet of the company conforms to the assets held by it), was merely part of a more extensive tort duty, under which the auditor was required to warn the company that investments were being made by directors on behalf of the company not in accordance with company policy. Some cases have effectively restricted the scope of the solicitor's obligations to the client to matters immediately arising from the retainer. For example, although a solicitor employed to transfer a liquor licence to clients had a duty to explain to them the existence and legal effect of a condition imposed by the Licensing Court, he had no obligation to warn them as to the possible financial effects of the condition: *Gallagher v Carman* [1990] Aust Torts Reports 81-011. A solicitor employed for the purchase of land owed no duty of care to the client in relation to a statement made by the solicitor about the value of an adjoining block which was for sale: *Orszalack v Hoy* [1989] Aust Torts Reports 80-293.

Contractual obligations towards third parties

[8.120] *Ross v Caunters* [1980] Ch 297 (see [8.110]) provides a clear example of a contractual obligation engineering a tortious duty of care towards a third party not a party to the contract. *Junior Books Ltd v Veitchi* [1982] 3 WLR 477 is another example, although now one that is treated in England with reservations. In that case, the defendant subcontractors had contracted with the main contractors to provide a floor for a factory to be constructed by the main contractors for the plaintiffs. The subcontractors were in a contractual relationship with the main contractors but not the plaintiffs. The floor provided by the defendants was of such poor quality that it either needed constant maintenance to render it serviceable or complete replacement. The plaintiffs sued the subcontractors in negligence, claiming as damages the cost of replacing the floor. This was pure economic loss – the floor was not damaged but was always defective. Nevertheless, the defendants were held to owe a duty of care in relation to the condition of the floor to the plaintiffs. Lord Roskill's judgment in the House of Lords is generally taken to constitute the best explanation of this decision. He emphasised the close degree of proximity between the plaintiffs and defendants. The defendants had been nominated as subcontractors by the plaintiff's architect acting as the plaintiff's agent. They knew this and therefore knew of the reliance placed on them by the plaintiffs. The relationship was as close as it could be "short of actual privity of contract": *Junior Books* at 491.

Lord Roskill's reasoning in *Junior Books* allows the case to be regarded, not as a case of an act causing pure economic loss, but of liability under the principle in *Hedley Byrne & Co v Heller* [1964] AC 465, based on the assumption of responsibility by the defendants and reliance on that by the plaintiffs. As has been consistently affirmed in recent House of Lords decisions, the broader principle on which *Hedley Byrne* liability is placed in the judgment of Lord Morris, allows for liability in tort for the negligent performance of voluntary services, at least where there is a relationship of reliance between the plaintiff and the service provider. This explanation of the decision in *Junior Books* also renders irrelevant criticisms of the decision that it allows in general an action for the negligent construction of real estate, a position that in England is now denied. There has been some attempt in England to effectively abrogate the decision in *Junior Books* by holding that a contractual duty cannot generate a tortious duty of care to persons outside the contract.[24] This approach, however, cannot explain *Ross*, nor the decision in *Smith v Eric S Bush* [1990] 1 AC 831 that a person who values a house for the purpose of obtaining a building society mortgage and who is under contract with the society, nevertheless owes a duty of care to purchasers of a house who foreseeably rely on the valuation.

---

[24]   *Greater Nottingham Cooperative v Cementation Piling & Foundations Ltd* [1989] QB 71 (CA); *Simaan v Pilkington (No 2)* [1988] QB 758 (CA). See Fleming, "Tort in a Contractual Matrix" (1995) 3 TLR 12; 33 Osg HLJ 661.

No dogmatic position is possible on whether a party to a contract should owe a duty of care as regards the performance of the contract to persons outside the contract who suffer economic loss by reasons of negligence. The question of duty depends upon the general principles of proximity and policy, although, since *Sullivan v Moody* (2001) 207 CLR 562, the concept of proximity must be treated with caution. The significance of these principles was recognised by the New Zealand Court of Appeal in *South Pacific Manufacturing Co Ltd v New Zealand Security Consultants Ltd* (2001) 207 CLR 562. The court in this case found that sufficient proximity existed between a firm of insurance assessors, acting on behalf of an insurance company in the investigation of a fire, and the insured person. On the other hand, reasons of policy in this situation determined there should be no duty of care, in particular that recognition of a duty tended to defeat the qualified privilege the firm enjoyed against liability in defamation in the absence of malice on its part, and the fact that the insured had a remedy against the insurance company itself by suing on the contract of insurance.

The decision in *Junior Books* as properly understood is therefore supportable, but the contractual nature of the defendants' obligation leaves certain questions uncertain. Lord Fraser in *Junior Books* held that the tort obligation could not go beyond the obligation in the contract. The defendants could not be liable for providing a low-quality floor, for example, if that is what the contract envisaged. The converse case causes difficulty. If the defendants had provided a reasonably serviceable floor but one falling below the standard required by the contract, the better view here would be that there could be no liability in tort. Another difficulty is what would have been the position had the defendants excluded their liability for negligence in the contract with the main contractors. On normal principles of privity of contract this would not have bound the plaintiffs. But if the basis of *Junior Books* is the *Hedley Byrne* principle, the difficulty about exclusion of liability disappears, since *Hedley Byrne* allows a unilateral exclusion.

Whatever its status in England, the decision in *Junior Books* was vindicated and even extended by the decision of the High Court in *Bryan v Maloney* (1995) 182 CLR 609. This decision concerned the liability of the builder of a house to a later purchaser in respect to defects in the building. Bryan, the defendant builder, had built a house under contract with its first owner. The house had been sold seven years later to its third owner, the plaintiff, Maloney. Six months after the purchase cracks began to appear in the walls of the house, later becoming extensive and necessitating repair work to the extent of some $34,000. It was common ground in the High Court that the cracks were due to the inadequacy of the footings of the house laid by the defendant and that the defendant was negligent in this regard. It was also clear that the loss in question was pure economic loss – the house was not damaged but was always defective. In these circumstances, the sole question was whether the defendant owed the plaintiff a duty of care. By a majority of 4:1 the High Court held that he did.

There follows an analysis of the salient points in the High Court's majority judgment (Mason CJ, Deane and Gaudron JJ). The majority emphasised at the start of its judgment that the question of whether a duty of care existed was dependent on the further question: whether a proximate relationship existed between defendant and plaintiff. But this was answered by considering a number of factors pertaining to (among other things) the justice and policy of the matter for determination:

- The majority was not troubled by the fact that Maloney was relying for her cause of action on the negligent performance of a contract with the first owner. The phenomenon of concurrent duties of care in contract and tort was well established. The majority approved a distinction made by a Canadian judge between what is required to be done by the contract and the manner in which it is required to be done: *Central Trust Co v Rafuse* (1986) 31 DLR (4th) 481 per Le Dain J at 521–522. Negligent performance of the former may give rise to a tort liability but not of the latter. So a mere non-compliance by the builder with the contractual specifications would not give rise to a liability in tort. In the present case, however, there was a breach of the fundamental obligation to build a sound house, clearly suitable for the imposition of a tort duty of care. This reasoning tends to answer the difficulty raised by Brennan J in his dissenting judgment, that it would be wrong to allow the plaintiff to enforce contractual standards imposed by a contract with a third party. Although the distinction between what is required to be done by the contract and how it is to be done may pose difficulty in its application, it is clear that a mere breach of contract would not confer a cause of action in tort on a third party. The liability in tort for negligence would be limited to failure to carry out a fundamental requirement of the contract, one that would generally arise from implied term rather than specific provision in the contract (as in *Bryan* itself).

• The majority adduced numerous policy reasons in support of its conclusion. There was no problem with indeterminacy since only the plaintiff Maloney was affected by the negligence. The problem that the builder's liability might last for an indeterminate time was answerable by reference to the requirement of reasonable foreseeability and by the judicial fixing of the content of the duty of care. The case concerned the purchase of a house as a residence, very often the most important commercial transaction a buyer will ever enter into. The builder "by virtue of superior knowledge, skill and experience in the construction of houses", was better qualified and positioned to avoid, evaluate and guard against the financial risk imposed by latent defect in the structure of the house. This emphasis on the builder's advantage over the purchaser in respect of latent defects suggests that in practice successful actions against builders will, in general, concern cases of defective footings. The majority also thought its conclusion to be supportable on the ground that it avoided the anomaly that where, through defects in its construction, the building presented a danger to person or property, the builder was liable if that injury or damage occurred, but not for the cost of repair work undertaken to avoid such injury or damage (although on the facts of *Bryan* there was no suggestion that the house presented such a danger). Brennan J also would allow the cost of repairs undertaken to avoid the risk of injury or damage to property posed by the defective house, but would limit the claim to those circumstances.

• The majority held that there was an assumption of responsibility by Bryan, the builder, to Maloney, the purchaser, and a reliance by Maloney on that assumption. This is the least supportable of the majority's conclusions. It is difficult to see how an assumption of responsibility to later purchasers totally unknown to the builder can be implied. Equally it is difficult to see how the purchaser can have placed reliance on a builder totally unknown to the purchaser. The purchaser has at most a reasonable expectation that the house has been properly built, which is a different matter from reliance.

- The majority supported its conclusion by reference to Canadian and New Zealand authority to the same effect (*Winnipeg Condominium v Bird Construction Co* [1995] 1 SCR 85; *Bowen v Paramount Builders* [1977] 1 NZLR 394), while recognising that there was a departure from two decisions of the House of Lords: *DF Estates v Church Commissioners* [1989] AC 177; *Murphy v Brentwood DC* [1991] 1 AC 398.

The application of *Bryan* was limited by the High Court decision in *Woolcock Street Investments Pty Ltd v CDG Pty Ltd* (2004) 216 CLR 515 which considered a similar predicament but in the context of a commercial building. A firm of consulting engineers (the second respondent) designed the foundations for a warehouse and offices in Townsville in 1987. At the time of design they requested geotechnical investigations but the original owner refused to pay for them so they proceeded without completed soil testing of the site. The complex was subsequently sold to the appellants. Of note is the fact that the contract for sale did not contain a warranty regarding the absence of defects and there was no assignment of rights to the purchasers. It soon became apparent that there was some damage to the building due to the settlement of the foundations and underlying material. The appellant sought recompense on the basis of breach of the duty owed to them by the respondents.[25]

In a 6:1 decision[26] the High Court denied that there was a duty of care owed in these circumstances. It is important to note that the court clearly resiled from the dominance of proximity as applied in *Bryan* due to the recognition that proximity no longer plays the dominant role that it did at the time of that decision.[27] Of significance therefore were the concepts of vulnerability, reliance and foreseeability. It was emphasised that when considering pure economic loss and the nature of commercial activity, it is never enough to simply show causation and foreseeability;[28] something more must be found. The concept of vulnerability was predominant in the considerations of all of the judges, along with assumption of responsibility, knowledge and existence of an ascertainable class. The procedure to follow in this "evolving area of law" was set out by Callinan J when he stated (at 231) that "cases will only be resolved by closely and carefully examining the facts to ascertain whether a sufficiency of factors of a sufficient degree of relevance and importance has been demonstrated". In these circumstances there was no vulnerability, as the original owners had declined to approve surveys and were not deemed to be in a position of vulnerability.[29]

Once again there are no generalities or certainties in this area. It is simply a process of identifying the "salient features" to be considered and applying them to the facts at hand.

---

[25]   The first respondent was an employee of the firm of consulting engineers.
[26]   Gleeson CJ, Gummow, Hayne and Heydon (joint judgment), McHugh and Callinan JJ all found that there was no duty. Kirby J was in dissent.
[27]   Refer Gleeson CJ, Gummow, Hayne and Heydon JJ at [18], McHugh J at [72] and Callinan J at [211].
[28]   Gleeson CJ, Gummow, Hayne and Heydon JJ at [21], Callinan J at [223].
[29]   The Supreme Court of New South Wales recently adopted the *Woolcock Street Investments* approach to vulnerability and the need for more than foreseeability in *Kirkland v Quinross Pty Ltd* [2008] NSWSC 286.

Figure 8.4: Tort and contract – factors to consider

> • Foreseeability (relevant but not enough to establish liability).
> • Vulnerability (a dominant consideration).
> • Assumption of responsibility.
> • Known reliance or dependence.
>
> Key: Consider each of these salient features and then apply them to the facts.

Liability for voluntary undertakings

[8.125] Lord Morris's wider ratio in *Hedley Byrne & Co v Heller* [1964] AC 465 imposes liability on the defendant for voluntarily undertaking to use skill on the plaintiff's behalf and reliance on that undertaking by the plaintiff. Liability for the negligent provision of advice or information was merely part of that wider ratio. The justification for this wider ratio was certain, relatively obscure, early case law.[30] Its status was in doubt for some time, but it has now been confirmed in England by a number of recent House of Lords decisions.[31] The objection to liability in tort in relation to voluntary undertakings is that it is making tort do the work of contract. The defendant is being held liable not for negligently promising to perform the service, but for negligently performing the service itself. Nevertheless, the House of Lords held in *Henderson v Merrett Syndicates Ltd* [1994] 3 All ER 506 that the defendants, Lloyd's managing agents, who were not in direct contractual relationship with the plaintiff "indirect names", nevertheless owed them a duty of care in relation to the management of underwriting business on their behalf,[32] on the basis of their assumption of responsibility to them, and the names' reliance on that assumption. The phrase "assumption of responsibility" cannot be taken to mean an assumption of legal responsibility, and in this context merely indicates a voluntary undertaking to use skill on the plaintiff's behalf. Another example is the New Zealand decision in *Meates v Attorney-General* [1983] NZLR 308. In that case, the New Zealand Government was held liable to the plaintiff shareholder for failing to carry out non-contractual assurances of financial aid to a company in which the plaintiff held shares, those assurances being made conditional on the company remaining in business. The assurances were not fulfilled, the company remained in business but suffered a total loss, its shares becoming worthless. The defendant government was held liable to the plaintiff for the loss of his shares.

The judgments of Lord Goff in *Hedley Byrne* and *Henderson* have clarified, and to some extent extended, the original ratio of Lord Morris. In *White v Jones* [1995] 1 All ER 691 he found that negligent performance of the undertaking included the case of total inaction – in that case the defendant solicitor never got around to the task of drawing up a replacement will. Since there was an assumption of responsibility, there could be

---

[30] *Shiells v Blackburn* (1789) 1 H B1 158; *Wilkinson v Coverdale* (1793) 1 Esp 75; *Banbury v Bank of Montreal* [1918] AC 626 at 689.

[31] *Henderson v Merrett Syndicates* [1994] 3 All ER 506; *Spring v Guardian Assurance plc* [1994] 3 All ER 129; *White v Jones* [1995] 1 All ER 691 (especially by the judgments of Lord Goff in those decisions).

[32] As opposed to the direct names who were in contractual relationship with the managing agents, already considered earlier in this chapter. Refer [8.115]ff.

liability for nonfeasance. Nonfeasance of this sort may, however, be distinguishable from a refusal to enter on the task at all, even though this may constitute a breach of contract with a third party such as the testator in *White* or the main contractor in *Junior Books Ltd v Veitchi* [1982] 3 WLR 477. In these circumstances there could hardly be actionable nonfeasance. Lord Goff extended the Lord Morris ratio by holding in *Spring v Guardian Assurance plc* [1995] 2 AC 296 that in appropriate circumstances it applied to a voluntary undertaking to apply knowledge of a non-skilled nature on the plaintiff's behalf (in that case the giving of a reference by the plaintiff's employer).

One difficult and unresolved question is whether there needs to be detrimental reliance on the undertaking by the plaintiff. On the one hand, requiring detrimental reliance would avoid the problem that gratuitous promises are not legally enforceable. Detrimental reliance would substitute for the missing element of consideration.[33] But a legally well-informed person would no doubt take advantage of the requirement of detrimental reliance by immediately incurring a detriment in reliance on the undertaking. In one situation at least, that of the disappointed beneficiary, the law dispenses with any requirement of detrimental reliance by the beneficiary.

Failure to advise or warn

[8.130] A number of examples have already been provided of situations in which a contractual relationship imposes an implied obligation to advise or warn or notify. It now needs to be considered what is the position in the absence of a contract. The question may be summed up in the following terms: in what circumstances is there a duty of care to speak, as opposed to a duty to speak carefully?

In the first place, there is no difficulty in holding that where a person has offered to give advice about a particular transaction, this must be full enough to enable the plaintiff to understand the effect of any obligations undertaken. In *Cornish v Midland Bank* [1985] 3 All ER 51 the court considered the responsibility of a bank which undertook to explain to a wife the effect of a mortgage she was executing over her property in favour of the bank for money lent by it to her husband. The court determined that the bank breached its duty of care to the wife in failing to point out that the particular mortgage extended to all future advances made by the bank to her husband. The various cases in which persons have sued banks for losses suffered by taking loans of money in offshore currency all turn on the issue of fact; that is, whether the bank was undertaking to advise as to the financial risks of the transaction or merely agreeing to make the loan facility available and to advise as to its terms.[34] *Royal Bank Trust Co v Pampellone* [1987] 1 Lloyds Rep 218 shows that it is important to distinguish according to whether the defendant is merely agreeing to provide information or to give advice. The bank in that case was held not liable because it had merely volunteered to provide information about a certain investment, which was accurate; not to advise on its safety.

Another clear case in which a duty to speak arises is that in which a person has without negligence made a statement to the plaintiff and has later discovered the

---

[33] For a comparable argument as to why contractual promises should be enforceable, see Atiyah, "Contracts, Promises and Obligations" (1978) 94 LQR 193.

[34] Cf *Foti v Banque Nationale de Paris* (1989) 54 SASR 354 (plaintiff successful) with *Lloyd v Citicorp Australia Ltd* (1986) 11 NSWLR 286; *McEvoy v Australia & New Zealand Banking Group Ltd* [1990] Aust Torts Reports 81-014 (plaintiffs unsuccessful).

statement to be incorrect. In these circumstances there is a duty of care to correct the statement where the defendant has reason to believe that the plaintiff is still capable of relying on it, and provided that it is not too late to avert such reliance: *Abrams v Ancliffe* [1978] 1 NZLR 420; *Richard Ellis (WA) Pty Ltd v Mullin's Investments Pty Ltd* [1995] Aust Torts Reports 81-319.

Apart from these two situations, the English courts have refused to impose positive duties to speak, in the absence of an assumption of responsibility to do so by the defendant. For example, insurance companies have been found to owe no duty of care (in the absence of a contractual term to that effect) to communicate to a prospective or an actual insured person circumstances indicating the possibility that the insurance cover would be placed at risk: *Banque Keyser Ullman SA v Skandia Insurance Co* [1990] QB 665. An employer was held to have no duty of care to inform an employee of the lack of insurance cover in Ethiopia against hit-and-run car accidents, so that the employee was left uncompensated when injured in such an accident while working in Ethiopia: *Reid v Rush & Tompkins Group plc* [1990] 1 WLR 212. Nor did a school owe a duty of care to a pupil to effect, or to advise the pupil's parents to effect, insurance against personal injury in a rugger game: *Van Oppen v Trustees of Bedford School* [1989] 1 All ER 273. Insofar as the English cases have concerned contractual relationships, the contracts have been regarded as of a different nature from that between solicitor and client, where positive obligations to offer various forms of advice may arise.

The position in Australia is uncertain. As we saw in *Hawkins v Clayton* (1988) 164 CLR 539, the majority differed as to the basis of the solicitor's duty to take reasonable steps to inform the executor of his appointment. Deane J thought it arose out of the contractual relationship between the solicitor and the testatrix, in particular on a reliance by the latter on the former's assumption of responsibility. Gaudron J (at 111) put the matter on a different basis, rejecting any reasoning based on reliance by the testatrix, but concluding instead that the executor had a reasonable expectation that the defendant would communicate to him information necessary for the exercise or enjoyment of his legal right. But in the absence of an obligation on the defendant's part to protect that right, this seems an unacceptably wide ratio.

Damages for negligent statement

[8.135] It now seems settled law that damages for negligent misstatement in a tort action are based on the tortious measure of damages – that is, the plaintiff is returned to the position he or she would have been in had the misstatement not been made – not the contractual expectation measure of damages, under which the plaintiff is put into the position he or she would have been in had the statement been true and by means of which the plaintiff is entitled to be compensated for lost profits that would have been made from the transaction in question: *L Shaddock & Associates Pty Ltd v Parramatta CC* (1981) 150 CLR 225 (where in fact no claim was made for loss of profits); *Kyogle SC v Francis* [1988] Aust Torts Reports 80-182. Where the plaintiff has acquired property in reliance on the statement, the measure of damages is the difference between the amount paid for the property and its actual value: *Carborundum Realty Pty Ltd v RAIA Archicentre Pty Ltd* [1993] Aust Torts Reports 81-228. But in *Rentokil Pty Ltd v Channon* (1990) 19 NSWLR 417 the plaintiff appears to have been allowed the difference between the value of the house as represented free of termites and its added value, that is the contractual measure. The plaintiff is also entitled to be compensated for consequential loss arising from the statement, for example in the *Shaddock* case the cost of council rates, water rates and additional stamp duty and solicitors' costs by reason of the inflated value placed on the land through the misstatement. That sort of consequential loss is required to be reasonably foreseeable: *Banque Bruxelles Lambert SA v Eagle Star Insurance Co Ltd* [1995] 2 All ER 993. In *Kyogle* Kirby P dissented on the ground that the plaintiff was entitled to be compensated for the profits that would have been made had the statement been true. Mahoney JA indicated an opinion that application of the tortious measure was not automatic, and the justice of the particular case might allow a successful claim for loss of profits to be made. This would allow a so-called expectation measure of damages, generally thought to be appropriate in cases of tort. If the plaintiff can prove that, but for the negligence, he or she would not have entered into the transaction at all, the plaintiff is entitled to damages for the loss of the use of the money invested: *Swingcastle v Gibson* [1991] 2 AC 223. That approach is in line with the decision of the High Court in *Hungerfords v Walker* (1989) 171 CLR 125, allowing compensation to be awarded for the loss of use of money of which the plaintiff is deprived by the negligence of the defendant.

Legislation imposing liability for statement

[8.140] Legislation following the English model imposing liability for misrepresentation exists in South Australia and the Australian Capital Territory: *Misrepresentation Act 1972* (SA); *Civil Law (Wrongs) Act 2002* (ACT). The liability is limited to misrepresentation by a defendant inducing the making of a contract between defendant and plaintiff. Substantively, the action has no obvious advantage over an action based on negligent misstatement, although it is for the defendant to disprove fault on his or her part in making the misrepresentation. However, the measure of damages may be more favourable to the plaintiff than that applying to the common law claim. Some English authority has allowed an expectation measure of damages to apply, that is, to put the plaintiff into the position he or she would have been in had the representation been true: *Watts v Spence* [1976] Ch 165. The better view supports the tortious measure, as for negligent misstatement (*Sharneyford Supplies v Edge* [1985] 3 WLR 1; *Ellul v Oakes* (1972) 5 SASR 377); that is, to put the plaintiff into the position as if a careful statement had been made. It is also possible that the measure of damages available under the action for deceit, rather than negligence, applies on the basis that the action is based on a fiction of fraud.[35] But this has not yet been clearly settled.

Section 52(1) of the *Trade Practices Act 1974* (Cth) is much more important. It provides that a corporation shall not, in trade or commerce, engage in conduct that is misleading or deceptive or is likely to mislead or deceive. This subsection, coupled with s 82(1), which allows an action to be brought for loss or damage suffered through contravention of s 52(1), creates a statutory tort of engaging in misleading or deceptive conduct. It is more limited than the common law action for negligent misstatement, in that the defendant must be a corporation and the conduct engaged in must be in trade or commerce. Otherwise, however, the claim is much wider than the common law claim. There is, for example, no need to prove a special relationship of proximity existing between defendant and plaintiff. The loss suffered need arise only by reason of the conduct and does not therefore have to be foreseeable. Even more important, there

CHAPTER 8

---

[35]   *McNally v Wellmade International Ltd* [1978] IRLR 490; *Royscot Trust Ltd v Rogerson* [1991] 3 All ER 294. The Court of Appeal in England applied the tortious measure.

is no requirement that the misleading conduct should be intentionally or negligently engaged in – the court is concerned with the effect of the conduct, not the state of mind of its perpetrator: *Hornsby Building Information Centre Pty Ltd v Sydney Building Information Centre Ltd* (1978) 140 CLR 216; *Parkdale Custom Built Furniture Pty Ltd v Puxu Pty Ltd* (1982) 149 CLR 191. Although s 53 and following sections go on to make provision for specific examples of misleading conduct, s 52(2) makes clear that these are not intended to limit the generality of s 52(1).

Negligent acts causing pure economic loss

[8.145] The original common law rule was that no duty of care existed in relation to negligent acts causing pure economic loss, a rule affirmed as the basic rule of English Law in *Leigh & Sillivan v Aliakmon Shipping Co Ltd* [1986] AC 785 (a decision of the House of Lords). As we shall see, the basic "exclusionary" rule is now subject to qualification in Australia. There are two main reasons for the basic rule. The first is that of indeterminacy. Negligent acts are on the whole even more fertile in producing widespread economic loss than negligent misstatements. Insofar as this economic loss is "pure", there is no obvious way of limiting it in order to avoid excessive liability on the defendant's part – foreseeability is not a sufficient limitation, neither is the need for a special relationship between defendant and plaintiff (as applies to liability for negligent statement) as it is is less easy to impose on negligent acts. The second factor behind the basic rule is that there may be sound policy reasons for letting the loss lie where it falls rather than transferring it to a negligent defendant. The plaintiff, in cases where pure economic loss is being asserted by way of a claim for damages, is very likely to be in a business and therefore able to "self protect", for example by taking out business loss insurance, by making provision in a contract with a third party as to who should bear the risk of the loss, or by transferring the loss to the public in the form of a higher charge for goods or services. The alternative – transferring the loss to the defendant by way of a tort action involving the proof of fault – has the disadvantage that high litigation costs are added to the initial costs of the accident. Also the desirable deterrence factor of allowing a negligence action to proceed is not noticeably lessened in the case of negligence causing pure economic loss, since in cases where the loss stems from damage to property or injury to person (that is, where the property damaged or the person injured is not the plaintiff, see [8.150]), a negligence action lies in respect of that damage or injury. That policy factors lie behind the basic rule is a confident assumption of writers on this subject, but these factors are seldom spelled out or relied on by courts. There are however exceptions to this with some judges being prepared to refer specifically to the relevant policy considerations. See for example the dissenting judgment of La Forest J in *Canadian National Railway v Norsk Pacific Steamship Co Ltd* (considered at [8.175]) and Gaudron J in *Perre v Apand* (1999) 198 CLR 180 when she lists two significant policy considerations of indeterminacy and the nature of the competitive commercial environment in which this kind of loss is ordinarily sustained (see [32]-[33]).

Concept of pure economic loss

[8.150] Pure economic loss may be defined as economic loss suffered by the plaintiff that is not consequential upon damage to property in which the plaintiff has a proprietary or possessory interest or upon personal injury to the plaintiff. Possessors of chattels such as bailees are therefore able to sue for damage to that property under the usual principles of suing for property damage. The same applies to the person who charters a ship under a voyage charter. On the other hand, a time charterer of a ship has no possessory interest in it and therefore economic loss to the time charterer through damage to the ship is pure economic loss rather than damage to property: *Candlewood Navigation Corp Ltd v Mitsui OSK Lines Ltd* [1986] AC 1. Thus, the buyer of a chattel to whom the risk but not the property has passed under the contract has, prior to delivery of the chattel, no proprietary or possessory interest in it, so that damage to the chattel is pure economic loss to the buyer. Where a chattel is defective through negligence in its manufacture, this is pure economic loss to the buyer of the chattel – the rule is otherwise if the chattel causes injury to the buyer or damage to the buyer's property. The same has now been settled to be the law as regards a defectively built house, although earlier case law had suggested that when the defects in the house caused it to become dangerous to its occupants, this was damage to property.[36]

The situations in which cases of pure economic loss arise present different features and may be divided into various types. The first is "relational" economic loss. This arises where the loss results from personal injury to another person with whom the plaintiff has an advantageous economic relationship or from damage to property on which the plaintiff's business is economically dependent. Australia continues to recognise a number of cases in which economic loss may be claimed arising from injury to another person, for example a spouse, a child or a "servant". There is also the well-established claim of a dependant for loss arising from the death of the person on whom the dependency exists. In general, however, the problem of a recovery for economic loss arising through death or injury to another person must face the conceptual difficulty that the loss is purely economic. Where the relational economic loss arises from damage to another person's property, the indeterminacy problem may be particularly acute – large numbers of people may be dependent on the existence of a railway or a ship or factory machinery. So the "ripple" effect of widespread economic loss may be countered. This is not invariably the case with pure economic loss arising from damage to property. For example, a buyer who has the risk but not the property in a chattel, may be the only person to suffer economic loss from the chattel's destruction – so also may a time charterer from damage to the ship. The cases of the negligent manufacture of a chattel or the building of a defective house are also cases where the loss is likely to be experienced by one person. The liability of the builder was considered earlier in this chapter (see [8.120]). The manufacturer's liability is considered at [8.185]. Finally, there are the cases where the loss is truly pure; that is, unrelated to damage or the defectiveness of property, or to personal injury. Examples are the liability for negligent misstatement (see [8.60]) and for the negligent exercise of statutory powers: see [8.240].

Indeterminacy

[8.153] A central concern of the cases in this area is the notion of indeterminacy of either class of plaintiff, amount of damages or time.[37] The problem of identifying and

---

[36]   *Anns v London Borough of Merton* [1978] AC 728 is overruled on this point by *Murphy v Brentwood BC* [1991] 1 AC 398, and was not followed by the High Court in *Bryan v Maloney* (1995) 182 CLR 609.

[37]   *Johnson Tiles Pty Ltd v Esso Australia Pty Ltd* [2003] Aust Torts Reports 81-692; [2003] VSC 27 at [909] per Gillard J.

quantifying these have taken up a significant amount of court time and it is important to understand the broad concept of indeterminacy before considering the specific decisions. In *Perre v Apand* (1999) 198 CLR 180, the High Court considered a claim for economic loss suffered when access to the lucrative Western Australian market was denied due to negligent exposure to a contaminated potato crop. All members of the court noted the significance of the issue of indeterminacy and went some way towards clarifying its role. Gaudron J emphasised that as a policy consideration as opposed to a rule of law, the inability to identify a particular class of plaintiff with any accuracy is not necessarily fatal to the claim (at [32]). McHugh J noted that liability is indeterminate only when it cannot be "realistically calculated" and depends upon "what the defendant knew or ought to have known of the number of claimants and the nature of their likely claims, not the [actual] number or size of those claims" (at [108]). And Gummow J emphasised that the inability to identify the class is not fatal to a claim. This position was clearly demonstrated in the judgment of Gillard J in *Johnson Tiles Pty Ltd v Esso Australia Pty Ltd* [2003] Aust Torts Reports 81-692; [2003] VSC 27 where the potential commercial claimants were estimated to be 43,161 (at [915]) and the potential domestic claimants 1,373,553 (at [924]). The significant volume of the class of claimant was recognised by his Honour who described indeterminacy as a control factor which was not, under these circumstances, sufficient to deny liability (at [936]). In short therefore, indeterminacy is a relevant policy consideration but the size of a class of claimants or damages award is not sufficient, on its own, to deny recovery.

Caltex Oil

[8.155] In *Caltex Oil (Aust) Pty Ltd v The Dredge "Willemstadt"* (1976) 136 CLR 529, the defendant's dredger fouled a pipeline situated on the ocean bed of Botany Bay. The action was based upon two negligent acts. The first defendant had navigated negligently and the second defendants, Decca, had supplied a plotter chart to the owners of the dredge which misplaced the position of the pipeline. Both defendants knew of the existence of the pipeline, and the chart showed that it led from an oil refinery on one side of Botany Bay to a terminal on the other. The refinery and pipeline belonged to AOR; the terminal to Caltex. The defendants admitted liability for the loss of oil already in the pipeline, but denied liability for the major loss suffered by Caltex, which was the cost of transporting oil from refinery to terminal by the overland route. The defendants argued that this was pure economic loss since it derived from damage to property – that is, the pipeline, which was not owned or possessed by Caltex. The High Court held unanimously that the plaintiff's action for negligence in respect of this loss should succeed against both defendants.

Although the High Court's decision was unanimous, there is considerable disparity of reasoning among the members of the court. However, three judgments betray the common thread of addressing objections based on indeterminacy in allowing the claim for pure economic loss. Gibbs J thought (at 555) that there were exceptional cases, of which this was one, in which "the defendant has the knowledge, or means of knowledge, that the plaintiff individually, and not merely as a member of an unascertained class, will be likely to suffer economic loss". Stephen J refused to lay down a rule but merely thought that sufficient proximity between defendant and plaintiff existed on the facts of the case. He stressed the defendant's knowledge, or means of knowledge from the charts, of the existence of the pipeline leading to the terminal and of the likely effect on the terminal owner of damage to the pipeline. He also thought it a relevant factor (at 576-577) that no claim was made by the plaintiffs for loss of profits but merely for out-of-pocket expenses, a limitation that does not appear in the other judgments. Mason J expressed the test to be applied by saying (at 593) that liability would arise when:

> a defendant can reasonably foresee that a specific individual as distinct from a general class of persons will suffer financial loss …This approach eliminates the prospect that there will come into existence liability to an indeterminate class of persons.

Jacobs J's conclusion, that the plaintiff's oil was effectively immobilised and that the case was tantamount to one of damage to property, is difficult to conform with the facts of the case itself – the oil could not go in any direction other than through the pipeline. Murphy J merely applied the test of reasonable foreseeability in determining the liability for the economic loss suffered – this has the attraction of simplicity but his view has attracted no support.

None of the three judgments containing a common element requires the defendant to foresee pure economic loss (as opposed to economic loss) to the plaintiff. This is not surprising because the defendants could not be expected to know the nature of the factors in the case rendering the loss to Caltex purely economic in character. However, this suggests that the test of knowledge, or means of knowledge of the plaintiff as a specific individual likely to suffer economic loss (Mason J's requirement of reasonable foreseeability must also depend on the possession of knowledge by the defendant) is stringent, requiring some degree of knowledge of the plaintiff's individual circumstances. Otherwise, it is arguable that the same result would have been reached in relation, for example, to any boat known by the navigators of the dredge to be in its vicinity and that was hit and damaged by the dredge. There remain, however, obscurities with regard to the issue of what amount of knowledge of the plaintiff's circumstances is required of the defendant, even if we accept that "means of knowledge" is limited to knowledge immediately available to the defendant at the time of the act in question, such as the knowledge available from the charts in that case.

Subsequent Australian case law

[8.160] The subsequent case law has accepted the "common" ratio of *Caltex Oil (Aust) Pty Ltd v The Dredge "Willemstadt"* (1976) 136 CLR 529 that there is no liability for pure economic loss where the person claiming is a member of an indeterminate class. So in *Johns Period Furniture Pty Ltd v Commonwealth Savings Bank* (1980) 24 SASR 224, the court held that no duty of care existed on the part of the defendant to warn traders of the theft of a quantity of blank bank cheque forms, by using one of which a rogue was enabled to obtain goods from the plaintiffs without paying for them. Insofar as the claim was based on *Caltex* principles, it failed because the class of persons who might be similarly defrauded was indeterminate. Again, in *Ball v Consolidated Rutile Ltd* [1991] 1 Qd R 524, the class of fishermen using an ocean bay for fishing purposes was insufficiently determinate for the court to recognise a duty of care owed to them by the defendants, whose operations on the shore had caused a deposit of vegetation in the bay which rendered fishing impossible.

However, even where no problem over indeterminacy existed, some courts have refused to impose a duty of care in relation to pure economic loss. In *Christopher v Motor Vessel "Fiji Gas"* [1993] Aust Torts Reports 81-202 the members of a fishing crew who suffered loss of earnings through damage to the fishing vessel on which they were employed were found to have no cause of action in negligence against the person who damaged the boat. The case supports a stringent test of the knowledge of the plaintiff's circumstances required of the defendant. Clearly the crew were an ascertained class – however, their identity was not known to the master of the defendant boat but was a matter of mere inference. Again, in *R G Anderson v Chamberlain John Deere Pty Ltd* (1988) 15 NSWLR 363 the defendant carriers were not liable for damage to goods in the course of transit to the plaintiffs, who were not owners of the goods at the time of the damage but who later, on becoming owners of the goods, sustained the loss. The carriers had neither the knowledge or means of knowledge of their identity. More surprising is the decision in *Foodlands Association v Mosscrop* [1985] WAR 215, in which it was held that no claim beyond the claim for loss of consortium could succeed on the part of a husband in respect of injury to his wife, even though the defendants had knowledge of the existence of a partnership between husband and wife.

More recently the Supreme Court of Victoria in *Johnson Tiles Pty Ltd v Esso Australia Pty Ltd* [2003] Aust Torts Reports 81-962, addressed the line of authority in this area and Gillard J, in a clear and persuasive judgment endeavoured to set out some clarifying principles. The ultimately unsuccessful claim was in response to a loss of gas supply to commercial and domestic premises for a period of approximately one week in 1998. In presenting his judgment Gillard J adopted a "three step methodology of reasoning" (at [745]):

1. *Reasonable foreseeability of injury;*

2. *Whether there is a relationship of proximity; and*

3. *Identification and consideration of competing salient features for and against the finding of a duty of care.*

The notion of proximity was described as a policy consideration (his Honour deferred to Kirby J in *Perre v Apand* at [281] on this point). The third step of the inquiry was crucial in Gillard J's eyes and he simplified this by asking the question as to whether the law ought to recognise a duty of care to avoid purely economic loss in the circumstances (at [753]). It was at the third stage of the inquiry that the plaintiffs in this context failed as they were aware that there was no guarantee of uninterrupted supply and they could have minimised the risk of harm to their interest; there was a clear contract chain between the suppliers and the consumers of gas and each party to the contract was aware of its rights, obligations and duties; and finally, the supply of services was described as a responsibility of the State and his Honour concluded that it really is up to the State to determine, "after proper consultation, investigation and consideration whether or not liability ought to lie" (at [1347]). The process is therefore one of considering the specific fact scenario, addressing the issue of indeterminacy and then applying some overt policy considerations.

Other jurisdictions

England

[8.165] In England the basic rule has been applied even in situations where no problem of indeterminacy exists. In *Leigh & Sillivan Ltd v Aliakmon Shipping Co Ltd* [1986] AC 785 the House of Lords held that a buyer of steel, to which the risk in the steel but not the property had passed under the contract, was unable to claim for damage to the steel inflicted on it in the course of loading by a firm of stevedores. In *Candlewood Navigation Corp v Mitsui OSK Lines* [1986] AC 1 the Privy Council held that a time charterer of a ship damaged by the alleged negligence of the defendants had no cause of action in respect of financial losses sustained in respect of the continuing obligation to pay rent under the charter party and loss of profits. Cases such as these have instigated the argument that the claim should be allowed on the ground that the position is essentially the same as a claim by the owner itself, except that the owner has in the one case transferred the risk to the plaintiff and in the other the beneficial use of the ship. But this transferred loss argument was considered and rejected in *Candlewood* on the ground that regarding damages as a "common fund" might require sub-charterers who had been relieved by the accident of a disadvantageous contract to contribute to the losses of those who had suffered, and also on the ground that allowing claims for loss of use by, for example, contractual passengers, would raise problems of indeterminacy.

The House of Lords in *Leigh* made no mention of its own previous decision in *Morrison SS Co v Greystoke Castle* [1947] AC 265. In that case, where a collision between ships occurred partly due to the negligence of the defendant ship, the owners of undamaged cargo, who had been required to make a payment by way of general average contribution to the loss suffered through damage to the ship and other cargo, were entitled to recover damages for this loss from the defendant. The case has been thought by some to be entirely limited to the case of general average contribution, but has also been rationalised (although not in the case itself) on the basis of a joint venture between the ship and the cargo owners. But the limits of joint venture are not clear. There was no attempt to apply the doctrine in *Candlewood* on the basis of any supposed joint venture between bareboat charterer (in possession of the ship) and time charterer; nor in *Leigh*, even though that case concerned the carrying of cargo; here however the damage was inflicted by the cargo carrier.

The English judges have expressed criticism of the decision in *Caltex Oil (Aust) Pty Ltd v The Dredge "Willemstadt"* (1976) 136 CLR 529. Goff LJ in the Court of Appeal in *Leigh* took the view that drawing a distinction between foreseeability of loss to a particular individual and to a class of persons was merely arbitrary: *Leigh* [1985] QB 350 at 395. Lord Fraser in *Candlewood* (at 24) thought that if members of an ascertained class could recover damages for pure economic loss, there was no guarantee that the class would be small, so that the defendant's liability could be very large.

New Zealand

[8.170] The *Caltex* decision has met with a more favourable reception in New Zealand. *New Zealand Forests Products v A-G* [1986] 1 NZLR 14 was a straightforward application of *Caltex* principles. In this case the defendant's employee negligently cut a cable supplying electricity to the plaintiffs' mill, so that the plaintiffs suffered a period of loss of production. The plaintiffs recovered damages for this from the defendant. The court applied *Caltex* reasoning, noting in particular that the plaintiffs were exclusive users of the cable and this fact was known to the defendant's employees. It is noted that the claim that succeeded was in effect one for lost profit. *Mainguard v Hilton Haulage* [1990] 1 NZLR 360, however, goes somewhat beyond the *Caltex* principles. Where an electricity pole was damaged by the negligence of the defendants' employee, and the plaintiffs' factory situated in the immediate vicinity of the pole suffered a 24-hour shut-down, damages for this were held to be recoverable from the defendants. Recoverability of damages was said to be limited to those persons in the near vicinity of the pole, but this goes beyond *Caltex* since there was no requirement that the employee need know of them as individuals.

Canada

[8.175] The Canadian Supreme Court gave exhaustive consideration to the pure economic loss rule in *Canadian National Railway v Norsk Pacific Steamship Co* [1992] 1 SCR 1020. Unfortunately, the result of this consideration is inconclusive. The case concerned damage to a bridge owned by PWC (in effect the state of Canada) caused by the admitted negligence of the defendants. The bridge was used by four railway companies of which the predominant user was the plaintiff (CN), having 85% of the rail traffic. The bridge and railway lines were owned by PWC, the rail companies' use being based on contract with PWC. Under the contract, CN furnished services such as repair, maintenance, consulting and inspection of the bridge, which were paid for by PWC; but it also rendered certain services voluntarily. From the defendants PWC recovered all its losses arising from the damage to the bridge. The four rail companies, however, suffered economic loss through having to make alternative arrangements for rail transport available to their users (and other similar loss). They claimed for this loss from the defendants (no claim was made for loss of profits). The claim as far as the rail companies were concerned was, of course, for pure economic loss. The action brought by CN was accepted by two rail companies and Norsk as the effective trial of the action (the fourth rail company made no claim). The existence of the bridge, its use by the plaintiff as a railway, and the fact that CN was the main user of that railway were known to Norsk's employee, the master of the tugboat that caused the collision. In fact, he thought that CN owned the bridge.

In the Canadian Supreme Court, CN's action succeeded by a 4:3 majority. The judgment of McLachin J in the majority was concurred with by two other judges. The judgment rests its conclusion in favour of CN on the finding of a joint venture between CN and PWC – there was a close proximity between the two, since the operations of CN were "closely allied to the operations of the party suffering the physical damage" (PWC). The conclusion in favour of CN was also supported by the fact that the floodgates were not being opened to indeterminate claims for economic loss, CN as main user of the bridge being obviously the predominant party affected.

Neither of these reasons is convincing. Although a close relationship existed between CN and PWC, it hardly merits the conclusion that there was a joint venture; there was no sharing of either profit or loss between the parties. The fact that CN was known by the defendants' employee to be the main user of the bridge would have justified an argument for liability based on *Caltex*, but the court simply relied on CN's status as main user of the bridge. Stevenson J on the other hand, giving a separate judgment in the majority, based his decision in favour of CN on a straightforward application of Mason J's reasoning in *Caltex*. The defendants' servant knew of the bridge and its use by CN as a railway; he also knew that CN was the principal user of the railway. In these circumstances no problem of indeterminacy arose.

The dissenting judgment of La Forest J (with which two other judges concurred) favoured applying the basic exclusionary rule to the case. In the course of his judgment La Forest J disposed of a number of possible circumventions of the basic rule. The transferred loss of use argument broke down by reason of the fact that damages for loss of use might exceed those suffered by an owner, for example where the owner suffered loss of a hire charge for the chattel and the user loss of profit. It also raised problems of indeterminacy where the use was transferred to a class of persons. The joint venture argument was of dubious standing.

Arguably, *Morrison SS Co v Greystoke Castle* [1947] AC 265 should be limited to cases of general average contribution. In any case there was no joint venture between CN and PWC because there was no pooling of risk – the relationship was purely contractual. The argument based on *Caltex* was also dismissed (at [282]):

> *Allowing CN's claim to be distinct from other contractual victims by virtue of its particular foreseeability as an individual victim would in my view give rise to an unjust rule owing to its sheer arbitrariness. It serves neither to distinguish particularly meritorious victims, nor to single out particularly careless tortfeasors. Its sole function is to reduce the class of claimants to a small group, a function that could be equally well performed by any other factual distinction.*

La Forest J also mentioned certain general considerations applicable to pure economic loss cases. The need for deterrence against negligence disappeared where an action lay to the owner of the property for damage to it. The insurance argument favoured allowing the loss to lie with the victims of it. In effecting business loss insurance, the nature of the risk was well known to the potential victim; this was not so in the case of the liability insurer. Liability insurance had the disadvantage that insurance was likely to be excessive, that the whole loss was placed upon one insurer, and that it failed to avoid double insurance since a potential victim could hardly depend on suffering loss by reason of an actionable tort. The victim could also be a self-insurer, for example by provision in the contract. Where, as in the present case, there was no such provision, this was significant since it suggested that the risk was already reflected in the contractual price.

These considerations might well suggest that La Forest J would support the absolute application of the exclusionary rule to negligent acts causing pure economic loss. However (somewhat illogically), he left the door open to a claimant who could overcome problems of indeterminacy and who could demonstrate an inability to self-protect against the apprehended economic loss.

Conclusion

[8.180] The area of negligent acts causing pure economic loss continues to be a developing area. The facts of each case are incredibly complex, and are usually in the commercial context with two or more plaintiffs. The role of policy is significant and will continue to limit the scope of liability. Courts have, in general, displayed a reluctance to develop a broad, principled approach preferring instead an incremental, case by case discussion. Gillard J's suggested three-step process may provide a road map for the future and it will be interesting to see what role, if any, this proposed methodology will play in addressing these difficult claims.

Manufacturer and consumer

[8.185] We saw earlier in this chapter (see [8.120]) that a builder of a house may now, under Australian law, owe a duty of care as regards the building of the house to a later purchaser of the house, with whom the builder was not in a contractual relationship. To some extent, similar considerations affect the question of whether a duty of care should be imposed on the manufacturer of goods towards a consumer of the goods. Of course, a duty of care already exists as regards personal injury or damage to property caused by the goods. The question therefore becomes whether the consumer is owed a duty of care by the manufacturer in relation to the mere defective state of the goods. As in the case of the loss suffered by the purchaser of a defective house, the loss in question is purely economic in character.

Initially, it is clear there are important differences between houses and goods. Houses are built to last and this point was emphasised by the High Court in *Bryan v Maloney* (1995) 182 CLR 609. Goods often wear out quite rapidly. The latter need not point to negligence in manufacture – the price paid for the product is relevant to its lasting quality. Goods are also more susceptible than houses to being damaged through mistreatment or neglect by their present owners. The conclusion may be drawn that courts would be reluctant to impose a duty of care on manufacturers towards the purchasers of second-hand goods. On the other hand, the court in *Bryan* saw no problem in recognising on the builder's part a duty of care in relation to the condition of a "second-hand" house.

These considerations would not exclude the possible imposition of a duty of care on the manufacturer as regards new goods. The fact that the buyer of such goods already receives substantial legal protection under the contract with the seller of goods (or against those that are corporations under the *Trade Practices Act 1974* (Cth)) does not seem a sufficient reason for excluding a duty of care on the manufacturer's part. The fact that the loss to the consumer is pure economic loss is answered in part by the argument that, as in the case of the house buyer, no problem of indeterminacy arises.

The High Court in *Bryan* expressly left open the issue of whether manufacturers should owe a duty of care to consumers of their products as regards the quality of the products.[38] Their argument about the central importance in most persons' lives of the transaction of house purchase might be another reason for distinguishing houses from goods; although, of course, substantial loss may be sustained through the purchase of defective goods. On the other hand, the argument accepted in *Bryan* – that one reason for allowing recovery to the house buyer of the cost of repairing the house was that if the house was dangerous the money spent on repairs might avoid later liability on the builder's part for personal injury or damage to property caused by the house – would also apply to dangerous goods. This was one of the reasons adopted in the dissenting judgment of Laskin J in the Canadian decision in *Rivtow Marine v Washington Ironworks* [1973] 6 WWR 692 for imposing liability on the manufacturer of a defective and dangerous crane for the cost of rendering the crane safe. The majority in that case, however, applied what was regarded as the normal rule of non-liability for negligent manufacture in the absence of personal injury or property damage caused by the crane. The majority did, on the other hand, impose liability on the manufacturer for not warning the buyer of the crane's defective state, even though the manufacturer had knowledge of it, thereby causing the crane to have to be withdrawn at the time of its peak user period.

Implied warranties under Trade Practices Act

[8.190] Implied warranties arise under s 74 of the *Trade Practices Act 1974* (Cth) as regards the suitability for a particular purpose of the goods, the correspondence of the goods with their description or with a sample, and their merchantable quality: see also *Manufacturer Warranties Act 1974* (SA). The warranties arise in favour of the consumer of the goods

---

[38]   Note that this issue was not considered in *Woolcock Street Investments Pty Ltd v CDG Pty Ltd* (2004) 216 CLR 515.

(that is their purchaser, although there are statutory limits on what sales are consumer sales) or of a person deriving title from the consumer. Action lies for loss or damage caused by breach of the warranty. Clearly, that loss may be of a pure economic nature.

Mental harm

[8.195] Physical and financial loss is relatively easy to identify and quantify; this is not always the case with mental harm (previously known as nervous shock).[39] The apparently intangible nature of mental harm has meant that the law in this area was slow to develop, the courts being reluctant to recognise an actionable injury unless the plaintiff was directly injured by the negligence of the defendant. In this context we are not considering the sense of loss or sadness that can occur at the death or injury of a third party; mental harm is something more than this. In order to be recognised as a head of damage for the purpose of establishing a cause of action in negligence, the mental harm must constitute a recognisable psychiatric illness:

> Sorrow does not sound in damages. A plaintiff in an action of negligence cannot recover damages for shock, however grievous, which was no more than an immediate emotional response to a distressing experience, sudden, severe and saddening. It is, however, today a known medical fact that severe emotional distress can be the starting point of a lasting disorder of mind or body, some form of psychoneurosis or psychosomatic illness. For that, if it be the result of a tortious act, damages may be awarded. It is in that consequential sense that the term nervous shock has come into the law.[40]

The law continues to maintain the distinction between distress on the one hand and actual mental harm on the other. Apart from that, the legal history of mental harm presents a picture of a gradually expanding field of recovery. The law has moved from total denial of recovery, through imposition of strict controls, to the recent removal of controls by the High Court and introduction of legislative considerations as a direct result of the Ipp Committee recommendations (which, in some jurisdictions, has perhaps seen a narrowing of principle once more): see [8.215]ff.

The important chronology of developments, which will form the basis of the discussion of mental harm, is set out in Figure 8.5.

---

[39]   The case law refers variously to psychological harm, nervous shock and mental harm. Recent statutory amendments in all jurisdictions have, in line with the Ipp Recommendations and trends from the courts, universally adopted the term "mental harm". The terms mental harm and psychological injury will be used throughout this text unless in the context of a direct quote.

[40]   *Mt Isa Mines Ltd v Pusey* (1970) 125 CLR 383 at 394 per Windeyer J.

Figure 8.5: Chronology of developments

> - Denial of recovery: *Victorian Railways Commissioners v Coultas* (1888) 13 App Cas 222.
> - Limited recovery: *Dulieu v White* [1901] 2 KB 669.
> - Creation and recognition of controls: *Mt Isa Mines v Pusey* (1970) 125 CLR 383.
> - Extension of immediate aftermath to the hospital and affirmation of controls: *Jaensch v Coffey* (1984) 155 CLR 549.
> - Controls become "relevant considerations": *Tame v New South Wales; Annetts v Australian Stations* (2002) 211 CLR 317; *Gifford v Strang Park Stevedoring* (2003) 214 CLR 269.
> - Ipp Committee considers "mental harm" and recommends statutory reform.
> - Legislative response in majority of Australian jurisdictions, and possible return of controls in some jurisidictions.

Sceptical courts

[8.200] In early law there was considerable medical doubt regarding the genuineness of mental harm where it was unaccompanied by any physical injury to the victim. An early decision denying recovery for shock was based on this scepticism, with the Privy Council finding that mental harm suffered by a woman after the experience of believing that the horse and buggy in which she and her husband were travelling was to be hit by a train, was too remote from the event: *Victorian Railways Commissioner v Coultas* (1888) 13 App Cas 222. The more recent Australian case demonstrating early scepticism is *Chester v Waverley Corporation* (1939) 62 CLR 1. In this case the High Court determined that a mother, who suffered mental harm after searching at great length for her son only to watch as his body was pulled from a ditch, could not recover as the injury was deemed to be unforeseeable. Not surprisingly *Chester* did not endure; in 1970 Windeyer J in the process of expressing the willingness of the court to recognise actionable mental harm was able to refer to "law, marching with medicine but in the rear and limping a little": *Mt Isa Mines v Pusey* (1970) 125 CLR 383 at 393. By 1984 Deane J was able to note that the judgment of the majority in *Chester* had not worn well with time: *Jaensch v Coffey* (1984) 155 CLR 549 at 590.

Recognition within guidelines: Mt Isa Mines and Jaensch

[8.205] With the High Court's recognition that there was no medical doubt that mental harm may be suffered by persons who are not themselves injured, came a willingness to recognise a legal claim in such circumstances. Early developments acknowledged liability when the harm was a foreseeable consequence of being put in fear of personal injury to oneself, or through the witnessing of an accident (there need be no actual injury provided it is reasonably apprehended by the plaintiff).[41] The latter class of case is

---

41   *Hambrook v Stokes Bros* [1925] 1 KB 141 – plaintiff observed runaway truck coming from direction towards which her children had just left. She recovered damages for nervous shock, although she did not actually see her child being hit by the truck.

exemplified by *Mt Isa Mines v Pusey* (1970) 125 CLR 383. The respondent in this case was an engineer working in the powerhouse of the appellant when two electricians, also employed by the appellant, suffered shocking burns as the result of a short circuit which led to an intense arc of heat and two loud explosions. The respondent rushed to their aid and assisted one of the electricians out of the building and to a waiting ambulance. He later learnt that the man he assisted died nine days after the incident. The respondent initially continued in his employment without any outward sign of distress or injury, but he ultimately suffered from depression and a severe schizophrenic reaction.

The key issue to be addressed by the High Court in this case was determining the scope of liability of the appellant with respect to:

- the lack of relationship between those who sustained physical injury and the respondent;
- the question of the relevance of the individual characteristics of the respondent; and
- whether the particular pathological condition needs to be foreseeable.

It was suggested by the appellant that there was a need to be able to foresee the precise psychological condition, and that the "schizophrenic reaction" was not only not foreseeable but was not causally connected as it was due in part to the brooding nature of the respondent. The court did not accept these arguments and in reaching a conclusion appealed to general negligence principles. The general principles clearly established in this case are set out in Figure 8.6.

Figure 8.6: Mt Isa Mines v Pusey (1970) 125 CLR 383

- It is sufficient that the class of injury, as distinct from the particular injury, is foreseeable: Barwick CJ at 390. The particular pathological condition need not be foreseeable: Windeyer J at 402.
- Sorrow does not sound in damages: Windeyer J at 394.
- There is no sound policy ground for limiting recovery for mental harm to those who are related to the party who suffers the physical harm: Windeyer J at 404.
- The court expressed misgivings about denial of recovery to those who were prone to "shock" as opposed to those of normal fortitude, but left the question open: Windeyer J at 404.
- If the sole cause of the injury is hearing about the event, then no action lies against either the bearer of bad tidings or those who caused the event of which the plaintiff is told: Windeyer J at 407.

The second case to consider in this context is *Jaensch v Coffey* (1984) 155 CLR 549. In this case the plaintiff was the wife of a person injured in a road accident. She developed a psychiatric illness, characterised by anxiety and depression, because of what she saw and heard in the hours following the accident. The key difference here is that she was not present at the location of the accident; her experience was limited to events at the hospital. The High Court, in a unanimous decision, held that she was entitled to recover damages for this in negligence.

The shock to Mrs Jaensch was clearly foreseeable shock but a question arose as to whether reasonable foreseeability of nervous shock was enough to establish liability. This issue had split the House of Lords in a contemporaneous decision, *McLoughlin v O'Brian* [1983] 1 AC 410. Two judges, Lords Bridge and Scarman, thought that the test of foreseeability was a sufficient one in all cases, including the difficult situations of shock to the casual spectator, or to a person who witnessed neither the accident nor its immediate aftermath. Two judges, Lords Wilberforce and Edmund Davies, thought that there were policy reasons for restricting claims for nervous shock, even where shock was foreseeable. The policy reasons related to the fear of excessive liability and the making of false claims. As regards the latter, the medical evidence would often be incapable of determining the genuineness of the mental harm claimed by the plaintiff. The symptoms of "shock" could easily enough be fraudulently simulated. Equally, one suffering from extreme distress rather than actual psychiatric illness might, at least for a time, exhibit symptoms characteristic of actual nervous shock. Accordingly, Lord Wilberforce considered (at 421–422) that claims for shock should be limited to the "plainest possible" cases: that is, where a sufficiently close emotional bond existed between the plaintiff and the victim, and the plaintiff witnessed the accident or its immediate aftermath. This would altogether exclude the casual spectator's claim and also the claim of one who suffered shock through receiving news of an accident to a close relative or friend.

In *Jaensch*, there were three differing approaches to the same problems. Gibbs CJ agreed with limitations proposed by Lord Wilberforce, although expressing the opinion that the need for a close emotional bond with the victim was the paramount factor. Brennan J, with whom Murphy J was in general agreement, adopted the approach of Lord Bridge, thinking that nervous shock cases turned entirely on issues of fact, that is, reasonable foreseeability and causation. But Brennan J's limitation of shock claims to those where shock is caused by a "sudden, sensory experience" seems to be one that derived at least in part from policy rather than wholly from reasonable foreseeability. This limitation was used by Brennan J as a reason for excluding a claim for nervous shock experienced as a result of hospital visits to the victim, as falling outside the immediate aftermath of the accident. Deane J applied principles of proximity in deciding the case. He found that Mrs Jaensch's claim succeeded because, by witnessing the immediate aftermath of the accident, she satisfied the requirement of causal proximity. But there are numerous references to policy in Deane J's judgment, leaving it open to question to what extent proximity was merely a means of giving a mechanical expression to what are really policy decisions. For example, Deane J while coming to a firm conclusion excluding the claim for nervous shock by a person whose shock develops slowly – through regular visits to the victim in hospital as opposed to witnessing the immediate aftermath, or through nursing the victims (on the ground of absence of causal proximity)[42] – expressed doubt about what rule of policy excluded the claim of a wife and mother who receives telephone information that her husband and children have been killed and who is too shocked to attend hospital: *Jaensch* at 608. Another difficulty with the causal proximity test proposed by Deane J is that it admits the claim of the casual spectator, a fact that Deane J himself (at 606) accepted.

---

[42]   As in *Pratt v Pratt* [1975] VR 378 – mother's claim for nervous shock through nursing injured daughter failed.

Controls become "relevant considerations"

[8.210] Following the decisions in *Mt Isa Mines v Pusey* (1970) 125 CLR 383 and *Jaensch v Coffey* (1984) 155 CLR 549, the general approach to cases involving mental harm remained stable for a number of years. The courts would strictly apply the requirements of sudden sensory perception of the accident or its aftermath and determine whether or not the plaintiff met these guidelines. If something in the fact scenario fell outside these requirements, then the case would, without any further consideration of specific facts and circumstances, fail.

Two more recent decisions of the High Court changed this. The first of these involved two separate cases which were considered together, *Tame v New South Wales; Annetts v Australian Stations Pty Ltd* (2002) 211 CLR 317. In the first of the two cases, Mrs Tame was driving a car which was involved in a minor accident. She rarely drank alcohol and in fact registered a 0 blood alcohol level. There was an initial mistake with respect to her blood alcohol level in the accident report; this was later corrected, but the copy of the report which was received by her insurance company contained the original error. When this was drawn to the attention of Mrs Tame and the police, the error was immediately rectified with full apologies from the police. Mrs Tame became obsessed with the error, however, and was convinced that the refusal of her insurer to pay for some specific treatment was based on the error (when in fact the insurer simply did not believe that she needed the treatment). Mrs Tame repeatedly referred to the error in conversation with her husband and friends and ultimately developed a depressive illness which was described as stemming from the impact of the original error on a particularly vulnerable personality.

In the second case, the Annetts' 16 year old son was employed as a jackeroo on a remote station. It was apparent that when he obtained his employment, the Annetts had sought (and received) certain undertakings regarding the safety of their son; these centred on assurances of close supervision. Two months after he arrived at the station, the son was sent to work as a caretaker at a remote area and it later emerged that he died of dehydration and exhaustion after his car became bogged in a sand dune. He was missing for a number of months and there was a prolonged and agonising search process. Ultimately both Mr and Mrs Annetts claimed to have suffered psychological illness, initially as a result of hearing the news that he was missing which was then exacerbated by the trauma of the prolonged search and the need to identify personal items and remains.

Neither of these cases fits within the required guidelines of sudden sensory perception of either the accident or the aftermath, and the case of Mrs Tame included the issue of whether or not normal fortitude was a requirement in such circumstances. The limitations of these cases provided the High Court with an opportunity to review the law with respect to mental harm and resulted in a clear rejection of the previously accepted rigid approach to determining liability. A more flexible approach was adopted, with the result being similar to that of general negligence with some special considerations when determining whether the injury was reasonably foreseeable.

The court was unwilling to accept that the strict controls continued to be of relevance, describing them as indefensible (per Gleeson CJ at 337), leading to anomalous and illogical consequences (per Gaudron J at 340) and operating in an arbitrary and capricious manner (per Gummow and Kirby JJ at 380). It was acknowledged by the court that the reason for the existing mechanisms was perhaps a reflection of the early scepticism surrounding any action in the absence of physical injury and the need to keep liability within practicable bounds: per Gummow and Kirby JJ at 380. This perceived need was, however, specifically rejected by the court as resulting in "unprincipled distinctions" which could only serve to bring the law into disrepute: per Gummow and Kirby JJ at 380. The correct role for each of these considerations was to simply operate as guidelines where relevant.

The basis of the appeal in the case of Mrs Tame was that the Court of Appeal had erred in determining that normal fortitude was a requirement with respect to foreseeability in the context of mental harm. The relevance of normal fortitude was clearly acknowledged by the court with a recognition that it would constitute an unreasonable constraint on human interaction if the law required us to take into account the impact of our actions on the most susceptible members of society. In reverting to general negligence principles, it was emphasised that the central inquiry is whether, in all the circumstances, the risk of the plaintiff suffering a recognised psychiatric illness was reasonably foreseeable, that is not far fetched or fanciful: per Gummow and Kirby JJ at 385. The relevance of normal fortitude is, therefore, found in the context of the test of reasonable foreseeability: if it is reasonably foreseeable that an individual will suffer mental harm, then the fact that the individual is not of normal fortitude will not be of relevance. Normal eggshell skull principles apply. In the case of Mrs Tame her reaction was described as extreme and idiosyncratic the risk of which was deemed to be far-fetched and fanciful: per Gummow and Kirby JJ at 397.

A relevant consideration in *Annetts* (especially in the judgment of Gleeson CJ) was the pre-existing relationship between the parents and the station owners. This left open the question as to whether it was this relationship that removed the requirement of sudden sensory perception of the accident. Furthermore, in the absence of such a relationship, would the strict controls be reinstated? The court was provided with an opportunity to address this specific question in *Gifford v Strang Park Stevedoring* (2003) 214 CLR 269. Mr Gifford was crushed to death by a forklift while at work and his three children were informed of his death later that day. There was no evidence of negligence in the manner in which the children received the news. All three claimed to have suffered psychiatric injury as a result of hearing of the death of their father. The question before the court turned on the issue of whether or not a duty of care was owed to the children in the absence of any pre-existing relationship.

It was noted that reasonable foreseeability involves more than mere predictability (per Gleeson CJ at 276) and the significance of the relationship between a father and his children was the turning point of the decision. McHugh J was the most generous in his consideration of the scope of the duty, indicating (at 281) that an "employer owes a duty to take care to protect from psychological harm, all those persons it knows (or ought to know) are in a close and loving relationship with its employee". The key to the duty lay not in any relationship between the employer and the children, but in that between the children and their father: at 288. This case re-emphasised the return to basic negligence principles in the context of mental harm, with Kirby and Gummow JJ recognising (at 293) that this was a result of the absolute rejection of the requirement of direct perception. There was a note of caution, however, sounded by Kirby and Gummow JJ (at 295). This was that it was erroneous to draw from *Tame and Annetts* the conclusion that reasonable foreseeability of mental harm is the only condition of the existence of a duty of care; on the contrary, all factors must be taken into account.

Ipp Committee recommends statutory reform

[8.215] As a part of its broader term of reference to consider the formulation of duties and standards of care, the Ipp Committee (chaired by the Hon David Andrew Ipp) carefully addressed the question of liability for mental harm and made some strong recommendations for statutory reform. The Committee clearly acknowledged the early reluctance of the courts to allow recovery for pure mental harm, identifying the reasons for this reluctance as being:

- difficulty of diagnosis;
- scope of plaintiffs; and
- limited resources, meaning that it was viewed as more important to compensate for physical harm than for mental harm.[43]

The first of the control mechanisms addressed by the Committee was the key requirement that the plaintiff suffer from a recognisable psychiatric illness. It was noted that there is currently a lack of forensic criteria of mental illness, and the Committee's dissatisfaction with this situation was clear. The recommendation stemming from this discussion involved the establishment of a panel of experts to develop a set of guidelines and forensic criteria.[44] (This recommendation has not been adopted by any jurisdiction.)

The main focus of the Ipp Report in this area was on the question of the duty of care. The Report clearly outlined the recent developments of *Tame v New South Wales; Annetts v Australian Stations Pty Ltd* (2002) 211 CLR 317,[45] and discussed the previous control mechanisms.[46] The conclusion of this discussion was the view that the fundamental proposition of *Tame and Annetts* is that reasonable foreseeability of mental harm is the only precondition and that normal fortitude is relevant to the question of reasonable foreseeability.[47] The basic concern of the Committee in this context was the fact that while mental and physical harm are entirely different forms of harm, the test as recently developed is essentially the same for both types of injury. The question of whether or not there should be further restriction on liability for mental harm was directly addressed, with the Committee expressing concern that the current law may not impose satisfactory limits.[48] In addressing this question the Committee considered some existing and proposed limitations on who could recover for mental harm.[49] The Committee appeared attracted by the notion of listing those who would be eligible, characterised on the basis of their relationship with the person who was injured or killed. It acknowledged, however, that it would be difficult to create a comprehensive list of recognisable relationships, and the Committee expressed its reluctance to do so.[50] The Committee also resiled from introducing an "evaluative concept" such as "close relationship", as this could bring the law into disrepute by requiring the courts to undertake a "forensic examination and assessment of the nature and quality of intimate human relationships".[51] Despite this reluctance, the Committee did provide an example

---

43   Australia, *Review of the Law of Negligence: Final Report* (September 2002) (hereafter "Ipp Report") p 135.
44   Ipp Report, p 136.
45   Ipp Report, p 137.
46   Ipp Report, pp 137-138.
47   Ipp Report, p 138.
48   Ipp Report, p 140.
49   Ipp Report, pp 140-141.
50   Ipp Report, pp 141-142.
51   Ipp Report, p 142.

of a list which may be included in legislation,[52] and this was one of the more universally accepted recommendations.

In conclusion to this discussion, the Committee introduced recommendation 34 which restates the law as established in *Tame and Annetts* and sets out some "relevant considerations" which directly mirror the old control mechanisms. The essence of the recommendation is as follows:

- mental harm *must* consist of a recognised psychiatric illness; and
- there will be no duty of care unless the defendant ought to have foreseen that a person of normal fortitude might, in the circumstances, suffer a recognised psychiatric illness.

When considering reasonable foreseeability, relevant circumstances include:

- whether the mental harm resulted from a sudden shock;
- whether the plaintiff was at the scene or its aftermath;
- whether the plaintiff witnessed the scene with unaided senses;
- whether there was a pre-existing relationship between the plaintiff and defendant; and
- the nature of the relationship between the plaintiff and the party injured, killed or put in peril by the defendant.[53]

These recommendations have been adopted to some extent in most jurisdictions, as set out in Figure 8.7. There now appears to be a lack of uniformity across the jurisdictions with regard to who can recover for mental harm. Recent judicial activity suggests that, in New South Wales at least, the requirement of actual presence at the scene has been reinstated (and will be strictly applied by the courts): see [8.218].

Figure 8.7: Ipp Commitee recommendations

Juris	Legislation	Sec	Provision
ACT	*Civil Law (Wrongs) Act 2002,* Pt 3.2 Mental Harm	s 33	Enables recovery for pure mental harm or nervous shock.
		s 34	Reasonable foreseeability based on normal fortitude. Relevant considerations as listed by Ipp Committee.
		s 35	Establishes requirement for recognisable psychiatric illness.
		s 36	Those who can recover are a parent, domestic partner or family member of the victim. Family member defined (in s 32) to include: • child (son, daughter, grandson, granddaughter, stepson or stepdaughter); and • parent (father, mother, grandfather, grandmother, stepfather or stepmother or someone acting in place of a parent).

---

[52] Ipp Report, p 142.
[53] Ipp Report, p 144.

Juris	Legislation	Sec	Provision
NSW	*Civil Liability Act 2002,* Pt 3 Mental Harm	s 28	Application of the Part.
		s 29	Enables recovery for pure mental harm or nervous shock.
		s 30	Limitation on recovery: • Plaintiff must have either witnessed the incident or be a close family member of the victim. • Damages are to be reduced to the same proportion as those to the victim on the basis of contributory negligence. • No damages to be paid to the plaintiff if the victim is excluded by law from recovery. Close family member defined as: • parent or person with parental responsibility; • spouse or partner; • child or stepchild of the victim or any person for whom victim has parental responsibility; • brother, sister, half-brother, half sister, stepbrother or stepsister of the victim.
		s 31	Establishes requirement for recognisable psychiatric illness.
		s 32	Reasonable foreseeability based on normal fortitude. Relevant considerations as listed by Ipp Committee, with the additional note that the section does not require the court to disregard what the court ought to have known about the fortitude of the plaintiff.
NT		s 23	Family member defined as: • wife, de facto partner, parent, child, brother, sister, half-brother or half-sister of that person; • child includes: son, daughter, grandson, granddaughter, step-son or step-daughter of that person, or a person to whom that person stands in loco parentis; • parent includes: father, mother, grandfather, grandmother, step-father or step-mother of that person, or a person standing in loco parentis to that person.

Juris	Legislation	Sec	Provision
ACT NT	*Law Reform (Miscellaneous Provisions) Act 1956*	s 25	Limitation on recovery: • person "put in peril or killed" must be a parent, husband, wife or de facto of the plaintiff, OR • a "member of the family" must be "put in peril or killed" within the sight of the plaintiff.
Qld	No mention.		
SA	*Civil Liability Act 1936*	s 33	Reasonable foreseeability based on normal fortitude. Relevant considerations as listed by Ipp Committee, with the additional note that the section does not affect the duty of care of a person (the defendant) to another (the plaintiff) if they know, or ought reasonably to know, that the plaintiff is a person of less than normal fortitude.
		s 53	Damages may only be awarded if injured or a parent, spouse or child of a person injured, killed or endangered. Introduces requirement of recognisable psychiatric illness.
Tas	*Civil Liability Act 2002,* Pt 8 Mental Harm	s 31	Enables recovery for pure mental harm or nervous shock.
		s 32	Limits liability to those present at the scene or a close family member of the victim. Close family member defined as: • parent or person with parental responsibility; • spouse (husband, wife or de facto spouse and where more than one person would qualify as a spouse, only the last person to so qualify can recover); • child, stepchild or any other person for whom the victim has parental responsibility; • brother, sister, half-brother, half-sister, stepbrother or stepsister.
		s 33	Establishes requirement for recognisable psychiatric illness.
		s 34	Reasonable foreseeability based on normal fortitude. Relevant considerations as listed by Ipp Committee, with the additional note that the section does not require the court to disregard what the court ought to have known about the fortitude of the plaintiff.

Juris	Legislation	Sec	Provision
Vic	*Wrongs Act 1958*, Pt XI Mental Harm	s 72	Reasonable foreseeability based on normal fortitude. Relevant considerations as listed by Ipp Committee, with the additional note that the section does not affect the duty of care of a person (the defendant) to another (the plaintiff) if they know, or ought reasonably to know, that the plaintiff is a person of less than normal fortitude.
		s 73	Limitation on recovery: • plaintiff must have either witnessed the incident or be in a close relationship with the victim; • no damages to be paid to the plaintiff if the victim is excluded by law from recovery.
WA	*Civil Liability Act 2003*, Pt 1B Mental Harm	s 5S	Reasonable foreseeability based on normal fortitude. Relevant considerations as listed by Ipp Committee, with the additional note that the section does not require the court to disregard what the court ought to have known about the fortitude of the plaintiff.

A narrowing of principle

[8.218] Post Ipp activity has, in certain cricumstances, seen a return to strict requirements for presence at the scene. In New South Wales, Tasmania and Victoria, in the absence of a family relationship, there is a clear requirement that the plaintiff actually witness the death or "peril" of the person. This legislative requirement has been given strict application by the Supreme Court of New South Wales: in *Burke v State of New South Wales* [2004] NSWSC 725 Master Malpass denied recovery for a plaintiff who claimed to suffer mental harm as a result of the landslide at Thredbo in 1997. The plaintiff claimed to have witnessed the destruction of Bimbadeen Lodge and stated that he knew all of those killed in the disaster, the most significant being his closest friend whom he had left at the lodge shortly before the incident. Master Malpass described the legislation as a "triumph for common sense" (at [58] in reference to the Second Reading Speech) and emphasised the prohibition of recovery unless the threshold requirements are satisfied (at [63]). It was acknowledged that the legislative expectations were narrower than what had been recommended by the Ipp Report (at [64]) but the expectation of perception by presence was adopted by the court (at [67]). This was more recently emphasised in *Wicks v Railcorp; Sheehan v State Rail* [2007] NSWSC 1346, which saw Malpass AJ rejecting the claims of two police officers who attended a rail disaster in 2003. The essence of their claim was that despite attending the crash site after the critical incident, they had met the requirements of the legislation through witnessing survivors who were either dead or seriously injured (and suffering progressive injury or aggravation of injury) (claim set out at [21]). Under previous common law provisions, this could perhaps have fallen into the category of "immediate aftermath", but such an avenue for recovery has, it would appear, been closed in some jurisdictions. In this instance, Malpass AJ clearly rejected the "aftermath" as an appropriate consideration (at [76]) and clearly stated that if the plaintiff is to be entitled to damages, then they must "witness, at the scene, the victim being killed, injured or put in peril" (at [77]). Such a position clearly limits the rights of the rescuer who comes across an accident scene. The wording of the New South Wales provision is mirrored in Tasmania and Victoria and it can be presumed that an equally narrow interpretation will be adopted. In the Australian Capital Territory and Northern Territory the legislative threshold is even tighter with recovery for family members (not including spouses) being limited to those who were within sight or hearing of the incident.[54]

Issues not addressed by reform

Victim as defendant

[8.220] In *Jaensch v Coffey* (1984) 155 CLR 549 Deane J placed a limitation on the right to sue for mental harm, namely that it did not apply where the victim was negligently responsible for his or her own death or injury, and was therefore the defendant in the action. This has been followed and applied in *Klug v Motor Accidents Insurance Board* [1991] Aust Torts Reports 81-134. Yet, although there is a degree of incongruence in allowing one partner, for example, to sue another in respect of the emotional deprivation caused by that other's death or injury, there is no clear logic in denying an action, and the other members of the High Court did not mention this as a limitation. Nor was it referred to as a limit in *Bourhill v Young* [1943] AC 92, where the situation was precisely raised on the facts of the case, although the claim for damages was made by a casual spectator.

Psychological damage through damage to plaintiff's property

[8.225] In *Attia v British Gas plc* [1987] 3 WLR 1101,[55] the Court of Appeal in England allowed a claim for mental harm where the injury was caused by the plaintiff's witnessing of damage to her property, rather than through fear of injury to herself or another person. The court upheld that the plaintiff would establish a claim for shock suffered on seeing her house burnt down through the defendant's negligence if she could prove her shock to be reasonably foreseeable. However, the application of a straightforward foreseeability test and the exclusion of difficult "policy" factors (such as whether a shock claim should be allowed for damage to property), was possible only because the defendants were in breach of their duty of care to the plaintiff in setting fire to the house. The question at issue, therefore, was one of remoteness of damage to which foreseeability alone was relevant. The approach of the Court of Appeal seems unsatisfactory in not treating as separate issues the duty of care in relation to the house, and in relation to the mental harm. Its effect, however, is that reasonable foreseeability is likely to be the sole determinant of the right to claim damages for mental harm caused by damage to property, since claims for such harm arising from damage to another person's property are unlikely to be made, and if they are made, are likely to fail without reference to any policy factors raised by the claim.

---

[54] See *Civil Law (Wrongs) Act 2002* (ACT), s 36(1)(c): "another family member of A, if A was killed, injured or put in danger within the sight or hearing of the other family member"; and *Law Reform (Miscellaneous Provisions) Act 1956* (NT), s 25(1)(b): "another member of the family of the person so killed, injured or put in peril, where the person was killed, injured or put in peril within the sight or hearing of that other member of the family".

[55] *Campbelltown CC v Mackay* (1989) 15 NSWLR 501 also admits the possibility of a successful claim for mental harm arising from damage to property.

Omission to act

[8.230] In limited circumstances a duty of care to engage in positive conduct may arise: liability may therefore be based on an omission to act (nonfeasance). Whilst it may be troublesome to the legal conscience, the situations in which a duty to act have been imposed do not extend to the failure to go to the rescue of another person in peril when some sort of rescue attempt could have been easily made. The usual example is that of the onlooker who sees a child drowning in a shallow pond, in the absence of a relationship between the parties, the common law imposes no duty to rescue that child.

Figure 8.8: Misfeasance/nonfeasance

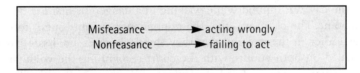

The notion of "omission" is not a simple one. The omission must be a "pure" omission. Omission to act in the course of positive conduct is not a pure omission and no difficulty arises over the imposition of a duty of care in relation to it. For example, a car driver may be held liable for causing damage through a failure to brake or give a signal. This is misfeasance on the car driver's part rather than nonfeasance (omission). The positive act required for misfeasance is the driving of the car, the "omission" being a wrongful performance of that act. On the other hand, positive conduct may in law amount to nonfeasance. For example, a failure to take any steps to avoid damage caused by a third party is nonfeasance; but the same applies to positive measures that fail to achieve the desired result. One very common example of this is nonfeasance in the exercise of statutory powers, which is considered in the next section.

Positive duties to act may be imposed where the defendant is in a pre-existing "protective" relationship with the plaintiff: examples being parent and child, educational authority or schoolteacher and pupil, employer and employee, occupier and visitor. (The duty of care existing in these "protective" relationships is examined further in Chapter 9.) The occupier is particularly affected. Where an occupier has created a situation in which alcohol is provided and they have identified the possibility of misbehaviour, a duty of care to protect all patrons arises. In *Club Italia (Geelong) Inc v Ritchie* (2001) 3 VR 447 the Victorian Court of Appeal found that the appellant club which had organised a ball at a licensed premises and employed insufficient security staff, failed to protect not only their patrons, but also two police officers who were savagely assaulted when they attempted to intervene in a brawl outside the venue. The key to the duty was the fact that the club ought to have realised that in the course of their business they were attracting potential trouble-makers to their premises and they ought to have taken steps to deal with the resulting danger of violent and other disorderly behaviour (at [35]). Similarly, in *Spedding v Nobles; Spedding v McNally* (2007) 69 NSWLR 100, the New South Wales Court of Appeal considered whether a hotel owed its patrons a duty of care to protect them from criminal assault by other patrons. It was determined that such a duty did exist but the court emphasised that the duty did not arise as a result of a special relationship between the patron and the hotel, but depended on the element of control exercised by the hotel over all patrons (at [50]). This is consistent with the High Court's position in *Modbury Triangle Shopping Centre Pty Ltd v Anzil* (2000) 205 CLR 254 in which there was no duty to protect customers from criminal assault in the carpark due to the lack of relationship between the shopping centre and the assailants and thus, lack of opportunity (or expectation) of control (for further consideration of the issue of control, refer [8.290]ff).

It is important to note that with an increasing emphasis being placed on personal responsibility and a shift away from the court's previous willingness to protect even those who failed to take care of themselves,[56] these decisions may not stand today. The recent High Court decision of *Cole v South Tweed Heads Rugby League Football Club Ltd* (2004) 217 CLR 469; [2004] HCA 29 is relevant in this context. The court considered the situation in which a plaintiff, who had been drinking at the respondent's premises for most of the day, was injured while walking in a dangerous manner down the road on the way home. The claim was that the respondent's servants ought to have refused to serve her earlier in the day and that they should have ensured safe passage home. Her claim failed on both counts, with the court recognising the voluntary nature of her behaviour (per Gleeson CJ at [3]) evidenced by the fact that she "systematically and deliberately drank herself into a state of intoxication" (per Callinan J at [131]). Her state of knowledge of the effect of alcohol was also recognised as a relevant factor (per Gummow and Hayne JJ at [73] and [78] and Callinan J at [112]). Previous recognition of a duty of care owed by owners of drinking establishments to patrons cannot, however, be conclusively disregarded on the basis of this decision, with Gummow and Hayne JJ (at [81]) declining to conclude whether or not a duty was owed and McHugh and Kirby JJ (in dissent) concluding that a duty of care did exist on the basis of occupier's liability.

Positive duties to act can be imposed by reason of the "status" of the defendant. Again the occupier is an example. *Goldman v Hargrave* [1967] 1 AC 64 held that an occupier owes a duty of care to persons outside the premises to deal with natural conditions arising on the land which threaten those persons. The defendant in that case was held liable for not extinguishing a fire which was caused by lightning striking his tree, when the fire spread to and damaged a neighbour's property. The duty here is not based on any pre-existing protective relationship with the neighbour, but by reason of the fact that the occupier is the only person capable of responding to the situation of danger. But the standard of care imposed on the occupier here is lower than the normal standard. In *Goldman* the danger could have been averted by the mere use of water, but if more than the trivial expense is involved and the means of the occupier are not easily able to accommodate this expense, the occupier's only duty may be to "invite the assistance of his neighbours" to solve the problem: cf *Leakey v National Trust* [1980] QB 485 (where, however, the occupier's means were more than adequate to remove the

---

[56]   Contrast the decision of *Nagle v Rottnest Island Authority* (1993) 177 CLR 423 where the respondent authority was found liable for injury sustained by a plaintiff who dived into a shallow rock pool, with the recent decisions of *Ballerini v Berrigan Shire Council* [2004] VSC 321 and *Wyong Shire Council v Vairy* [2004] Aust Torts Reports 81-754; [2004] NSWCA 247 where on the one hand liability was reduced by 80% and, on the other, no liability at all was recognised on the basis of plaintiffs who failed to care for their own safety. Vairy was appealed to the High Court, *Vairy v Wyong Shire Council* (2005) 223 CLR 422 and the appeal was dismissed on the basis that it was unreasonable to expect the placing of signs. Ballerini was also appealed, *Berrigan Shire Council v Ballerini* (2005) 13 VR 111; [2005] VSCA 159 and upheld – with the 30% contributory negligence affirmed. Special leave to appeal to High Court was denied.

danger). This duty along with the standard has now been enshrined in statute in some jurisdictions, as set out in Figure 8.9.

Figure 8.9: Occupiers' liability

Juris	Legislation	Provision
ACT	*Civil Law (Wrongs) Act 2002*	s 168
NSW	No mention	
NT	*Personal Injuries (Liabilities and Damages) Act 2003*	s 9 • Specifically excludes liability for any loss or injury suffered by those who are entering or have entered premises with the intent to commit an offence punishable by imprisonment. • For general occupiers' liability the common law stands.
Qld	No mention	
SA	*Civil Liability Act 1936*	Pt 4, ss 19-22
Tas	No mention	
Vic	*Wrongs Act 1958*	Pt IIA, ss 14A-14E
WA	*Occupier's Liability Act 1985*	s 5(1) and (2) • Limits liability for harm suffered as a result of risks willingly assumed or if the entrant is engaged in an offence punishable by imprisonment.

Reliance by the plaintiff on previous conduct by the defendant may give rise to a positive duty of care on the defendant's part to continue that conduct. A prime example is *Mercer v South Eastern Railway Co* [1922] 2 KB 549. In that case the defendants had a practice known to the plaintiff of locking the gates of a level-crossing on the approach of a train. On one occasion the gates were left open through the negligence of a railway employee and the plaintiff on entering the crossing was struck by a train. The defendants were held liable to the plaintiff for his injuries. It is arguable that *Mercer is* not a true case of omission – the defendants' conduct had caused the plaintiff to act to his own loss, a similar liability to that arising from a negligent misstatement. Reliance is also important in relation to the negligent exercise of statutory powers, at least in the case where nonfeasance in the exercise of those powers is alleged. A duty of care may arise in relation to this failure but, as will be seen when considering this liability, the notion of reliance is more extensive than that present in *Mercer*.

Duty owed when acting

[8.235] Where no antecedent duty of care to act exists, a person who acts is merely under a duty not to make things worse, not a duty to improve matters by, for example, averting a danger or preventing it from arising. In *Horsley v McLaren* [1972] SCR 441 the two plaintiffs were guests and passengers on the defendant's boat on a Canadian lake. The first plaintiff, Matthews, fell overboard without fault on the defendant's part. The defendant reversed the boat in his direction to attempt a rescue. The second plaintiff, Horsley, seeing the likely failure of the rescue dived in in an attempt to rescue the first plaintiff. Both plaintiffs were drowned. In the action of their estates against the defendant, the majority in the Canadian Supreme Court found that a duty of care to attempt a rescue existed towards the first plaintiff, as a passenger on the boat, but that the defendant had committed no breach of duty of care since his chosen method of rescue, although not the approved one, was in the emergency situation not negligent. The majority's decision on negligence made it unnecessary to consider the defendant's liability against Horsley, the second rescuer; although it was stated that liability could only be established if the defendant has created a new situation of peril that induced the second rescuer to act. It seems, therefore, that a mere failure to achieve a rescue, even though negligent, would not have rendered the defendant liable to Horsley. This is in accordance with the generally accepted principle of no liability for nonfeasance. However, Laskin J – who considered the defendant negligent in the method he adopted in order to attempt rescue – thought that a duty of care existed to both plaintiffs, and that there was liability to Horsley even though the negligent attempt had not made Matthews' position worse. This contravenes the nonfeasance principle, since there was clearly no duty of care owed to Horsley to rescue Matthews, and the duty of care owed to Matthews appears irrelevant.

The duty of care to the first plaintiff in *Horsley* was based on the antecedent relationship with the defendant as occupier of the boat. Where such a relationship is not present, there is no duty of care to attempt the rescue of persons in danger; nor is there any duty when rescuing except not to make the plaintiff's position worse. The latter could be achieved not only by creating a new danger but also, arguably, by deterring rescue attempts by other persons. The general position taken by the law here has been criticised on the ground that where a means of rescue is easily available to the defendant there should be a positive duty of care to go to the rescue.[57] Against this it is arguable that there may be such a variety of valid reasons for not acting that the imposition of the duty might acquire a dimension of arbitrariness. There is also the fact that if a duty of care exists to rescue, then a duty will also exist to take care to achieve a rescue once started; and granted the public-spirited nature of rescuers, this would create a feeling of injustice. Some alleviation of this could be provided by imposing a duty of care, but reducing the standard of care owed by the rescuer.

The suggestion of Lord Morris in *Hedley Byrne & Co v Heller* [1964] AC 465 at 495 – that a doctor who treats an unconscious accident victim is under a duty of care to improve the patient's condition if that is possible, based on the doctor's voluntary undertaking to use skill on the patient's behalf – is open to the fundamental objection that it is likely to deter rescue by medically skilled persons. As mentioned at [8.230], the lack of a positive duty to rescue someone has troubled the legal conscience; so too has the fact that the common law may find the rescuer liable if the rescue goes horribly wrong. Such an approach discourages the "good samaritan" who may stop and consider potential liability before attempting to help someone who is in trouble. The response to this has been the introduction of legislative protection for the good samaritan in some jurisdictions (see Figure 8.10), with the overarching requirement in most provisions being that the "samaritan" was acting in good faith.

---

[57]   Weinrib, "The Case for Duty to Rescue" (1980) 90 Yale LJ 247.

Figure 8.10: Protection of the good samaritan

Juris	Legislation	Provision
ACT	*Civil Law (Wrongs) Act 2002*	s 5
NSW	*Civil Liability Act 2002*	
NT	*Personal Injuries (Liabilities and Damages) Act 2003*	Pt 8, ss 55–58
Qld	No mention	
SA	*Civil Liability Act 1936*	s 8
Tas	No mention	
Vic	*Wrongs Act 1958*	Pt VIA, ss 31A–31D
WA	*Civil Liability Act 2003*	Pt 1D, ss 5AD–5AE

Statutory powers

[8.240] The question of liability for the negligent exercise of statutory powers may raise the omission/nonfeasance problem, although the fact that a statutory duty rather than a power is imposed on the defendant does not remove the case from the nonfeasance area – given that the issue is whether a common law duty of care to act should be recognised, rather than whether an action exists for breach of statutory duty. Where the issue is one of nonfeasance in relation to the statutory power, the High Court in *Sutherland SC v Heyman* (1985) 157 CLR 424 regarded the imposition of a duty of care, at least on the facts of that case, as turning on establishing some form of reliance by the plaintiff. On the other hand, the actual exercise of a statutory power could constitute misfeasance, and to this question the matter of reliance is irrelevant.

A special feature of the recognition of a duty of care in relation to statutory powers is the judicial acceptance that an action for negligence is inappropriate in relation to decisions by public bodies or officials of a planning or policy nature. The grounds for this is the difficulty of applying negligence principles to decisions requiring a discretionary balancing of conflicting interests. Thus, in *Commonwealth v Eland* [1992] Aust Torts Reports 81-157,[58] the court refused to impose a duty of care on the Commonwealth of Australia as regards its non-enactment of legislation to relieve the problem of alcoholism among Aborigines in Australia, on the ground of the high level of policy at which such a decision would need to be taken.

---

[58] See also *Skuse v Commonwealth* (1985) 62 ALR 108 – no duty of care to provide protection in a courtroom against threats of shooting in the court, which were carried out against the plaintiff barrister; cf *Unilan Holdings Pty Ltd v Kerin* (1993) 44 FCR 481 – not settled whether statements by government Minister as to future policy could create a duty of care on the Commonwealth.

Figure 8.11: Operation/policy

- Courts will not interfere in the pure policy decisions of statutory authorities.
- More likely to intervene in pure operational decisions (where the policy decisions are implemented).

On the other hand, where the decision-maker has moved out of the area of policy into the operational area of the statutory power, an action for negligence is possible. Mason J in *Heyman* (at 469) drew a distinction between policy decisions dictated by:

> *financial, economic, social or political factors, which should be subject to immunity from a negligence action, and discretionary decisions which were merely the product of administrative direction, expert or professional opinion, technical standards or general standards of reasonableness*

where no immunity would arise. Deane J, in the same case, thought it necessary to confer immunity as a matter of assumed legislative intent on policy-making decisions and on functions of a quasi-legislative character. He considered the powers and functions of a local government authority, in relation to the inspection of houses under construction in its area, to be of a routine administrative or "operational" character. It is clear also, as Lord Wilberforce pointed out in *Anns v London Borough of Merton* [1978] AC 728, that a broad distinction may be drawn between decision-making, where policy factors may play a large role, and implementation of decisions, where the role of the person implementing the decision is likely to be largely operational.

Statutory powers cover a vast complex of factual situations, not all of which are suitable for the imposition of a common law duty of care. English courts have in recent years consistently refused to impose duties of care in relation to the exercise of public powers for a variety of reasons, although the underlying reason appears to be an unwillingness to recognise private duties of care arising in relation to the exercise of public functions.[59] Australian courts, however, have proved more willing to impose duties of care in relation to statutory and other public powers. Apart from the policy/operational divide, the issue of whether a duty of care should exist depends on matters relevant to the issue of duty of care in general, such as the relationship between the parties, the nature of the defendant's conduct and the nature of the loss suffered. Overlaid on factors such as these in relation to statutory powers is the question of the purpose of the legislation. This has been recognised as a relevant factor,[60] but its determination is just as elusive a matter as determining the intent of the legislature for the purpose of the tort of breach of statutory duty, in that the legislative purpose or

---

[59]   *Calveley v Chief Constable* [1989] AC 1228 – no duty of care as regards the holding of a police disciplinary inquiry to the police involved; *Yuen Kun Yew v A-G of Hong Kong* [1988] AC 175 – no duty of care owed by Commissioner of Deposit-taking Companies to depositors in relation to the powers of refusal of registration or re-registration of those companies; *Davis v Radcliffe* [1990] 1 WLR 821 – no duty of care owed by Bank of England to commercial bank to exercise its powers of supervision to prevent imprudent investments by the commercial bank (followed in *Alinories Finance Ltd v A Young* [1989] 2 All ER 105).

[60]   *Egger v Gosford CC* (1989) 67 LGRA 304 – right of appeal under statutory scheme showed legislation intent not to allow a common law action; see also *Jones v Dept of Employment* [1989] QB 1.

intent is seldom clearly spelled out. In some cases the courts determine the issue of a duty of care of a body exercising statutory powers on ordinary principles of duty of care without reference to the fact that statutory powers were being exercised. Thus in *Glasheen v Waverley Corporation* [1990] Aust Torts Reports 81-016 the court held that the defendants, who, acting under statutory powers, had set up a flagged area on a beach that was patrolled by its safety inspectors, owed a duty of care to a surfboard rider who was hit and injured by a surfboard of another surfer who was not allowed in that stretch of water. The conclusion was not based on the reliance principles in *Heyman* but on the defendants' assumption of responsibility for the safety of swimmers and surfers in that area. In effect, the defendants' exercise of their statutory power of control put them into a position tantamount to that of an occupier.

Statutory powers and duties

[8.245] In considering negligence in the exercise of statutory powers, it should be pointed out that for the purpose of deciding whether an action for common law negligence is available, no difference exists between statutory power and statutory duty. Indeed, Mason J in *Sutherland SC v Heyman* (1985) 157 CLR 424 did not clearly classify the statutory powers he was considering as creating a duty, although the tenor of his judgment relates to statutory powers. The only difference between power and duty for the purpose of an action in tort is that an action for breach of statutory duty may be available in relation to the statutory duty. This depends entirely upon express or presumed parliamentary intention to create such a right of action, whereas that intention, although relevant in the case of the power, is only one of a number of relevant factors in considering whether a duty of care arises in the exercise of the power.

Sutherland SC v Heyman

[8.250] In *Sutherland SC v Heyman* (1985) 157 CLR 424 the High Court of Australia decided that a local government authority owed no duty of care in relation to the exercise of its statutory powers of inspection of the footings of a house under construction in its area, to the purchaser of the house. The purchaser suffered loss when cracking occurred in the house structure because of inadequate footings laid by the builder. In deciding this, the High Court decided not to follow the decision of the House of Lords in *Anns v London Borough of Merton* [1978] AC 728. However, the reasons given by the various members of the court contained considerable variation. Gibbs CJ and Wilson J accepted the decision in *Anns* but found that since no actual inspection by a Council inspector of the footings was shown to have taken place, and since a failure to inspect had not been shown to be outside the discretionary immunity conferred by the power, no duty of care had been established on the facts of the case. The "majority" in the case took a different view of the facts and on the basis of that view decided not to follow *Anns* as a matter of law. The finding of the majority judges was that either inspection had taken place, in which case it was clearly negligent, or no inspection had taken place at all, which was also negligent.

Mason J emphasised the importance of reliance by the plaintiff on the defendant in establishing a duty of care in the exercise of statutory powers. Such reliance could either be a specific reliance by the plaintiff on the defendant, which might require specific conduct on the defendant's part to engender it, and/or a detrimental reliance by the plaintiff (by acting to his own loss); although Mason J expressly stated that neither condition was necessary in all cases. Alternatively, the plaintiff could succeed by establishing a general public reliance on the exercise of the power by the defendant. On the facts of *Heyman* he found neither form of reliance existed. Mason J's judgment draws no clear distinction between nonfeasance in the exercise of a statutory power (of which *Heyman* was an example, since the actual damage was caused by the builder) and misfeasance in its exercise. Brennan J, however, held the Council not liable because nonfeasance in the exercise of a statutory power was in general not actionable – although it would be different if the Council had adopted a practice of "so exercising its powers that it induces a plaintiff reasonably to expect that it will exercise them in the future". Deane J based his judgment in part on the fact that no relationship of reliance existed between the defendant Council and the plaintiff; but also on the facts that the case was one of omission, the loss was purely economic in character, and there was nothing in the relevant statute or ordinances indicating a legislative intent to protect the buyer of the house against that sort of loss. The classification of the loss suffered in *Heyman* as purely economic in character is clearly correct, and is supported by the later decision of the High Court in *Bryan v Maloney* (1995) 182 CLR 609 (in the majority judgment in which Deane J participated). But in that case, the distinction between physical damage to the house and diminution in value of the house through the inadequacy of its footings was said to be "essentially technical". Perhaps, therefore, Deane J has changed his view on this. Certainly the loss suffered by a person compelled to live in a crumbling house seems to be pure economic loss of a special kind.

There are clearly some fundamental differences between the three majority judges in *Heyman*. One common factor to all three, however, is an acceptance of the fact that reliance may play a part in establishing the existence of a duty of care. Mason J's concept of general reliance is not referred to by the other members of the majority. Brennan J refers only to a specific reliance induced by the conduct of the Council. Deane J emphasises the total lack of any contact or relationship between the defendant Council and Heyman. All three judges mention that if the plaintiff had obtained a certificate of compliance with the requirements of the ordinances as regards footings prior to purchase, this form of reliance would have been sufficient to establish a duty of care on the Council's part. The High Court decision in *Crimmins v Stevedoring Industry Finance Committee* (1999) 200 CLR 1 confirmed that general reliance is no longer the determinant. Following on from its decision in *Perre v Apand Pty Ltd* (1999) 198 CLR 180, the High Court held that there needs to be known vulnerability.

Parramatta CC v Lutz

[8.255] *Parramatta CC v Lutz* (1988) 12 NSWLR 293 concerned the discretionary/operational distinction and also the issue of reliance. In that case, the plaintiff had complained to the defendant Council on frequent occasions of the existence of a vacant and derelict house next door to her own, and of its being frequented by vagrants with consequent dangers of various kinds including a fire risk to her own property. The Council eventually served a s 317B (*Local Government Act 1991* (NSW)) notice on the owners of the house giving them 60 days to repair or demolish it. On the expiration of the 60 days the Council itself had a power to enter the premises and demolish it. The 60 days expired without any action on the owners' part and the plaintiff continued to complain frequently to the Council. Some months later a fire was started by vagrants in the derelict property and spread to and destroyed the plaintiff's cottage. The Council was held liable in negligence to the plaintiff. Two members of the New South Wales

Court of Appeal, Kirby P and McHugh J, based their judgments on negligence in the exercise of the statutory powers by the Council, Mahoney J deciding the case on the basis of liability for negligent misstatement. Kirby P found that a duty of care arose to the plaintiff, based on her specific reliance on the Council and the Council's knowledge of this. On the policy/operational distinction, he found that although the Council had a discretion whether to exercise its power to demolish the vacant house on the expiration of 60 days, it had a duty to take the decision expeditiously and to inform the plaintiff promptly if a decision against demolition was taken so that "she could pursue any other causes of action open to her and her friends". There was, therefore, detrimental reliance on the Council by the plaintiff. McHugh JA, although agreeing with Kirby P on the result, differed on both aspects of the case as to his reasons. First, he found no indication that the plaintiff had relied on the Council's assurances to her detriment, since there was no effective action she could have taken herself to remedy the situation, and he appeared to think a detrimental reliance was necessary (differing from Mason J in *Sutherland SC v Heyman* (1985) 157 CLR 424). Nevertheless, the case fell within Mason J's concept of general reliance since there were a number of factors supporting the presence of a general public reliance; and in the case of general public reliance there was no need to show reliance on the exercise of the power by the plaintiff herself, nor any detrimental reliance. Thus, once the notice to repair or demolish had expired, the Council had no further discretion vested in it in the circumstances of this case. Its duty was to take action to secure immediate demolition of the vacant house. In other words, the Council had moved from the discretionary into the operational area. However this distinction is questionable when *Crimmins v Stevedoring Industry Finance Committee* (1999) 200 CLR 1 is examined.

In that case, the High Court detailed the guiding principles to determine whether or not a duty of care is owed by a statutory authority:

- Was it reasonably foreseeable that a failure to exercise a statutory power would result in an injury to the plaintiff? If no, then there is no duty.
- By reason of its statutory powers, did the authority have the power to protect the interests of a specific class of people (including the plaintiff) rather than the public at large? If no, then there is no duty.
- Was the plaintiff vulnerable in the sense that he could not protect his own interests? If no, then there is no duty.
- Did the defendant know, or ought the defendant to have known, of a risk of harm to a specific class of people of which the plaintiff was a member, if it did not exercise its powers? If no, then there is no duty.
- Would such a duty impose a liability with respect to the authority's *core policy making* or *quasi-legislative* functions? If yes, then there is no duty.
- Are there any other policy reasons, for example imposing a liability would be inconsistent with the statutory scheme, or imposing a liability for pure economic loss? If yes, then there is no duty.

This case broadens a statutory authority's potential liability to members of the public.

It should also be noted that where statutory bodies have attempted to protect themselves from liability in tort by inserting exclusions clauses in legislation, such clauses will be strictly interpreted so that they remove this protection: eg *Puntoriero v Water Administration MC* (1999) 199 CLR 575.

Other situations

[8.260] Since *Sutherland SC v Heyman* (1985) 157 CLR 424, a number of further duty of care situations have been recognised (or at least not denied) in relation to the exercise of statutory powers. Safety inspectors, for example of mines (*Gordon v James Hardie* [1982] Aust Torts Reports 80-133) or of meat-cutting equipment (*Hurling v Haines* [1987] Aust Torts Reports 80-103),[61] have been held to be capable of owing a duty of care to employees within those industries. A Council when approving a development application was held to owe a duty of care to a developer who purchased land in reliance on the approval and then discovered the land to be contaminated and unsuitable in that state for the development: *Curran v Greater Taree CC* [1992] Aust Torts Reports 81-152. The court found it to be immaterial that the loss suffered by the developer was purely economic. A local authority maintaining a rubbish dump under statutory authority was held to owe a duty of care to local residents in relation to a fire risk presented by the dump: *F S Evans Ply Ltd v Delaney* (1985) 58 LGRA 405. In *Northern Territory v Deutscher Klub* [1994] Aust Torts Reports 81-275 the court held the fire service liable for the negligence of its officers in failing to detect and remove the danger presented by a sawn-off gas pipe that later caused a gas explosion injuring the plaintiff boy. The court found there to have been no reliance placed by the plaintiff on the officers, but stated that *Heyman* did not hold that reliance was always necessary to establish a duty of care in relation to statutory powers. Reliance as a necessary condition of a duty of care was also not required in *Swan v South Australia* [1994] Aust Torts Reports 81-281. In that case a convicted paedophile who had been released by the Parole Board on parole committed assault and rape on the plaintiff. The court found there to be no duty of care as regards the decision to release on parole, nor in the setting of its conditions, since these were in the area of policy. Nor was there any duty on the part of the Board to exercise a general supervision of the acts of the parolee. On the other hand, a duty of care arose when the Board received specific information that the parolee was committing breaches of parole conditions by associating with minors. Significantly, as will all other areas of negligence, it is difficult to make generalisation that apply to all situations. This was emphasised by Hayne J in *Vairy v Wyong Shire Council* (2005) 223 CLR 422 when he noted that it would not be a useful exercise to define the "content of the Councils' duty of care more precisely". He described the duty owed by a statutory body to those who enter land (at [118]) as: "not being a duty to ensure that *no* harm befalls the entrant ... beyond that it is not possible to amplify the content of the duty without reference to particular facts and circumstances. In each case, the content of the duty will turn critically upon the particular facts and circumstances." Thus the starting point of the duty inquiry may differ from the general inquiry (that is, it begins with a consideration of the categorisation of the defendant as a statutory body) but the end point, which is close analysis of the facts, remains the same.

Police officers

[8.265] A number of recent decisions, English and Australian, have explored the duty of care owed by members of the police force to members of the public. Clearly there is no general immunity for the police from liability in negligence.[62] But *Hill v Chief Constable*

---

[61] See also *McAuley v Hamilton Island* [1987] Aust Torts Reports 80-119 – duty of care of Commonwealth as regards safety of airport runway.

[62] For example, in driving a police vehicle: *Gaynor v Allen* [1959] 2 QB 403; *Commonwealth v Winter* [1993] Aust Torts Reports 81-212.

of West Yorkshire Police [1989] AC 53 established that, for reasons of policy, the police owed no duty of care to members of the public to apprehend a particular criminal. This was followed in *Osman v Ferguson* [1993] 4 All ER 344, which observed that the *Hill* rule was not confined to policy as opposed to operational decisions by the police and that such a distinction as regards police work would be "utterly artificial and impossible to draw". A duty of care on the part of the police to protect individual members of the public against dangerous road conditions has also been denied in England, on the ground that the recognition of such a duty would conflict with the general duties of the police.[63] Another public policy limitation on police liability, established in *Hughes v National Union of Mineworkers* [1991] 1 ICR 669, related to "on the spot operational decisions taken by senior police officers in the course of attempts to control serious public disorder". The same case, however, expressly reserved the position where there was specifically identified antecedent negligence, and this was applied in the Victorian decision in *Zalewski v Turcarolo* [1994] Aust Torts Reports 81-280. In that case the police officer had been called out to deal with a case in which a paranoid schizophrenic had retired to a room with a gun, threatening to shoot himself. On opening the door and entering the room, the officer shot and injured the plaintiff in what was found to have been justifiable self-defence by the jury, on the ground that the plaintiff, immediately after the police entry, pointed the gun at the police officer. Nevertheless, the police officer was found to have been negligent and therefore liable to the plaintiff through the act of opening the door, which was an antecedent act of negligence and one not falling within any public policy limitation on police liability. The court left open the question whether the English position outlined in the above cases provided acceptable limits to police liability for negligence.

Highway authorities

[8.270] For many years those who were responsible for the maintenance of roads, such as councils and main roads departments, were not held to owe a duty to act positively in relation to road users. However, in *Brodie v Singleton SC* (2001) 206 CLR 512 the High Court abolished the highway immunity for non-feasance.

Discretionary immunity

[8.275] The question arises: is it for the plaintiff to prove that the defendant was acting within the operational, rather than the policy, area of the statutory power? Or is it for the defendant to prove that the relevant action or inaction was within the area of a policy decision? Although this would create an exception to the normal rule that the legal burden of proving all aspects of negligence rests on the plaintiff, it is suggested that it ought to be for the defendant to establish the nature of the decision taken, since the defendant is in a far better position than the plaintiff to know this. However, what authority there is places the burden of proof on the plaintiff. For example, Gibbs CJ and Wilson J held in *Sutherland SC v Heyman* (1985) 157 CLR 424 that the action failed because the plaintiff had failed to prove that non-inspection of the footings by the inspector had not occurred through the bona fide exercise of a policy decision not to inspect that particular house. Hodgson J in *Sasin v Commonwealth* (1984) 52

---

[63]   *Ancell v McDermott* [1993] 4 All ER 355; see also *Clough v Bussan* [1990] 1 All ER 431 – no duty of care to take action on failure of traffic lights; *Alexandrou v Oxford* [1993] 4 All ER 328 – no duty of care arising out of failure to respond to burglar alarm.

ALR 299 assumed that the choice of a particular safety-belt for use in planes by the Director-General of Aviation represented a policy choice and was therefore immune from an action of negligence – even though the actual basis of the decision to choose that particular belt was not before the court. If the decision had been based on safety factors alone, these would appear quite capable of being examined by the court in order to decide whether the decision was negligent.

Ultra vires decisions

[8.280] The policy immunity applies only to intra vires decisions. If the decision reached is ultra vires the decision-maker, the immunity disappears and an action for negligence becomes possible. Of course, negligence must be established – the mere invalidity of the decision is not enough to create liability. In *Dunlop v Woollahra MC* [1982] AC 159, the defendant Council was not held liable to the plaintiff for invalidly imposing on him a building line and for invalidly limiting the number of storeys the plaintiff was allowed to build, on the ground that in making these decisions the Council had taken the legal advice of a solicitor and was therefore not negligent. The plaintiff in *Dunlop* would, it seems, have had no difficulty in establishing a causal connection between the invalid decision and his loss, since he was complaining of having his money tied up while he fought the decision. However, where the substantive merits of the decision are in issue in the negligence action, the plaintiff may have difficulty in establishing causal connection between the decision and the loss suffered. This is because a discretion that is improperly exercised (for example, a decision that is invalidated by the taking into account of irrelevant factors) might be validly decided in the same way when based on the relevant factors. Furthermore, the court will normally refuse to speculate on what the proper decision should be, since that would involve the court itself exercising the discretion. These difficulties disappear where the decision is regarded as being in the operational area, since here only one decision is possible. A clear example of this is McHugh J's determination that the Council in *Parramatta CC v Lutz* (1988) 12 NSWLR 293 had no further discretion to exercise after the expiration of the 60-day notice period in that case. Another example is the decision of the New Zealand Court of Appeal in *Takaro Properties Ltd v Rowling* [1986] 1 NZLR 22. The court there held that once the irrelevant factor taken into account by the Minister (that land owned by Takaro should revert to New Zealand control) was excluded from the decision, consent to a share issue to a Japanese company could not validly have been refused by him on any other ground.

Injury or damage caused by third party

Negligence of third party

[8.285] A duty of care may, in certain circumstances, arise to anticipate and guard against negligence by third parties causing injury or damage to the plaintiff. The essence of a duty to protect an individual from the actions of a third party is often found in either a pre-existing relationship or a situation of control. A common situation in which such a duty has been found is where the behaviour of children was the responsibility of a defendant. *Haynes v Harwood* [1934] 1 KB 146 provides an example of a duty to take care to avoid the mischievous actions of children.[64] Another example is *Carmarthenshire County C v Lewis* [1955] AC 549, in which the defendant school authority was held liable for taking insufficient care to prevent very young children from escaping from the school on to the public highway. A gate was incorrectly secured and this enabled small children to leave the school premises and run onto the road. The plaintiff's husband, who was driving a truck, swerved to miss them and was killed in the resulting accident. A duty of care may also arise in regard to the acts of older children. In *Smith v Leurs* (1945) 70 CLR 256,[65] the court held that parents who had entrusted their 13-year-old son with a shanghai owed a duty of care to other persons as regards the son's use of the weapon based on their special relationship of control over the boy. (The standard of care is, however, set quite low with the court determining that their seeking of assurances from him that the weapon would not be used outside the house meant that they were not in breach of duty to a person injured by the son's use of the shanghai.)

Deliberate act by third party

[8.290] Whether a duty of care is owed to a plaintiff in respect of injury or damage deliberately inflicted by a third party is a question of considerable legal difficulty. In *Home Office v Dorset Yacht Co Ltd* [1970] AC 1004, the defendant's employees had seven young offenders (Borstal boys) under their care and supervision whilst they were doing some work on an island. During the night the boys escaped. For the purposes of the judgment, allowing the boys to escape was assumed to be negligent. The plaintiff's yacht was moored offshore and the boys entered and damaged the yacht. The House of Lords held by a 4:1 majority that on proof of these facts a duty of care to the plaintiffs would arise. The judgments contained different opinions as to the nature of the duty in these circumstances.

Lord Reid based his judgment on the finding that in these circumstances the damage to the boat was "very likely" to happen. Lords Morris and Pearson thought the crucial element in the recognition of a duty was the controlling relationship between the defendant and the prisoners. Lord Diplock recognised a duty of care based on the reasonable foreseeability of the damage caused on escape, but limited the duty as a matter of law to damage in the vicinity of the prison immediately after escape. For reasons of policy, no duty of care existed as regards further damage inflicted by the escapees while they remained at large.

A similar question was recently before the Court of Appeal of the Supreme Court of New South Wales in the case of *New South Wales v Godfrey* [2004] Aust Torts Reports 81-741; [2004] NSWCA 113. The facts of the case were that Barry Hoole escaped from Bathurst Gaol at the end of July 1990 and in early October he committed an armed robbery at a newsagency in Western Sydney (located near his parents' home). During the robbery he pointed a shotgun at the face of the first respondent (Mrs

---

[64]   In this case the defendant's employee negligently left unattended a two-horse van in the public highway. A schoolboy threw a stone at the horses, causing them to bolt. The plaintiff, a police constable on duty at the time, in order to prevent injury to a woman and some children standing in the path of the horses, seized the offside horse and brought the van to a stop, but was injured when one of the horses fell on him. The Court of Appeal held the defendant liable to the plaintiff in negligence. The act of the child in throwing the stone did not interrupt causation since it was the very risk the employee should have anticipated.

[65]   See also *Hogan v Gill* [1992] Aust Torts Reports 81-182; *Pask v Owen* [1987] 2 Qd R 421; *Curmi v McLennan* [1994] 1 VR 513.

Godfrey) and threatened to shoot her if anyone moved. At that time Mrs Godfrey was an employee at the newsagency and was 23 weeks pregnant. She subsequently experienced stomach cramps and in the days following gave birth to the other respondent (Andrew Godfrey). Mrs Godfrey suffered severe anxiety and was unable to look at her son for a number of days after his birth. In addition, Andrew Godfrey suffered many health and developmental problems associated with premature birth.

The basis of the claim was that the State of New South Wales, through the Department of Correctional Services, had failed to secure Mr Hoole, and was liable for the subsequent injuries suffered by the plaintiffs as a result of the armed robbery. Two fundamental questions were identified: first, whether there was in fact a duty of care owed to the plaintiffs; and second, the scope of that duty. The question of breach of duty was resolved as the defendant had, for the purposes of the proceedings, acknowledged negligence in allowing Mr Hoole to escape. At first instance a duty of care was recognised and liability established. This decision was overturned on appeal on the basis that no authority has ever gone so far as to impose such an onerous duty (per Spigelman CJ at [20]) and that once the prisoner had escaped and travelled such a significant distance over a period of time, the control of the prison authority no longer existed: per Spigelman CJ at [48]. Also of relevance was the indeterminate nature of the scope of liability, which rendered the imposition of duty in these circumstances impractical and too onerous: per Spigelman CJ at [55].

Also of relevance in this context is the High Court decision of *Modbury Triangle Centre Ltd v Anzil* (2000) 205 CLR 254, which concerned an attack in a shopping centre carpark. The appellant in this instance owned the shopping centre and leased shops to various tenants. One of the tenants ran a video shop which closed at 10.00 pm each night. The carpark lights were turned off at 10.00 pm and there was no illumination of the carpark after that time. An employee of the video shop was attacked while walking to his car after the shop closed and the lights were turned off. The basis of the claim was that the appellant owed a duty of care to protect tenants from injury and that they failed in this duty by turning off the lights. In allowing the appeal, the court identified situations in which a duty to protect others from the actions of third parties may rely: generally these involve a relationship of control or perhaps reliance (per Gleeson CJ at 264); alternatively (or additionally) they involve situations where there is a special vulnerability or assumption of responsibility: per Gaudron J at 270. In this instance, the inability to either foresee or control the criminal activities of parties who were strangers to both the appellant and respondent meant that a duty to protect another from these activities could not be found.

Another possible situation in which a duty of care may arise in relation to the infliction of deliberate damage or injury is where a protective relationship exists between defendant and plaintiff. Occupiers of drinking establishments have been found to owe a duty of care to protect their patrons against acts of drunken aggression by other patrons: *Chordas v Bryant* (1988) 92 FLR 401; *Wormald v Robertson* [1992] Aust Torts Reports 81-180; and *Spedding v Nobles; Spedding v McNally* (2007) 69 NSWLR 100 (discussed above at [8.230]). The keeper of a prison owes prisoners a duty of care to protect them from violent acts of other prisoners: *L v Commonwealth* (1976) 10 ALR 269; *Nada v Knight* [1990] Aust Torts Reports 81-032; *New South Wales v Bujdoso* (2005) 227 CLR 1. A restaurateur was found to have a duty of care to an employee to so arrange the task of depositing the restaurant's takings with the bank as to avoid the risk of the employee being mugged: *Chomentowski v Red Garter Restaurant* (1970)

92 WN(NSW) 1070. A driver's duty of care towards a passenger, while driving in the highlands of Papua New Guinea, was held to include a duty not to injure a native, because of the risk of instant retribution: *Papua New Guinea v Moini* [1978] PNGLR 184. A relationship of reliance between defendant and plaintiff may also engender a duty of care to prevent a deliberate act of a third party. In *Stanshie v Troman* [1948] 2 KB 48 it was held that a contractor, who had been left alone in the plaintiff's house with the understanding that he would lock the door on leaving the house, was held liable for the theft of the plaintiff's jewellery that occurred when he left without locking the door. The risk of theft was small, but it was the very thing the contractor was relied on to prevent. On the other hand, no duty of care has been imposed on occupiers or employers to safeguard the property of their visitors or employees against theft during the period of the visit or working hours: eg *Pert v Camden LBC* [1984] QB 342.

Where there is neither a controlling relationship between the defendant and third party, nor a protective relationship between the defendant and plaintiff, a duty of care in relation to deliberate acts of the third party is more difficult to establish. For example, the trend of authority was to deny any duty of care on the part of an occupier to take care to render the property safe from entry by vandals, thereby avoiding the risk of damage to a neighbouring property. Yet in *Smith v Littlewoods Ltd* [1987] AC 241, the majority in the House of Lords accepted that in these circumstances an occupier might owe a duty of care to an adjoining owner. In *Smith* the defendants owned a cinema building that had been left vacant for a period of time. There was evidence that vandals had forced entry into the building and caused damage there, but it was found as a fact that this was not known to the defendants. Finally, vandals obtained entry and caused a fire in the building that spread and damaged the plaintiff's property. The defendants were held to owe the plaintiff no duty of care in respect of this damage. Lord Mackay's judgment admitted the possibility of a duty of care in these circumstances, but the test of reasonable foreseeability necessary to establish such a duty required likelihood of the third party's entry, which on the facts known to the defendant in this case did not exist. The other members of the House, apart from Lord Goff, also accepted the possibility of a duty of care arising in this sort of situation, while agreeing that on the facts it did not. Lord Goff was in favour of applying the basic principle of no liability for nonfeasance in this situation, although in two exceptional circumstances a duty of care would arise: where the occupier himself had created or allowed to arise a source of danger on the land in circumstances where entry and activation of the danger by a third party was foreseeable; or where the occupier knew or ought to have known of the creation of a danger by a third party on the land.

Whichever formulation is followed, the likelihood of an occupier actually being held liable to a neighbour is remote. Even if the likelihood of entry is satisfied, the standard of reasonable care required of the occupier to discharge the duty will inevitably be a low one. It will normally be sufficient – even in the case of a vacant house, where the likelihood of entry is higher – to keep the house locked up and in proper repair. *Parramatta CC v Lutz* (1988) 12 NSWLR 283 applied the test of reasonable foreseeability rather than likelihood of entry by vandals in determining the duty of care owed by the Council; but there was abundant evidence known to the Council of likely entry by vandals.

Legal advocate

[8.295] As a matter of public policy, the barrister or solicitor is immune from liability for negligence in relation to the conduct of the case in court, or in relation to such pre-trial matters as are:

> *so intimately connected with the conduct of the case in court that it can be fairly said to be a preliminary decision affecting the way the case is conducted when it comes to a hearing.*[66]

The "advocate's" immunity applies to both barristers and solicitors.

The leading High Court case, in which the policy reasons for the immunity were outlined, is *Giannarelli v Wraith* (1988) 165 CLR 543. The main reasons given by the High Court were:

- the existence of a duty to the court owed by the advocate that may conflict with the interests of the client;
- the need to ensure freedom of speech on the advocate's part in the same way as this is enjoyed by other participants in the legal process such as judges, jurors and witnesses;
- the possible waste of court time by an advocate presenting unnecessary arguments to the court through fear of a negligence action by the client; and
- the undesirability of allowing collateral challenge to legal decisions in other proceedings where a different result may be reached on different evidence, creating a lack of confidence in the legal process.

The first two reasons of policy seem to run together. Clearly an advocate could not be held negligent when performing the duty to the court by, for example, presenting evidence or accepting a legal point contrary to the client's interest. The fact that the duty to the court and the client's interest may be in conflict does not seem to be sufficient reason for altogether ruling out liability for court work. The need to confer the same immunity on the advocate as is possessed by other participants in the legal process is also not obvious – those other participants are performing a purely public function in the administration of justice whereas the advocate has a private interest to protect. The argument about the waste of a court's time by the presentation of unnecessary argument seems fanciful, since the court may stop the advocate pursuing a particular point. The last argument has force. The later civil proceedings will not undo the earlier decision if a contrary conclusion is reached. The later court has the task (which in some cases will be impossible) not of deciding the case itself but of deciding how the earlier court would have decided the case had the advocate properly performed the task of advocacy.[67] On the other hand, there undoubtedly exist cases where that task presents no real difficulty. One method of outflanking the last argument of policy was accepted in *Laird v Mossenson* [1990] Aust Torts Reports 81-058. The court there held that where the plaintiff's claim accepted the correctness of the first decision but claimed damages for loss of the chance of its being decided differently through the negligence of the advocate, this did not amount to a collateral attack on the first decision. This is because the later court was not bound to reach a conclusion as to whether the case was rightly decided, but merely as to the chance that it would have been decided differently. That

---

[66] *Bees v Sinclair* [1974] 1 NZLR 180 at 187.

[67] *Somosundaram v M Julius Melchior* [1989] 1 All ER 129, an English decision, held that a collateral challenge by civil action to another court's decision will generally be struck out as an abuse of court process.

again may present a difficult question for the court. The decision also accepts that damages may be claimed for the loss of a chance to succeed in litigation; even of a less than 50% chance. But this is regarded as acceptable in an action in contract against a solicitor, where the breach is established without the need to show a probability of loss arising from the breach (as would be the case in a tort action for negligence), and the basis of the contract is to provide the plaintiff with the chance of succeeding.[68]

In *Boland v Yates Property Corp Pty Ltd* (1999) 167 ALR 575, the High Court had another opportunity to consider whether the immunity should continue. In that case, Yates sued a firm of solicitors and a barrister whom he had engaged to act in a compensation claim before the Land and Environment Court of New South Wales. The High Court held that there was no negligence on the part of the legal team, so the question of immunity was not resolved. Kirby J suggests that the court may be amenable to abolishing this immunity in the future. Since that case, the House of Lords in *Arthur JS Hall v Simons* [2000] 3 All ER 673, decided to end barristers' immunity in civil and criminal proceedings.

Child and parent at pre-natal stage

[8.300] It is accepted law that a duty of care may be owed to a child while it is in the foetus stage awaiting birth: *Watt v Rama* [1972] VR 353; *Lynch v Lynch* [1991] Aust Torts Reports 81-142. This raises no theoretical difficulty of principle over whether the foetus has sufficient legal personality to qualify as a plaintiff in a tort action. Clearly a duty of care may be owed to persons unborn at the time of the negligent act but who suffer damage through the continuing consequences of that act. There is no difference in principle where the damage is sustained immediately by the foetus. The actual damage necessary to sustain an action for negligence occurs when the child is born alive suffering from the defect caused by the injury to the foetus. This was the rationale adopted by the Victorian Court in *Watt* for allowing an action for negligence by the plaintiff in relation to an injury suffered prior to birth. The consequence of this approach is that no action is available unless there is a live birth; no issue of the legal personality of a stillbirth arises. Successful actions have been brought by plaintiffs against a person who caused an accident to the mother during pregnancy (*Watt*; *Lynch*) and against a doctor who failed to diagnose syphilis in the plaintiff's mother with the consequence the plaintiff was born infected: *X v Pal* (1991) 23 NSWLR 26. In *Lynch* a successful claim was brought against the mother herself for causing a road accident through negligent driving, thereby causing injury to her yet-to-be-born child. It is one thing to hold the parent liable for negligent driving in these circumstances – effectively the defendant is an insurance company, and the duty situation is clear. It is, however, doubtful whether a duty of care would be recognised in relation to the "parental lifestyle" exposure of the unborn child to danger, such as excess smoking, alcohol, drugs or dietary indiscretion. The claim of the child based on foetal injury must be distinguished from that for unwanted birth (a "wrongful birth" claim). Here the claim, generally against a medical practitioner, is not made for the suffering of injury, but for not taking steps to terminate the pregnancy, knowing of the likelihood of the child being born with defects. However the merits of the claim may be assessed, the law has refused to allow it on the basis that it is impossible to make an assessment by

---

[68] Following *Kitchen v Royal Air Force Association* [1958] 1 WLR 563; see also *Scott v Echegaray* [1991] Aust Torts Reports 81-120.

way of damage based on the difference between an (allegedly) miserable life and no life at all: *McKay v Essex Area Health Authority* [1982] QB 1166; *Bannerman v Mills* [1991] Aust Torts Reports 81-079; *Harriton v Stephens* (2006) 226 CLR 52.[69]

No doubt the mother of a child born with birth deformities through the defendant's negligence would have a claim for nervous shock suffered as a result of this. In cases where actionable nervous shock has been suffered by a mother, the courts have been ready to compensate for a miscarriage or the birth of a child with deformities caused by that shock.[70] There seems no reason to doubt that compensation would be afforded in the converse case, that is where a miscarriage or birth of a deformed child caused shock, even in those cases where there was no trauma associated with the circumstances giving rise to the miscarriage or deformity.

The parent's claim in respect of "wrongful life" differs from that of the child. An action in contract or tort is available to parents of a child born through the negligence of a medical practitioner in failing in his or her duty to the parents to prevent the child having being conceived. The parental remedy in this situation is now established by a number of decisions.[71] However the courts have limited damages to the financial costs of bringing up the child, no damages being awarded in respect of the time and trouble involved in rearing the child, still less for emotional disturbance through having the child, the latter being outweighed by the joy of being parents to a healthy child. This issue was resolved when the High Court delivered its judgment in *Cattanach v Melchior* (2003) 215 CLR 1. The question in this case was whether damages in failed sterilisation cases should include the costs of child rearing, or whether such costs constitute an allowable category of damages for economic loss. In this instance, the court determined that such damages should extend to the cost of child rearing until the age of 18. There was some strong reaction to this decision, largely centred around the apparent commodification of human life, with three jurisdictions introducing legislative amendment to ensure limitation of damages in such situations.[72]

The failure by a mother to seek an abortion in these circumstances is not an unreasonable failure to mitigate damage.[73] However, the ordinary principles of remoteness of damage have denied a remedy in a case where the claim was for rearing expenses; the purpose of a failed sterilisation was to avoid the danger of childbirth

---

[69] Fleming, *Law of Torts* (1992), p 169 argues against this on the ground that the real reason is that it is: "repugnant to our cultural ethos to complain about the circumstances of one's conception. Otherwise one might envisage even claims by the child against its own parents for causing the birth under some prejudice, like illegitimacy, poverty or a physical imperfection". The cases suggested seem fairly easily answered on the basis that the law would not impose a duty of care. The courts' rationale seems entirely correct. How does one measure the gap in financial terms between existence and non-existence? Or indeed, how does one answer such a question in philosophical terms? It is perhaps as the High Court has said, best left to philosophers and theologians as they are "as persons better schooled than courts in apprehending the ideas of non-being, nothingness and the afterlife": *Harriton v Stephens* (2006) 226 CLR 52 at [252] per Callinan J.

[70] *Stevenson v Basham* [1992] NZLR 225; *Bourhill v Young* [1943] AC 92 – miscarriage by mother; *Dulieu v White* [1901] 2 KB 669 – shock causing birth of deformed child.

[71] *Udale v Bloomsbury Area Health Authority* [1983] 1 WLR 1098; *Emeh v Kensington Area Health Authority* [1985] QB 1012; *Thake v Maurice* [1986] QB 644.

[72] *Civil Liability Act 2002* (NSW), s 71 (limitation of the award of damages for the birth of a child) which prohibits the award of damages for costs associated with the rearing or maintaining of the child, including loss of earning capacity; and *Civil Liability Act 2003* (Qld), ss 49A and 49B (as per the New South Wales legislation this includes a prohibition on recovery of damages for child rearing costs and covers failed sterilisation procedures as well as failed contraceptive procedure or contraceptive advice); similarly *Civil Liability Act 1936* (SA), s 67 (specifically excludes recovery for the ordinary costs of bringing up a child, conceived as a result of failed sterilisation procedures, contraceptive procedures etc).

[73] *Stevenson v Basham* [1992] NZLR 225; *Bourhill v Young* [1943] AC 92; *Dulieu v White* [1901] 2 KB 669.

to the mother; or to obviate the risk of a disabled child, although the child was born healthy: *Harthe v McKelway* 707 F 2d 1544 (1983).[74]

Guide to Problem Solving

NEGLIGENCE

Do the facts fit into one of the established categories?

Otherwise:

1. **DUTY OF CARE (Chapters 8 and 9)** – The neighbour principle (Is there a duty owed to the person who has been injured?)

   Reasonable foreseeability
   * Would the reasonable person in the defendant's position have foreseen that there was a real risk that carelessness on his or her part could cause loss/harm to PEOPLE in the plaintiff's position?
   * What CLASS OF PEOPLE might possibly be put at some risk of injury in some way if the defendant failed in some way to take reasonable care?
   * Is the plaintiff one of those people?

   Vulnerability
   Was there a vulnerable relationship (position of reliance)?
   * Was the defendant in such a position of power (through resources, knowledge, legal duty or right) AND KNEW this?
   * Was the plaintiff in a position of powerlessness such that the defendant could be said to be responsible for protecting the plaintiff's vulnerability?

   Policy
   Can operate to exclude liability.
   "Policy" considerations can include value judgments as to fairness and consequentialist or utilitarian arguments. Also considerations of whether a duty would lead to indeterminate liability; and the restraining of legitimate business activities (concerns about social and economic ramifications).

2. **BREACH OF DUTY (Chapter 10)**

   Standard of care
   * What standard of care is owed? (Question of law)
   * The standard of care owed by the reasonable person in the circumstances.
   * What would the reasonable person do in the defendant's position?

   Failure to meet standard (breach of duty)
   * Did the defendant's actions or omissions breach that standard? (Question of fact)
   * Was the RISK of injury to the plaintiff REASONABLY FORESEEABLE?
   * Degree of risk (how foreseeable was the RISK of harm to the plaintiff?)
   * Gravity of harm.
   * Probability.

   IF SO,
   Was the RESPONSE of the defendant to this risk REASONABLE?
   Consider:
   * Burden of precautions.

---

[74] See further Fleming, *Law of Torts* (1992) p 170.

* Utility or justifiability of defendant's activity (emergency).
* Any relevant professional, customary or statutory standards.

Res ipsa loquitur

An evidentiary rule that might help when there is no other explanation for the accident.

3. **DAMAGE**

(Must be actual damage)

Recognisable categories

* Physical
* Economic
* Psychological

4. **CAUSATION (Chapter 11)**

Factual: Is there a relationship between the defendant's breach and the plaintiff's injury?

* Would the damage have happened "but for" the defendant's actions (if he/she had not done what he/she did)?
* Common sense: all things considered, was the negligent breach a materially contributing factor OR did it materially increase the risk of this kind of harm?

Novus actus interveniens

A new intervening act by the plaintiff or a third party which comes after the defendant's act which may break the chain of causation.

(Novus actus and remoteness are usually raised by the defendant)

Legal: REMOTENESS

* Reasonable foreseeability: could the defendant have reasonably foreseen that kind of LOSS?

5. **DEFENCES (Chapter 12)**

(For the defendant to prove on the balance of probabilities)

Contributory negligence

* Any failure on the part of the plaintiff to take care for his/her own care which contributed to either the event of damage occurring, or the level of damage suffered. It is not a complete defence. If it is proved, then the damages are apportioned according to the level of comparative negligence.
    - Was the plaintiff acting as a reasonable person and with reasonable care? (Judged against the standard of reasonable care.)
    - Did the plaintiff contributorily cause his/her damage?

Volenti non fit injuria

Voluntary assumption of risk (total defence)

* Did the plaintiff perceive the existence of danger?
* Did the plaintiff fully appreciate the danger?
* Did the plaintiff voluntarily accept the risk?

Illegality

6. **DAMAGES**

Award of damages $$$$

NEGLIGENT STATEMENT

DUTY OF CARE

Reasonable foreseeability

Proximity

* Physical: How close in time were the words to the plaintiff's reliance on them?
* Circumstantial (Trust and reliance) [Control]

–Statement must relate to SERIOUS MATTER

–Person making the statement must realise or ought to realise his/her ADVICE is being RELIED ON (Person ASSUMES RESPONSIBILITY) [Vulnerability]

–Whether it is REASONABLE in the circumstances that the other PARTY RELIED.

* Causal: How direct is the plaintiff's loss to the defendant's words? [Did some other information negate his/her words?]

England   special skill needed

Australia   assumption of responsibility (no need for special skill)

Policy

* Balancing public interest issues

Other factors for consideration

Financial interest by the defendant? Disclaimer (is it effective?); Special skill/expertise; Setting/manner of advice; Defendant induced the plaintiff; Did the plaintiff have an alternative source of information? Request for information.

MENTAL HARM

DUTY OF CARE

Reasonable foreseeability – relevant considerations:

* Of psychological harm (normal plaintiff)
* Caused by a SHOCK (stressor/series of events)
* Resulting in recognisable illness

Proximity

* Relational – sufficiently close relationship of love or dependence with the physically injured victim; or
* Geographical/temporal – plaintiff must at least have personally witnessed the accident or its immediate aftermath (important to remember the variation in relevant legislative provisions).

Practice Questions

Revision Questions

8.1 Plaintiffs are now being awarded damages for pure economic loss. What is "pure economic loss"?

8.2 Mental harm (previously known as nervous shock) has a somewhat chequered past, with the courts initially being reluctant to impose liability for pure "nervous shock". The situation has changed over time and while primary victims of accidents who suffer psychological harm can obtain compensation, the situation for secondary victims is much more difficult. Who are "secondary" victims (include in your answer the definition from your relevant statute)?

8.3 What is a statutory authority?

Problem Questions

8.1 The 2000 Sydney Olympic Games produced some unexpected heroes. In particular, Eric from Equatorial Guinea rose to fame because of his extraordinary swim. It was not his speed that impressed, but his sheer determination when it was obvious that he was not particularly adept. Because of Eric's efforts he was given a sum of $50,000 by Speedo at a celebratory function after the closing ceremony of the Games. The money was a gift. Eric did not have to do anything for the money but when he received it he expressed the wish to use the money over the next four years to allow him to pursue his swimming seriously. He wanted the money to be able to provide his accommodation and food so that he could do some serious training.

During the function, George Pinch, an accounting lecturer who was also an athlete, approached Eric and commented that he had heard Eric's remarks and said that he could possibly help him. It was noticeable that George Pinch had consumed quite a few cocktails by now, but nevertheless Eric was keen to hear what he had to say. George introduced himself as a well-respected academic who had published extensively on insider trading issues in corporations. He said that he would have no trouble at all advising Eric on what he could do with his $50,000.

Eric reiterated his concern that the money would need to support him over the next four years so that he could train. George advised that he had received, only today, a prospectus for a new company which he believed would be the answer for Eric. He suggested that Eric buy the shares in the new company and reap the benefits. Eric said that he knew nothing about shares but that he also knew that to just put the money in a bank would not give him the return he needed for his purposes. George said "Trust me mate – I am an expert but give me a call tomorrow and I will give you more accurate details". The next day Eric decided to follow George's advice and invested in the shares. The broker questioned the new company saying that he had not heard much about it. Eric said that he had been given some very reliable information and that he wished to make the purchase.

Secure in the knowledge that his financial worries were over, Eric decided to have the next day off and go to Bondi Beach. He really felt that he needed to have some fun after working so hard in his preparation for the Olympics. He decided to have a go on a jet ski. It was a very windy day causing the waves to be very choppy and so the participants were told to maintain a tight grip on their handles to keep control of their skis. They were also told to stay within a certain area which was marked by buoys. Eric was quite careful but noticed that Dennis, one of the riders, was a daredevil who seemed to enjoy terrorising the other riders. While rushing past Eric, Dennis called out to him "Watch this!" With that Dennis tried to splash John, a 12-year-old boy, but went too close and rammed the boy's leg. The fright and the pain made John loosen his grip on the handles and he strayed beyond the buoys into a group of swimmers that had been carried out of the swimming area by the rip. Sam, one of the swimmers, was injured by the jet ski. Both Sam and John were seriously injured and rushed to hospital. Eric acted very quickly and was instrumental in getting the unconscious Sam to the beach. He also tried to comfort John who was very distressed at running into Sam. When the ambulances finally arrived, the officers decided to take Eric to the hospital as well as it was obvious that he was suffering from shock. He was later diagnosed with post-traumatic stress. A couple of days later, Eric was discharged from the hospital but on the way out of the hospital he saw the headlines in the

Sydney Herald which reported that the new company in which he had invested was now going through bankruptcy proceedings.

(a) Under Australian law, advise Eric of his chances of pursuing a negligence claim against George.

(b) Advise John, the 12-year-old boy, of his chances of pursuing a negligence claim against Dennis.

(c) Advise Sam, the swimmer, of his chances of pursuing a negligence claim against Dennis.

(d) Advise Eric of his chances of pursuing a claim for nervous shock against Dennis.

8.2 Mean So & So is a large retail firm trading in all States of Australia. It employs hundreds of people. In January of this year, it contracted with Wheal Fire Emm, efficiency consultants, to examine the whole of its establishment with a view to streamlining its operations. Rupert, the well-respected purchasing manager of the Queensland arm of the business, aged 60 years, has been with the retail firm for 13 years.

On completion of the report, Oswald, the chief consultant of Wheal Fire Emm, recommended to the owners a number of changes. In particular, he recommended to Mean So & So that all the State purchasing managers should be offered redundancy packages and that a National Manager should be given the overall responsibility for purchasing. The package included pro-rata long service leave. In other words, even though someone like Rupert ordinarily would not be eligible to draw the whole amount of long service leave of 15 weeks' pay because he had not worked for 15 years with the company, the package would make it possible for him to draw a sum equivalent to 13 weeks' pay as long service leave. Mr Mean indicated to Oswald that he was happy with the proposals.

Since Oswald is a personal friend of Rupert, he determined to make it his business to talk to Rupert at a party they were both attending on the following weekend, to forewarn him of the situation. On that occasion, while Oswald and Rupert were enjoying a quiet drink by the pool, Oswald broached the subject with Rupert. He told Rupert that he knew that Mean So & So would soon be offering a redundancy package to him, drawing his attention to the fact that the package would include pro-rata long service leave.

Rupert questioned the inclusion of the pro-rata leave since he had not heard of this possibility before. Oswald assured him that Mr Mean was in favour of the recommendation and that the pro-rata long service leave was a part of the redundancy package being offered to all the State purchasing managers.

Rupert was thrilled with this news and immediately told Oswald that now he would be able to visit his daughter in New York for an extended time. He also told Oswald that he would be making plans immediately to finish at the time being suggested – in four weeks. Oswald had heard Rupert's ramblings about wishing to visit his daughter many times, and so he was only partly listening to these plans.

The following Monday, Mr Mean mentioned the redundancy package to Rupert. Rupert enthusiastically agreed to the proposal and said that he would leave at the suggested date in four weeks' time, even though he had not seen any documents. The next four weeks passed very quickly and during that time

Rupert signed a lease to rent his house for 12 months and he purchased his ticket to New York. His final day at work came and while Rupert saw it as the beginning of a new life, he was shocked and bitterly disappointed when he was presented with his final cheque from Mr Mean and the documentation on the package. The cheque did not include the expected amount for the pro-rata long service leave, and there was no mention of this in the documents. Rupert queried this with Mr Mean. He said he was going to use the long service leave to pay for his expenses while in New York. Mr Mean said that there could be no pro-rata long service amount included in the package, since the legislation in Queensland did not provide for that to be included.

Rupert has rung you, as his solicitor, to see whether there is anything that he can do. He tells you that this has affected and will affect his finances very detrimentally. Is Rupert able to claim negligent misstatement against Oswald?

Answers to Practice Questions

Revision Questions

8.1 The text defines "pure economic loss" as "economic loss suffered by the plaintiff" which is not consequential upon injury to the plaintiff or damage to the plaintiff's property. This kind of loss is different to the pecuniary losses associated with personal injuries. In personal injury matters, plaintiffs can suffer economic loss but that is associated with the fact that they cannot work or that their car has been damaged.

8.2 "Secondary" victims are those people who have not been involved in the accident personally but witness the "aftermath". These people may be close relatives, co-workers or even rescuers (see Figure 8.7 for references to relevant legislation).

8.3 Statutory authorities are local councils; specific governmental instrumentalities with regulatory roles (eg ASIC); and private bodies vested with public powers (eg law societies). Statutory authorities are considered differently to private bodies because of their unique situation. They (a) are created by statute and so their powers are limited and they are bound to act within their powers; (b) perform public duties and are ultimately answerable to citizens through the government; and (c) are funded by public money – therefore the payment of this money raises questions of whether the purpose is a deserving one and whether funding it is an appropriate and efficient allocation of the moneys available.

Problem Questions

(Remember to include relevant case law and legislative provisions in your response.)

8.1 **(a)** *Eric v George*: This is an economic loss matter.

        Issue: Does George owe Eric a duty of care?

        R/f: Eric would argue that George would have reasonably foreseen that

Eric would be harmed economically if he did not take care in giving his advice.

George would argue that he had said that he was an accounting academic and that he wouldn't have expected Eric to have acted solely on his advice in an area that was not his specialty.

Proximity

Statement serious

Eric: The matter was a serious one since he needed to invest the money in such a way that it would provide him with financial support for the next four years. Eric repeated his dependency on the money.

George: Eric is only talking about $50,000, and after all people should only invest in shares with extra money – not money upon which they are absolutely dependent. George would argue that the timing of the discussion suggests that Eric was just making conversation – the discussion took place at a party and they were drinking cocktails. George would also suggest that Eric knew he had consumed quite a few cocktails.

Assumption of responsibility

Eric: George knew of his circumstances and he said to trust him and so he was inviting Eric to rely on his advice. Eric also voiced his concerns about shares, stating that he knew nothing about them. So he was vulnerable. As far as Eric was concerned he saw George as someone with knowledge and expertise.

George: He would suggest that his drinking made him sound more sure of himself than normal and that this should have alerted Eric to the fact that he could have been talking rubbish.

Reasonable to rely?

Eric: George had the knowledge of accounting matters; he is an accounting academic.

George: He was drunk; he was not an expert in shares (only in insider trading). He had just received the company's prospectus, like anyone else. George did tell Eric to call tomorrow and he would clarify matters and give more accurate details: this should have alerted Eric to ring for more information. Eric should also have been conscious of some concerns when the broker questioned his choice.

It is more probable in this situation that it would be found that it was not reasonable for Eric to rely on George and so George would not be held liable for the economic loss suffered by Eric.

(b)   *John v Dennis*: This part of the question would need to be dealt with very briefly. It aims at having the reader recognise that only reasonable foreseeability needs to be considered to determine that a duty of care exists.

Issue: Has Dennis been negligent?

D/care: John has suffered a physical injury; thus a duty of care is assumed if it is reasonably foreseeable that Dennis's actions would hurt John (this is so).

Breach: Obviously.

Causation: Caused by Dennis.

Damage: Yes, physical.

(c) *Sam v Dennis*

D/care: Physical damage – was in the water and physically close to the activity so probably will owe a duty of care. The question is whether it would it be reasonably foreseeable that a swimmer would be hurt? Maybe not.

Breach: Yes.

Causation: Perhaps a skier could harm a swimmer (even without the collision) if swimmers are in their area. Perhaps John did something that caused this (novus actus).

Cont/neg: Outside the swimming area.

There would probably be an award for Sam, but it would be reduced because of his contributory negligence. Maybe Dennis and John would be held jointly liable.

(d) *Eric v Dennis:* Psychological damage.

R/f: Was it reasonably foreseeable that an accident of this type (skiers banging together and then hurting a swimmer) would produce psychological harm in a person present? Possibly. Was the shock caused by the event? Probably. Recognised illness? Yes – post-traumatic stress.

Proximity

Relational:	No relationship.
Geographical:	Personally witnessed the accident or its immediate aftermath. Yes.

8.2 Issue

The main hurdle in cases where pure economic loss has been suffered involves establishing a duty of care. The other elements for negligence tend to be subsidiary to this. Most questions asked of you in this area require you to focus mainly on the duty of care – and in most cases you are asked that particular question.

Here the question was phrased broadly but it still requires you to dwell primarily on the duty of care question.

Reasonable foreseeability

Would Oswald reasonably foresee that if he gave advice carelessly, Rupert could be harmed?

Rupert

* Rupert would say that because of his position as consultant to his firm, Oswald should have foreseen that Rupert expected him to know what was happening and that he would act on Oswald's inside information.

Oswald
- Oswald would say that he was just a consultant: he was not expecting Rupert to act solely on the information he was giving. It was up to the firm to make their decision in relation to his recommendations. Oswald was only on contract to the firm for a particular project.
- Oswald would also argue that he made these statements at a party, by a pool, while having a drink with Rupert. This was a social event, at which people's conversations are usually on a very informal basis.

Proximity (need for special relationship)
Rupert
- Their discussion was of a serious matter: retrenchment, retirement and redundancy packages. Ceasing to have a pay packet.
Oswald
- Retirement is something that most people talk about when they get to this age. They had spoken of this often, particularly Rupert. Oswald was only forewarning Rupert that he may be affected by the firm's streamlining operations.

Assumption of responsibility/knew or ought to have known that advice was being relied upon
Rupert
- Oswald and Rupert were close friends and trusted each other.
- Rupert questioned Oswald about the inclusion of the pro-rata component of the redundancy package. AND Oswald reassured Rupert that the pro-rata deal would be in the package. Oswald gave the assurance without any qualification (no disclaimer) and thus seemed to be guaranteeing the accuracy of his information.
- Oswald ought to have known that Rupert would rely on his advice. Rupert knew him as a friend and Oswald had heard him speak many times of his desire to have an extended visit with his daughter in America. AND Rupert spoke positively about taking up the offer (he talked of his plans). Rupert then went on to take these steps at his first opportunity (the following Monday).
- Oswald ought to have known that the redundancy package, and particularly the added bonus of the pro-rata component, would allow Rupert to carry out these plans.
Oswald
- Oswald was only forewarning his friends.
- Oswald had heard about Rupert's plans plenty of times before and now he turned off to Rupert's "ramblings".
- Oswald had only made recommendations. Mr Mean was in favour of these BUT he is not the whole company. We are not sure exactly what his position is, but it seems to be a company or at least a partnership.

Reasonable reliance
Rupert
- Believed he was getting information from someone with knowledge of the firm's movements AND the legislation involved.

- Rupert believed that Oswald has "special skill". He is the person that Mean & Co have asked to advise them on efficiency matters; he holds a particular position (ie chief consultant) in his firm. Oswald's company and Oswald himself are efficiency consultants, it is their area of expertise. They were contracted to advise Mean So & So on this very issue (streamlining the operations of R's firm).
- It would be expected that Oswald would know the relevant legislation and could be relied on when he assured Rupert that the pro-rata long service leave would be included.

Oswald

- Setting was informal ie pool, party and drinking (not necessarily alcohol but probably implied).
- Merely advising Mean So & So.
- Informing Rupert as a friend.
- Rupert should have checked on the details before committing himself.
- Oswald was only forewarning Rupert as a friend.

Tutorial Questions

Discussion Questions

8.1 Can you list some policy arguments the courts are using to limit liability?

8.2 Do you think the courts are treating policy arguments separately to, or are their discussions concerning policy subsumed within, the guise of other elements – particularly proximity?

8.3 Do you think the Australian courts would have come to the same decision as was held in *Alcock v Chief Constable of South Yorkshire Police* (1992) 4 All ER 907?

8.4 Do you think that statutory reform will lend clarity to negligence law in general?

CHAPTER 9

Special Duty of Care Situations

Reading

Sappideen, Vines, Grant and Watson, *Torts: Commentary and Materials*, Chapter 11.

Objectives

This chapter will examine the duty of care of:

- parent of child towards the child and third parties;
- educational authorities or school teachers towards pupils;
- occupier towards persons present on the land or premises;
- transferor of premises as regards their safety;
- transferor of defective chattels causing injury or death;
- medical practitioners towards patients; and
- employers towards employees and independent contractors.

Principles

Introduction

[9.05] In Chapter 8 the general principles governing duty of care were considered. This chapter will continue the duty discussion in a different context. We will turn our attention to specific situations in which it is clear that, as a matter of law, a duty of care exists but it is one to which special considerations apply. The duty may, for example, be one that is or has been subject to legal restriction, or one that is or has been subject to special formulation. Also included in this chapter are duties of care arising from "protective" relationships recognised by the law, the special feature of which is that the law imposes a duty of care to take positive action. Examples of such relationships include the occupier's duty of care to lawful visitors and the duty owed by a hospital to its patients. An area which has attracted a great deal of judicial debate, was closely considered by the Ipp Committee and is now subject to legislative control, is the special protective relationship between a doctor and their patient. This duty will be considered in some detail with developments clearly outlined and explained.

Parent's duty to child and third parties

Duty to child

General duty

[9.10] As regards liability to the child, *a parent is of course liable for their negligent acts which cause injury to their child*. This has been accepted in cases concerning negligent driving of a motor vehicle by the defendant. In such cases, an insurance company stands behind the parent satisfying their liability. The issue is not quite as clear when one moves out of the context of a situation covered by insurance into the ordinary, day-to-day conduct of family life. It has been broadly accepted that a parent should not owe the child any general duty of care to supervise its activities. An illustrative case in this context is *Robertson v Swincer* (1989) 52 SASR 356. The respondents in this case were the parents of a four-year-old boy who was injured when he ran across the road. The family had been visiting some friends and were preparing to leave when the small boy crossed the road to the family car then attempted to return to his parents. It was on this second attempt at crossing the road that he was struck by a car driven by the appellant. In determining whether or not the supervision of children should attract a duty recognised by the law,[1] emphasis was placed on policy considerations including the social consequences of such a legal rule, the need to spread loss across society and the "alarming personal implications" of parents' assets being at risk.[2] The practical reality of situations such as these is that claims against the parent are very often made not by the child itself, but by a third party seeking contribution from the parent for damages payable to the child. Enforcing a contribution claim may be tantamount to making a

---

[1]   It was readily acknowledged by the court that a moral duty exists; the question was under what circumstances this moral duty should be converted to a legal one.

[2]   Consider the comments of King CJ at 359-361.

deduction from damages payable to the child, since the child may be assumed to have an interest in the parent's assets. The law will therefore not allow a "sword of Damocles duty of care" to hang over the parental head at all stages of a child's life as this would create an "unwarranted burden": per Legoe J at 369.

Specific duty

[9.15] It is important to note that these policy considerations are not enough to avoid the imposition of a duty of care as regards negligent acts of the parent injuring the child. In such a situation, the general rules of negligence apply.

A situation outside the normal rules of negligence arises in special circumstances when a parent may have a positive duty to supervise the child. An example is found in *Rogers v Rawlings* [1969] Qd R 262. A child was injured during a day of water skiing and the negligent party was seeking contribution from the mother. The court found that the mother had failed to adequately supervise the child and to warn the owner and driver of the boat of the level of inexperience of her child. Her position of knowledge regarding the particular skill level of her daughter was sufficient to attract a duty in this situation. In *Dickinson v Dickinson* (1986) 3 SR (WA) 233, liability was determined to exist when a father left a four-year-old and a two-year-alone in a car. The two-year-old suffered serious burns when the older child found some matches between the front seats and set the floor mat alight. The older child was able to escape from the car, but the younger was asleep at the time and was rescued by a passer-by. The lack of supervision in the presence of danger was sufficient to attract liability.

Of significance in this decision were the "allurements" which can be found in a motor car, and which were described as numerous and potentially dangerous. The "incipient danger" was deemed to be compounded by the protracted absence of the father: Sadleir J at 240. The significance of the particular circumstances was echoed in *Robertson v Swincer* (1989) 52 SASR 356 at 359 when King CJ recognised that a duty to protect a child from harm may arise, irrespective of blood relationship, if the parent acted in such a way as to create a risk of injury.[3] This rule is not limited to parents; circumstances may arise which warrant the imposition of a duty of care on a person, other than the parent, having care of the child. In *Bye v Bates* (1989) 51 SASR 67, the the children of another family were under the care and supervision of the defendant. When the defendant had to leave his house, he simply instructed the children to go home and failed to take further steps to ensure that they left his premises as directed. The plaintiff child did not leave and was injured when he clutched the live element of a vaporiser that had been left on the back verandah. The defendant was held liable. The special circumstances were the total withdrawal of supervision and the accessibility to the plaintiff of the dangerous vaporiser. The key to such situations, therefore, is either the absence of supervision in a situation containing an inherent risk or the actual creation of a risk.[4]

This point was further emphasised in *Smith v Leurs* (1945) 70 CLR 256 when the High Court had to determine whether the parents of a child were to be held responsible for the actions of their son when he injured the plaintiff with a slingshot. The court was

---

[3]   Of significance in this decision was the statement in the judgments that if the parents had either called or taken the child onto the road, then the outcome would have been different.

[4]   See also *Towart v Adler* (1989) 52 SASR 373 – defendant landlord who negligently placed double bunk bed near a window, was liable to the plaintiff six-year-old child who, whilst using the window sill to climb onto the upper bunk, fell through the window. Plaintiff's father was not liable to make contribution, even though he had opened the window – the circumstances were not such as to take the case outside the rule that the parent owes the child no duty of care of general supervision.

clear in identifying a duty to control dangerous activities encouraged and introduced by the parents but stopped short of holding them responsible for the activities of their son when he was not with them. Thus, there was no vicarious liability (nor was there any breach of primary duty to control and protect third parties, to be discussed further below).

Duty to protect third parties

[9.20] The remaining question is whether or not a parent owes a duty of care to protect others from the dangerous activities of their children. In *Robertson v Swincer* (1989) 52 SASR 356 at 362 King CJ emphasised that the discussion in that case bore no relation to the question of a duty of "custodians" to protect third parties from harm as a result of the failure to supervise. While a comparison of the formulation of the duty of a school or teacher in terms of that of a parent was rejected by King CJ (at 362), the comparison has attracted judicial discussion and can be illustrative of how the courts may deal with a situation involving the question of duty to protect others.

In the leading House of Lords decision of *Carmarthenshire CC v Lewis* [1955] AC 549 the defendant school authority was held liable in relation to the escape from a school which was under its authority of a four-year-old child onto the public highway. The plaintiff truck driver swerved to miss the child and was killed. The basis of liability was the inadequacy of the school gates to prevent exit by four-year-old children, a matter that was a breach of the personal duty of care applying to the Council, rather than to any failure of supervision by the teaching staff. Considered in the context of the *Robertson* discussion, and in the absence of any other authority, an analogy between this situation and that of parents may well be misplaced and it is likely that the teacher owes a more onerous duty of care than the parent.

To illustrate further, consider *Smith v Leurs* (1945) 70 CLR 549 where the court determined that it was sufficient for the parents to have warned the child about the dangers of the shanghai, there was no positive duty to remove it from their son's possession or actively protect other children. In rejecting vicarious liability as an option, the High Court held that tortious liability may only be established on the basis of personal fault on the parent's part. The duty clearly exists, but the standard of care is not onerous and is clearly lower than that expected of a school authority.[5]

Figure 9.1: Duty of care of parent of child

- Liability for any negligent acts causing injury to their child.
- No duty of care of general supervision of their child's activities.
- Duty may arise if the parent either fails to supervise an inherently dangerous activity or they themselves create the danger.
- Not vicariously liable for their child's torts.

---

[5]   See further on the liability of parents for allowing their children access to guns: *Pask v Owen* [1987] 2 Qd R 421; *Hogan v Gill* [1992] Aust Torts Reports 81-182; *Curmi v McLennan* [1994] 1 VR 513.

Educational authority's duty to pupils

[9.25] The duty to protect others arises out of the identification of a protective relationship and such a relationship clearly exists between a school and its students. As noted at [9.20], there has been some attraction to drawing an analogy between the protective relationship between parent and child and that between a school authority (and its teachers) and pupils at the school,[6] at least as regards their physical safety. However, as also noted, the expectations of active protection is higher in the context of the school. When considering school premises the expectation is that individual students will be protected from their own carelessness as well as the carelessness (and in some instances cruelty) of others. With such an high expectation of protection, the analogy between the parent and the school authority or its teachers, though having some support, seems now imperfect[7] and it is more productive to avoid analogies, turning instead to the specific nature of the relationship between students and the school.

Extent of duty

[9.30] The duty is an onerous one and exists wherever there is a relationship of care and control between teachers and pupils. Students are to be protected from:

- other students using play equipment (student pulled from a flying-fox and injured, whilst breach was not found it was clear that a duty was owed: *Trustees of the Roman Catholic Church for the Diocese of Canberra and Goulburn (as Saint Anthony's Primary School) v Hadba* (2005) 221 CLR 161);
- use of equipment in the classroom (student injured when using a belt sander in an industrial design class: *Parkin v ACT Schools Authority* [2005] ACTSC 3);
- state of the yard (student put his foot in a pothole whilst playing sport and suffered an injury, clear duty to maintain sports fields identified: *Bujnowicz v Trustees Roman Catholic Church* [2005] Aust Torts Reports 81–824);
- fixtures in the schoolyard (student injured when he and some friends lifted a heavy grille covering the long drain: *Victoria v Subramanian* [2008] VSC 9); and
- bullying by other students (student suffering from ongoing, significant psychological harm as a result of serious bullying during his first year at school: *Cox v State of New South Wales* [2007] Aust Torts Reports 81–888).

This duty has been found to extend beyond the confines of the school and school hours.

- Where the school has adopted a practice of allowing its pupils into school premises before the commencement of teaching, a duty of care to exercise supervision arises: *Commonwealth v Introvigne* (1982) 150 CLR 285.[8]
- Where a five-year-old child was discharged early from school before the expected arrival of his parent and was then injured in a traffic accident, the

6   For further discussion consider Heffey, "The Duties of School and Teacher to Protect Pupils from Injury" (1985-86) 11 Mon LR 1.
7   Though supported by statements of McTiernan J in *Ramsay v Larsen* (1964) 111 CLR 16. In *Commonwealth v Introvigne* (1982) 150 CLR 285 Murphy J thought the better analogy to be the duty of care owed by a hospital or factory (or their staff) towards patients or employees.
8   Also consider *Geyer v Downs* (1977) 138 CLR 91.

school authority was held liable to the child even though the accident occurred off the school premises: *Barnes v Hampshire CC* [1969] 1 WLR 1563.[9]

- It is clear also that teachers who take children on school trips or holiday outings owe them a duty of care to supervise their activities: *Gugiatti v Servite College* [2004] Aust Torts Reports 81-724.[10]

- A duty of care may exist to supervise boarding arrangements on buses provided by the school or as regards behaviour on those buses. Generally, however, once the pupils have left the school premises the duty of care terminates: *Stokes v Russell* (unreported, Supreme Court, Tas, 18 January 1983, No 2/1983).[11]

- If, however, the school through its staff members has become aware of a particular danger to its pupils after leaving school, it has a duty to take reasonable protective measures. Thus, a school authority was held liable where the school had failed to offer protection against bullying of its pupils by older boys after school, and the plaintiff pupil had been hit and injured by a missile thrown by an older boy: *Trustees of the Catholic School of Bathurst v Koffman* [1996] Aust Torts Reports 81-398.

Figure 9.2: Extent of the duty of care includes –

- school hours while the pupils are on the premises;
- before and after school hours, to exercise supervision if the school allows pupils onto school premises or allows them to remain;
- proper supervision of pupils on school trips or holiday outings which are part of school activities;
- supervision of boarding arrangements on buses provided by the school and behaviour on those buses;
- where the school becomes aware of a particular danger to its pupils outside school hours;
- where the school is aware that a parent is to pick up the pupil but fails to ensure that the pupil remains on the school premises.

Breach of duty

[9.35] Whilst the duty of care of general supervision owed by the school and its teachers has at times been an onerous one it has more recently evolved into a practical consideration of facts and circumstances. The general duty was considered by the High Court in *Commonwealth v Introvigne* (1982) 150 CLR 285. In this case there was an

---

[9]   This was extended in *Reynolds v Haines* (unreported, Supreme Court, NSW, 27 October 1993, 15185/1988) to the case where a school boy, situated immediately outside the school premises and just before commencement of school hours, threw fruit at the plaintiff boy, who was riding his bike on the public highway on his way to school, and damaged his eye beyond repair. The school was found liable on the basis that it had assumed responsibility for supervision in these circumstances.

[10]   Steytler J relied on *Commonwealth v Introvigne* (1982) 150 CLR 285 at [19] to emphasise that the duty moves beyond the schoolyard and when on a trip outside the school (in this instance a Year 12 leadership camp) the duty continues "unabated". Also consider *Munro v Anglican Church of Australia* (unreported, Court of Appeal, NSW, 1415/89, No 490/1985).

[11]   In this instance it was held that no duty of care was owed as regards the boarding of an ordinary service bus by a pupil after school had finished.

extraordinary staff meeting called prior to the commencement of school and during the meeting a student was struck by a halyard which fell from a flag pole when another student was swinging on it. Whilst it was before school, students were allowed on the premises at this time of day. The High Court emphasised that there is a duty to ensure that reasonable care is taken to ensure the safety of students on the premises during the hours when the school is open (per Mason J at 269). The court concluded that the accident was foreseeable and that there was negligence on the part of the school in failing to provide supervision at the time it occurred. On the other hand, the duty is one of general rather than constant supervision. As Mason J points out in *Introvigne* (at 265), the school teachers' duty does not require that 15-year-old boys be kept under constant observation and supervision, and the High Court has emphasised that the duty extends to taking reasonable care for the safety of the students but not to prevent all kinds of harm: *New South Wales v Lepore* (2003) 212 CLR 511 per Gaudron J at [103] and Gleeson CJ at [31].[12] More recently, the Victorian Supreme Court has noted that the expectation is that reasonable care is taken for the safety of students and that it is not a duty of "insurance against all harms": *Victoria v Subramanian* [2008] VSC 9 per Cavanough J at [10].

The standard of care, consistent with the general standard inquiry (to be covered in more detail in Chapter 10), is fact driven and can vary according to knowledge of the particular student and the nature and location of the activity: *Parkin v ACT Schools Authority* [2005] ACTSC 3. If the students are in a classroom there is an expectation of close supervision as evidenced in the decision of *Richards v Victoria* [1969] VR 136 when a teacher was found negligent for failing to take steps to prevent fighting known to be occurring in the class. If we move the events to the playground and shift the timing to recess or lunch time, there is a lower expectation with the recognition that it would require an "army of supervisors" to prevent all potentially harmful incidents: *Australian Capital Territory v El Sheik* [2000] Aust Torts Reports 81-577 at [25] per Wilcox J when considering a fact scenario involving injuries sustained when a "play fight turned serious". This position was highlighted in *Parkin* when Master Harper emphasised the higher expectation of control and protection within the classroom environment. In this instance, the plaintiff was a known risk taker and was injured when using a belt-sander in his industrial design class. An earlier report to his parents had raised concerns regarding his behaviour and the existence of this report combined with the presence of the belt-sander served to heighten the expected standard of care. The failure to provide adequate supervision (and to inform a relief reacher of the plaintiff's pattern of behaviour) was deemed to be negligent. Thus, under certain circumstances the standard of care continues to be an onerous one but it is tempered by pragmatic considerations.

Nature of duty of school authority

[9.40] As regards the liability of the school authority for the negligence of schoolteachers, this proceeds on normal principles of vicarious liability on the part of an employer for the negligence of an employee in the course of employment. It is also relevant to note that the duty is a non-delegable duty which can exist in the absence of employee negligence. There are therefore primarily two levels of duty. There is the personal non-delegable duty of the Commonwealth (or school authority) which is to provide

---

12   While the case is illustrative in this context, it is important to note that the consideration of the court was centred around the intentional torts of physical and sexual abuse.

a safe environment and employ capable staff members. There is also the possibility of negligence of staff members which may result in the Commonwealth (or school authority) being held vicariously liable for these actions. While non-delegable duties and vicarious liability as potential sources of liability are similar in many respects and can operate together (as they did in *Commonwealth v Introvigne* (1982) 150 CLR 285), they can also exist independently.[13] There is also a potential third source of liability with the State (or School Authority) bearing responsibility as an occupier of the premises, although it has been pointed out that this adds nothing new to the inquiry unless a plaintiff is injured when entering the school yard out of school hours and independently of the school.[14]

Duty of care towards third parties

[9.45] *Haines v Rytmeister* (1986) 6 NSWLR 529 establishes that a duty of care may arise on the part of a school teacher towards a third party injured on the premises by the acts of pupils. The teacher was liable in that case for failure to give adequate instructions to pupils as to the carrying and depositing of heavy boxes. The consequence of that failure was injury to the plaintiff, a visitor to the school premises. In appropriate circumstances, a similar duty of care would no doubt arise to school teachers themselves, whether on the part of another teacher or of the school authority.

Occupier's duty to persons on premises

[9.50] From quite early on the occupier of land and premises (hereafter "premises") has been held to owe a duty of care as regards the state of the premises towards persons lawfully present on them. The duty imposes a positive obligation to act to take care for the safety of the entrant, and arises from a protective relationship between occupier and visitor. The formulations of this duty originally drew distinctions between two classes of entrant, the invitee and the licensee. The invitee was regarded as a person present on the premises with the permission of the occupier and whose entry was in the occupier's material interest. The licensee was a person merely permitted to be present on the premises. The occupier owed the invitee a duty of care to safeguard the invitee against unusual dangers of which the occupier was or should have been aware. The duty owed to the licensee was to warn or otherwise give notice of concealed dangers of which the occupier knew. Both relationships gave rise to a duty to take positive action. Running parallel to these duties was a general or overriding duty of care based on foreseeability of harm to the entrant under the application of *Donoghue v Stevenson* principles. This general duty was particularly associated with liability for acts or current activities carried out by the occupier on the land or premises. Now, as a result of the decision of the High Court in *Australian Safeway Stores v Zaluzna* (1987) 162 CLR 479, applying the earlier judgment of Deane J in *Hackshaw v Shaw* (1984) 155 CLR 614 and the judgments of Mason and Deane JJ in *Papatonakis v Australian Telecom* (1985) 156 CLR 7, it has become settled law that there is only one duty of care owed to lawful entrants on the premises by the occupier. That duty of care is the general one, which has superseded the specially formulated duties.

---

[13]   For further discussion regarding the nature of the duty, consider *Commonwealth v Introvigne* (1982) 150 CLR 285 at 271 per Mason J, at 274-275 per Murphy J and at 279 per Brennan J.

[14]   This topic was briefly introduced in Chapter 8. Refer to Figure 8.9.

Figure 9.3: General principles in relation to the duty of care of an occupier

- The general duty of care of an occupier is based on the danger to the entrant being reasonably foreseeable.
- The defendant should manifest a degree of physical presence on the premises and control over them.
- The standard of care will depend on the circumstances of the case.
- Children require greater protection than adults.
- The standard of care owed by an occupier to a trespasser on the land remains a largely unresolved matter with some limited legislative consideration (refer Figure 9.4).[14]

The general duty of care of the occupier arises under the normal criterion of establishing a duty of care: *that the danger to the entrant is reasonably foreseeable* and extends to nonfeasance as well as misfeasance. The duty covers all lawful entrants on the land; for example, invitees, licensees, entrants as of right, contractual entrants and even, arguably, trespassers though this case requires separate consideration. *Papatonakis* and *Zaluzna* were both cases concerning invitees but there is nothing in them to indicate that the High Court was limiting the application of the general duty to invitees. *Zaluzna* illustrates the point concerning nonfeasance. In that case, action was brought by a shopper who had suffered injury through slipping on the supermarket floor which had become wet and slippery in wet weather, allegedly through failure on the part of the defendants to remove the moisture.[15] The High Court held that a duty of care was capable of arising on these facts and remitted the matter to the trial court for consideration of whether there was a duty of care and breach on the facts of the case.

While it is clear that oocupiers owe lawful entrants to their land a duty of care, the extent and nature of the duty is subject to different factors such as relationship between the occupier and entrant, purpose of entry and type of premises.

What is occupation?

[9.55] Occupation of premises is a question of fact. There is no need to prove that the defendant was in occupation under any form of legal title. Nor is it necessary to establish possession on the defendant's part. What is necessary is that the defendant should manifest a degree of physical presence on the premises and control over them. The factual state of occupation may therefore be exercised jointly with persons in actual possession of the premises. For example, in *Wheat v Lacon* [1966] AC 552, the private living quarters of a public house tenant, who lived in them under licence from a brewery and who was therefore not in possession of them, were held to be occupied jointly by the tenant and the brewery (which had actual possession). In *Hartwell v Grayson Docks* [1947] KB 901 a contractor, who was converting a ship into a troopship in dry dock, was an occupier, though clearly that occupation was enjoyed jointly with

---

14   Occupier's liability was also discussed in Chapter 8: refer to Fig 8.9 for the relevant legislative provissions.

15   The South Australian Supreme Court reiterated the importance of owners of commercial premises ensuring a safe and clean environment for shoppers in *Ragnelli v David Jones (Adelaide) Pty Ltd* (2004) 90 SASR 233; [2004] SASC 393 (2 December 2004).

the shipowner. A number of more recent Australian decisions have extended the duties of occupiers to persons having the statutory care, control and management of public reserves, though it is arguable that in cases of this sort the test of occupation would be satisfied: eg *Wallis v Town of Albany* [1989] Aust Torts Reports 80-283; *Randel v Brisbane CC* [1989] Aust Torts Reports 80-284; *Saroukas v Sutherland SC* [1992] Aust Torts Reports 81-149. Of significance in the cases in this context is the level of control exercised by the "occupier" over the land and facilities.[16] It should be noted that the rules of occupier's liability are applied also in relation to the static condition of "occupiable" chattels such as ships or airplanes.

Standard of care required

[9.60] The standard of care required of the occupier depends on the circumstances of the case. *Nagle v Rottnest Island Authority* (1993) 177 CLR 423 (considered in Chapter 10) shows that the occupier may be required to make provision against even slight risks, in that case the risk of swimmers making dangerous dives into an area where the presence of dangerous rocks below the surface of the water was apparent. The relevant breach of duty in that case was the failure to post a suitable warning notice of the danger; in many cases the occupier's duty will be discharged by the posting of warning notices, the provision of adequate lighting and so forth. As noted above, the requsite standard is established by consideration of both the purpose of the entry and the nature of the premises. Usually, commercial premises will have a higher standard than private or domestic dwellings. Consider *Lanahmede Pty Ltd v Koch* [2004] SASC 204, for example, where the Supreme Court of South Australia found that proprietors of a hotel are expected to maintain their grounds and be aware that entrants may be intoxicated and not take due care for themselves and in *Skulander v Willoughby City Council* [2007] NSWCA 116 it was emphasised that the occupier of a bus interchange must accept the reality of the distracted commuter. In contrast, the High Court in *Neindorf v Junkovic* (2005) 80 ALJR 341 held that a reasonable response to a risk on domestic premises may well be to do nothing.

The decision and reasoning in *Nagle* must now be considered in the light of the statutory amendments and decisions with respect to "obvious" and "inherent" risks.[17] In the past the courts have applied a stringent standard of care to occupiers because of their position of control and authority. Some relevant cases to consider in this context include *Saroukas v Sutherland SC* [1989] Aust Torts Reports 80-291 in which it was held that warning notices of dangers on the land should be in pictorial as well as verbal form, in recognition of the fact that persons who could not read English might be present on the land. In *Conors v Western Railways* [1992] Aust Torts Reports 81-187, the defendant occupier was held liable for giving inadequate notice of trains approaching a railway crossing, even though a warning sign had been posted. There has been a shift in recent years towards a more pragmatic approach with the post-Ipp era seeing a focus on personal care and responsibility. It is a clear fact driven inquiry and, as outlined above, the

---

[16]   Consider the diving and swimming cases discussed in Chapter 10 for further detail on the importance of the element of "control" and also *Romeo v Conservation Commission of the Northern Territory* (1998) 192 CLR 431; *Mulligan v Coffs Harbour City Council* (2005) 223 CLR 486, *Vairy v Wyong Shire Council* (2005) 22 CLR 422; *Clarke v Coleambally Ski Club Inc* [2004] NSWCA 376 (18 October 2004); *Ballerini v Berrigan Shire Council* [2004] VSC 321.

[17]   Refer discussion at [10.30]ff. These decisions are further discussed in Chapter 12 in the context of the defence of volenti and the statutory introduction of the concept of obvious and inherent risks.

standard will be adjusted according to the expected activities of the entrants, the nature of the premises and practical realities including potentially drunk entrants and their specific vulnerabilities, including age (see *Brock v Hillsdale Bowling & Recreation Club Ltd* [2007] NSWCA 46 when it was deemed relevant that the entrants to a bowling club were elderly).

The occupier is required to provide a greater measure of protection for children than for adults on the ground that they are less able to take care for their own safety. In the case of premises open to the public, however, this duty might be discharged by restricting entry by children to those accompanied by an adult. The occupier is entitled to expect older children on the premises to be able to recognise and avoid obvious dangers.[18] The additional care requirement for such children is sometimes expressed in terms that the occupier must not have present on the land attractions or allurements to children which contain concealed dangers (such as poisonous berries in a public park): *Glasgow Corporation v Taylor* [1922] 1 AC 44 or a derelict boat on the grounds of council flats: *Jolley v Sutton London Borough Council* [2000] 3 All ER 409. To the very young child, however, almost anything on the premises represents a danger. The court in *Phipps v Rochester Corporation* [1955] 1 QB 450 held an occupier not liable to a five-year-old child who fell into a trench on the land, the danger of which would have been apparent to an adult or older child. The ground for this decision was that it was not reasonably foreseeable that the plaintiff would be present on the land unaccompanied by an adult or responsible older child.[19]

The key in all situations is, therefore, the nature of the relationship between occupier and entrant and the facts and circumstances of the situation.

Delegability of duty

Contractual entrant

[9.65] The duty of care owed to the contractual entrant is based on an implied warranty that the premises are as safe for entry as the exercise of reasonable care on the part of anyone can make them, a rule confirmed by the High Court: *Calin v Greater Union Organisation Pty Ltd* (1991)173 CLR 33; *Morawski v State Rail Authority (NSW)* (1988) 14 NSWLR 374. This formulation does not extend the personal duty of the occupier beyond that which applies under the general duty of care established in *Australian Safeway Stores v Zaluzna* (1987) 162 CLR 479.[20] Its effect is to make it clear that the duty is non-delegable; that is, it is incapable of being discharged by the employment of an independent contractor. Even so, lack of care on the part of the contractor must be established.

There is authority in the judgment of Windeyer J in *Voli v Inglewood SC* (1963) 110 CLR 74 that the non-delegability of the duty of care owed to persons who enter under contract with the occupier is not limited to persons in actual contractual relationship

---

[18] *Perry v Wrigley* [1955] 1 WLR 1164 – hole in the ground not an "allurement". Cf *Cough v NCB* [1954] 1 QB 191 – slow moving railway trucks amounted to a concealed danger.

[19] For statutory regulation of the standard of care of the occupier, see *Civil Law (Wrongs) Act 2002* (ACT), s 168; *Personal Injuries (Liabilities and Damages) Act 2003* (NT), s 9; *Civil Liability Act 1936* (SA), Pt 4, ss 19–22; *Wrongs Act 1958* (Vic), Pt IIA, ss 14A–14E; and *Occupiers Liability Act 1958* (WA) Pt IIA, ss14A–14E. Also refer Figure 8.9.

[20] Though an argument could be made, based on the formulation in the text, that a professional rather than amateur standard of care is owed by the occupier to the contractual entrant. In other words, the decision in *Wells v Cooper* [1958] 2 QB 265 is not applicable. The matter awaits decision.

with the occupier, but extends to those who enter under the terms of a contract made with another person.

Towards other lawful entrants

[9.70] A decision of the House of Lords which held an occupier liable to an invitee for the negligence of an independent contractor (*Thomson v Cremin* [1956] 1 WLR 103) has been qualified by later decisions limiting the liability to cases where the task entrusted to the contractor requires no technical skill. In *Woodward v Mayor of Hastings* [1945] KB 174, the occupier was held liable for a school cleaner's failure to properly clean the school steps of snow and ice.[21] A New South Wales decision is to the same effect: *Vial v Housing Commission* [1976] 1 NSWLR 388. The occupier has been held not liable in cases where the contractor's task required technical skill or knowledge.[22] The rationale of this distinction is, however, obscure. It can hardly be explained on the basis that the occupier is expected to personally perform tasks of a non-technical nature.

Occupier's duty of care to trespassers

[9.75] The original common law rule concerning the liability of the occupier towards a trespasser injured on the land was that the occupier was liable only for intentionally or recklessly injuring the trespasser: *Addie v Dumbreck* [1929] AC 358. No duty of care was owed to the trespasser as such. This rule was never completely accepted by Australian courts, which evolved the concept of an overriding duty of care based on normal principles of reasonable foreseeability, which could in appropriate circumstances operate in favour of the trespasser (although this was rare). The fundamental consideration addressed by Australian courts was the foreseeability of the trespass combined with the foreseeability of harm to the trespasser. The most obvious application of the "overriding duty of care" concept was in relation to an act or continuing activity of the occupier carried out on the land or premises. The possibility of the duty applying in these situations was recognised by Dixon CJ in *Commissioner for Railways v Cardy* (1960) 104 CLR 274 at 286 in which liability was imposed for injury to a trespasser caused by hot ashes beneath a crust of earth:

> *The rule remains that a (person) trespasses at his own risk and the occupier is under no duty to him except to refrain from intentional or wanton harm to him. But it recognises that nevertheless a duty exists where to the knowledge of the occupier premises are frequented by strangers or are openly used by other people and the occupier actively creates a specific peril seriously menacing their safety or continues it in existence.*

Other Australian judges went even further in regarding the occupier's duty of care to the trespasser as being based on normal *Donoghue v Stevenson* principles. Under these a duty of care arose if harm to the trespasser was reasonably foreseeable, whether by reason of the static condition of the premises or the activities of the occupier thereon. The leading example is the judgment of Fullagar J in *Cardy*.

Cardy and earlier Australian cases which established the concept of an overriding duty

---

21 See also *Green v Fibreglass Ltd* [1958] 2 QB 245.
22 *Haseldine v Daw* [1941] 2 KB 434 – occupier not liable for negligent repair of a lift by the contractor; *Occupiers' Liability Act 1985* (WA), s 6(1) considered – occupier generally not liable for the negligence of an independent contractor.

of care owed to trespassers, were overruled under the then prevailing rules of precedent by the Privy Council decision in *Commissioner for Railways v Quinlan* [1964] AC 1054. However, the High Court, being no longer bound by Privy Council decisions, reopened the issue of the duty of care towards trespassers in *Hackshaw v Shaw* (1984) 155 CLR 615. That case concerned the liability of an occupier who deliberately fired at a car containing the plaintiff, and hit and injured her. The plaintiff and her friend had been trespassing on the property in order to steal petrol from the defendant. The defendant shot at the engine of the car in an attempt to disable it. He was unaware of the presence of anyone in the car except the driver, the plaintiff being slumped in the front seat and not visible from outside the car. The High Court held by a majority that the defendant was liable to the plaintiff for negligence. Gibbs CJ and Wilson J emphasised that the factual situation was wholly outside the normal one in which the issue of liability of the occupier toward the trespasser arose: here the occupier deliberately fired shots in the plaintiff's direction. Dawson J dissented on the ground that *Quinlan* precluded liability towards the trespasser except when the occupier intentionally or recklessly injured the trespasser. Deane J held that the previous overriding duty of care towards trespassers established by cases such as *Cardy* should now be regarded as the sole test for duty of care. The duty of care based on normal principles of foreseeability should not distinguish between dangers arising from the static condition of the premises and from activities of the occupier carried out there. The judgment of Fullagar J in *Cardy* received Deane J's approval. In determining the existence of a duty of care, however, the special circumstances attendant to entry of a trespasser would be relevant. Deane J said (at 662-663):

> All that is necessary is to determine whether in all the relevant circumstances, including the fact of the defendant's occupation of premises and the manner of the plaintiff's entry upon them, the defendant owed a duty of care under the ordinary principles of negligence to the plaintiff ... where the visitor is on the land as a trespasser, the mere relationship of occupier and trespasser ... will not satisfy the requirement of proximity. Something more will be required. The additional factor or combination of factors which may, as a matter of law, supply the requisite degree of proximity or give rise to a reasonably foreseeable risk of relevant injury are incapable of being exhaustively defined or identified. At the least they will include either knowledge of the actual or likely presence of the trespasser or reasonable foreseeability of a real risk of his presence.

While the nature of the duty of care owed by an occupier to a trespasser at common law remains a largely unresolved matter, the current trends of the High Court can prove illuminating. The court, consistent with the views of the Ipp Committee, is increasingly interested in placing a higher level of responsibility on the plaintiff: for further discussion see [10.25]ff. If a plaintiff willingly and knowingly trespasses, placing themselves at risk, the court is less likely to attach liability to the occupier of the land. This view is supported by the decision of *Wilmot v South Australia* [1993] Aust Torts Reports 81-259. In this instance the plaintiff had entered, as a trespasser, a portion of unalienated Crown land for the purpose of trail bike riding. She was injured when she took a trail on which the track fell away sharply and she and her bike went over a cliff. The defendants were aware of the practice of trail bike riding on the land but had taken no precautions against the occurrence of injury arising from it. The Full Court assumed the existence of a duty of care owed by the defendants to the plaintiff but found there to have been no breach of it. Whatever precautions might have been taken would have proved futile to prevent the accident. Fencing the land would not have deterred entry. Warning notices would have been vandalised or removed and in any case would not have deterred the trail bike riders who had full knowledge that the practice was dangerous, indeed it was one of its attractions.[23] Consistent with this approach is the position adopted by the New South Wales Court of Appeal in *Rundle v State Rail Authority* [2002] Aust Torts Reports 81-678 when it found that the plaintiff had recklessly engaged in an inherently dangerous activity, using the railway carriage in a manner that was so far removed from the way it was intended that it came close to being self-inflicted harm. There was no duty to protect those engaged in such unlawful and reckless activities.[24]

There is now some legislative consideration of the relationship between occupiers and trespassers: In the Northern Territory an occupier (of both domestic and commercial premises) owes no duty of care to those who enter their premises with the intention of committing an offence punishable by imprisonment; in South Australia there is no duty owed by an occupier to a trespasser unless the presence of the trespasser and the injury sustained were foreseeable and measures for protection ought to have been taken; and in Western Australia the duty to trespassers extends only to refraining from acting in a manner either to deliberately or recklessly cause harm.

Figure 9.4:

Juris	Legislation	Provision
NT	*Personal Injuries (Liabilities and Damages) Act 2003*	ss 9-10
SA	*Civil Liability Act 1936*	s 20(6)
WA	*Occupiers' Liability Act 1985*	s 5(2), (3)

Duty of transferor of premises

[9.80] The rule still applies at common law that one who sells or lets real property has no duty of care, by reason of the mere sale or lease, towards persons on the premises who are injured as a result of the premises' defective state: *Bottomley v Bannister* [1932] 1 KB 458; *Otto v Bolton & Norris* [1936] 2 KB 46 (vendor); *Robbins v Jones* (1863) 15 CB (NS) 221; *Cavalier v Pope* [1906] AC 428. A remedy might lie in contract to the buyer or the lessee. For example, an implied warranty of "habitability" arises on a lease of furnished premises: *Smith v Marrahle* (1843) 152 ER 693; *Wilson v Finch Hatton* (1877) 2 Ex D 336. But no similar warranty applies in the case of the lease of unfurnished premises or on the sale of a house. On the other hand, a duty of care to persons injured on the premises arises where the vendor or lessor (or their agents) has, by work on the premises prior to their transfer, been responsible for creating their defective condition. *Sharpe v Sweeting* [1963] 1 WLR 665 was interpreted in this sense by decisions of the House of Lords in *Anns v London Borough of Merton* [1978] AC 728 and *Murphy v*

---

[23] As to the standard of care towards the trespasser, see also *Bryant v Fawdon Pty Ltd* [1993] Aust Torts Reports 81-204 – plaintiff failed either because her presence on the premises was not reasonably foreseeable, or because, even if it was, the cause of her injury was not reasonably foreseeable.

[24] In this instance the plaintiff had squeezed his upper body through a small window of a railway carriage and was injured when he was sitting, with his torso out of the window, whilst the train was moving, spray painting graffiti on its roof.

Brentwood District [1991] AC 398. Again, a lessor of property who was responsible for its defective design was held liable to a person who received injury on the premises by reason of that defect: *Rimmer v Liverpool CC* [1985] QB 1. The authority of the basic rule was to some extent further undermined by the judgments of Brennan CJ and Gaudron J in *Northern Sandblasting v Harris* (1997) 188 CLR 313. In this case they held that a landlord has a duty of care to inspect the premises for safety purposes prior to letting them, and was therefore liable to the child of a tenant for failing to correct an electrical fault which caused the child injury, where the fault existed on the premises at the commencement of the lease, and where careful inspection would have revealed it. But the remainder of the Full Bench of the High Court did not accept this basis of the landlord's liability. A lessor who enters and does repairs after the commencement of the lease is liable for negligently creating a dangerous condition on the premises to a person injured as a result, whether or not the lessor has a duty to repair under the lease: *Billings (AC) v Riden* [1958] AC 240. On the other hand, a lessor who had undertaken a duty under the lease to keep the premises in good repair was held not liable to the wife of the tenant who received injury when she fell through the floor of the premises. The wife, not being a party to the lease, could not take advantage of the covenant to repair and no general duty of care as regards the state of the premises existed on the part of the lessor: *Cavalier v Pope* [1906] AC 428. However, in *Parker v South Australian Housing Trust* (1986) 41 SASR 493[25] the South Australian Full Court refused to follow *Cavalier* in a case in which the tenant's daughter received injury through a defect in a boiler forming part of the premises which the defendant had covenanted to keep in good repair. The absence of privity of contract between the daughter and the defendant was no objection after the decision in *Donoghue v Stevenson* [1932] AC 562 and the defendant's covenant to repair created a relationship of reliance between the daughter and the Housing Trust. On the basis of the approach taken by the South Australian court in this case, a similar result would apply in the case of the letting of furnished premises. The lessor's implied warranty as to the condition of the premises at the commencement of the lease would extend the duty to those who may be present on the premises but not a party to the warranty. *Parker* was approved in principle by the High Court in *Northern Sandblasting*, but Toohey and McHugh JJ went further in holding that the landlord's duty to keep the premises in good repair was non-delegable and could therefore not be discharged through an independent contractor. Again, however, the remainder of the High Court was against this conclusion.

The position in *Northern Sandblasting* was clarified by the High Court in *Jones v Bartlett* (2000) 205 CLR 166 when Gummow and Hayne JJ noted that the landlord's duty was "conterminous with a requirement that the premises be reasonably fit for the purposes for which they are let" (at [171]) with an expectation that the landlord act "in a manner to reasonably remove risks" (at [173]). Thus the standard of care expected of a lessor is consistent with general negligence principles to take reasonable care. This does not extend to a positive undertaking that the tenant (or their family) will not be injured in the house, neither does it extend beyond a duty to keep the premises in safe repair (per Gaudron J at [92]).

---

[25] For statutory confirmation of the duty of care in tort of the landlord who has undertaken the obligation to repair, towards persons injured on the premises, see: *Civil Liability Act 1936* (SA), s 21; *Occupiers' Liability Act 1985* (WA), s 9(1). The *Wrongs Act 1958* (Vic), s 14B(3), (4) extends the landlord's liability to the case where he or she has a right to enter and repair.

Duty of transferor of defective chattels

[9.85] The distinction which the law formerly drew between chattels dangerous in themselves and those dangerous by reason of their defective state no longer applies. As regards the former type of chattel, ordinary principles of negligence operated; as regards the latter, knowledge of the defect on the part of the defendant had to be proved. The distinction was expressly rejected in the Victorian case of *Todman v Victa* [1982] VR 849.[26] The court held it to be irrelevant whether a defective lawn mower fell within the class of objects dangerous in themselves. In any case the distinction was inconsistent with the principles laid down in *Donoghue v Stevenson* [1926] AC 562 as to the duty of care of the manufacturer of products towards their consumers. In that case Lord Atkin said (at 599):

> *A manufacturer of products, that he sells in such a form as to show that he intends them to reach the ultimate consumer in the form in which they left him with no reasonable possibility of intermediate examination, and with the knowledge that the absence of reasonable care in the preparation of putting up of the products will result in injury to the consumer's life or property, owes a duty to the consumer to take that reasonable care.*

The so-called narrow ratio of *Donoghue* concerning the duty of care of the manufacturer has been extended to other persons who put chattels into circulation; for example, repairers,[27] distributors[28] and retailers.[29] Indeed it is now apparent that the narrow rule in *Donoghue* is merely one aspect of the general duty of care binding those who put chattels into circulation in circumstances where the chattel may cause injury or damage. This is borne out by *Stennett v Hancock* [1939] 2 All ER 578, a case decided soon after *Donoghue*. In *Stennett* the plaintiff who had been hit and injured by a flange of a tyre which fell off a moving car, recovered damages from the repairer of the car. The plaintiff, a mere pedestrian on the highway, could in no sense have been considered a "consumer" of the car. He had merely been foreseeably injured by it. Another reason for supporting the view that the narrow rule is merely an application of the general principles of negligence, is that this allows the restrictions placed upon the duty of care by Lord Atkin to be regarded not as legal restrictions on the duty of care but as factors to be borne in mind when considering issues of breach of duty and causation. The fact that the chattel is in some way to change form before it reaches the consumer should not automatically rule out the existence of a duty; it is relevant to breach. Likewise the possibility of intermediate examination may or may not excuse the manufacturer. For instance, in *Taylor v Rover Car Co* [1966] 1 WLR 1491 the act of a foreman in keeping in use a hammer known by him to be defective was held to be an intervening act sufficient to negative liability on the part of the manufacturer; likewise the act of a purchaser in continuing to use on his vehicle a defective trailer coupling after discovering the defect in it: *Lambert v Lewis* [1982] AC 225. On the other hand, in *Sousaari v Steinhardt* [1989] 1 Qd R 477, it was held that where an employer had continued to use a defective pawl and cylinder which eventually injured an employee did not constitute a new cause since the employer had given instructions to the employee as to how to use the defective

---

[26] For rejection of the distinction, see also *Griffiths v Arch Engineering Co Ltd* [1968] 3 All ER 217.

[27] *Stennett v Hancock* [1939] 2 All ER 578; *Haseldine v Daw* [1941] 2 KB 343; *J Bull v Wilson & Horton* [1968] NZLR 88; *Andrews v Hopkinson* [1957] 1 QB 229.

[28] *Watson v Buckley* [1940] 1 All ER 174; *Vacwell Engineering Co Ltd v BDH Chemicals* [1971] 1 QB 88; *Cuckow v Polyester Reinforced Chemicals Pty Ltd* (1970) 19 FLR 143.

[29] *Andrews v Hopkinson* [1957] 1 QB 229; *Herschtal v Stewart & Arden* [1940] 1 KB 155.

equipment (though since these instructions were faulty the employer was also negligent). In *Voli v Inglewood SC* (1963) 110 CLR 74 the High Court held that an architect who had designed a stage which had collapsed and injured the plaintiff was liable to the plaintiff, even though the stage had to be approved by the Council's safety inspectors and inspectors failed to notice that it did not comply with the relevant by-laws.

Granted that there is a general duty of care owed by persons who put chattels into circulation, differences between the types of defendant will be reflected in differences in the standard of care imposed. A higher standard is imposed on manufacturers[30] or repairers of the chattel than on distributors or retailers. The latter would in general not be expected to test the safety of the product, although circumstances might arise in which this was required; for example, a requirement by a manufacturer that the distributor should test the product.[31] Private persons who distribute the chattel in the course of a private transaction are subject to a much lower standard of care than commercial dealers: possibly a mere duty to warn of known defects. In *Pivovaroff v Chernabaeff* (1978) 21 SASR 1 it was held that the gratuitous lender of an onion sorting machine had sufficiently discharged his duty of care by warning the borrower against allowing children to operate the machine. In *Hurley v Dyke* [1979] RTR 298 some members of the House of Lords thought that a person who had entered a second hand car in an auction sale on terms that it was sold "as seen with all faults" would have discharged his duty of care even as regards known defects rendering the vehicle dangerous to drive (no such knowledge was on the facts brought home to the defendant).

Statutory strict liability

[9.90] Under provisions of the *Trade Practices Act 1974* (Cth) (see also *Manufacturers Warranties Act 1974* (SA)), strict liability for injury or damage caused by a defective chattel may be incurred. The relevant liability is that of a corporation which either has manufactured the chattel, or holds itself out as the manufacturer, or is its importer (where the manufacturer has no place of business in Australia). Under s 74 of the *Trade Practices Act* a number of implied warranties arise on the supply of goods to a consumer on the part of the manufacturer or importer. (Note that the Act places limits on the concept of "consumer" transactions.) The most relevant warranty for present purposes is that arising under s 74D: that the goods be of merchantable quality. If they are not, there is liability for loss or damage caused to the consumer or to a person deriving title from the consumer. That loss or damage covers personal injury or damage to other property of the consumer. Liability is strict but no liability exists:

- where the defect in the goods is caused by a person not a servant or agent of the corporation or from a cause independent of human control;
- as regards defects specifically drawn to the consumer's attention; or
- if the consumer examines the goods prior to contracting to purchase them, as regards defects which the examination should have revealed.

---

[30] But not enough to hold a manufacturer of tampons liable as regards toxic shock syndrome: *Thompson v Johnson & Johnson Pty Ltd* [1989] Aust Torts Reports 80-278 – the medical knowledge available to the defendant was not such that a warning should have been given to the medical profession advising of damages associated with use.

[31] *Andrews v Hopkinson* [1957] 1 QB 229 – used car dealer had duty of care to test car prior to sale; *Kubach v Hollands* [1937] TLT 1024 – distributor had duty of care to carry out test stipulated by the manufacturer.

Section 75AD imposes liability on corporate manufacturers or importers of defective goods for personal injury caused by the defect in the goods they supply. Again, liability is strict and is wider than that under s 74 since it does not require supply of goods to a consumer; nor need the plaintiff be, or derive title from, a consumer. The liability extends to any person injured because of the defect in the goods. Section 75AE extends the liability to loss suffered by an individual other than the one injured. The loss must be suffered as a result of that injury or the death of the injured individual from the injury. That loss, however, must not arise from a business relationship between the injured individual and the person suffering the loss. Sections 75AF and 75AG extend the liability to damage caused to other goods and to land and buildings. Section 75AK establishes the defences:

- that the defect did not exist at the time the goods were supplied;
- that the defect existed only because of the defendant's compliance with a mandatory standard;
- that the state of scientific or technical knowledge at the time of the goods' supply by the actual manufacturer was not such as to enable the defect to be discovered; or
- that the goods were comprised in other finished goods and the defect was attributable to the design of the finished goods, or their markings, or the instructions or warnings given by the manufacturer of the finished goods.

Liability of the manufacturer or other persons under ss 74 and 75 is incapable of being excluded by contractual provision: s 68(1), though this is limited to some extent by s 68A.

Medical practitioner's duty to patient

[9.95] There is of course no doubt about the existence of the duty of care owed by a medical practitioner to a patient.[32] There has, however, been significant judicial and legislative activity around the question of the appropriate standard of care. In Australia there was originally an acceptance of the "*Bolam* test" which was rejected in the seminal decision of *Rogers v Whitaker* (1992) 175 CLR 479 and then revised by the Ipp Committee and given a modfied legislative voice in the Civil Liability Acts. It is important therefore to begin with *Bolam v Friern Hospital Management Committee* [1957] 1 WLR 582 when McNair J explained the professional standard of care in the following terms (at 587):

> *A doctor is not guilty of negligence if he has acted in accordance with a practice accepted as proper by a responsible body of medical men skilled in that particular art ... a doctor is not negligent if he is acting in accordance with such a practice, merely because there is a body of opinion that takes a contrary view.*[33]

Therefore there are two elements to the test: acceptance by a responsible body of peers and secondly, the existence of a contrary view will not result in a negligence finding.

---

[32]   This area was closely considered by the Ipp Committee. In order to understand the recommendations and subsequent statutory amendment, an understanding of the development of the common law is required.

[33]   The facts of this case involved the plaintiff suffering fractures during the administration of electro-convulsive therapy. The alleged negligence involved the lack of restraints and relaxants during the procedure as well as the lack of warning of the risks involved.

In rejecting the *Bolam* test, the High Court in *Rogers v Whitaker* found it unsatisfactory that the medical profession should determine the standards applicable to it in questions of legal liability.[34] The abandonment of *Bolam* by the High Court has been interpreted as a general one, applying to matters of diagnosis and treatment as well as to disclosure of risks.[35] This interpretation is despite the fact that the leading joint judgment draws a distinction between the former two categories and the third (a distinction which becomes more important when considered in the light of the Ipp Report). The question of what risks are to be disclosed is, according to the High Court, one on which lay opinion is as entitled to form an opinion as the medical profession. In matters of diagnosis and treatment, however, the question of whether the proper standard of care has been observed is one on which responsible medical opinion will have "an influential, often a decisive role to play": Mason CJ, Brennan, Dawson, Toohey and McHugh JJ. It was emphasised however, that the ultimate decision is for the court, not the profession. Significantly, the High Court did not reject the importance of professional evidence, it simply relegated it to one of the many relevant considerations: "The relevance of professional practice and opinion was not denied, what was denied was its conclusiveness": *Rosenberg v Percival* (2001) 178 ALR 577 at [7] per Gleeson CJ.

Duty to warn of risks

[9.100] The rejection of the *Bolam* test in the context of the giving of advice prior to treatment was, however, emphatic and clear. Such provision of information was viewed as a question removed from medical standards and practices: Mason CJ and Brennan, Dawson, Toohey and McHugh JJ. It was firmly stated that the standard of reasonable disclosure of the risks of treatment is to be determined by the court and turn on questions of what the individual patient would deem important (at 491):

> *A doctor has a duty to warn a patient of a material risk inherent in the proposed treatment; a risk is material if, in the circumstances of the particular case, a reasonable person in the patient's position, if warned of the risk, would be likely to attach significance to it, or if the medical practitioner is or should reasonably be aware that the particular patient, if warned of the risk, would be likely to attach significance to it. This duty is subject to the therapeutic privilege.*

It may be noted that the first part of the test is stated objectively; the second part is related to the practitioner's knowledge of the characteristics of the particular patient. Thus it is an objective test tempered by subjective considerations.

On the question of how to determine what risks should reasonably be disclosed to the patient, the court quoted King CJ in *F v R* (1983) 33 SASR 189 to the effect that the matter depended on a broad ranging inquiry including consideration of: the nature of the matter to be disclosed, the nature of the treatment, the desire of the patient for information, the temperament and health of the patient and the general surrounding circumstances. In *F v R* itself there was found to be no breach of duty in failing to inform the patient about the risk of re-canalisation after a tubal ligation, since the operation created no risk to health, was the only acceptable method at the time of sterilisation of a female and was performed in response to a "vehement request": see also *Petronic*

---

[34] *Rogers v Whitaker* (1992) 175 CLR 479 concerned the duty of care of a practitioner in advising a patient as to the risks of a certain operation (the facts and details of the decision are considered in [9.100]).

[35] See, eg, *Lowns v Woods; Procopis v Woods* [1996] Aust Torts Reports 81-376.

v Barnes [1988] Aust Torts Reports 80-147. In *Rogers v Whitaker* the operation to be performed was a largely cosmetic one on a previously injured eye. The risk in question (of sympathetic ophthalmia causing blindness in the other eye) was assessed at one in 14,000. In determining whether this risk was a material one, the court considered the cosmetic nature of the surgery, the catastrophic nature of the risk if it materialised and the obvious concern of the patient to protect her good eye, concluding that the doctor was negligent in his failure to inform the patient of this risk. As the concerns of the patient were clear in this instance the court was not obliged to decide how the second branch of its formulation should be applied. But it indicated that a question about a specific risk must be answered truthfully. The Canadian decision in *Reibl v Hughes* (1980) 114 DLR (3d) 1 received the approval of the High Court in *Rogers v Whitaker*. In *Reibl* there was a finding that the 10% chance of a stroke from a particular operation should have been disclosed. *Battersby v Tottman* (1985) 37 SASR 524 shows, somewhat controversially, the continued existence of the therapeutic privilege. In that case it was held that the risk to the plaintiff's sight of the administration of a certain drug need not have been disclosed, because the plaintiff was in a suicidal state through mental illness and the drug would relieve that condition. The risk of suicide was reasonably regarded as the more serious by the practitioner, acting on the assumption that disclosure of the risk to sight would have led to the patient refusing the drug.

Battery or negligence?

[9.105] The question of what risks of treatment should be disclosed by the practitioner to the patient is a question of breach of duty of care in the tort of negligence. Even where disclosure is found to be inadequate, consent to the treatment is still present and no action of battery is possible. This was emphasised in *Rogers v Whitaker* when the majority held that battery is negatived by the patient being advised in broad terms of the nature of the procedure to be performed (at 490). Where, on the other hand, the nature of the treatment is not disclosed or is inadequately disclosed to the patient, there is no consent and battery is available.

Even though a patient is able to establish a breach of duty through inadequate disclosure of the risks of certain treatment, this alone is not enough to establish a cause of action in negligence. The patient must also show that if the risk had been disclosed he or she would not have undergone the treatment. The issue of causation this raises is considered in Chapter 11.

Ipp Committee recommendations

[9.110] The terms of reference provided to the Ipp Committee[36] highlighted the need to reconsider the approach adopted in *Rogers v Whitaker* (1992) 175 CLR 479. The Committee acknowledged the difference between treatment and provision of information and stated that the law should deal with these activities in different ways. The question (as identified by the Committee) with respect to treatment is whether the court is to be deemed the ultimate arbiter or to defer to a designated body of opinion

---

[36]   Australia, *Review of the Law of Negligence Final Report: September 2002* (hereafter Ipp Report): Term of Reference 3(d) directed the Committee to develop and evaluate options for a requirement that the standard of care for professionals (including medical professionals) accords with the generally accepted practice of the relevant profession at the time of the negligent act or omission.

within the medical profession.[37] The approach in *Bolam v Friern Hospital Management Committee* [1957] 1 WLR 582 was considered and the opinion of the Committee was that a modified version of the *Bolam* rule should be introduced.[38] In order to overcome the perceived limitations of the *Bolam* test (and indeed the *Rogers v Whitaker* test) and to ensure compliance with the terms of reference, the Committee recommended a rule that a defendant could not be held liable where the court is satisfied that the conduct in question was in accordance with an opinion widely held by a significant number of respected practitioners in the relevant field.[39] The Committee also noted that it is necessary to provide guidelines as to circumstances in which a court is justified in not deferring to medical opinion[40] and recommended the adoption of the *Bolitho*[41] proviso that there was no requirement to accept medical opinion if the court considered that opinion to be "irrational".[42]

These recommendations have been endorsed by statute in most jurisdictions, as set out in Figure 9.5. It is important to note that there are subtle, but perhaps significant differences in the wording of each of the relevant sections. The significance of these differences awaits judicial interpretation. There has been limited discussion of the relevant legislative provisions with the Supreme Court of New South Wales noting that in applying s 5O of the *Civil Liability Act 2002* the defendant professional must establish that they were acting in accordance with a manner accepted by a professional opinion and that in contesting this evidence, it is not sufficient for the plaintiff to seek expert evidence of an alternate path of treatment; something more than a differing opinion is needed: *Walker v Sydney West Area Health Service* [2007] Aust Torts Reports 81-892 at [167] per Simpson J.

It is important to note that in each jurisdiction adopting the legislative reformulation of the *Bolam* test there is a clear statement to the effect that the section does not apply in the context of the giving of advice prior to medical treatment. The materiality test therefore remains on foot in its original, narrow form.

Employer's duty to employees

[9.115] The employer's duty of care for the safety of employees is one of the most important "protective" relationships recognised by the common law and one which clearly may entail for its proper discharge positive action on the employer's part. However, the considerable extension of workers' compensation legislation which confers a right to compensation on the employee independently of the employer's fault has caused some diminution in the importance of the common law action, and even its replacement in whole or in part in some States by the statutory scheme: see Chapter 2. Strict liability on the part of the employer towards the employee may also exist at common law under the tort of breach of statutory duty. The "safety" of employees protected by the common law duty of care extends to their property, though the practical importance of this is not great.

---

[37] Ipp Report, [3.2].
[38] Ipp Report, [3.5]. This opinion was basically founded on the negative response to the question whether the court should defer to medical opinion.
[39] Ipp Report, [3.14].
[40] Ipp Report, [3.17].
[41] *Bolitho v City Hackney Health Authority* [1998] AC 232.
[42] Ipp Report, [3.18]. It is important to note that the Committee acknowledged at [3.19] that it would be rare to identify instances of treatment that are both irrational and in accordance with an opinion widely held by a significant number of respected practitioners in the field.

Figure 9.5: Professional standards

Juris	Legislation	Provision
ACT	*Civil Law (Wrongs) Act 2002*	No mention.
NSW	*Civil Liability Acts 2002* Div 6	s 5O Standard of care for professionals: • A person practising a profession does not incur liability if it is established that the person acted in a manner that (at the time the service was provided) was widely accepted in Australia by peer professional opinion as competent. • Peer professional opinion cannot be relied on if the court considers it to be irrational. • The existence of differing peer professional opinions does not prevent any one or more of those opinions being relied upon for the purposes of this section. • Universal acceptance is not required. s 5P Division 6 does not apply to duty to warn of risk.
NT	*Personal Injuries (Liabilities and Damages) Act 2003*	No mention.
Qld	*Civil Liability Act 2003* Div 5	s 20 Defines professional as a person practising a profession. s 21 Proactive and reactive duty of doctor to warn of risk: • Requires a doctor to warn a patient of risks by providing information that a "reasonable person in the patient's position, would require in order to make a reasonably informed decision". • This includes information that the doctor knows or ought reasonably to know the patient wants to be given before making the decision (essentially adoption of the *Rogers v Whitaker* test). s 22 Standard of care for professionals: • No breach in provision of a professional service if it is established that the professional acted in a way that (at the time the service was provided) was widely accepted by a significant number of respected practitioners in the field as competent professional practice. • No reliance required if the peer professional opinion is considered to be irrational or contrary to written law. • The existence of differing peer professional opinions does not prevent any one or more of those opinions from being relied upon for the purposes of this section. • Universal acceptance is not required.

Juris	Legislation	Provision
		• The section does not apply to liability arising in connection with the giving of (or the failure to give) a warning, advice or other information in relation to the risk of harm to person. **Also note:** s 15 No proactive duty to warn of obvious risk: • No duty of care to warn of an obvious risk; unless P has requested advice from D about the risk, or D is required by law to warn, or risk is inherent in professional service provided by D. • Doesn't apply to doctors.
SA	*Civil Liability Act 1936* Pt 6, Div 4	s 40: • Establishes the standard of care required of a person holding themselves out as possessing a particular skill is to be determined by reference to what could reasonably be expected of a person professing that skill and the relevant circumstances at the date of the alleged negligence. s 41 Standard of care for professionals: • No liability is attached to a professional service provider if it is established that the provider acted in a manner that (at the time) was widely accepted in Australia by members of the same profession as competent professional practice. • No reliance required if the peer professional opinion is considered to be irrational. • The existence of differing peer professional opinions does not prevent any one or more of those opinions being relied upon for the purposes of this section. • Universal acceptance is not required. • Does not apply to liability arising in connection with the giving of (or failure to give) warning, advice or other information in respect of a risk of death or injury.
Tas	*Civil Liability Act 2002* Div 6	s 21 Proactive and reactive duty of registered practitioner to warn of risk: • Requires a doctor to warn a patient of risks by providing information that a "reasonable person in the patient's position would require in order to make a reasonably informed decision". This includes information that the doctor knows or ought reasonably to know the patient wants to be given before making the decision (essentially adoption of the *Rogers v Whitaker* test). • Provides protection for the medical practitioner by excluding the application of the section from situations where the medical practitioner has to act promptly to avoid serious risk to the life or health of the patient and the patient is not able to hear or respond to warning and there is not sufficient time to contact a person responsible for making a decision for the patient.

Juris	Legislation	Provision
		s 22 Standard of care for professionals: • No liability is attached to a professional service provider if it is established that the provider acted in a manner that (at the time) was widely accepted in Australia by members of the same profession as competent professional practice. • No reliance required if the peer professional opinion is considered to be irrational. • The existence of differing peer professional opinions does not prevent any one or more of those opinions being relied upon for the purposes of this section. • Universal acceptance is not required. • Does not apply to liability arising in connection with the giving of (or failure to give) warning, advice or other information in respect of a risk of death or injury.
Vic	*Wrongs Act 1958* Div 5	s 57 Defines a professional as an individual practising a profession. s 58 The standard of care required of a person holding themselves out as possessing a particular skill is to be determined by reference to what could reasonably be expected of a person professing that skill and the relevant circumstances at the date of the alleged negligence. s 59 Standard of care for professionals: • No breach in provision of a professional service if it is established that the professional acted in a way that (at the time the service was provided) was widely accepted by peer professional opinion by a significant number of respected practitioners in the field as competent professional practice in the circumstances. • No reliance required if the peer professional opinion is considered to be unreasonable. • The existence of differing peer professional opinions (of a significant number of respected practitioners in the field) does not prevent any one or more of those opinions from being relied upon for the purposes of this section. • Universal acceptance is not required. • If a court determines peer professional opinion to be unreasonable, it must specify in writing the reasons for that determination (this does not apply where there is a jury). s 60 Duty to warn of risk: • Does not apply to liability arising in connection with the giving of (or failure to give) warning, advice or other information in respect of a risk of death or injury.

Juris	Legislation	Provision
WA	*Civil Liability Act 2002*	s 5PA Defines health professional. s 5PB Standard of care for health professionals:
		• No liability for an act or omission by a health professional if it is in accordance with a practice which, at the time of the act or omission, is widely accepted by the health professional's peers as competent professional practice. • Does not apply in relation to informing a person of a risk of injury or death associated with the treatment proposed for a patient or a foetus being carried by a pregnant woman or a procedure proposed to be conducted for the purpose of diagnosing a condition of a patient or a foetus being carried by a pregnant patient. • Applies even if another practice that is widely accepted by the health professional's peers as competent professional practice differs from or conflicts with the treatment. • Does not exclude liability where the health professional acted in a manner which was so unreasonable that no reasonable health professional in that position and those circumstances would have acted (or omitted to act) in that manner. • Universal acceptance not required. • The plaintiff always bears the onus of proof.

Practice Questions

Revision Questions

9.1 Discuss the extent of the duty of care owed by teachers and education authorities to school children.

9.2 In what ways, if any, has tortious liability been supported by statutory strict liability for injury or damage caused by defective goods? Discuss.

9.3 Explain the professional duty of care.

Answers to Practice Questions

Revision Questions

9.1 There is no question about the existence of the duty of care during school hours while the pupils are on the premises. But the duty may extend beyond that. Where the school has adopted a practice of allowing its pupils onto school premises before the commencement of teaching, a duty of care to exercise supervision arises: *Commonwealth v Introvigne* (1982) 150 CLR 285; *Geyer v Downs* (1977) 138 CLR 91. Where a five-year-old child was discharged early from school before the expected arrival of his parent and was then injured in a traffic accident, the school authority was held liable to the child even though the accident occurred off the school premises: *Barnes v Hampshire CC* [1969] 11 WLR 1563.[43] It is clear also that teachers who take children on school trips or holiday outings owe them a duty of care to supervise their activities: *Munro v Anglican Church of Australia* (unreported, Court of Appeal, NSW, 1415/89, No 490/1985); and *Gugiatti v Servite College* [2004] Aust Torts Reports 81-724. Again a duty of care may exist to supervise boarding arrangements on buses provided by the school or as regards behaviour on those buses. Generally, however, once the pupils have left the school premises the duty of care terminates: *Stokes v Russell* (unreported, Supreme Court, Tas, 18 January 1983, No 2/1983) (no duty of care owed as regards the boarding of an ordinary service bus by pupil after school had finished). Where, however, the school through its staff members has become aware of a particular danger to its pupils after leaving school, it has a duty to take reasonable protective measures. So a school authority was held liable where the school had failed to offer protection against bullying of its pupils by older boys after school, and the plaintiff pupil had been hit and injured by a missile thrown by an older boy: *Trustees of the Catholic School of Bathurst v Koffman* [1996] Aust Torts Reports 81-398.

The expected level of supervision of students can vary depending upon the location of the activity with the classroom generally requiring closer supervision than the schoolyard: *Parkin v ACT Schools Authority* [2005] ACTSC 3; and *Australian Capital Territory v El Sheik* [2000] Aust Torts Reports 81-577. Knowledge of a pattern of behaviour can also impact on the expected response: *Parkin v ACT Schools Authority* [2005] ACTSC 3. There is a clear duty to protect students from bullying behaviour of other students: *Cox v State of New South Wales* [2007] Aust Torts Reports 81-888.

9.2 Discussion should centre on the provisions of the *Trade Practices Act 1974* (Cth) and also the *Manufacturers Warranties Act 1974* (SA). Both Acts provide strict liability for injury or damage caused by defective goods. Liability attaches to the corporation which either has manufactured the goods, or holds itself out as the manufacturer or is its importer (where the manufacturer has no place of business in Australia). Under s 74 of the *Trade Practices Act*, there are a number of implied warranties in relation to the supply of goods to a consumer on the part of the manufacturer or importer, but note the limits on the concept of "consumer" transactions:

* Section 74D requires that goods be of merchantable quality. If they are not, there is liability for loss or damage caused to the consumer or to a person deriving title from the consumer. That loss or damage covers personal injury or damage to other property of the consumer. Liability is strict but no liability exists:

  — where the defect in the goods is caused by a person not a servant or agent of the corporation or from a cause independent of human control;

  — as regards defects specifically drawn to the consumer's attention; or

---

[43] See also *Reynolds v Haines*, above, n 9.

— if the consumer examines the goods prior to contracting to purchase them, as regards defects which the examination should have revealed.

- Section 75AD imposes liability on corporate manufacturers or importers of defective goods for personal injury caused by the defect in the goods they supply. Liability is strict and is wider than that under s 74 since it does not require supply of goods to a consumer; nor need the plaintiff be, or derive title from, a consumer. The liability extends to any person injured because of the defect in the goods.

- Section 75AE extends the liability to loss suffered by another individual than the one injured, as a result of that injury or the death of the injured individual from the injury. That loss, however, must not arise from a business relationship between the injured individual and the person suffering the loss.

- Sections 75AF and 75AG extend the liability to damage caused to other goods and to land and buildings. Section 75AK establishes a number of defences.

9.3   The professional standard of care has evolved from the UK position stated in *Bolam v Friern Hospital Management Committee* [1957] 1 WLR 582 in which the actions of professionals were measured against their peers. This test was deemed inappropriate by the High Court of Australia on the basis that it placed responsibility for the ascertaining of appropriate behaviour in the hands of the very profession under consideration. The materiality test was developed in the decision of *Rogers v Whitaker* (1992) 175 CLR 479 which placed the emphasis on expectations of the patient. The test was originally developed in the context of the giving of advice prior to treatment but was given broad application by the courts: *Lowns v Woods; Procopis v Woods* [1996] Aust Torts Reports 81-376. The Ipp Committee addressed the question of professional standards and as a result of its recommendations the *Bolam* test has been given legislative form. The legislation refers to professionals generally with a significant exception when considering the provision of advice prior to medical treatment. If there is a risk of either injury or death in a particular course of medical treatment then the legislation does not apply, instead the *Rogers v Whitaker* materiality test remains the relevant legal measure with respect to the provision of advice.

Tutorial Questions

Discussion Questions

9.1   Should parents be vicariously liable for the torts of their children?

9.2   In *Rogers v Whitaker* (1992) 175 CLR 479 the court said that:

> *A doctor has a duty to warn a patient of a material risk inherent in the proposed treatment; a risk is material if, in the circumstances of the particular case, a reasonable person in the patient's position, if warned of the risk, would be likely to attach significance to it, or if the medical practitioner is or should reasonably be aware that the particular patient, if warned of the risk, would be likely to attach significance to it. This duty is subject to the therapeutic privilege.*

Does this standard place too high a burden on the medical profession? Discuss (remembering that this test now only applies in the context of the giving of advice prior to treatment).

9.3   Should an employer be vicariously liable for the actions of an independent contractor in the same way that they are vicariously liable for the actions of their employees?

9.4   Should an occupier owe a duty of care towards trespassers? Discuss, including in your discussion some commentary on *Hackshaw v Shaw* (1984) 155 CLR 614 and the relevant legislative provisions.

CHAPTER 10

Breach of Duty of Care

Reading

Sappideen, Vines, Grant and Watson, *Torts: Commentary and Materials*, pp 447-516.

Objectives

This chapter will explain:

- the concept of a breach of duty generally;
- reasonable foreseeability of the risk of harm (including consideration of the notion of obvious and inherent risks);
- relevant factors as to the foreseeability of the risk of harm;
- relevant considerations as to the reasonableness of the defendant's conduct;
- the objective standard of the reasonable person;
- relevance of the defendant's subjective characteristics; and
- relevance of professional and community standards of conduct.

Principles

Establishing breach of duty of care

[10.05] In Chapter 8 we considered the preliminary question of whether or not the defendant owes the plaintiff a duty of care. Once duty is established, the second step in determining liability is to address the question of whether or not the defendant is in breach of that duty. To determine breach there are two factors to consider:

- the degree of foreseeable risk created by the defendant's conduct; and
- the reasonableness or otherwise of the defendant's response to that risk.

Central to these considerations is the notion of the standard of care required by the defendant in the circumstances. If the defendant has failed to meet the requisite standard of care, then breach will be established.

The first factor looks at the *degree of foreseeable risk*, rather than the foreseeability of the risk itself. The higher the degree of risk the less reasonable it will be for the defendant to fail to take steps to prevent it occurring. The second factor addresses the issue of the reasonableness of the defendant's response to the risk. This matter is determined by reference to a variety of factors including the cost and burden imposed on the defendant in having to attempt to remove the risk, and the public or social utility of the defendant's conduct associated with the creation of the risk. These factors in combination are referred to as the "calculus of negligence".[1]

It is essential to note that the process does not involve a strict, formulaic application of the law. Decisions on whether there has been a breach do not create binding precedents, but are limited to their own facts,[2] or as Gleeson CJ and Kirby J explain it: "the issue of breach of duty framed in negligence is one of fact. Results are fact sensitive".[3] In any consideration of breach of duty, however, it is appropriate to begin with a consideration of the issue of reasonable foreseeability and the nature of the risk. The reason for this approach was explained by Gummow J in *Roads and Traffic Authority of NSW v Dederer* (2007) 238 ALR 761 when he stated that "it is only through the correct identification of the risk that one can assess what a reasonable response to that risk would be" (at [59]).

---

[1] The case most often cited as authority for the calculus of negligence is *Wyong SC v Shirt* (1980) 146 CLR 40. For a demonstration of the calculus and how it is applied see *Romeo v Conservation Commission (NT)* (1998) 192 CLR 431.

[2] For example, cf *Sydney CC v Dell 'Oro* (1968) 89 WN Pt 1 (NSW) 168 and *Bus v Sydney CC* (1989) 167 CLR 78, where the fact situations were very similar but different decisions were reached. See also *Qualcast Wolverhampton Ltd v Haynes* [1959] AC 743 – no rule of law that employers must ensure that their employees wear the protective clothing provided – everything depended on the particular factual situation. Also note the comment in *Vairy v Wyong Shire Council* (2005) 223 CLR 422 at [3] that the decision in *Nagle* (discussed in [10.25]) is not authority for the proposition that the coastline of Australia should be ringed with signs warning of the danger of invisible rocks.

[3] *Vairy v Wyong Shire Council* (2005) 223 CLR 422 at [2].

Figure 10.1: General principles

> Was the RISK of injury to the plaintiff REASONABLY FORESEEABLE?
>
> IF SO, was the RESPONSE of the defendant to this risk REASONABLE?
>
> CONSIDER: Did the defendant meet the requisite STANDARD OF CARE?
>
> IF NOT: BREACH of duty.

The reasonable person

[10.07] The first step of the standard inquiry begins, as with duty, at the reasonable person. The start point is covered with a deceptively simple statement: standard is to be determined in accordance with what the "reasonable person, in the defendant's position (with the knowledge that they either had or ought to have had) would have done in the circumstances out of which the harm arose'.

Figure 10.2

Juris	Legislation	Provision
ACT	*Civil Law (Wrongs) Act 2002*	s 42
NSW	*Civil Liability Act 2002*	Mentioned in context of contributory negligence, s 5R
NT	No mention.	
Qld	*Civil Liability Act 2003*	General standard provisions only, refer Fig 10.7
SA	*Civil Liability Act 1936*	s 31(1)
Tas	*Civil Liability Act 2002*	General standard provisions only, refer Fig 10.7
Vic	*Wrongs Act 1958*	Mentioned in context of contributory negligence, s 62
WA	*Civil Liability Act 2002*	Mentioned in context of contributory negligence, s 5K

This is of course, only the preliminary step which becomes more complicated once the issue of what constitutes the reasonable person or a reasonably foreseeable risk is raised. It is this discussion which will form the focus of the remainder of this chapter.

Reasonable foreseeability

[10.10] In determining whether or not a breach of duty has occurred, the first step is to determine whether or not the risk was reasonably foreseeable. It is important to remember that this is only a preliminary step, as Kirby J explained in *Romeo v Conservation Commission (NT)* (1998) 192 CLR 431 at 480:

It is quite wrong to read past authority as requiring that any reasonably foreseeable risk, however remote, must in every case be guarded against. Such an approach may result from the erroneous conflation of the three separate inquiries: duty, scope of duty and breach of duty.

Within this preliminary step there are some significant factors to take into account:

- a risk that is not "far fetched or fanciful" (now given legislative form as "not insignificant");
- the imprudent plaintiff; and
- obvious and inherent risks.

Risk not "far fetched or fanciful"

[10.15] Even slight risks of harm may be regarded as reasonably foreseeable. Clearly some events are absolutely unforeseeable in general, or regarded as foreseeable given the knowledge of the particular defendant: see [10.90]. However the slightness of risk may not be enough to discharge the defendant if it is a real risk; it is the nature of the risk that is of relevance to the courts, not the likelihood of it occurring. In *The Wagon Mound (No 2)* [1967] 1 AC 617 the Privy Council held that the possibility of furnace oil that had been discharged from the defendant's ship catching fire on the waters of Sydney Harbour, though a slight risk, was nevertheless a reasonably foreseeable risk. This was because "a reasonable man having the knowledge and experience of the chief engineer of the Wagon Mound would have known there was a real risk of the oil on the water catching fire in some way": Lord Reid at 641.

The same point was made by the High Court in *Wyong SC v Shirt* (1980) 146 CLR 40 in holding that the Council was negligent in placing "Deep Water" signs in shallow water alongside a deep water channel for boats, thereby engendering a belief in the plaintiff water-skier that the water was generally safe for water-skiing. The Council was held responsible for the plaintiff's injury caused by his falling from the skis into shallow water and hitting his head on the bottom. Mason J stated (at 47):

A risk of injury which is remote in the sense that it is extremely unlikely to occur may nevertheless constitute a foreseeable risk. A risk which is not far-fetched or fanciful is real and therefore foreseeable.

The plaintiff is further assisted in establishing reasonable foreseeability of harm by the rule that the "precise concatenation of circumstances" need not be foreseeable. Provided the individual elements of the "concatenation" are foreseeable, their operation in combination does not need to be. A well-known example of this is the decision of the High Court in *Chapman v Hearse* (1961) 106 CLR 112. The defendant, Chapman, negligently drove his car into the rear of another car and was thrown out of his car into the centre of the roadway. Some short time afterwards Dr Cherry, who was driving past, stopped to render medical assistance to Chapman. The weather conditions were dark and wet and there was no-one available to give warning to oncoming traffic. While rendering assistance Dr Cherry was hit and killed by a car driven by Hearse. Chapman's argument – that he owed no duty on the facts to Dr Cherry on the ground that the events were not reasonably foreseeable – was dismissed by the High Court. The combination of events was unusual but each event was by itself foreseeable and the plaintiff did not need to show that the "precise manner in which his injuries were sustained was reasonably foreseeable": Dixon CJ, Kitto, Taylor, Menzies and Windeyer JJ at 121.

The rule just stated is clearly established but, when considered in combination with the rule that even slight risks may be reasonably foreseeable, it throws doubt on the proposition that events or combinations of this sort are such that the reasonable person actually bears them in mind when directing his or her mind to the activity being conducted. Rather, the relevant test of reasonable foreseeability appears to be whether the reasonable person would accept that events of this sort were not altogether unlikely consequences of the act in question, if asked about it at the time of the act:

> It is not necessary to show that this particular accident and this particular damage were probable; it is sufficient if the accident is of a class that might well be anticipated as one of the reasonable and probable results of the wrongful act.[4]

That test is one of hindsight rather than foresight,[5] and in respect of the unusual risk that seems to be how the law operates. In some cases, however, the combination of factors and the unusualness of those factors, are so freakish that a reasonable person even with the benefit of hindsight would regard them as unpredictable. A famous example is the American case of *Palsgraf v Long Island Railway* 248 NY 339 (1928). The plaintiff was a passenger on the defendant's railway line standing on the platform awaiting a train. A man carrying a package wrapped in newspaper attempted to board a moving train, but was in some difficulty and was assisted by two of the defendant's guards, one attempting to pull him on the train and the other pushing him from behind. In the course of this, the package, which proved to contain fireworks, was dislodged from the man's grasp and fell upon the rails. This caused the fireworks to explode. The shock of the explosion threw down some scales some feet away from where the fireworks fell. The scales struck and injured the plaintiff.

The court held that even if there were negligence on the part of the guards, there was no actionable negligence towards the plaintiff since the injury to her was not reasonably foreseeable. This conclusion, which seems entirely correct, may be based on the non-foreseeability of the individual factors; for example, that the innocent looking package should contain fireworks (the point particularly emphasised by Cardozo CJ) or of an explosive force being released sufficient to upset scales at some distance, or of these factors operating in combination.[6]

Risk "not insignificant"

[10.17] The Ipp Committee considered the test of foreseeability set out in *Wyong SC v Shirt* (1980) 146 CLR 40 (that a foreseeable risk is one which is not far fetched or fanciful) and expressed concern that this test could encourage lower courts to ignore the elements of the calculus of negligence.[7] The suggested improvement was to replace "far fetched or fanciful" with a term indicating a risk with a higher degree of probability of

4   *Haynes v Harwood* [1935] 1 KB 146 per Greer LJ at 156 (cited with approval in *Chapman v Hearse* (1961) 106 CLR 112 at 120).

5   Support for a test of reasonable foreseeability based on hindsight rather than foresight is contained in the judgment of Lord Jauncey in the House of Lords decision in *Page v Smith* [1995] 2 All ER 736 at 750, quoting Lord Wilberforce in *McLoughlin v O'Brian* [1983] 1 AC 410 at 420.

6   This case is also often cited as authority for the concept of the unforeseen plaintiff. In these circumstances it was found that the reasonable person would not have foreseen injury to Mrs Palsgraf.

7   Australia, *Review of the Law of Negligence Final Report: September 2002* (hereafter Ipp Report), p 105.

and the Committee settled on the term "not insignificant".[8] Recommendation
embodied this term and suggested that the elements of the calculus of negligence
be clearly identified and specifically included in the legislation.[9]

Whilst the response has been consistent in most jurisdictions; the practical impact
of the change in phraseology is yet to be considered by the courts.

Figure 10.3: Risk "not insignificant"

Juris	Legislation	Provision
ACT	*Civil Law (Wrongs) Act 2002*	s 43(1)(b)
NSW	*Civil Liability Act 2002*	s 5B(1)(b)
NT	No mention	
Qld	*Civil Liability Act 2003*	s 9(1)(b)
SA	*Civil Liability Act 1936*	s 32(1)(b)
Tas	*Civil Liability Act 2002*	s 11(1)(b)
Vic	*Wrongs Act 1958*	s 48(1)(b)
WA	*Civil Liability Act 2002*	s 5B(1)(b)

Interplay of factors: Bolton v Stone and Wagon Mound (No 2)

[10.20] The leading case *Bolton v Stone* [1951] AC 850 illustrates the situation in which
a risk, while foreseeable, may be deemed to be so unlikely that it does not constitute
a breach if no steps are taken to prevent it. The plaintiff in *Bolton* was standing on the
highway outside a cricket ground and was struck and injured by a cricket ball hit out of
the ground. The number of times such a hit had occurred previously was estimated at
some half a dozen times in the previous 30 years and the particular hit was considered
quite exceptional. The House of Lords held the defendants not liable, not because
the injury was not reasonably foreseeable, but because in view of the slightness of the
risk the defendants were justified in taking no precautions whatsoever to prevent its
occurrence. One of the problems facing the plaintiff in this case was to suggest a feasible
means of eliminating the risk; as Lord Normand suggested, the only practical method
of avoiding the danger would have been to stop playing cricket in the ground.

More recently, in *Roads and Traffic Authority of NSW v Dederer* (2007) 238 ALR 761
in which a 14-year-old boy was rendered a partial paraplegic after diving off the bridge,
the High Court found it significant that the bridge had been there and people of all ages
had been diving off it for over 40 years and there had been no other incident. Whilst
this was not deemed to be determinative, it was certainly a relevant consideration.

This point was explained (with reference to *Bolton*) taken up by Lord Reid, giving
the judgment of the Privy Council in *The Wagon Mound (No 2)* [1967] 1 AC 617, the
facts of which have already been considered. Lord Reid stated (at 642-643):

> *It does not follow that, no matter what the circumstances may be, it is justifiable to
> neglect a risk of such a small magnitude. A reasonable man would only neglect such
> a risk if he had some valid reason for doing so: for example that it would involve*

---

[8]   Ipp Report, p 105.
[9]   The "calculus of negligence" and its legislative form is considered further below, at [10.40]ff.

considerable expense to eliminate the risk. He would weigh the risk against the difficulty of eliminating it. If the activity which caused the injury to Miss Stone had been an unlawful activity there can be little doubt but that Bolton v Stone would have been decided differently. In their Lordships' judgment Bolton v Stone did not alter the general principle that a person must be regarded as negligent if he does not take steps to eliminate a risk which he knows or ought to know is a real risk and not a mere possibility which would never influence the mind of a reasonable man. What that decision did was to recognise and give effect to the qualification that it is justifiable not to take steps to eliminate a real risk if it is small and if the circumstances are such that a reasonable man, careful of the safety of his neighbour, would think right to neglect it. In the present case there was no justification whatever for discharging the oil in to Sydney Harbour. Not only was it an offence to do so, but also involved considerable loss financially. If the ship's engineer had thought about the matter there could have been no question of balancing the advantages and disadvantages. From every point of view it was both his duty and his interest to stop the discharge immediately.

Figure 10.4: Reasonable foreseeability

Key to reasonable foreseeability = Nature of the risk, not the likelihood of the event.

"When we speak of a risk of injury as being foreseeable we are not making any statements as to the probability or improbability of its occurrence."[10]

Imprudent plaintiff

[10.25] The behaviour of the plaintiff has become increasingly relevant to the courts when determining the outer boundaries of foreseeability. Until recently the High Court has readily found that it is necessary to foresee and guard against extremely foolhardy conduct by the plaintiff, even when such behaviour is deemed to be unlikely. An example is the failure to take adequate precautions by an electrician in performing a task unaided in the vicinity of live wires, the existence of which he knew: *Bus v Sydney CC* (1989) 167 CLR 78. Another example is a motorist through extreme drunkenness failing to see and avoid a clearly visible obstruction in the highway: *March v E & MH Stramare Pty Ltd* (1991) 171 CLR 506. Yet another is a swimmer diving into a rocky coastal basin and hitting his head on a rock, where some danger (though not the exact nature of it) must have been apparent to the swimmer: *Nagle v Rottnest Island Authority* (1993) 177 CLR 423. A State decision also illustrates the point. In *Kelly v Smith* (1986) 42 SASR 13 the defendant had left a bottle of clear cleaning fluid in a transparent bottle marked "Poison" on the top of the refrigerator in a hotel. The plaintiff, mistaking it for water, drank from it and suffered internal injury. The defendant was held liable for these injuries.

There is, of course, the possibility of a substantial reduction of damages for contributory negligence in cases of this kind.[11] In other cases, however, the plaintiff's knowledge of the risk has been found sufficient to discharge the defendant from liability. In *Phillis v Daly* (1988) 15 NSWLR 65 the plaintiff was injured when she

---

[10] *Wyong Shire Council v Shirt* (1980) 146 CLR 40 at 47 per Mason J.
[11] To be considered in detail in Chapter 12.

slipped while walking over some ornamental logs in the grounds of the defendant's hotel. Although the protuberances on the logs, where branches had been, created a risk of slipping, the risk was obvious and the defendant was entitled to expect that persons such as the plaintiff would avoid it by going round the logs or by taking reasonable care when walking over them. The plaintiff's injury was therefore not reasonably foreseeable. Again, in *Delahunt v Westlake* [2000] Aust Torts Reports 81-542, the master of an apprentice electrician was held not liable to the apprentice who had fallen from a roof and injured himself while working on a TV aerial. The fall was caused by improper use by the apprentice of the safety harness; but since he had been fully instructed as to its use by the master, and since he had used it safely under supervision for nine months, the master was not liable for his injuries.

In other cases, however, knowledge of the risk on the part of the plaintiff has not been enough to excuse the defendant. In *Rowes Bus Service v Cowan* [1999] Aust Torts Reports 81-515 the defendant bus company was held liable for continuing to allow its buses to stop at a place where road traffic conditions were known to be dangerous. On the occasion in question the plaintiff, a 17-year-old passenger, had alighted safely onto the footpath but then when crossing the road had been struck and injured by a car. In *Anderson v Mt Isa Basketball Association* [1997] Aust Torts Reports 81-451 the defendants were held to be in breach of their duty of care to the plaintiff, a novice referee, for failing to instruct her to avoid running backwards on the concrete surface on which the game was played; even though, as the dissenting judge pointed out, the danger of running backwards was obvious and on occasions during the game would be necessary. Recent judicial and legislative trends have, however, turned away from the imprudent plaintiff.

Obvious and inherent risks

[10.30] An increasingly relevant consideration in the context of foreseeability and breach is the categorisation of a risk as either obvious or inherent. This trend is clearly illustrated in the High Court decision of *Woods v Multi-Sport Holdings Pty Ltd* (2002) 208 CLR 460. The majority of the Court (Gleeson CJ, Hayne and Callinan JJ) found that the risk of a participant in a game of indoor cricket being hit in the face was so obvious that the lack of either specific warnings or provision of protective head gear did not constitute a breach of duty.

Some more recent activity in superior State courts and the High Court has reflected this trend and clearly demonstrated the significance of the recognition of obvious risks. The courts have retreated from the position in *Nagle v Rottnest Island Authority* (1993) 177 CLR 423 and have placed personal responsibility on those who dive into water which they know (or ought reasonably know) is either shallow or rocky. This position is clearly demonstrated in a collection of decisions: *Vairy v Wyong Shire Council* (2005) 223 CLR 422; *Mulligan v Coffs Harbour City Council* (2005) 223 CLR 486;[12] *Clarke v Coleambally Ski Club Inc* [2004] NSWCA 376;[13] *Berrigan SC v Ballerini* [2005] VSCA

---

[12]   Both plaintiffs suffered serious injuries after diving into water at popular swimming sites. There were no signs warning of the risks of diving into water at either location and this was argued to constitute a breach of duty owed by the defendant Councils. In denying liability, the court acknowledged the shift towards personal responsibility for conduct, especially in the context of sporting and recreational pursuits where the risk is obvious.

[13]   In this instance the plaintiff swung out over the water on a rope and attempted a somersault into the water. He landed on his head instead of his feet and sustained serious injury. Ipp JA at [24] noted that this action was so obviously dangerous that no person, taking reasonable care for his or her safety, would do such a thing. Special leave to appeal to the High Court was refused, [2006] HCATrans 008.

159.[14] Also of note is the House of Lords decision in *Tomlinson v Congleton BC* [2004] 1 AC 46 in which the clear obviousness of the risk played a significant role in the determination of the court. It is important to note, however, that while a risk that is obvious may be a significant consideration when determining whether or not there has been a breach of duty, it is not a decisive factor; rather it is merely one factor to be taken into consideration by the court.[15]

Ipp Committee considers relevance of nature of risk

[10.35] The Ipp Committee recognised this trend and discussed it under the heading of the defence of voluntary assumption of risk.[16] However, it is included here as a component of foreseeability; this is where the courts have addressed the issue of obvious risk and it is therefore relevant at this stage of the inquiry. It is important to note, however, that it will also be a relevant consideration at the defence stage, as here in the context of breach, it is one of the many factors to take into account. As a defence, however, it is a factor to be considered on its own.

The recommendations of the Ipp Committee in this context will be discussed in detail when considering the defence of volenti. For present purposes, it is sufficient to note that the Committee recommended that obvious and inherent risks be given statutory recognition.[17]

In direct response to this, most jurisdictions now provide some protection for defendants when a plaintiff is injured by an "obvious" or "inherent" risk: see Figure 10.5. Of significance in the current context is the legislative protection provided to defendants when there is an obvious risk. In such circumstances there is no duty to warn.

---

[14] This case differed from the others in that a duty of care was found on the basis of the danger being less obvious than in the other situations and the swimming hole had a reputation as a safe area. However, the award of damages was reduced on the basis of contributory negligence.

[15] Refer *Clarke v Coleambally Ski Club Inc* [2004] NSWCA 376 per Ipp JA at [17] and *Wyong Shire Council v Vairy* [2004] Aust Torts Reports 81-754; NSWCA 247 per Tobias JA at [195].

[16] This defence, referred to as volenti non fit injuria, is discussed in more detail in Chapter 12.

[17] Ipp Report, Recommendation 32.

Figure 10.5: Obvious and inherent risks

Juris	Act	Obvious risks	Inherent risks
ACT	*Civil Law (Wrongs) Act 2002*		Limited to inherent risks in equine activities, s 3.
	Civil Liability Act 2002	s 5F Meaning of "obvious risk": • Defines obvious risk in terms of a reasonable person in the same position. Includes risks that are common knowledge, have low probability of occurring, and are not physically observable. s 5G Injured persons presumed to be aware of obvious risks: • Presumed to be aware of obvious risks unless proven not aware (on balance of probabilities). s 5H No proactive duty to warn of obvious risk: • No duty of care to warn of an obvious risk unless P has requested advice from D about the risk, or D required by law to warn, or risk is inherent in professional service provided by D.	s 5I No liability for materialisation of inherent risk: • An "inherent risk" cannot be avoided by the exercise of reasonable care and skill. • No liability in negligence for harm resulting from the materialisation of an inherent risk, but does not exclude a duty to warn.
NT	*Personal Injuries (Liabilities and Damages) Act 2003*	No mention	No mention.
Qld	*Civil Liability Act 2003*	s 13 Meaning of "obvious risk": • Defines obvious risk in terms of a reasonable person in the same position. • Includes risks that are common knowledge, have low probability of occurring, and not physically observable. • Not an obvious risk if created by a failure to operate or maintain the thing, unless the failure itself is an obvious risk.	s 16 No liability for materialisation of inherent risk: An "inherent risk" cannot be avoided by the exercise of reasonable care and skill. No liability in negligence for harm resulting from the materialisation of an inherent risk, but does not exclude a duty to warn.

Juris	Act	Obvious risks	Inherent risks
		s 14 Persons suffering harm presumed to be aware of obvious risks: • Presumed to be aware of obvious risks unless proves not aware (on balance of probabilities). • Awareness includes the type of risk not the exact risk. s 15 No proactive duty to warn of obvious risk: • No duty of care to warn of an obvious risk unless P has requested advice from D about the risk, or D required by law to warn, or risk is inherent in professional service provided by D. • Doesn't apply to doctors.	
SA	*Civil Liability Act 1936*	s 36 Meaning of obvious risk: • Defines obvious risk in terms of a reasonable person in the same position. • Includes risks that are common knowledge, and have low probability of occurring. s 37 Injured persons presumed to be aware of obvious risks: • Presumed to be aware of obvious risks unless proves not aware (on balance of probabilities). • Awareness includes the type of risk not the exact risk. • A defence of voluntary assumption of risk, requires establishing that a reasonable person in the same position would have taken steps (which P did not in fact take) to avoid it. s 38 No duty to warn of obvious risk: • No duty of care to warn of an obvious risk unless P has requested advice from D about the risk, or D required by law to warn, or risk is inherent in professional service provided by D.	s 39 No liability for materialisation of inherent risk: • An "inherent risk" cannot be avoided by the exercise of reasonable care and skill. • No liability in negligence for harm resulting from the materialisation of an inherent risk, but does not exclude a duty to warn.

Juris	Act	Obvious risks	Inherent risks
Vic	*Wrongs Act 1958*	s 53 Meaning of obvious risk: • Defines obvious risk in terms of a reasonable person in the same position. • Includes risks that are common knowledge, have low probability of occurring, and not physically observable. • Not an obvious risk if created by a failure to operate or maintain the thing unless the failure itself is an obvious risk. s 54 Voluntary assumption of risk: • Presumed to be aware of obvious risks unless proves not aware (on balance of probabilities). • Except where damage relates to a professional service or health service, or associated with work done for another. s 50 Duty to warn of risk: • A duty to warn is satisfied if D takes reasonable care in giving that warning or other information.	s 55 No liability for materialisation of inherent risk: • An inherent risk cannot be avoided by the exercise of reasonable care. • No liability for the materialisation of an inherent risk, but does not exclude a duty to warn of a risk. s 56 Plaintiff to prove unawareness of risk: • P is required to prove, on balance of probabilities, was not aware of the risk or the warning. • Doesn't apply when associated with work done for another.
WA	*Civil Liability Act 2002*	s 5F Meaning of obvious risk: • Defines obvious risk in terms of a reasonable person in the same position. • Includes risks that are common knowledge, have low probability of occurring, and not physically observable. • No duty of care to warn of an obvious risk unless P has requested advice from D about the risk, or D required by law to warn, or risk is inherent in professional service provided by D.	s 5E Interpretation: • "Inherent risk" means a risk of something occurring that cannot be avoided by the exercise of reasonable skill and care. s 5P No liability for harm from inherent risk: • No liability in negligence for harm resulting from the materialisation of an inherent risk, but does not exclude a duty to warn.
		s 5H No liability for harm from obvious risks of dangerous recreational activities: • No liability for harm or presumption of a duty to warn from obvious risks of dangerous recreational activities whether P aware of the risk or not; unless P has requested advice from D about the risk, or D required by law to warn. s 5I No liability for recreational activity where risk warning:	

Juris	Act	Obvious risks	Inherent risks
		• No duty of care for recreational activity where risk warning (oral or written) of the general nature of the risk given to P, or competent parent (or other person) of a child, by D (or person organising the activity). Warning must be reasonably likely to be effective but D does need to establish that receiver understood (or was capable of understanding) the warning. Warning cannot be relied upon by D if: – harm resulted from a contravention of the law; – the warning was contradicted by or on behalf of D; – P was required to engage in the activity by D; – harm resulted from a reckless act or omission; or – warning to an incompetent person. • A risk warning does not establish an obvious or inherent risk, or a duty of care. s 5N Injured person presumed to be aware of obvious risk: • Presumed to be aware of obvious risks unless proves not aware (on balance of probabilities). • Awareness includes the type of risk not the exact risk. s 5O No duty to warn of obvious risk: • No duty of care to warn of an obvious risk unless P has requested advice from D about the risk, or D required by law to warn, or risk is inherent in professional service provided by D.	

Juris	Act	Obvious risks	Inherent risks
Tas	*Civil Liability Act 2002*	s 15: Defines obvious risk in terms of a reasonable person in the same position. Includes risks that are common knowledge, have low probability of occurring, and not physically observable. However, not an obvious risk merely because a warning has been given. Persons suffering harm presumed to be aware of obvious risks. s 16: Presumed to be aware of obvious risks unless proves not aware (on balance of probabilities). Awareness includes the type of risk not the exact risk. s 17 No proactive duty to warn of obvious risk: No duty of care to warn of an obvious risk unless P has requested advice from D about the risk, or D required by law to warn, or risk is inherent in professional service provided by D. Doesn't apply to doctors. No liability for harm suffered from obvious risks of dangerous recreational activities. s 20:	No mention.

Relevant interrelating factors

Balancing factors

[10.40] The determination of foreseeability is an often complex consideration of interrelated factors which go beyond the basic consideration of the nature of the risk. The court may also be influenced by:

- the magnitude of harm;
- the cost and burdensomeness of precautions; and
- public or social utility.

These three factors in combination are referred to as the "calculus of negligence" and the case most often cited as authority for the significance of these factors in this combination is *Wyong SC v Shirt* (1980) 146 CLR 40. This authority has been recently affirmed with the High Court declining to reconsider the *Wyong SC v Shirt* approach in *New South Wales v Fahy* (2007) 81 ALJR 1021.

Figure 10.6: Negligence "calculus" in standard of care

- Likelihood of the injury
- Seriousness of the risk and the gravity of the injury
- Utility of the defendant's act
- Cost of avoiding the harm
- Peculiar background of the defendant
- Dangerous nature of the activity
- Current state of knowledge
- Prevailing safety standards

Exculpatory factors of the sort here under consideration are not defences to negligence. The defendant no doubt has an evidential burden of showing that one or more of the various factors may apply, but the legal burden of proof remains throughout with the plaintiff.

Magnitude of harm

[10.45] The House of Lords in *Paris v Stepney BC* [1951] AC 367 laid down that the gravity of the foreseeable consequences of the defendant's conduct is a relevant factor in determining the existence of a breach of duty of care. As it is sometimes stated, the risk of greater injury is relevant as well as the greater risk of injury. In *Paris* the plaintiff employee, a one-eyed man, was blinded when a chip from a rusty bolt he was hammering flew off and entered his good eye. The House of Lords by 3:2 majority found the defendant employers negligent in not providing him with protective goggles, the plaintiff's one-eyed state being known to them. Lord Macdermott observed (at 389-390):

> [T]he known circumstance that a particular workman is likely to suffer a greater injury than his fellows from the happening of a given event is one which must be taken into consideration in assessing the nature of the employer's obligation to his workmen.

The House assumed, without deciding, that a similar obligation would not be owed to a two-eyed man because of the slightness of the risk of injury.

Paris is not a very satisfactory decision. Granted that the degree of risk was the same for two-eyed as well as one-eyed workmen, it is difficult to see why the loss of an eye should not be regarded as a grave injury, as would indeed be the case with almost any form of personal injury. Cases in which the ratio in *Paris* will have an operation are likely to be few.

In *Ward v Hertfordshire CC* [1970] 1 All ER 535 the plaintiff schoolboy suffered a serious injury to his head when he fell against a wall in the schoolyard and his head struck a piece of flint on the wall, the wall being a flint wall with jagged edges. The plaintiff's argument that the school authority was negligent in having such a wall in the schoolyard failed. The basis of this argument was that the wall was likely to cause a greater injury; the danger of falling against any sort of wall was the same. However, the Court of Appeal dismissed the argument without reference to *Paris*, on the ground that there was no reasonably foreseeable risk of injury. It is, of course, clear that knowledge of an employee's disabilities and illnesses may increase the obligations of the employer towards that employee. But that is generally because of the increased likelihood of the employee suffering injury. This may extend to the case where the plaintiff's disability is not known to the defendant but should have been foreseen.

In *Haley v London Electricity Board* [1965] AC 778 the plaintiff, a blind man, had fallen into a hole in the public highway excavated by the defendants, and suffered injury. The defendants had taken steps to protect sighted persons from falling into the hole but these were of no use in protecting blind persons. The House of Lords held the defendants liable on the ground that the risk of blind persons being present near the hole, though relatively slight, was nevertheless reasonably foreseeable.

It is not only the plaintiff who is in a specific sub-class of potential plaintiffs who constitutes a relevant consideration at this point in the inquiry; all foreseeable plaintiffs are relevant. When discussing the risks of falling off a cliff (which included death and quadriplegia) the court in *Romeo v Conservation Commission (NT)* (1998) 192 CLR 431 readily acknowledged the extreme magnitude of the risk, but this alone was not sufficient to determine breach. Similarly, in *Road Traffic Authority of NSW v Dederer* (2007) 238 ALR 761 both Gummow J (at [71]) and Callinan J (at [273]), whilst acknowledging the gravity of the risk, declined to address it as a determinative consideration.

Cost and burdensomeness of precautions

[10.50] *Romeo v Conservation Commission (NT)* (1998) 192 CLR 431 once again proves to be illustrative when considering the relevance of the cost or difficulty of taking adequate precautions to protect all potential plaintiffs. The plaintiff, aged nearly 16, had, with a group of friends, entered as a visitor as of right a nature reserve occupied by the defendants. The reserve contained cliffs with a sheer drop, but their presence was obvious to visitors and known to the plaintiff. Access to the cliffs was possible from the visitors' carpark, there being no fencing at that or any other point along the cliff face. The plaintiff, who had drunk one-fifth of a bottle of rum, gained access to the cliffs from the carpark, and then in some way fell over them and was seriously injured.[18]

Although the members of the High Court were unanimous in holding that the injury to the plaintiff was reasonably foreseeable (applying the test in *Wyong SC v Shirt* (1980) 146 CLR 40), the majority of the court found that there had been no breach of duty to the plaintiff in failing to fence off access to the cliffs from the carpark. Bearing in mind the very low risk of the occurrence of the plaintiff's injury, it would not have been reasonable to require fencing, since this would have entailed the need to place fencing along the whole line of the cliffs, and arguably to fence any other dangerous parts of the reserve. Kirby J also raised the need to preserve the aesthetic environment of the reserve, which would be diminished by unsightly fencing. The dissenting minority in the High Court denied the need to fence at any other point than at the carpark, which would be a simple matter involving little expense.

Caledonian Collieries Ltd v Speirs (1957) 97 CLR 202 illustrates how the factor of cost can result in a finding that there was a breach. In that case, the defendants' runaway rolling stock entered a mainline belonging to the defendants from a private line also belonging to the defendants, and caused a fatal accident at a level crossing. The High Court upheld a jury finding of negligence against the defendants by reason of their

---

[18] Neither the plaintiff, nor the friend who fell with her, had any clear recollection of how they came to fall from the cliffs to the beach below. It was accepted by the court, however, that they may have mistaken a cleared area for a path.

not having installed catch points to prevent entry onto the main line. The court held the jury to be entitled to come to its conclusion that cost in the form of delay in rail services created by the catch points was outweighed by the risk of accidents of the sort which had occurred. The factor – that a decision to install catch points here would lead to the necessity of their being installed countrywide – was found to be irrelevant to the decision: the jury could only be expected to reach a decision on the facts before them. The likelihood is, therefore, that an argument on these lines is rarely likely to succeed.

The fact that the defendants had installed catch points immediately after the accident was thought to be a legitimate consideration for the jury, but not as an admission of negligence. Finally, the danger of the catch points derailing a runaway truck (a factor going to utility rather than cost) was found to have been legitimately thought by the jury to be outweighed by the danger of such a truck entering the main line.

There seems to be no real conflict between the majority conclusion in *Romeo* and the High Court's earlier decision in *Caledonian Collieries*. The risk in the latter case was of a much higher order and was created by the defendants. *Romeo*, on the other hand, concerned the question whether the occupier of a reserve to which the public had access as of right should have to take positive steps to protect the public against an obvious danger presented by a natural phenomenon. An argument based on the mere financial cost of removing the danger is unlikely to succeed where the defendant is responsible for creating the danger.

Ultra-hazardous activity

[10.55] Where an activity is unacceptably dangerous the defendant has the option of ceasing the activity or spending money to remove the danger. For example, cost played no part in the arguments placed before the court in *Mercer v Commissioner for Road Transport and Tramway* (1936) 56 CLR 580 as to why the defendants were not negligent in failing to install a "dead man's handle" in their trams. The purpose of the device was to avoid the danger of the collapse of the driver at the wheel while driving the tram (as happened in that case). The main considerations relied on by the defendants were the increased strain placed on the driver where these devices were in use, and the increased danger of rear-end collisions where the handle had operated (both factors of utility rather than cost). The High Court upheld a jury decision of negligence against the defendants in failing to install the device. This must now be considered in the context of "inherent risks": refer Figure 10.5.

Course of employment

[10.60] In *Vozza v Tooth & Co Ltd* (1964) 112 CLR 316 the defendant's employee's hand was cut in the process of removing a broken bottle from a pasteuriser in the course of employment. The court found that no practicable safe means of removing the bottle fragments existed – whether by means of mechanical handling or the provision of thicker gloves – and a breach of duty of care was negatived. But there is a concealed element of volenti non fit injuria (voluntary assumption of risk) about a decision of this sort. An employee impliedly consents to those dangers that are a necessary part of employment and that cannot be practicably removed.

Creating a nuisance on land

[10.65] With respect to nuisances arising naturally on the defendant's land, *Goldman v Hargrave* [1967] 1 AC 645 held that the means and resources available to the occupier to deal with the nuisance are relevant matters in deciding on the extent of the occupier's obligations towards persons affected by the nuisance.

Public or social utility

[10.70] The public or social utility of the defendant's conduct is a relevant factor in determining whether there has been a breach of duty of care. There is tacit recognition of the relevance of utility to the standard of care in the fact that the mere use of motor vehicles or of dangerous machinery in factories is not regarded as negligent itself, even though their total elimination would largely reduce serious accidents. The law is therefore that negligence must be established by reference to the operation, construction or maintenance of the vehicle or machine. In relation to matters such as these, the factor of utility is generally unlikely to have relevance.

The necessity for undertaking life-saving measures has in certain cases excused the carrying out of a dangerous operation. In *Watt v Hertfordshire CC* [1954] 1 WLR 835 the plaintiff fireman had been called to assist in an emergency in which a person had become trapped under a heavy vehicle. The only transport available for transporting a heavy lifting-jack was a truck unsuitable for the purpose, the suitable truck being out on call. During the course of the journey the jack moved on to the plaintiff and injured him. There was found to be no negligence in the use of the vehicle by the defendants because of the emergency situation. The issue of the cost of maintaining a sufficient fleet of suitable vehicles to answer all likely emergencies was not considered by the court.

Social utility has been given broad interpretation.[19] In *Haris v Bulldogs Rugby League Club Ltd* [2006] Aust Torts Reports 81-838, for example, Santow J considered the useful social purpose of attending football matches when addressing the question of whether further steps ought to have been taken to protect a spectator from injury (the appellant was struck in the eye by a firework), whilst in *Road Traffic Authority v Dederer* (2007) 238 ALR 761, the public benefit of being able to "walk across the bridge, enjoy the view and to pause and lean in comfort on a flat surface of a top rail as they did so", was raised by Callinan J (at [275]).[20] This does not, of course, detract from the more obvious issues of public health and public benefit, such as the availability of blood stocks which was deemed relevant in *E v Australian Red Cross* (1991) 31 FCR 299. Clearly, the concept of "social utility" is a broad one and the courts are prepared to consider any possible benefit to the community. Once again, this is but one of the factors under consideration.

Sport and associated physical risk

[10.75] The factor of utility may also relate to questions of negligence in the case of sporting activities carried on in schools and similar institutions. Hence, there is no negligence on the part of a school merely in organising sports and games carrying an element of risk, provided the activity in question carries with it no undue or unnecessary element of danger and adequate supervision is provided.

---

[19]   Social utility has, at times, been overlooked in the classic common law statement of the calculus of negligence, but is now given legislative form. See Figure 10.7.

[20]   In addressing social utility, Santow J was referring to the *Civil Liability Act 2002* (NSW), s 32(2)(b); thus we are seeing a gradual introduction of the new legislative provisions into the judicial consideration of negligence.

The physical risk in the activity is outweighed by the utility involved in participation in the sport or game. In *Kretschmar v Queensland* [1989] Aust Torts Reports 80-272 the plaintiff was injured during a game of "fetching and carrying" played by intellectually-handicapped children. The game involved no undue risk of physical injury to the children, was adequately supervised and conducive towards the development of manipulative skills and team spirit among the pupils. The benefits involved in the game combined with the care taken in the conduct of the activity to support a conclusion that no breach of duty had occurred.

A school authority is, however, liable for exposing school children to an unreasonable degree of risk arising from participation in a sport, as in *Watson v Haines* [1987] Aust Torts Reports 80-094. The court determined that the education authority should have been aware of the danger to a child with a long thin neck of playing as hooker in a rugby scrum and was liable in negligence for failing to give warning to schools of the danger. In *Bujnowicz v Trustees of the Roman Catholic Church* [2005] Aust Torts Reports 81-824 the game of rugby itself was not deemed dangerous but the presence of a pothole in the playing field was. The benefits of the game did not outweigh the expectation of the provision of a safe playing field; significantly, however, the court noted that "it may be accepted that the mere fact that a serious injury may occur to a student who was playing a game of touch football at the College will not automatically result in a finding of breach of the duty of care even though the risk was foreseeable" (at [39] per Tobias JA). Thus the nature of the game is not determinative and neither is the advent of injury. Once again we see the courts emphasising the process of weighing each relevant consideration against the others.

Ipp Committee considers calculus of negligence

[10.80] The significance of the calculus of negligence in determining whether or not a breach has occurred was acknowledged and supported by the Ipp Committee. The Committee emphasised that no individual factor is decisive and that the process involves a weighing of factors against each other.[21] Foreseeability is considered as a matter of knowledge at the time of the event, described as a matter of inference and not a scientific process.[22] This position is consistent with the High Court approach expressed in *Road Traffic Authority of NSW v Dederer*, with Gummow J pointing out (at [69]) that "what *Shirt* requires is a contextual and balanced assessment of the reasonable response to a foreseeable risk" and then (at [79]) that it is about a "reasonable response, and the law demands no more and no less".

As outlined above at [10.17] the main area of concern for the Committee was the uncertainty of the phrase, "far fetched or fanciful". In general, however, there was strong support for the existing common law approach and as a result, the calculus, as expressed in *Wyong Shire Council v Shirt* has, with the exception of the concept of "far fetched and fanciful", now been given legislative voice: see Figure 10.7

---

[21] Ipp Report, p 103.
[22] Ipp Report, p 103.

Figure 10.7: Precautions against risk (calculus of negligence)

Juris	Legislation	Provision
ACT	*Civil Law (Wrongs) Act 2002*	s 43 Precautions against risk – general principles: • No negligence unless risk was foreseeable, significant, and a reasonable person would have taken precautions. • Factors for the court to consider re taking precautions include: – the probability of harm without precautions taken; – the likely seriousness of the harm; – the burden of taking precautions; and – the social utility of the activity creating the risk of harm. s 44 Precautions against risk – other principles: • the burden of taking precautions includes the burden of taking precautions to avoid similar risks; • risk avoidance by doing something in a different way does not affect liability for the way in which it was done; and • the subsequent taking of action that would have avoided a risk does not affect liability; nor is it an admission of liability.
NSW	*Civil Liability Act 2002*	s 5B General principles: • No negligence unless risk was foreseeable, significant, and a reasonable person would have taken precautions. • Factors for the court to consider re taking precautions include: – the probability of harm without precautions taken; – the likely seriousness of the harm; – the burden of taking precautions; and – the social utility of the activity creating the risk of harm.
NT	*Personal Injuries (Liabilities and Damages) Act 2003*	No mention.
Qld	*Civil Liability Act 2003*	s 9 General principles: • No negligence unless risk was foreseeable, significant, and a reasonable person would have taken precautions. • Factors for the court to consider re taking precautions include: – the probability of harm without precautions taken; – the likely seriousness of the harm; – the burden of taking precautions; and – the social utility of the activity creating the risk of harm. s 10 Other principles: • the burden of taking precautions includes the burden of taking precautions to avoid similar risks; • risk avoidance by doing something in a different way does not affect liability for the way in which it was done; and • the subsequent taking of action that would have avoided a risk does not affect liability nor is it an admission of liability.

Juris	Legislation	Provision

SA	*Civil Liability Act 1936*	s 32 Precautions against risk:
		• No negligence unless risk was foreseeable, significant, and a reasonable person would have taken precautions.
		• Factors for the court to consider re taking precautions include:
		  – the probability of harm without precautions taken;
		  – the likely seriousness of the harm;
		  – the burden of taking precautions; and
		  – the social utility of the activity creating the risk of harm.

Tas	*Civil Liability Act 2002* Division 2: Standard of care	s 11 General principles:
		• No negligence unless risk was foreseeable, significant, and a reasonable person would have taken precautions.
		• Factors for the court to consider re taking precautions include:
		  – the probability of harm without precautions taken;
		  – the likely seriousness of the harm;
		  – the burden of taking precautions; and
		  – the social utility of the activity creating the risk of harm.
		s 12 Other principles:
		• risk avoidance by doing something in a different way does not affect liability for the way in which it was done; and
		• the subsequent taking of action that would have avoided a risk does not affect liability nor is it an admission of liability.

Vic	*Wrongs Act 1958*	s 48 General principles:
		• No negligence unless risk was foreseeable, significant, and a reasonable person would have taken precautions. (Insignificant risks include far-fetched or fanciful risks.)
		• Factors for the court to consider re taking precautions include:
		  – the probability of harm without precautions taken;
		  – the likely seriousness of the harm;
		  – the burden of taking precautions; and
		  – the social utility of the activity creating the risk of harm.
		s 49 Other principles:
		• the burden of taking precautions includes the burden of taking precautions to avoid similar risks;
		• risk avoidance by doing something in a different way does not affect liability for the way in which it was done; and
		• the subsequent taking of action that would have avoided a risk does not affect liability nor is it an admission of liability.
		s 50 Duty to warn of risk – reasonable care:
		• a duty to warn is satisfied if D takes reasonable care in giving that warning or other information.

Juris	Legislation	Provision
WA	*Civil Liability Acts 2002*	5B General principles: • No negligence unless risk was foreseeable, significant, and a reasonable person would have taken precautions. (Insignificant risks include far-fetched or fanciful risks.) • Factors for the court to consider re taking precautions include: – the probability of harm without precautions taken; – the likely seriousness of the harm; – the burden of taking precautions; and – the social utility of the activity creating the risk of harm. s 5C General principles: • Fault was a necessary condition of harm occurring; and appropriate for scope of liability to extend to the harm caused. • Court to consider both whether and why responsibility imposed; and whether and why the harm should be left to lie where it fell.

Objective standard: the reasonable person

[10.85] Implicit in the considerations outlined above is the question of what was a reasonable response to the risk. The test for determining the reasonableness of the defendant's response is an objective standard: that of the reasonable person. The question is asked: what would the reasonable person have done in the situation with which the defendant is presented? The issue of the determination of breach is for the court itself and not delegated to any supposed reasonable person, though evidence may be called from witnesses who are capable of assisting the court in fixing the standard of reasonableness. The standard of care may also be variable on the basis of personal characteristics of the defendant, level of experience or nature of the activity. It is important to emphasise that this continues to be an objective test based on broad characteristics such as age as opposed to specific, subjective characteristics such as temperament.

Figure 10.8: Standard of care

> To establish a duty of care it is not enough to establish negligence. It must also be proved that the duty of care has been breached.
> • What standard of care is owed?
> • Did the defendant's actions or omissions meet that standard? (Refer to the calculus factors at [10.40]ff.)
> • If not, then breach of duty.

Relevant characteristics of defendant

[10.90] While the standard of care is ostensibly that of the reasonable person, circumstances may exist which make it relevant to take account of differences between persons in determining what actions would be reasonable. Relevant characteristics could include age, fitness and health, intellectual capacity and sanity of the defendant. Matters such as gender and ethnicity could also conceivably play a part; as could the level of experience of the defendant (for example whether they are a professional or an amateur or otherwise qualified or unqualified for the task to be performed). It is generally true that a person should not undertake a task known to involve danger to other persons if that person has knowledge of his or her incompetence to perform it; so that in such a case the differing standards become irrelevant. Also of relevance is the level of knowledge of the plaintiff: if the plaintiff was aware of the limitations in the defendant's skill then the expected standard may reflect the reality of the skill level.

Figure 10.9: Test for standard of care

> **Test:** The care owed is that of the reasonable person in the circumstances.
> **Objective test:** Whether the defendant took the same amount of care that a reasonable person would have taken.
> The test may vary according to the type of defendant.

Children

[10.95] The age of the defendant may be a relevant factor in determining the standard of care required. For example, young children are not expected to observe the same standard as adults. There is no minimum age for tortious capacity, such as exists in the criminal law, but it may be assumed that a very young child would be held to have committed a tort requiring fault only in very unusual circumstances. In the case of older children, although there is no difficulty in holding them liable for their negligence, the standard of care expected of them must take account of their age, and it continues to be objectively determined.

In *McHale v Watson* (1966) 115 CLR 199 a 12-year-old child who threw a pointed metal rod at a tree causing it to glance off and hit the plaintiff in the eye, was cleared of liability. Kitto J thought (at 212) the standard to be applied was that of an "ordinary child of the relevant age" and noted that this was appealing to a standard of ordinariness and therefore an objective test. Owen J (at 231) thought the standard should be that of a child "of like age, intelligence and experience". Menzies J dissenting, thought that the age of the child was irrelevant to the question of liability for negligence, but was a relevant factor in determining an issue of contributory negligence: at 224. It is now clear that Menzies J's view does not represent the law. Significantly, Windeyer J (at first instance) noted that "childhood is not an idiosyncrasy": *McHale v Watson* (1964) 111 CLR 384 at 396 and it was this position that was accepted by the majority.

As between the different tests of Kitto and Owen JJ, that proposed by Kitto J seems preferable and was accepted by the majority of the South Australian Supreme Court in *Griffiths v Wood* [1994] Aust Torts Reports 81-274, though Olsson J preferred the formulation of Owen J. By a majority, the court acquitted the plaintiff, a six-year-old, of contributory negligence in riding his bike out from a car park into the path of a semi-trailer driven negligently by the defendant. The plaintiff had been engrossed in a game played with his fellows and had merely acted impulsively in the manner to be expected of one of his age.

The following cases have established liability in negligence on the part of older children: *Gorely v Codd* [1967] 1 WLR 19 (use of air rifle by 16-year-old); *Johns v Minister of Education* (1981) 28 SASR 206 (12-year-old held liable for discharging a ball point pen with a catapult at the plaintiff); *H v Pennell* [1987] Aust Torts Reports 80-112 (15-year-old defendant injured plaintiff by flicking a car aerial with force in plaintiff's direction).

On the issue of contributory negligence, a Canadian decision was surprisingly lenient to the plaintiff child in *Yachuk v Oliver Blais Co Ltd* [1949] AC 346. A nine-year-old child had obtained petrol from an attendant at a service station by telling a false story, and had then used it for lighting a torch in the course of which he received burns. The child was held not to be contributorily negligent in his action against the owner of the service station on the ground of his limited knowledge of the inflammatory characteristics of petrol. In some Australian cases, the courts have made reductions for contributory negligence in the case of very young children, who might have been found very unlikely to have committed the tort of negligence itself.[23]

Old age

[10.100] Unlike childhood, old age has featured very rarely in decisions on standard of care. This is undoubtedly because the old person, though possibly lacking in physical agility, possesses, if healthy, the necessary understanding of the risks involved and will generally be expected to take steps to ensure that he or she is not placed in a position where physical agility is required to avert danger to other persons. In *Daly v Liverpool Corporation* (1939) 160 LT 128 the court acquitted an old person of contributory negligence in crossing the street and then being hit by the defendant's bus, basing its decision on the fact that the old person is not expected to possess the same agility as the young person. However, there was no suggestion in the case that the plaintiff had been negligent in attempting the crossing at the time and place he did.

Disease and disability

[10.105] It is not possible to lay down any general principle as regards the effect upon the standard of care of disease or disability, subject of course to the general proposition that a person who understands the nature of the incapacity must not create danger for other persons. Even actual insanity is no necessary bar to liability for negligence. In *Adamson v Motor Vehicle Insurance Trust* (1957) 58 WALR 56 an ill person suffering from an irrational fear that his workmates were about to kill him, stole a car and hit and injured the plaintiff at an intersection by driving into the intersection against a traffic policeman's signal. He was held liable in negligence because his condition did not render him unable to appreciate the wrongfulness of his conduct in taking the car and ignoring the policeman's instructions.

---

23   See *Wiech v Amato* (1973) 6 SASR 328; *Bullock v Miller* (1987) 5 MVR 55 (both five-year-olds); cf *Beasley v Marshall* (1976-78) 17 SASR 456 – no deduction in the case of a four-year-old. See also *Jones v Homeister* (1976) 14 SASR 328 – 50% deduction in the case of a boy of eight who ran backwards into a truck on the highway, and cf the treatment of the plaintiff in *Griffiths v Wood*, dealt with above; *Chan v Fong* (1973) 5 SASR 1 – deduction in the case of a seven-year-old; may be compared with *Delphin v Savoleinen* (1989) 10 MVR 293 – no deduction when seven-year-old suddenly stepped into the highway. In the case of a schoolgirl cyclist of unstated age, who caused an accident by riding into the path of a motor cyclist, the deduction was 70%: *Lacy v Schneider* (1989) 9 MVR 512.

Intellectual impairment or physical disability

[10.110] There is very little in the way of decided cases on the effect of conditions such as intellectual impairment or physical disability caused by disease or trauma, apart from *Finbow v Domino* (1957) 11 DLR (2d) 493, a Canadian decision. This decision acquitted a child aged eight with a mental age of three of contributory negligence, thus supporting a subjective relaxation from the norm. There are a number of decisions about the sudden onset of disabling illness in car drivers, the result of which is that where some degree of consciousness and ability to control the car remains after the onset of the attack, the normal standard of care continues to apply. In *Roberts v Ramsbottom* [1980] 1 WLR 823 a driver who suffered a stroke which impaired his driving and rendered him unaware of the impairment, was held liable in negligence on the ground that the stroke did not render him an automaton, because he retained some degree of consciousness. In *Leahy v Beaumont* (1981) 27 SASR 290 a fit of coughing eventually produced unconsciousness in the driver, but he was held negligent because he should have taken steps to stop the car while conscious. In *Scholz v Standish* [1961] SASR 123 a driver who was stung by a bee and then drove into a tree a few feet away was not negligent, since the immediate loss of control was unavoidable; though he would have been expected to bring the car under control soon afterwards.

Some cases have investigated the question of whether the driver ought to have recognised the symptoms of the illness before it manifested itself, but in none of these has the driver been held liable on this ground: *Waugh v James K Allan Ltd* [1964] SC 102 (heart attack); *Smith v Lord* [1962] SASR 88 (sudden loss of vision); *Robinson v Glover* [1952] NZLR 669 (sudden fainting at wheel not negligent although defendant had had prior illness).

Inexperience

Professional inexperience

[10.115] Where the defendant has the necessary professional qualifications, it seems generally true that the standard of care required is that of the normally competent member of that profession, without allowance being made for inexperience.[24] For example, lawyers in private practice who have no hierarchical structure, and who will be more or less experienced or more or less successful as the case may be, will be judged by the same standard of care. The same would no doubt apply to accountants.

Medical practitioners

[10.120] The medical profession, on the other hand, recognises distinctions (for example, between general practitioner, junior or senior house surgeon and consultant) with the standard of care required reflecting these distinctions. In *Wilsher v Essex Area Health Authority* [1986] 3 All ER 801 an inexperienced junior house doctor (the equivalent of an intern in the Australian context) had caused a catheter to be inserted into the plaintiff's vein, rather than an artery. The catheter in consequence failed to register properly the amount of oxygen in the blood. Mustill LJ thought that the standard of care of the junior doctor was that of the "averagely competent and well-informed junior houseman", though of such a person who offers "highly specialised advice".

---

[24] The standard of care required by professionals in general, and medical practitioners in particular, has some specific detailed requirements. These were considered in Chapter 9.

Glidewell LJ agreed with this, saying expressly that the inexperience of the junior house doctor in question was irrelevant to the standard of care required of him. The junior doctor was absolved from blame by the majority in this particular case because he had sought the opinion of the senior registrar as to the position of the catheter after it was inserted in the patient; he had acted appropriately in seeking further advice. It was, however, agreed by all members of the Court of Appeal that a higher standard of care attached to the senior registrar and that he was in breach of his duty of care towards the plaintiff.

Learner drivers

[10.125] Until recently, the High Court decision of *Cook v Cook* (1986) 162 CLR 376 stood as authority that the standard of care owed by a learner driver to the instructor is reduced to reflect the level of inexperience of the driver. The reasoning of the court was based upon the view that the "special circumstances" of the relationship removed it into a "distinct category of case". The requisite standard was deemed to be "that which is reasonably to be expected of an unqualified and inexperienced driver in the circumstances in which the pupil is placed" (at 383-384). In coming to this conclusion the High Court expressly refused to follow the English Court of Appeal in *Nettleship v Weston* [1971] 2 QB 691, imposing the normal standard of care on the learner driver. This situation has now changed, however, with the High Court specifically overruling *Cook* in *Imbree v McNeilly* [2008] HCA 40 (28 August 2008).

The appellant in *Imbree* allowed the (then) 16-year-old respondent to drive a 4WD along an unsealed road in the Northern Territory. The respondent was, with the full knowledge of the appellant, unlicensed and inexperienced. When he saw some tyre debris on the road he swerved to miss it, over-corrected and rolled the vehicle, rendering the appellant a tetraplegic. The main judgment was delivered by Gummow, Hayne and Kiefel JJ and the principle of *Cook v Cook* was clearly rejected as a "departure from fundamental principle [which] achieved no useful result" (at [72]). The learner driver therefore must take the same care as that of the reasonable driver (at [72]).[25]

Figure 10.10: Pre-existing knowledge of defendant's incapacity

> The plaintiff's pre-existing knowledge of the defendant's incapacity could allow the defendant to plead:
> • voluntary assumption of risk;
> • diminished standard of care; or
> • contributory negligence.

---

[25] The instructor's knowledge of the inexperience is of continued relevance in the context of contributory negligence, with the damages here reduced by 30%. Of further note in this decision was Kirby J's consideration of the additional factor of compulsory third party insurance (at [107]ff) and Heydon J's view that there was no need to revisit *Cook v Cook* as the overruling of the earlier decision was not, in his view, a "necessary step in the reversal of the Court of Appeal's decision" (at [191]).

Professionals and amateurs

[10.135] It is an obvious proposition that more is required in terms of knowledge and skill of the professionally qualified person[26] than of the amateur. In terms of knowledge, the point is made by comparing *The Wagon Mound (No 2)* [1967] 1 AC 617 with *Caminer v Northern Investment Trust* [1951] AC 88. In the former case it was held that a ship's engineer ought to know of the unlikely possibility of furnace oil igniting on water, knowledge which would not be expected of the layman. In the latter case, it was held that the degree of knowledge expected from a private landowner of diseases in trees on the estate lay "somewhere between that of an urban observer and a scientific arborculturalist". But the landowner was held liable in that case because he ought to have known that elm trees possess special hazards and the tree in question overhung the public highway.

Amateur persons are subject to the general rule that they ought not to undertake work which involves danger to the public and which they are not competent to perform. That proposition yields to the qualification that where the absence of professional skill is known to the particular member of the public concerned, that person is not entitled to expect such skill in the performance of the work. This explains the case of *Phillips v William Whitely* [1938] 1 All ER 566 where an ear-piercing operation was carried out in the jewellery department of the defendant's store, the passing of the needle through a flame prior to the operation was an adequate discharge of the defendant's standard of care, even though the wound became infected; the plaintiff was not entitled to expect the sterilisation procedures of a hospital.

This does not explain *Wells v Cooper* [1958] 2 QB 265. In this case it was held that the standard of care required of a person who fitted a new door handle onto his door was that of the reasonably competent domestic carpenter, rather than that of the professional carpenter. The defendant had complied with the latter standard by using three-quarter-inch screws, even though the professional person might have thought it better to use one-inch screws. The defendant therefore was not liable to the plaintiff who fell from some steps having pulled the door against a strong wind and the handle having come off in his hand. Since the evidence does not appear to have shown that the professional carpenter would have regarded the three-quarter-inch screws as unsafe, the case perhaps does not unduly expose the public to dangers caused by do-it-yourself activities. Had that been otherwise, it would be difficult to defend, since a minimum requirement of ensuring reasonable safety for normal uses appears desirable.

Participants in sport

[10.140] Australian courts have refused to accept limitations proposed by the judgment of Diplock LJ in *Wooldridge v Sumner* [1963] 2 QB 43. The case held that a person engaged in a sporting contest and using his or her best endeavours as a competitor in the contest, is liable only for reckless disregard of the safety of fellow competitors, or of other persons such as spectators at the contest who may also be regarded as privy to the risks of the contest. This standard has also now been departed from in England in a later Court of Appeal decision, *Condon v Basi* [1985] 1 WLR 866, in which a foul tackle in a football game was held to be negligent.

---

[26] For the general standard of care of professionals, see Figure 9.5.

In *Rootes v Shelton* (1967) 116 CLR 383 the High Court held that the defendant was liable for negligence in taking the plaintiff water skier too close to a boat with which he was in collision. The court did so on the basis that care was required of the defendant in his navigation of the pulling boat. Barwick CJ observed (at 385) that the participants in a sport or pastime "may be held to have accepted risks which are inherent in that sport or pastime"; but Kitto J stated (at 389):

> *It seems that when a judge is directing a jury as to the acceptance of risk which a plaintiff's participation in a sport has implied, it is not satisfactory for him to confine their attention to the risks, "inherent" in the sport, or the risks that are "recognised" (in the sense of "perceived") in it; for not only are these expressions imprecise – they may refer, for example, to risks necessarily incurred, or reasonably to be expected, or obviously possible. The question to be decided should be regarded by the common law rather from the defendant's point of view: was the defendant's conduct which caused injury to the plaintiff reasonable in all the circumstances, including the inferences fairly to be drawn by the defendant from the plaintiff's participation in what was going on at the time.*

It is doubtful whether there is much practical difference between the two formulations. The main point is that the standard of care imposed on participants must take account of the risks of the game. This is not because of any actual subjective consent to those risks, but because of legal imposition of the requisite standard. So, in *Johnston v Fraser* [1990] Aust Torts Reports 81-056, the defendant jockey was held liable for negligence in crossing dangerously close to two other horses having overtaken them, thereby causing the plaintiff's horse to fall and the plaintiff to suffer injury.

In *Shelton* Barwick CJ and Kitto J were in agreement that the rules of the sport have some evidentiary value as to the standard of care to be required of participants in sport but are not determinative of the issue, Kitto J stating (at 389):

> *Non-compliance with such rules, conventions or customs (where they exist) is necessarily one consideration to be attended upon the question of reasonableness; but it is only one, and it may be of much or little or even no weight in the circumstances.*

Some foul tackles, for example, may be completely harmless; others dangerous.[27] Clearly the introduction of obvious and inherent risks into the legislation (see Figure 10.5) lends support to these conclusions and may in fact lead to more rigorous protection of defendants on the sporting field. It of course remains to be seen how the courts will interpret and apply the legislation.

Figure 10.11: Acceptance of risk and the right of action

- The plaintiff's acceptance of risk may not necessarily preclude his or her right of action.
- The plaintiff retains the right of action with respect to the defendant's negligence beyond the inherent risk the plaintiff may have accepted as being associated with a particular activity.

---

27 *Morris v West Hartpool Steam Navigation Co Ltd* [1956] AC 552; *Cavanagh v Ulster Weaving Co Ltd* [1960] AC 145; *Waterwell Shipping v HIH Insurance* [1997] Aust Torts Reports 81-444.

Compliance with professional or community standards

[10.145] The question here is whether it is enough for the defendant to show compliance with some professional or other generally prevailing standard in order to discharge the standard of care. The answer is that, in general, such compliance is relevant evidence and no more that the defendant acted reasonably. A community practice may nevertheless be a negligent practice: *Brown v Rolls Royce Ltd* [1960] 1 WLR 210.

Failure to adopt a community standard is not necessarily negligent.[28] A community standard, if originally acceptable, may become negligent in the course of time. In a case in which the defendants had acted in accordance with a common practice among employers of ignoring the risk of hearing loss to employees caused by the noise of work in their shipyards, this was originally held to be no breach of duty of care. But later, in the light of greater medical knowledge of the risk and greater availability of medical advice and warnings to employers, it became so.[29]

The former deference paid to the standards of the medical profession in determining questions of medical negligence no longer prevails in Australia. The matter was dealt with in Chapter 9.

Practice Questions

Revision Questions

10.1 For negligence to be established the tortfeasor must be found to be at fault. How is this fault determined?

10.2 If a defendant has failed to meet a regulation or a safety standard stated in a piece of legislation does this automatically establish negligence?

BREACH OF DUTY

Standard of care
- What standard of care is owed? (Question of Law)
- The standard of care owed by the reasonable person in the circumstances.
- What would the reasonable person do in the defendant's position?

Duty breached
- Did the defendant's actions or omissions fail to meet that standard? (Question of fact)
  - Was the RISK of injury to the plaintiff REASONABLY FORESEEABLE?
  - Degree of risk *(how foreseeable was the RISK of harm to the plaintiff)*
  - Magnitude of harm

IF SO,
- Was the RESPONSE of the defendant to this risk REASONABLE?

---

[28] See also *Agar v Hyde* [2000] Aust Torts Reports 81-569 – refusal to impose a duty of care on the members of the International Rugby Board towards amateur rugby players injured during the course of a breach of the rules of the game.

[29] *Thompson v Smith Ship Repairers Ltd* [1984] QB 405; see also *Hughes v Australian Telecom* [1997] Aust Torts Reports 81-428 – employer should have been aware of irritant symptoms caused by the use of carbonless copy paper in a telex machine when those symptoms were displayed by the employees using the machine.

- Apply the calculus of negligence (now given legislative form)
  AND where relevant
  Consider
  - reasonability of precautions;
  - utility or justifiability of defendant's activity (emergency); and
  - any relevant professional, customary or statutory standards.

Problem Questions

10.1 At the height of the snow season at Perisher the ski slopes were littered with enthusiastic skiers, many of whom were participating in lessons with instructors. However, the snow fall had been poor necessitating the use of the snow-making machines. Nevertheless, the snow tended to be hard and/or icy, although usable. Kannot Stop was a beginner who had had a number of lessons and was now at Level 6 (the group that could be described as those who were sometimes able to turn and stop). On 10 August, Know Itall, a European ski instructor who could only speak a little English, intended to teach the students how to "ski in snowplough position". Know Itall took the students on the chairlift to the top of Easy Slope and arranged them at the top of the slope. After he had shown them how to snowplough without using stocks he positioned himself about 12 metres below the students and called for the first student to snowplough down to him. Kannot Stop was the first student to go.

Kannot noticed that a group of people were standing about six metres behind Know Itall. Although Kannot tried to emulate Know Itall's instructions, he found that his skis kept moving with a grating sound over the snow. He tried to stop near Know Itall but found that he couldn't do so. He continued on past Know Itall, eventually colliding with one of the people in the group. Kannot hit the ground with a thud and the person whom he struck fell on top of his left leg. Doctors have found that Kannot will have long-term consequences caused by the injury. Kannot maintains that Know Itall failed to allow a sufficient runout area for beginners. Know Itall should have known that he was a beginner and needed a lot of space in which to stop. In other words, Know Itall should have allowed a much longer space between himself and others so that the beginner skiers had plenty of area within which to stop if they could not manage to stop near the instructor.

Has Know Itall breached his duty of care to Kannot Stop?

Note: assume that a duty of care has been established between the ski instructor and the students.

10.2 Janet Pringle, a girl in her teens, decided to have a party. She went to the corner store to purchase four bottles of ginger-ale. These were kept on the top shelf of the fridge, 1m 80cm above the floor level, arranged in a single line from front to back. Janet said that the floor was clean and "glossy" and that her thongs squeaked as she walked over it. Since Janet was only 1m 60cm tall she had to reach for the bottles. While holding the door of the fridge open with her right hand she reached up for the bottles with her left hand. She placed three bottles in her trolley but each bottle required her to reach further back and so by the time she went to grasp the fourth bottle she had to stretch up on tiptoe. Just as she managed to clasp the fourth bottle she slipped over and fell with the bottle which smashed, causing her a nasty cut to her right hand. The ensuing mayhem of liquid, broken glass and blood caused Janet to faint. Janet has since been told that the cut has caused major damage to the nerves in her hand. Janet maintains that the store failed to arrange the bottles in such a way that she as a customer could make the purchases safely.

Has the store breached its duty of care to Janet?
Note: assume that there is a duty of care owed by the store to the customers.

Answers to Practice Questions

Note: The legislative reform is not considered in these general answers. When responding to these questions, include considerations of the legislation relevant to your jurisdiction.

Revision Questions

10.1 A plaintiff must prove that the defendant was at fault by showing that the defendant failed to meet a reasonable standard of care appropriate to the circumstances. If the person couldn't reasonably have acted otherwise, then fault is not established even though that person caused the damage. It is important to note that the concept of fault does not equate to or impose a judgment of moral culpability.

10.2 No. Codes of practice, safety standards and procedures provide guidelines on best practice and suggest what would be considered to be reasonable behaviour, but the courts treat them as only persuasive in relation to negligence actions. However a breach of these may found other torts (eg the tort of breach of statutory duty).

Problem Questions

10.1 **Standard of care:** A breach of a duty of care will only be proved if it can be shown that the defendant failed to meet the appropriate standard of care. In these circumstances the standard is that of the reasonable ski instructor. That is, the reasonable person in the defendant's position (reference here to the standard of care as currently stated in the legislation, Figure 10.7). This now has the added complexity of the legislative standard, in some jurisdictions, expected of a "person with a special skill" (refer Figure 9.5).

Should the standard be lowered because Know Itall does not speak fluent English? This would not be taken into account since Know Itall's lack of English would not affect what we would expect of him at all. It is his positioning himself in the particular place he did that is important here, not his ability to speak English.

It is well known that many ski instructors on the snow–fields come from different countries and so this would be accepted by students.

Therefore Know Itall should be expected to do what a reasonable ski instructor would do: that he would consider the skills or lack thereof of his students and position himself so that the beginner skiers could stop in the space that he makes available.

Standard met?: Did Know Itall's actions or omissions breach that standard? See the factors set out in *Wyong v Shirt* (1980) 146 CLR 40 (ie the calculus of negligence, legislative provisions set out Figure 10.7).

Risk? Was the risk of injury to Kannot Stop reasonably foreseeable?
Know Itall would know that Kannot Stop might have difficulty stopping by the fact that he was taking a Level 6 class and these students are described as those who "are sometimes able to turn and stop". So the risk of Kannot Stop in fact not being able to stop and so hitting other skiers was not far-fetched or fanciful but real and foreseeable.

Magnitude of risk? The risk of injury involved in skiing is inherent and quite probable, particularly on poor snow, which was the circumstance on 10 August.

Response? Were the actions of Know Itall reasonable in relation to the risk identified?

Precautions? In congested areas, like beginners' slopes, it would seem that ski instructors would be continually visually assessing the area within which they were conducting their classes. In this respect, Know Itall should have seen the group of people six metres beyond him and realised that they were too close. The students in the Level 6 class may not be able to stop and so the people presented a hazard. Know Itall could have warned the students about their presence or have asked the group of people to move or indeed could have positioned himself differently so that there was ample room behind him in which the students could attempt to stop. None of these possible precautions would have involved any significant expense, difficulty or inconvenience.

Customary practice? We are not given any information concerning customary practice, but even if we were it is persuasive only.

Conclusion: It seems that Know Itall did not take reasonable care to ensure that the runout area he allowed was adequate. Thus, in failing to meet the requisite standard of care, he breached his duty of care.

10.2 **Standard of care**: A breach of a duty of care will only be proved if it can be shown that the defendant failed to meet the appropriate standard of care. In these circumstances the standard is that of the reasonable shopkeeper.

Standard met? Has the shopkeeper's placing of the bottles met the standard of the "reasonable shopkeeper"? See the factors set out in *Wyong v Shirt* (1980) 146 CLR 40, now given legislative voice (refer Figure 10.7).

Risk? Was the risk of injury to Janet Pringle foreseeable? The risk of people dropping the bottles is foreseeable but it is perhaps not probable that anyone would be hurt.

Magnitude of risk? Even if it could be foreseen that bottles would be dropped, the risk does not seem to be grave.

Response? Were the actions of the shopkeeper reasonable in relation to the risk identified? It should be noted that Janet managed to retrieve three bottles without mishap; the question of negligence only seems to relate to the difficulty in removing the fourth bottle.

Precautions? Should all the bottles in the shop be placed at a comfortable height for every customer? Janet is said to be 1m 60cm tall: does the shopkeeper need to keep in mind all the customers who are not even as tall as this? Do the bottles need to be brought further to the front to accommodate the heights of all people? Couldn't Janet have asked for help?

Conclusion: It would seem that Janet would not succeed in showing that the shopkeeper had acted unreasonably.

Tutorial Questions

Discussion Questions

10.1 Is the High Court becoming more conservative in determining reasonable care in recent years?

10.2 Should the standard of care be modified for children according to age or mental ability?

10.3 Has the legislative re-statement of the "calculus of negligence" added anything to the process of determining breach of duty?

CHAPTER 11

Causation and Remoteness of Damage in Negligence

Reading

Sappideen, Vines, Grant and Watson, *Torts: Commentary and Materials*, Chapter 14.

Objectives

This chapter will explain:

- the difficult concept of causation;
- the two limbs of causation (including consideration of Ipp Committee recommendations and subsequent reform);
- how the law addresses the situation when there are multiple possible causes;
- the effect of intervening causes;
- the difficulties with the "but for" test; and
- the recent interest in the developing recovery for the loss of a chance.

Principles

Introduction

[11.05] The underlying principle of the law of negligence is that no-one can be held responsible for loss or damage that does not flow from their actions. Consistent with this principle is the third step in the process of determining liability:[1] the issue of causation. Even where there is duty and breach, the court will not attach liability unless the loss or injury was incurred as a direct result of that breach of duty. This question is not as straightforward as it may at first appear.

Implicit in any discussion of causation is the issue of remoteness of damage. It is important to note from the outset that despite the fact that courts frequently fail to separate them in terms of nomenclature (using either "causation" or "remoteness" to cover both concepts) they are distinct and separate issues. They may be distinguished in the following way:

- The issue of causation is concerned with the question of whether the defendant's conduct has caused the interference required by the tort of which the plaintiff complains. The issue is sometimes described as that of "factual causation", the relevant question being: was the act (or omission) part of the history/story?

- The issue of remoteness of damage arises once causal connection has been established. It is concerned with whether the damage, or other interference complained of, is too remote from the conduct of the defendant to allow the defendant to be held liable for it. This issue is sometimes referred to as that of "causation in law" or, more recently, "scope of liability", the relevant question being: ought that act (or omission) which was a part of the story attract liability?

Figure 11.1: Introduction

> **Factual causation**
> - Whether the defendant's carelessness, on the balance of probabilities, materially contributed to or increased the harm to the plaintiff.
>
> **Legal causation**
> - Could the defendant have reasonably foreseen that kind of loss, or is it too remote?

The recent review of the law of negligence and subsequent statutory amendments have sought to lend some clarity to the application of the principles of causation and remoteness. This chapter will consider the common law as it currently stands, then provide a brief outline of the findings of the Ipp Committee and set out the legislative response.

---

[1] The first step (duty) was discussed in Chapters 8 and 9 and the second step (breach) in Chapter 10.

Causation

[11.10] The plaintiff has the burden of proving that the defendant's negligence caused his or her loss or damage. This so-called "factual causation" issue is generally addressed by asking whether the plaintiff would have received the injury or damage but for the defendant's negligence.[2] If the answer is "yes", the action fails even though the plaintiff can establish negligence by the defendant. So in *Barnett v Chelsea Hospital Management Committee* [1969] 1 QB 428 a hospital doctor, in clear breach of his duty of care, refused to examine a person who had attended an outpatients clinic complaining of vomiting. The patient was suffering from arsenic poisoning and died soon afterwards. In these particular circumstances it was determined that even had the doctor properly carried out his duty of examination, it would have been too late for effective treatment to have been administered. As the loss did not flow from the refusal of treatment, there was deemed to be no liability. In *McWilliams v Arrol Ltd* [1962] 1 WLR 295[3] a workman was killed in an accident at work. The defendants had, in breach of duty, failed to supply safety-belts, the wearing of which would have prevented the injury the plaintiff suffered. Nevertheless, the action failed because the evidence failed to convince the court that he would have worn the belt had it been provided. In *Cutler v Vauxhall Motors* [1971] 1 QB 418 the plaintiff, an employee of the defendants, grazed his ankle in an accident at work for which the defendants were liable in negligence. The graze caused ulceration of the leg necessitating an immediate operation for the removal of varicose veins. The plaintiff was unable to recover damages for having to have the operation because the court found that he would have needed to have the same operation within five years. The proof accepted by the court as to the likely need for the later operation was on the balance of probabilities. Now, however, following the decision of the High Court in *Malec v Hutton* (1990) 169 CLR 638, if there had been any chance that the plaintiff would not have needed the operation, he would have been entitled to compensation for the loss of that chance.

Figure 11.2: Causation

In the absence of a clear causal link, even negligent behaviour will not attract liability.
Question to ask: Did the act or omission make a difference to the outcome? If not, no liability.

Difficulty in establishing factual causation

[11.15] Determination of causation (not just causation at law but also factual causation), is not always straightforward. In some situations, there may be a selection of possible contributing factors; while in others, the current state of scientific or medical knowledge may make it impossible to separate one possible cause from another. In such circumstances there may clearly be two or more breaches of duty which may,

---

[2]   The "but for" test was once the determinative test for establishing causation, but there have been problems identified with this test, and it has now been rejected as determinative. Refer *March v E & MH Stramare* (1991) 171 CLR 506.

[3]   See also *Forbes v Olympic General Products* [1989] Aust Torts Reports 80-301 – no liability on manufacturer for failing to warn consumer, since consumer would not have heeded the warning.

or may not, have led to the loss or injury. The only certainty is that the negligence of at least one party led to that loss or injury. In such situations the courts have demonstrated a willingness to adjust the test of causation on the grounds that to do otherwise "would be deeply offensive to instinctive notions of what justice requires and fairness demands": *Fairchild v Glenhaven Funeral Services Ltd* [2003] 1 AC 32 per Lord Nicholls at 68.

Two (or more) possible causes

[11.20] It may not always be possible to pinpoint one individual cause where there exist different factors which could each, individually, have led to the loss or injury. This difficulty is clearly recognised by the courts and a number of cases show that the courts will draw inferences favourable to the plaintiff, even though absolute proof of causal connection is lacking. In *Bonnington Castings v Wardlaw* [1956] AC 613 the plaintiff had contracted a lung disease through exposure to noxious fumes, for some of which his employers were liable. The plaintiff was found to have discharged the burden of establishing causal connection between his disease and those fumes for which the employer was to blame. The House of Lords found that these fumes had "materially contributed" to the plaintiff's disease. This amounts to an inferential finding in the plaintiff's favour that the non-tortious fumes were probably not a sufficient cause of the disease. In *Bonnington* the damage due to the non-tortious fumes was regarded as not severable from that arising from the tortious. A different result was reached in *Thompson v Smiths Shiprepairers (North Shields) Ltd* [1984] QB 405 in which the court was able to apportion damage to hearing resulting from an earlier non-tortious exposure to noise by distinguishing it from that caused by a later tortious exposure.

On the rather special facts of the Canadian decision of *Cook v Lewis* [1952] 1 DLR 1, a transfer of the legal burden of proof to the defendant on the causation issue was accepted by the court. In that case, two defendants had negligently discharged their guns in the direction of the plaintiff at the same time and one had hit him. The court held that since both were in breach of a duty of care towards the plaintiff, and since the effect of that breach was to make it impossible for the plaintiff to prove which shot had hit him, he was entitled to succeed against both defendants, unless either of them could show his was not the culpable shot.

This possible shift in evidential onus is briefly discussed in Chapter 13 and continues to be the subject of some debate in the courts. The New South Wales Court of Appeal recently described any "mechanical application of a rule that the evidential onus shifts once a breach has occurred" as being in "conflict with ... basic principles of the common law". In this instance it was noted that such a "radical change" in the law must be based upon an "unequivocal" statement by the High Court (which is yet to occur): *Flounders v Millar* [2007] NSWCA 238 at [36] per Ipp JA.[4] Continued and clear support for a shift in evidential onus is perhaps best described as doubtful.

---

[4]   Indeed, in his comprehensive exploration of this issue in his judgment, his Honour outlines evidence of the somewhat equivocal approach of the High Court to the question of shifting evidential onus. Decisions referred to include: *Betts v Whittingslowe* (1945) 71 CLR 637; *Bennett v Minister of Community Welfare* (1992) 176 CLR 408; *Chappel v Hart* (1998) 195 CLR 232; and *Naxakis v Western General Hospital* (1999) 197 CLR 269. Also refer discussion in Chapter 13 at [13.10].

Defendant creating the risk

[11.25] In some situations, the defendant may have been responsible for creating a risk of injury, but within the facts at hand, it is not possible to determine whether it was this creation of the risk that caused the injury, or the presence of another factor. The difficulties of such situations are clearly demonstrated in two leading English cases, *McGhee v National Coal Board* [1973] 1 WLR 1 and *Wilsher v Essex Area Health Authority* [1988] AC 1074. In *McGhee*, the plaintiff worked in kilns and was subject to prolonged exposure to brick dust. It was claimed that the defendants had failed in their duty of care to the plaintiff by not providing shower facilities at the workplace. The plaintiff contracted dermatitis, allegedly as a result of the inability to shower and remove the dust. It was found that the condition had been caused by that negligence even though the medical aetiology of dermatitis is not yet clearly established, so that it might have been caused by something quite separate from brick dust (such as the friction of riding his bike home, or a cut sustained while riding home).

Wilsher saw the House of Lords correcting some of the indications in the judgments in *McGhee* (in particular that of Lord Wilberforce) that the plaintiff need establish only a breach of duty by the defendant's creating a risk of a certain harm occurring, and that, if that harm occurred, the defendant had the burden of proving the harm had another cause. In this instance, *McGhee* was explained as being simply an example of a favourable inference of causal connection being drawn by the court; there was at no point a transfer of any burden of proof to the defendant. The plaintiff in *Wilsher*, an infant born prematurely, had had a surplus of oxygen administered to him negligently by the defendants' medical staff and had become blind. Blindness in prematurely born children may occur spontaneously from a number of causes including a surplus of oxygen. The House of Lords ordered a new trial on the issue of causation, since the Court of Appeal had applied the erroneous Wilberforce reasoning in *McGhee*. Ultimately, as the surplus of oxygen was only one of many possible causes of blindness (including the premature birth) there was insufficient basis for a determination of causation in this instance.

It is essential to note, however, that the High Court has recently re-emphasised that the mere creation of a risk and failure to fulfil a duty is not sufficient. *Roads and Traffic Authority v Royal* (2008) 245 ALR 653; [2008] HCA 19 involved a two-car collision at an intersection with a history of accidents, indeed it was a designated "Black Spot". In this instance there was evidence of carelessness on the part of both drivers and whilst the problems with the intersection *may* have contributed to the accident, the majority of the court (Gummow, Hayne and Heydon JJ with Kirby J in dissent)[5] held that the fact that there had been 20 crashes at the intersection between 1993 and 2001 was relevant to the identification of a breach of duty but not necessarily to the issue of causation (at [26]). In this instance the court took the opportunity to emphasise that "breach alone is not sufficient" (at [26]). On the facts before the court, the most significant causal factor was the failure of the driver "to drive sufficiently carefully to avoid the risk of a collision" (at [33]). Thus, the failure to ensure a clear line of sight (which was the identified breach of duty) was little more than a coincidence, it merely established that there would not have been an intersection of this kind, not that there would not have been "a collision between drivers as careless as the defendant and the plaintiff" (at [33]).

---

5   The dissenting opinion of Kirby J will be considered further below under the heading, "Role of policy".

Inferences of causation

[11.30] The facts can sometimes lead to a situation of uncertainty which can only be addressed by the court drawing inferences of causation. Examples of favourable inferences to the plaintiff being drawn by Australian courts are found in *Tubemakers of Australia Ltd v Fernandez* (1976) 10 ALR 303 and *Chance v Alcoa of Australia* [1990] Aust Torts Reports 81-017. In *Fernandez* the plaintiff had received a blow on the hand for which his employer was liable. The injury caused painful swelling of the hand. Some months later the plaintiff developed Dupuytren's contracture of a finger on the hand (finger pulled down towards the palm). The nature of the causal element in Dupuytren's remains uncertain, though there was evidence that repeated blows to the hand might produce it. Nevertheless, the High Court held the initial blow to the hand to be the cause of the later condition in the absence of other explaining evidence. In *Chance* the plaintiff suffered caustic soda burns to both eyes and later developed "dry eye" condition in both. Although there was evidence that it was unusual for a caustic soda burn to produce the dry eye condition after a period of time of this sort, the court interpreted this to mean that it was not impossible and held causal connection to have been established. Nevertheless, Mahoney JA in the New South Wales decision in *X v Pal* (1991) 23 NSWLR 26, warned against a presumptive approach to causation based on a post hoc propter hoc line of argument (because it follows it, it must have been caused by it). In that case, the court refused to find causal connection between the non-treatment for syphilis of the plaintiff's mother and the plaintiff's birth with deformities (since these deformities had not been shown to be a result of the plaintiff's congenital syphilis). The evidence did not make it possible to sustain that conclusion. Also in *Pickford v ICI* [1998] 3 All ER 462,[6] the House of Lords held that the plaintiff had failed to prove that repetitive typing during her employment causing strain on her wrist had caused her RSI condition. The evidence before the court had left unresolved the question whether the source of this condition was physical or psychogenic.

Whilst an inference may well result in a positive outcome for a plaintiff, it is important to recognise that an element of certainty must be present; the courts will not determine causation based upon mere speculation. This was emphasised by Ipp JA in *Flounders v Millar* [2007] NSWCA 238 at [35] when he concluded that: "the choice between conflicting inferences must be more than a matter of conjecture. If the court is left to speculate about possibilities as to the cause of the injury, the plaintiff must fail."

Asbestos cases

[11.35] Asbestos-related diseases have involved the courts in a task of considerable difficulty caused by imperfect medical understanding of the way in which exposure to asbestos works on the body to cause disease. Where there is only one known exposure, the court is usually ready to infer that that has caused the disease: *CSR v Young* [1998] Aust Torts Reports 81-468 (exposure to blue asbestos during first 27 months of childhood caused mesothelioma at age 34). Most of the difficulties centre around cases where there is more than one exposure caused by different defendants. In two of these cases, the person responsible for the last exposure was held not liable on the ground that the probability was that that exposure had not materially contributed to the disease: *ICI v Walsh* [1997] Aust Torts Reports 81-452; *Bendix Pty Ltd v Barnes* (1997) 42 NSWLR 307. But in *Baldwin Pty Ltd v Plane* [1999] Aust Torts Reports 81-499, where substantial

---

[6] *Phipson Nominees v French* [1988] Aust Torts Reports 80-196 was to the same effect.

quantities of asbestos dust had been inhaled by an employee during his work, and there was also a source of exposure in substances contained in brake-blocks supplied by the second defendants, the court inferred dual causation. In the absence of anything to persuade it otherwise, the court held the second defendants and the employer equally liable for causing the disease. In this case, it was stated that epidemiological studies conducted under laboratory conditions were only relevant to showing a possible link between certain types of exposure to asbestos and a related disease; they could not establish a probability of causation.

The most recent of these cases has brought a level of certainty to the debate. *Fairchild v Glenhaven Funeral Services Ltd* [2003] 1 AC 32 involved the House of Lords hearing three cases together. In each case, the plaintiffs had been exposed to asbestos dust in the course of their employment by more than one employer. The court emphasised the material contribution of each employer and made references to "substantial" and "significant" contribution to the risk of injury. Emphasis was placed on the concept of a just outcome (eg Lords Bingham and Nicholls at 68, Lord Hoffmann at 73) and the need to ensure that the inability to "prove the unprovable" (Lord Bingham at 44) did not result in a plaintiff being unable to recover in the face of clear negligence. The key to the decision was the material contribution. Whether this can be extended to other situations in which there are multiple possible causes is yet to be determined by the courts, but it was an issue considered at some length by the Ipp Committee.[7]

Causation and the loss of chances

[11.40] In many instances where loss or injury is sustained by a plaintiff, considerations move beyond the initial loss suffered to loss of a chance. Examples may include loss of a chance for full recovery or to exploit a lucrative contract. While this potential loss may be readily recognisable it is not always possible to quantify and, in general, the doctrine of compensation in relation to the loss of a chance does not apply. In *Hotson v East Berkshire Health Authority* [1987] AC 750 the plaintiff had suffered an injury for which he was treated by the defendants, who failed to discover that a serious injury to the hip had occurred. It was found that had this been correctly diagnosed and given proper treatment, the plaintiff would have had a 25% chance of complete recovery from the injury. Instead the plaintiff suffered a permanent deformity of the hip. The House of Lords held that the plaintiff was not entitled to compensation for the loss of the 25% chance of complete recovery. In order to establish liability on the defendants' part, proof on the balance of probabilities was necessary.

Hotson is still accepted law as far as establishing matters of historical fact necessary to prove the cause of action is concerned. It has been thrown into doubt in cases where the plaintiff's case depends on showing not what happened but what might have happened, of which, of course, *Hotson* was one example. In *Sellars v Adelaide Petroleum NL* (1994) 179 CLR 332 Adelaide Petroleum had withdrawn from contractual negotiations with Pagini Resources NL in order to enter into negotiations with Poseidon, with which it then entered into a contract. Poseidon later withdrew from the contract on the ground that its agent, Sellars, had exceeded his authority in entering into it. Adelaide Petroleum then entered into a contract with Pagini, but on less favourable terms than it might have

---

7   The reasoning in *Fairchild v Glenhaven Funeral Services Ltd* [2003] AC 32; [2002] 3 WLR 89 continues to clearly be of relevance, however, with the legislature in South Australia taking the interesting step of including it as a footnote to s 34 of the *Civil Liability Act 1936* (SA).

obtained had the original contractual negotiations with Pagini proceeded to fruition. It was found as a fact that the chance of Adelaide's obtaining the more favourable terms from Pagini at the time it concluded the contract with Poseidon was of a lower order than a 51% probability (in fact some 40%). Nevertheless, the High Court of Australia held that Adelaide Petroleum was entitled to succeed against Poseidon for loss of this chance in an action brought under the trade practices legislation for misleading or deceptive conduct by Poseidon. The majority in the High Court found that Adelaide Petroleum had established a probability of loss of some sort in losing the original contract with Pagini, since commercial opportunities have value. It was therefore entitled to compensation based on the actual chance the plaintiffs had of entering into that contract. This reasoning causes difficulty. While it is true that mere chances of financial gain have value – lottery tickets, options to sell shares etc may be bought and sold – it is difficult to see that the lost commercial opportunity in the case itself was anything other than the 40% chance of gaining the more favourable contract with Pagini. Although the High Court spoke only in terms of lost commercial opportunities, it is hard to see why the doctrine laid down should be limited in this way. The chance of wearing the safety-belt could be seen as having value to the plaintiff in *McWilliams v Arrol Ltd* [1962] 1 WLR 295, even though he could not show a probability of his having worn one if it had been provided. The chance of refusing consent to an operation, if the patient had been warned of a certain risk, could be seen as of value to that patient even though the patient was unable to show a probability of refusal of consent if warned of the risk: see [11.10].

Figure 11.3: Last chance?

Plaintiff compensated for a loss of chance to gain a favourable outcome or avoid a detrimental event (<50%)
- Recover for the percentage of the loss: *Sellars v Adelaide Petroleum NL* (1994) 179 CLR 332
- Only 40% chance that contract would have been successfully concluded

The Court of Appeal in England reached a similar conclusion to that in *Sellars* in *Allied Maples v Simmons* [1995] 4 All ER 907. In this case, the plaintiffs claimed that the defendant solicitors had been negligent in failing to advise them about the risk (which materialised) of incurring substantial "first tenant" liabilities on their acquisition of a group of companies. They claimed that had they known of this risk, they would have negotiated with the sellers to obtain protection against possible liabilities in the form of a warranty; but they were unable to show a probability that they would have succeeded in this. However, the Court of Appeal held that they only needed to show a probability that they would have had recourse to the sellers in order to negotiate. Having shown that, they were entitled to damages in tort based on the chance of their succeeding. The novel point about the decision is that the court treated the claim as being one in tort rather than for breach of contract, in which (as we saw in Chapter 8) solicitors have been held liable for loss of less than probable chances, such as those of succeeding in litigation.[8]

---

[8]   *Kitchen v Royal Airforce Assn* [1958] 1 WLR 563. The case law on loss of chances compensation in actions against solicitors is set out at [8.295]. Loss of less than probable chances is clearly available for breach of contract: *Chaplin v Hicks* [1911] 2 KB 786.

Where the plaintiff has established on the balance of probabilities a cause of action in tort against the defendant, there is no problem about awarding compensation for contingencies affecting the valuation of the claim which are less than probable to occur. *Malec v Hutton* (1990) 169 CLR 338 (considered at [11.60]) illustrates the point.

Two special cases of "but for" causation

Whether plaintiff would have refused consent if properly informed

[11.45] Chapter 9 showed that a breach of duty of care may be established against a medical practitioner by showing that the practitioner failed to disclose the risks of an operation to be performed on the plaintiff. Should the undisclosed risk materialise in the course of the operation, the plaintiff has a cause of action against the practitioner, but only if the patient were able to prove a probability that he or she would not have undergone the operation if properly informed of the risk. The law is clear that on this matter the court is concerned with what the actual patient would have decided, not what a reasonable person in the patient's position would have decided. The question then becomes one of extreme difficulty since every plaintiff will swear under oath that he or she would not have had the operation given the relevant knowledge. For a decision concluding against the plaintiff despite such an assertion, see *Rosenberg v Whitaker* (2001) 205 CLR 434; *Zaltron v Raptis* [2001] SASC 209; and *Bustos v Hair Transplant* (unreported, NSWCA, 15 April 1997). The plaintiff in *Rogers v Whitaker* (1992) 175 CLR 479, on the other hand, was able to demonstrate a probability that she would not have had the operation had she been informed of the risk of total blindness.

The subjective test of causation has proved to be a difficult one to meet with sceptical courts rejecting the claims of plaintiffs that they would not have proceeded with the treatment if warned of the risk. The reason for the scepticism is usually based upon something in the facts which means that it is highly unlikely that advice would have made any difference: the focus of the patient on positive outcomes (a succesful hair transplant in *Bustos*), an established relationship of trust in and reliance on the doctor (*Smith v Barking, Havering & Brentwood Health Authority* [1994] 5 Med LR 285) or the severity of the condition (*Smith v Salford Health Authority* [1994] 5 Med LR 321).

Chappel v Hart (1998) 195 CLR 232 raised a novel question in this area. The plaintiff had been advised by the defendant consultant surgeon that she needed an operation to remove a pharyngeal pouch in her oesophagus which was interfering with her swallowing. She asked about the risks of the operation, indicating she did not wish to end up with a croaking voice like the former Premier of New South Wales. The defendant failed to warn her of the possible risk of an oesophageal tear during the operation and the consequent, very much less likely, risk of an infection of the oesophagus occurring, and of it seriously affecting her voice. The plaintiff contended that had she known of the risk, she would not have had the operation at that time but would have consulted a more experienced consultant. During the course of an operation conducted by the defendant, the undisclosed risk manifested without any negligence on the defendant's part. As the condition was a degenerative one, the trial judge found as a fact that the plaintiff would inevitably have needed the operation at some time, and that the same risk would have applied. She then went on to successfully appeal this decision with a 3:2 majority in the High Court.

This decision is hard to support. Clearly the defendant was negligent in failing to disclose the risk to the plaintiff. Equally, on a simple "but for" approach to causation in the case, he caused her injury, since her evidence disclosed that had she known of the risk she would not have had the operation performed at that time or by the defendant, but would have consulted a more experienced surgeon. This approach seems to have been the basis of the majority decision in her favour. The majority judges could find no sufficient ground of common sense or policy to reject the "but for" conclusion. To some extent Kirby and Gaudron JJ were influenced by the fact that the risk with a more experienced surgeon would have been less, but this was mere speculation and contradicted the finding of fact of the trial judge. On the other hand, the fact that she would have needed the operation at some time despite disclosure of the risk, and that there was no evidence to suggest that the risk would have been less with another surgeon, weighed with the judges in the minority. The negligence of the defendant had placed the plaintiff in a position of no greater risk than she was in already.

Reliance in cases of negligent statement

[11.50] The plaintiff in an action for negligent statement must establish not only a relationship of reliance between plaintiff and defendant, but also that the plaintiff actually relied on the statement. In order to prove reliance the plaintiff must satisfy the "but for" test of causation; that is, would the loss have been suffered but for the occurrence of the breach? The special meaning of this question in relation to negligent statements must be emphasised. The question is not what the plaintiff would have done in the absence of a statement, but in the presence of a careful statement. If despite there being a careful statement on the matter in question the plaintiff would still have acted in the same way, then reliance is not proved. Thus in *JEB Fasteners Ltd v Marks & Bloom* [1983] 1 All ER 583 the plaintiffs were held to be unable to prove reliance on false statements in the accounts of a company prepared by the defendant accountants. This was because the court found, as a fact, that their main reason for buying the company was to obtain the services of two of its directors and, therefore, they would still have bought the company had they known of its true financial position.

Where two or more negligent statements have been made to the plaintiff by different persons, the application of *JEB Fasteners* and the "but for" test may produce the result that the plaintiff is able to succeed against neither person, since when applied to each statement the conclusion is drawn that the plaintiff would still have relied on the other person's statement. This is unsatisfactory and falls within the disapproval of the "but for" test in its application to two or more independent, sufficient causes of the loss, which was expressed by Mason CJ in *March v E & MH Stramare Pty Ltd* (1991) 171 CLR 506. The likelihood is therefore that in the situation posed, both defendants would be held liable to the plaintiff.

A further question concerning liability for negligent statements is whether it is necessary that the loss suffered by the plaintiff should fall within the risk to which the defendant's advice was relevant; a point relevant to remoteness of damage rather than causation. If, for example, the plaintiff has been negligently advised to buy a certain share for more than its worth, but the share has then suffered a further loss in a stock market crash, it is arguable that the defendant is not liable for this loss because it is unrelated to the matter on which the defendant gave advice. On the other hand, on a simple application of "but for" principles, the plaintiff should be able to recover damages in respect of the market fall, if it can establish that it would not have bought the shares had it known the true position. In *Banque Bruxelles v Eagle Star* [1997] AC

191 the House of Lords held that falls in the property market were not part of the risk to which a property valuation related; so that in the case of a negligent overvaluation, the valuer's liability was limited to the difference between the amount lent and the property's actual value at the time of the valuation. In *Kenny & Good v MGICA* (1999) 199 CLR 413, the High Court reached a different conclusion, but one best explained by the particular facts of the case. In that case the valuer had not only overvalued the property but also indicated to the plaintiffs that it was suitable for the investment of trust funds for a period of three to five years. The plaintiffs, who had insured a bank's mortgage of the property on the strength of the valuation, were able to rely on that provision in a case brought for misleading or deceptive conduct under the trade practices legislation to obtain additional damages for a fall in the property market. The advice that the valuation would remain good for the period during which the market fell was certainly the basis of the judgments of McHugh and Gummow JJ, though less clearly the joint judgment of Kirby and Callinan JJ. Their stressing that the case was limited to its own facts and gave rise to no general principles concerning market falls suggests they were of the same opinion as McHugh and Gummow JJ.[9] On the other hand, the award in *L Shaddock & Associates v Parramatta CC* (1981) 150 CLR 225 of damages for consequential loss (such as the payment of rates and telephone charges on the property purchased) shows that the plaintiff is entitled to be indemnified against all the ordinary occupational expense incurred in the occupation of land, where (as in *Shaddock*) they are able to satisfy the court they would not have bought the land except for the defendant's negligence. In line with the decision in *Banque Bruxelles*, the same would not apply if the loss had occurred through a natural event such as a landslip.

Criticism of "but for" test

[11.55] In *March v E & MH Stramare Pty Ltd* (1991) 171 CLR 506 the High Court of Australia expressed reservations about the "but for" test as a test of factual causation. As the court pointed out, the test is inadequate to deal with the case where there is more than one cause of the damage, each sufficient to cause it; also the case where the defendant's negligence has merely placed the plaintiff in the position in time and place where he or she receives a later injury. The court also criticised it on the ground that its application may produce too wide a field of compensation. These criticisms will now be dealt with in turn.

Independent sufficient causes of damage

[11.60] Where there are two (or more) causes of damage, each sufficient to cause that damage, the "but for" test is incapable of being satisfied by the plaintiff in relation to any of the causes, since when applied to any of them the answer will be given that the plaintiff would still have suffered the damage. This does not necessarily rule out liability on the part of the defendant. In *Baker v Willoughby* [1970] AC 825 the plaintiff had received an injury to his leg through the defendant's negligence, and the leg was partially disabled as a result. Later, the plaintiff was shot in the leg by another person and the leg was in consequence amputated. The need for amputation did not arise because of the existing disability in the leg. Nevertheless, the House of Lords held that the plaintiff should recover compensation from the defendant on the basis of a

---

[9] That there is no general liability for consequential loss is in line with *Potts v Miller* (1940) 64 CLR 282 – racehorse bought after fraudulent misrepresentation became diseased and died – seller not liable for the death if this was simply a coincidental development.

continuing disability in the leg arising from the earlier injury. Lord Reid's explanation of the decision was that the later event merely operated as a concurrent cause of the plaintiff's disability along with the earlier injury. It did not "obliterate" the effects of that injury. There were two causes of the plaintiff's disability. Only if it improved the plaintiff's condition, therefore, would the later event be causally relevant. Lord Pearson based his judgment on the injustice that would arise if the plaintiff received less than full compensation from the first defendant for his injury. The first defendant would have to pay damages only up to the time of the second injury; the second defendant would have to pay damages only for causing the loss of an already damaged leg, since it is settled law that the so-called thin skull rule (see [11.90]ff) operates in favour of defendants as well as against them. Though injured by two torts, the plaintiff would receive less in compensation than the whole value of the leg.

In explaining his reasoning, Lord Pearson intimated that a difference might exist where the later event was not a tort. There was indeed authority for this point prior to *Baker* in *Carslogie Steamship Ltd v Royal Norwegian Government* [1952] AC 292, a case confirmed by the House of Lords' decision in *Jobling v Associated Dairies* [1982] AC 794. The plaintiff had sustained an injury to his back at work which had reduced his working capacity by 50%, and for which his employer, the defendant, was liable to compensate him. Before trial he developed spondylotic myelopathy (a compression of the spinal cord in the neck) quite independently of the first injury. This condition destroyed his working capacity altogether. The House of Lords unanimously upheld the verdict of the Court of Appeal that the later natural event must be taken into account in awarding damages; the effect being that no damages were awarded for the loss of working capacity after the onset of the myelopathy. All the members of the House of Lords were in agreement that Lord Reid's explanation of *Baker* based upon the idea of successive concurrent causes was not supportable. Later detrimental events were relevant to causation because in general the courts in awarding damages make some deduction for the so-called "vicissitudes of life", these being thought to work on the whole adversely to the plaintiff. If one such vicissitude has actually occurred at the date of the trial, it would be wrong to ignore it. This reasoning throws considerable doubt upon the decision in *Baker* itself, but no member of the House actually stated that that case was wrongly decided, and there was some support for Lord Pearson's view that the case turned on the fact that the plaintiff's injuries had been caused by successive torts. The distinction between a later tort and a later natural event seems therefore to have won the guarded approval of the House of Lords. The *Baker/Jobling* problem only arises in the case where each event is by itself a sufficient cause of the damage which the plaintiff suffers. Where the defendant's negligence needs to act in combination with a later act of negligence in order to produce the relevant damage, there is no difficulty in finding factual causation established in regard to both acts of negligence.

The Australian position on this particular problem has not been clearly established. *Baker* has been applied in Australia in *Nicholson v Walker* (1979) 21 SASR 481. But in *Faulkner v Keffalinos* (1970) 45 ALJR 80 two members of the High Court (Windeyer and Gibbs JJ) thought that a subsequent motor accident, which would have been partly responsible for producing the same effect as the first accident, must be taken into account in assessing damages. Here, however, since the circumstances of the later accident were unknown and there was no alleged tortfeasor before the court, it was presumably treated as accidental, so that *Faulkner* belongs within the *Jobling* category of case rather than under *Baker*. In *Malec v Hutton* (1990) 169 CLR 338 *Jobling* was distinguished by the High Court. In that case the plaintiff had suffered brucellosis for which his employer was liable and which rendered him unemployable. The trial court had held that on the balance of probabilities, a spinal condition unassociated with brucellosis would also have rendered the plaintiff unemployable after a certain date, and refused the plaintiff damages for loss of wages after that date. The High Court held this to be mistaken. Even if the spinal condition was proved to be likely to have had the effect suggested on the balance of probabilities, the plaintiff was still entitled to be compensated for the residual contingency that it would not have occurred. Thus it is only if the proof of likelihood was 100% would the plaintiff go uncompensated. The situation before the High Court in *Malec* was not the same as that in *Jobling*. In *Jobling* the myelopathy had occurred at the time of trial. In *Malec* the future development of the plaintiff's spinal condition was uncertain. *Malec* may operate in the defendant's favour also, by allowing reduction in respect of known contingencies, which are probably unlikely to occur.[10]

Figure 11.4: General principles

> **Subsequent tortfeasor:** *Baker v Willoughby* [1970] AC 825
> - Original tortfeasor: liability continues at same level as though subsequent tort had never occurred
> - Subsequent tortfeasor liable for any additional loss sustained
>
> **Subsequent non-tortious event (independent and certain to happen):** *Jobling v Associated Dairies* [1982] AC 794
> - Liability extends only to the point at which the subsequent event occurred, ie loss of earning capacity only to be paid until the illness intervened and the plaintiff would have had to discontinue work (this subsequent event is totally independent of the original tort)
> - A tortfeasor is only liable for the extent of the loss which was caused by his or her negligence
>
> **Subsequent non-tortious event (independent and only a chance it will happen):** *Malec v Hutton* (1990) 169 CLR 338
> - Liability reduced by the percentage of likelihood that the illness would have overtaken the plaintiff
> - Plaintiff compensated for the residual contingency that the additional loss would not have occurred

Too great a field of compensation

[11.65] Where there is more than one cause of damage, but each cause is insufficient by itself to cause the damage, the "but for" test may be satisfied in relation to each cause. The causes are said to be concurrent. Whether the responsibility in relation to the first cause extends to damage inflicted by the second depends on whether the latter is a novus actus interveniens (intervening act). The doctrine is one of considerable legal difficulty.[11] The problem arises because, even though the "but for" test may be satisfied and the loss or damage may be reasonably foreseeable, the court may not accept that it *should* be legally recoverable. The approach favoured by Mason CJ, Deane and Toohey JJ in the High Court decision in *March v E & MH Stramare Pty Ltd* (1991) 171 CLR

---

10   See, eg, *Wynn v NSW Insurance* [1996] Aust Torts Reports 81-371 – deduction of 12.5% from damages for future economic loss included a deduction for the contingency that a previous injury might cause future earning loss.

11   This is particularly so in relation to human conduct and will be discussed in this context in this chapter.

506 was to reject the automatic application of the "but for" test as a determinant of causation in fact in relation to the earlier "cause", even though the test is satisfied as regards that cause. Rather, causation in fact must to some extent be assessed by regard to the dictates of common sense. McHugh J, on the other hand, favoured the retention of the test as a determinant of causation in fact in all but the special cases considered above, but regarded the question whether a later event is a novus actus as depending on a policy choice to be made by the court. In his view, common sense was not an appropriate criterion for determining the limited question of the existence of causal connection, which should not depend upon a decision of a discretionary nature. The approach of the majority in the case appears at the moment to be in the ascendant, though the differences between the two are more apparent than real. In particular, it is hard to see how the "but for" test can be applied in a commonsense fashion. If it is understood that common sense may reject the results of its mechanical application, that is not far from the stance adopted by McHugh J. The problems with the commonsense test were highlighted by the Ipp Committee and are reflected in subsequent legislative amendments: see [11.170].

Role of "policy"

[11.67] The causative inquiry involves more than a mere consideration of the factual history of events. Of relevance are some "intangible" considerations, referred to as normative, or "policy" based considerations. The significance of the "normative" inquiry was demonstrated in *New South Wales v Godfrey* [2004] Aust Torts Reports 81–741[12] in which the decisive consideration was the potential for indeterminant liability. Thus despite the historical link between the breach of duty to ensure that prisoners did not escape and the later robbery, the appeal in this instance was successful, based upon a need to clearly set boundaries.

The importance of a broad inquiry has been acknowledged by the High Court with some recent discussion regarding the role of policy. In *Allianz Australia Insurance Ltd v GSF Australia Ltd* (2005) 221 CLR 568, McHugh J noted that causation always involves a "normative" decision and in *Travel Compensation Fund v Tambree* (2005) 224 CLR 627, Gleeson CJ acknowledged that normative considerations have a role to play in judgments about issues of causation but cautioned that this is not an open invitation to judges to engage in value judgments "at large" (at 639). Such a caution is appropriate as an appeal to what is "just" or "appropriate" in given circumstances can perhaps divert attention from the question which lies at the heart of causation: did the breach make any difference to the outcome? An illustrative example can be found in Kirby J's dissenting judgment in *Roads and Traffic Authority v Royal* (outlined above at [11.25]ff). The majority decision turned upon the significant fact that mere breach of duty is not sufficient to establish causation, there is a need for a clear and decisive link between that breach and the subsequent loss or damage. In this particular instance, the majority determined that a change in the design of the intersection would not have impacted on the careless driving of the parties involved in the accident. Kirby J on the other hand, turned his mind to the important public role played by the Roads and Traffic Authority and appealed to the objectives of tort law which, in his view, extended beyond the mere provision of compensation to the imposition of "monetary sanctions" (at [114]).

---

[12] The facts of this case are set out in Chapter 8 at [8.290].

To attribute responsibility to the Roads and Traffic Authority would be appropriate as it would provide stimulus for risk assessment and measures of accident prevention and safer highways (at [117]). The causative inquiry is therefore more than a mere historical consideration of events, and this was emphasised in the Ipp Report and is reflected in the legislative reform to be considered below at [11.170].

Remoteness of damage

[11.70] The relevance of "intangible" considerations becomes more apparent when the courts are called upon to turn their minds to the issue of remoteness of damage. The question here becomes what was a foreseeable outcome of the breach of duty and did the damage suffered fall within the scope of foreseeability or is it "too remote"? The test for remoteness of damage in negligence is that laid down in the decision of the Privy Council in *The Wagon Mound (No 1)* [1961] AC 388. As pointed out already, the test is that of reasonable foreseeability. The case was an appeal from the courts of New South Wales. As such, the Privy Council decision bound all Australian courts (that being the effect of a Privy Council decision at the time) but not the courts of England where Privy Council decisions are of a mere persuasive authority. In fact, the decision in *Wagon Mound (No 1)* ran contrary to an earlier English authority in the Court of Appeal decision in *Re Polemis* [1921] 3 KB 560 which in theory at least bound all English courts except the House of Lords. Despite this the Privy Council decision was immediately accepted by English courts and remains the law of Australia.

A comparison between the decisions in *Re Polemis* and *Wagon Mound (No 1)* remains instructive, because it brings out the central issue for decision, and one that perplexed and divided lawyers for a number of years. That question may be expressed as whether there ought to be a difference between the rule relating to the establishing of culpability and that relating to compensation (that is, what damage or injury the defendant should have to answer for). *Re Polemis* gave the answer that there ought to be different tests, that culpability must be established by what the defendant should have foreseen, but that foreseeability was not relevant as regards compensation. In *Re Polemis* the servants of the defendants, who were charterers of the plaintiffs' ship, while shifting cargo negligently let a plank fall into the hold of the ship, where a fire broke out causing damage to the ship. The findings of fact, by the arbitrator in the dispute, were that the cause of the fire was the ignition of petrol vapour present in the hold through leakage from drums stored there, the ignition being caused by a spark set off by the falling plank; and that though some damage to the fabric of the ship through the fall of the plank was foreseeable, damage through fire caused in this way was not. Accepting these findings, the Court of Appeal found the defendants liable because the fire was a direct result of their breach of duty to the plaintiffs; and the fact that it was not a foreseeable consequence did not matter.

In *Wagon Mound (No 1)* the employer of the defendants had carelessly allowed the discharge of a quantity of furnace oil from the defendants' ship onto the waters of Morts Bay, Sydney. The oil had spread to the plaintiffs' wharf where welding operations were being carried out on a ship, the "Corrimal". The oil congealed on the slipways in such a way as to have a damaging effect. The plaintiffs' wharf manager suspended welding on the "Corrimal" before taking advice that it was safe to continue. The oil, which has an ignition point of 170°F was, however, ignited in the course of welding, the trial judge finding that floating objects on the oil (such as cotton waste) had probably acted as a wick. In the ensuing fire considerable damage was done to the wharf and to the "Corrimal". In the New South Wales courts, *Re Polemis* was applied to hold the defendant charterers liable to the wharf owners. Although the ignition of the oil was not foreseeable, damage by fouling of the plaintiffs' wharf's slipways was foreseeable and the fire was a direct consequence of the defendants' employees' breach of duty in allowing the oil to escape. These decisions in favour of the plaintiffs were reversed on appeal to the Privy Council. The defendants were liable only for the foreseeable consequences of the escape of the oil. The unchallenged finding of fact by the trial judge that the ignition of the oil was not reasonably foreseeable therefore determined the result of the case.

As between the positions in *Wagon Mound (No 1)* and *Re Polemis* there is what appears to be an absolute philosophical divide. At the level of legal decision-making, however, the difference between the test of direct and of foreseeable consequences has produced little if anything by way of practical difference. This is because of three main factors. First, *Re Polemis* applied only to direct, physical consequences. Where the damage was not physical or was indirect, reasonable foreseeability was always the test for remoteness. Second, foreseeability at the remoteness level has, in post-*Wagon Mound (No 1)* decisions, been given an extensive meaning in much the same way as in the case of breach, even allowing recovery in some cases for harm classified as not reasonably foreseeable. Finally, the thin skull rule, under which the victim's pre-existing weak condition was not required to be foreseeable by one in breach of duty to the victim, has been held to be of continuing force. The result is that it is hard to identify a decision which would have been decided in a different way had *Re Polemis* rather than *Wagon Mound (No 1)* been the appropriate rule to apply.

Breach of duty distinguished

[11.75] According to the decision in *The Wagon Mound (No 1)* [1961] AC 388, foreseeability determines not only the issues of culpability and compensation, but also of breach of duty and remoteness of damage. Granted that there is no apparent difference in the test of foreseeability to be applied to breach and remoteness, this raises the difficulty of distinguishing the two concepts. The difference is that the question, as regards breach, is whether the defendant has unreasonably created or allowed to arise a foreseeable risk of harm to the plaintiff. Remoteness requires foreseeability of the actual harm suffered by the plaintiff, and the question of unreasonableness of the defendant's conduct does not enter into it. There is, however, undoubtedly a tendency by courts to conflate the two issues, so that the question becomes a consideration, first, of whether the actual damage suffered was reasonably foreseeable and, second, whether the defendant's response to the risk of that damage had been reasonable. This generally causes no great problem, but it does obscure the point that breach may be established by showing the creation of an obvious risk which has not materialised. The question of liability for any unusual damage which has occurred, is a question of remoteness of damage, requiring no balancing of the risk against the reasonableness of the defendant's conduct.[13]

---

[13] As is most apparent in the decisions based on the application of *Hughes v Lord Advocate* [1963] AC 837, considered at [11.85].

Foreseeability

General principles

[11.80] The nature of the foreseeability required of the defendant has been examined in Chapter 8 in relation to duty of care and breach of duty. What was said there broadly relates to remoteness of damage also. To sum up the earlier statement:

- The risk must be one which would occur to a reasonable person as a possible, and not fantastically improbable, consequence of his or her negligence.
- Nevertheless, in some cases the courts may appear to be applying a test of hindsight rather than foresight where the consequence is one which is unlikely to have occurred even to a reasonable person at the actual time of his or her act.
- Provided the damage is, broadly speaking, within the risk of what may be expected to arise, the precise sequence of events by which it arises does not need to be foreseeable.

The last principle clearly applies in relation to remoteness of damage. It was best expressed by Lord Denning MR in *Stewart v West African Air Terminals* (1964) 108 SJ 838:

> *It is not necessary that the precise concatenation of circumstances should be envisaged. If the consequence was one within the general range which any reasonable person might foresee (and was not an entirely different kind which no one would anticipate) then it is within the rule that a person who is guilty of negligence is liable for the consequences.*

There is less objection to applying a test of hindsight, rather than foresight, in relation to remoteness of damage as opposed to breach of duty. In the issue of remoteness, the court is not judging whether the defendant has been negligent (that has already been established); it is merely deciding what are the foreseeable consequences of that negligence. The High Court ruled, in a decision turning on issues of duty on the facts and breach, that the precise concatenation of events need not be found to be reasonably foreseeable: *Chapman v Hearse* (1961) 106 CLR 112. The same applies a fortiori to issues of remoteness of damage. This has of course been subject to review, and we await the court's interpretation of recent statutory amendments.

Damage or injury a mere variant of the foreseeable

[11.85] In *Chapman v Hearse* (1961) 106 CLR 112 itself, all the individual events in the "concatenation" were clearly foreseeable. The question becomes a little more complicated when one or more of those events is not foreseeable. In *Hughes v Lord Advocate* [1963] AC 837 the defendants' servants had left a manhole shelter unattended. Four lighted paraffin lamps were placed at the corners of the shelter. The plaintiff, a boy aged eight, took one of the lamps into the shelter to explore the manhole. The plaintiff dropped the lamp into the hole and an explosion occurred through the ignition of vapourised paraffin from the lamp. The plaintiff received severe burns. The findings of the court were as follows:

- the defendants were in breach of their duty of care to the plaintiff, since the lamps were an allurement and a danger to children, creating a risk of their being burned if a lamp broke; and

- the actual manner in which the plaintiff was injured (by explosion through ignition of vaporised paraffin) was not reasonably foreseeable.

Despite the latter finding, the House of Lords held that the defendants were liable in negligence. Since the effect of the negligence was to create a foreseeable risk of the plaintiff being burned, and since the plaintiff actually received burns, it did not matter that the precise manner in which he received the injury was unforeseeable. The actual damage was not different in kind from the foreseeable.

This broad approach to the remoteness issue drew some support from an earlier statement by Lord Denning, which received the approval of the Judicial Committee in *The Wagon Mound (No 1)* [1961] AC 388. He said "the test of liability for shock is foreseeability of shock": *King v Phillips* [1953] 1 QB 429. At one stage lawyers inclined to the view that the acceptance of Lord Denning's statement by the Privy Council together with the judgments of the House of Lords in *Hughes* might mean that provided the broad kind of damage that occurred was foreseeable, the manner in which it occurred need not be. For example, *Re Polemis* [1921] 3 KB 560 would still, under *Wagon Mound (No 1)*, produce a decision against the plaintiffs, since fire damage was not a foreseeable risk. However, it seems clear that the present state of the law does not support any broad test of foreseeability under which only the kind of damage need be foreseeable without regard to the manner of occurrence of the damage. In the case of psychological injury itself, foreseeability of shock may arise whenever the plaintiff is physically endangered by the defendant's negligent conduct; yet it does not follow that liability always exists where shock is suffered. *Rowe v McCartney* [1976] 2 NSWLR 72[14] shows that the manner of occurrence of the shock is relevant. There the plaintiff was injured in an accident caused by the negligent driving of the defendant, but suffered shock through her guilt feelings in allowing the defendant to drive the car. Her shock was held to be not reasonably foreseeable. There would also be problems in classifying the "type" of damage required to be foreseen. What of bodily disease, for example? If all bodily diseases were regarded as one type of damage, this would take the risk principle a long way, bearing in mind that disease with broadly similar effects may have quite distinct origins. But there is no evidence that this is the law; indeed, there is authority against it in the case of *Tremain v Pike* [1969] 1 WLR 1556.

In many cases, therefore, it will not be possible to ignore the issue whether particular harm happened in the way in which it was foreseeably likely to happen. In *Doughty v Turner Manufacturing Co* [1964] 1 QB 518 the following question arose before the Court of Appeal: whether (assuming a breach of duty by the defendants' servant in knocking an asbestos cover into a bath containing a molten chemical liquid at very high temperature, thus subjecting the plaintiff to the risk of receiving burns by splashing) the defendants were liable for the plaintiff's burns received when an unforeseeable chemical reaction took place and the liquid erupted and burned the plaintiff. The Court of Appeal found that this was not a mere variant of the foreseeable risk, but (in the words of Lord Reid in *Hughes*), "the intrusion of a new and unexpected factor". Yet the effect on the plaintiff was the same in the case of either splashing or eruption; that is, burn. The key to the decision was the extent of the splashing and the manner in

---

[14]   Cf *Nader v Urban Transport Authority* [1985] Aust Torts Reports 80-724.

which it occurred. If the lid had merely fallen into the bath of molten chemical then those in close proximity were likely to be splashed. The plaintiff in this instance was, however, beyond the risk of the foreseeable splash (he was standing in a doorway) and was only injured when the previously unforeseen chemical reaction occurred resulting in the splashing spreading to him. The new and intruding factor being the unforeseen chemical reaction.

Therefore, the law in this area cannot be stated more precisely than by saying that the actual way in which the harm occurs, if unforeseeable, must be not too dissimilar to that which is foreseeable. Indications are that in answering this question the courts are adopting a broad approach and are not too narrowly particularising the risk according to manner of occurrence. Thus the risks produced by exposure to extreme cold have been held to include the unforeseeable risk of frostbite: *Bradford v Robinson Rentals* [1967] 1 WLR 337. The risk of causing intestinal disease in pigs has been held to include the unforeseeable risk of e-coli infection: *Parsons v Uttley Ingham & Co Ltd* [1978] QB 791. And the risk caused by the spread of fire has been held to include the "unusual" risk of asphyxiation through smoke: *Cuckow v Polyester Products Pty Ltd* (1970) 19 FLR 122. But the foreseeable perils of rat infestation (disease caused by rat bite or food contamination) do not extend to the unforeseeable risk of Weil's disease, which is caused by contact with rat urine: *Tremain v Pike* [1969] 1 WLR 1556. This decision seems dubious in the light of cases previously considered. The remoteness question may turn on how broadly the initial foreseeable risk is classified, and judicial minds may differ on this. For example, in *Jolley v Sutton London BC* [2000] 3 All ER 409 the Court of Appeal regarded the risk to teenage boys attracted by an abandoned boat left in a recreational area under the defendants' authority, as that of the danger presented by rotting timber inside the boat. The court held that this risk did not extend to injury caused to the plaintiff boy when the boat fell on him after he and others had propped it up in order to make it sailable. This was reversed on appeal to the House of Lords, which regarded the initial foreseeable risk as including attempts by the boys to reproduce adult behaviour in dealing with the boat. Even on the most generous classification of risk, however, the decision in *Eaton v Pitman* (1991) 55 SASR 386 seems unduly favourable to plaintiffs. The plaintiff, a nurse, had gone to the assistance of a person injured in a road accident caused by the defendant's negligence, and in the course of bending down to assist the victim had reactivated a former back condition. The court held that since physical injury to the plaintiff was reasonably foreseeable, the defendant was liable since the precise manner in which the injury occurred need not be reasonably foreseeable. It seems questionable, however, whether the way in which the injury was suffered bore any relation to the foreseeable risks to a rescuer in this situation.

In the converse problem to that posed by *Hughes*, that is where the harm that eventuates is not of the type constituting the main class of foreseeable risk but happens in a foreseeable way, there is no problem about establishing liability. For example, the risk of drowning would tend to be excluded as one of the likely risks arising from negligent driving in the main street of a town. But in *Versic v Connors* [1969] 1 NSWLR 481 the plaintiff was flung out of his truck after an accident caused by the defendants' negligence. His head became caught in a gutter. This caused a flood (the day being very wet) and he was drowned. Jacobs JA held the defendants liable on the basis that the manner of occurrence of the death here was foreseeable, even though death by drowning is not one of the more obvious risks of careless driving.

Herron CJ held that even though death by drowning may have been unforeseeable, the defendants were nevertheless liable under the *Hughes* principle. Holmes JA agreed with both judgments.

Thin skull rule

[11.90] The rule in *Re Polemis* [1921] 3 KB 560 operated to allow the plaintiff to recover damages for an infliction or aggravation of an injury produced by some pre-existing condition of his or her own. That physical condition was not required to be foreseeable. *The Wagon Mound (No 1)* [1961] AC 388 threw doubt upon the continued existence of the thin skull rule in cases where the plaintiff's condition was unforeseeable; but subsequent cases in England, Australia and other Commonwealth jurisdictions have held that the rule is unchanged. The first English decision since *Wagon Mound (No 1)* is a typical example of the rule in operation. In *Smith v Leech Brain* [1962] 2 QB 405,[15] the plaintiff had received an injury to his lip through burning by molten metal. Because the lip was in a pre-cancerous condition, the plaintiff contracted cancer and died. His death was held to be not too remote. Only the initial injury needed to be reasonably foreseeable. Thereafter the defendant "took the plaintiff as he found him". The rule can apply to psychological trauma triggered by the injury where this arises from a pre-disposition to such trauma.[16] Problems have arisen concerning the development of a tendency to alcoholism. *McCoy v Watson* (1976) 13 SASR 506 ruled against recovery for this. But in *Havenaar v Havenaar* [1982] 1 NSWLR 626, Glass JA supported the application of the thin skull rule in these circumstances; and Hutley JA thought that damages for the alcoholism should be recoverable, provided the drinking arose through involuntary addiction rather than voluntary recourse. Only Reynolds JA ruled out liability altogether. A later New South Wales court, in a matter concerning the plaintiff's development of throat cancer caused by a resort to tobacco and alcohol in response to the injury, held that the thin skull rule applies only where the unforeseeable damage is of the same kind as the foreseeable. Since the throat cancer was not of the same kind as the original injury, the plaintiff had to prove that it was foreseeably caused by that injury: *Commonwealth v McClean* (1996) 41 NSWLR 389. This view of the thin skull rule is difficult to accommodate with *Leech Brain*, which was referred to by the court; also with *Telstra Corp v Smith* [1998] Aust Torts Reports 81-487 (a suicide attempt after the initial injury causing further injury to a plaintiff with a fragile psyche was covered by the thin skull rule).

Relevance of surrounding circumstances

[11.95] In general, the thin skull rule does not apply to the victim's surrounding physical circumstances. Otherwise *Re Polemis* [1921] 3 KB 560 would be still decided in the same way (that is, the petrol vapour in the hold would not need to be foreseeable). The case of *Great Lakes SS v Maple Leaf Milling* (1924) 41 TLR 21 does not conflict with this. In that case the extra damage to a negligently grounded ship caused by its coming to rest on a submerged anchor was held to be recoverable. Here both the type and manner of damage were foreseeable (that is, impact damage), and it was not

---

[15]   See also *Warren v Scruttons* [1962] 1 Lloyds Rep 497; *Sayers v Perrin (No 3)* [1966] Qd R 89.

[16]   For a more detailed discussion of this issue refer [8.210] and the discussion regarding *Tame v New South Wales*; *Annetts v Australian Stations Pty Ltd* (2002) 211 CLR 317.

to the point that the damage may have been unforeseeably great in extent. As we saw earlier in this chapter, the extent of foreseeable damage need not be reasonably foreseeable: *Vacwell Engineering Co v BDH Chemicals* [1971] 1 QB 88. On the other hand, there is a difference of opinion about the application of the rule to the victim's family circumstances, where these have aggravated the victim's psychological damage. An English decision has refused to apply the rule here; but one of the grounds for the decision of McHugh JA in *Nader v Urban Transport Authority* (1985) 2 NSWLR 501[17] in favour of the plaintiff was to allow the victim's surrounding family circumstances and the preoccupation with the victim's condition to be taken as they were found.

Basis of the rule

[11.100] The juridical basis of the thin skull rule, in the light of the remoteness of damage rule established by *The Wagon Mound (No 1)* [1961] AC 388 is uncertain. A simple answer is that it survives as an exception to the *Wagon Mound (No 1)* principles, not having been expressly removed by the Privy Council. The rule can hardly be accommodated within the foreseeability principle, since, although some predisposing physical states such as blindness are reasonably foreseeable, many others are not. A further suggestion is that the rule forms part of the measure of damages to which foreseeability is irrelevant. That was the express justification given by the court for its decision in *Smith v Leech Brain* [1962] 2 QB 405. It also accords with the rule about extent of damage, which also may be explained on this basis. A case worth considering in this context is *Stephenson v Waite Tileman Ltd* [1973] 1 NZLR 152. In that case, in a judgment of considerable force and persuasion, Richmond J held that where an initial hand injury had produced a later unforeseeable condition of virtual paralysis in the plaintiff, the employer if liable for the initial injury, was liable for the later state of the plaintiff whether this resulted from the unforeseeable entry of a virus into the wound or because of compensation neurosis resulting from the plaintiff's previous vulnerable personality. The advantage of this approach is that it removes the present advantage which thin skull plaintiffs possess over normal persons upon whom bodily injury works in an unforeseeable way. But *Stephenson* runs contrary to the New South Wales decision in *Beavis v Apthorpe* (1963) 80 WN NSW 852, which held that the question whether there was liability for the tetanus infection of a wound depended on the reasonable foreseeability of the infection.

The explanation of the rule based on measure of damages fails to explain cases where the thin skull condition combines with the injury and a later event to produce a distinct injury: *Wieland v Cyril Lord* [1969] 3 All ER 1006 (inability to adjust to wearing of bifocal lenses through initial injury caused later injury in a fall); *Robinson v Post Office* [1974] 1 WLR 1176 (initial injury caused administration of a tetanus injection to which the plaintiff was allergic and he suffered paralysis). These cases seem to require the later injury to be foreseeable, granted the plaintiff's thin skull condition. It also seems necessary to support the measure of damages explanation of the rule that there should be an initial foreseeable injury, though the rather slender authority of an obiter dictum of a first instance judge in *Bradford v Robinson Rentals* [1967] 1 WLR 337 would deny even this: according to that judge, if the plaintiff in that case had caught frostbite only through his abnormal susceptibility to extreme cold, he would still have recovered damages under the thin skull rule. But prior to contracting frostbite the plaintiff suffered no injury other than exposure to extreme cold. If the mere combination of breach of

17   Cf *McLaren v Bradstreet* (1969) 113 SJ 471.

duty of care and thin skull condition to produce injury is enough, it seems hard to give the rule a rational basis consonant with *Wagon Mound (No 1)* principles.

Where the condition of the plaintiff is such that there is some chance that it will arise independently or by some other accidental triggering event, the damages awarded to the plaintiff must be reduced to reflect that contingency. The tortfeasor in effect takes both the benefit and burden of the plaintiff's pre-existing condition. If a defendant wishes to suggest that the plaintiff's injury (for which the defendant would otherwise be held wholly liable) is due in whole or in part to some predisposing condition, the defendant must adduce evidence of that condition; but the legal burden of proof remains with the plaintiff throughout: *Watts v Rake* (1960) 108 CLR 158; *Purkess v Crittenden* (1965) 114 CLR 164. In accordance with the decision of the High Court in *Malec v Hutton* (1990) 169 CLR 638, even if a court were to conclude on a balance of probabilities that the thin skull condition is likely to produce by itself in the future the same effect as the defendant has produced, the plaintiff is still entitled to be compensated in respect of the residual contingency that it would not have had this effect.

Intervening causes

[11.105] In some situations, something or someone may intrude on the events set in motion by the negligence of the defendant. These intervening circumstances may either contribute to the loss sustained or, in some cases, completely change the course of events so that they can be said to be the true cause of the loss or injury sustained by the plaintiff. When this occurs, the intervening events are described as a novus actus interveniens (intervening event) which operates to "break the chain of causation". The issue then becomes one of determining who, or what, truly caused the loss or injury.

Figure 11.5: Intervening causes

Plaintiffs or third parties may commit an act which gives a fresh origin to the after consequences: *Haber v Walker* [1963] VR 339.

An intervening occurrence is either:
• human action that is properly to be regarded as either voluntary; or
• a causally independent event (a coincidence).

Liability for intervening causes

[11.110] There may occur, between the defendant's breach of duty and the damage or injury suffered by the plaintiff, an intervening act or event. If both the breach of duty and the later event satisfy the "but for" test of causation as regards the damage they cause, the two will normally operate as concurrent causes of the plaintiff's damage. But the majority of the High Court in *March v E & MH Stramare Pty Ltd* (1991) 171 CLR 506 held that satisfaction of the "but for" test by the plaintiff will not be accepted as establishing causation, if that result is contrary to the common sense of the court. Where the intervening event is the act of an irresponsible person (such as a child) or an animal or is a natural event, there is generally no problem about applying the usual tests for factual causation and remoteness of damage. The test of remoteness to be applied is that of reasonable foreseeability. Thus in *Haynes v Harwood* [1935] 1 KB 146 the act of a child in throwing a stone at the defendant's unattended horse was foreseeable and did not prevent liability arising. *Beavis v Apthorpe* (1963) 80 WN NSW 852, even though it was questioned earlier, is at least authority for the proposition that the occurrence of a disease, if it is not to operate as a new cause, must merely be reasonably foreseeable.

More problems arise where the later event is the act of a responsible human being. Here it will be seen that applying the "but for" test to determine causation, and the test of reasonable foreseeability to determine remoteness, will not be adequate to solve all the problems that may arise. The test to be applied depends on the nature of the human act and there is no all-embracing formula to cover all the cases. The law in general draws distinctions between later deliberate actions and later negligent actions, and between acts of the plaintiff and acts of third parties.

Whether the later act is that of the plaintiff or of another tortfeasor, if it does not interrupt the chain of causation some means of apportioning responsibility for the plaintiff's damage between (on the one hand) the plaintiff and defendant, and (on the other) the defendant and the later tortfeasor, is required. This is provided in the contributory negligence and contribution among tortfeasors legislation present throughout the States and Territories of Australia: see Chapter 12.

Human conduct

[11.115] Questions of novus actus interveniens (intervening event) as regards later human conduct are particularly appropriate for the application of the commonsense approach adopted by the High Court in *March v E & MH Stramare Pty Ltd* (1991) 171 CLR 506. This issue is discussed in more detgail in Chapter 12.

Deliberate conduct of plaintiff

"Unreasonable" conduct

[11.120] Where the plaintiff has deliberately chosen to face a risk, this will normally be regarded as a new cause terminating the liability of the defendant. According to the House of Lords in *McKew v Hannen Holland & Cubitts Ltd* [1970] AC 20, the issue was not whether the plaintiff's conduct was reasonably foreseeable, but whether it was reasonable. That was because many unreasonable actions are reasonably foreseeable, so that to adopt foreseeability as a test would unfairly extend the scope of liability. In *McKew* the plaintiff had a weakened leg caused by an injury for which the defendants were liable. He chose to descend some steps without a handrail, holding the hand of his daughter and neglecting to seek any help from his adult relatives walking behind him. He suffered further injury when his leg collapsed beneath him and he fell down the steps. The House of Lords denied him recovery of damages for the further injury because his method of descending the steps was deemed to be unreasonable. It is unfortunate that the leading judgment of Lord Reid in the House of Lords does not make it clear whether the plaintiff's action was regarded as a deliberate incurring of the risk or a mere negligent failure to appreciate it. The likelihood is the former, because a mere negligent failure to appreciate the risk in what the plaintiff was doing, though unreasonable, should not have been regarded as interrupting causation. The appropriate solution in that case would have been an apportionment of damages for the further injury between the defendant and plaintiff. *McKew* was used by Mason J in *March v E & MH Stramare Pty Ltd* (1991) 171 CLR 506 as an example of a case in which "but for" reasoning establishing factual causation was rejected as a matter of common sense. But that was not the approach adopted by the House of Lords, which is more akin to the views of McHugh J in *March*.

"Reasonable" conduct

[11.125] The reasoning in *McKew v Hannen Holland & Cubitts Ltd* [1970] AC 20 will not apply where the plaintiff is compelled to take the risk of further injury as part of his or her employment. In *GIO v Oakley* [1990] Aust Torts Reports 81-003, the plaintiff nurse had received an injury to her right arm and shoulder in a motor accident caused by the defendant's negligence. This left her with a residual disability causing her to rely only on the left arm in lifting patients. In lifting a geriatric patient she suffered further injury when the patient slipped and fell, pulling down on the plaintiff's left arm as she did so. The defendant motorist responsible for the first injury was held responsible as to 50% of the later injury, since the first injury was a factor contributing to it. Even a voluntary withdrawal from employment where this is the result of injury does not necessarily operate as a novus actus (intervening event), thereby depriving the injured person of any claim to damages for loss of earning capacity after the resignation. So a university professor who, as a result of the injury suffered due to the negligence of the defendant, took early retirement because he felt that he was unable to satisfactorily combine his duties of teaching and research was held to be entitled to damages for loss of earning capacity for the remainder of his working term: *Medlin v SGIC* (1995) 182 CLR 1. The majority of the High Court stated that the retirement must be reasonable as between the plaintiff and defendant. Granted that the plaintiff was through no fault of his own unable to work to his own satisfaction, reasonableness on his part seems readily enough established. The additional requirement that it should be reasonable as between plaintiff and defendant may take account of the fact that the plaintiff was already near to retirement when he left. Perhaps a difference would apply in the case of a much younger employee.

Suicide and refusal of medical treatment

[11.130] Not every voluntary act of self-exposure to injury by the plaintiff will be regarded as a deliberate and unreasonable incurring of the risk. The prime example of this is the case of suicide as a result of depression induced by the injury inflicted by the defendant. The act of the person who commits suicide in these circumstances is not regarded as truly voluntary, so that the test of unreasonableness in *McKew v Hannen Holland & Cubitts Ltd* [1970] AC 20 is not satisfied. The suicide cases are considered in relation to the action for wrongful death in Chapter 21. Similar problems arise in relation to the refusal to accept medical treatment. The test applied appears to be whether the plaintiff's refusal is, in the circumstances, reasonable. In *Walker-Flynn v Princeton Motors Pty Ltd* (1960) SR(NSW) 488 it was held to be relevant evidence for the jury to consider that the plaintiff's refusal to use contraceptives to mitigate the damage that further pregnancies would cause to her crushed pelvis arose because the plaintiff was a Catholic and rejected birth control. The jury concluded she acted reasonably. In *Boyd v SGIC* [1978] Qd R 195, however, a decision by a Jehovah's Witness's son to refuse a blood transfusion in order to placate his father was found to be an unreasonable failure to mitigate damage. The cases are not readily distinguishable, and demonstrate the difficulty faced by the courts when there is a need to draw on individual value judgments. Perhaps the plaintiff's actions in *Walker-Flynn* were viewed as more reasonable as they were based not only upon a religious conviction but also a more readily acceptable human desire to procreate. The result of the refusal to follow medical advice was to create life as opposed to endangering it. The question of the defendant's liability for voluntary self-infliction of harm by thin skull plaintiffs has already been considered at [11.90].

Inappropriate response

[11.135] Where the plaintiff's act may be seen as an inappropriate response to difficulties caused by an earlier injury, causation of the additional loss raises some particular difficulties. In *Yates v Jones* [1990] Aust Torts Reports 81-009 the plaintiff, who had suffered serious injuries in a road accident, was allegedly denied painkillers by hospital staff and then resorted to taking heroin which was offered to her by an acquaintance visiting her in hospital. The majority in the New South Wales Court of Appeal held the defendant, who had caused her initial injury, not liable for the plaintiff's state of heroin addiction, either on the ground that the course of events leading to the taking of heroin was not reasonably foreseeable (Samuels JA) or that the plaintiff's act in taking the heroin was deliberate and voluntary (Meagher JA). On the other hand, the court distinguished and approved its own previous decision in *Grey v Simpson* (unreported, Court of Appeal, NSW, 3 April 1978) where the plaintiff fell into addiction as a direct result of psychological problems stemming from his original physical injury. A somewhat less controversial decision was that of the majority of the same court in *State Rail Authority v Wiegold* [1991] Aust Torts Reports 81-148 in which it was held that where the victim of a tort took to a life of crime because of financial difficulties imposed on him by reason of his injury, the defendants were not liable for the loss of his job which resulted from his conviction. In England it was held that a person who changed from being a minor criminal to being a violent rapist as the result of a brain injury was able to recover damages for the change in his personality (*Meah v McCreamer* [1985] 1 All ER 367) but not for the financial consequences of being held civilly liable for two rapes committed by him after experiencing that change: *Meah v McCreamer (No 2)* [1986] 1 All ER 943.

Fraud of the plaintiff

[11.140] On a commonsense view of causation, fraud of the plaintiff will almost inevitably operate as a novus actus (intervening event). But on the particular facts in *Krakowski v Trenorth* [1996] Aust Torts Reports 81-401 an exception to that position was recognised. The directors in the plaintiff company had given knowingly false replies in connection with a sale of the company's property to a third party, causing the sale to be set aside for fraudulent misrepresentation. These replies had been given on the advice of a solicitor employed by the defendants concerning the directors' duty of disclosure under the transaction. The fraud was found to be of a technical nature, there being no intention to deceive on the directors' part. In these circumstances it was held that the company should obtain an indemnity from the solicitors for their negligent advice, and that the company's fraud did not interrupt causation. In *Duke Group v Pilmer* [1999] Aust Torts Reports 81-507 it was held that, where directors of a company had used a negligently made valuation report to the asset value of a company in order to fraudulently obtain the consent of the shareholders of the company to a takeover of the other company, the directors' fraud did not insulate the valuer from liability to the company in negligence.

Negligence of the plaintiff

[11.145] Negligence on the plaintiff's part will in most cases be regarded as reasonably foreseeable and therefore not a novus actus interveniens (intervening event). The mere fact that negligence is "unreasonable" will not affect this, though of course a reduction of damages for contributory negligence will be made. *March v E & MH Stramare Pty Ltd* (1991) 171 CLR 506 illustrates the point. In that case the plaintiff was guilty of a considerable degree of fault in driving in a drunken state into the defendant's truck which, though properly lighted, had been negligently parked in the centre of the highway. The negligent act of someone such as the plaintiff driving into the truck was the very thing the defendant's employee should have foreseen. It was, therefore, not a novus actus. The extreme degree of negligence shown here by the plaintiff was reflected in a large reduction of the damages award, that is by 70%.[18] English courts, in comparable situations, have felt able to classify the later driving as "reckless", and have held that it operates as a new cause: *Wright v Lodge* [1993] 4 All ER 299 (truck driver's act in driving at 60 mph on the motorway in conditions of poor visibility through fog was reckless and operated as a novus actus).[19]

Damage caused by third party

Deliberate conduct of third party

[11.150] As in the case of acts of the plaintiff, the conduct of a third party,[20] though deliberate, may not be truly voluntary and may therefore be reasonable in the circumstances and not a novus actus interveniens. An example is *The Oropesa* [1943] P 32. Through its negligent navigation, the "Oropesa" was in collision with the "Manchester Regiment". The captain of the latter decided to put to sea in a lifeboat, along with other members of the crew including the plaintiff, to discuss the possibility of salvaging the "Manchester Regiment". The lifeboat capsized in heavy seas and the plaintiff was drowned. His estate recovered damages for his death from the owner of the "Oropesa". The captain's act in putting to sea in the lifeboat was a reasonable one in the situation of the peril created by the defendants and could not be regarded as a deliberate braving of the risk. It was therefore not a novus actus.

To regard any act of deliberate and unreasonable infliction of damage by a third party as a novus actus would produce too restricted a field of compensation, whereas a test of reasonable foreseeability might go too far in the opposite direction. It is pre-eminently in this area of the law that the approach of the High Court in *March v E &*

---

[18] The reasoning behind this was based on the partial defence of contributory negligence, which is considered in more detail in Chapter 12.
[19] See also *Rouse v Squires* [1973] 2 All ER 903.
[20] It is important to remember that often these situations will not move beyond the duty stage of the discussion. Refer discussion at [8.290] regarding *Modbury Triangle Centre Ltd v Anzil* (2000) 205 CLR 254; *New South Wales v Godfrey* [2004] Aust Torts Reports 81-741; [2004] NSWCA 113; and *Home Office v Dorset Yacht Co Ltd* [1970] AC 1004.

MH Stramare Pty Ltd (1991) 171 CLR 506 seems likely to be applied, whether through modification of the "but for" test on commonsense principles (as suggested by Mason CJ and Deane J) or by regarding the issue of novus actus interveniens as turning on matters of policy (as suggested by McHugh J).[21] Policy underlay the decision of Lord Denning MR in *Lamb v London Borough of Camden* [1981] 2 WLR 1038. In that case the defendant local authority had, through the negligence of its employees, broken into a water main outside the plaintiff's house, causing the house to be flooded and the plaintiff to have to vacate it. The house was then occupied by two sets of squatters who caused considerable damage to it. The question at issue was the liability of the defendant for the damage caused by the squatters. Lord Denning rejected the test proposed by Lord Reid in *Home Office v Dorset Yacht* [1970] AC 1004, that the question turned on whether the third party's act was likely. He also rejected the criterion of reasonable foreseeability. Policy reasons should dictate the conclusion in cases of this sort, but the ground of policy he gave for denying the plaintiff's claim (that she herself had failed to take effective measures to safeguard the house against the entry of squatters) seems better explained on the basis of an unreasonable failure to mitigate damage on the plaintiff's part. Oliver LJ thought that the test to be applied was that of reasonable foreseeability, but that, in the context of damage caused deliberately by a third party, this required likelihood. The damage here, however, was unlikely; the reasonable worker swinging his pickaxe in the vicinity of the water main would not anticipate the likely need for the vacation of a house in the vicinity. Two points may be made about Oliver LJ's position. First, in the case of remoteness of damage even more than in that of breach, the test for reasonable foreseeability (including likelihood) should arguably turn on reasonable hindsight rather than foresight. Of course the consequence of his conduct would not occur to the worker at the time of his act, but that should not be enough to exclude liability for them. Second, the likelihood of an event is so much a question of degree that the question appears to contain a concealed policy choice; though of course cases may arise where likelihood is too apparent to admit argument to the contrary. Social conditions prevailing in London at the time of *Lamb* could well have produced the response in a reasonable person that invasion by squatters of a vacant house was likely.[22]

Later negligence by third party

[11.155] If, as a result of negligence on the part of the defendant, the plaintiff enters some form of relationship (for example medical or contractual) and that in turn is performed negligently, it is likely to be deemed to be reasonably foreseeable and the later negligence will generally not constitute a novus actus interveniens (intervening act). Where the defendant has created a risk of harm to the plaintiff the defendant will not be excused by the fact that a third party has, by later negligence, failed to eliminate the risk. In *Grant v Sun Shipping Co Ltd* [1948] AC 549 the plaintiff was injured when he fell into the hold of a ship. The danger was created when the repairers of a ship removed and failed to replace the hatch covers over the hold. The shipowners' employees failed to notice this and the hold remained uncovered at the time the plaintiff fell into it and

---

[21]   For a detailed discussion regarding the role of policy, refer above, [11.67], "Role of policy".

[22]   See also *Ward v Cannock Chase DC* [1986] Ch 546 where vandal damage was held not too remote, but there was the additional factor that the defendants were not only liable for the initial damage but also for failure to repair it. Also the district was not residential, so the risk of intrusion was found to be higher than in *Lamb*, and this was known at the time of the failure to repair.

was injured. The House of Lords held that the repairers were not relieved from liability to the plaintiff by reason of the later negligence of the shipowners' employees. A similar decision was that of the High Court in *Bennett v Minister of Community Welfare* (1992) 176 CLR 408. The plaintiff was a State ward of court who had lost some fingers while using an unfenced machine in the Department's workshop. In these circumstances the Department owed a duty of care to enable him to obtain independent legal advice as to his legal position, but they had not carried out this duty. After leaving the Department the plaintiff obtained the advice of a barrister to the effect that he had no legal claim against the Department, advice which was erroneous because there was a clear likelihood of a successful claim. The plaintiff's claim subsequently became statute-barred. The High Court held the Department liable to the plaintiff for its failure to provide him with independent legal advice. The barrister's advice, even if negligent, did not operate as a novus actus. The High Court's decision went one stage further than that of the House of Lords in *Grant*. The duty of the Department was only to provide independent rather than sound legal advice and this the barrister had provided. In these circumstances the finding that the Department had contributed to the barrister's mistake by the advice it provided him with may be a necessary part of the decision, though Mason CJ thought this not to be the case.

Where later negligence has activated, rather than failed to eliminate, a risk created by the defendant the negligence is unlikely to operate as a novus actus. In *Philco Radio Ltd v Spurling* [1949] 2 KB 33 the defendant carriers had negligently and by mistake delivered a package containing highly-inflammable film scrip to the plaintiff's premises. An employee of the plaintiff had approached the package with a lighted cigarette and caused a fire in which the plaintiff's premises were extensively damaged. The Court of Appeal held the defendants liable on the basis that the employee's action was negligent rather than deliberate. A deliberate action would have been outside the foreseeable risk created by the defendants.

Plaintiff placed in situation of ordinary risk

[11.160] On the other hand, in cases such as *Baker v Willoughby* [1970] AC 825, the courts have rejected the logical application of the "but for" test in a situation where the defendant's wrongdoing has merely put the plaintiff into a situation carrying with it no more than the ordinary risks of everyday life, and the plaintiff has then been injured or damaged as the result of the negligence of another person, or of the plaintiff. As Mason CJ pointed out in *March v E & MH Stramare Pty Ltd* (1991) 171 CLR 506 the application of the "but for" test here would produce absurd consequences. If, however, the situation in which the plaintiff has been placed by the defendant's wrongful conduct is one of heightened risk, and that risk has materialised, then causal connection will be established. The distinction between a situation of ordinary risk and one of heightened risk may be observed by a comparison between two decisions concerning ships. In *SS Singleton Abbey v SS Paludina* [1927] AC 16 the "Paludina" fell upon and thereby caused the "Singleton Abbey" (which was docked in Valetta Harbour, Malta) to be cast adrift. The "Singleton Abbey" then did the same thing to the "Sara". Both ships were manoeuvring to regain their positions when, 20 minutes after the original event, the "Sara" negligently collided with the "Singleton Abbey" and was sunk. The "Paludina" was found to be not liable for the later collision. The "Sara" was not disabled; it was under the control of its crew and had the whole of the harbour in which to negotiate its return. It was as if it were on a normal voyage. But in *The Calliope* [1970] P 172 the "Carlsholm" collided negligently with the "Calliope". The latter had to execute an exceptionally difficult turning manoeuvre to resume its voyage, but did so negligently and was further damaged. The "Carlsholm" was held liable in part for the further damage: the "hand of the tortfeasor was still heavy on the ship".

One very clear case in which the plaintiff has been placed in a situation of heightened risk by the defendant's negligence is where the plaintiff has, through negligence, received personal injury requiring remedial hospital treatment. A question to consider in this context is: what is the position if through negligence the hospital fails to treat the wound properly, aggravating or failing to improve it? A general proposition is that this should not operate as a new cause; the situation is one of heightened risk. This has been generally accepted by Australian courts: *Moore v AGC (Insurances)* [1968] SASR 389. However where the medical advice or treatment is "inexcusably bad" this operates as a novus actus interveniens: *Mahony v Kruschich (Demolitions) Pty Ltd* (1985) 156 CLR 522.[23] Where the medical negligence does not operate as a novus actus, the result will be an apportionment of the later injury between the earlier tortfeasor and the medical defendant. In *Scout Association of Queensland v Central Regional Health Authority* [1997] Aust Torts Reports 81-450 the Authority's failure, through its doctors, to correctly diagnose the nature of the plaintiff's injury, was not sufficiently gross to operate as a novus actus. The Association was not relieved from liability in relation to the consequent complications experienced by the plaintiff,[24] but it was found to be 70% responsible for the further injury.

The basis of the test that emerges from the judgment of the High Court in *Mahony* appears to be foreseeability: inexcusably bad medical treatment is not a foreseeable consequence of the initial injury. But *Vieira v Water Board* [1988] Aust Torts Reports 80-166 shows that it may be possible to decide the matter on principles of causation without the need for categorisation of the medical negligence. In *Vieira* the plaintiff had received an injury to his hand for which he sought treatment. The surgeon, suspecting (mistakenly or not) that the plaintiff was suffering from a condition of the elbow, operated to relieve that condition. The hand injury improved spontaneously but the elbow thereafter caused the plaintiff recurrent pain. The defendant who was responsible for the hand injury was held not liable for the elbow condition since the injury to the hand had not caused it. The court reserved the position of what would have been the case had the surgeon thought that by operating on the elbow he would alleviate the problem with the hand.

Another situation of heightened risk that has been recognised is where the defendant's wrong has created in the plaintiff a predisposition to later injury or to suffering more serious effects of that injury. In *GIO v Aboushadi* [1999] Aust Torts Reports 81-531[25] the court held that where the later injury would not have happened at all but for the pre-existing condition, the earlier wrongdoer was responsible for the later injury. If, on the other hand, it happened to one in a normal state of health and fitness, the earlier wrongdoer was liable only for the greater effects the earlier injury caused.

---

[23]   In this instance the court recognised that if an injury is exacerbated by medical treatment, this amounts to a foreseeable consequence of injuring someone. The key here is that the seeking of medical treatment must be reasonable *and* that treatment must not be grossly negligent or experimental in nature. Further examples include *Martin v Isbard* (1946) 48 WALR 52 (novus actus); *Lawrie v Meggitt* (1974) 11 SASR 5 (not novus actus).

[24]   Necrosis of the hip.

[25]   Applying principles laid down in *Fishlock v Plummer* [1950] SASR 176.

Multiple causation

[11.165] The principles outlined in this chapter show that damage or injury suffered by the plaintiff may be caused by, and therefore ascribed to, more than one and possibly several wrongful acts constituting torts.

Figure 11.6: Joint/several tortfeasors

> **Jointly liable**
> * responsible for the same tort.
>
> **Separate concurrent tortfeasors**
> * responsible for the same damage.

The legal recognition of the phenomenon of multiple causation raises a difficulty over the respective liabilities of the various defendants. Where two or more persons are liable in tort for causing the same damage, each may be held personally liable for the whole of that damage. It would clearly be unjust, however, for one tortfeasor to be found responsible for the whole of the damage. Justice demands a mechanism for apportioning responsibility among the various persons liable, while preserving the right of the plaintiff to obtain full compensation for the injury or damage. The mechanism is contribution.

The claim for contribution is in effect a statutory right of a quasi-contractual nature. A separate claim by a tortfeasor to enforce the right to contribution is, however, a rarity. Normally, all possible defendants will be before the court, either because the plaintiff has joined them as defendant or because the person sued has issued third-party notices on other persons whom he thinks should be defendants compelling their appearance before the court. In either case, the court will apportion responsibility among the various persons held liable without the necessity for separate contribution proceedings.

The first point to note is that contribution in no way impacts on the position of the plaintiff who is entitled to one, indivisible amount of damage. Of significance is the point that the right to seek contribution arises where the tortfeasors are liable "in respect of the same damage, whether as joint tortfeasor or otherwise". If two or more tortfeasors have caused different damage (for example, one has caused the loss of the plaintiff's arm, the other of a leg) there is no case for contribution. Each tortfeasor must pay for the damage he or she has caused. A question of contribution arises only where the damage inflicted by the various tortfeasors is indivisible, for example where the plaintiff is killed by the combined negligence of two motorists. Where tortfeasors have combined to produce the same damage, the law draws a distinction between the case where the tortfeasors are joint tortfeasors and the case where they are not, although the practical impact of this difference is limited.

Persons who are joint tortfeasors commit the same tort. That sort of liability arises in the following circumstances:

* The employer of an employee who has committed a tort in the course of employment is a joint tortfeasor with the employee. The same applies in other cases of vicarious liability.

* Where there has been concerted action in the furtherance of a common

design, those participating are joint tortfeasors.[26] Conspirators are therefore joint tortfeasors; so too are the author, publisher and printer of a libellous work.

- A person who has instigated or authorised the commission of a tort by another person is a joint tortfeasor with that person.

Persons who have by their torts caused damage that is indivisible, and who are not joint tortfeasors, are conveniently described as "separate, concurrent tortfeasors". The right of contribution is an essential consideration when addressing the position of the defendant, and where possible, should be sought in order to mitigate the liability of the defendant.

Ipp Committee recommendations

[11.170] In directing its attention to causation, the Ipp Committee emphasised the importance of the underlying principle that no-one can be held liable for harm they did not cause. The lack of guidance provided by the courts in applying the "commonsense" test of causation was lamented by the Committee and the need for more certainty recognised. The main focus of the discussion was on the situations in which there are "evidentiary gaps" characterised by factual situations in which it is unclear which of two or more factors directly caused the harm.[27]

A central focus of the Committee's discussion in this context was the decision in *Fairchild v Glenhaven Funeral Services Ltd* [2003] 1 AC 32 and the recognition that the position taken by the House of Lords would be "widely considered to be fair and reasonable".[28] The Committee concluded that a problem with the "material contribution" test is the normative issue of determining which sort of cases warrant the relaxing of the normal requirements of proof of causation. The conclusion was that detailed criteria should be left for common law development, but there were some considerations recommended to be included in legislation:

- whether and why responsibility for the harm should be imposed (mirroring some of the "policy" considerations discussed above at [11.67]; and
- whether and why the harm should be left to lie where it fell (with the plaintiff).

A final issue in this context was the fact that in some limited circumstances, in an attempt to address "evidentiary gaps", courts have shifted the onus of proof from the plaintiff to the defendant. In the Committee's opinion this did not address the issue but tended to "mask it". To ensure that this did not occur, it was recommended that there be a clear legislative statement that the plaintiff bore the onus of proof with respect to causation.[29]

A further area of interest to the Committee was those situations in which a causal link may depend upon the plaintiff's hypothetical reaction. The example used to illustrate such a situation was *Chappel v Hart* (1998) 195 CLR 232 (discussed at [11.45]) in which it was accepted that the plaintiff would not have undertaken the operation if she

---

[26] *Brooke v Bool* [1928] 2 KB 578 – negligent concerted design by defendants to explore a gas leak with a lighted match.

[27] Australia, *Review of the Law of Negligence Final Report: September 2002* (hereafter Ipp Report), [7.28]-[7.36]. The following is a summary of the discussion in these paragraphs.

[28] Ipp Report, [7.32].

[29] Ipp Report, [7.34].

had been made fully aware of the risk. The Committee recognised that there are two possible approaches to the hypothetical question: subjective (what the plaintiff would have done) and objective (what the reasonable patient would have done). It was noted that in Australia (as opposed to Canada) the courts have adopted the subjective test, and it was accepted that this was the appropriate approach.[30] However, in some jurisdictions there are limitations imposed on the role of plaintiff evidence, with legislation stating that: "any statement made by the person after suffering the harm about what he or she would have done is inadmissible except to the extent (if any) that the statement is against his or her interest".[31]

The remainder of the discussion centred around the "two pronged" test of causation and concerns about the tendency of the courts to fail to distinguish clearly between the factual and normative questions in the context of causation. The Committee further noted the perception that the courts are too willing to impose liability for consequences considered to be only "remotely" connected with the conduct; the concern being that the net of liability is being cast too wide. The Committee recommended that some statutory certainty be introduced to provide some guidance.[32]

There was, as in other areas discussed throughout this text, subsequent legislative activity which has been subject to limited judicial scrutiny. So far, comments have been limited to acknowledgment of the two stages of the inquiry. In *Cox v New South Wales* [2007] Aust Torts Reports 81-888; [2007] NSWSC 471, Simpson J (at [115]) acknowledged that the legislative provision exists and (at [116]) described it as reflecting the common law as enunciated in *Ruddock v Taylor* (2003) 58 NSWLR 269; [2003] NSWCA 262. Similarly, in *Graham v Hall & AMP* (2006) 67 NSWLR 134; [2006] NSWCA 208 per Ipp JA (at [78]) referred to the Review of Negligence and the legislative response, and emphasised that it is a two-stage inquiry with "a finding that the negligent conduct was a necessary condition of the harm does not, itself, justify a conclusion that the defendant ought to be held liable". His Honour went on to emphasise the importance of the normative stage of the inquiry.

In essence therefore, we now have a clear, legislative statement of the two stages of the inquiry which many argue has been the accepted common law approach for many years. The impact on current approaches has been questioned by academic scholars and there is a strong school of thought that the causative provisions will be interpeted in accordance with existing common law principles set out in this chapter.[33] Determination of causation is not, therefore, a straightforward process with the situation nicely summarised in the Supreme Court of Canada: "Much judicial and academic ink has been spilled over the proper test for causation in cases of neligence": *Resurface Corp v Hanke* [2007] 1 SCR 333. At this point, the impact of the legislative provisions continues to be opaque and perhaps more judicial and academic ink will be spilt until the High Court is given the opportunity to enunciate the appropriate interpretation of the legislation.

---

[30] Ipp Report, [7.37]-[7.40].

[31] See *Civil Liability Act 2002* (NSW), s 5D(3)(b); *Civil Liability Act 2003* (Qld), s 11(3)(b); *Civil Liability Act 2002* (Tas), s 13(3)(b). The legislation in Western Australia takes this one step further and provides that "evidence of the injured person as to what he or she would have done if the *tortfeasor* had not been at fault is inadmissible": *Civil Liability Act 2002* (WA), s 5C(3)(b).

[32] Ipp Report, [7.41]-[7.49].

[33] For further discussion on this see Bartie, "Ambition Versus Judicial Reality: Causation and Remoteness Under Civil Liability Legislation" (2007) 33 UWA L Rev 415.

Figure 11.7: Causation

Juris	Legislation	Provision
ACT	*Civil Law (Wrongs) Act 2002* Pt 4.4	s 45 General principles: • Causation comprises two elements: – factual causation; and – scope of liability (refers to "appropriateness" of extension of scope). • Where plaintiff exposed to similar risk by a number of different people and it is not possible to assign responsibility to any one or more of them: – the court may continue to apply the common law principle to assign responsibility; but – it must consider the position of each defendant individually and state reasons for bringing the defendant within the scope of the liability. • In determining the scope of liability, the court must consider whether or not, and why, responsibility for the harm should be imposed on the negligent party. s 46 Plaintiff bears the burden of proving any fact relevant to the issue of causation.
NSW	*Civil Liability Act 2002*	s 5D General principles: • Causation comprises two elements: – factual causation; and – scope of liability (refers to "appropriateness" of extension of scope). • In determining in an exceptional case whether negligence exists that cannot be established as a necessary condition (ie factual causation) the court must consider whether or not, and why, responsibility for the harm should be imposed. • If it is relevant to the determination of factual causation to determine what the person who suffered the harm would have done if the negligent person had not been negligent (ie *Chappel v Hart* situation): – the matter is to be determined subjectively; and – any statement made by the person who suffered the harm is inadmissable except to the extent that the statement is against his or her interests. • In determining the scope of liability, the court must consider whether or not, and why, responsibility for the harm should be imposed on the negligent party. s 5E Plaintiff bears the burden of proving any fact relevant to the issue of causation.
NT	*Personal Injuries (Liabilities and Damages) Act 2003*	No mention.

Juris	Legislation	Provision
Qld	*Civil Liability Act 2003* Ch 2, Pt 1, Div 2	s 11 General principles: • Causation comprises two elements: – factual causation; and – scope of liability (refers to "appropriateness" of extension of scope). • In determining in an exceptional case, whether negligence exists that cannot be established as a necessary condition (ie factual causation) the court must consider whether or not, and why, responsibility for the harm should be imposed. • If it is relevant to the determination of factual causation to determine what the person who suffered the harm would have done if the negligent person had not been negligent (ie *Chappel v Hart* situation): – the matter is to be determined subjectively; and – any statement made by the person who suffered the harm is inadmissable except to the extent that the statement is against his or her interests. • In determining the scope of liability, the court must consider whether or not, and why, responsibility for the harm should be imposed on the negligent party. s 12 Plaintiff bears the burden of proving any fact relevant to the issue of causation.
SA	*Civil Liability Act 1936* Pt 6, Div 4	s 34 General principles: • Causation comprises two elements: – factual causation; and – scope of liability (refers to "appropriateness" of extension of scope). • Where plaintiff exposed to similar risk by a number of different people and it is not possible to assign responsibility to any one or more of them: – the court may continue to apply the common law principle to assign responsibility (note: SA has taken the unusual step of citing *Fairchild v Glenhaven Funeral Services Ltd*) at this point; but – it must consider the position of each defendant individually and state reasons for bringing the defendant within the scope of the liability. • In determining the scope of liability, the court must consider whether or not, and why, responsibility for the harm should be imposed on the negligent party. s 35 Plaintiff bears the burden of proving any fact relevant to the issue of causation.

Juris	Legislation	Provision
Tas	*Civil Liability Act 2002* Div 3	s 13 General principles: • Causation comprises two elements: – factual causation; and – scope of liability (refers to "appropriateness" of extension of scope). • In determining in an exceptional case whether negligence exists that cannot be established as a necessary condition (ie factual causation), the court must consider whether or not, and why, responsibility for the harm should be imposed. • If it is relevant to the determination of factual causation to determine what the person who suffered the harm would have done if the negligent person had not been negligent (ie *Chappel v Hart* situation): – the matter is to be determined subjectively; and – any statement made by the person who suffered the harm is inadmissible except to the extent that the statement is against his or her interests. • In determining the scope of liability, the court must consider whether or not, and why, responsibility for the harm should be imposed on the negligent party. s 14 Plaintiff bears the burden of proving any fact relevant to the issue of causation.
Vic	*Wrongs Act 1958* Pt X, Div 3	s 51 General principles: • Causation comprises two elements: – factual causation; and – scope of liability (refers to "appropriateness" of extension of scope). • In determining in an exceptional case, whether negligence exists that cannot be established as a necessary condition (ie factual causation) the court must consider whether or not, and why, responsibility for the harm should be imposed. • If it is relevant to the determination of factual causation to determine what the person who suffered the harm would have done if the negligent person had not been negligent (ie *Chappel v Hart* situation): – the matter is to be determined subjectively; and – any statement made by the person who suffered the harm is inadmissible except to the extent that the statement is against his or her interests. • In determining the scope of liability, the court must consider whether or not, and why, responsibility for the harm should be imposed on the negligent party. s 52 Plaintiff bears the burden of proving any fact relevant to the issue of causation.

Juris	Legislation	Provision
WA	*Civil Liability Act 2002* Pt 1A, Div 3	s 5C General principles: • Causation comprises two elements: – factual causation; and – scope of liability (refers to "appropriateness" of extension of scope). • In determining in an exceptional case whether negligence exists that cannot be established as a necessary condition (ie factual causation), the court must consider whether or not, and why, responsibility for the harm should be imposed. • If it is relevant to the determination of factual causation to determine what the person who suffered the harm would have done if the negligent person had not been negligent (ie *Chappel v Hart* situation): – the matter is to be determined subjectively; and – any statement made by the person who suffered the harm is inadmissible except to the extent that the statement is against his or her interests. • In determining the scope of liability, the court must consider whether or not, and why, responsibility for the harm should be imposed on the negligent party. s 5 Plaintiff bears the burden of proving any fact relevant to the issue of causation.

Guide to Problem Solving

CAUSATION

In the absence of further guidance, the common law principles are set out below, based upon an assumption that the legislative approach will (as early indications appear to suggest) essentially follow the common law reasoning process.

Factual (First limb of the legislative test)
Is there a relationship between the defendant's breach and the plaintiff's injury?

- Would the damage have happened "but for" the defendant's actions (if the defendant had not done what he or she did)?
- Common sense: all things considered, was the negligent breach a materially contributing factor OR did it materially increase the risk of this kind of harm?

Normative (Second limb of the legislative test)
Involves policy considerations, normative inquiries: ought the defendant be held liable for the plaintiff's injury?

Novus actus interveniens
A new intervening act by the plaintiff or a third party which comes after the defendant's act and which may break the chain of causation.

[novus actus and remoteness are usually raised by the **defendant**]

Remoteness
Reasonable foreseeability: could the defendant have reasonably foreseen that kind of LOSS?

Practice Questions

Revision Questions

11.1 The test of "reasonable foreseeability" figures in the determination of the duty of care, the breach of the duty of care, and remoteness. Can you distinguish their use in each of these elements?

11.2 The "but for" test has been acknowledged as effective at screening out certain causes, but there are problems when the test is used on its own. Can you identify the circumstances in which the test would not be a safe guide?

Problem Questions

11.1 Tom, Dick and Harry went on a weekend camping trip to the Springbrook Falls, part of the Springbrook National Park. The Park boasted some very challenging four-wheel-drive terrain and walking tracks. More importantly for these nature lovers, the Park was famous for its very old trees which were the subject of an environmental study. The study was investigating the effect of the re-routing of a river in the area which resulted in many of the trees having their roots submerged. Their visit, disappointingly, coincided with some very windy weather but they went ahead with their plans because they realised it would be quite a while before they would all be able to find another free weekend.

After breakfast on the Saturday morning Tom and Dick went for a swim in the creek a short distance from their camping site. The swimming hole was very popular because it was located at the termination point of the two main vehicular tracks, it was adjacent to the camping spot, and it was the start of one of the two major walking tracks. Harry decided to meet Tom and Dick at the swimming hole so he loaded up the vehicle. The track was a little bumpy and so Harry's water bottle fell to the floor of the vehicle. Harry slowed the vehicle to a crawl. In his efforts to retrieve the bottle Harry loosened his grasp on the wheel and the vehicle veered into one of the trees that had its roots in the water. To Harry's horror, and despite his warning shouts to his two friends, the tree fell on Tom and Dick. Tom was killed and Dick suffered very serious injuries to his back, ribs, foot and spleen.

Assume Harry has breached his duty of care and discuss the issues concerning causation.

11.2   Lavinia, a 40-year-old woman, was injured while working at a factory. A heavy box of bottles fell on her causing injuries to her neck and right arm. After the incident she had great difficulty caring for her very long hair. She eventually decided to cut her hair short. Her husband was very upset with her for doing this and he left her, ending the marriage. Lavinia is now suing the owner of the factory for her physical injuries and her psychiatric injuries resulting from the break-up of her marriage.

Advise Lavinia. Was her decision to cut her hair a novus actus?

Answers to Practice Questions

Revision Questions

11.1   Reasonable foreseeability in relation to duty of care refers to the defendant being able to foresee a particular *class of people* of which the plaintiff is one. In the breach element, it is questioned whether the defendant would reasonably have foreseen the *risk* to the plaintiff? In the area of remoteness, it is questioned whether the defendant could reasonably have foreseen the *kind of loss* to the plaintiff?

11.2   There are many instances when it can be see that the "but for" test is inadequate, for example:

- Where there are multiple causes. As suggested in the text, if X and Y simultaneously shoot Z and each shot has the capability of killing Z, then X could argue that even if he had not fired, Z would have been killed by Y. Y could also argue that even if he had not fired, Z would have been killed by X. The "but for" test could be used by either of them to deny responsibility for Z's death.

- Where a plaintiff's harm could be considered to be purely coincidental and really the result of a risk incidental to everyday life.

- Where the damage to the plaintiff could have happened even if the breach had not occurred (for example, as the result of an undiagnosed condition).
- Where there are later acts by plaintiffs or third parties leading up to the trial.
- Where there is some conduct not legally relevant to the action (for example, an unlicensed driver may have driven very competently and could not be held liable for the event that caused the damage).

Problem Questions

11.1 The question here is: what would have happened if Harry had not been negligent? Would the injuries have happened anyway?

While it is established that Harry is negligent, can it also be said that he is responsible for the injuries? There is no clear answer to the question of whether this would have happened even if Harry had not hit the tree. This shows us that the "but for" test is not reliable when there are other possible causes. The court in *March v E & MH Stramare Pty Ltd* (1991) 171 CLR 506 has established that commonsense factors need to be applied. When the facts are considered, could it be said that Harry's negligent act materially contributed to the injuries to Tom and Dick, or materially increased the risk of this harm? The facts state that the weather conditions were windy and also that the trees in the area now have their roots in water. While we are not told the results of the environmental study, it can be assumed that it is investigating the effect of the water on the health of the trees. This kind of moisture, it can be supposed, could make the roots of the tree very pliant and weaken its strength to withstand any kind of force. We are also told that the car had slowed to a crawl and in fact when it hit the tree it could have just been a bump. But the combined bump of the car and the weakening of the roots by the moisture has caused the tree to fall. It may even be possible to argue that the tree would have fallen at some time even without the bump. So Harry's negligence may not be the cause at all; or alternatively it is certainly not the sole cause of the injuries.

The kind of harm that occurred is not too remote. It could certainly be foreseen that a falling tree could result in the kind of loss that occurred, the death of Tom and the injuries to Dick.

Conclusion: It is quite likely that the combined effect of the wind and the moisture weakening the tree contributorily caused the injuries. The car hitting the tree was too negligible.

11.2 The issue here is whether Lavinia's cutting of her hair was a voluntary act or an act that is totally independent of the earlier injury to her. On one view, it could be thought to be a voluntary action on her part since beauty decisions are made all the time by women. This determination would result in her actions being classified as a novus actus interveniens (intervening act), thereby alleviating the factory owner from any responsibility for her psychiatric illness.

Alternatively it could be argued that the act of having her hair cut was necessitated by her efforts to reduce her pain in looking after her hair. So it could be argued to be the product of the tortiously-created pain and discomfort under which she was labouring. So the pain caused her to have her hair cut, which led to the displeasure of her husband, the break-up of her marriage and her consequent psychiatric illness.

(A relevant case in this context is *Medlin v SGIC* [1995] 182 CLR 1.)

Conclusion: The action of her cutting her hair does seem to have been fashioned by the initial event and so the factory owner would be held responsible for all her injuries both physical and psychiatric.

Tutorial Questions

Discussion Questions

11.1 In *March v E & MH Stramare Pty Ltd* (1991) 171 CLR 506 at 524, Deane J said that in determining whether a defendant's conduct is a cause of the injury, a court needs to make "value judgment(s) involving ordinary notions of language and common sense". Again, in *Bennett v Minister of Community Welfare* (1992) 176 CLR 408 at 412-413, Mason, Deane and Toohey JJ said: "In the realm of negligence, causation is essentially a question of fact, to be resolved as a matter of commonsense."

Can you think of situations or cases where the use of the "but for" test then common sense has been applied with shifting meanings? In other words, there is evidence of judicial discretion and the infusion of value judgments or policy.

11.2 What do you believe will be the impact of the legislative amendments on the practical application of the test for causation in negligence?

CHAPTER 12

Defences to Negligence

Reading

Sappideen, Vines, Grant and Watson, *Torts: Commentary and Materials*, Chapter 17.

Objectives

This chapter will outline:

- the avenues available to defendants to limit or eliminate their liability;
- particularly, the defences of:
  - contributory negligence;
  - volenti non fit injuria (voluntary assumption of risk); and
  - illegality.

Principles

Introduction

[12.05] The preceding chapters have taken us through the steps required to establish liability in negligence. Once negligence is established, it is appropriate to consider whether there are any defences available to the defendant. A defence in negligence involves a consideration of all the surrounding circumstances including the behaviour of the plaintiff. The defences in general tend to reflect an endeavour by the courts to balance the liability equation and impose an expectation that individuals with be aware of their own safety. It is important to remember that the recent trend of the court is to expect a higher level of personal responsibility, and this is reflected in the Ipp Report and subsequent legislative amendments.

The defences to be dealt with in this chapter may operate as defences to straightforward negligence as well as in situations where negligence is the gist of the action, such as employers' liability, occupiers' liability and liability for chattels. The burden of proof of establishing the defence lies on the defendant.

Figure 12.1: Defences

- Defences recognise that the law requires ALL persons to act reasonably.
  - Both the defendant and plaintiff can be negligent.
- The defendant has the onus of proof.
- Defences are raised by defendants trying to limit or eliminate their liability.

Contributory negligence

Historical development

[12.10] In its original form, the defence of contributory negligence operated as a complete defence, with the result that the plaintiff was denied recovery if contributory negligence was found. The modern manifestation of the defence operates to apportion liability between the plaintiff and defendant – that is, it operates as a partial defence. If a clear understanding of the defence is to be attained, it is illustrative to consider the background development and thereby gain some insight into the underlying rationale of contributory negligence as a defence.

It was recognised from early on in the development of negligence that fault of the plaintiff might bar the recovery of damages against the defendant. Thus in *Butterfield v Forrester* (1809) 103 ER 926 the defendant was held liable where the plaintiff rode his horse into a pole which the defendant had wrongfully placed across the highway. Although it was dusk, the pole was visible some 100 metres away, and the plaintiff's own lack of care was found to be wholly responsible for his accident.[1] However, in

---

[1] It is interesting to compare this decision with a modern equivalent, *Carey v Lake Macquarie City Council* [2007] Aust Torts Reports 81-874, in which the New South Wales Court of Appeal considered both volenti and

Davies v Mann (1842) 152 ER 588 the plaintiff had negligently turned his donkey loose on the public highway. The defendant, driving his coach and horse faster than he should have done, hit and killed the donkey. For this he was held liable in damages despite the earlier fault on the part of the plaintiff. In cases of this sort, the courts were asking a question along the lines of "whose fault principally caused the damage?" Although most people would accept that the defendant in the *Butterfield* case and the plaintiff in the *Davies* case were to some extent responsible for the damage, the courts were unable to give legal expression to this in a system in which the defendant could only be held liable for the whole of the damages or for nothing at all. Thus the defence of plaintiff's fault, which during the course of the 19th century became described as contributory negligence, was originally a complete defence, defeating the plaintiff's action altogether.

With the present day universal recognition of the phenomenon of multiple causation embodied in legislation allowing the apportionment of damage according to fault has come a more realistic approach with contributory negligence now operating as a partial defence.

In both these earlier cases, it will be noticed that the later act of negligence was chosen as the effective cause of the damage. In the earlier editions of his book on tort, Sir John Salmond advanced the view that the person who had the last opportunity of avoiding the accident must be held to blame for it; the so-called "last opportunity rule". Had this "rule" merely been accorded the status of an application to facts of causal principles, it would at least have caused no conceptual problems. In both *Butterfield* and *Davies*, for example, a considerable period of time elapsed between the earlier negligence and the later. However, for a time the courts seemed to be applying the rule as a mechanical rule of law. The courts even extended the rule to cases of so-called "constructive last opportunity". That is, cases where the defendant was precluded from having the last opportunity by his or her negligence, even though it preceded in time that of the plaintiff: *British Electric Railway Co v Loach* [1916] 1 AC 719 (in which the defendant started out with defective brakes). The rule was particularly inappropriate in the case of joint negligence producing collisions between motor vehicles, where split seconds might intervene between the two acts of negligence. In such circumstances, both the High Court and the House of Lords ruled the "last opportunity rule" to be inapplicable: *Alford v Magee* (1952) 85 CLR 437; *Swadling v Cooper* [1931] AC 1. The effect of this was, however, to worsen the position of the unfortunate plaintiff, since in cases of this sort where no clear line could be drawn between negligence of the plaintiff and defendant, the plaintiff's action failed entirely because contributory negligence was a complete defence. The force of reasoning demanding a judicial power to apportion damage between plaintiff and defendant had been recognised in England, as early as 1911, in the case of collisions between ships: *Maritime Conventions Act 1911* (UK), s 1. Finally, in 1945, the United Kingdom legislature introduced a general power of apportionment in cases of combined fault of plaintiff and defendant causing injury to the plaintiff, and abolished the rule that the plaintiff's contributory negligence operates as a complete defence: *Law Reform (Contributory Negligence) Act 1945* (UK). Section 1(1) of the Act provides as follows:

---

contributory negligence in the context of a plaintiff who rode his bicycle into a bollard placed in a pathway by the Council. This decision is discussed further below at [12.125], it is sufficient to point out that similarly to the plaintiff in *Butterfield* contributory negligence was identified by the court. Thus, basic principles continue to have similar outcomes.

> *Where any person suffers damage as the result partly of his own fault and partly of the fault of any other person or persons, a claim in respect of that damage shall not be defeated by reason of the fault of the person suffering the damage, but the damages recoverable in respect thereof shall be reduced to such extent as the court thinks just and equitable having regard to the claimant's share in the responsibility for the damage.*

"Fault" was defined in the definition section of the Act to mean: "negligence, breach of statutory duty or other act or omission which gives rise to a liability in tort, or which would, apart from this Act, give rise to the defence of contributory negligence".

Virtually identical legislation has been passed in the six Australian States, highly similar legislation in one Territory, and a comparable Act in the other.[2] This legislation clearly paved the way for recognition of contributory negligence as a partial defence to be routinely considered by the courts.

Contributory negligence and breach of contract

[12.15] As noted in [12.10] the definition section of the *Law Reform (Contributory Negligence) Act 1945* (UK) defines fault as: "negligence, breach of statutory duty, or other act or omission which gives rise to a liability in tort or would, apart from this Act, give rise to the defence of contributory negligence".

The definition section excludes liability for breach of contract from the apportionment provisions. Even where the breach of contract is negligent, the use of the word "other" before "act or omission giving rise to liability in tort" indicates that it must be negligence giving rise to tortious liability. Furthermore, prior to the Act, it was the law that contributory negligence could not be used as a defence to an action for breach of contract. This was so even though the plaintiff's conduct might ground other defences (such as failure to mitigate damages) or show absence of causation between the breach of contract and the damage. Negligence of the plaintiff did not, therefore, give rise to a defence in actions of contract "apart from this Act".

The Australian law, prior to *Astley v Austrust* [1999] Aust Torts Reports 81-501, allowed the defence where the breach of contract in question gave rise to a concurrent liability in tort, since the defendant's conduct here fell within the first part of the definition. This is also the English position.[3] But in *Astley*, the High Court refused to allow the defence in an action against a firm of solicitors whose liability arose in both tort and contract. This position has now been reversed by amendments to

---

[2]   The English model has been followed in these jurisdictions: *Civil Law (Wrongs) Act 2002* (ACT), s 101; also see *Law Reform (Miscellaneous Provisions) Act 1955* (ACT), s 14; *Law Reform (Miscellaneous Provisions) Act 1965* (NSW), s 9; *Workers' Compensation Act 1987* (NSW), s 151N(4); *Wrongs Act 1958* (Vic), s 26; *Law Reform Act 1995* (Qld), s 10; *Wrongs Act 1936-1975* (SA), s 27A (this section has since been repealed and the *Wrongs Act* is now the *Civil Liability Act 1936* (SA), s 50 which sets out how a case is to be dealt with, while preceding sections set out principles of contributory negligence); also refer *Law Reform (Contributory Negligence and Apportionment of Liability) Act 2001* (SA); *Tortfeasors and Contributory Negligence Act 1954* (Tas), s 4; *Law Reform (Miscellaneous Provisions) Act 1956* (NT), s 16. Western Australia is furthest from the English model. Section 4 of its *Law Reform (Contributory Negligence and Tortfeasors' Contribution) Act 1947* introduces apportionment in the case of joint fault. It achieves this by abolishing the last opportunity, but only insofar as the last opportunity is that of the plaintiff. The current status of legislation with respect to contributory negligence is set out in Figure 12.6.

[3]   *Forsikringsaktieselskapet Vesta v Butcher* [1989] AC 852; *Rains Harding v McCredie* (1988) 13 NSWLR 437. And on the closely analogous situation of whether a concurrent tortfeasor may claim contribution based on a concurrent liability in tort and contract, see *Macpherson v Kevin J Prunty* [1983] 1 VR 573 and *Aluminium Products Pty Ltd v Hill* [1981] Qd R 33 (both allowing the claim).

the appointment legislation in all States and Territories except Western Australia. Th legislation effectively now considers a "wrong" as including a breach of a contractual duty of care that is concurrent with a duty of care in tort. This legislation now allows the damages in an action for a breach of a contractual duty of care to be reduced if there is contributory negligence on the part of the plaintiff. This gave weight to the second part of the definition section quoted above, rather than the first. Although it is clear that prior to the Act contributory negligence was not available as a defence to a contract action, it is by no means clear that this applied in the case of concurrent liability in contract and tort. As concurrent liability is limited to liability for negligence, the contributory negligence defence seems appropriate, whichever cause of action is asserted. *Astley* now settles the law against this view.

Contributory negligence or mitigation of damages?

[12.17] An interesting question arose in the recent decision of *Ackland v Commonwealth of Australia* [2007] Aust Torts Reports 81-916; [2007] NSWCA 250 when the possibility of contributory negligence was raised in connection with post-accident alcohol abuse. The excessive drinking of the appellant was said to exacerbate the original injury suffered as a result of a collision between HMAS Voyager and HMAS Melbourne. The jury at trial were directed to consider whether there was contributory negligence in relation to the appellant's alcohol abuse and this was raised as a matter of appeal. As discussed in Chapter 11 such post accident behaviour ordinarily sits under the rubric of causation, with the operative question being: can the subsequent actions of a plaintiff, which impact on the original injury, be viewed as an intervening act? In *Ackland*, Santow JA stood alone in his willingness to apply contributory negligence principles to the question of post accident exacerbation of injury. Both Ipp JA and McColl JA preferred to adopt the mitigation of damages approach. Ipp JA drew a clear analogy between the appellant's actions and those of plaintiffs who unreasonably refuse medical treatment (at [145]). See, for example, *Fazlic v Milingimbi Community Inc* (1982) 150 CLR 345. In such cases the courts have adopted a mitigation of damages approach and considered whether the plaintiff has taken "reasonable steps" to mitigate loss, whilst contributory negligence is more appropriately concerned with "blameworthiness and causal potency" (per Ipp JA at [146]).[4] Thus contributory negligence is focused on pre-accident behaviour which either contributes to the cause of the accident or results in an injury which was more serious than it otherwise would have been. The focus is on the plaintiff's pre- as opposed to post-accident behaviour.

Proving contributory negligence

[12.20] The defence of contributory negligence is based on the principle that an individual has a duty to protect their own interests and that, conversely, we can conduct our daily affairs on the presumption that this is so. There are two key considerations which are fundamental if the court is to determine that the relevant conduct of the plaintiff constituted contributory negligence: first, that the plaintiff failed to meet the appropriate standard of care; and second, that the conduct contributed to the loss or injury.

---

[4]   Special leave was denied by the High Court: *Ackland v Commonwealth of Australia* [2008] HCATrans 167 (18 April 2008).

Figure 12.2: Contributory negligence – elements

> • Failure to meet the duty of care required:
>   – that the plaintiff failed to take the precautions a reasonable
>   person would have taken for their own protection (failure to
>   meet standard).
> • Causation:
>   – that the damage was reasonably foreseeable and was
>   contributed to by the plaintiff's act.

Standard of care

[12.25] In proving contributory negligence, the task of the defendant is equivalent to that of the plaintiff in proving negligence. Thus the defendant must show that the plaintiff has failed to observe the requisite standard of care and that that failure contributed to the damage the plaintiff suffered. The basic principle was succinctly stated by McHugh J in *Joslyn v Berryman* (2003) 214 CLR 552 at [16]:

> *At common law, a plaintiff is guilty of contributory negligence when the plaintiff exposes himself or herself to a risk of injury which might reasonably have been foreseen and avoided and suffers an injury within the class of risk to which the plaintiff was exposed.*

As in the case of the tort of negligence, most cases will turn on decisions of fact and no binding precedents will be created by them. The "fault" on the part of the plaintiff consists in a failure to look after her or his own safety and there is no requirement that this should endanger other persons, though clearly it might do so. Similar problems to those arising in negligence concern the issue of persons who have characteristics that render it difficult or impossible for them to comply with the objective standard of care of the reasonable person. There is, in general, no difference in principle between standard of care cases and those of contributory negligence with the test being an objective one "independent of the idiosyncrasies of the individual": at [16]. The court has, however, acknowledged that there may be characteristics of the individual which render a slightly adjusted standard appropriate – such as in the situation of children and perhaps the aged: at [32] and [35].[5] In short, the plaintiff is "expected to take as much care of themselves as they would expect others to take of them": *Carey v Lake Macquarie City Council* [2007] Aust Torts Reports 81-874 per McColl J at [10].

Conduct must contribute to loss or injury

[12.30] A fundamental requirement of contributory negligence is that the action specifically contributed to the loss or injury. In the words of Lord Denning in *Froom v Butcher* [1976] 1 QB 286 at 292: "The question is not what is the cause of the accident. It is rather, what was the cause of the damage."

The point is well illustrated by *Froom*, in which the plaintiff suffered multiple injuries when he was involved in a motor vehicle accident caused by the defendant's negligence. The plaintiff was not wearing a seatbelt at the time of the accident and many of his injuries were attributed to that lack of personal care. He suffered a broken

---

[5]   Although it is important to remember that the test in these circumstances continues to be an objective one; that is, the standard of the reasonable person of that age, independent of individual differences.

finger, which the court determined would not have been prevented by the wearing of a seatbelt, and this was therefore the only injury which was not deemed to be caused by the contributory negligence of the plaintiff.[6]

Children

[12.35] The reduction in the standard of care required of children has already been considered in Chapter 10. The same principles apply to contributory negligence on the part of children.

Momentary thoughtlessness by employee

[12.40] In *Staveley Iron and Chemical Co v Jones* [1956] AC 627 Lord Tucker suggested that in cases of liability for breach of statutory duty brought against an employer by his employee, not every "risky act due to familiarity with the work or some inattention due to noise or strain" amounted to contributory negligence, even though it might amount to negligence for the purpose of maintaining an action in tort against the worker or the employer. Lord Tucker's opinion was stated in relation to breach of statutory duty on the employer's part, but there is no reason for not also applying it to an action against the employer for common law negligence. This was accepted by the High Court in *Commissioner for Railways v Ruprecht* (1979) 142 CLR 563[7] in which the court took similar factors into account in deciding whether the plaintiff had been guilty of contributory negligence in an action against the employer, based on his vicarious liability for the common law negligence of another employee.

Failure to observe statutory regulations/highway rules

[12.45] As in the case of breach of a duty of care, this is merely evidence of negligence (*Foxcroft v Duncan* [1956] St R Qd 136) and not conclusive as to contributory negligence. Equally, compliance with such rules is not conclusive that care has been taken: *Sibley v Kais* (1967) 118 CLR 424 (in which a plaintiff who had the right of way at an intersection was, nevertheless, contributorily negligent).

Agony of the moment

[12.50] This refers to the case where the plaintiff, through negligence by the defendant, has been presented with two or more alternatives, all of which are attended with some risk, and, acting in "the agony of the moment" selects the alternative which leads to the injury. In such a case the plaintiff's action will not be regarded as contributory negligence. The formulation here is drawn from the facts of the decision in *Jones v Boyce* (1816) 171 ER 540. In this case, the plaintiff was a passenger in the defendant's coach. Because of the breaking of a defective coupling-rein, the plaintiff was presented with the alternatives of remaining in the coach and exposing himself to the danger of it overturning or jumping off. He chose the latter and was injured. His action was found not to be contributory negligence, even though the coach remained upright. The reasonableness of the plaintiff's decision had to be determined in the light of the facts as he saw them, not of after events, and the emergency in which he acted had to be taken into account. Where the plaintiff has been presented with a similar dilemma of risky alternatives not involving agony of the moment, an erroneous choice on his or her part is even here not necessarily contributory negligence. The choice has to be

[6]   This situation has now been abrogated by legislation in some Australian jurisdictions.
[7]   *Sungravare Pty Ltd v Ateani* (1964) 110 CLR 24 at 37.

unreasonable in the circumstances that were presented to the plaintiff, though here the chances of its being found unreasonable are higher. *Jones v Boyce* was carried one stage further by the decision of the High Court in *Caterson v Commissioner for Railways* (1973) 128 CLR 99. In this case a father jumped off a slowly moving train in order to be with his 14-year-old son who was being left behind at the station, and to avoid being taken to another stop 80 miles away. The court found that even though the alternative of pulling the communication cord existed, there was no contributory negligence. Here the alternative presented no risk to the father whatsoever, although there was a risk to the son, who otherwise would have been left alone 40 miles from home.

Seatbelts/crash helmets

[12.55] There are two difficulties with the application of the principles of contributory negligence to the problem of seatbelts and crash helmets. The first is, there is very little doubt that a failure on the plaintiff's part to take action that would merely have mitigated the plaintiff's damage, rather than have prevented it altogether, would not have constituted contributory negligence before the *Law Reform (Contributory Negligence) Act 1945* (UK) and therefore would not fall within the statutory definition of fault. This difficulty has been ignored by the case law, which establishes a defence of contributory negligence as regards failure to wear a seatbelt or crash helmet: *Froom v Butcher* [1976] 1 QB 286; *O'Connell v Jackson* [1972] 1 QB 270. The second difficulty is determining how much reduction of damages is appropriate. The apportionment should be made only in relation to the additional damage that wearing the seatbelt would have prevented, a matter virtually incapable of proof. In *Froom* the deduction was 25% if the wearing of the seatbelt would have prevented all injury; 15% if it would have limited it.[8] On the other hand, no deduction is made where the court concludes that wearing a seatbelt would not have prevented or diminished the injury that occurred: *Wieben v Wain* [1990] Aust Torts Reports 81-051. In the Australian Capital Territory, New South Wales and South Australia, there is a legislative presumption of contributory negligence if the injured person was not wearing a seatbelt or motorcycle helmet.[9]

Rescuers (good samaritans)

[12.60] In the past there has been some concern regarding the situation of rescuers or "good samaritans". Agony of the moment may excuse a rescuer who has, for example, chosen a method of rescue which would otherwise be regarded as unreasonable, or for an inefficient performance of what would otherwise be a reasonable rescue operation. This, however, failed to prevent a reduction of the plaintiff's damages in *Harrison v British Railways Board* [1981] 3 All ER 679. The plaintiff, a guard on an electric train, attempted to assist another employee who was trying to board a train as it was leaving the station. In the course of doing so, he was pulled onto the line and injured. He had ignored a rule of his employment that in such circumstances the train's emergency brake must be applied, and this was found to be contributory negligence on his part.

Whilst not directly addressing the defence of contributory negligence it is timely to pause and consider the potential liability of the rescuer. What if the behaviour of

---

[8]   A tariff reduction of this sort was opposed in *Hallowell v Nominal Defendant* [1983] Qd R 266, but no clear alternative basis for reduction has been established in Australia.

[9]   *Civil Law (Wrongs) Act 2002* (ACT), s 97; *Motor Accidents Act 1988* (NSW), s 74; *Civil Liability Act 1936* (SA), s 49.

the rescuer exacerbates or causes injury to another person? There has been concern that the likelihood of legal liability will deter individuals from coming to the aid of others and there has been a strong legislative response to this concern. The law in most jurisdictions now offers protection to those who act in good faith and without recklessness.

Figure 12.3: Good samaritan protection

Juris	Legislation	Provision
ACT	*Civil Law (Wrongs) Act 2002*	s 5: • Overarching requirement of good faith. • No liability if assisting or giving advice about the assistance to be given to a person who is injured or in need of emergency medical assistance. • No protection if covered by compulsory third party or capacity significantly impaired by a recreational drug.
NSW	*Civil Liability Act 2002*	s 56 Definition of good samaritan: key is no expectation of payment, acting in good faith comes to the assistance of a person who is injured or at apparent risk of injury. s 58 No protection if: • it was the good samaritan's negligent or intentional act or omission which gave rise to the situation in the first place; • impaired by a drug voluntarily taken (can be prescription as well as recreational); • no due care and skill; or • representing as having skills (ie health care) that he or she does not have.
NT	*Personal Injuries (Liabilities and Damages) Act 2003*	s 8: • Over-arching requirement of good faith and without recklessness. • Covers emergency assistance and specifically covers a good samaritan with medical qualifications giving advice about treatment of a person being given emergency medical assistance. • No protection if intoxicated. • Defines emergency assistance (life or safety endangered or in need of emergency medical treatment) and good samaritan (key is no expectation of payment).
Qld	*Civil Liability Act 2003*	No mention.

Juris	Legislation	Provision
SA	*Civil Liability Act 1936*	s 74: • Defines emergency assistance and good samaritan. • No liability if done in good faith and without recklessness in rendering aid to a person apparently in need of emergency assistance. • Does not apply if covered by compulsory third party insurance or if capacity to exercise due care and skill significantly impaired by alcohol or some other recreational drug.
Tas	*Civil Liability Act 2002*	No mention.
Vic	*Wrongs Act 1958*	s 31B: • Protects rendering of assistance in an emergency situation (good faith and without recklessness). s 31B(1) defines good samaritan in similar terms to other Acts. s 31B(3) in contrast to NSW applies even if the situation was created by the good samaritan.
WA	*Civil Liability Act 2002*	s 5AB defines emergency assistance, good samaritan and medical qualifications. s 5AD protects: • good samaritan if acting at the scene of an accident in good faith and without recklessness; and • medically qualified good samaritan who gives advice in good faith and without recklessness. s 5AE specifically excludes those whose ability to exercise reasonable care and judgment was significantly impaired by self-induced intoxication from drugs or other alcohol.

Intoxication

[12.65] The issue of intoxication of a plaintiff has been addressed by the courts in the context of both volenti and contributory negligence. The most recent consideration was, however, in relation to contributory negligence and the High Court took the opportunity to clarify the position (at common law) of the intoxicated plaintiff. In *Joslyn v Berryman* (2003) 214 CLR 552 both the plaintiff and the defendant had been drinking until at least 4.00 am with the plaintiff then sleeping for a few hours in his car, and the defendant on the ground adjacent to the car. When they both woke up they decided to drive to a town 20 minutes away for breakfast. When they were returning after breakfast the plaintiff was seen to be falling asleep behind the wheel so the defendant took over driving. The defendant had previously lost her licence for driving under the influence and the plaintiff was aware of this. A few minutes later the car rolled and the defendant sustained injuries. The question considered by the court was whether or not an intoxicated plaintiff is subject to an adjusted standard of care due to their incapacity to make sound judgments.

The subjective test was rejected by McHugh J (at [35]) and the court denied the relevance of the level of intoxication of the plaintiff. McHugh J raised the example of an intoxicated person walking down the street and falling down an open manhole that would have been readily apparent to a sober person: at [39].[10] The reasonable person in this circumstance is deemed to be a sober person – and the test one of whether a sober person would have foreseen that accepting a lift from an intoxicated person was exposing them to a risk: McHugh J at [38].

This position is now widely reflected in legislation, as set out in Figure 12.4.

Figure 12.4: Intoxicated plaintiff – presumption of contributory negligence

Juris	Legislation	Provision
ACT	*Civil Law (Wrongs) Act 2002*	s 95 Presumption of contributory negligence where injured person is intoxicated. s 96 Presumption of contributory negligence where injured person is relying on intoxicated person.
NSW	*Civil Liability Act. 2002*	No mention. However note *Motor Accidents Act 1988* s 74
NT	*Personal Injuries (Liabilities and Damages) Act 2003*	s 14 Presumption of contributory negligence if injured person is intoxicated. s 15 Presumption of contributory negligence if reliance on intoxicated person.
Qld	*Civil Liability Act 2003*	s 47 Presumption of contributory negligence if person who suffers harm is intoxicated. s 48 Presumption of contributory negligence if person who suffers harm relies on care and skill of person known to be intoxicated.
SA	*Civil Liability Act 1936*	s 46 Presumption of contributory negligence where injured person is intoxicated. s 47 Presumption of contributory negligence where injured person relies on care and skill of person known to be intoxicated. s 48 Evidentiary provision relating to intoxication.
Tas	*Civil Liability Act 2002*	s 5 Presumption of contributory negligence where injured person is intoxicated.
Vic	*Wrongs Act 1958.*	No mention
WA	*Civil Liability Act 2002*	s 5L Presumption of contributory negligence where injured person is intoxicated.

Foreseeable consequence of the negligence

[12.70] Again, the principles are the same as those relating to causation and remoteness of damage in the tort of negligence itself. As well as being caused by the plaintiff's negligent conduct, the damage must be reasonably foreseeable. In relation to the requirement of foreseeability, it seems necessary that the plaintiff's conduct should have unreasonably exposed him or her to the type of risk that actually materialises.

---

[10] He also noted that in other areas of contributory negligence a plaintiff cannot plead ignorance of the facts.

This is illustrated by *Gent-Driver v Neville* [1953] QSR 1. The plaintiff had accepted a lift at night in the pillion car of a motorcycle driven by the defendant, knowing the lights were defective. A collision occurred with another vehicle. There was a finding of fact that this happened because the defendant had failed to keep a proper lookout and had been on the wrong side of the road, not because of the defective lighting. The defence of contributory negligence failed; the defective lighting on the vehicle in which he was travelling had not contributed to the accident. In *Jones v Livox Quarries* [1952] 2 QB 608, on the other hand, the plaintiff workman was, in breach of instructions, standing on the back of an excavator when a dumper truck driven by a fellow employee ran into the back of it and injured him. The instruction in question was aimed at preventing workmen falling off and being trapped in the excavator machinery. Nevertheless, the plaintiff was found partly to blame for his injury, since standing in the position he did unnecessarily increased the risk of his receiving injury in the way he did, and the plaintiff should have foreseen this. Denning LJ gave an example of an event that would be quite outside the foreseeable risk created by the plaintiff; that of his being hit while on the excavator by a shot fired by a negligent sportsman. Singleton LJ added the example of the person who negligently sits on an unsafe wall and is injured when struck by the defendant's car negligently driven into the wall.

Basis of apportionment

[12.75] As noted at [12.10], contributory negligence provisions allow that the plaintiff's damages shall be reduced "to such extent as the court thinks just and equitable having regard to the claimant's share in the responsibility for the damage". Despite some initial academic protest,[11] it appears now settled that in assessing the extent of the plaintiff's contribution, the court must take into account not only the plaintiff's culpability but also the so-called "causative potency" of his conduct. The former arguably should comprise both the issue of moral blameworthiness and degree of departure from the objective standard of care; but the decisions seem to indicate that only the latter is relevant: *Pennington v Norris* (1956) 96 CLR 10 at 16; *Watt v Bretag* (1981) 27 SASR 301. The second relevant factor may be particularly applicable in cases, for example, where the defendant is in charge of dangerous machinery or is carrying out an ultra-hazardous activity. In such a case the defendant might have to bear a large part of the damages, even though the defendant's culpability is relatively small. Causative potency is also relevant where the defendant has committed a tort of strict liability, especially breach of statutory duty. Indeed if it were not relevant, the court could not apportion at all in such a case where no fault is proved. Very few cases have produced any conflict between the two factors.[12] It is suggested that courts also, though tacitly, take into account other factors, in particular the qualitative difference between a negligent failure to look after one's own safety and negligently causing injury. In *Pennington v Norris* (1956) 96 CLR 10, for example, the plaintiff, a pedestrian, stepped out into a road and was hit by a car negligently driven by the defendant. The night was dark and rainy and the street crowded but the defendant's speed was only some 50km per hour. The plaintiff's damages were reduced by 20% by the High Court, on appeal from an original reduction of 50%. The "blameworthiness" element of fault on the part of the plaintiff

---

[11] Chapman, "Apportionment of Liability between Tortfeasors" (1948) 64 LQR 26 at 28: "causation is difficult enough; degrees of causation would really be a nightmare".

[12] But see *Cavanagh v London Transport Executive* (23 October 1956) The Times in which culpability alone yielded a 50/50 result; causative potency a 20/80; and the court reduced damages by 33.3%.

here looks at least as great as that committed by the defendant. Recently, the High Court has ruled that a finding of 100% contributory negligence is inappropriate, since it amounts to a finding that the case is not one of causation through joint fault: *Wynbergen v Hoyts Corp* (1997) 149 ALR 25. This latter finding has been directly challenged by the Ipp Committee and is subject to some legislative intervention.

Figure 12.5: Contributory negligence – apportionment of damages

> - Damages award is reduced to the extent that the plaintiff's carelessness contributed to the damage.
> - Apportionment of liability between the parties is expressed in percentage terms.
> - Apportionment is a measure of the departure from the standard of care of the reasonable person.

Ipp Committee considers contributory negligence

[12.80] The general approach of the Ipp Committee with respect to contributory negligence was consistent with the overall tone of the review and was grounded in the perceived need to move away from the overly generous approach of the courts. The Ipp Report addressed the current common law situation and then noted three relevant questions:

- Should the standard of care applicable to contributory negligence be the same as that applicable to negligence?
- Should particular types of contributorily negligent conduct attract a minimum reduction of damages fixed by statute?
- Should the law allow apportionment for contributory negligence in such a way as to deny the contributorily negligent person any damages at all?[13]

Each question was addressed individually.

Standard of care

[12.85] The Ipp Committee emphasised that the principle embodied in contributory negligence is that people should take reasonable care for their own safety as well as for that of others, and also emphasised that it is an objective concept.[14] The Committee noted the community expectation that people will take as much care for themselves as they expect others to take for them, and a perception (which the Committee observed may reflect reality) that many lower courts are "more indulgent to plaintiffs than defendants".[15] The Committee declined to support any differential expectations and recommended a legislative amendment emphasising the objective standard of care and including the essence of the calculus of negligence.[16]

---

[13]   Australia, Review of the Law of Negligence Final Report: September 2002 (hereafter Ipp Report) [8.4].
[14]   Ipp Report, [8.6].
[15]   Ipp Report, [8.9]-[8.10].
[16]   Ipp Report, [8.13]-[8.14].

Minimum reduction of damages

[12.90] The Committee addressed the concept of establishing categories of contributory negligence which automatically result in a minimum reduction of damages. Examples of such categories would be the non-wearing of seatbelts or intoxication.[17] Such an approach was rejected by the Committee which described it as arbitrary and unprincipled, and likely to result in an increase in the possibility of injustice. The Committee recommended that courts retain their wide discretion to apportion damages.[18]

Assumption of risk and 100% contributory negligence

[12.95] There has been a general reluctance to reduce damages by more than about 90% on the basis that to do so would be incompatible with a finding of negligence. The Committee lamented this reasoning, noting that the defence of volenti (discussed at [12.100]) operates as a complete defence but does not deny the negligence. While the Committee noted that findings of contributory negligence over 90% would be rare, it noted that a provision that a court is entitled to reduce a contributorily negligent plaintiff's damages by 100% would be a desirable reform of the law.[19] The (sometimes fine) line between contributory negligence and volenti is outlined at [12.110].

Figure 12.6: Contributory negligence – general principles

Juris	Legislation	Provision
ACT	*Civil Law (Wrongs) Act 2002*	s 27 Contributory negligence is not a defence in relation to death. If death is the result of the negligence, contributory negligence is not available. s 47 Contributory negligence can defeat claim. Provides for 100% reduction in damages if the court determines that it is just and equitable to do so.
NSW	*Civil Liability Act 2002*	s 5R Standard of contributory negligence: the same principles applicable in determining negligence apply in determining whether the person who suffered harm has been contributorily negligent. For that purpose: • standard required is that of a reasonable person in the position of the person who suffered harm; and • to be determined on the basis of what the person knew or ought to know at that time.

---

[17] Ipp Report, [8.15]. An example of an existing category is found in the *Civil Liability Act 1932* (SA), s 49(3), in which presumed contributory negligence on the basis of not wearing a seatbelt results in a statutory reduction of 25%.

[18] Ipp Report, [8.22]-[8.25].

[19] Ipp Report, [8.22].

Juris	Legislation	Provision
NT	*Personal Injuries (Liabilities and Damages) Act 2003*	No general provisions regarding standard, but in addition to the presumptions (s 14 Presumption if injured person intoxicated and s 15 Presumption if reliance on intoxicated person), there are two procedural provisions: s 16 Evidentiary provisions. s 17 Amount of reduction in contributory negligence established.
Qld	*Civil Liability Act 2003*	s 23 Standard of care in relation to contributory negligence: the same principles applicable in determining negligence apply in determining whether the person who suffered harm has been contributorily negligent. For that purpose: • standard required is that of a reasonable person in the position of the person who suffered harm; and • to be determined on the basis of what the person knew or ought to know at that time. s 24 Contributory negligence can defeat claim. Provides for 100% reduction in damages if the court determines that it is just and equitable to do so.
SA	*Civil Liability Act 1936*	s 44 Standard of contributory negligence: • principles applicable in determining negligence also apply in determining whether the plaintiff has been contributorily negligent. • unlike other jurisdictions, this legislation does not provide any further guidance regarding how that standard is to be determined. s 45 Contributory negligence in cases brought on behalf of dependants of deceased person. In direct contrast to ACT, specifically provides that the defence is available even when the plaintiff dies. Includes procedural provision: s 50 How case is dealt with where damages are liable to reduction on account of contributory negligence.
Tas	*Civil Liability Act 2002*	s 23 Standard of contributory negligence: the same principles applicable in determining negligence apply in determining whether the person who suffered harm has been contributorily negligent. For that purpose: • standard required is that of a reasonable person in the position of the person who suffered harm; and • to be determined on the basis of what the person knew or ought to know at that time.

CHAPTER 12

Juris	Legislation	Provision
Vic	*Wrongs Act 1958*	s 26 General principles for determination of liability based upon what is "just and equitable": • specifically provides that contributory negligence is not available where the negligence has caused death. s 62 Standard of contributory negligence: the same principles applicable: • in determining negligence apply in determining whether the person who suffered harm has been contributorily negligent. For that purpose: • standard required is that of a reasonable person in the position of the person who suffered harm; and • to be determined on the basis of what the person knew or ought to know at that time. s 63 Contributory negligence can defeat a claim. Provides for 100% reduction in damages if the court determines that it is just and equitable to do so.
WA	*Civil Liability Act 2002*	s 5K Standard of contributory negligence: the same principles applicable in determining negligence apply in determining whether the person who suffered harm has been contributorily negligent. For that purpose: • standard required is that of a reasonable person in the position of the person who suffered harm; and • to be determined on the basis of what the person knew or ought to know at that time.

Volenti non fit injuria

General principles

[12.100] Volenti non fit injuria (voluntary assumption of risk) operates as a complete defence to negligence.[20] The essence of the defence lies in a plaintiff's willingness to assume a risk which the plaintiff knew existed in a particular activity. It is relevant to note at this point that the use of the defence is in decline and courts have narrowed the application of the defence to the point that, in its current form, it is extremely onerous to establish. However, whilst it may be a "highly endangered species it is not yet extinct",[21] thus it is of continued relevance. If the defence is to succeed it must be shown that the plaintiff not only perceived the existence of the risk but that he or she fully appreciated the nature and extent of that risk and voluntarily accepted that specific risk. The defence does not extend to an awareness of the general nature of the risk; it is narrowly confined to that specific risk. This limitation of the defence was addressed by the Ipp Committee whose recommended (and adopted) developments are considered at [12.140]. The clarity and value of these amendments have been challenged by the courts, discussed at [12.143].

---

[20]   It is important to read [12.100]-[12.140] in conjunction with [10.30] (discussion of obvious and inherent risks); see also Figure 10.5.

[21]   *Leyden v Caboolture Shire Council* [2007] QCA 134 per Jerrard JA at [41]. The defence of volenti was successful in this case and is discussed in more detail at [12.125].

Figure 12.7: Volenti non fit injuria – elements

> - The plaintiff perceived the existence of the danger.
> - Fully appreciated it.
> - Voluntarily accepted the risk (can be inferred by conduct).

Distinguishing volenti from other defences

Consent

[12.105] Consent and volenti are in effect the same defence. Consent is the defence where the plaintiff consents to the actual invasion of his or her interest; volenti where the plaintiff has consented to the *risk* of such invasion. This means that "consent" is the name given to the defence in the case of the intentional torts; "volenti" in the case of the unintentional torts (more particularly negligence). Although a subjective consent is necessary in both defences, it need not be expressly conferred but may be inferred from the plaintiff's conduct.

Contributory negligence

[12.110] As outlined above, contributory negligence requires that the plaintiff should have failed unreasonably to safeguard his or her own safety, rather than that the plaintiff should have consented to the risk of harm. Nevertheless, where consent is alleged to have arisen by way of an inference from the plaintiff's conduct, there is a clear possibility of overlap with contributory negligence.[22] For the defendant's purposes, volenti or consent is clearly the more advantageous defence since it operates as a complete defence.

Novus actus interveniens

[12.115] Volenti must be distinguished from the concept of novus actus interveniens (intervening event). Novus is not a defence, since the plaintiff must prove causation of injury or damage. Where a novus is established there is a break in the chain of causation such that there is no negligence. Volenti on the other hand, operates to override the impact of negligence; there is no denial of negligence.

Reduced standard of care

[12.120] Another defence which may overlap with volenti is that of reduced standard of care. This was recognised as a legal defence in the judgment of Dixon J in *Insurance Commissioner v Joyce* (1948) 77 CLR 39. Difficulties as to which defence applies in the case of passengers travelling with drunken drivers are further considered at [12.130]. For the moment it need only be stated that the defence differs from volenti in that its operation leaves open the possibility of negligence being established, and that it

---

[22] This overlap is clearly demonstrated in the intoxicated driver situations. Also refer *Carey v Lake Macquarie City Council* [2007] Aust Torts Reports 81-874 in which McClellan CJ at CL closely considered volenti and rejected it, opting instead to find contributory negligence. The other two judges did not consider volenti as it was not argued before the primary judge (McColl JA at [2]).

requires not a consent to run the risk of negligence occurring (as in volenti), but mere knowledge that it may occur.

Volenti as inference from plaintiff's conduct

[12.125] Courts during the 19th century were quite willing to find volenti proved on the inference of consent to be drawn from the fact that an employee, knowing of the commission of a negligent practice by the employer in the place of work, nevertheless chose to remain in the job. In *Smith v Baker* [1891] AC 325, however, the House of Lords refused to draw the inference from facts of that nature. The plaintiff, along with other employees, had complained of the employer's practice of lifting and swinging heavy stones from a cutting over their place of work, but the practice continued. One day a stone fell on to the plaintiff and injured him. The House of Lords held that the defence of volenti failed. The reasons of the members of the House are divergent, but it is suggested that the reasoning of Lord Herschell is most cogent; that merely to remain in one's employment knowing of a negligently created risk does not justify an inference of consent to that risk. In order to establish the defence, the consent must be a genuine one, and this is not the case where an employee remains in the job for reasons of economic necessity. The case is sometimes explained on the basis that it established that the defence is volenti non fit injuria, not scienti non fit injuria (to the knowing there is no injury). It is true that the House of Lords held that the defence could not be rested on the workman's knowledge on these particular facts. Where, however, there is no compulsion to remain in the employment, economic or otherwise, mere knowledge of the risk may logically justify the inference of consent if the plaintiff chooses not to remove himself or herself from it. However, it is clear that the relevant knowledge must be a full appreciation of the risk.[23]

The nature of knowledge was carefully addressed by McClellan CJ at CL in *Carey v Lake Macquarie City Council* [2007] Aust Torts Reports 81-874. The appellant in this instance was a cyclist who, when riding along a pathway in a public park at 5.20 am (thus reduced light) rode into a bollard and sustained injuries. His Honour emphasised that knowledge alone is not sufficient to make out the defence of volenti (at [76]) and that the plaintiff must fully appreciate the nature and likely manifestation of the risk. The defence will fail if the plaintiff had a genuine belief that the risk will not materialise (at [82]); in this instance, the injured cyclist simply did not turn his mind to the risk of riding into the bollard. It was accepted that whilst he may have been aware of the existence of the bollard on the path, he did "not consciously accept the risk, rather, he simply did not think about it" (at [101]). Such careless riding is not sufficient to support a conclusion of volenti, but it demonstrated that the rider was, of course, sufficiently careless of his own safety to reduce the damages by 50% for contributory negligence. Thus, whilst knowledge of the existence of a risk is relevant, it is merely a "step on the way to proof that a plaintiff has voluntarily assumed the risk" (at [106]).

Effective knowledge thus extends beyond the mere existence of a risk to an acceptance of materialisation of that risk. The House of Lords decision of *ICI v Shatwell* [1965] AC 656 is illustrative here. In that case, two brothers who were employees of the defendants decided to test a detonator by direct application of the leads of the galvanometer, in breach of the defendants' instructions and of their own statutory duty. The employee

---

[23]   Emphasised in the judgment of King CJ in *Banovic v Perkovic* (1982) 30 SASR 34 – mere knowledge the defendant has had some amount of drink does not establish consent to drunken driving on his part.

who was injured in the ensuing explosion sought to make the defendants liable to him vicariously for the negligence of his brother. The action failed because of volenti. The plaintiff not only had full appreciation of the risk but was a participant in his brother's negligence at the time it was occurring. More recently, in *Leyden v Caboolture Shire Council* [2007] QCA 134, the Queensland Court of Appeal found that volenti defeated the claim of a 15-year-old boy who was injured at a BMX track. There was a practice of modifying the jumps at the track and in response to these modifications, the Council had implemented a weekly inspection regime. The appellant had successfully gone over the modified jump (which ultimately led to his injuries) at least five times before the fateful jump and was aware of the need for extra speed and a specific approach. Whilst Jerrard JA noted the relevance of the appellant's knowledge of the jump and need to "increase speed like to 100 percent" (at [8]) he was swayed by his age and on that basis, declined to find volenti, preferring instead to opt for a 50% reduction for contributory negligence. The other two judges were not, however, prepared to rely so heavily upon his age. Emphasis was placed on the fact that he had been riding bikes since he was four or five and went to the track three to five times a week (Mckenzie J at [32]). The knowledge of the appellant extended to actual knowledge of the risks involved in going over the altered jump: he was able to clearly describe the preferred technique and the fact that it was "almost inevitable" if the landing was not correct that the rider would be thrown over the handlebars and injured (at [35]). Helman J recognised that successful application of volenti is rare but in instances such as this, where the appellant was both fully aware of the risk and voluntarily took it (indeed such a risk was part of the allurement of the activity) the defence should apply (at [42]).

There has been some discussion regarding the application of volenti to sporting activities and events. As demonstrated in *Woods v Multi-Sport Holdings Pty Ltd* (2002) 208 CLR 460 this is now dealt with under the rubric of duty and breach (see discussion regarding "obvious and inherent risks" in Chapter 10 at [10.30]ff).

Drunken drivers and passengers

[12.130] In the case of drunken driving, courts have generally proved reluctant to allow the volenti defence against the passenger.[24] This is because the effect of the defence is to cause the plaintiff's action to fail altogether. As a matter of justice the more serious fault seems to be that of the driver, who should have to bear some responsibility for the plaintiff's injury. This is achieved by applying a defence of contributory negligence. Certainly in the "non-pub crawl" cases (that is, where the plaintiff and defendant are not engaged in a joint drinking bout) volenti is unlikely to be applied as a defence.[25] An extreme example of this is *Dann v Hamilton* [1939] 1 KB 509. The plaintiff, though sober herself, allowed herself to be driven by the defendant in a highly drunken state, and after a number of near escapes received injury in an accident caused by the defendant's negligent driving. Despite the fact that the plaintiff had opportunities of leaving the car but had continued with the journey, the court found that the volenti defence failed. Less extreme examples of the same point are *Banovic v Perkovic* (1982) 30 SASR 34 and *Weston v Woodroffe* (1985) 36 NTR 34. In both cases the plaintiff and defendant had

---

[24]   In reading [12.130] it must be remembered that there is a strong overlap with contributory negligence and that the legislature has intervened in some jurisdictions to impose a presumption of contributory negligence where the driver and/or the passenger is drunk: refer Figure 12.4.

[25]   Hogg, "Guest Passengers: A Drunk Driver's Defences" (1994) 21 TLJ 37.

been drinking together at the same social gathering but not in each other's company. In both, the defence of volenti failed because the plaintiff did not have a sufficiently full appreciation of the defendant's condition to make him volens (aware) to the risk of negligence, even though in both cases the plaintiff knew the defendant had had some drink (contributory negligence was also found not to be present on the facts in both cases). In *Banovic* King CJ pointed out that if the plaintiff had drunk himself into a condition in which he was incapable of assessing the defendant's capacity to drive, this would not go towards establishing either defence, where there was nothing to indicate to the plaintiff while sober that the defendant would be unfit. To hold otherwise would interfere with reasonable arrangements under which the members of a drinking party left the driving to one person who was expected to remain sober.

Where plaintiff and defendant are engaged in a pub crawl, the argument against applying volenti is not so clear: the joint enterprise of the two should allow the plaintiff ample warning of the defendant's condition. Whether to apply volenti or contributory negligence will depend on the degree of knowledge and appreciation by the plaintiff of the defendant's condition. The position is further clouded by the fact that some judges have thought the case suitable for the reduced standard of care defence, and this may make a difference because the defence depends upon knowledge of the defendant's condition rather than on willing assumption of risk. In *Insurance Commissioners v Joyce* (1948) 77 CLR 39, a case of a joint drinking bout between defendant and plaintiff, Latham CJ thought that all three defences were applicable on the facts with no difference in the result. The reduced standard of care defence would inevitably produce a decision in the defendant's favour, since the drunken driver could not be expected to show any care in the driving of the car, and at the time of the decision contributory negligence was a complete defence, whereas now it is not. Dixon J thought on the other hand that the appropriate defence in drunken driving cases of this sort was reduced standard of care.

At common law there continues to be some debate regarding the appropriate approach as between volenti and reduced standard of care. *Roggenkamp v Bennetts* (1950) 80 CLR 292, a case decided soon after *Joyce,* held that volenti was the appropriate defence in a case of a drinking reunion between two wartime RAAF pilots. That defence was applied also in *Hanson v Motor Accidents Board* [1988] Aust Torts Reports 80-155. In *Jeffries v Fisher* [1985] WAR 250 the Western Australian Supreme Court divided three ways: one judge applying volenti, another reduced standard of care and the third reducing damages for the plaintiff's contributory negligence. The Victorian decision in *Radford v Ward* [1990] Aust Torts Reports 81-064 rejected the application of reduced standard of care as a matter of law, on the ground that it leads to the impossible task of fixing the standard of care of the drunken driver. There being no submission of volenti applying, damages were reduced for contributory negligence. The High Court went some way towards clarifying the matter in *Joslyn v Berryman* (2003) 214 CLR 552 with McHugh J pointing out at [27] that:

> *Since the introduction of apportionment legislation, contributory negligence has been the preferred characterisation of the conduct of the plaintiff who accepts a lift from a driver known to be intoxicated.*

There has been legislative intervention in this area with the Australian Capital Territory, New South Wales and South Australia all introducing legislation specifically excluding volenti as a defence where a passenger relies on an intoxicated driver.[26] In the other jurisdictions volenti is still available, "at least theoretically" (*Joslyn v Berryman* (2003) 214 CLR 552 per McHugh J at [28]), though perhaps unlikely.

Exclusion of liability based on express agreement

[12.135] Whatever may be the position regarding volenti based on inferential consent it is quite clear that consent based on express agreement may operate to license future negligence in advance. The agreement may be a contractual one, though this is not necessary. The contractual doctrine under which exclusionary terms of which reasonable notice has been given to the other party form part of the contract may apply outside the contractual sphere. The court in *Scanlon v American Cigarette Co Pty Ltd* [1987] VR 289 distinguished the defence of exclusion by notice from that of volenti as a matter of principle. All that was necessary to establish the former defence was that the defendant had done what was reasonably necessary to give notice of the exclusionary provision to the plaintiff.[27] Volenti on the other hand requires an actual consent. These points may be observed in the case of *Birch v Thomas* [1972] 1 WLR 294. The plaintiff was a passenger in a car driven by the defendant. Prior to the journey, the defendant had told the plaintiff that he was not covered by insurance for liability to passengers and on entry into the car he had pointed to a legible notice on the windscreen exempting him from liability for negligence to passengers. It was held that he had given sufficient notice of the exempting term, and that the plaintiff's action against him for negligent driving causing injury therefore failed, whether or not the plaintiff had read or understood the notice. The ground stated was volenti non fit injuria but that defence requires an actual consent, whereas the defence in question here merely requires that the defendant should have given reasonable notice of the exclusion clause. For example, the giving of reasonable notice of an exclusion clause is all that is required of an occupier for protection against liability to a visitor (considered in Chapters 8 and 9). However, the Court of Appeal in England has held that the display of a notice, to the effect that parked vehicles will be wheel-clamped, creates only a factual presumption that vehicle owners know of, and consent to, this provision, allowing them (as in the case itself) to prove ignorance of it, and therefore absence of consent: *Vine v Waltham Forest LBC* [2000] 4 All ER 169. So the consent requirement under this decision continues to be subjectively defined. There is support for this in the decision in *Burnett v British Waterways Board* [1973] 1 WLR 700, which held the plaintiff not to be bound by the terms of an exclusion clause displayed outside premises which the plaintiff was bound by his contract of employment to enter. Further, it is clear that the ability to exclude liability by the giving of reasonable notice is a doctrine of limited extent. In the absence of a contract between plaintiff and defendant, it should be limited to cases where some consensual arrangement exists between them.

The same principles governing the construction of contractual exemption clauses will apply to agreements excluding liability in tort, whether contractual or not. Such agreements are strictly construed and contra proferentem (against the party relying on

---

[26]   *Civil Law (Wrongs) Act 2002* (ACT), s 96(5); *Motor Accidents Act 1988* (NSW), s 76; and *Civil Liability Act 1936* (SA), s 47(6).

[27]   This may be observed also in the "ticket" cases in contract *Parker v South Eastern Railway* (1877) 2 CPD 416 (railway ticket); and in the case law on exclusion of liability by an occupier of premises: *Ashdown v Williams* [1957] 1 QB 409.

them). Thus ambiguities will be resolved in favour of the other party. So, where there are two possible grounds for liability, one based on negligence and one on strict liability, a general exclusion of liability clause was held to apply only to the strict liability: *White v Warwick* [1953] 1 WLR 1285. Where negligence is the only possible source of liability, a general exclusion will apply to it: *Alderslade v Tendon* [1945] KB 189. But the court must be satisfied that it is an exclusion clause and not a mere warning of non-liability in the absence of legal liability: *Hollier v Rambler Motors* [1972] 2 QB 71.

Ipp Committee considers volenti

[12.140] The defence of volenti is thus extremely narrow and was described as "more or less defunct" by the Ipp Committee.[28] The current narrow application of the defence was explained by the Committee as reflecting a lack of willingness by the courts to find that plaintiffs actually knew of the risk and freely and voluntarily accepted that risk. The result of this reluctance was explained as being a tendency to narrowly define risks at a high level of detail. The Committee recommendation was that courts be encouraged to make greater use of the defence by making it easier to establish.[29] The Committee identified some ways in which this could be achieved. The essence of the recommendations follow:

- Reverse the burden of proof on the issue of awareness of risk in relation to obvious risks (where a risk is deemed to be obvious there would be a presumption that the person was aware of the risk).

- Provide that the plaintiff need only be aware of the type of the risk, not its precise nature, extent or manner of occurrence.

- No provision should be made with respect to voluntariness. The Committee felt that this was an evaluative question, making it difficult to make satisfactory general provisions.[30]

The legislative response was quite strong in most jurisdictions, as set out in Figure 12.8.[31]

Figure 12.8: Obvious risks

Juris	Legislation	Provision
ACT	*Civil Law (Wrongs) Act 2002*	No mention.
NSW	*Civil Liability Act 2002*	s 5G Injured person presumed to be aware of obvious risks unless proves not aware (on balance of probabilities). Awareness includes the type of risk, not the exact risk.
NT	*Personal Injuries (Liabilities and Damages) Act 2003*	No mention.

---

[28] Ipp Report, [8.28].
[29] Ipp Report, [8.28]-[8.29].
[30] Ipp Report, [8.3]-[8.32].
[31] Figure 12.8 is incomplete as it does not include definitions of obvious and inherent risks and duty of care with respect to such risks: these issues are discussed in Chapter 10.

Juris	Legislation	Provision
Qld	*Civil Liability Act 2003*	s 14 Person suffering harm presumed to be aware of obvious risks unless proves not aware (on balance of probabilities). Awareness includes the type of risk, not the exact risk.
SA	*Civil Liability Act 1936*	s 37: • Injured persons presumed to be aware of obvious risks unless proves not aware (on balance of probabilities). Awareness includes the type of risk, not the exact risk. • A defence of voluntary assumption of risk requires establishing that a reasonable person in the same position would have taken steps (which the plaintiff did not in fact take) to avoid it.
Tas	*Civil Liability Act 2002*	s 16 Presumed to be aware of obvious risks unless proves not aware (on balance of probabilities). Awareness includes the type of risk, not the exact risk.
Vic	*Wrongs Act 1958*	s 54 Voluntary assumption of risk: Presumed to be aware of obvious risks unless proves not aware (on balance of probabilities) except where the damage relates to a professional service or health service, or is associated with work done for another.
WA	*Civil Liability Act 2002*	s 5N Injured person presumed to be aware of obvious risks unless proves not aware (on balance of probabilities). Awareness includes the type of risk not the exact risk.

Judicial response

[12.143] The response to the legislative enunciation of volenti has not been enthusiastic with the statutory scheme being described as lacking in clarity (*Carey v Lake Macquarie City Council* [2007] Aust Torts Reports 81-874 at [71] per McClellan CJ at CL). His Honour went on to acknowledge that prior to the amendments to the *Civil Liability Act 2002* (NSW) the defendant "faced a difficult task" to establish the defence (at [86]) and that the amendments were designed to address this difficulty (at [87]). In his Honour's view, however, the mere existence of an "obvious risk" does not trigger the defence, rather it raises a rebuttable presumption that the plaintiff was aware of the risk (at [90]) and, of course awareness of the risk is not sufficient to constitute acceptance of that risk. The rebuttable presumption interpretation was also adopted in *CG Maloney Pty Ltd v Hutton-Potts* [2006] NSWCA 136 (per Santow JA at [101]). Interestingly, the defence, considered under the statutory scheme, failed in both of these cases yet was successful when considered under common law principles in *Leyden v Caboolture Shire Council* [2007] QCA 134.

Illegality

[12.145] The considerations which cause an action to fail for illegality of the plaintiff have already been mentioned in relation to the intentional torts. Of particular note are the closeness of connection between the criminal or otherwise illegal enterprise and the cause of action in tort, and the nature of the illegality in question. Some earlier Australian authority applied similar considerations to the question whether an action for negligence is available to a participant in a joint illegal enterprise. In *Smith v Jenkins* (1970) 119 CLR 397 the plaintiff and defendant had stolen a man's car keys and driven away in his car. Later the plaintiff was injured in the course of negligent driving by the defendant. The High Court dismissed his action for negligence, either on the ground that the court simply refused to make its remedies available to one engaged in serious criminal conduct (per Kitto J), or that as a matter of policy no duty of care arose between plaintiff and defendant: favoured by Windeyer J. It should be noted that no especial danger of accident existed at the time the plaintiff received injury, and the car was not being pursued by the police.[32] Nevertheless the negligent driving was thought to be sufficiently closely associated with the earlier conduct to deny the plaintiff a remedy. Windeyer J observed that something might turn on the nature of the illegality and that in particular mere traffic law violations might not have the same effect. This was put to the test in *Jackson v Harrison* (1978) 138 CLR 438 where, however, the High Court applied a different approach to the problem. In that case both plaintiff and defendant were disqualified drivers. They obtained the defendant's car from his parents by means of deceit, and in the course of its being driven by the defendant the plaintiff received injury through the negligence of the defendant. The High Court held the plaintiff to be entitled to recover damages for this negligence. The plaintiff's illegal conduct in participating in the illegal driving of the car did not prevent the court from fixing a standard of care, this being a ground of distinction from *Smith v Jenkins*. The same approach had been adopted in *Progress & Properties Ltd v Craft* (1976) 135 CLR 651. This case held that the illegal conduct of the plaintiff in travelling on a hoist (the use of which was confined by statutory regulation to the raising and lowering of goods) did not prevent the court from assessing whether the hoist operator had acted negligently, and the plaintiff's action succeeded.

Both the latter cases were decided before the High Court laid down the general requirement of proximity for determining duty of care, but *Gala v Preston* (1991) 172 CLR 243 has adopted their approach in considering the issue of proximity in this situation. In *Gala* the plaintiff and defendant had been engaged in a joint drinking bout as a result of which both were well over the legal alcohol limit for driving. They then broke into and took away a vehicle, a criminal offence under the *Queensland Criminal Code*. Later, as a result of the defendant's allegedly negligent driving, the plaintiff received injury. The trial judge held that neither the defence of volenti non fit injuria nor that of reduced standard of care was made out on the facts, a finding categorised as surprising by the High Court, though one which was allowed to stand. Nevertheless the trial judge held the defence of illegality to be made out, a finding on which he was reversed by the Full Court but which was restored unanimously by the High Court. The majority of the High Court proceeded on the basis that the criminal nature of the enterprise, together with the large amount of alcohol consumed by the participants, meant that the parties were not in a relationship of proximity: it would not be "possible

---

[32] As was also the case in *Godbolt v Fittock* (1963) 63 SR(NSW) 617 – plaintiff injured in the course of cattle rustling by truck.

or feasible" to determine what was an appropriate standard of care.

There were three dissentients to the approach taken by the majority of the High Court in *Gala*. Brennan J thought that the case raised no difficulty about proximity apart from the joint criminal activity of plaintiff and defendant since they occupied the positions of passenger and driver; nor was it impossible to fix a standard of care in relation to the driving of the motor vehicle. The plaintiff's action failed on the ground that the breach of criminal law concerned was one which the criminal law could not condone, in particular because to allow a civil remedy would be to weaken the force of the criminal sanction. Dawson J, though not accepting the latter point, agreed with Brennan J that the unwillingness of the law to set a standard of care "is not because it is impossible to do so but because it is repugnant to the law to do so". The action must therefore fail for the policy reasons mentioned by Windeyer J in *Smith v Jenkins* (as a matter of policy "the law refuses to exact a duty of care"). Toohey J regarded *Smith v Jenkins* as "sound law" which should be followed: "A duty of care is held not to exist, not because of the difficulty of fixing a standard of care but because of the participation by the parties in a criminal activity which resulted in the injury."

It is difficult to disagree with Brennan J's conclusion that *Gala* raised no difficulty about proximity as regards the question of duty of care. The relationship between the parties was the simple one of driver and passenger. It is true that because of the drunken state of the driver, it would have been difficult to fix a standard of care, though that seems more pertinent to the reduced standard of care defence which had been negatived. If, however, it is accepted that the intrinsically dangerous nature of the illegal activity is a relevant factor in the court's decision that a standard of care cannot be fixed, and that therefore a defence of illegality applies, the question arises as to what the position is when the illegal enterprise is not dangerous. In such a case it may be perfectly "possible or feasible" to fix a standard of care. The question arose before the Federal Court in *Italiano v Barbaro* (1993) 114 ALR 21. In this case the plaintiff was a participant in a fraudulent enterprise of staging a road accident so as to falsely claim damages from an insurance company. The whole object of the exercise was that no-one should receive an actual injury, but the plaintiff was injured allegedly as a result of negligent driving by the defendant, a fellow participant in the enterprise. The majority of the court (Neaves and Whitlam JJ) found as a fact that the plaintiff received his injury in the course of actually staging the accident. It held that, while it might be possible or even feasible to fix a standard of care in these circumstances, it was not "appropriate" to do so; therefore, the defence of illegality was made out. The High Court in *Gala* had not intended to draw a distinction between safe and unsafe criminal enterprises so far as the fixing of the standard of care was concerned. This goes most of the way towards restoring the previously understood law in *Smith v Jenkins* and *Godbolt v Fittock* (1963) 63 SR(NSW) 617, in both of which no particular danger existed at the time of the negligent driving. The approach of the other two judges (Black CJ and Beasley J) was different, although they also concluded that the plaintiff's claim failed because of illegality. Their conclusion of fact was that the accident occurred before the intended staging of the accident but in the process of preparatory driving searching for a suitable place to stage the accident. In these circumstances it was not appropriate to fix a standard of care, because that standard would have to take into account the conflicting demands of the criminal enterprise. It might be, for example, that "the mere driving to the scene of a proposed crime would not involve any transformation of the relationship of driver and passenger".

Where action is being brought by a participant in an illegal enterprise against one who was not party to that enterprise, the principles laid down by the majority of the High Court in *Gala* appear to indicate that this will not affect the success of the plaintiff's action. There is no necessary difficulty in such a case in determining the standard of care of the defendant and as a matter of policy it is arguable that the mere criminality of the plaintiff's conduct should not place him or her beyond the protection of the civil law. This is borne out by *Commonwealth v Winter* [1993] Aust Torts Reports 81-212. The plaintiff was a disqualified driver who was driving at excessive speed in a police chase and was injured when he drove into a police car placed as a road block. It was held that the police owed him a duty of care despite his criminal conduct and were in breach of that duty, there being no reason to expose the plaintiff to the risk of serious injury through the placing of the road block merely in order to apprehend him.[33]

The relationship between illegality and negligence has now been addressed by legislation in most jurisdictions with the availability of damages being limited according to the seriousness of the offence and the "material contribution" of the illegal conduct to the actual injury.[34]

A final note

[12.150] The discussion throughout this section of the text has emphasised the signficance of the Ipp Report and subsequent legislative amendments, cautioning that we are yet to be certain of the overall impact on the law of negligence. Indeed, inherent in much of the discussion has been an assertion that perhaps little will in fact change. It is timely to turn to the judiciary for guidance. Bryson JA in *CG Maloney Pty Ltd v Hutton-Potts* [2006] NSWCA 136 (at [177]) sought to summarise the import of the shifting of negligence from the common law into the legislative framework:

> *There is no general statement of purposes or of objectives in either Act [referring to the principal and amending Act]. Some of the provisions may have been intended to restate or declare parts of the law of negligence while others change parts of that law. I have not observed any overall purpose or scheme of the amendments which can be brought to bear on the construction of any particular provision. The application of each particular provision should be considered in its statutory context and in relation to the facts of each particular case in which a litigant claims to rely on it. Broad views and insights based on them should be deferred until there has been a significant accumulation of judicial experience on the operation of these provisions.*

The appropriate way forward then? View each situation on the facts before the court within the context of the specific claim and the legislative framework. This appears to be somewhat similar to the approach adopted by the courts under the rubric of the common law – with some additional considerations set out in the legislation. In short, we just wait and see whether the legislative enunciation of negligence heralds more clarity or sweeping changes (or perhaps, a mix of both).

---

[33] *Marshall v Osmond* [1983] QB 1034 – policeman driving a car in police chase owed duty of care to person pursued but was not negligent as regards the error of judgment which caused that person injury. The court took into account in fixing the standard of care the "circumstances" of the driving, namely the police chase.

[34] *Civil Law (Wrongs) Act 2002* (ACT), s 38 (refers only to acts of terrorism); *Civil Liability Act 2002* (NSW), s 54; *Personal Injuries (Liabilities and Damages) Act 2003* (NT), s 10; *Civil Liability Act 2003* (Qld), s 45; *Civil Liability Act 1936* (SA), s 43; *Civil Liability Act 2002* (Tas), s 6; *Wrongs Act 1958* (Vic), s 14G.

Practice Questions

Revision Questions

12.1 How does the "agony of the moment" affect the standard of care in determining contributory negligence?

12.2 Negligence is a person's carelessness in breach of duty to others. To prove contributory negligence does a defendant have to show that the plaintiff's conduct put anyone else at risk or that the plaintiff breached a duty of care owed to someone else? What is the key question in contributory negligence?

Problem Questions

12.1 Jake fancied himself as a bit of a charmer. He often went to the local swimming pool to show the girls "true perfection". Jake's belief in himself did not reflect reality and he spent most of his time gazing at the girls and attempting to get their attention. He was walking along the edge of the pool one day, looking hopefully at a group of girls who were training in the pool, when he fell over a pile of kick boards left lying around by the swim coach. He suffered a badly bruised knee and some cuts to his hands.

Are there any defences available to the coach or the swimming centre?

12.2 Don and Denise owned a beautiful home on a canal. In September they went on a cruise leaving their son Damian to caretake the house. One Saturday evening, Damian went "on the town" with his friend Carl. They didn't return to the home until the early hours of the morning, completely inebriated. Carl slept for an hour or so and then woke up feeling very hot. He decided to take a refreshing dip in the canal.

The night was dark because there was a lot of cloud cover, but Carl was very familiar with the property because he had visited there many times. He walked past the pool and stood on the low fence separating the pool from the canal and dived into the canal. Since the canal was no more than a metre deep he suffered paraplegia.

Assume that the owners have breached their duty of care by not providing warning signs and a higher fence. Discuss to what extent contributory negligence would be found against Carl.

Answers to Practice Questions

Revision Questions

12.1 Courts apply the standard of care more leniently to plaintiffs whose conduct occurs in a situation of risk created by the defendant's negligence. This is called the "agony of the moment" – where the defendant's negligence has placed the plaintiff in a position of imminent personal danger, causing the plaintiff to choose a course of action while under pressure.

12.2 Contributory negligence is simply a *failure by the plaintiff to take reasonable care for her or his own safety*. The defendant does not need to show that the plaintiff's conduct put anyone else at risk or was necessarily a breach of a duty of care owed to someone else. The court in *Froom v Butcher* [1976] 1 QB 286 stated:

> Negligence depends on a breach of duty, whereas contributory negligence does not. Negligence is a man's carelessness in breach of duty to others. Contributory negligence is a man's carelessness in looking after his own safety. He is guilty of contributory negligence if he ought reasonably to have foreseen that, if he did not act as a reasonable prudent man, he might hurt himself.

The key question to ask when considering contributory negligence is, to use the words of Lord Denning in *Froom*, "not what is the cause of the accident [but] what was the cause of the damage".

Problem Questions

12.1 When walking around a pool, especially at a time when squads are training, it would be expected that a person would be paying attention to where they put their feet. The fact that Jake was looking at the girls in the pool could be argued by a defendant that he was not doing this and so acted carelessly – failing to take the precautions necessary for his own safety.

Was the damage reasonably foreseeable and did his breach cause the damage?

It could further be argued that it could be foreseen that his carelessness could result in him hurting himself in the way he did, and that his carelessness helped cause the injuries he suffered.

12.2 Carl would certainly be found to be contributorily negligent but it is always difficult to assess the extent of that apportionment. Each State has apportionment legislation (eg *Law Reform Act 1995* (Qld), s 10) that requires a court to apportion damage on the basis of what it believes to be "just and equitable [given] the claimant's share of responsibility". If the defendant is successful, the plaintiff's damages may be reduced according to the degree of departure from the standard of care of the reasonable man in the plaintiff's position. Consideration is given to the "relative importance of the acts of the parties in causing the damage: *Pennington v Norris* (1956) 96 CLR 10; *Podrebersek v AIS & S* (1988) 59 ALJR 492.

Assuming negligence on the part of the defendants, the degree of fault that will be attributed to Carl in our facts could be quite high. In this respect the court would probably find in the vicinity of 70% contributory negligence on the part of Carl. Of relevance here is *Ballerini v Berrigan SC* [2004] VSC 321 discussed in Chapter 10.

Tutorial Questions

Discussion Questions

12.1 Do you believe that an apportionment of damages by a jury, where contributory negligence is involved, should be open to amendment by a higher court? Refer to the discussion of the judges in the High Court in *Liftronic Pty Ltd v Unver* (2001) 75 ALJR 867.

12.2 Contributory negligence acknowledges that a plaintiff can be partially to blame and so it provides a mechanism whereby plaintiffs must also be personally responsible for their actions. Do you think that the recent High Court cases are taking this concept more seriously and this is resulting in more defendant-friendly decisions?

12.3 Does the increased role of legislation lend clarity to the operation of defences?

CHAPTER 13

Proof in Civil Trials: Proof of Negligence

Reading

Sappideen, Vines, Grant and Watson, *Torts: Commentary and Materials*, pp 566-583.

Objectives

This chapter will:

- examine who has the burden of proving negligence;
- recognise the importance of res ipsa loquitur (the thing speaks for itself); and
- consider the conditions necessary for the operation of res ipsa loquitur.

Principles

Introduction

[13.05] In civil actions the plaintiff has the burden of proof and must demonstrate that, on the balance of probabilities, there is a case against the defendant.

The burden of proof rule operates in the following way. The plaintiff must establish that there is a probability that the defendant has committed the tort alleged. In theory, this means that the plaintiff must establish a 51/49 chance that the defendant has committed that tort (though it is very unusual for courts to quantify probabilities in that way). In other words, it must be demonstrated that it is more likely than not that the tort was committed. The defendant may contest the plaintiff's action in one of three ways:

- **Demurrer.** The defendant may claim that the plaintiff's statement of claim discloses no cause of action in tort. This type of defence is often referred to as a "demurrer". Since an issue of law is involved, the question cannot be resolved by reference to the burden of proof, although both parties must be heard on the issue of law.

- **Traverse (denial).** The defendant may simply deny the allegations of fact in the plaintiff's statement of claim. This type of defence is referred to as a "traverse". If the defendant relies on this defence, there is no effect upon the burden of proof which remains with the plaintiff.

- **Excuse/defence.** The defendant may admit the plaintiff's allegations of fact, and that they constitute a tort, and yet set up other facts which in law constitute an excuse. The defendant may, for example, allege that he or she was acting in self-defence and was therefore not liable in battery. This type of defence is referred to as a "confession and avoidance" and the legal burden of proof in establishing the facts on which it is based rests with the defendant. The "defences" to torts referred to throughout this book are all cases of confession and avoidance.[1]

Apart from the third case (excuse/defence), the plaintiff's evidence must establish the probability that the defendant committed the tort which is represented by the facts alleged by the plaintiff. In doing so, the plaintiff's evidence must establish at the end of the case, that it is more likely than not that the defendant did commit the tort. The balance of probabilities rule must not be interpreted as a balance of *possibilities* rule. The mere fact that the defendant's tort is the most likely possibility arising from certain facts and giving rise to several other possibilities, clearly does not mean that the court should draw the conclusion that the defendant committed the tort.

Although the plaintiff has the ultimate legal burden of proof, the effect of the plaintiff's evidence may be such that the case made out is likely to succeed unless the defendant calls evidence to rebut it. A so-called prima facie (at first sight) case exists, requiring an answer.

It is said that the effect of this is that an evidential burden of proof passes to the defendant, the legal burden remaining with the plaintiff. It is most unusual, however,

---

[1] It is worth noting at this point that the burden of proof can sometimes be reversed where there is a possible defence. These situations were addressed in Chapter 12.

for a finding of a shift of an evidential burden of proof to be made in the course of the trial. It is much more likely that this conclusion would be drawn by a judge when giving judgment, or in giving directions to the jury in a jury trial. However, at the close of the plaintiff's evidence, a submission of no case to answer may be made by the defendant. This requires the court to determine whether there is a case to answer; that is, whether (in a jury trial) there is a case to be left to the jury. Even in the case of a decision in favour of the plaintiff on this point, however, the jury should be directed that it is possible for it to return a verdict in the defendant's favour. Having a case to answer which is not answered is not inevitably to be equated with the plaintiff's having satisfied the legal burden of proof: *Davis v Bunn* (1936) 56 CLR 256 at 267-269 per Evatt J. Where, however, the submission of no case to answer is made to a judge sitting alone, it seems certain that a failure on the submission will lead to the plaintiff's success in the action. In this situation the submission amounts to an election on the defendant's part to call no evidence: *Alexander v Rayson* [1936] 1 KB 169; *Parry v Aluminium Corp* [1940] WN 246. In the case of jury trial, on the other hand, the judge may allow evidence to be called by the defendant, despite the failure of the submission: *Young v Rank* [1950] 2 KB 510; *Payne v Harrison* [1961] 1 WLR 1455 (though Evatt J in *Davis* seemed of the opinion that here the defendant may call evidence without the leave of the court).

The transfer of an evidential burden of proof to the defendant is, however, normally tantamount to a requirement that it must provide some cogent evidence in rebuttal or lose the case. The High Court in *Purkess v Crittenden* (1965) 114 CLR 164 at 168 pointed out that where a defendant was seeking to show that an injury which prima facie was caused by the defendant's negligence was in fact due to some pre-existing condition of the plaintiff, the defendant must lead evidence to that effect rather than merely suggest the existence of some such condition. That being done, however, it was for the plaintiff to prove to the court's satisfaction that the injury arose not out of a pre-existing condition but through the defendant's negligence.

Figure 13.1: Proving and defending a case

The burden of proof is on the plaintiff to prove its case (that the defendant committed the tort alleged) on the balance of probabilities.

The defendant may:

- claim the plaintiff's statement of claim discloses no cause of action in tort – a demurrer;
- deny the allegations of fact in the plaintiff's statement of claim – a traverse; or
- admit the plaintiff's allegations of fact but present other facts which in law constitute an excuse – confession and avoidance.

Proof of negligence

[13.10] The plaintiff bears the legal burden of proof on all the issues involved in a negligence action; that is, on the issues of fact arising in relation to duty of care, breach of duty and causation and remoteness of damage. There has been some discussion in the courts following an apparent shift in evidentiary onus in *Chappel v Hart* (1998) 195

CLR 232 which has resulted in some confusion as to whether such a shift ought to occur. This opaque position has been reinforced in the High Court: in denying special leave to appeal from *Zaltron v Raptis* [2001] SASC 209 (24 July 2001), Gaudron J noted that there was a difference of opinion with respect to the evidential onus in *Chappel v Hart* (1998) 195 CLR 232, but stated that it was not an appropriate vehicle to solve that difference and Kirby J mentioned the "verbal formulae" but declined to pursue it further because the decision had been made on a factual basis.[2] Evidential onus has been specifically considered in recent legislative amendments;[3] thus whilst we await further clarification from the courts it is appropriate to suggest that the evidential onus does not shift in the causation stage of the inquiry. In some torts, which may overlap with negligence, the burden of proof on the fault issue is on the defendant. So in an action for trespass occurring off the highway, the plaintiff merely has to prove the direct contact with his or her person or property arising from the defendant's act, and where that is proved the defendant has the burden of proving inevitable accident: see Chapter 3. In detinue, the plaintiff who is suing for loss of the chattel by the defendant need prove only the bailment of the chattel to the defendant and its loss. The defendant then has the legal burden of proving that the loss occurred without fault on its part: *Houghland v RR Low (Luxury Coaches) Ltd* [1962] 1 QB 694; *Nibali v Sweeting* [1989] Aust Torts Reports 80-258. Proof of non-fault is here a confession and avoidance defence.

The plaintiff in negligence must prove his or her case on the balance of probabilities. The legal effect of requiring proof on the balance of probabilities is set out in this passage from the judgment of Gibbs J in the High Court decision in *TNT Management Pty Ltd v Brooks* (1979) 23 ALR 345 at 349-350:

> *Of course, as far as logical consistency goes, many hypotheses may be put which the evidence does not exclude positively. But this is a civil and not a criminal case. We are concerned with the probabilities, not with possibilities. The difference between the criminal standard of proof in its application to circumstantial evidence and the civil is that in the former the facts must be such as to exclude reasonable hypotheses consistent with innocence, while in the latter you need only circumstances raising a more probable inference in favour of what is alleged.*

Proof of negligence may be by direct evidence (for example, eye-witness accounts) or by circumstantial evidence (where the court infers the probability or otherwise of negligence from the proof of certain facts). Cases of the latter sort often give rise to considerable difficulty, and may produce split decisions. A leading example is *Holloway v McFeeters* (1956) 94 CLR 470. The proved facts were that the deceased was hit and killed at night by a car driven by a hit-and-run driver who was never identified. The state of the road showed that the plaintiff was hit at the centre of the road, that there were tyre marks for some 14 metres indicating hard braking, and that the plaintiff was carried that distance by the car. The plaintiff had been last seen in a normal state of health and sober an hour before the accident, although a medical test taken after death indicated the presence of alcohol in the plaintiff's blood. The majority of the High Court upheld the jury finding that the facts proved raised a probability of negligence on the part of the driver. Dixon and Kitto JJ dissented on the ground that this inference

---

[2]   *Zaltron v Raptis* (2002) 23 (7) Leg Rep SL2, A29/2001 (19 April 2002).

[3]   *Civil Law (Wrongs) Act 2002* (ACT), s 46; *Civil Liability Act 2002* (NSW), s 5E; *Civil Liability Act 2003* (Qld), s 12; *Civil Liability Act 1936* (SA). s 35; *Civil Liability Act 2002* (Tas), s 14; *Wrongs Act 1958* (Vic), s 52 and *Civil Liability Act 2002* (WA), s 5 all provide that the plaintiff bears the burden of proving any fact relevant to causation.

was not reasonably open to the jury, since it was no more than conjecture, and numerous possibilities not consistent with fault on the driver's part could not be excluded. The two dissenting judges arrived at a similar conclusion in a later case, although here forming part of a 3:2 majority of the High Court: *Luxton v Vines* (1952) 85 CLR 352 (in which the plaintiff was struck by an unknown vehicle while walking along the edge of the road on a dark wet night; the action failed).

Figure 13.2: Legal burden of proof

> The plaintiff bears the legal burden of proof on all the issues
> involved in a negligence action, that is:
> • on the issues of fact arising in relation to duty of care;
> • breach of duty; and
> • causation and remoteness of damage.

Res ipsa loquitur

[13.15] A special method of proving negligence by means of circumstantial evidence is the evidentiary principle known by the Latin phrase res ipsa loquitur (the thing speaks for itself). Where this applies, its effect is that the mere occurrence of the accident (the "thing") constitutes evidence of negligence. The earliest cases concerned the dropping of barrels from the upper storey window of the defendants' warehouses on to the plaintiff situated below: *Byrne v Boadle* (1863) 2 H & C 722; 159 ER 299; *Scott v London & St Katherine Docks* (1865). In both cases it was held that the doctrine of res ipsa loquitur applied. The court in the latter case laid down the following conditions for the operation of the doctrine:

- the accident must be such as would not happen in the normal course of events without negligence on the part of someone;
- the thing being under the control of the defendant, the facts point to negligence by the defendant or those for whom the defendant is responsible; and
- the actual cause of the accident must not be known.

These requirements will be examined in turn.

Figure 13.3: Res ipsa loquitur

> • The thing speaks for itself.
> • Where it applies, its effect is that the occurrence of the
>   accident constitutes evidence of negligence.
> • The following conditions apply:
>   – the accident must raise the presumption of negligence;
>   – the thing must be under the control of the defendant; and
>   – the actual cause of the accident must not be known.

Accident must raise presumption of negligence

[13.20] The doctrine of res ipsa loquitur has been applied in a number of situations, though there is of course no finite list of cases in which it applies. As stated at [13.15], the earliest cases concerned the falling of objects from the upper storeys of buildings on to persons beneath.[4] Another very common case is that of vehicles being driven on the highway going out of control in some excessive way, for example by mounting the footpath: *Laurie v Raglan Building Co* [1942] 1 KB 152; *GIO v Best* [1993] Aust Torts Reports 81-210. The rule has also been applied to manufactured products; for example, to a stone found in a commercially produced bun (*Chaproniere v Mason* (1905) 21 TLR 633) and to sulphites found in manufactured underwear: *Grant v Australian Knitting Mills* [1936] AC 85. It has been applied in medical cases; for example, where swabs were left in a patient after an operation (*Mahon v Osborne* [1939] 2 KB 14) and where a plaintiff operated on for two stiff fingers ended up with a useless hand: *Cassidy v Minister of Health* [1951] 2 KB 343. But it did not apply where a piece of a complicated machine detached itself while the machine was operating, and struck and injured the plaintiff: *Schellenberg v Tunnel Holdings* [2000] Aust Torts Reports 81-553. A breakdown of a machine of this sort can occur without negligence on the part of those in control. In a decision criticised by Professor Fleming, the High Court found res ipsa loquitur inapplicable in the case of a piece of wood being flung out of a circular saw and entering the plaintiff's eye: *Mummery v Irvings* (1956) 96 CLR 99.[5] The court refused to apply res ipsa loquitur in the absence of any evidence from the plaintiff on the basis of which they could determine the characteristics of circular saws. A more recent Australian decision has refused to apply the doctrine to the mechanical failure of flashing lights at a level crossing: *Houston v Queensland Railways* [1995] Aust Torts Reports 81-324.

Thing must be under defendant's control

[13.25] The relevance of this requirement is that the accident must point to negligence on the defendant's part. Where the negligence must have been that of an employee of the defendant, there is no difficulty in holding the defendant liable, even though the particular employee may not be identified: *Grant v Australian Knitting Mills* [1936] AC 85. Nor does it help the defendant in this situation to show that it has taken care to eliminate risks by instituting a safe system, if the probability is of negligence in working that system: *Grant*; *Hill v Crowe* [1978] 1 All ER 812. On the other hand, there are difficulties if one or more of the presumed negligent persons is an independent contractor of the defendant, since vicarious liability for a contractor's negligence only applies in certain situations: see Chapter 14. If, however, the situation is one in which there is a non-delegable duty of care binding the employer, it makes no difference that the presumed negligence could be that of a contractor. A hospital, for example, owes a non-delegable duty of care in regard to the medical treatment of its patients.[6] Therefore, if something goes wrong in the course of an operation, pointing to negligence by someone engaged in its performance, it is not necessary for the plaintiff to identify the negligent person as a servant of the hospital rather than an independent contractor of the hospital (such as a surgeon).

---

[4]   See also *Fitzpatrick v Cooper* (1935) 54 CLR 200 – bag of plaster falling from skip on building.

[5]   Fleming, *Law of Torts* (9th ed, LBC Information Services, 1998), p 354 (pessimum exemplum).

[6]   Confirmed by the High Court in *Burnie Port Authority v General Jones Pty Ltd* (1994) 179 CLR 520.

Where the negligence established as probable could be that of one of several persons who are independent of each other, the plaintiff must show the likelihood that the negligence was that of a defendant to the action. In *Kilgannon v Sharpe Bros* (1986) 4 NSWLR 600 res ipsa loquitur was applied to establish negligence as regards an explosion of a bottle of soft drink. The court held that the plaintiff would be entitled to succeed against the bottler by showing a probability that a defect existed in the bottle at the time of bottling (whether caused by the manufacturer or the bottler itself) and that a careful system of bottle inspection would have detected the fault. Proof of these facts would clearly be insufficient against the manufacturer.

Actual cause of accident must not be known

[13.30] Where the cause of the accident is sufficiently established in the course of a trial, it is not possible for the plaintiff to rely on res ipsa loquitur. The proper course in this instance is for the court to determine whether it can conclude from the known facts that there was negligence by the defendant. In *Barkway v South Wales Transport* [1950] AC 185 the defendants' coach, containing passengers including the plaintiff's husband, had left the road and crashed, killing the husband. These facts by themselves would have called the principle into operation. However, the trial court determined that the cause of the accident was a burst tyre on the coach, so that the sole question became whether the plaintiff's evidence satisfied the court that there was defective maintenance of the vehicle by the defendants. The House of Lords found that the evidence established a faulty system of inspection by the defendants so that negligence was established. Inability to rely on res ipsa loquitur did not prejudice the plaintiff in this case, but in some cases it may do so. In *Nominal Defendant v Haslbauer* (1967) 117 CLR 448 the defendant drove her car into the back of the plaintiff's parked car. Res ipsa loquitur would normally apply in such a situation, but the defendant relied on the fact that her brakes failed immediately prior to the accident and there was evidence to support this contention. The High Court held that, if the defendant's brake failure was accepted by the jury as the cause of the accident, res ipsa loquitur did not apply. The plaintiff must show that the defendant was negligent despite the brake failure, or was to be held responsible in some way for the defective condition of the brakes. The plaintiff's action failed on this issue. The plaintiff, however, is not required to elect between reliance on direct proof of negligence and on res ipsa loquitur. If, for example, the plaintiff alleges and attempts to prove a certain explanation of the accident pointing to the defendant's negligence, he or she may still fall back on res ipsa loquitur if that attempt fails: *Anchor Products v Hedges* (1966) 115 CLR 493; *Jazairy v Najjar* [1998] Aust Torts Reports 81-478.

Effect of res ipsa loquitur applying

[13.35] The effect of res ipsa loquitur applying is to require the defendant to provide an explanation of the occurrence consistent with absence of negligence on the defendant's part. This the defendant may do in one of two ways: either by showing a cause of the occurrence for which he or she was not responsible, or by showing that the defendant took all reasonable care. The latter is merely a variant of the first method: care having been proved, it may be inferred the accident has another cause. But its limits have already been noted – it is not enough for the defendant to show the institution of a careful system designed to avoid accidents if the reasonable inference may be drawn that a person for whom the defendant is responsible was negligent in the operation of that system.

Res ipsa loquitur transfers a mere evidential burden of proof, rather than a legal burden, to the defendant.[7] The effect is that if, as a result of the defendant's explanation, the probabilities are equally balanced as between negligence and no negligence on the defendant's part, the defendant is entitled to succeed. There is authority based on decisions in jury trials that the defendant may be entitled to succeed even in the absence of any explanation on his or her part: *The Kite* [1933] P 154; *GIO v Fredrichberg* (1968) 118 CLR 403; *Fitzpatrick v Walter E Cooper Pty Ltd* (1935) 54. In a jury trial, the jury must be informed that res ipsa loquitur creates only a prima facie case of negligence by the defendant and in these circumstances it is legitimate for the jury to reject the case, even without explanation by the defendant. Where the trial is before a judge alone, however, this hardly seems possible. The judge can scarcely at one and the same time find that the defendant is required to provide an explanation and then find the defendant not negligent in the absence of an explanation.

The suggestion that the effect of res ipsa loquitur is to transfer a legal burden of proof to the defendant to prove itself not negligent rested on some unsatisfactory and inconclusive English authority: *Barkway v South Wales Transport* [1948] 2 All ER 460 at 471 per Asquith LJ (Court of Appeal); *Moore v Fox* [1956] 1 QB 596. This idea is inconsistent with principle, since it would create a difference between res ipsa loquitur and direct evidence of negligence, in the case of which it is clear that at no stage is there any transference of the legal burden of proof to the defendant. A Privy Council decision (*Ng Chun Put v Lee Chuen Tat* (1988) 132 Sol Journal 1244; [1988] RTR 298) was to the effect that when res ipsa loquitur applies, only an evidential burden passes to the defendant. And the New South Wales Court of Appeal's decision in *GIO v Best* [1993] Aust Torts Reports 81-210 has confirmed the trend of the earlier High Court authority in adopting that position. The "spillage" cases[8] also proceed on the basis that the defendant has only an evidential burden, although the opinion was expressed in them that it would be preferable to place a legal burden of proof on the defendant in accordance with the English position.[9] But the English position on this matter has changed in accordance with the Privy Council decision, and in any case the spillage cases raise difficulties of principle which require resolution by the High Court.

Two special problems

Spillage cases

[13.40] The various "spillage" cases[10] have caused problems both of principle and application. The evidentiary basis of these cases is that where the plaintiff has proved the presence of a dangerous substance on the floor of a supermarket or like place

---

[7]   Per Evatt J in *Davis v Bunn* (1936) 56 CLR 256 at 267-269; per Windeyer J in *Anchor Products v Hedges* (1966) 115 CLR 493 at 500; contra, Latham CJ in *Fitzpatrick v Cooper* (1935) 54 CLR 200 at 207-208.

[8]   That is, spillage on supermarket floors: *Brady v Girvan Bros* (1986) 7 NSWLR 241; *Sleiman v Franklin Food Stores* [1989] Aust Torts Reports 80-266; *Shoeys Pty Ltd v Allan* [1991] Aust Torts Reports 81-114.

[9]   See *Brady v Girvan Bros* (1986) 7 NSWLR 241 at 244; *Sleiman v Franklin Food Stores* [1989] Aust Torts Reports 80-266 at 68,828-68,829; *Shoeys Pty Ltd v Allan* [1991] Aust Torts Reports 81-114 at 68,941.

[10]   *Brady v Girvan Bros* (1986) 7 NSWLR 241; *Sleiman v Franklin Food Stores* [1989] Aust Torts Reports 80-266; *Shoeys Pty Ltd v Allan* [1991] Aust Torts Reports 81-114.

(and that injury to the plaintiff was suffered through slipping etc), the defendant must then lead evidence showing that a careful system of floor inspection was in force and operating at the relevant time. If the defendant discharges this burden, the plaintiff's case fails; but even if the defendant does not discharge this burden, the plaintiff may still fail for inability to establish causal connection between the injury and the presumed breach of duty (since the court must reach a conclusion as to how long the substance has been on the floor in order to decide whether a system of careful inspection would have removed it). If the court is unable to decide this, the plaintiff's action fails. The "spillage" cases are not true examples of res ipsa loquitur since the mere presence of the substance on the floor is not something which would not happen in the absence of negligence by the defendant. They must be regarded as concessions to the plaintiff, no doubt arising from the extreme difficulty of establishing negligence in this type of case. But their principle needs consideration by the High Court.

In some analogous situations, courts have been able to determine the issue of negligence because of other evidence before them. In *Staines v Commonwealth* [1991] Aust Torts Reports 81-106, the court was able to conclude that a concealed hole in some grass in an area used as access to playing fields had been in existence for some time because the grass in the hole was of the same height as the grass in the surrounding area. On the other hand, in *Gaetani v Christian Brothers* [1988] Aust Torts Reports 80-156, the court was able to conclude that a school bag, which was left on the floor of a school passage and on which the plaintiff tripped and injured himself, was left there immediately prior to the accident, since a master was actually in charge at the time and would have noticed the bag had it been there for any length of time.

Collisions between vehicles

[13.45] A collision between motor vehicles may occur in circumstances such that there is no independent evidence of negligence. For example, both drivers may have been killed and the position of the vehicles on the road leads to no inference as to who was to blame. In such a case the High Court in *Nesterczuk v Mortimore* (1965) 115 CLR 140, rejecting some English authority,[11] held that it is not possible to apply res ipsa loquitur to find both drivers equally at fault. On the other hand the circumstances may be such that joint equal fault may be inferred; for example "where a collision between two vehicles travelling in opposite directions on an otherwise empty road is known to have occurred in the centre of the road": Owen J at 158. This inference of joint equal fault on the part of both drivers was drawn by the High Court on the facts of *TNT Management Pty Ltd v Brooks* (1979) 23 ALR 345 in which both drivers were killed in a head-on collision and there were no independent witnesses. This, however, is not res ipsa loquitur but an inference of negligence drawn from the circumstances of the case.

Practice Questions

Revision Questions

13.1 In what ways may a defendant contest the plaintiff's action? Discuss.

13.2 In proof of negligence, discuss the burden of proof that confronts the plaintiff.

13.3 What conditions must subsist before res ipsa loquitur operates? Discuss.

---

11 *Baker v Market Harborough DC* [1953] 1 WLR 1472.

Answers to Practice Questions

13.1 The defendant may contest the plaintiff's action in one of three ways:

- by claiming that the plaintiff's statement of claim discloses no cause of action in tort (a demurrer). Since an issue of law is involved, the question cannot be resolved by reference to the burden of proof, although both parties must be heard on the issue of law.

- by denying the allegations of fact in the plaintiff's statement of claim (a traverse). If the defendant relies on this defence, there is no effect upon the burden of proof which remains with the plaintiff.

- by admitting the plaintiff's allegations of fact, and that they constitute a tort, and yet setting up other facts which in law constitute an excuse, for example self-defence rendering the defendant not liable in battery (confession and avoidance). The legal burden of proof in establishing the facts on which confession and avoidance is based rests with the defendant.

13.2 The plaintiff bears the legal burden of proof on all the issues involved in a negligence action; that is, on the issues of fact arising in relation to duty of care, breach of duty, and causation and remoteness of damage. The plaintiff in negligence must prove his or her case on the balance of probabilities. Proof of negligence may be by direct evidence (for example, eye-witness accounts) whether that of the parties to the case or of third parties; or by circumstantial evidence, where the court infers the probability or otherwise of negligence from the proof of certain facts.

13.3 The court in *Scott v London & St Katherine Docks* (1865) 3 H & C 595 laid down the following conditions for the operation of the doctrine:

- the accident must be such as would not happen in the normal course of events without negligence on the part of someone;

- the thing being under the control of the defendant, the facts point to negligence by the defendant or those for whom the defendant is responsible; and

- the actual cause of the accident must not be known.

Tutorial Questions

Discussion Questions

13.1 What is the defendant's responsibility in a res action? Discuss.

13.2 Discuss the procedural effect, if any, that a plaintiff gains from the use of res ipsa loquitur.

SECTION

4

Torts of Strict Liability

Torts of strict liability are torts that are capable of being committed without fault on the defendant's part. The defendant is therefore liable in the absence of intent, recklessness or negligence on their part.

There is no systematic principle of strict liability in tort in the common law, and no clear common ground among the various cases in which it arises.

Breach of statutory duty is a tort that applies most particularly in the industrial context, in that it is especially, though not exclusively, associated with statutory provisions imposing safety standards on employers for the protection of employees against personal injury. The statutory standards are generally an attempt to define what can reasonably be expected from employers in terms of protection, and quite often the tort merely operates as statutory negligence. But a non-negligent failure to comply with the statutory provision may be actionable, depending on the terms of the provision.

It is now accepted that the strict vicarious liability of employers for the torts of their employees is imposed for reasons of policy to be considered in Chapter 15. The vicarious liability imposed on employers for the torts of their independent contractors is rarely found and rests on the existence of a non-delegable duty of care binding the employer. Where such a non-delegable duty has been found, the difficult question (particularly acute under the present ruling in *Burnie Port Authority v General Jones Pty Ltd* (1994) 120 ALR 42) is what governs the imposition of such a duty.

Nuisance now seldom operates as a tort of strict liability. It is true that it requires unreasonable rather than negligent behaviour. But the vast majority of nuisances are committed knowingly, or at least negligently, so that in practical terms strict liability is unlikely to arise. But some isolated cases of genuine strict liability in nuisance may continue to exist.

Strict liability imposed on the keeper of a known dangerous animal for injury or damage it causes (whether the animal is of a known dangerous kind or the particular animal is known to be dangerous) is justified because of the extra-hazardous nature of the activity of keeping it. Strict liability for cattle-trespass, on the other hand, is justified by the fact that a system of mutual give-and-take, under which each person pays for damage inflicted by that person's cattle independently of fault, serves best the needs and wishes of the agricultural community.

The concept of an extra-hazardous activity was sometimes used to explain strict liability under the tort of *Rylands v Fletcher* (1868) LR 3 HL 330 for damage caused by the escape of dangerous things from the defendant's land, but that tort has been removed from Australian law by the High Court decision in *Burnie Port Authority*.

Strict liability as regards the defamatory content of a defamatory statement reflects the high degree of importance the law attaches to reputation.

As pointed out earlier in this book, torts such as trespass or conversion, although requiring an intentional invasion of the plaintiff's interest, may operate as torts of strict liability since at common law reasonable mistake is not a defence.

It should not be assumed that strict liability torts cannot be defended, or liability cannot be avoided once the defendant's conduct is found to be actionable. Defences such as voluntary assumption of risk, consent and act of God are available, but difficult to establish. While contributory negligence is not available as a defence to an action founded on strict liability (*Higgins v William Inglis & Son Pty Ltd* [1978] 1 NSWLR 649), it is available in limited circumstances for an action founded on breach of statutory duty. In the case of public authorities, a number of jurisdictions, as part of their reforms to the laws of negligence based on the Ipp recommendations, now provide statutory protection against a claim for damages for an alleged breach of statutory duty by a public authority in connection with the exercise of, or a failure to exercise, a function of the authority.[1]

---

[1]   ACT: *Civil Law (Wrongs) Act 2002*, Ch 8; NSW: *Civil Liability Act 2002*, Pt 5; Qld: *Civil Liability Act 2003*, Pt 3, Div 1; SA: *Civil Liability Act 1936*, Pt 6, Div 5 (limited to road authorities); Tas: *Civil Liability Act 2002*, Pt 9; Vic: *Wrongs Act 1958*, Pt XII; WA: *Civil Liability Act 2002*, Pt 1C.

CHAPTER 14

Breach of Statutory Duty

Reading

Sappideen, Vines, Grant and Watson, *Torts: Commentary and Materials*, Chapter 18.

Objectives

This chapter will explain:

- that a private action may be inferred from a statute;
- the elements necessary to establish a tort of breach of statutory duty;
- the defences available; and
- the effect of a statutory duty upon a plaintiff employee.

Principles

Inferring private cause of action from statute

[14.05] In certain circumstances, a plaintiff may succeed in an action in tort where he or she has suffered damage in consequence of the breach of a statutory duty imposed on the defendant. Two initial points need to be made:

- First, the law has never countenanced the position that the breach of every statutory duty gives rise to a cause of action in tort. Whether it does or does not do so is a matter of construction based upon the intention of the Parliament which enacted the statute. This does not cause a problem where the legislature has expressly manifested its intention that an action in tort should lie. In most cases, however, the statute is silent and here, the inference of intent must be drawn by the court. The courts have proved especially willing to allow the action in the case of the breach of industrial safety provisions in statutes and regulations, but have been much more reluctant to allow it in the case of other statutes.

- Second, it is important to realise that we are here concerned with the liability for failing to perform a statutory duty, not with an action for common law negligence arising from a failure to perform the duty.[1] The latter type of liability, which is available in relation to both statutory duties and powers, has already been considered in Chapter 8.

Case law on breach of an industrial safety provision proves illustrative when identifying typical features of the action for breach of statutory duty. The availability of the action is of considerable assistance to the plaintiff here. The statutory provision will often spell out in advance, and in considerable detail, the obligations of the defendant. If the plaintiff was confined to bringing an action in negligence the obligations of the defendant may well be less clear as the courts prefer a fact driven inquiry. True, the statute may merely detail what the court eventually would determine the defendant's obligations to be if negligence were the cause of action, but the very existence and application of the statute precludes argument as to what those obligations are and provides a firmer foundation for the argument of the plaintiff. There may be further advantages to the plaintiff in relying on breach of statutory duty. If liability for failure to comply with the statutory standard is strict (that is, it can be seen to amount to the imposition of an absolute duty), the defendant will not succeed by showing that it was impossible to have complied with it, still less that compliance with it was very difficult. *Doval v Anka Builders Pty Ltd* (1992) 28 NSWLR 1 illustrates the latter point. The employer in question was under a statutory duty to "maintain lighting ... sufficient for the illumination of all work places". Because of a general power failure, lights at the workplace failed for a period of ten minutes and during this period the plaintiff employee stumbled and fell on some steel mesh and was injured. The majority of the New South Wales Court of Appeal held the employers liable for breach of statutory duty. The statute clearly established an expectation of "sufficient" lighting and to ensure compliance with the statute a back-up lighting system should have been provided. The assertion by the employer that this would have involved inordinate expense being

---

[1] *Millard v Serck Tubes Ltd* [1969] 1 WLR 211.

dismissed, one of the considerations of the calculus of negligence became irrelevant (see [10.40]ff) and breach easier to satisfy.

Breach of statutory duty is a hybrid: it is not necessarily a tort of strict liability though it often operates as one. The nature of liability turns on the interpretation of the relevant statutory provisions. Thus, as demonstrated by the industrial safety cases, there is a spectrum of possibilities. At one end of the spectrum there is a liability which is just about absolute (where a strict duty is imposed to provide some safety measure which the standard of reasonableness in the tort of negligence would not require).[2] At the other end of the spectrum sit the cases where the duty is indistinguishable from a common law duty to take care or is an even lesser obligation: *Bux v Slough Metals* [1973] 1 WLR 1358.

Requirements

[14.10] In any action for breach of statutory duty, the starting point in determining whether there is a cause of action lies in ascertaining the intention of Parliament, that is, did it intend to confer a civil remedy in tort for its breach? This is a question of construction. If it appears that Parliament did intend to confer such a right, the requirements of the tort of breach of statutory duty are then essentially the same as those of the tort of negligence: there must be a duty, a breach of that duty and damage resulting from that breach. Nevertheless, the statutory overlay upon the action for breach of statutory duty makes the two torts readily distinguishable; interpretation of the statute is necessary at all points in the tort of breach of statutory duty in order to determine the success of the plaintiff's action. Bearing this in mind, the essential features of the tort are as set out in Figure 14.1.

Figure 14.1: Breach of statutory duty – elements

- Statutory duty in question must have been expresssly **intended** by Parliament to confer a civil remedy in tort for its breach.
- The **duty** must be laid upon the **defendant** and the defendant must be in breach of that duty.
- The plaintiff is within the class of persons who are intended to be protected by the statute.
- Plaintiff must be a person within the **protection** of the statute.
- Damage that the plaintiff has suffered must be **caused** by the defendant.

Each of these elements depends upon construction of the statute.

---

[2] See, eg, *Peitsos v Hamandos* [1984] Aust Torts Reports 80-524; *Transfield Pty Ltd v Fallavolita* (1984) 154 CLR 431; *Doval v Anka Builders Pty Ltd* (1992) 28 NSWLR 1.

Was statute intended to confer civil remedy in tort?

[14.15] The leading authority on this matter in Australia is the judgment of Dixon J in *O'Connor v S P Bray Ltd* (1937) 56 CLR 464[3] at 478 in which he said:

> *Where there is a provision prescribing a specific precaution for the safety of others in a matter where the person upon whom the duty is laid is, under the general law of negligence, bound to exercise due care, the duty will give rise to a correlative private right, unless from the nature of the provision or from the scope of the legislation of which it forms part a contrary intention appears.*

Kitto J suggested that the correct approach when determining whether a failure to comply with a statutory provision gives a right to a private cause of action in *Sovar v Henry Lane Pty Ltd* (1967) 116 CLR 397 at 405 was to consider the document in the light of all its surrounding circumstances.

This presumptive intention approach explains the general availability of the action in relation to statutory duties concerning industrial safety, but is not limited to duties of that sort. For example, in *JD Bell Ltd v Shortland CC* [1991] Aust Torts Reports 81-139, it was held, applying the Dixon J formulation, that a statutory duty to prevent an aerial conductor from coming into contact with trees created a civil right of action in favour of a person whose property was damaged by a fire (which would not have occurred had the duty been properly performed). A different approach to *Bell* is seen in those cases which have denied a remedy for breach of statutory duty on the ground that the statutory duty is for the protection of the public generally, rather than a particular class of it: *Evenden v Manning MC* (1930) 30 SR (NSW) 52 (in which no action lay for failing to attach a lifeboat to a ferry punt). So, for example, the cause of action has been denied where the statute is aimed against the creation of dangers in the highway (*Dennis v Brownlee* [1964] NSWR 455; *Tassone v Metropolitan Water Board* [1971] 1 NSWLR 207) or is by way of road or air traffic regulation: *Tucker v McCann* [1948] VLR 222; *Abela v Giew* (1965) 65 SR (NSW) 485; *Martin v Queensland Airlines Pty Ltd* [1956] St R Qd 362.

The court has also denied the existence of a remedy for breach of statutory duty in cases where a common law duty of care is already in existence, and it is inappropriate to add to that duty, a duty of strict obligation which would run directly counter to the principles laid down by Dixon J. An example is *Hopewell v Baranyay* [1962] VR 311,[4] in which no action lay for breach of a statutory duty, where regulations required that no person should drive a car which was not in good mechanical condition, since the common law should not be extended by creating a strict obligation. On the other hand, the courts' refusal to find that statutory duties of a general nature give rise to a civil cause of action[5] is justified by the express formulation in *O'Connor*. So too is the courts' refusal to find a cause of action where no common law duty of care exists, or is dubious. Thus, in *Grand Central Car Park Pty Ltd v Tivoli Freeholders* [1969] VR 62 it was held that

---

[3]   See also *McDonald (t/as B E McDonald Transport) v Girkaid Pty Ltd* [2004] Aust Torts Reports 81-768.

[4]   Compare, however, *Anderson v McKellar CC* (1968) 69 SR (NSW) 444 – ordinance requiring underpinning of land gave rise to a cause of action since it extended the common law right to support of buildings.

[5]   *Smith v Macquarie Stevedoring Co* (1965) 8 FLR 435 – general duty to ensure safety of stevedoring operations was not a specific precaution as required by Dixon J in *O'Connor v Bray*; *Bennett v Orange CC* (1967) 67 SR (NSW) 426, *X v Bedfordshire CC* [1995] 3 All ER 353 – social welfare legislation imposing wide discretionary powers and duties on councils did not give a right of action for breach of statutory duty to children affected by the actions of the council in question.

no action for breach of statutory duty lay for running an unlicensed car park thereby causing loss to a licensed competitor.[6] And in *Byrne v Australian Airlines Ltd* (1995) 185 CLR 410, the High Court decided that provisions of the *Industrial Relations Act 1988* (Cth), which imposed a penalty for breach of an award, did not create a cause of action for damages for breach of statutory duty as its scope and purpose did not disclose any intention to benefit or protect employees or any other class of persons by conferring on them a right of action for breach of statutory duty (in this case breach of an award obligation).[7] On the other hand, a successful action was brought in *Monk v Warbly* [1935] 1 KB 75 for breach of statutory duty on the part of a motorist in failing to have third party insurance on his car; also in *Owen v Kojonup* [1965] WAR 3 against an authority for failing to insure a firefighter against economic loss arising from injury in the course of firefighting.[8]

Statutory duty laid upon defendant

[14.20] An action for breach of statutory duty will only lie against the party upon whom the legislation places a duty to take a specific precaution or measures for the benefit of others.[9] Where the statutory duty is laid by the statute upon an employer who is the defendant in the case (for example, the employer of a worker), there is no problem. Where it is interpreted to lie upon an employee, the High Court has held that vicarious liability on the part of the employer does not exist: *Darling Island Stevedoring v Long* (1957) 97 CLR 36. The issue of whether there should be vicarious liability here is considered in Chapter 16. The problem of an employee injured by reason of his or her own breach of statutory duty is considered at [14.55].

Breach of duty

[14.25] The question of breach of statutory duty begins with a consideration of the relevant statutory provision. Where the statutory duty is interpreted as being strict (that is, as imposing an absolute duty) the defendant's breach will be established without showing any sort of fault on their part. So, in *Galashiels Gas Co v Miller* [1949] AC 275 it was held that the defendants' statutory duty to maintain a lift in good repair was a strict one. When the lift fell to the bottom of the shaft and injured the plaintiff, the defendants were liable, even though no fault on their part was established. A similar decision was reached by the Victorian court in *Kirkpatrick v Lewis Construction* [1964] VR 515. In *John Summers v Frost* [1955] AC 740[10] it was held that the duty to securely fence "every dangerous part of any machinery" was a strict one. The employers were in breach of that duty in failing to fence a grindstone even though the effect of fencing

---

[6]   In fact private actions are generally not available for a breach of a statute which requires the defendant to be licensed: *Leask Timber and Hardware Pty Ltd v Thorne* (1961) 106 CLR 33.

[7]   In fact an examination of the Act reveals a contrary intention by providing a means for the enforcement of awards which does not contemplate the existence of private rights enforceable by way of an action for damages.

[8]   But see also *Richardson v Pitt Starley* [1995] 2 WLR 26 – failure by directors to effect compulsory insurance against injury to employees did not give rise to an action for breach of statutory duty by an injured employee.

[9]   *O'Connor v SP Bray Ltd* (1937) 56 CLR 464; *John Pfeiffer Pty Ltd v Canny* (1981) 148 CLR 218.

[10]   Although in the common law action for negligence this would be a relevant consideration: *Retsas v Commonwealth* (1976) 44 ALJR 52.

CHAPTER 14

the machine was to make it unusable. Australian case law suggests that the duty to fence or guard dangerous machinery is strict: *Bouronicos v Nylex* [1975] VR 120. A breach was established in that case even though the plaintiff worker had prematurely removed a protective guard on a piece of machinery. These cases may be compared with *Austral Bronze Company Pty Ltd v Ajaka* (1970) 44 ALJR 740. The High Court held there, that a statutory provision for the floors of a factory to be maintained "in good order, condition and repair" did not impose a strict duty on the defendant in relation to the removal of oil or grease on the floor, but merely a duty to take reasonable care. Generalisations beyond the significance of the interpretation of the statute are almost impossible in this area. All will depend upon the interpretation given by the court to the particular provision in the light of the given circumstances.

It is important to recognise that a statutory duty will not always be strict. The addition of the words "so far as reasonably practicable" to the employer's duty is a clear indication that a strict duty is not imposed: *Australian Oil Refining Pty Ltd v Bourne* (1980) 54 ALJR 192; *Levesley v Thomas Firth* [1953] 1 WLR 1206.[11] Even so, the burden of showing impracticability rests on the employer: *Kingshott v Goodyear Tyre & Rubber Co Australia Ltd (No 2)* (1987) 8 NSWLR 707; *Slivak v Lurgi (Australia) Pty Ltd* (2001) 205 CLR 304. But the more specific the statutory obligation, the more likely it is that the court will infer that it was intended to confer a private right of action: *McDonald (t/as BE McDonald Transport) v Girkaid Pty Ltd* [2004] Aust Torts Reports 81-768; [2004] NSWCA 297.

The court must be satisfied that the statutory language as precisely interpreted, applies to the case before it. So in *Eaves v Morris Motors* [1961] 2 QB 285,[12] the plaintiff failed to show a breach of the fencing requirement in s 14(1) of the *Factories Act 1937* (UK) since that requires only the fencing of dangerous parts of machinery and not of materials that are inserted into the machines. Under the same section, there is no duty to fence when what is dangerous is the machine as a whole and not its parts; otherwise there would be a duty to fence motor vehicles.

Plaintiff must be within statutory protection

[14.30] There are two facets of this rule:

(a) the plaintiff must show that he or she is one of those persons for whose benefit the statutory provision was enacted; and

(b) the harm suffered must be of the type against which the statute was intended to guard.

---

[11]   In *Slivak v Lurgi (Australia) Pty Ltd* (2001) 205 CLR 304, all members of the High Court held that a provision of the *Occupational Health, Safety & Welfare Act 1986* (SA), which turned on the phrase "ensure so far as reasonably practicable", created a private cause of action (at [27]–[29] per Gleeson CJ, Gummow and Hayne JJ, at [50] per Gaudron J, at [87] per Callinan J). For other non-absolute duties, see *Milankovic v Discount Manufacturers Pty Ltd* [1974] 2 NSWLR 1 – duty to stack goods in a manner "which will best ensure their stability"; *Waugh v Kippen* (1986) 160 CLR 156 – duty to ensure adult employees did not have to lift excess weight; *McDonald (t/as BE McDonald Transport) v Girkaid Pty Ltd* [2004] Aust Torts Reports 81-768; [2004] NSWCA 297 – duty under the *Dangerous Goods Act* and Regulations where the Regulations required the defendant to take "all practicable steps" and "all practicable precautions" sufficiently identified specific precautions or measures to support the conclusion that, taken with the purpose of the dangerous goods legislation, those regulations created a private cause of action.

[12]   But cf *Dairy Farmers Co-op Ltd v Azar* (1990) 170 CLR 293 where the relevant Act required the defendant to securely fence "all dangerous parts of the machinery". The High Court noted that the Act used the broader word "machinery" instead of "machines", which meant that if any part of the machinery (that is, part of the machine or the machine itself) was dangerous then it had to be fenced.

Both questions again raise issues of statutory interpretation. The question as to whether the plaintiff falls within the ambit of the protection provided by the legislation is distinct from that of whether the statute was intended to create a cause of action in tort. The latter question may be answered in the affirmative and yet the plaintiff may be found to be incapable of suing if he or she does not fall within a sufficiently defined class protected by the legislation. In *Hartley v Mayoh* [1954] 1 QB 383 the plaintiff fireman was electrocuted in fighting a fire at the defendants' factory and this had happened because of the faulty state of the wiring in the factory, this being a breach by the defendants of their duty under factory legislation. The defendants, nonetheless, were held not liable for breach of statutory duty since the legislation expressly referred to the risk of bodily injury to "persons employed" and the plaintiff was not such a person. So, also, an independent contractor was denied recovery in breach of statutory duty on the ground that he was not a "workman employed" by the defendant: *Herbert v Harold Shaw* [1959] 2 QB 138. Where the statute itself does not limit the ambit of the duty, the duty has been held to extend to persons generally: *Bonser v County & Suburban Stock Feed Pty Ltd* [1964-65] NSWR 1749 (in which a duty to fence extended to all persons lawfully working in the factory including the plaintiff, an employee of a sub-contractor); *Quilty v Bellambi Coal Co Pty Ltd* (1966) 67 SR (NSW) 193 (similar).

If the plaintiff is within the protected class, it does not matter that he or she was acting outside the course of the employment; nor that the plaintiff was trespassing upon the employer's machinery or premises: *Smith v Supreme Wood Pulp* [1968] 3 All ER 753; *Uddin v Associated Portland Cement* [1965] 2 All ER 582; *Westwood v Post Office* [1974] AC 4. Such conduct may, of course, give rise to a reduction of damages for contributory negligence.[13] However, in *Westwood* no deduction was made where the plaintiff had trespassed into a part of his employer's premises, since such trespass did not indicate lack of reasonable care for his own safety.

In relation to the type of harm, the leading case of *Gorris v Scott* (1874) LR 9 Ex 125 laid down the rule that the harm that occurs must be that which the statute is designed to prevent, that is "within the contemplation of the statute". It is not enough to show that the harm suffered was a reasonably foreseeable consequence of the breach of statutory duty. In that case, the defendant was transporting the plaintiff's sheep on his ship. He had infringed a statutory order under which the animals were to be divided into pens. The sheep were washed overboard and drowned and it was found that this would not have occurred had the defendant performed his statutory duty to pen the sheep. Nevertheless, the plaintiff's action for breach of statutory duty failed. The purpose of the penning order was to prevent the spread of disease, not to prevent animals being washed overboard. There have been numerous applications of the rule. In *Mummery v Irvings Pty Ltd* (1956) 96 CLR 99 it was held that the purpose of requiring the fencing of a circular saw was to prevent human contact with the blades, not to prevent pieces of wood being flung out in the sawing process. The plaintiff, who was unable to establish negligence, was therefore also unable to succeed in a claim for breach of statutory duty in relation to an eye injury sustained when a piece of wood was emitted from the defendants' unfenced saw. Also, in *Graham v Mascot Galvanising Works Pty Ltd* [1965] NSWR 1402 it was held that the purpose of requiring fencing of vats, pans and tanks was not to prevent the escape of liquids. Where the precise harm against which the statute is intended to guard occurs, the defendant is unlikely to succeed in an argument

---

[13]   As in *Uddin* where there was an 80% reduction of damages.

that it occurred in an unforeseeable way. The principle established in *Hughes v Lord Advocate* [1963] AC 837 applies. For example, in *Millard v Serck Tubes* [1969] 1 WLR 211,[14] the plaintiff's arm was caught in a machine which the defendants, in breach of their statutory duty, had failed to fence. The defendants were held liable, although the way in which the plaintiff's arm became caught in the machine was not foreseeable.

Damage in action for breach of statutory duty

[14.35] Actual damage, in the form of personal injury or damage to property, for example, is a necessary ingredient of an action for breach of statutory duty in the *majority* of cases, and particularly in relation to actions brought by workers against employers for breach of industrial safety regulations. This does not, however, operate as a universal rule as demonstrated in *Ashby v White* (1704) 2 Ld Raym 938; 92 ER 126 where an interference with the plaintiff's right to vote was in that case sufficient to ground the action. With respect to the awarding of damages, *Collings Constructions Co Pty Ltd v ACCC* (1998) 43 NSWLR 131 suggests that aggravated damages may be awarded for breach of statutory duty.[15]

Defences

Voluntary assumption of risk

[14.40] Voluntary assumption of risk (or "volenti non fit injuria") is not a defence to an action by a worker for breach of statutory duty laid upon the employer: *Wheeler v New Merton Board Mills* [1933] 2 KB 669. Policy demands that employers should not be able to contract out of the performance of their statutory duties by agreement, contractual or otherwise, with employees. Where, however, the statutory duty is laid on an employee, volenti is a defence to a claim for breach of statutory duty by that employee, where the plaintiff has consented to the breach, and was not in a position of subordination to the employee who committed the breach: *ICI v Shatwell* [1965] AC 656 (though only mentioned in obiter dicta). This makes little difference in Australia, where the employer itself is not vicariously liable for the breach other than in New South Wales.[16]

Contributory negligence

[14.45] Contributory negligence may operate as a partial defence in all States and the Northern Territory for breach of statutory duty, and in each case it will be a matter of

---

[14] There are suggestions, however, in the judgments of Lords Reid and Diplock in *Boyle v Kodak Ltd* [1969] 1 WLR 661 that the plaintiff need only establish causal connection between the breach of a statutory duty and his injury. See also *Millard v Serck Tubes Ltd* [1969] 1 WLR 211.

[15] But cf *Cullen v Chief Constable of the Royal Ulster Constabulary* [2004] 2 All ER 237.

[16] *Darling Island Stevedoring v Long* (1956-57) 97 CLR 36. In New South Wales, s 7 of the *Law Reform (Vicarious Liability) Act 1983* provides that an employer will be vicariously liable in respect of any tort committed by employees while carrying out an "independent function" in the course of their employment or incidental to the employer's business. "Independent function" is broadly defined in s 5(1) as a function conferred or imposed on an employee by common law or statute. Section 10 further provides that any statutory exemption from liability available to an employee is to be disregarded when considering the vicarious liability of the employer.

fact taking into account all the relevant circumstances in each case.[17] The operation of the defence is limited by the need to have regard to the fact that the worker should not be held contributorily negligent for momentary error or inattention in the performance of a routine task.[18] Apportionment legislation in all State and Territory jurisdictions applies to reduce damages for the plaintiff's contributory negligence.[19]

Statutory defence

[14.50] Where the breach of a statutory duty is the basis for a civil action for damages, and the statute contains a statutory defence, it does not automatically follow that the statutory defence will be available to a defendant in a civil action. The defendant who wishes to rely on such a statutory defence must be able to establish that it was not only intended to exonerate them from criminal liability but also prevented a civil action from arising.[20]

In the case of a public authority, a number of jurisdictions have provided statutory protection to public authorities where it has been alleged that there has been a breach of statutory duty in connection with the exercise of, or a failure to exercise, a function of the authority.[21] Liability will continue to arise where there is an absolute duty to do or not to do a particular thing but in all other cases it is a defence for a public authority to show that the act or omission in all the circumstances was a reasonable exercise of their functions.[22]

Statutory duty of plaintiff employee

[14.55] Where the statutory duty is laid upon the plaintiff employee, who is injured through breaching it, *Darling Island Stevedoring v Long* (1957) 97 CLR 36 is authority for the proposition that this is enough to hold the employer not liable to the plaintiff, since there is no vicarious liability for the plaintiff's breach of statutory duty in these circumstances.[23] The action for breach of statutory duty lies only against the person upon whom the duty is imposed. But there is another reason for holding the plaintiff

CHAPTER 14

---

17   *Kakouris v Gibbs Burge & Co Pty Ltd* (1970) 44 ALJR 384; cf *Sherman v Nymboida Colliery Ltd* (1963) 109 CLR 580, but note that the court had to decide one way or the other between the defendant and plaintiff, contributory negligence being no defence to an action for breach of statutory duty in New South Wales. Now that this defence is available, similar facts would produce an apportionment of damage between defendant and plaintiff.

18   *Sungravure Pty Ltd v Meani* (1964) 110 CLR 24; *Davies v Adelaide Chemical and Fertilizer Co Ltd* (1946) 74 CLR 541; *Piro v W Foster & Co Ltd* (1943) 68 CLR 313.

19   The apportionment legislation applies to "wrongs" which include actions for breach of statutory duty: ACT: *Civil Law (Wrongs) Act 2002*, ss 101, 102(2); NT: *Law Reform (Miscellaneous Provisions) Act 1992*, s 15; NSW: *Law Reform (Miscellaneous Provisions) Act 1965*, s 8 and *Workers Compensation Act 1987*, s 151N(3); Qld: *Law Reform Act 1995*, s 5; SA: *Law Reform (Contributory Negligence and Apportionment of Liability) Act 2001*, ss 3, 4(c); Tas: *Wrongs Act 1954*, s 2; WA: *Law Reform (Contributory Negligence and Tortfeasors' Contribution) Act 1947*, s 3.

20   In *Sovar v Henry Lane Pty Ltd* (1967) 116 CLR 397 a majority of the High Court held that the statutory defence only protected the defendant from criminal liability.

21   The standard is that of a reasonable statutory authority instead of the reasonable person: ACT: *Civil Law (Wrongs) Act 2002*, ss 111, 112; NSW: *Civil Liability Act 2002*, ss 43, 44; Qld: *Civil Liability Act 2003*, ss 35, 36; Tas: *Civil Liability Act 2002*, ss 38-41; Vic: *Wrongs Act 1958*, ss 83-85; WA: *Civil Liability Act 2002*, ss 5W-5Y.

22   In *Great Lakes Shire Council v Dederer* [2006] Aust Torts Reports 81-860; [2006] NSWCA 101, one of the issues was whether the Council, in failing to exercise its enforcement powers, had acted so unreasonably that it gave rise to civil liability under the *Civil Liability Act 2002* (NSW). The court considered that, taking into account all the circumstances, the failure by the Council to enforce the prohibition signs was not unreasonable and that the Council could rely on the protection provided under the legislation.

23   In the UK Court of Appeal case of *Majrowski v Guy's & St Thomas's NHS Trust* [2005] IRLR 340, the court held that an employer could be vicariously liable for the harassment of an employee by his supervisor in breach of the *Protection for Harassment Act 1997* (UK). The conduct of the supervisor was sufficiently closely connected to the employment and there was nothing in the statute which negated the court from finding vicarious liability.

unable to recover damages in this case, which is that the plaintiff is in effect suing him or herself: there is no breach on the part of the employer which is not equally that of the plaintiff. The force of this reasoning applies in two other situations to which *Darling Island Stevedoring* is not applicable. The first is where the statutory duty is laid upon both the plaintiff employee and the employer, but is breached by the action of the employee. *Ginty v Belmont Building Supplies* [1959] 1 All ER 414 held that in these circumstances the plaintiff's action against the employer failed. The second situation is where the statutory duty is laid upon the employer but performance of it is delegated to the plaintiff. An example is *Shedlizki v Bronte Bakery* (1970) 92 WN (NSW) 151. In this case the statutory duty in question lay upon a company of which the plaintiff employee was controlling shareholder and managing director. It was held by the majority that the plaintiff could not succeed against the company for breach of statutory duty, since for that breach the plaintiff was wholly responsible. It was successfully argued that the actions of the plaintiff could not be distinguished from that of the defendant but in *Andar Transport Pty Ltd v Brambles Ltd* (2004) 217 CLR 424 the High Court agreed with the dissenting observations of Mason JA that the company was a legal entity and distinct from its plaintiff.[24]

Apportionment of damage for contributory negligence will not be available where, as *Ginty* put it, the injury was not partly the fault of the plaintiff and partly that of the defendant, as required by the contributory negligence legislation, but wholly the fault of both (fault being defined in the contributory negligence legislation to include breach of statutory duty). On the other hand, where there is some independent fault on the part of the employer, the proper result is an apportionment of damage between the parties. In *Ross v Associated Portland Cement Manufacturers Ltd* [1964] 1 WLR 768,[25] where the defendants had delegated to the plaintiff employee their statutory duty of making safe a work fence, they were held liable for two-thirds of the relevant compensation for injuries received by the plaintiff through failing to make the fence safe. The ground for this decision was that the delegation had been made without proper instructions being given to the plaintiff, who was not fully qualified for the task. The House of Lords in *Boyle v Kodak Ltd* [1969] 1 WLR 661 established another case of independent fault on the part of an employer, where there had been a failure to instruct the employee as to the steps to be taken to avoid the commission of a breach of statutory duty binding both employer and employee.[26]

It also appears that if the actions of the employee put the employer in breach and nothing could have been done by the employer to stop the employee from disobeying instructions, the negligent employee will be unable to recover damages in such circumstances.[27]

---

[24]   In *Andar's* case, the High Court found that Andar Transport had failed to take reasonable steps to ensure that the loading and unloading by an employee, Wall, who was one of the employer's two directors, was carried out in a safe manner. See also *Texcrete Pty Ltd v Khavin* [2003] NSWCA 337 where the first respondent was employed to fix a piece of machinery and this could only be done with the guard removed which was in breach of the occupier's statutory duty; the court concluded that the occupier's removal of the guard implicitly invited that plaintiff to test the machine with the guard off with the result that the respondent was in breach of their statutory duty (although the plaintiff's damages might be reduced in such circumstances for contributory negligence).

[25]   *Tonelli v Electric Power Transmissions Pty Ltd* [1967] 1 NSWR 584; *Armstrong v Virenius* (1981) 58 FLR 77.

[26]   Mason J in *H C Buckman v Flanagan* (1974) 133 CLR 422 at 441-443 thought that the basis of the rule in *Ginty* and similar decisions was to avoid absurdity.

[27]   In *Sherman v Nymboida Collieries Pty Ltd* (1963) 109 CLR 580, the plaintiff was the mine deputy with responsibility to check whether ventilation in the mine was sufficient to dispel any gas. The plaintiff was found dead in the mine with a lamp and a cigarette lighter beside it following an explosion. The mine owner was held not liable because there was no causal connection between acts or omissions of the mine owner and the plaintiff's injuries when the plaintiff's conduct in apparently lighting a cigarette lighter in a gas filled area was

Guide to Problem Solving

TORT OF BREACH OF STATUTORY DUTY

NB: This action is often pleaded with negligence.

In taking an action for tort of breach of statutory duty, the following process should be adopted:

1. **Is there a right to sue?**
   - This is an interpretative exercise.
   - Are there other actions available: does negligence provide an adequate action? [Negligence has been found to be adequate for road accidents.]
   - There is a presumption that there is a private action intended in relation to safety issues.
   - There is a presumption that if the Act provides a remedy then a private action was not intended.
   - What was the purpose of the Act? Perhaps the Second Reading Bill or Notes to the Bill may help.
   - Policy considerations.

2. **Is the statutory duty laid on the defendant?**
   - An action only lies against the person upon whom the duty is imposed by the statute.
   - If the duty is owed by the employer then that person will be vicariously liable for the employees; however, if one of the employees is the person nominated by the statute, then the employer is not vicariously liable: see *Darling Island Stevedoring v Long* (1957) 97 CLR 36.

3. **Has the duty been breached?**
   - This depends on the preciseness of the standard in the words of the statute.
   - If the legislation imposes an absolute duty then it does not matter if the plaintiff has taken reasonable care or not.
   - However, if the statute requires a "reasonable standard" then it is up to the defendant to show that the obligation has been satisfied.

4. **Is the plaintiff a member of the protected class?**
   - What is the protected class? And is the plaintiff one of those?
   - Courts are more likely to allow a private action when the legislation is meant to protect a particular class of person as opposed to where the protection is for the public benefit.

5. **Was the statute directed at preventing the kind of harm suffered by the plaintiff?**

6. **Has the plaintiff's damage been caused by the breach?**
   - The plaintiff needs to have suffered personal injury, property damage or an inference with a right.

---

taken into account. It was the separate and independent act of the employee that brought about the liability. In this case, the employee was the one responsible for ensuring that the statutory duty was fulfilled, that is to say, making sure that the mine was properly ventilated. See also *Millington v Wilkie Plumbing Services* (2005) 62 NSWLR 322; [2005] NSWCA 45 where the employee was injured performing an act which the employer had expressly prohibited him from doing, causing the employer to breach their statutory duty. The court found that by performing the act, the employee was also breaching his statutory duty and as the employee was alone at the time, and there was nothing that the employer could have done to stop him from disobeying orders, the employee was unable to recover damages.

- The damage needs to have been caused by the defendant's breach (similar principles to those in negligence). In this respect there may be an intervening act.
7. **Are there any defences available to the defendant?**
   - Volenti non fit injuria.
   - Contributory negligence.
   - Statutory defences.

Practice Questions

Revision Questions

14.1 Do all statutes confer on plaintiffs a civil right to sue?

14.2 Do you think it is more difficult to prove a tort of breach of statutory duty as compared to negligence?

Problem Questions

14.1 Ork Ward is an employee of Captain Cook Cruises, a business operating only in Queensland. Ork is a deck hand on "MV Heave", a ferry which transports passengers and cars between Brisbane and Southport. The journey takes two days. All the employees are employed on a 28 days on and 28 days off roster. While the employees are on duty they live on board. During their days off they return to their homes. Ork lives in Brisbane.

Since the employees spend a lot of time on board, Captain Cook Cruises tries to encourage them to exercise. Up until six months ago there was a gymnasium on the ship, but due to the need to make the business more viable this has been converted into more car spaces. However, in response to an industrial dispute between the employees and Captain Cook Cruises, there is an arrangement whereby private gym facilities in Brisbane are paid for by Captain Cook Cruises. In this respect Captain Cook Cruises is subject to the *Workplace Health and Safety (Miscellaneous) Regulations 1995* (Qld) which provide as follows:

> *Fitness for duty — recognition of working in confined spaces*
> **333.** An employer or self-employed person who has employees who work in confined spaces must ensure that they are fit to carry out the tasks assigned to them. This may mean that certain equipment should be provided at their workplace to allow them to exercise.

The "MV Heave" arrived in Southport ahead of schedule on 4 June and since Ork had completed all his duties, he decided to go for a jog. The ferry was due to depart on its return journey to Brisbane later that evening. While it was not the practice of the employees to go jogging in between trips, Ork felt he had to get some exercise as he had been feeling tense and "hemmed in". Ork has an invigorating run, but just as he is about to run up the gangplank onto the "MV Heave" he collapses, gasping for breath. Later, a doctor at the Southport Hospital diagnoses Ork as suffering from an asthmatic condition that is triggered by stress.

Advise Ork. NB: Only consider the tort of breach of statutory duty.

Answer to Practice Questions

Revision Questions

14.1 No. Some statutes include a right to sue so they expressly give that right, but many statutes are silent on whether or not a person has a right to sue. In the case of the latter a plaintiff, in claiming the tort of breach of statutory duty, must first show that the statute implies such a right. This is achieved by an interpretive process taking into account the purpose of the Act.

14.2 In both negligence and the tort of breach of statutory duty, the plaintiff will need to prove duty, breach of that duty and damage caused by the breach that is not too remote. But the tort of breach of statutory duty requires more initially. Before these elements are considered the plaintiff must first of all establish that the statute confers this right and that the Act applies to the plaintiff. The construction of the relevant legislation is of particular importance and each of the elements must be considered in this light. Where there is a strict liability the hurdle of breach is passed with ease and elements which are relevant in an action in negligence become irrelevant (refer discussion at [14.05] regarding the calculus of negligence and expense and/or difficulty of protecting against the risk).

Problem Questions

14.1 The section of the Act applies to Ork since he is an employee who is required to work in confined spaces.

Is there a right to sue? This is really a question of construction or interpretation. The answer depends on a consideration of the Act and the circumstances in which it was enacted. Certain presumptions apply in relation to this question. It seems that if the Act is concerned with safety then it may be presumed that a private right of action applies. This presumption was established in *O'Connor v S P Bray Ltd* (1937) 56 CLR 464. However there is another presumption that operates here. If the Act creates an obligation, penalty or other enforcement mechanism then the courts will presume that the statute has provided the sanction and that it was not intended that there should be a private action for individuals: *Doe d Murray, Lord Bishop of Rochester v Bridges* (1831) B&Ad 847. On the facts provided there does not appear to be any penalty included in the Act which concerns safety matters and therefore it could be argued that a right to sue can be implied.

Is the duty laid on the defendant? The Act imposes the duty on the employer and so Captain Cook Cruises would be responsible.

Is the duty breached? The Act requires that certain equipment may need to be provided for employees who work in confined spaces. The wording of the section does not impose an absolute duty. The words used are quite general and it could be argued that the word "may" allows the employer some discretion and so the standard is that ordinarily used in negligence: that the employer should do whatever is reasonable in the circumstances. However, the section also says that employees need to be kept fit and suggests that to do this the employer may need to provide certain equipment at the workplace. We see from the facts that Captain Cook Cruises tries to encourage employees to exercise and that up until six months ago there was a gymnasium on the ship. However, this has now been removed because of economic pressures. The company has provided private gym facilities in Brisbane but this provides only a partial solution. It could be argued then that the duty has been breached. The standard once set by Captain Cook Cruises when it had a gym on board suggests that it saw that that was what it had to do, and now that is no longer available.

Is the plaintiff a member of the protected class? Ork is an employee and he does work in a confined space and so he is part of the class that the Act is trying to protect.

Was the statute directed at preventing the kind of harm suffered by the plaintiff? Ork has been "feeling tense and 'hemmed in'" and, as a result of that, went for a run. He then collapsed and was diagnosed as "suffering from an asthmatic condition that is triggered by stress". It would seem that the Act is trying to guard against this kind of harm (employees feeling trapped in the confined space and then needing to take some action to improve their fitness). It could be said that the feeling of being confined might produce some psychological concerns, as opposed to an asthmatic attack. Yet alternatively, asthma has been suggested to be the result of stress.

Has the plaintiff's damage been caused by the breach and is the damage not too remote? Because there was no gym on board Ork had to take a run and the run directly caused his illness. The asthma attack is the kind of harm that could be reasonably foreseen as occurring.

Defences? There is no real evidence of contributory negligence but perhaps it could be argued that he had over-exerted himself in that he had undertaken a much longer run than he could adequately cope with.

Conclusion It would seem that Ork could establish that Captain Cook Cruises did breach its statutory duty and therefore he should be awarded damages.

Tutorial Questions

Discussion Questions

14.1   Do you think that the implication of civil liability into a statute is needed? Wouldn't those who formulated the statute have thought of this?

14.2   Many statutes have now excluded the individual's right to a private action (for example *Occupational Health and Safety (Commonwealth Employment) Act 1991* (Cth), s 79 and many State equivalents) although the South Australian Act preserves "any civil right or remedy". Is there any utility in allowing this tort?

14.3   Luntz and Hambly ask why this tort is necessary. They suggest that it is a form of insurance for the employee at the expense of the employer. But why should this be necessary when the Workers Compensation Acts do this?

14.4   Fleming criticises the presumption that has evolved that if the duty is owed to the public then it is not protecting a particular class. He states: "If the duty is owed to everybody, it is owed to nobody." What are your thoughts?

CHAPTER 15

Vicarious Liability

Reading

Sappideen, Vines, Grant and Watson, *Torts: Commentary and Materials*, Chapter 16.

Objectives

This chapter will examine:

- the situations in which vicarious liability will arise;
- who is a servant;
- when a servant is said to be acting in the course of employment;
- what is a "frolic" of the servant's own;
- when an employer may be held liable for the acts of an independent contractor; and
- the position of principal and agent for the purposes of vicarious liability.

Principles

Introduction

[15.05] The term "vicarious liability" refers to the case where one person is held liable for a tort committed by another person.[1] The outstanding example is that of the liability of an employer for the torts of employees committed in the course of their employment.[2] Whilst this is the most common form of this type of liability, there are other categories which will be considered in this chapter, some examples being: the liability of a partner for the act of another partner committed in the course of the partnership business; the liability of the owner of a motor vehicle for the negligence of those who drive the vehicle with their permission: *Soblusky v Egan* (1960) 103 CLR 215 (see further this chapter at [15.90]). However, the High Court has not extended its decision in *Soblusky* to boats (*Frist v Warner* (2002) 209 CLR 509) or aircraft (*Scott v Davis* (2002) 204 CLR 333). See also "Vicarious liability of owners of vehicles" at [15.90]. The liability therefore turns on the nature of the relationship between the two "responsible" parties.[3]

Vicarious liability is *always strict liability* and must be distinguished from personal liability, which generally requires fault on the defendant's part. For example, an employer who is held liable for the negligence of an employee because of the employer's negligence in selecting that employee for the task to be performed, is personally rather than vicariously liable. So is the person who instructs or authorises another person to commit a tort. It is true that vicarious liability for the acts of employees has been explained in some past cases on the basis that the employee is committing a breach of the employer's own duty of care (in the case of negligence, for example). But the employer's tort explanation of vicarious liability for the acts of employees is unsatisfactory. If it were true, it would not appear to matter whether the tort was committed through the medium of an employee or an independent contractor. Yet it is clear that the law distinguishes between acts of employees and of independent contractors in deciding whether liability should be imposed on the employer.

The concept of vicarious liability is also relevant to the relationship of principal and agent. For present purposes the term "agent" has two meanings. The first is a person who performs a service on one's behalf. Insofar as such a person is an independent contractor, the principles of liability for contractors apply. It must be noted here that the vicarious liability of a principal for their agent is limited to those situations where it can be established that it is the intention of the principal to sue an independent contractor to bring about legal relations between the principal who engages them and a third party: *Sweeney v Boylan Nominees Pty Ltd t/as Quirks Refrigeration* (2006) 226 CLR 161 at 170-171. Where the agent is not a contractor, there is no general principle of vicarious liability for the acts of the agent. The second meaning of agent is a person employed

---

[1]   A person who is vicariously liable for the tortious conduct of another is protected by any immunity that is available to the wrongdoer: *Commonwealth v Griffiths* (2007) 245 ALR 172; [2007] NSWCA 370; *Bell v Western Australia* (2004) 28 WAR 555; [2004] WASCA 205; *Parker v Commonwealth* (1965) 112 CLR 295; *Darling Island Stevedoring and Lighterage Co Ltd v Long* (1957) 97 CLR 36.

[2]   There have been some technical discussions regarding the appropriate language to be used in this context, originally (and technically) the terminology was that of "master and servant". This chapter will, however, employ the common terminology of the courts (employer and employee).

[3]   That is: the negligent party and the party who attracts liability for that negligent act.

to represent the principal in dealings with third parties and to bring about contractual relations with those parties. Here, vicarious liability on the part of the principal is limited to acts done or representations made within the scope of the agent's authority, actual or ostensible.[4] There is no general vicarious liability for torts committed by such an agent.

Employer and employee

Policy justifications

[15.10] The liability of the employer is based in policy, and the policy reasons received recognition in the dissenting judgment of La Forest J in *London Drugs Ltd v Kuehne International Ltd* [1992] 3 SCR 299. Those reasons may be summed up as follows: the desirability of providing a solvent defendant (the employee being generally unlikely to be worth suing); the capacity of the employer to absorb the cost of liability as part of the costs of the enterprise (for which tax relief is available); the justness of the conclusion that profit-making enterprises should be made to compensate for losses inflicted by the enterprise on third parties, where those losses are caused by persons within the enterprise; and the encouragement provided by vicarious liability to employers to institute proper safety standards within the enterprise, so that vicarious liability is consistent with a theory of deterrence.

There are two persistent survivors from the early, technical applications of vicarious liability and the "master's tort theory of vicarious liability". In *Darling Island Stevedoring and Lighterage Co v Long* (1957) 97 CLR 36 the High Court held that a master was not vicariously liable for the breach by a servant of a statutory duty placed on that servant. The only clear basis for this holding appears in the judgments of Kitto and Taylor JJ, namely the master's tort theory. The master, not being subject to the duty, cannot be held liable for its breach. The decision runs counter to the policy justifications of vicarious liability stated above, in particular the solvent defendant and enterprise liability justifications. It has been statutorily reversed in New South Wales: *Law Reform (Vicarious Liability) Act 1983*, s 7. Apart from this, the practical significance of the decision is limited, granted the fact that statutory duties are generally placed on masters rather than servants and that the master will be vicariously liable if the servant's breach of statutory duty also amounts to common law negligence.

The second unfortunate survival is the rule that where an independent discretion rests in the employee (servant), the employer (master) is not vicariously liable for acts done in the exercise of that discretion. Since the employee in this case is not subject to the employer's control, the employer is not considered to have committed a tort through the medium of the employee. Again, however, in the light of the policy justifications for imposing vicarious liability for the acts of employees, this rule has become anomalous. In its main area of operation, in relation to vicarious liability for the acts of police officers, the rule has been removed by statute in most parts of Australia.[5] But it has a

CHAPTER 15

---

[4] See, for example, *Colonial Mutual Life Assurance Society Ltd v Producers and Citizens Co-Operative Assurance Co of Australia Ltd* (1931) 46 CLR 41.

[5] *Australian Federal Police Act 1979* (Cth), s 64B; *Law Reform (Vicarious Liability) Act 1983* (NSW), s 8; *Police Service Administration Act 1990* (Qld), s 10.5; *Police Act 1998* (SA), s 65; *Police Service Act 2003* (Tas), s 84; *Police Regulation Act 1958* (Vic), s 123; *Police Act 1892* (WA), s 137; *Police Administration Act 1978* (NT), s 163.

wider operation, having been applied to a collector of customs,[6] a tax commissioner,[7] a legal aid officer,[8] and a ship's pilot.[9]

Figure 15.1: Justification for vicarious liability of employers

- Desirability of providing a solvent defendant.
- Servant being generally unlikely to be worth suing.
- Capacity of employer to absorb the cost of liability as part of the costs of the enterprise (for which tax relief is available).
- Justness of the conclusion that profit-making enterprises should be made to compensate for losses inflicted by the enterprise on third parties, where those losses are caused by persons within the enterprise.
- Deterrent to encourage employers to institute proper safety standards within the enterprise (per La Forest J in *London Drugs v Kuehne International*).

Who is an employee?

[15.15] The difficulty in deciding whether a person is an employee or something else is found in deciding whether there is sufficient control by the employer to be able to say that an employment relationship has been created. In any given case, this is a question of fact based on an objective assessment of what the facts reveal.[10] This is an important question, granted that vicarious liability invariably applies to the acts of employees but not invariably to those of independent contractors. An independent contractor is generally regarded as a principal and liable for his or her own wrongful acts. The question has also become of increasing importance in recent years in the light of the fact that both parties to the employment relationship have often found it advantageous to establish an independent contractor rather than a service relationship. The employee has generally done this in order to exploit tax loopholes, though these to some extent have been closed. The non-service relationship presents a number of advantages to the employer, ranging from a greater ability to exclude unions to the capacity to avoid the various imposts to which the State subjects persons who employ servants (or which are regarded as normal features of contracts of service, such as a right to sick pay and holiday allowance). So there has been an increase in self-employment and labour-only sub-contracting (where the labour is provided by a third party who may or may not be the employer of the persons provided).

As regards the test for distinguishing employees from independent contractors, the first point to note is that there is a linguistic distinction that has played a role in

---

[6]   *Baume v Commonwealth* (1906) 4 CLR 97.

[7]   *Carpenter's Investment v Commonwealth* (1952) 69 WN (NSW) 175.

[8]   *Field v Nott* (1939) 62 CLR 660.

[9]   *Oceanic Crest v Pilbara* (1986) 160 CLR 626.

[10]   See *Rowe v Capital Territory Health Commission* (1982) 39 ALR 39 – the ACT Health Commission stopped treating its student nurses as employees and paying award rates of pay, changing their status to students and paying them at a lower rate. The Federal Court held that the students were still employees as they provided services and therefore fell under the award.

determining the difference between the two. The employer/employee relationship has been referred to as a "contract *of* service", whilst the employer/independent contractor relationship is based upon a "contract *for* services". It is a fine, yet significant distinction that points to the fundamental difference between the two relationships. It is also relevant to note that it is not for the parties themselves to determine the nature of the relationship by express contractual provision, although the way the parties view the relationship is relevant evidence of the nature of the contract: *Australian Mutual Provident Society v Chaplin* (1978) 18 ALR 385. Mason J, in *Stevens v Brodribb Sawmilling Co Pty Ltd* (1986) 160 CLR 16,[11] confirmed the existence of two tests, the test of control[12] and that of integration into the enterprise, the two tests operating together for the determination of the matter but the control test in his opinion having priority. In *Hollis v Vabu Pty Ltd (t/as Crisis Couriers)* (2001) 207 CLR 21, the High Court suggested that the proper approach was to consider the totality of the relationship between the parties (a "multi-facet" text).

The control test

[15.16] As regards control, Mason J pointed out that this meant the *right to control the activities of the employee* under the contract, not the actual exercise of that control. Nor was the difficulty or otherwise of exercising control relevant. An employee performing the most difficult technical task with which there was little likelihood of the employer interfering might nevertheless be subject to contractual control, in the sense that if the employer chose to tell the employee how to perform the task, the employee would be in breach of contract in failing to comply with the instruction. In *Stevens* the owner of a sawmill had employed three sets of persons to conduct logging operations on its behalf: one set to cut the trees, another to push them into place for transportation and another to transport the wood by truck. The defendant employers undertook responsibility for co-ordinating the activities of the three sets of persons and setting up their system of work but left them alone to operate that system unaided. By the negligence of a person engaged in the second task of loading the logs, the plaintiff, a truck driver was injured. The High Court held that the relationship between the employers and the three sets of persons was that of employer and independent contractor. The persons employed were wholly outside the employer's control in the way in which they performed their tasks. The employer's control ceased once the system of cutting and removing timber had been set up. The consequence of this was that the rules relating to liability for the acts of independent contractors, not servants, were applicable: see [15.60]. The employers were held not liable.

The control test has difficulties in its application, as is apparent on the facts of *Stevens*. While it may be satisfactory in the case of unskilled workers, it is unrealistic to say that an employer can control the nature and manner of work done by a highly skilled employee, who may have more expertise in how the work should be carried out than the employer. Nor is the contract itself likely to provide, expressly or impliedly, for the factor of control, so that (as in *Stevens*) the court looks more at the practice of the parties than the contract itself.

---

[11] The question of the legal determination of the nature of the relationship was explored at some length in the judgment of Mason J (with whom Brennan and Deane JJ concurred).

[12] The test was first formulated by Denning LJ in *Stevenson v Macdonald* [1952] 1 TLR 101 at 111.

The "integration" or "organisation" test

[15.17] A supplementary test to that of control is whether the individual is sufficiently integrated into the organisation to be regarded as its employee.[13] The integration test asks the question whether *the employee is "part and parcel" of the organisation* by reference to matters such as the working of fixed hours, the presence of holiday and sick pay entitlement, the presence of a notice requirement to terminate the contract and so on. Wilson and Dawson JJ in *Stevens* thought that the integration test had equal primacy with that of control in determining service: the ultimate question was one of degree which no particular test could solve. Mason J, while not denying the relevance of integration factors, thought they went towards the existence of control by the employer. On the facts in *Stevens* there was no difference of opinion that the men in question were not sufficiently integrated. They provided their own equipment, set their own hours of work, made their own tax arrangements, and were paid by results with no guarantee of work.

It is, however, possible for the control and integration tests to provide different answers to the question of whether there is a contract of service. It is suggested that despite the assertion of the primacy of the control test by Mason J in *Stevens*, it would still be possible for a court to hold that a completely controlled individual was none the less insufficiently integrated in the organisation to be its employee,[14] or that an incompletely controlled individual was so well integrated into the employer's organisation as to be its employee.[15] Problems of this sort are particularly likely to arise in the case of borrowed employees, where the issue is one of determining which employer is liable for the tortious conduct of the employee because only one employer can be vicariously liable for the tortious conduct. The onus is on the employer which lends the employee to show a transfer of control.[16] In *Mersey Docks & Harbour Boards v Coggins & Griffiths Ltd* [1947] AC 1 the harbour authority had hired out a mobile crane, along with its operator, to a stevedoring company and in the course of operations the crane driver had through negligent operation of the crane injured a stevedore. Despite a provision in the contract of hire that the crane driver was an employee of the hirer during the period of hire, the House of Lords concluded that the driver remained an employee of the harbour authority, which was therefore liable for his negligence.[17] This

---

[13] Though the case law has generally produced the result that casual employees of this sort are servants: *Hackshall's Ltd v Pritchard* 1934 AR (NSW) 290; *Re Nicol Bros* (1942) CAR 331; *Re Shop Assistants (Metropolitan) Award* 1957 AR (NSW) 337.

[14] See in particular *Zuijs v Wirth Bros Pty Ltd* (1955) 93 CLR 561; and *Humberstone v Northern Timber Mills* (1949) 79 CLR 389.

[15] *Stevenson, Jordan & Harrison Ltd v MacDonald & Evans* [1952] 1 TLR 101. In *Federal Commissioner of Taxation v Barrett* (1973) 129 CLR 395, land salesman had total freedom as to how he performed his task of finding purchasers, but enjoyed a permanent relationship with employer, and had to report daily to the employer. The court held he was a servant. Stephen J observed that control was "only one of a number of indicia" of service.

[16] A general employer seeking to shift vicarious liability for the tortious acts of its employees when lent to a third party will have to establish exceptional circumstances: see the observations of Ashley J in *Deutz Australia Pty Ltd v Skilled Engineering Ltd* (2001) 162 FLR 173 while the Queensland Law Reform Commission in its report, *Vicarious Liability* (QLRC 56, December 2001) in Recommendation 3.4 recommended that legislation should be passed to ensure the general employer remains vicariously liable for the negligence of their employees when lent to a third party.

[17] See also *McDermid v Nash Dredging Ltd* [1987] AC 906 – employee of parent company was working as skipper of a boat belonging to the subsidiary – held that he remained the employee of the parent company since he continued to be paid by them, the subsidiary was performing the parent's work and gave him no instructions as to the performance of that work; *McDonald v Commonwealth* (1945) 46 SR (NSW) 129 – where the driver of a

was based on the authority's continuing control over the way in which he performed his work, a conclusion regarded with some scepticism by academic writers.[18] The case illustrates a tendency on the part of the courts to hold the general rather than the temporary employer vicariously liable, a conclusion reached also by the High Court in *Kondis v STA* (1984) 154 CLR 672. So far, the courts have rejected the possibility of finding both employers vicariously liable, on the ground that a servant cannot have two employers.

The "multi-facet" test

[15.18] In 2001 the High Court held in *Hollis v Vabu Pty Ltd (t/as Crisis Couriers)* (2001) 207 CLR 21 that the proper approach for determining whether a worker was an employee or an independent contractor involved a consideration of a range of factors which could be best described as a "multi-facet" test. Not every factor will be relevant, nor will all be given the same weight. The extent to which each factor is relevant will depend upon the particular facts and circumstances of each case and while control remains the central element, this test requires the court to consider the totality of the relationship between the parties.

Upon close consideration it can be seen that all of these tests are subsets of each other, each requiring a close consideration of the nature of the relationship between the parties and the contractual terms of their activities. A recent, practical example of the process is found in *Sweeney v Boylan Nominees* (2006) 226 CLR 161. The High Court was called upon to determine liability for injuries sustained by the the plaintiff when she opened the door to a refrigerator at a service station. The door had been negligently secured by a refrigeration mechanic and liability turned on whether or not he was an employee of, or an independent contractor for, the company which assigned the job to him. In reaching its conclusion that the mechanic was an independent contractor the High Court considered the invoicing arrangements, responsibility for the workers' compensation and public liability insurance and supply of tools. It was, quite simply, a fact finding exercise. Such an approach is entirely consistent with the earlier High Court decision of *Stevens v Brodribb Sawmilling Co Pty Ltd* (1986) 160 CLR 16 which set out relevant indicia of an employer/employee relationship as: "the right to have a particular person do the work, the right to suspend or dismiss the person engaged, the right to the exclusive services of the person engaged and the right to dictate the place of work, hours of work and the like". An employer/independent contractor relationship on the other hand could, according to the High Court, be evidenced by such factors as: "work involving a profession, trade or distinct calling on the part of the person engaged, the provision by him of his own place of work or of his own equipment, the creation by him of goodwill or saleable assets in the course of his work, the payment by him from his remuneration of business expenses of any significant proportion and the payment to him of remuneration without deduction for income tax" (at [11] per Wilson and Dawson JJ).

---

vehicle was hired out by his employer with the vehicle to the Commonwealth in time of war for an indefinite period and during that period being subject to the entire control of the Commonwealth, he became at the relevant time its employee.

[18] Grunfeld, "Master and Servant, General and Temporary Employers" (1947) 10 MLR 203.

Figure 15.2: Tests for distinguishing servants from independent contractors

- Main test is **multi-facet test** of which the **control test** is still the central element.
- The extent to which each factor is relevant will depend upon the particular facts and circumstances of each case but requires the court to consider the totality of the relationship between the parties.

Course of employment

[15.20] In order that the employer be held vicariously liable for the servant's act, *the employee must have been acting in the course of his or her employment*. The legal test for determining the matter is clear: was the employee carrying out the work he or she was employed to do, taken in the context of all the surrounding circumstances? If the answer is yes, then the employer is vicariously liable even though the work is being carried out in an unauthorised or improper manner: *Commonwealth v Connell* (1986) 5 NSWLR 218.[19] It is no longer relevant that any benefit might have accrued to the employer through the employee's wrongful act. The difficulty lies in applying that test to the facts of particular cases and this is a question of fact and dependent upon the circumstances in each case. In *Century Insurance Co Ltd v Northern Ireland Transport Board* [1942] AC 509 the House of Lords held that a truck driver who caused a fire by striking a match while transferring petrol from the truck to the plaintiffs' underground tank was acting in the course of his employment even though the lighting of the matches was strictly forbidden by his employer in these circumstances. The truck driver was performing in an unauthorised way that which he was employed to do. There follows an account of a number of situations in which the application of the test has caused difficulty.

Figure 15.3: Course of employment

- Employer vicariously liable for acts of employee only where employee acting in the course of employment.
- Was employee doing what he or she was employed to do?
- An employer is not vicariously liable for the independent wrongful acts of an employee.

Express prohibition by employer

[15.25] *Century Insurance Co Ltd v Northern Ireland Transport Board* [1942] AC 509 shows that the breach of an express prohibition by the employee will not automatically place the employee outside the course of employment. It will only have that effect if the nature of the prohibition is by way of a delimitation of the sphere of employment rather than of the manner in which it is to be performed. This type of prohibition is unusual, the sphere of employment generally being defined positively by the contract rather than through prohibition. Racing a bus against another bus in the course of its service

---

[19] However, an employer is not vicariously liable for independent wrongful acts of employees: *Owston v Bank of New South Wales* (1879) 4 App Cas 270.

operations contrary to the employer's instructions has been held to be within the course of employment: *Limpus v London General Omnibus Co* (1862) 1 H & C 526; 158 ER 993. So also, the driving of a vehicle by an unauthorised person for the purposes of the employer has been regarded as within the course of the employment, though there are conflicting decisions.[20] In *Ilkiw v Samuels* [1963] 2 All ER 879 Diplock LJ took the persuasive view that the prohibition against permitting anyone else to drive the truck in the course of loading it was a prohibition on the mode of carrying out the job; that is, a prohibition against conduct "within the sphere of employment". The employer was therefore held liable for the negligence of the employee in entrusting the driving of a truck to an unqualified driver.

Prohibitions also raise difficulties in relation to employees who give unauthorised lifts to third parties in their employer's vehicle. Whether the employer is to be held vicariously liable is based on whether the employee was acting in the course of his employment.[21] In *Rose v Plenty* [1976] 1 All ER 97 a milk roundsman had, contrary to the instructions of his employer, made use of the services of a 13-year-old boy in assisting him to deliver milk. The plaintiff was injured by the negligent driving of the float by the roundsman. All three members of the Court of Appeal treated the question as turning on whether the roundsman was acting in the course of his employment; the plaintiff's status as a trespasser on the float did not affect the duties owed by the roundsman towards him. A majority of the Court of Appeal held the defendant liable on the ground that the boy's services were being used for the purposes of the business.

"Frolic" of employee's own

[15.30] An employer may be able to absolve itself from liability if it can be established that the actions of the employees were not "reasonably incidental" to their duties. This raises issues of fact and degree when trying to determine whether the employee has stepped outside the boundaries of the employment relationship. In *Harvey v O'Dell* [1958] 2 QB 78 the conclusion was drawn that workers who took an unauthorised lunch break and who caused an accident while driving to it were nevertheless acting within the course of their employment; that conclusion being supported by the fact that they were not advised to take lunch with them and were paid subsistence money by their employer.[22] However, in *Hilton v Thomas Burton* [1961] 1 WLR 705 workmen, who decided that they had completed their work for the day, repaired to a cafe and on the way caused an accident. This was held to be outside the course of their employment.[23] It is also possible to find unduly restrictive the conclusion in *General Engineering Services Ltd v Kingston* [1988] 3 All ER 867 that a fire station crew who were engaged in an industrial go-slow in proceeding to a fire were not acting in the course of their employment. The fact that the crew was in deliberate breach of contract appears irrelevant and the driving of the vehicle clearly had a connection with their employment.[24]

---

[20]   *Ilkiw v Samuels* [1963] 2 All ER 879; *LCC v Carrermole Garages Ltd* [1953] 1 WLR 997; *Kay v ITW* [1968] 1 QB 140 – employers held liable; *Beard v London General Omnibus* [1900] 2 QB 530; *Iqbal v London Transport Executive* (1973) 16 KIR 329 – employers not liable.

[21]   And one earlier decision: *Twine v Bean's Express* (1946) 175 LT 131.

[22]   See also *Bugge v Brown* (1919) 26 CLR 110 – roustabout who was authorised to take lunch but who took it at an unauthorised place and there caused a fire was acting in the course of his employment; he was doing an authorised activity in an unauthorised place. Thus he was still acting within the scope of his employment. However, note the lamentable decision in *Crook v Derbyshire Stone* [1956] 2 All ER 447 – worker entitled to take lunch breaks was nevertheless outside the course of employment when crossing the road to buy food during a break.

[23]   A similar outcome occurred in *McClure v Commonwealth* [1999] NSWCA 392; two infantrymen took home an unexploded shell in breach of army regulations. Subsequent occupiers of the house were injured when they found the shell and one of them dropped it. It was held that the Commonwealth was not vicariously liable as the infantrymen were on a frolic of their own when they took the shell home.

[24]   Very often the contest in these motoring cases is between the employer's liability insurer and the car insurer.

Temporal limits of employment

[15.35] The period of employment begins at the moment the employee starts work. It is settled law that an employee driving to or home from work is not acting in the course of employment. But reasonable extensions beyond the limits of working hours have been recognised; for example, the leaving on of taps in a washroom by an employee who had completed his working day was found to be in the course of employment: *Ruddiman & Co v Smith* (1889) 60 LT 708.

Travel in the course of the employee's duties from one workplace to another has caused difficulties. In *Commonwealth v Cocks* (1966) 115 CLR 413 it was held that a public servant who had been posted from Canberra to Melbourne was not driving in the course of employment while travelling to his new place of employment, even though being paid mileage allowance for the move. But in *Smith v Stages* [1989] AC 928, it was held that travel by an employee back from a temporary place of work to the main workplace was within the course of employment where lost time through travel was paid for at the wage rate, even though the mode and to some extent the date and time of travel were left to the employee.

Assault by employee

[15.40] Where the assault by the employee is merely an excessive mode of performing his or her duty to the employer, the employer will be held vicariously liable for it. So in *Poland v John Parr* [1927] 1 KB 236 where the employee struck and caused injury to a boy whom he thought to be stealing sugar from his employer's wagon, the employer was held liable on the basis that the employee's act was an excessive performance of the duty to protect the employer's property. Similarly, in *Petterson v Royal Oak Hotel* [1948] NZLR 136 a customer who had been refused drink at the bar of the defendants' hotel, threw a glass at the barman, shattering the glass. The barman picked up some of the glass and threw it at the customer, hitting him and causing a piece of glass to enter the plaintiff's eye. The act of the barman was held to be in the course of his employment, being an excessive mode of the barman's duty to keep order in the bar.[25] However, in *Deatons Pty Ltd v Flew* (1949) 79 CLR 370 the High Court regarded the act of a barmaid who flung a glass in the direction of a customer who had attacked her as a private act of retaliatory self-defence. Her actions were not connected with, or within the scope of, either her specific duties or with maintaining order in the bar. In *Warren v Henley's Ltd* [1948] 2 All ER 935 a garage attendant suspected the plaintiff of leaving without paying and accused him of this. Later, when the plaintiff had paid, the attendant assaulted him. This was found to be outside the course of the attendant's employment. *Canterbury Bankstown Rugby League Football Club v Rogers* [1993] Aust Torts Reports 81-246 held that a foul and dangerous tackle in a rugby game was within the player's course of employment, since its object was to stop an opponent, rather than being an act of totally gratuitous violence.[26]

---

[25]   In *Ryan v Ann St Holdings Pty Ltd* [2006] 2 Qd R 486, a nightclub security guard assaulted a patron inside the nightclub after closing time. Both at first instance and on appeal, the nightclub was found to be vicariously liable for the injuries inflicted on Ryan by the security guard. A similar finding was made by the New South Wales Court of Appeal in *Zoron Enterprises Pty Ltd v Zabow* [2007] NSWCA 106, where the question arose as to whether s 3B(1) of the *Civil Liability Act 2002* excluded the operation of the Act in relation to vicarious liability of an employer for an intentional tort by its employee. The court held that a nightclub was vicariously liable for injuries to the respondent intentionally caused by one of its bouncers.

[26]   A decision of the British High Court in *Gravil v Carroll* [2008] EWCA Civ 689 appears to have abolished the distinction between full-time and part-time employees when it comes to the question of the employer being vicariously liable for a player's actions. As long as there is a contract in place between the club and the player, the court is prepared to adopt the position that it is only "fair and just" to hold the club liable for an intentional tort committed during the course of play, even if the game is not their main or full employment.

Horseplay by employee

[15.45] The retention by an employer of an employee given to dangerous horseplay may constitute a breach of the employer's personal duty of care to provide proper staff: see further Chapter 10. But the horseplay may be found to be within the course of employment, thus rendering the employer vicariously liable. In *Petrou v Hatzigeorgiou* [1991] Aust Torts Reports 81–071, a case concerning the vicarious liability on the part of one partner for the act of another, the plaintiff had been doused with paint thinner in the course of horseplay at the workplace. He was approached by a partner in the business with a lighted cigarette lighter and was severely burned as a result when the paint thinner ignited. The act of the partner was intended as part of the horseplay. His fellow partner was held to be vicariously liable for the plaintiff's injuries, since the act was committed in the course of the partnership business. To similar effect are *Hayward v Georges Ltd* [1966] VR 202, in which the slapping of a waitress in the back caused her to fall and suffer injury within the course of employment; and *Commonwealth v Connell* (1986) 5 NSWLR 218, in which the pushing of a naval apprentice off a bridge in the course of skylarking was within the course of employment.

Dishonesty by employee

[15.50] Again, the test is whether the employee's dishonest act may be regarded as a wrongful mode of performing what the employee is employed to do (in which case it is within the course of employment) or whether it has no connection with the performance of the employee's duties (in which case it is not). There must be some nexus between the dishonest act of the employee and the circumstances of the employment for the employer to be liable. In *Morris v Martin & Sons Ltd* [1966] 1 QB 716 the plaintiff entrusted her mink stole for cleaning to a furrier who, with the plaintiff's permission, sent it for cleaning to the defendant cleaners. The stole was stolen by an employee of the defendants to whom the cleaning of the stole had been entrusted. The Court of Appeal held the defendants liable on the ground that the theft of the stole was a wrongful mode of performance of the employee's duty of cleaning it. Diplock LJ arrived at this conclusion by the application of the normal principles that apply to determine what is within the course of an employee's employment. Lord Denning MR, however, justified the same conclusion on the basis of a non-delegable duty of care owed by the defendants as sub-bailees of the stole to the plaintiff. On neither judgment would the defendant have been liable had the fur been stolen by an employee to whose care it had not been entrusted. Another case which is relevant to liability for the employee's dishonesty is *Ffrench v Sestili* (2007) 98 SASR 28; [2007] SASC 241 where the plaintiff, a quadriplegic, depended on carers provided by the defendant. One of the carers stole the plaintiff's credit and ATM cards and used them. The court held that the defendant was vicariously liable on the grounds that the carer's fraudulent conduct was sufficiently connected to her conduct which was authorised by the defendant to make the defendant vicariously liable for that conduct.[27] See also *Lloyd v Grace Smith & Co* [1912] AC 716, although that case is best explained on agency principles and is therefore discussed at [15.85].

[27] In *Ffrench's* case, the carer was employed to do the plaintiff's shopping and required to pay for that shopping with either the plaintiff's credit or ATM card. The unauthorised withdrawals were so closely connected to the authorised withdrawals that the court was able to justify the imposition of vicarious liability.

Serious criminal conduct by employee

[15.51] Where the employee's conduct amounts to a serious criminal offence, vicarious liability may still arise if it can be established that there is a sufficient connection between the employee's criminal conduct and what the employee was employed to do. In *Lister v Hesley Hall Ltd* [2001] 2 All ER 769, the House of Lords held that a school be held vicariously liable for the sexual assaults committed against students by the warden employed by the school at its boarding house. In this case, the House of Lords looked more broadly at the job, which was to care for the children, and came to the conclusion that as the employer had undertaken to care for the children through the services of the warden there was a very close connection between the torts of the warden and his employment.[28]

Contribution

[15.55] Where an employer is held to be vicariously liable for the torts of an employee committed in the course of employment, the direct liability of the employee at common law is not extinguished. But, as noted earlier,[29] for a number of policy reasons the employer makes a better defendant as they are better able to satisfy a claim than the employee ([15.10]). However, while the injured plaintiff may not wish to pursue the employee, the employer may wish to bring a claim against the negligent employee for contribution, indemnity only being available where it can be established that there is no independent fault on the part of the person seeking an indemnity.

Both contribution and indemnity are, in some jurisdictions, subject to statutory bars. Section 66 of the *Insurance Contracts Act 1984* (Cth) prevents the employer's insurer from having the right to be subrogated to the rights of the insured against the employee.[30] Statute law in New South Wales, South Australia and the Northern Territory[31] also prevents an employer from seeking a contribution or an indemnity from an employee whose tortious acts have left the employer vicariously liable, unless the employee has committed serious and wilful or gross misconduct in the course of employment.

Employer and independent contractor

[15.60] The topic of the employer's liability for the acts of an independent contractor requires certain distinctions to be made for the purpose of comprehension. While an

---

[28] In *New South Wales v Lepore; Samin v Queensland; Rich v Queensland* (2003) 212 CLR 511, each case involving sexual abuse of students by their teachers, the High Court held that a school could be held vicariously liable for the criminal conduct of its teachers (in this case the sexual assaults). In *Trustees of Roman Catholic Church v Ellis* (2007) 63 ACSR 346; [2007] NSWCA 117, the court had to consider whether the Trustees of the Roman Catholic Church for the Archdiocese of Sydney were vicariously liable for the sexual abuse of Ellis by an assistant priest when Ellis was a young altar server. The court found that the organisation was an unincorporated association and so did not exist as a juridical entity. As a result, difficulties about attributing vicarious liability remain personal with the members who formed the committee who were in office at the time. The court held that in this case the relationship between individual office holders in the church and the members of the church as a whole was too diffuse to establish members' liability as principals in contract or their vicarious liability in tort.

[29] *Mersey Docks & Harbour Boards v Coggins & Griffiths Ltd* [1947] AC 1.

[30] The House of Lords in *Lister v Romford Ice & Cold Storage Co Ltd* [1957] AC 555 held that an insurer, who had paid out a claim to the employer, could recover from the negligent employee on the basis of subrogation.

[31] *Employees Liability Act 1991* (NSW), ss 3, 5, 7; *Civil Liability Act 1936* (SA), s 59(1), (3); *Law Reform (Miscellaneous Provisions) Act 1956* (NT), s 22A.

independent contractor is generally regarded as a principal, and therefore liable for his or her own torts, there are occasions where an employer may be personally liable for a tort committed through the medium of an independent contractor. So the employer may have instructed or authorised the contractor to commit a tort, or may be negligent in the choice of the contractor, or in the instructions given to the contractor; or the employer may have committed through the contractor a tort of strict liability. The clearest example of the last type of liability is the tort of *Rylands v Fletcher* (1868) LR 3 HL 330, now defunct in Australia, though the point being made here applies to other torts of strict liability. In that case contractors who had been engaged to build a reservoir on the defendant's land came upon some disused mine shafts on the land which, unknown to the contractors, connected with mines on the plaintiff's land. The contractors having failed to seal up the shafts, water from the reservoir entered and flooded the plaintiff's mines. For this the defendant was held liable to the plaintiff. The judgments in the case made it clear that the liability imposed was not a vicarious one for the negligence of the contractor but a personal one based on the defendant's collection of water on his land and its escape to the plaintiff's. The liability imposed was strict, not being dependent on the negligence of the contractor.

There are a number of situations where the employer of an independent contractor is held liable for the contractor's negligence. Liability here is essentially vicarious rather than personal. However, the courts have chosen to rationalise it on the basis of the employer's breach through the contractor of a non-delegable duty of care binding the employer. The concept of the non-delegable duty of care is mainly a convenient means for courts to rationalise a conclusion that the situation is one in which liability for the acts of an independent contractor may arise. The formulation conceals a choice by courts as to whether to impose liability on the employer, a choice to be made in conformity with criteria laid down by the High Court in *Burnie Port Authority v General Jones Pty Ltd* (1994) 179 CLR 520.

The considerations attendant on the issue whether to impose a non-delegable duty of care have produced the following formulation in *Burnie*. The duty arises where:

> the person on whom the duty is imposed has undertaken the care, supervision or control of the person or property of another or is so placed in relation to that person or his property as to assume a particular responsibility for his or its safety ... It will be convenient to refer to that as the "central element of control". Viewed from the perspective of the person to whom the duty is owed, the relationship of proximity giving rise to the non-delegable duty of care is marked by special dependence or vulnerability on the part of that person.

Protective relationships

[15.65] The non-delegable duty of care arising in protective relationships such as employer and employee, school authority and pupil[32] and hospital and patient[33] fits well into the *Burnie* criteria. The undertaking of care for a class of persons and the special dependency of that class are clearly apparent here. Another relationship that may be regarded as protective, that of occupier towards lawful visitor, is less easy to fit within the criteria and the High Court expressly left open the question whether the occupier's

---

32 *Commonwealth v Introvigne* (1982) 150 CLR 258. For more detail on this relationship refer Chapter 9, [9.25]ff.
33 *Samios v Repatriation Commission* [1960] WAR 219.

duty of care was non–delegable (though for no very convincing reason the contractual entrant is still owed a non-delegable duty of care by the occupier): *Calin v Greater Union Organisation* [1991] Aust Torts Reports 81–110.

The High Court in *Burnie Port Authority v General Jones Pty Ltd* (1994) 179 CLR 520 stated in unqualified terms the non-delegability of the duty of care owed by a hospital to its patient.[34] The advantage of this approach towards the liability of hospitals is that it avoids the question whether the particular person offering treatment to the patient is an employee of the hospital so as to attract vicarious liability on the hospital's part. It is likely that a distinction drawn in two New South Wales decisions prior to *Burnie* will survive that case's clear recognition of the hospital's non-delegable duty to provide careful treatment. *Ellis v Wallsend District Hospital* (1989) 17 NSWLR 553 found that the hospital was not liable for the negligence of a surgeon who was not an employee of the hospital in circumstances where the surgeon had been privately consulted by the patient and the hospital had merely lent its facilities and support staff to the surgeon for carrying out an operation. The earlier case of *Albrighton v Royal Prince Alfred Hospital* (1980) 2 NSWLR 542 was distinguished on the ground that in that case the plaintiff went directly to the hospital both for advice and treatment, and could therefore be regarded as an employee of the hospital.[35]

Another category of non-delegable duty of care may be loosely fitted within the general head of protective relationships: where the duty arises in a situation analogous to contract (contractual duties themselves are of course generally incapable of being delegated). The non-delegable duties of care of bailees and sub-bailees for reward are examples of this category: *Morris v CW Martin & Sons Ltd* [1966] 1 QB 716; *BRS v Critchley* [1968] 1 All ER 811. Closely analogous to this case is the liability of a carrier of cargo at sea towards the cargo owner for the negligence of a contractor employed by the carrier.

A number of jurisdictions have now legislatively deemed "non-delegable duty claims" to be based on vicarious liability notwithstanding that the work that caused the injury might have been carried out by a person who was not an employee or agent of the defendant.[36]

At the heart of these relationships is the assumption of responsibility, viewed as a willing acceptance of potential liability for any wrongdoing: *Burnie Port Authority* at [36].

---

[34]   Whilst this case was focusing on other forms of relationships giving rise to a non-delegable duty, the relationship between a hospital and its patients was listed as a straightforward example of non-delegability.

[35]   *Ellis v Wallsend District Hospital* (1989) 17 NSWLR 553 was followed in *John James Memorial Hospital Ltd v Keys* [1999] FCA 678.

[36]   *Civil Liability Act 2002* (NSW), s 5Q; *Civil Liability Act 2002* (Qld), Sch 2; *Civil Liability Act 2002* (Tas), s 3C; *Wrongs Act 1958* (Vic), s 61; *Law Reform (Miscellaneous Provisions) Act 1956* (NT), s 22A.

Figure 15.4: Protective relationships

> Non-delegable duty of care arises in protective relationships such
> as:
> - employer and employee;
> - school authority and principal; and
> - hospital and patient.
>
> It has also been extended to:
> - occupier and lawful visitor or contractual entrant;
> - *Rylands v Fletcher* situations; and
> - bailees and sub-bailees.
>
> Employer is not liable for collateral or casual negligence of
> contractor in carrying out work.

Other situations of non-delegable duty

[15.70] The High Court in *Burnie Port Authority v General Jones Pty Ltd* (1994) 179 CLR
520 recognised another situation of non-delegable duty as regards work done outside
the plaintiff's land causing a withdrawal of lateral support to that land or damaging a
common wall. This liability is considered in Chapter 16 where it is pointed out that
there is also liability for a nuisance created by an independent contractor, where the
work commissioned creates a particular risk of the creation of a nuisance. The High
Court in *Burnie* has added the *Rylands v Fletcher* situation to the list of non-delegable
duties of care, replacing the former strict liability which existed in that situation. The
principle in *Rylands v Fletcher* (1868) LR 3 HL 330 applied where the occupier of
land had brought onto the land something likely to cause harm if it escaped, and the
thing had escaped and caused damage outside the land. In *Burnie* the defendants were
held liable for breach of the non-delegable duty of care which arises in the *Rylands
v Fletcher* situation. They had "collected" on their premises cardboard cases of Isolite,
a substance difficult to ignite but likely to burn destructively if it did, that collection
being in the vicinity of welding work which they had commissioned to be carried
out by their contractor. They were therefore liable for the contractor's negligence in
allowing sparks from the welding to ignite the cardboard and then the Isolite, causing a
fire which spread to and caused damage on the plaintiff's premises. The commissioned
work created a special danger for which they were responsible, and the plaintiffs were
particularly vulnerable to that danger.

   Rylands v Fletcher liability had no necessary connection with "ultra-hazardous"
activities, although these quite often fell within the rule. Any general form of strict
liability for the carrying on of an ultra-hazardous activity was denied by the House
of Lords in *Read v Lyons Ltd* [1947] AC 156 (no liability for explosion in defendants'
munitions factory causing injury to the plaintiff inside the factory since the plaintiff
was unable to establish an escape of the explosive sufficient to create liability under
Rylands v Fletcher). The High Court in *Stevens v Brodribb Sawmilling Co Pty Ltd* (1986)
160 CLR 16 rejected the concept of the ultra-hazardous operation as having any
relevance in establishing vicarious liability for the negligence of contractors, so that the

suggested hazardous nature of logging operations could not found an argument that the employers in that case owed a non-delegable duty of care in relation to logging work carried out by independent contractors. The majority in *Stevens* expressly approved the rejection in Australian case law of cases such as *Honeywill & Stein Ltd v Larkin Brothers Ltd* [1934] 1 KB 191 in which it was found that the taking of flashlight photographs inside a cinema was an especially hazardous operation and that therefore the defendants were liable for their contractor's negligence in starting a fire while carrying out that work. Now, however, it appears that the concept of the especially dangerous operation has reappeared, though seemingly limited to the *Rylands v Fletcher* situation.

Dissatisfaction with the *Burnie* criteria is emerging as courts attempt to apply them to particular situations. The High Court in *Northern Sandblasting v Harris* [1997] Aust Torts Reports 81-419 divided 5:2 on whether a landlord owed a non-delegable duty of care in relation to the repair of an electric stove carried out by an electrician to the plaintiff, a child of the tenant. The electrician's negligent failure to carry out the repair properly had catastrophic effects in the form of personal injury to the plaintiff. The majority denied the existence of a non-delegable duty here. As far as occupants are concerned, a landlord's duty goes no further than to engage a reasonably competent independent contractor.[37] There was also a difference of opinion in the New South Wales Court of Appeal in *Newcastle Entertainment Security v Simpson* [1999] Aust Torts Reports 81-528 (the respondent had been injured whilst crowd surfing at a concert): two members of the court held that the promoter of the concert and the manager/ operator of the centre at which the concert was held had effectively delegated to a security firm their duty of care, in relation to dangers to patrons caused by the dancing, while the third member of the court dissented on this point. Non-delegable duties of care have been denied on the part of a head contractor on a construction site in relation to the negligence of a sub-contractor towards a workman on the site: *Hetherington v Mirvac* [1999] Aust Torts Reports 81-514. They have also been denied on the part of a courier service firm in relation to the negligent driving of its couriers who were independent contractors: *Hollis v Vabu* [1999] Aust Torts Reports 81-535 (though this was later overturned by the High Court, *Hollis v Vabu* (2001) 207 CLR 1 with emphasis placed upon the wearing of uniforms, lack of skill and inability to determine mode of work practices). In *Simpson v Blanch* [1998] Aust Torts Reports 81-458 the court held that in principle an occupier of land owed motorists a non-delegable duty of care to fence the land to prevent the escape of animals onto the highway, though the actual decision in favour of the motorist in that case turned on the fact that no delegation to a competent fencing contractor had been made.[38]

In the case of the three protective relationships where the non-delegable duty of care is clearly established, there seem to be sound policy reasons to support this conclusion, though the *Burnie* criteria seem intended to exclude reference to policy. In all three cases, the defendant will be a financially responsible person fully aware of its responsibilities towards the class of persons in question; is already vicariously liable for the fault of its own staff; and will undoubtedly possess insurance against that liability.

---

[37] Nor will an occupier of premises owe a non-delegable duty to an entrant who is injured on the premises by a dangerous cleaning process used by an independent contractor if the occupier has no knowledge, or is not in a position to know, of the danger: *McVicar v S & J White Pty Ltd* (2007) 97 SASR 160.

[38] Nor does a highway authority owe road users a non-delegable duty in relation to the maintenance of road works as long as the authority acts with reasonable care when it comes to appointing and supervising the work of an independent contractor. If the contractor is negligent, then it is the contractor who is liable: *Leichhardt Municipal Council v Montgomery* (2007) 233 ALR 200.

The addition of vicarious liability for independent contractors does not seem to add much to its overall position in terms of liability or the cost of insurance. The policy arguments in relation to those other cases considered above are not by any means as clear-cut. The *Burnie* criteria do not contain the non-delegable duty of care within a sufficiently clear ambit. They seem to be capable of applying to the commissioning of any work which creates a danger to other persons if negligently performed.

Collateral or casual negligence

[15.75] The employer is not liable for the collateral or casual negligence of the contractor in carrying out the work. The doctrine has some affinity with that of the course or scope of employment in placing a limit on the liability of the employer but its effect is to render that liability narrower than that applying to the acts of employees. There is an initial difficulty in resolving the question, "collateral to what?" The answer seems to be that this depends on the particular duty situation in question. As regards the second category of non-delegable duty situations considered above, the answer seems to be, "collateral to the risk engendered by the work commissioned". That explains, for example, the liability of the defendant in *Burnie Port Authority v General Jones Pty Ltd* (1994) 179 CLR 520, since the contractors by negligence had activated the very risk that the employers in commissioning the work had created; that is, the risk of fire extending to a neighbouring property. In the first category (the duties of care based on protective relationships) it is suggested that collateral negligence means negligence collateral to the performance of the personal duty of care of the employer. *Kondis v STA* (1984) 154 CLR 672 provides an example. In that case the negligence of a borrowed crane-driver (in law an independent contractor) in dropping a metal rod from his crane onto the plaintiff's head was not collateral negligence, since the crane-driver was participating in a system of work which required the plaintiff to stand underneath the crane and which was therefore unsafe. In the same way a school authority employing a contractor to repair the school premises would not be liable for the negligent driving of the contractor in the schoolyard.

Principal and agent

[15.80] As pointed out in [15.05], the relationship of principal and agent is generally irrelevant to questions of vicarious liability.[39] But vicarious liability on the part of the principal for the acts of the agent may be established where the agent has been appointed to represent the principal in dealings with third parties. In this case the principal is liable for acts of the agent that are within the scope of the authority, actual or apparent, entrusted to that agent.

Scope of authority test

[15.85] First it should be noted that the scope of authority test is narrower than the course of employment test applicable to employees. In general, the principal's liability arises only in relation to acts done with reference to carrying out that authority. It is not enough that at the time of the act the agent was engaged on the principal's business.

---

[39] See, for example, *Ramsey v Vogler* [2000] NSWCA 260 where the court discusses the question of the vicarious liability of a principal for the agent.

In practice, the liability arises only in relation to statements or representations made by the agent, these giving rise to a number of possible torts such as deceit, defamation, negligent misstatement or statutory misrepresentation. In *Colonial Mutual Life Assurance Society Ltd v Producers Co-operative Assurance Co of Australia Ltd* (1931) 46 CLR 41 the defendant company was held liable for defamatory statements made by its insurance agent about a rival company while attempting to gain business for the defendants. The agent had been expressly prohibited from making defamatory statements by the terms of his employment, so that the statements were outside the agent's actual authority. The High Court held the defendants liable on the ground that the statements were made in the exercise of the general, apparent authority entrusted to the agent to represent his employers. However, in *Colonial Mutual Life Assurance Society Ltd v Macdonald* [1931] AD 412 (South Africa), the defendants were held not liable for an injury suffered by the plaintiff medical practitioner who was being driven by the defendants' insurance agent to a location to conduct medical examinations for the purpose of life insurance proposals, and who was injured by the negligent driving of the agent. The decision illustrates the difference between the scope of authority test and the course of employment test. The agent was driving the car on the principal's business, but driving a car had nothing to do with the authority entrusted to the agent.

The principles regarding scope of authority apply to employees as well as to agents, where the employee is performing the functions of an agent in representing the employer in dealings with third parties. A leading example is *Lloyd v Grace Smith & Co* [1912] AC 716. The defendants, a firm of solicitors, were held liable for the fraud of their conveyancing clerk, who had induced the plaintiff to convey to him two cottages which she wished to sell, representing falsely that this was necessary for a transaction concerning the sale of the cottages to go ahead. The clerk had no actual authority to act as he did, but by allowing him to perform conveyancing the defendants had clothed him with apparent or ostensible authority in the matter in question. Apparent authority also exists where the act performed is within the usual class of acts performed by an employee or agent of that kind. A limitation on the latter type of authority as a means of rendering the principal liable was recognised in *Kooragang Investments Pty Ltd v Richardson & Wrench Ltd* [1982] AC 462. That case held that it must be known by the plaintiff that the person the plaintiff is dealing with is an employee or agent of the employer or principal. In *Kooragang* the defendants' employee was accustomed as part of his employment to perform valuations of property on their behalf, but had been expressly instructed not to perform valuations for the plaintiff company. Nevertheless he performed valuations for them, and upon these proving to be inaccurate, the plaintiffs sued the defendants on the basis of his negligence. The defendants were held not liable. No actual or ostensible authority had been conferred on the employee to perform this valuation, and the plaintiffs could not rely on his usual authority as an employee accustomed to perform valuations since there was nothing to tell them he had any connection with the defendants.[40]

---

[40] See also *Armagas Ltd v Mundogas SA* [1986] AC 248 – agent authorised to sell ship and charter the ship back to its previous owners for 12 months, fraudulently entered into a charter-back agreement with the plaintiff purchasers for 36 months. The defendants were not liable for the agent's fraud since he had no actual or ostensible authority to enter into such a contract, nor was the charter agreement within the usual authority of that sort of agent, as the plaintiffs in fact knew.

Figure 15.5: Principal's liability under scope of authority test

- Narrower than the course of employment test applicable to employees.
- Generally only arises in relation to acts done with reference to carrying out *their* authority.
- Arises only in relation to statements or representations made by agent.

Vicarious liability of owners of vehicles

[15.90] The owner of any vehicle (including horse-drawn carriages) who delegated the driving of the vehicle to another person, but remained in the vehicle while it was being driven, was liable for the negligence of the driver of the vehicle on the basis that the owner retained control over the driving of the vehicle by the capacity to give directions to the driver. The liability of the owner arises here rather on the basis of identification of the owner with the driver's negligence than on vicarious liability. The earlier decision of the High Court in *Soblusky v Egan* (1960) 103 CLR 215, in which a car owner, who remained in the car while another person was driving it but fell asleep in the course of the journey, was held liable for the driver's negligence. Soblusky had been held liable on the basis that when Lewis had been driving the car, he was doing so as the agent of Soblusky and at the time of the accident was acting within the scope of his authority. While the decision in *Soblusky* was approved in *Scott v Davis* (2001) 204 CLR 33, it was to be confined to motor vehicles.[41] Gummow J expressed the view that it rested on "insecure and unsatisfactory foundations of principle", and would not be extended. In *Scott* itself the defendant had allowed his airplane to be used for a pleasure flight piloted by another person with the plaintiff boy as a passenger. The plane crashed, through the pilot's negligence, and the plaintiff was injured. Applying the principles stated above, the court held the defendant not liable for the negligence of the pilot. The defendant had no control over the flying of the plane, and there was no doctrine of vicarious liability for an agent's negligence, even if it could be shown that the flight was for the defendant's purposes. As far as the negligent driving of motor vehicles causing personal injury is concerned, under the relevant legislation the compulsory insurer is liable whether or not the car is driven with the owner's consent, and even in the absence of insurance cover: see Chapter 2 for the legislation. Its importance is therefore limited to the case of property damage caused by the negligent driving of the motor vehicle.

---

[41] See also *Gutman v McFall* (2004) 61 NSWLR 599; [2004] NSWCA 378 – whether an agency relationship had arisen which could be caught by the *Soblusky* principle where the plaintiff was injured by an outboard motor on a dinghy. The court unanimously agreed that *Soblusky* was confined by the High Court in *Scott* to motor vehicles.

Practice Questions

Revision Questions

15.1 When will a principal be liable for the acts of its agent?

15.2 When will a non-delegable duty of care arise out of a protective relationship?

15.3 What kind of relationship must exist between the parties before a special non-delegable duty of care will be imposed?

15.4 When will an employer be liable for the negligence of an independent contractor?

15.5 What is the test used by the courts in order to determine whether an employee has committed a tort "in the course of employment"?

15.6 How do the courts determine whether a person is an employee or an independent contractor?

Problem Questions

15.1 Jonas is a medical student doing his internship at a public hospital. Sam visits the Emergency Centre at the hospital, complaining of severe stomach cramps. Jonas conducts a brief examination of him while the Registrar is treating another patient, without informing Sam that he is not a fully qualified doctor. Jonas tells Sam that he has a 24-hour virus, gives him two aspirin and tells him that he should go home to bed. On his way home, Sam collapses at the wheel of his vehicle and hits a parked car, causing a lot of damage to both vehicles. Sam is rushed back to the hospital where it is shown that he has severe internal bleeding from a ruptured ulcer which could have been diagnosed and treated by a competent doctor.

Advise Sam.

Answers to Practice Questions

Revision Questions

15.1 The principal's liability will only arise in relation to acts done with reference to the agent carrying out the principal's authority (actual or apparent) and generally only in relation to statements or representations made by the agent.

15.2 The law recognises three protective relationships:

- employer and employee;
- school authority and pupil; and
- hospital and patient.

In all three cases the defendant will be a financially responsible person fully aware of their responsibilities towards the plaintiff.

15.3 The High Court in *Burnie Port Authority v General Jones Pty Ltd* (1994) 179 CLR 520 at 551 suggested a non-delegable duty of care would arise if a plaintiff could show a special dependence or vulnerability on the part of that person:

> *the person on whom [the duty] is imposed has undertaken the care, supervision or control of the person or property of another or is so placed in relation to that person or his property as to assume a particular responsibility for his or its safety ..". It will be convenient to refer to that common element as the "central element of control". Viewed from the perspective of the person to whom the duty is owed, the relationship of proximity giving rise to the non-delegable duty of care in such cases is marked by special dependence or vulnerability on the part of that person.*

15.4 Where an employer engages an independent contractor, while the work is done at the employer's request and for their benefit, it is considered as an independent function of the independent contractor who has undertaken it. This means that as a general rule there is no vicarious liability for the negligence of an independent contractor. However, employers are under a personal, non-delegable duty to take reasonable care to avoid exposing their employees to any unnecessary risk of injury which means providing a safe system of work. If the wrongful act of an independent contractor causes an injury to an employee, the employer will be personally liable for the breach of duty of care, whether or not the contractor is also liable. The question of vicarious liability does not arise: see *Kondis v STA* (1984) 154 CLR 672.

15.5 The test established by the House of Lords in *Century Insurance Co Ltd v Northern Ireland Transport Board* [1942] AC 509 asks the question whether the employee was carrying out the work he or she was employed to do. If the answer is affirmative, then the employer is vicariously liable even though the work is being carried out in an unauthorised or improper manner.

15.6 The courts principally use two tests to determine the nature of the relationship. The primary test is control; that is, the right of the employer to control the activities of the employee under the contract. A supplementary test is the integration test; here the courts consider whether the employee is sufficiently integrated into the organisation to be regarded as an employee by looking at factors such as the working of fixed hours, holiday and sick leave entitlements and a notice requirement to terminate the contract.

Problem Questions

15.1 If Jonas was employed by the hospital, the hospital may find itself vicariously liable for Jonas's negligence as it appears that he was acting in the course of his employment with the hospital at the time when he saw Sam. There is a non-delegable duty of care arising out of a protective relationship such as hospital and patient: see *Burnie Port Authority v General Jones Pty Ltd* (1994) 179 CLR 520 at 551. In such a case Sam would be advised to sue the hospital for damages for Jonas's negligence rather than Jonas, who is still only a student.

CHAPTER 15

Tutorial Questions

Discussion Questions

15.1 In *Canterbury Bankstown Rugby League Football Club Ltd v Bugden* [1993] Aust Torts Reports 81-246, why was the Canterbury Football Club found vicariously liable for compensatory damages?

15.2 Hayward operated a hotel. Flew, a customer at the hotel had arrived at opening for a long drinking session to drown his sorrows over the loss of his job the previous day. During the course of the day, he became increasingly offensive towards one of the barmaids. He ignored her requests to refrain from making suggestive and offensive comments to her. An argument developed late in the afternoon between them over his behaviour and he attempted to attack her. She flung the contents of a glass of beer in Flew's face and then threw the glass in his direction, striking him in the face and causing him to lose the sight of an eye.

Discuss.

CHAPTER 16

Nuisance

Reading

Sappideen, Vines, Grant and Watson, *Torts: Commentary and Materials*, Chapter 19.

Objectives

This chapter will explain:

- the torts of private and public nuisance;
- the factors that go to establishing the torts;
- the defences and remedies available; and
- the relationship between the two torts.

Principles

Introduction

[16.05] The term nuisance is shared by two torts which have the common feature that the defendant must in some way have acted to the annoyance (the annoyance being substantial and unreasonable) of another person or persons but which in other ways are quite distinct.

Figure 16.1: Nuisance

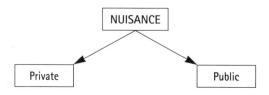

Private nuisance is a tort protecting the plaintiff's interest in the enjoyment of land. It derives from the action on the case, and is relied on where the invasion is indirect or where the invading "thing" is intangible.[1] So noise or an offensive sight will give rise to an action in nuisance.

Private nuisance grew up as a means of regulating the mutual obligations of neighbouring landowners. It is still necessary for the plaintiff in private nuisance to show an interest in land, though it is now clear that there is no need for the defendant to be shown to be in possession or occupation of land in order to commit the tort.[2]

Public nuisance, on the other hand, derives from the criminal law. It is a common law misdemeanour to commit acts to the annoyance of the general public such as obstruction of the highway or of a navigable river, pollution of the public water supply or of the waters of a harbour, or the keeping of a common gaming house. Civil proceedings may be taken by the Attorney-General to restrain the nuisance by an injunction under the power as parens patriae to act in the public interest. Private individuals may also maintain an action in tort in relation to the nuisance, but only if they can establish special damage to themselves above and beyond that suffered by the public generally.

---

[1] *Hollywood Silver Fox Farm v Emmett* [1936] 2 KB 468 (noise); *Phillips v California* (1960) 31 WWR 311 – escape of vibrations not trespassory.

[2] *Hubbard v Pitt* [1975] 2 WLR 254 (from highway); see also *Dollar Sweets Pty Ltd v Federal Confectioners Association of Australia* [1986] VR 383; *Boral Bricks v Frost* [1987] Aust Torts Reports 80-077; *Animal Liberation (Vic) v Gasse* [1991] 1 VR 51; cf *Thompson-Schwab v Costaki* [1956] 1 WLR 151 – misuse of premises caused nuisance on highway; *Bernstein v Skyviews* [1978] 1 QB 478 – repeated surveillance of plaintiff's land by air flights over it could amount to a nuisance.

Private nuisance

General features

[16.10] Private nuisance requires a substantial and unreasonable interference by the defendant with the plaintiff's enjoyment of his or her land.[3] An action in private nuisance requires an initial examination of the nature of the interference on the one hand and the defendant's conduct in producing it on the other, followed by a determination of reasonableness by striking a balance between the two.[4]

As in negligence, unreasonableness is a central determinant of liability for private nuisance, but the question of reasonableness differs as between the two torts. Negligence requires proof of actual damage or injury, and since the plaintiff's interest is in most situations regarded as worthy of protection against actual damage, the focus is almost entirely on the reasonableness or otherwise of the defendant's conduct in producing that damage. Nuisance protects against an interference with the enjoyment of land, and questions of degree will arise as to whether there has been a sufficiently substantial interference with that enjoyment, as well as on the nature of the defendant's conduct in producing it.

The use or enjoyment of the land protected by private nuisance may be the normal one of residing there and putting it to domestic use, but it is possible for nuisance to protect agricultural or commercial use. The plaintiff cannot succeed where he or she has put the land to a special extra-sensitive use requiring a greater degree of protection than the general community expects. The tort extends to numerous invasions, whether of tangibles such as fire,[5] flood[6] and dust[7] or of intangibles such as electricity,[8] noise[9] or offensive sights.[10] However, the tort has been held to cover cases where there has been no invasion, for example, where the defendant's activity outside the plaintiff's land had caused a power failure on that land: *British Celanese v Hunt* [1969] 1 WLR 959. Two New Zealand cases have questionably held that nuisance may even be committed by an activity of the defendant on the land itself: *Clearlite v Auckland CC* [1976] 2 NZLR 729; *Paxhaven Holdings Ltd v Attorney-General* [1974] 2 NZLR 185 (these decisions are labelled "questionable" as, ordinarily, private nuisance requires an indirect interference and thus usually flows from outside the land). It is also worth noting that nuisance need not be committed from private land, it can be committed from the highway or from the air space above the plaintiff's land: *Bernstein v Skyviews* [1978] QB 479.

The protection afforded by the action of private nuisance does not extend to conferring on the occupier a monopoly of view of what takes place on the land. The broadcast of commentaries of horse racing held on the plaintiff's land viewed from a

CHAPTER 16

---

[3]   See, eg, the definition of an actionable nuisance by Harris J in *Oldham v Lawson (No 1)* [1976] VR 654 at 655; *Don Brass Foundry Pty Ltd v Stead* (1948) 48 SR 482 at 485.

[4]   *Challen v McLeod Country Golf Club* [2004] Aust Torts Reports 81-760 – frequent incursion of golf balls from adjoining course onto appellant's land.

[5]   *Spicer v Smee* [1946] 1 All ER 489.

[6]   *Radstock Co-operative & Industrial Society v Norto-Radstock Urban DC* [1968] Ch 605; *Corbett v Pallas* [1995] Aust Torts Reports 81-329.

[7]   *Andreae v Selfridge* [1938] Ch 1; *Matania v NPB* [1936] 2 All ER 633.

[8]   *Bridlington Relay v Yorkshire EB* [1965] Ch 436.

[9]   *Halsey v Esso Petroleum* [1961] 1 WLR 683 (also acid smuts damaging clothing).

[10]   *Thompson-Schwab v Costaki* [1956] 1 WLR 151.

vantage point outside the land was deemed not to be a nuisance: *Victoria Park Racing v Taylor* (1937) 58 CLR 479. Nor does nuisance protect against merely being observed from outside the land: *Bathurst City Council v Saban* (1985) 2 NSWLR 704; *Bernstein v Skyviews* [1978] 1 QB 478. However extensive or repeated observance could well constitute nuisance: *Bernstein*. Again, nuisance does not protect the plaintiff's view from the land, nor the enjoyment of light, though the creation of an offensive sight may constitute nuisance as in *Thompson-Schwab v Costaki* [1956] 1 WLR 151 where the defendant used his premises as a brothel and the prostitutes repeatedly paraded on the highway outside the plaintiff's premises.[11] But in *Broderick Motors Pty Ltd v Rothe* [1986] Aust Torts Reports 80-059 the display of a car with an offensive message attached to it outside the premises of a car dealer did not constitute a nuisance.[12]

Cases such as these turn to some extent on the degree as well as the nature of the interference suffered by the plaintiff. Under a different principle, certain rights of land use attaching to land ownership are regarded as absolute and may be exercised whatever the effect on neighbouring land and whatever the motive for their exercise. In *Elston v Dore* (1982) 149 CLR 480 the High Court held that the defendant committed no tort by blocking two artificial drains on his land, thereby causing the plaintiff's land, from which water had previously passed through the drains, to become flooded. Nor was the defendant's motive for this action relevant. The matter would have been different had the defendant blocked a natural watercourse flowing through his land, but the plaintiff had no right to the preservation of the drains for his benefit.[13]

An important feature of private nuisance, though one that applies also to public nuisance, is that its continuance may be restrained by the issue of an injunction. The remedy is an important one since many nuisances are of a continuing nature.

It finally remains to note that New South Wales has introduced a statutory scheme under the *Trees (Disputes Between Neighbours) Act 2006*, which provides that no action may be brought in nuisance[14] by giving the Land and Environment Court jurisdiction (rather than Local Courts) power to make orders to remedy, restrain or prevent damage to property or to prevent injury to any person caused by a tree on adjoining land. The court must be satisfied that certain preconditions have been met before it can make an order under the Act. It must also consider specified matters in determining the application, and if it decides an application in favour of the applicant, it is given a wide charter to make orders to remedy, restrain or prevent specified harm as a consequence of the tree the subject of the application.[15] The court cannot make an order unless it is satisfied:

- that the applicant has made a reasonable effort to reach agreement with the owner of the land on which the tree is situated;
- if the requirement to give notice has not been waived, that the applicant has

---

[11] See also *Laws v Florinplace* [1981] 1 All ER 659 – sex shop in residential area was nuisance.

[12] Cf *Teamay v Severin* (1988) 94 FLR 47.

[13] *South Australia v Simionato* (2005) 143 LGERA 128 – did the extension of roots of plants from neighbouring property causing dessication and cracking constitute a nuisance.

[14] *Trees (Disputes Between Neighbours) Act 2006* (NSW), s 5.

[15] There is no restriction in the tort of nuisance to vegetation meeting the description of a tree. However, the definition of tree in s 3(1) of the *Trees (Disputes Between Neighbours) Act 2006* is more restrictive which means that the scope of application of the Act is restricted: see, for example, *Buckingham v Ryder* [2007] NSWLEC 458 where a vine, the pink trumpet vine, Podranea ricasoliana, which was not self-supporting, was not a tree for the purposes of the Act. The Act contains no limitation on bringing common law actions in trespass or negligence, regardless of whether the tree concerned is one to which the *Trees (Disputes Between Neighbours) Act 2006* applies: *Robson v Leischke* (2008) 159 LGERA 280.

given notice of the application in accordance with the Act; and

- that the tree concerned has caused, is causing, or is likely in the near future to cause, damage to the applicant's property; or is likely to cause injury to any person.[16]

Figure 16.2: Private nuisance – elements

- Unlawful interference with someone's interests in land:
  - physical (property) OR enjoyment damage.
- Unreasonable interference of recognisable rights:
  - balancing the rights of "neighbours";
  - neighbours must expect a certain amount of give and take.
- Invasion is usually indirect or intangible.

Equation of reasonableness

[16.15] As mentioned at [16.10], establishing private nuisance entails an examination of the effect of the alleged nuisance on the plaintiff and the nature of the defendant's conduct in producing it. These are not considered in isolation: each impinges on the other. The court may find the interference produced to be so intolerable that the defendant is liable, even though the defendant shows that there is no reasonable means of eliminating or mitigating it. In that case, the defendant must cease altogether engaging in the nuisance-producing activity: *Rapier v London Street Tramways* [1893] 2 Ch 588. In other cases the interference might not be sufficient to establish nuisance, were it not for the fact that the defendant has acted maliciously or negligently.

It is convenient to start with a consideration of the defendant's conduct in producing the interference.

Defendant's conduct

State of mind

[16.20] Liability runs from that point in time when the defendant knew or ought to have known of the nuisance. It is a relevant factor that the defendant has taken all reasonable steps to eliminate the nuisance, though this may not be enough to preclude liability: *Rapier v London Street Tramways* [1893] 2 Ch 588.[17] It is also a relevant factor that the defendant could have eliminated the nuisance by some reasonable expenditure or precaution. Malice is relevant and, where present, may elevate even the slightest interference to actionable nuisance. In *Hollywood Silver Fox Farm v Emmett* [1936] 2 KB 468 the defendant discharged guns on his land in order to interfere with the breeding of the plaintiff's valuable silver foxes, and he achieved this result. He was held liable in nuisance. The defendant argued that the degree of interference by noise through commission of an isolated act of this sort was not enough to constitute nuisance; also that the plaintiff was complaining of interference with an extra-sensitive use. No doubt

---

[16] *Trees (Disputes Between Neighbours) Act 2006* (NSW), s 10.
[17] See also *Challen v McLeod Country Golf Club* [2004] Aust Torts Reports 81-760.

this would have been sufficient to protect the defendant had his act been other than malicious. The same principle applies to retaliatory gestures engaged in as a protest against activities of the defendant.[18]

Domestic user

[16.25] Any ordinary or reasonable activity (done without malice or negligence) deemed to be consistent with the the common and ordinary use and occupation of land and houses is unlikely to support an action in nuisance. This was stated as a rule of law in *Bamford v Turnley* (1862) 122 ER 27, with Bramwell B providing as examples of acceptable use the burning of weeds, the emptying of cesspools and the making of noises during repairs. The application of the rule in *Clarey v Women's College* [1953] ALR 850 meant that there was no actionable nuisance for the noise created by those living in a residential college since it was merely incidental to occupation. The House of Lords confirmed the domestic user rule in *Southwark LBC v Mills* [1999] 4 All ER 449, where the plaintiff tenants complained of excessive noise created by ordinary domestic use of an adjoining flat caused by inadequate soundproofing of the intervening wall. The House held that the acts of the neighbours were not nuisances in themselves because of the domestic user rule. The plaintiffs could not succeed against the landlord because of the rule that the tenant takes the condition of the premises as it is found at the commencement of the lease,[19] the significant point here being the pre-existing status of the premises. An illustrative contrast is found in *Sampson v Hodgson-Pressinger* [1981] 3 All ER 710 which imposed liability in nuisance on a landlord for noise created by domestic use in an upstairs flat. In this case the problem arose after the lease had commenced when the landlord converted the upstairs flat by installing a tiled terrace, creating excessive noise in the downstairs flat.

Public interest

[16.30] The law seems reasonably clear that the public interest in the commission of the alleged nuisance is an irrelevant factor and that the courts will not allow it to determine whether a nuisance has been committed, nor whether an injunction should be granted: *Kennaway v Thompson* [1980] 3 All ER 329.[20] There is no reason why private interests should be sacrificed to those of the public at large, in the absence of statutory authority allowing it. So the private interest of the person affected prevailed over the interests of the employees of a firm who might lose their jobs if the nuisance was restrained by injunction: *Pennington v Brinsop Hall* (1877) 5 Ch D 769. Similarly, the interests of persons affected by a nuisance by smell, caused by the keeping of horses for milk deliveries, prevailed over those of consumers of milk, who would be affected if the defendant was restrained from keeping horses: *Munro v Southern Dairies* [1955] VLR 332.[21]

---

[18]   *Christie v Davey* [1893] 1 Ch 316 – defendant held liable in nuisance for noise created by banging pans and utensils as a protest against the noise of music coming from the plaintiff's premises, although the court found the degree of noise created might have been found reasonable if there had been no malicious intent of the defendant; cf *Fraser v Booth* (1950) 50 SR (NSW) 113 – some retaliatory measures did not constitute an unreasonable interference; *Pratt v Young* (1952) 69 WN (NSW) 214 – purposeful creation of conditions for rabbits to enter plaintiff's land was nuisance.

[19]   See to the same effect *Baxter v Camden LBC* [1999] 1 All ER 237.

[20]   See also *Lester-Travers v City of Frankston* [1970] VR 2 – nuisance through frequent incursion of golf balls onto plaintiff's land.

[21]   See also *Attorney-General v Birmingham Corporation* (1858) 4 K & J 528 – public interest in effective discharge of sewage did not excuse nuisance by discharging it into a river.

Effect of interference on plaintiff

[16.35] In *Walter v Selfe* (1851) 64 ER 849 Knight Bruce VC stated the test to be whether the interference was an:

> *inconvenience materially interfering with the ordinary comfort physically of human existence, not merely according to dainty modes and habits of living, but according to plain and sober and simple notions among the English people.*

Questions of degree must be resolved in order to decide whether the interference is sufficiently serious to constitute nuisance. In estimating degree, a further consideration is important. In *St Helens Smelting Co v Tipping* (1865) 11 HL Cas 642 Lord Westbury LC drew a distinction between a nuisance causing material damage to property and one that merely interferes with the occupier's comfort and enjoyment. The locality in which the alleged nuisance is committed is only relevant in the latter case, and here the question of degree becomes important, but not in the former.[22] The character of a neighbourhood may change and this process may be hastened by planning decisions taken by a planning authority. In *Gillingham BC v Medway (Chatham) Dock Co* [1992] 3 All ER 923 it was held that where planning approval had been given to convert a naval dockyard near a residential area into a commercial port, a public nuisance could not be established in relation to noise caused by heavy goods vehicles using the port between the hours of 7.00pm and 7.00am. This was due to the planning approval changing the character of the neighbourhood, and the fact that access to the port was only available through the residential area. Unlike the case of domestic user, locality is merely a relevant factor to reasonableness; not an absolute rule.

The relevance of location was discussed in *Colls v Home & Colonial Stores* [1904] AC 179 and Lord Halsbury explained (at 185):

> *What may be called the uncertainty of the test may also be described as its elasticity. A dweller in towns cannot expect to have as pure air, as free from smoke, smell, and noise as if he lived in the country, and distant from other dwellings, and yet an excess of smoke, smell, and noise may give a cause of action, but in each of such cases it becomes a question of degree, and the question is in each case whether it amounts to a nuisance which will give a right of action.*

It is thus a question of fact, a point emphasised in *Polsue v Rushmer* [1907] AC 121 (in which the above passage was cited with approval). In *Polsue* the respondent had carried out the business of a "dairyman" in Fleet Street, a district "devoted to the printing and allied trades". The appellant had set up a printing press in the neighbouring house to the respondent and the operation of the press during the night was at the heart of the action. Whilst the Lords acknowledged the relevance of the nature of the area it was not deemed to be decisive, and in this instance even a printing press in Fleet Street caused sufficient noise to constitute a nuisance.

It is clear that by "material damage to property" Lord Westbury (in *St Helens Smelting*) was referring to actual physical damage rather than loss in value of the property. Otherwise, the distinction would lose its significance since it is clear that the value of property is detrimentally affected by nuisances such as noise or smell. It is generally accepted that the temporary nature of the interference is a relevant factor in deciding

---

[22]   In *Halsey v Esso Petroleum* [1961] 1 WLR 683, Vaisey J found nuisance established by the mere proof of damage to clothing caused by acid smuts.

whether a nuisance has been committed. For example, a person may be expected to put up with noise and other discomfiture produced by his neighbour during temporary building operations, where the interference is no more than reasonable: *Andreae v Selfridge* [1938] Ch 1. On the other hand, it has been judicially stated that the loss of one night's sleep is a serious interference: *Andreae v Selfridge* [1938] Ch 1 accepted by Sholl J in *Munro v Southern Dairies* [1955] VLR 332. The relevance of the timing of the noise was emphasised in *Halsey v Esso Petroleum* [1961] 1 WLR 683, holding that there was a distinction between noise at night and day, "night being the time when ordinary men took their rest" (at 698). The court in *Halsey* determined that the plaintiff was entitled to an injunction between 10pm and 6am, with no limitation placed on the noise during daylight hours.

Unusually sensitive plaintiffs

[16.40] The defendant may in certain cases successfully argue that the plaintiff is unduly sensitive to the particular interference. "A man cannot increase the liabilities of his neighbour by applying his own property to special uses, whether for business or pleasure."[23] The rule operates both in relation to the extra-sensitivity of the plaintiff's property as well as to undue sensitivity on the part of the plaintiff, such as neurotic over-sensitivity to noise. Also, it is not necessary here to distinguish between interference with the enjoyment of land and physical damage to property. For example, in *Robinson v Kilvert* (1889) 41 Ch D 88 the plaintiff was found to be unable to recover damages in nuisance for damage done to his business stock of manufactured brown paper (an exceptionally sensitive trade) by heat from the defendant's pipes. The House of Lords in *Hunter v Canary Wharf* [1997] 2 All ER 426[24] unanimously held that interference with television reception caused by the erection of a tall building does not constitute nuisance. The residents in *Hunter* were not complaining about the building's erection but were merely seeking compensation for the interference with their enjoyment of television, the elimination of which did not require demolition of the building.

The rule in *Robinson v Kilvert* only applies where the interference with the extra-sensitive use is the only means of proving nuisance. If Robinson could have established that the heat was a substantial interference with his comfort, or that the heat caused damage to his property which was not extra-sensitive, he would, subject to the rules of remoteness of damage, have recovered for the damage done to his brown paper. In *McKinnon Industries v Walker* [1951] 3 DLR 577, where a nuisance was established by the invasion of poisonous chemical fumes, the plaintiff recovered for damage to his highly sensitive orchids caused by those fumes.

Damage

[16.45] Private nuisance lies for any unreasonable and substantial interference with the plaintiff's use and enjoyment of land. No actual damage, whether physical or financial, need be shown.[25] Substantial interference with the enjoyment of land is itself damage.

---

23   *E & SA Telegraph v Cape Town Tramways* [1902] AC 381 – plaintiffs' use of submarine cable for receipt of telegraphic messages was too sensitive to require protection against electrical interference.
24   But cf the Canadian case *Nor-Video Services v Ontario Hydro* (1978) 84 DLR (3d) 221.
25   *McCombe v Read* [1955] 2 QB 429; *Peisley v Ashfield Municipal Council* (1970) 21 LGRA 243; *Barton v Chibber* [1988] Aust Torts Reports 80-185.

Or, as it is sometimes put, the court presumes damage, and makes an award of general damages: *South Australia v Simionato* (2005) 143 LGERA 128; [2005] SASC 412.[26]

Private nuisance does not appear to be available for the recovery of personal injury. An influential passage from the judgment of Lord MacMillan in *Read v Lyons* [1947] AC 156 at 173 (though spoken about in the context of *Rylands v Fletcher* rather than nuisance) suggests that it is not available. It is clear law, however, that the plaintiff may recover damages for damage done to chattels on the land by the nuisance, as *Halsey v Esso Petroleum* [1961] 1 WLR 683 indicates.

Title to sue

[16.50] The plaintiff in nuisance must be in possession of the land under some proprietary or possessory title[27] to it, whether arising at law or in equity. Thus actual possession without legal title is sufficient.[28] An owner out of possession cannot sue in nuisance, although the owner is entitled to maintain proceedings on the case for damage to his or her reversionary interest in the land. Also the owner of an easement or profit à prendre may sue in nuisance for interference with the exercise of the right, without having to satisfy a requirement of possession: *Nicholls v Ely Beet Sugar Factory* [1931] 2 Ch 84.[29] A mere licensee, having neither possession nor any interest in the land cannot sue in nuisance. This means that a tenant can bring the action; but the tenant's spouse and children cannot (though a spouse's matrimonial interest would probably now allow the decision): *Malone v Laskey* [1907] 2 KB 141; *Oldham v Lawson (No 1)* [1976] VR 654.[30] The key point here is that the title to sue in nuisance rests on having the relevant interest in the land subject to the nuisance.

A more liberal approach to the question of who may bring an action in nuisance was adopted by the majority of the Court of Appeal in *Khorasandjian v Bush* [1993] QB 727.[31] In that case, the action was allowed to be brought by the daughter of the occupier, who had no possessory interest in the premises, but this case was overruled by the House of Lords in *Hunter v Canary Wharf* [1997] 2 All ER 426 (see [16.40]) where the law was stated in its original form.

---

[26]   *Asman v MacLurcan* [1985] 3 BPR 9592 at 9594. The cause of action will ordinarily accrue on proof of damage occurring: *McCombe v Read* [1955] 2 QB 429; *Peisley v Ashfield Municipal Council* (1970) 21 LGRA 243 (reversed on appeal but on a different point); *Peisley v Ashfield Municipal Council* (1971) 23 LGRA 166; *South Australia v Simionato* (2005) 143 LGERA 128; *Lister v Hong* [2006] NSWSC 1135.

[27]   *Foster v Warblington Urban DC* [1906] 1 KB 648 – plaintiff established he was engaged in an occupancy of a substantial nature. It would have been different if he had been a mere licensee: *Malone v Laskey* [1907] 2 KB 141.

[28]   *Newcastle-under-Lyme Corporation v Wolstanton* [1947] Ch 92; *Vaughan v Shire of Benalla* (1891) 17 VLR 129 – holder of a grazing licence had right to sue, even though he had no legal estate, interest or right to possession.

[29]   Also the holder of a riparian right pertaining to land: *Van Son v Forestry Commission of NSW* [1995] Aust Torts Reports 81-333.

[30]   But it would be different if the licensee had exclusive occupation together with an equity to remain binding the owner: *Dillwyn v Llewellyn* (1862) De G F 517; *Inwards v Baker* [1965] 2 QB 29.

[31]   Following *Motherwell v Motherwell* (1976) 73 DLR (3d) 62.

Figure 16.3: Private nuisance – who can sue?

> • Those with a proprietary interest: *Oldham v Lawson (No 1)*
>   [1976] VR 654.
> • What about family members?
>   – *Khorasandjian v Bush* [1993] QB 727 (UK): yes.
>   – *Hunter v Canary Wharf Ltd* [1997] 2 All ER 426 (UK):
>   overrules *Khorasandjian*.
>   – *Motherwell v Motherwell* (1976) 73 DLR (3d) 62 (Canada):
>   yes.

Strict liability and negligence

[16.55] Nuisance is sometimes stated to be a tort of strict liability. The defendant may of course be held liable in nuisance in circumstances where no reasonable care or precautions on his or her part will remove the nuisance, at least where the nuisance is continuing.[32] Here, however, the defendant is merely presented with the alternative of desisting from the activity causing the nuisance; to hold the defendant liable for failure to do so hardly imposes strict liability on the defendant.

The fact that most defendants know of the nuisance they have created by reason of its continuing nature does not prevent nuisance from being a tort of strict liability. A tort may be one of strict liability even though most people held liable for it are at fault. The question whether nuisance is a tort of strict liability resolves itself into whether the defendant may be held liable in nuisance for an interference which was neither known about by the defendant nor reasonably foreseeable.

As a starting point the present attitude of the higher courts, though not conclusive on the matter, suggests that nuisance will no longer be allowed to operate as a tort of strict liability. The decision of the High Court in *Burnie Port Authority v General Jones Pty Ltd* (1994) 120 ALR 42[33] is significant on this matter. In that case the defendant engaged contractors to do work involving welding in the roof of a cold-store building owned by the defendant. Sparks fell in the course of the welding onto some cartons containing a material, Isolite, which though initially difficult to ignite, will burn fiercely. It was established that the sparks from the welding ignited the Isolite and in the ensuing fire (which spread to the plaintiffs' adjoining premises) the plaintiffs' fruit and vegetables were destroyed. The High Court refused to apply the rule in *Rylands v Fletcher* (1868) LR 3 HL 330 or the old special rule concerning liability for fire on these facts, holding that both had become outmoded and no longer applied in Australia. That represented a decisive rejection by the High Court of two former torts of strict liability. Liability in these circumstances therefore depended on establishing negligence. The defendant Authority was held liable on the ground that the contractors were at fault, and the defendant owed the plaintiffs a non-delegable duty of care. Liability for nuisance was not considered even though there was previous authority that nuisance

---

[32] In *Rapier v London Street Tramways* [1893] 2 Ch 588 in which a nuisance of smell by the collection of horses was complained of, Lindley CJ said: "If they cannot have 200 horses together, even where they take proper precautions, without committing a nuisance, all I can say is they cannot have so many horses together."
[33] See also *Brodie v Singleton SC* (2001) 206 CLR 512.

was available in relation to isolated escapes of fire (as in this case) and that liability in nuisance in these circumstances was strict: for example, *Spicer v Smee* [1946] 1 All ER 489; *Midwood v Manchester Corporation* [1905] 2 KB 597. Whilst illustrative of the possibility of strict liability, it is important to remember that *Burnie* was not concerned with liability in nuisance and the position as regards strict liability for isolated escapes remains unsettled.

Liability in nuisance for damage caused by spreading tree roots has in some cases been held to be strict: *Davey v Harrow Corporation* [1958] 1 QB 60; *Barton v Chibber* [1988] Aust Torts Reports 80-185.[34] But the better view seems to be that no liability exists unless the defendant knows or ought to know of the spread: *Proprietors of Strata Plan No 14198 v Cowell* (1989) 24 NSWLR 478; *Solloway v Hampshire CC* (1981) 79 LGR 449.[35] The Supreme Court of South Australia, in discussing the encroachment of roots onto neighbouring land, noted (at [53]) that "in general terms it may be said that a person who creates a nuisance is liable for the damage caused by it and there is a sense in which his liability is a strict liability", thus it is open to some interpretation. A Tasmanian decision, *Kraemers v Attorney General (Tas)* [1966] Tas SR 113, held the Crown strictly liable for a nuisance created when it removed a bank of soil on another person's land with the consequence that water moved onto the plaintiff's land and flooded it.[36] On the other hand, it is clear that fault on the part of the defendant is necessary for liability to arise in nuisance caused by a natural event or the act of a third party: see [16.60].

One case in which strict liability for nuisance does exist is that of withdrawal of support for a neighbour's land by acts committed on the land of the defendant: *Dalton v Angus* (1881) 6 App Cas 740 at 791; *Fennell v Robson Excavations Pty Ltd* [1977] 2 NSWLR 486. At common law the liability does not extend to causing a withdrawal of support for neighbouring buildings (unless there is an easement of support for the building). However where support for land has been withdrawn, damages will be recoverable for the collapse of buildings on the land: *Pantalone v Alouie* (1989) 18 NSWLR 119. There is some doubt whether there is even a duty of care to prevent withdrawal of support for buildings: *Kebewar Pty Ltd v Harkin* (1987) 9 NSWLR 738. This was resolved in favour of the plaintiffs in *De Pasquale v Cavanagh Biggs* [1999] Aust Torts Reports 81-521. That case confirmed that liability exists on the part of those who work on or commission work on the land, such as a contractor or (as in *De Pasquale*) an architect. Whether nuisance by the withdrawal of support will continue to impose strict liability is now doubtful in the light of the majority judgment of the High Court in *Burnie*. There are clear indications there that the case is appropriate for the imposition of a non-delegable duty of care, rather than strict liability.

A further case of strict liability in nuisance relates to the collapse of buildings situated on the public highway due to want of repair. This rule is almost certainly limited to public nuisance and is dealt with under that heading.

---

[34] See *Sparke v Osborne* (1908) 7 CLR 51 at 71 where Isaacs J (as he then was) stated: "The respondent's case rests upon the contention that every landowner is bound at his peril to prevent damage to his neighbour by reason of plants of any kind extending over his boundary, and irrespective of whether their growth and development are entirely the work of nature or not."

[35] *Lister v Hong* [2006] NSWSC 1135.

[36] Subject to the exception in *Chasemore v Richards* (1859) 7 HL Cas 349, that is, water running in a known and defined subterranean channel, the removal of water from beneath the surface of one's own land, even if it causes damage to the plaintiff, does not give rise to liability to the plaintiff in nuisance: *South Australia v Simionato* (2005) 143 LGERA 128; *Xuereb v Viola* [1990] Aust Torts Reports 81-012.

To say that nuisance is no longer a tort of strict liability does not mean that it is identical to negligence. In particular, negligence does not protect against interference with the comfort and enjoyment of an occupier of land in the absence of physical damage caused by the interference. Where there is such damage, however, the two torts appear to be identical at least as regards liability for the infliction of the damage. It is true, as Lord Goff pointed out in *Cambridge Water Co v Eastern Counties Leather plc* [1994] 2 AC 265, that nuisance requires unreasonable rather than careless use of land on the defendant's part. But it is hard to see how unreasonable use in the case of isolated escapes or those not known to the defendant can mean anything other than fault.

Natural events and act of third party

[16.60] For an occupier to be held responsible for a nuisance for which, initially, he or she is in no way responsible there must be either actual or imputed knowledge of the nuisance. Such situations arise when a nuisance is created by a third party (whether a contractor, invitee or trespasser) or by natural forces. In *Sedleigh-Denfield v O'Callaghan* [1940] AC 880 the House of Lords held that an occupier of land who had knowledge of a nuisance created there by a trespasser, had a duty of care to remove it once he knew or ought to have known of it. A failure to remove the nuisance would give rise to liability for either "continuing or adopting the nuisance". "Continuing" the nuisance means failure to remove it. "Adopting" it means using it for one's own purposes. The nuisance in question was removable by the simple and inexpensive means of placing a grating over a culvert pipe. In *Goldman v Hargrave* [1967] 1 AC 645 the defendant, a landowner in Western Australia, discovered that a redgum tree on his land had been struck by lightning and caught fire. He decided to fell the tree and let the fire burn itself out. A sudden change of wind caused the fire to increase and spread to the plaintiff's land on which it caused damage. The fire could easily have been extinguished at minimal expense by the use of water. The Privy Council held the defendant liable here both in nuisance and negligence. Indeed liability in the two torts was here legally indistinguishable. A duty to take careful action to remove the nuisance had to be established. Such a duty might be found to exist in a case where the condition arose naturally on the land without any fault on the part of the defendant. However, the standard of care required of the defendant in taking steps to remove the nuisance must take into account the defendant's resources, both physical and financial. If expensive work was required, the only duty might be to invite the assistance of neighbours in removing the nuisance.

A further question is whether an occupier of land should be held liable for the actions of persons who have trespassed on their land and then committed nuisances on neighbouring properties. In accordance with the above cases some amount of knowledge and tolerance of the presence of those persons on the part of the occupier is necessary to establish liability. But further questions as to the reasonableness of the defendant's behaviour will arise in relation to whether it can be shown that the defendant has adopted the nuisance.[37] Clearly therefore, once the occupier becomes aware of the nuisance on their land, it is no defence to argue that they did not create the nuisance. The law imposes a positive duty to act to remove or, at the very least, minimise the nuisance.

---

[37] See, eg, *Page Motors v Epsom BC* (1983) 80 LGR 337 – council had adopted the nuisance by providing gypsies with a variety of services; cf *Lippiatt v South Gloucestershire CC* [1999] 3 WLR 137 – element of adoption not present.

Creator

[16.65] A person who creates a nuisance will be liable,[38] but the creator need not be in occupation of land.[39] So the tort may be committed by an independent contractor (for example, *Wherry v KB Hutcherson Pty Ltd* [1987] Aust Torts Reports 80-107) or a trespasser on another person's land: *Southport v Esso Petroleum* [1953] All ER 1204 per Devlin J at 1207 (dicta).

Liability can continue for the person who creates the nuisance even after he or she has disposed of the land and even if they possess no ability to abate the nuisance: *Roswell v Prior* (1700) 88 ER 1570; *South Australia v Simionato* (2005) 143 LGERA 128. If more than one person contributes to a nuisance, all are individually liable notwithstanding that the contribution of any one of them would be insufficient on its own to constitute a nuisance: *Bonnici v Ku-ring-gai Municipal Council* (2001) 121 LGERA 1.[40]

Figure 16.4: Private nuisance – who is liable?

- Person who creates the nuisance:
  - not necessarily the owner or occupier.
- May be sued for the actions of others if:
  - adopts or passively permits interference to continue;
  - knows or ought to be aware of it; and
  - is able to take reasonable precautions to bring the interference to an end.

Authorisation of nuisance

[16.70] Any person, entitled to control the use of land, who authorises a use of that land which results in a nuisance, is responsible for that activity and will be held liable. So a landlord who let land, knowing it was to be used for the purpose of a lime quarry, was held liable for authorising the nuisance created by the quarry: *Harris v James* (1876) 45 LJQB 545. Here it seems that the nuisance was treated as an inevitable result of quarrying. The case may be compared with *Smith v Scott* [1973] 1 Ch 314 where a local authority let property to a family known to be a "problem" family. The local authority was not liable in nuisance in respect of physical damage to the plaintiff's property and noise committed by the members of the family. The tenancy agreement had actually prohibited the commission of a nuisance by the tenant; in any case nuisance was not inevitable but was merely foreseeable.[41] Interestingly, foreseeability was held to be enough to constitute liability for a nuisance in *De Jager v Payenham Lodge* (1984) 36

---

[38] *Fennell v Robson Excavations Pty Ltd* (1977) 2 NSWLR 486 – defendant liable for creating a nuisance on plaintiff's land; see also *Paxhaven Holdings Ltd v Attorney-General* [1974] 2 NZLR 185.

[39] *Cambridge Water Co v Eastern Counties Leather plc* [1994] 2 AC 264 per Lord Goff of Chieveley at 300; *South Australia v Simionato* (2005) 143 LGERA 128.

[40] See, eg, *Thorpe v Brumfitt* (1873) 8 Ch App 650 at 656; *Blair & Sumner v Deakin; Eden & Thwaites v Deakin* (1887) 57 LT 522 at 525; *Pride of Derby & Derbyshire Angling Association Ltd v British Celanese Ltd* [1952] 1 All ER 1326 (per Harman J at 1331-1333).

[41] Pennycuick V-C's statement of the law relating to a lessor's liability for a nuisance created by a tenant in *Smith v Scott* was referred to with approval in *Wilkie v Blacktown City Council* (2002) 121 LGERA 444 and his comments on the absence of a duty of care on a landlord in selecting tenants were endorsed in *W D & HO Wills (Aust) v SRA* (1998) 43 NSWLR 338.

SASR 498. In this instance the owner and occupier of a suburban hall let it out for functions and, despite their best efforts to prevent inappropriate use the hirers would, on occasion, create a nuisance through excessive noise. Liability attached on the basis of foreseeability of the nuisance. The requisite level of foreseeability does not, however, require actual knowledge. In *R v Shorrock* [1993] 3 All ER 917, the defendant had let a field to three people and gone away for the weekend. The field was then used for an "acid house party" attended by in excess of 3,000 people and was the subject of 275 individual complaints.[42] The defendant was held liable for the nuisance on the ground that he ought to have known it would be created. In other words there were sufficient facts known to the defendant, at the time of letting, to put him on notice of the likely creation of a nuisance.

Continuation/adoption of nuisance

[16.75] This has already been considered in relation to the decision in *Sedleigh-Denfield v O'Callaghan* [1940] AC 880: see [16.60]. The question often arises in relation to nuisances created by predecessors in title of the occupier. In one such case, the occupier was held not liable for the flooding of the plaintiff's land caused by the condition of a downpipe on the defendant's premises, since the condition had been caused by the defendant's predecessor, and the defendant neither knew nor ought to have been aware of it.[43] In other words, the defendant will only be liable where he or she knew or ought to have known of the existence of the nuisance and failed to take reasonable steps to abate it in a timely fashion.[44] In *Torette House Pty Ltd v Berkman* (1939) 62 CLR 637, Dixon J (at 659) emphasised that fault by a land holder in respect of the commission of a nuisance is essential: "to enter into occupation of land upon which a potential source of nuisance or of mischief to others exists is not enough to impose liability for the consequences upon the new occupier. Some element of fault on his part is necessary." These cases demonstrate once again that nuisance is not always tort of strict liability.

Vicarious liability

[16.80] Where the nuisance has been created by the defendant's employee, the defendant is liable provided *the employee was acting in the course of the employment*. There is vicarious liability for a nuisance created by an independent contractor where the work commissioned creates a particular likelihood of a nuisance being created;[45] also where the contractor's work causes a withdrawal of support from neighbouring land: *Dalton v Angus* (1881) 6 App Cas 740.

---

[42] This was, in fact, a case in public nuisance but the position with respect to knowledge is relevant here.

[43] See also *Montana Hotels Pty Ltd v Fasson Pty Ltd* [1987] Aust Torts Reports 80-109; *Torette House Pty Ltd v Berkman* (1940) 62 CLR 618; *St Anne's Well Brewery v Roberts* (1928) 149 LT 1.

[44] See, eg, *Wilkins v Leighton* [1932] 2 Ch 106; *Sedleigh-Denfield v O'Callaghan* [1940] AC 880; *Morgan v Khyatt* [1964] AC 475; *Goldman v Hargrave* (1966) 115 CLR 458; *Cartwright v McLaine & Long Pty Ltd* (1979) 143 CLR 549; *Proprietors of Strata Plan No 14198 v Cowell* (1989) 24 NSWLR 478; *Richmond City Council v Scantelbury* [1991] 2 VR 38; *Valherie v Strata Corporation No 1841 Inc* (2003) 86 SASR 245. An occupier who knows or ought to know of a nuisance and that there is the possibility of danger occurring as a result, must take such positive action as a reasonable person, in his or her position and circumstances, would consider necessary to eliminate the nuisance: *Sedleigh-Denfield v O'Callaghan* [1940] AC 880; *Montana Hotels Pty Ltd v Fasson Pty Ltd* (1986) 61 ALJ 282; *City of Richmond v Scantelbury* [1991] 2 VR 38; *Delaware Mansions Ltd v Westminster City Council* [2002] 1 AC 321; *South Australia v Simionato* (2005) 143 LGERA 128.

[45] *Matania v National Provincial Bank* [1936] 2 All ER 633 – building work creating nuisance by noise and dust.

Landlord and tenant

[16.85] The tenant as occupier is liable under the normal principles of nuisance. The landlord is liable if the nuisance existed on the premises at the time of letting, and the landlord knew or should have known of its existence: *Brew Bros Ltd v Snax (Ross) Ltd* [1970] 1 QB 612.[46] In such a case it is no defence for the landlord to show that the lease placed the obligation to repair the premises on the tenant: *Brew Bros*. The landlord is also liable for nuisances arising from disrepair of the premises, where he or she has covenanted to repair[47] or where he or she has reserved the right to enter and do repairs.[48] In the above cases the liability for the nuisance is not strict.

Defences

Prescription

[16.90] The privilege to commit a nuisance may only be acquired if the right amounts to an easement by prescription; that is, by 20 years' continuous exercise of the conduct constituting the nuisance by the defendant. The conditions under which the defence may be established are the following:

- The content of the nuisance must be capable of being made the subject of a grant by the owner of the servient estate. The interpretation of this seems to be that it must be sufficiently specific. Thus an easement might arise to emit smoke through a party wall but not a nuisance to emit smoke generally: *Jones v Pritchard* [1908] 1 Ch 630.
- The prescriptive period does not begin to run where the defendant's act is done secretly or under protest from the plaintiff. Also it must acquire the character of a nuisance before the prescriptive period begins to run.[49]

Conduct or consent of plaintiff

[16.95] It is not a defence that the plaintiff has "come to the nuisance". *Sturges v Bridgman* (1879) 11 Ch D 852 shows that this rule applies also to the case where the nuisance arises from a change in the use of the plaintiff's land by the plaintiff. This point was confirmed by the decision in *Proprietors of Strata Plan No 14198 v Cowell* (1989) 24 NSWLR 478 in which the plaintiff was allowed to succeed in an action brought for a nuisance caused by tree roots, the damage having been sustained when the plaintiff built units at the boundary of his land. *Miller v Jackson* [1977] QB 966 threw doubt on the rule about coming to the nuisance. In *Miller*, while the defendant's activity was considered unreasonable and substantial such as to entitle the plaintiff to a verdict

---

[46] In *Peden Pty Ltd v Bortolazzo* [2006] 2 Qd R 574 the Queensland Court of Appeal held that a lessor was not responsible for the creation of a nuisance created by a tenant unless the lessor let the premises for a purpose calculated to cause a nuisance. See also *Montana Hotels Pty Ltd v Fasson Pty Ltd* [1987] Aust Torts Reports 80-109 where the Privy Council upheld a decision of the Full Court of the Victorian Supreme Court that the defendant occupier of the adjoining building was not liable in nuisance because the occupier had not known of the defective downpipe and there was no reason why it should have known.

[47] *Wringe v Cohen* [1940] 1 KB 229 – the case concerned liability in public nuisance for a house situated on the highway, but it is assumed the same liability would apply in private nuisance.

[48] *Wilchick v Marks* [1934] 2 KB 56; *Mint v Good* [1951] 1 KB 517 – again these were public nuisance cases arising out of a danger to the highway, but their principle presumably extends to private nuisance.

[49] *Sturges v Bridgman* (1879) 11 Ch D 852 – the prescriptive period did not begin to run until the plaintiff set up consulting rooms at the bottom of his garden and found that the noise interfered with their use.

and damages, the defendant's activity which caused the interference was considered reasonable enough in the circumstances to deny an injunction. Effectively, the court was saying that the defendant may continue the activity, but must pay the plaintiff for the interference it causes.

Consent may operate as a defence to an action in nuisance. Clearly an express consent puts the matter beyond doubt. Merely tolerating the nuisance does not establish the defence. In *Kiddle v City Business Properties* [1942] 1 KB 269 consent was found to have been established on the part of an occupier of a shared building to a nuisance caused by a shared facility, in this case a common water supply.

Contribuory negligence

[16.100] If the nuisance has been established as a result of the defendant's negligent actions, it may be possible to raise the defence of contributory negligence. This possibility was raised in *White v Humphries* (1984) 1 MVR 426 (in the context of an obstruction on the highway following an accident) but was not specifically resolved.

Conformation of the land

[16.105] A defendant may plead that their activity did not alter the conformation of the land (that is, its general shape or form) and that they were therefore not responsible for creating the nuisance, but it is submitted that it is a difficult defence to successfully plead unless the defendant can establish that they had no knowledge of its existence.[50]

Statutory authority

[16.110] In establishing a defence of statutory authority the defendant's first task is to show that the statutory provision applies to the act in question. In *Allen v Gulf Oil Refining* [1981] 2 WLR 188, Gulf Oil was empowered by statute to acquire certain land for the purpose of establishing an oil refinery at a particular location. The Court of Appeal held Gulf Oil liable for a nuisance caused by the operation of the refinery since the power to operate it was not expressly conferred by the statute. This decision was reversed by the House of Lords. The power to establish the refinery carried with it by necessary implication the power to operate the refinery.

As regards the availability of the defence where the statutory provision covers the activity in question, the rules have been stated and restated on numerous occasions, but the result has generally been confusion. The following is a statement of the present position arrived at in Australia:

- Where there is negligence in the execution of the power or duty, liability in nuisance arises. The burden of proving no negligence lies on the defendant: *Geddis v Bann Reservoir* (1878) 3 App Cas 430.

- Where there is no negligence in the execution of the power or duty, the defendant succeeds by showing that the creation of the nuisance was the inevitable result of carrying into execution the statutory power or duty: *Tock v St John's Metropolitan Area Board* [1989] 2 SCR 1181 at 1214 (Canada); *Bonnici*

---

[50] In *Sedleigh-Denfield v O'Callaghan* [1940] AC 889; *Goldman v Hargrave* [1967] 1 AC 645; and *Leakey v National Trust for Places of Historic Interest* [1980] QB 485, the court recognised that in each case there existed a liability in the land owner for damage caused to an adjoining land owner by reason of things which occurred on their land, even though they occurred as a result of natural causes or the actions of a trespasser. In each case, the occupier was held liable for failing to take reasonable means to eradicate the nuisance, after he had knowledge of its existence.

v Ku-ring-gai Municipal Council (2001) 121 LGERA 1; [2001] NSWSC 1124. "Inevitability" in this context means that the literal terms of the power or duty sanctions the interference: *Melaleuca Estate Pty Ltd v Port Stephens Council* (2006) 143 LGERA 319; [2006] NSWCA 31.

- Where a specific work is commissioned by the statute but the defendant is left with a measure of discretion as to how to achieve it, the defendant is liable in nuisance unless it is shown that it was practically impossible to avoid creating a nuisance. Proving inevitability lies on the defendant, and this burden is no light one. In *York Bros (Trading) Pty Ltd v Commissioner for Main Roads* [1983] 1 NSWLR 391, the court held that the statutorily authorised building of a bridge over a navigable river must not be done so as to prevent navigability, even though the cost of a lift-span bridge to allow navigation would have been 66% higher and the plaintiffs were the only persons whose navigation would have been interrupted.

  Where a general power is conferred by the statute, it must not be exercised so as to create a nuisance. Proof of the inevitability of creating a nuisance is in effect impossible. In *Metropolitan Asylum District v Hill* (1881) 6 App Cas 193 the House of Lords held that the existence of a general statutory power to build hospitals did not legitimise the building of a smallpox hospital in a situation where it gave rise to a nuisance. A general power of this nature must be exercised so as not to interfere with private rights.

If the Parliament is to deny an applicant relief against actionable private nuisance committed by the Crown, it must do so in clear words: Hodgson J in *Attrill v Richmond River Shire Council* (1993) 30 NSWLR 122 at 127; Gzell J in *Alamdo Holdings Pty Ltd v Bankstown City Council* (2003) 134 LGERA 114.

Figure 16.5: Private nuisance – defences

- Burden of proof generally lies on defendant.
- Defences include:
  - prescriptive right to continue the interference complained of (must be continued interference for more than 20 years);
  - conduct or consent of the plaintiff;
  - contributory negligence;
  - conformation of the land;
  - statutory authority.
- Ineffective defences include:
  - plaintiff came to the nuisance;
  - activities complained of benefit the public;
  - benefit to the public outweighs detriment to the plaintiff.

Remoteness of damage

[16.115] The issue of remoteness is relevant when the nature of damage (and thus a damages claim) is under consideration but it does not form part of the inquiry into whether there has been an interference with the use or enjoyment of the land. *Cambridge Water Co v Eastern Counties Leather plc* [1994] 2 AC 265 (see [16.55]) has settled the rule for English law that the damage must be a reasonably foreseeable consequence of the nuisance; nor is there any reason to doubt that this is the Australian position also.

Remedies

[16.120] There are three possible remedies for private nuisance: abatement of the nuisance,[51] damages and an injunction to prevent the continuance of the nuisance. The first remedy was considered under defences to intentional torts in Chapter 7. It remains to consider whether the remedies of damages and injunction may be sought in conjunction with each other. The damages awarded will depend upon the court's willingness to issue an injunction, since the court has power to award damages in lieu of an injunction: see [16.140]. Where this is done, damages will cover both past and future loss; where an injunction is awarded, only past loss will be compensated. Damages for depreciation in the value of property will not generally be awarded where an injunction is granted. The court may quantify the interference with the land according to reasonable and unreasonable interference, awarding damages only for the latter: *Andreae v Selfridge* [1938] Ch 1.

Damages may cover actual losses, such as property damage, or financial loss through interference with trade or depreciation in the value of the land affected. Damages may also be awarded for an interference with the enjoyment of land even where no actual damage is suffered. These are difficult to assess; nevertheless the court must attempt the task. In *Bone v Seale* [1975] 1 WLR 797, UK£1,000 damages were awarded for a nuisance by smell caused by a pig farm, the nuisance lasting two years. In *Oldham v Lawson (No 1)* [1976] VR 654 the plaintiff was awarded $500 in respect of one year's interference by noise. In *Challen v McLeod Country Golf Club* [2004] Aust Torts Reports 81-760 the plaintiff was awarded $12,000 for a nuisance caused by the entry of golf balls onto her property over a 10-year period.

Proprietors of Strata Plan No 14198 v Cowell (1989) 24 NSWLR 478 raised the issue of the award of damages to a person who has taken reasonable steps to abate the nuisance. Here, the principle that the plaintiff is able to recover the costs of mitigation from the defendant as damages prevailed. So the plaintiffs in that case were able to recover the costs of mitigating a nuisance caused by tree roots.

In limited circumstances exemplary damages may be awarded but there must be evidence of either contemptuous disregard of, or arrogant indifference to, the plaintiff's rights.[52]

In numerous cases the court has had to decide whether to award damages rather than issue an injunction, that award being intended as the final resolution of the action, so that the damages compensate for both past and future losses. The courts are notably reluctant to refuse an injunction and compensate by damages, since to do so would

---

[51]   New South Wales aside (because of the *Trees (Disputes Between Neighbours) Act 2006* (NSW)), if the nuisance involves branches and/or roots, even though actual damage has not yet occurred, the neighbour has a right to abate by cutting away at the boundary so much of the branches and/or roots that encroach: *Lemmon v Webb* [1894] 3 Ch 1; *Smith v Giddy* [1904] 2 KB 448; *Mills v Brooker* [1919] 1 KB 555; *Butler v Standard Telephones & Cables Limited* [1940] 1 All ER 121; *Young v Wheeler* [1987] Aust Torts Reports 80-126; *Robson v Leischke* (2008) 159 LGERA 280. However, the occupier does not have a right to cut away branches or roots growing between the tree and the boundary as this would amount to trespass as they are still part of the property of the owner of the land on which the trees grow: *Gazzard v Hutchesson* [1995] Aust Torts Reports 81-337. The neighbour who cuts away the branches or roots should return them to the tree owner to avoid liability for conversion: *Mills v Brooker* [1919] 1 KB 555.

[52]   *Commonwealth v Murray* [1988] Aust Torts Reports 80-207.

amount to an expropriation of the plaintiff. The relevant principles are those laid down by A L Smith LJ in *Shelfer v City of London Electric Lighting* [1895] 1 Ch 287. In that case, he said that damages would be awarded in lieu of an injunction only in an unusual case. For the award of such damages, four conditions had to be met:

- the injury to the plaintiff's rights must be small;
- the injury must be one which is capable of being estimated in money;
- the injury must be one which can be adequately compensated by a small monetary payment; and
- the case must be one where it would be oppressive to the defendant to grant an injunction.

The power to award damages in addition to, or in lieu of, an injunction was conferred by the *Chancery Amendment Act 1858* (UK) (*Lord Cairns' Act*), the original courts of equity having no power to award damages. *Lord Cairns' Act* is replicated under statutory provisions throughout Australia. Its main effect is to enable courts to award damages in respect of threatened future loss arising from the nuisance, a power not available at common law. Although damages are awarded in lieu of an injunction, there is still power to award damages even though the court would refuse an injunction on the facts of the case: *Barbagaflo v J & F Catelan Pty Ltd* [1986] 1 Qd R 245 at 251. It should be noted that the combination of *Lord Cairns' Act* and the ability of the court to grant a quia timet injunction[53] against the threatened commission of a tort by the defendant means that the court has power to award damages in lieu of an injunction for that threatened tort: *Leeds Industrial Co-operative Society v Slack* [1924] AC 851.[54]

Figure 16.6: Private nuisance – remedies

- Abatement (summary removal of nuisance by person affected without recourse to legal proceedings).
- Injunction to restrain continuation of the interference in the future.
- Damages in respect of past interference.

Public nuisance

[16.125] A public nuisance was defined by Romer LJ in *Attorney-General v PYA Quarries* [1957] 2 QB 169 at 184 as:

---

53 A quia timet injunction might lie to restrain apprehended or impending damage to a neighbour's property, for example, by encroaching tree branches or roots, but only if there is proof that it is imminent or likely to occur in the near future and is very substantial or almost irreparable: *Fletcher v Bealey* (1885) 28 Ch D 688; *Hooper v Rogers* [1975] Ch 43; *Robson v Leishke* (2008) 159 LGERA 280. Such an injunction should not be granted prematurely and while there should be a real appreciable probability of irreparable damage, this is not an absolute standard. Ultimately, what should be aimed at is justice between the parties, having regard to all the circumstances: *Hooper v Rogers* [1975] Ch 43 at 50.
54 See also Hodgson CJ in *Wallace v Powell* (2000) 10 BPR 18,481.

any nuisance which materially affects the reasonable comfort and convenience of life of a class of Her Majesty's subjects. The sphere of the nuisance may be described generally as the "neighbourhood".

What comprises a sufficient number of persons to constitute a class of "the public" is a question of fact in every case. It is sufficient if there is a representative cross-section of the class that has been so affected: *Baulkham Hills SC v Domachuk* (1988) 66 LGRA 110; *Farley & Lewers Ltd v A-G (NSW)* (1962) 63 SR (NSW) 814.

A private citizen may only sue in the tort of public nuisance where he or she can establish special damage above and beyond that suffered by other members of the affected section of the public. The requirement of special damage relates both to the ability to claim damages in this tort and to proceed for an injunction.

Figure 16.7: Public nuisance – general principles

> - Protects the shared rights of the public.
> - Consists of interference with any rights shared by the public.
> - Interference must be substantial and unreasonable:
>   – to public land;
>   – obstructing highway/polluting river/discharging oil in sea;
>   – must consider realities of business and commercial life.
> - Is a criminal offence at common law and under statute (in those jurisdictions that have codified the criminal law).

Basis of liability

[16.130] As in the case of private nuisance, public nuisance is generally not a tort of strict liability. Unreasonable behaviour on the part of the defendant must be established in relation to the creation of the nuisance, and such behaviour will contain an element of fault.[55] But what is unreasonable must take account of the realities of business and commercial life. It is not public nuisance to run such a successful business in a business premises on the highway that a crowd collects there at certain times of the day, thereby obstructing the highway, even though the gathering of such a crowd is reasonably foreseeable: *Silservice v Supreme Bread* (1949) 50 SR (NSW) 127. It is a different position where the defendant could have so arranged the business that no such crowd need have collected, whether by arranging the time of the services (*Lyons v Gulliver* [1914] 1 Ch 631) or by ensuring that they were offered off the highway: *Fabbri v Morris* [1947] 1 All ER 315. Leaving a broken-down and unlit vehicle on the public highway is, without negligence, not a public nuisance: *Maitland v Raisbeck* [1944] KB 689. In such a case the nuisance is not created immediately, but only if the defendant "allows the obstruction to continue for an unreasonable time or in unreasonable

---

[55] *R v Shorrock* [1994] QB 279 – landowner/occupier liable for a public noise nuisance, of which he knew or ought to have known, created on his land by his licensees.

circumstances": *Parish v Judd* (1960) 3 All ER 33. Unreasonable time or unreasonable cirumstances were relevant in the decision of *Volman t/as Volman Engineering v Lobb; Mobil Oil Australia Pty Ltd v Lobb* [2005] NSWCA 348 in which public nuisance was proved against both Mobil and Volman after a Mobil station site was demolished and the footpaths alongside the site were covered with mud for a period of weeks. This was deemed to constitute a substantial and unreasonable interference with the public's right to pass along the footpath, and thus a public nuisance.[56] With respect to the leaving of a vehicle on a roadway, there is a difference between a truck and a car. In *Dymond v Pearce* [1972] 1 QB 496, public nuisance was found where the truck was parked for some hours at night on a public highway. This was so even though the truck had adequate illumination and there was plenty of room for other traffic to pass. The truck still constituted an unreasonable obstruction of the highway. But in *Trevett v Lee* [1955] 1 WLR 113, where the defendant had left a hosepipe across the public highway in conditions of drought and the plaintiff had tripped over it and been injured, it was found that the defendant's use of the highway in these circumstances was not an unreasonable one.

Public nuisance and negligence

[16.135] We saw in Chapter 10 that in *The Wagon Mound (No 2)* [1967] 1 AC 617 the Privy Council held the defendants liable for a spillage of oil onto the waters of Sydney Harbour and the consequent damage by fire to the plaintiffs' ship which was moored in the harbour. Although the view may legitimately be held that the question of liability for the fire damage was one of remoteness of damage once a public nuisance by oil pollution of the waters of the harbour had been established, the actual reasoning of Lord Reid in the Privy Council does not support this conclusion. He tested the slight risk of fire against the conduct of the defendant in producing that risk, finding the latter to have acted unreasonably. This was to treat the matter as one of breach rather than remoteness of damage. The creation of a public nuisance was merely one factor in showing the unreasonableness of the defendant's conduct. This approach appears to deny public nuisance the status of a tort separate from negligence. However, proving a public nuisance will almost invariably preclude argument as to whether the defendant has behaved reasonably, so that the question of liability for damage caused by the nuisance becomes one of remoteness of damage.[57] And there remains an advantage to suing in public nuisance rather than negligence: the tort allows recovery for pure economic loss, and for other loss not covered by negligence. It is relevant to note that the tort of public nuisance in the context of public authorities (in particular, highway authorities) was recognised as being subsumed by negligence law in the High Court decision of *Brodie v Singleton SC; Ghantous v Hawkesbury CC* (2001) 206 CLR 512 (see [16.145] and [16.150]).

---

[56] Volman, as the creator of the nuisance, was liable for its foreseeable consequences, including personal injury to a person slipping on the mud: *Fennel v Robson Excavations Pty Ltd* [1977] 2 NSWLR 486. While the nature of the operations being carried out did not give rise to a non-delegable duty on the part of an occupier, Mobil nevertheless had a duty to ascertain from time to time whether those activities were causing a nuisance and should have known of the hazard at a time when reasonable steps to deal with the hazard would have prevented the accident.

[57] *Dymond v Pearce* [1972] 1 QB 496 treated the question of liability in public nuisance for personal injury caused by the parked truck as one of causation, though the result of this (that there was no liability because the parking of the truck created no foreseeable risk of the accident which occurred) could just as easily have been reached had the action been treated as one of negligence.

Special damage

[16.140] The plaintiff in public nuisance must show damage to himself or herself exceeding that suffered by members of the general public. Personal injury, which unlike the case of private nuisance is undoubtedly recoverable in public nuisance, is an obvious example of special damage. So is damage to property.[58] Interference by noise is recoverable provided it exceeds that inflicted on the general public who are subject to the nuisance.[59] Economic loss arising from an interference with the plaintiff's right to use the highway or a navigable river is recoverable as special damage. So in *Rose v Miles* (1815) 4 M & S 101; 105 ER 773[60] a barge-man succeeded in his action against the defendant who had wrongfully moored his boat across a navigable river, causing the plaintiff to have to unload his cargo and transport it overland.[61] Economic loss arising from interference with business customers' access to premises arising from an obstruction of the highway is also recoverable.[62]

Mere inconvenience arising from an obstruction of the highway has been held to be recoverable in public nuisance. In *Boyd v GN Railway* [1895] 2 IR 555 the plaintiff, a doctor, recovered damages for being held up for 20 minutes at a level-crossing because his time had a pecuniary value. *Walsh v Ervin* [1952] VLR 361 took the matter one stage further. The plaintiff complained that through the defendant's obstruction of the highway over a three-year period he had been deprived of access to his property by motor-vehicle and had been forced to transport his sheep by a more indirect route. He received damages for this in public nuisance, although the court did not treat the inconvenience as having a pecuniary effect.

Figure 16.8: Public nuisance – who can sue?

- No need for proprietary rights.
- Ordinarily the state (director of public prosecutions or attorney general).
- Private individual:
  - if individual can show he or she suffered a "particular" or "special" loss or a greater loss than the public.

---

[58] *Castle v St Augustine's Links Ltd* (1922) 38 TLR 615 – golf balls smashed the windscreen of the plaintiff's taxi which was on the highway.

[59] *Halsey v Esso Petroleum* [1961] 1 WLR 683; *Nitschke v McEntee* (1976) 15 SASR 330; whatever the nature of the interference, it must exceed that to the public at large: *Teamay v Severin* (1988) 94 FLR 47 at 51 – selling alcoholic liquor to members of an Aboriginal community was not actionable by the plaintiffs as a public nuisance, since the damage was to the community as a whole, and the plaintiffs had established no damage beyond that.

[60] See also *York Bros Trading v Commissioner of Main Roads* [1923] 1 NSWLR 391; *Tate & Lyle Industries Ltd v CLC* [1983] 2 AC 509; but cf *Ball v Consolidated Rutile Ltd* [1991] Qd R 524 – no public nuisance where defendant had caused the collapse of sand dunes into the sea.

[61] See also *Lyons v Gulliver* [1914] 1 Ch 631; *Wilkes v Hungerford Market* (1835) 132 ER 110.

[62] *Taylor v City of Perth* [1988] Aust Torts Reports 80-191 – council liable in public nuisance to plaintiff who owned a shop in an arcade adjacent to the highway, as it had no power to block the highway to pedestrians; but cf *Silservice Pty Ltd v Supreme Bread Pty Ltd* (1949) 50 SR (NSW) 127; and *Grand Central Car Park Pty Ltd v Tivoli Freeholders* [1969] VR 62 – in both cases an obstruction created by a queue was not a public nuisance.

Special cases

Buildings and projections on/over highway

[16.145] Public nuisance is constituted by, among other things, interference with the public right of passage along a public road or highway, and this interference extends to the dangerous condition of premises situated on the road or highway. It seems probable that under the High Court's approach to strict liability in tort in *Burnie Port Authority v General Jones Pty Ltd* (1994) 120 ALR 42 and the subsequent subsuming of public nuisance in highway cases to negligence in *Brodie v Singleton SC; Ghantous v Hawkesbury CC* (2001) 206 CLR 512 by applying the reasoning in the *Burnie* case, that what now exists is the imposition of a non-delegable duty of care.

Defective state of highway

[16.150] This matter has been considered in connection with the duty of care of public authorities. A claim for public nuisance was often added to a claim for negligence where it was sought to impose liability on a highway authority for injury or damage caused by the defective state of the highway. However, following the decision of the High Court in *Brodie v Singleton SC; Ghantous v Hawkesbury CC* (2001) 206 CLR 512, the tort of public nuisance in highway cases has now been subsumed by the law of negligence. The court formulated a duty of care, to apply in cases of non-feasance as well as misfeasance, being a duty to take reasonable care that the exercise of or failure to exercise the powers by such authorities does not create a foreseeable risk of harm to road users.[63]

Access to or use of the highway

[16.155] Generally, speaking, a substantial and unreasonable interference upon the free and uninterrupted use of a public road by members of the public may confer a cause of action for public nuisance upon the plaintiff. However, as in other cases of public nuisance, whether it does will depend upon whether the plaintiff can show that he or she has incurred some "particular" or "special" damage over and above the ordinary inconvenience or annoyance suffered by the public at large.[64] Thus, processions may use a public road for passage on lawful occasions for lawful objects provided that the use is reasonable, but a static demonstration or picket which threatens obstruction of the roadway and causes persons who wish to use the road to hesitate through fear to proceed constitutes an unreasonable obstruction amounting to a public nuisance[65] and

---

[63] Some jurisdictions, as part of their civil liability reforms of the laws of negligence, have restricted the liability of authorities for a failure to carry out work unless they had actual knowledge of the facts creating the risk: *Civil Liability (Wrongs) Act 2002* (ACT), Ch 8; *Civil Liability Act 2002* (NSW), s 45; *Civil Liability Act 2003* (Qld), ss 35, 36; *Civil Liability Act 1936* (SA), s 42; *Civil Liability Act 2002* (Tas), s 42; *Civil Liability Act 2002* (WA), s 5Z.

[64] For example, in *McFadzean v Construction Forestry Mining and Energy Union* [2007] VSCA 289, a claim arising out of an anti-logging demonstration and an opposing pro-logging picket which resulted in barricading in some of the anti-logging demonstrators on a roadway into the logging area. The appellants' claim that they had been subjected to a public nuisance by being prevented by the loggers from leaving via the road failed, notwithstanding that the court found that the action of the loggers was such as to cause a public nuisance but that they did not have a right of action in respect of that cause of action as they did not sustain particular substantial and direct damage beyond that suffered by the general public.

[65] *BLF v J-Corp Pty Ltd* (1993) 42 FCR 452 at 457.

an interference with private rights.[66] It amounts to an unreasonable restriction upon the right of an individual to free movement on a roadway. A public road is primarily for free passage of the public for all reasonable purposes.

Defences and remedies

[16.160] A defendant may raise statutory authorisation to the nuisance but it must be expressly or impliedly authorised. If the activity can be carried out without creating a nuisance, the defence is not available. In *Cohen v City of Perth* (2000) 112 LGERA 234, although the council had a statutory obligation to collect garbage, Roberts-Smith J was not convinced that the council had done all that it reasonably could to ensure that excessive noise would occur at a time when it would cause least inconvenience.

A defendant may raise a defence of contributory negligence to prevent a careless plaintiff improving their position in relation to damage by basing their claim in nuisance rather than negligence: *McMeekin v Maryborough Council* [1947] QSR 192.

As with private nuisance (see [16.120]), remedies for public nuisance (criminal law aside) are: abatement of the nuisance;[67] proved general damage such as inconvenience and delay (provided that it is substantial, direct and appreciably greater in degree than any suffered by the general public). Aggravated or exemplary damages may also be awarded in an appropriate case. The final remedy is an injunction to prevent the continuance of the nuisance. It is important to remember that the remedies are not mutually exclusive and may be awarded in combination.

Relationship between public and private nuisance

[16.165] While the torts of public and private nuisance are different, they also have a number of similarities. Both are concerned with an interference with rights caused by an activity or condition. The question of reasonableness is common to both torts and is governed by the same principles. The law as to defences and remedies, and as to who is liable for the nuisance, is largely the same, although prescription is not a defence to public nuisance. The distinction between them lies in the nature of the rights which are infringed. Private nuisance consists of the infringement of rights relating to the ownership or occupation of land. Public nuisance, on the other hand, is not so much concerned with the infringement of rights related to land but rather the interference with any right enjoyed by the public at large.

Practice Questions

Review Questions

16.1. Would a court recognise a right to a view?

16.2. Detail any differences you can detect between private and public nuisance.

---

[66] *Dollar Sweets Pty Ltd v Federated Confectioners Association of Australia* [1986] VR 383 at 388-389; *BLF v J-Corp Pty Ltd* (1993) 42 FCR 452 at 457; *Broome v Director of Public Prosecutions* [1974] AC 587.

[67] The right to self-help in public nuisance is more limited than in private nuisance because of the need of the person abating to show that they have suffered greater damage than the rest of the community: *Alexander v Mayor and Corporation of Sydney* (1861) 1 SCR (NSW) 6.

Problem Question

16.1   Bill and Ben own a home at 9 Ernest Street, Northport. Clive and Carla are the owners of the property at 6 Bertha Street, Northport. Clive and Carla's property adjoins the property owned by Bill and Ben.

Clive and Carla are very security conscious and have installed on their property floodlights and camera surveillance equipment. The floodlights and surveillance equipment are so positioned that they illuminate Bill and Ben's backyard and may record on video tape everything that occurs there.

Bill and Ben use their backyard for hanging up their clothes, doing their gardening, sitting and listening to the radio. They say they have become distressed since July this year when the electronic equipment was installed, and no longer feel that they can use their backyard as they had previously. The floodlight system appears to be activated by a sensor, which switches the floodlights on with movement or noise, such as movement in the backyard or perhaps even a dog barking. When the equipment is activated the lights come on (and remain on for 10 minutes) and the camera may be activated because there is sufficient light to film what is happening. Bill and Ben contend that they are suffering real health problems as a result of the continued illumination of their land.

Advise Bill and Ben.

Answers to Practice Questions

Revision Questions

16.1   No. Aesthetic values, such as a pleasing view, are not protected. It would be advisable for a homeowner to consult the town planning rules or consider the use of a restrictive covenant.

16.2   Private nuisance is a tort but public nuisance tends towards criminal law. However, public nuisance is a tort where there is damage suffered by an individual. An action for private nuisance may only be brought in relation to land but public nuisance is available where other interests are involved. Those with a proprietary interest may sue in private nuisance but in relation to public nuisance the state is usually the plaintiff; plaintiffs do not need property rights.

Problem Question

16.1   Bill and Ben would be advised to take an action for private nuisance against Clive and Carla. They would be arguing that the installation of the lights and the surveillance equipment presents an unlawful interference with their interest in the land. In an action for nuisance it is apparent that in many instances the court is balancing the rights of "neighbours". Here Clive and Carla are wishing to ensure their security, while Bill and Ben wish to use their backyard.

Who can sue – and who should be sued?

Bill and Ben have a right to sue since they have the requisite interest in the property. Clive and Carla are the parties to be sued since they have created the nuisance.

Interference with enjoyment

Bill and Ben argue that their ability to use their backyard has been seriously interfered with.

Lights: Because the lights and the surveillance equipment are triggered by noise the interferences are frequent. The locality is residential and so the strong lights are very obtrusive and therefore unreasonable.

Surveillance equipment: As a general rule, if someone can see something then they can photograph it: *Victoria Park Racing v Taylor* (1937) 58 CLR 479. While in Australia there is not a right to privacy it would seem that if the circumstances were such that it could be argued that Bill and Ben felt that they were being watched, then this is much more serious. Bill and Ben would argue that there is a deliberate attempt by Clive and Carla to pry and record their movements. Young J in *Raciti v Hughes* (1995) 7 BPR 14,837 suggested that videotaping a neighbour's backyard with a motion-activated video might amount to an invasion of privacy. Dicta in *ABC v Lenah Game Meats Pty Ltd* (2001) 208 CLR 199 has also opened the door to a tort of invasion of privacy but to date the matter has not been decided conclusively one way or the other in a superior court. However, to date the cause of action has only been recognised in Queensland in the District Court in *Grosse v Purvis* [2003] Aust Torts Reports 81-706.

Bill and Ben would also contend that the interferences are affecting their health.

Defences

Clive and Carla would defend their right to install the lights and surveillance equipment on their property. They might refer to recent break-ins in the area. They would certainly refute the idea that there is any malice in what they are doing and argue that their actions are reasonable.

Conclusion

It would seem that each of the component parts (the lights and the surveillance equipment) would give Bill and Ben an action for nuisance. The two together present an even stronger case, and this is really the situation, since it could be argued that the stronger lights allow the surveillance to take place.

Bill and Ben could be granted an injunction and/or damages. However it is possible that this situation would be settled by an agreement of some sort. Perhaps Clive and Carla might agree to having their equipment adjusted (for example, fitting the lights with weaker bulbs or adjusting the trigger for the equipment so that it is not so sensitive).

Tutorial Questions

Discussion Questions

16.1 Should the tort of private nuisance be available to families of the person who has a proprietary interest in the land?

16.2 Is the tort of nuisance still relevant in light of the growing body of planning and environmental legislation?

Problem Question

16.3 Warren planted a row of willow trees along the boundary between his place and that of his neighbour, Liz. As the trees grew, they began to cause Liz great distress when their branches began to hang over into Liz's yard. This caused loss of light into her backyard and covered it with leaves and branches. The roots also got into the sewerage pipes and underneath her pool, causing the pipes to block up and the pool to lift and crack.

Advise Liz whether there is anything she can do about the problem.

CHAPTER 17

Liability for Animals

Reading

Sappideen, Vines, Grant and Watson, *Torts: Commentary and Materials*, Chapter 20.

Objectives

This chapter will:

- consider the circumstances under which scienter liability is imposed;
- examine the essential features of cattle trespass;
- note the liability for the acts of one's dogs; and
- consider the liability for negligence of an occupier who keeps domestic animals.

Principles

Introduction

[17.05] A person may be held liable for damage or other interference caused by animals under torts not specifically applying to animals; for example, negligence or private or public nuisance. The principles under which a person may be held liable in negligence for the acts of their animals are considered later in this chapter. There are, however, torts which are specifically associated with the acts of animals. These are scienter liability for the acts of a dangerous animal, cattle trespass, and the statutory liability that applies in the various States for the acts of dogs. It should be noted that all three impose a form of strict liability. The reasons for this are, however, divergent but they were developed at a time when arable agricultural interests predominated in England and there was no liability for stock wandering on to highways or from highways onto adjacent land.

Scienter liability is based upon the special risk created by the keeping of a dangerous animal, and on the fact that the defendant has done so voluntarily with knowledge of the dangerous characteristic. The same seems to be true of liability for dogs: the potentiality of the dog for causing harm is manifested by the near universality of the statutory provisions. Strict liability in cattle trespass is attributed not to the particular risk created, but rather to the acceptance by the agricultural community that strict liability conveniently allocates the damage caused by trespassing cattle, whereas negligence liability encourages expensive litigation. Despite the general move away from strict liability in tort,[1] it survives as regards the acts of animals in all Australian States and Territories, except New South Wales, South Australia, Western Australia and the Australian Capital Territory,[2] in all of which liability is now dependent on negligence (though liability for dogs is an exception). For example, Western Australia has retained scienter liability and cattle trespass, while imposing liability in negligence for damage caused by animals straying on the public highway: *Highways (Liability for Straying Animals) Act 1983* (WA), s 3(3).

Scienter liability

[17.10] Scienter is merely Latin for "with knowledge". Liability is therefore imposed on the keeper of a dangerous animal with knowledge of its characteristics. That liability is imposed under the following conditions:

- A distinction is drawn between wild animals (ferae naturae) and tame or domesticated animals (mansuetae naturae). In the case of the former, liability is strict. In the case of the latter, liability is only strict if the animal has a propensity to be dangerous and the keeper has knowledge of those characteristics. *The basis of the classification of an animal as ferae naturae is the propensity of the species to attack human beings or other animals.* So the bear,[3] the

---

[1]   The High Court's decision in *Burnie Port Authority v General Jones* (1994) 179 CLR 520 resulted in the strict liability common law rule in *Rylands v Fletcher* (1868) LR 3 HL 330 being subsumed by negligence. However, some jurisdictions have statutorily abolished the rule: *Animals Act 1977* (NSW), s 4; *Civil Law (Wrongs) Act 2002* (ACT), s 215.

[2]   Abolition of scienter liability and cattle trespass: *Animals Act 1977* (NSW), s 7(2); *Civil Liability Act 1936* (SA), s 18(1), (9); *Civil Liability (Wrongs) Act 2002* (ACT), s 214; *Highways (Liability for Straying Animals) Act 1983* (WA), s 3.

[3]   *Besozzi v Harris* (1858) 1 F & F 92; 175 ER 640.

elephant,[4] the zebra,[5] the chimpanzee,[6] and the leopard[7] have been found to be ferae naturae. Kangaroos[8] and bees[9] have been held mansuetae naturae. Animals which merely have the propensity to damage property (such as the Colorado beetle) or to spread disease (such as the mosquito or rat) are not ferae naturae. The distinction between animals ferae naturae and mansuetae naturae is not quite the same as that between wild and domesticated animals. Domestication of the species throughout the world is, however, relevant evidence that it is not ferae naturae. So a camel has been classified as mansuetae naturae: *McQuaker v Goddard* [1940] 1 KB 687; *Nada Shah v Sleeman* (1917) 19 WALR 687. The partial domestication of some members of the species does not, however, preclude a finding that it is ferae naturae. Thus, the Indian elephant is regarded as ferae naturae: *Behrens v Bertram Mills Circus* [1957] 2 QB 1. So too was the dingo in *Fischer v Stuart* (1979) 25 ALR 336, despite the fact that the dingo is semi-domesticated in parts of Australia.

- The knowledge that is relevant in the case of *animals mansuetae naturae is knowledge of the vicious characteristic of the particular animal*. Knowledge that that type of animal may commit an attack is insufficient, even in the case of an animal such as a bull. Also, knowledge of the cat's propensity to attack birds is insufficient: *Buckle v Holmes* [1926] 2 KB 125. So also is that of fillies to commit playful sorties on persons in their enclosures: *Fitzgerald v Cook Bourne (Farms)* [1964] 1 QB 249. Knowledge of heightened aggressiveness of particular members of a species (such as German shepherd dogs) is equally insufficient to establish scienter. Illogically, however, courts have allowed the action to succeed where the animal was acting aggressively in the course of a periodical sexual tendency shared by the species as a whole.[10]

- The necessary knowledge in the case of *animals mansuetae naturae is actual knowledge*. The courts however, "impute" the knowledge of employees to their employer. In *Eather v Jones* (1979) 49 ALJR 254 the High Court refused to extend the doctrine of imputation to the knowledge possessed by the defendant's son. In any case, the court found that the knowledge possessed by the son did not establish a vicious propensity on the part of the animal.

- There is *no need to show an escape of the animal from the defendant's control*. On this point the New South Wales Court of Appeal (in *Higgins v William Inglis* [1978] 1 NSWLR 649) refused to follow the decision of the English Court of Appeal in *Rands v McNeil* [1955] 1 QB 253 which has now been removed in England by statute. In *Higgins*, both defendants were held liable for an injury caused by a bull while inside its pen prior to an auction.

---

[4]   *Filburn v Peoples Palace* (1890) 25 QBD 258; *Behrens v Bertram Mills Circus* [1957] 2 QB 1.

[5]   *Marlor v Ball* (1900) 16 TLR 239.

[6]   *James v Wellington City* [1972] NZLR 970; but not all species of monkey are ferae: *Brook v Cook* (1961) 105 Sol Journal 684 – small African grass monkey not ferae.

[7]   *Sylvester v Chapman* (1935) 79 Sol Journal 777.

[8]   *Lake v Taggart* (1978) 1 SR (WA) 89.

[9]   *Stormer v Ingram* (1978) 21 SASR 93.

[10] *Jackson v Smithson* (1846) 15 M & W 563; 153 ER 973 – butting ram; *Barnes v Lucille Ltd* (1907) 96 LT 254 – bitch with pups; *Howard v Bergin* (1925) 2 IR 110 – frightened bullocks; *Powell v Sloss* (1919) 13 QJPR 81 – no need to show scienter as it was in the nature of grown bulls to fight.

- Where the animal has been classified as ferae, any foreseeable damage which it causes is recoverable, even though this does not take place in the course of an attack. This broad approach to the remoteness of damage issue was taken by Devlin J in *Behrens*. Two circus midgets were injured by the actions of circus elephants in the course of attacking a dog which had barked and snapped at them. The damage was found not to be too remote. The general tenor of the judgment suggests that it would have made no difference if the damage had not resulted from an attack, provided it was foreseeable.[11] It is doubtful whether the same liberal approach would apply to an animal mansuetae naturae with a known vicious tendency where the damage did not arise through the exhibiting of that tendency.

The liability under scienter is placed upon the keeper of the animal. It is abundantly clear that a mere possessor of the animal is liable, though not shown to have any title to the animal. An employer is liable for the acts of animals whose charge has been entrusted to an employee. This is not so, however, where the employee was allowed by the employer to keep the animal as a private pet: *Knott v LCC* [1934] 1 KB 126. Strict liability continues to exist where the animal is in the charge of an independent contractor such as an auctioneer. On the other hand the contractor, despite having possession of the animal as a bailee, is not its keeper and is therefore liable only for negligence: *Higgins* (in which the auctioneer was held liable for negligence in failing to prevent an injury caused by a bull). An employee will in general enjoy no independent possession of the employer's animal and will not be regarded as its keeper.

Figure 17.1: General principles

Scienter liability is imposed with the following conditions in mind:
- Is the animal classified as a wild animal, ie does it have a propensity to attack human beings or other animals (ferae naturae) or tame or domesticated (mansuetae naturae)?
- If the animal is ferae naturae, the scienter on the defendant's part is conclusively presumed; but if it is mansuetae naturae the plaintiff has to prove that the defendant has knowledge of the dangerous characteristics of the particular animal.
- In the case of animals mansuetae naturae, does the defendant have *actual knowledge* of the vicious characteristics of the particular animal?
- There is no need to show an escape.
- If the animal is classified as ferae, any foreseeable damage is recoverable.
- Liability under scienter is placed upon the *keeper* of the animal, who may or may not be the owner.

---

[11] Note the judge's statement that if a person wakes up in the middle of the night and finds an escaped tiger on his bed, and suffers a heart attack, it would not matter that the tiger's intentions were quite amiable: *Behrens v Bertram Mills Circus* [1957] 2 QB 1 at 18–19.

Defences to scienter liability

[17.15] The defences to scienter liability are not well defined. Volenti non fit injuria (voluntary assumption of risk) may operate as a defence in appropriate circumstances.[12] The availability of act of God, though it was accepted as a defence in *Rylands v Fletcher* (1868) LR 3 HL 330, has been doubted in relation to scienter liability.[13] The New South Wales Court of Appeal has denied that contributory negligence could operate as a defence, on the ground that it was not so before the enactment of the contributory negligence legislation: *Higgins v William Inglis* [1978] 1 NSWLR 649.[14] This means that it is necessary to find alternative bases for decisions prior to that legislation in which the plaintiff failed because he had approached too near the animal[15] or had provoked it[16] (in terms, for example, of the plaintiff causing his own loss). It has generally been accepted that the act of a third party is not a defence, but the decision in question concerned the act of a servant and cannot be regarded as conclusive on this point: *Baker v Snell* [1908] 2 KB 825. On the other hand, negligence on the part of the owner's independent contractor does not prevent liability arising on the owner's part: *Higgins*. It would also appear that a person who goes unlawfully onto premises, ie, as a trespasser, and is bitten, cannot complain as his own fault led to the injuries (*Simpson v Bannerman* (1932) 47 CLR 378, per Starke J at 384; at this point in the judgment his Honour took care to note that whilst the rule is stated in absolute terms, it must be considered within the circumstances "under which the injury was sustained"). As a generalisation therefore, it would appear that defences (like the "offence" itself) turn on an element of knowledge.

Cattle trespass

[17.20] Cases involving the strict liability tort of cattle trespass are rare.[17] This tort is committed by a person in possession of animals of the class of "avers" (that is, oxen, horses, donkeys, sheep goats, and pigs; also fowls, ducks and geese,[18] but not dogs[19] or cats) which escape and thereafter trespass upon the plaintiff's land.[20]

---

[12]   As against a person who had intervened in a dog fight: *Smith v Shields* (1964) 108 Sol Journal 501; or is an animal keeper: *Sylvester v Chapman* (1935) 79 Sol Journal 777; or has entered premises in the knowledge they contain a vicious guard dog: *Cummings v Granger* [1977] QB 397.

[13]   By Bramwell B in *Nichols v Marsland* (1875) LR 10 Ex 255 at 260 and approved of by Cozens Hardy J in *Baker v Snell* [1908] 2 KB 825. Bramwell B expressed doubt whether the owner of a tiger which escaped because lightning broke its chain would have a defence.

[14]   *Mary Aird v Grantham* [1998] WASCA 254 also held that contributory negligence was not available. However, the Privy Council in obiter dictum seems to assume that the plea of contributory negligence is available: *Forbes v M'Donald* (1885) 7 ALT 62.

[15]   *Marlor v Ball* (1900) 16 TLR 238; *Sycamore v Ley* (1932) 147 LT 342.

[16]   *Filburn v People's Palace* (1890) 25 QBD 258.

[17]   Cattle trespass has been abolished in some jurisdictions, eg, *Civil Liability (Wrongs) Act 2002* (ACT), s 212; *Animals Act 1977* (NSW), s 4; *Civil Liability Act 1936* (SA), s 18 but still exists as an independent tort in other jurisdictions such as Queensland: see, eg, *Lade & Co Pty Ltd v Black* [2007] QSC 385. Whether it survives post *Burnie Port Authority v General Jones Pty Ltd* (1994) 179 CLR 520 remains to be seen.

[18]   *Edwards v Rawlins* [1924] NZLR 333.

[19]   The non-liability in cattle trespass for entry by a dog (or cat) was confirmed in *Jones v Linnett* [1984] 1 Qd R 570. However, the dog in that case had several times caused injury to the plaintiff's dog, so scienter was established and an injunction granted against future repetition of the attacks. See also *Chittenden v Hale* [1933] NZLR 836.

[20]   *Lade & Co Pty Ltd v Black* [2007] QSC 385.

The following are the essential features of cattle trespass:

- *Liability is strict.*[21] Indeed it is as strict as is found anywhere in the law of tort. There is, for example, no need to show any knowledge of the propensity of the cattle to trespass nor of circumstances likely to produce that trespass.

- As a survival of the action on the case, the tort requires *proof of damage.*

- Liability is that of the *possessor* of the cattle.[22] The owner out of possession is not liable.

- As in trespass, the *plaintiff must show a possessory interest in the land*, although an early Victorian decision (*Rutherford v Hayward* (1877) 3 VLR (L) 19) allows a licensee to sue, and the strictness of this rule has yielded to allow the grantee of the crops of land or of an exclusive right of pasture over it to succeed: *Wellaway v Courtier* [1918] 1 KB 200.

- *A trespass to land must be proved.*[23] Where the defendant's mare was put into a field with the consent of the owner of the field and then kicked the plaintiff's horse so severely that it had to be destroyed, cattle trespass was not committed.[24] In *Lade & Co Pty Ltd v Black* [2007] QSC 385 de Jersey CJ found cattle trespass existed when cattle strayed onto the plaintiff's land by their own volition.

- The damage that is recoverable in this tort includes damage to the land itself and to crops on the land, and to causing a depasturing of cattle present there. Also recoverable is damage to chattels, injury to animals and even personal injury. In all cases, of course, the plaintiff must be a person able to satisfy the test for bringing cattle trespass (see above). Damage to animals extends to damage to animals caused by physical attack, or by infection or insemination. In *Wormald v Cole* [1954] 1 QB 614[25] the plaintiff recovered damages in cattle trespass for her personal injuries through being knocked down and trampled upon by the defendant's trespassing heifer. That sort of damage was a foreseeable result of the trespass. Exemplary damages may be awarded if it can be established that there is a "conscious wrong-doing in contumelious disregard of the plaintiff's rights".[26]

- In addition to volenti non fit injuria (*Park v Jobson* [1945] 1 All ER 222) and act of a third party (*Sutcliffe v Holmes* [1947] KB 147), two particular defences need mention. The strict liability in cattle trespass does not apply where the defendant's animal has escaped from the public highway, on which it was lawfully present, onto the adjoining land or premises of the plaintiff. Liability in these circumstances for damage caused by the animal depends on proof of negligence.[27] The second particular defence is that the trespass was the result of a breach of duty owed by the defendant to the plaintiff; for example, a duty to fence the plaintiff's land (though the defence is not available where the plaintiff is merely in breach of a fencing statute).[28]

---

[21] *Wormald v Cole* [1954] 1 QB 614.

[22] "Cattle" includes sheep and pigs.

[23] Cattle trespass is closely related to trespass to land. The person who drives their cattle deliberately on to the land of another may face an action in trespass to land: *League Against Cruel Sports Ltd v Scott* [1986] QB 240.

[24] *Manton v Brocklebank* [1923] 2 KB 212 – the trespass need only be technical or partial; *Ellis v Loftus Iron Co* (1874) LR 10 CP 10 – defendant liable when his horse kicked the plaintiff's mare through a fence.

[25] This case was decided at a time when directness of consequence rather than reasonable foreseeability was the remoteness rule.

[26] *Gray v Motor Accident Commission* (1998) 196 CLR 1 at 9.

[27] *Tillett v Ward* (1882) 10 QBD 17 – ox in an ironmonger's shop.

[28] *Rutherford v Hayward* (1877) 3 VLR (L) 19 – in other words the duty to fence must be owed to the plaintiff.

Defences to cattle trespass

[17.21] The defences available to a defendant to an action in cattle trespass include volenti non fit injuria, act of God, an act of a third party over whom the defendant has no control and the plaintiff's own default, for example, failing to fence when under a statutory obligation.[29]

Figure 17.2: Cattle trespass – general principles

Cattle trespass applies only to animals of the class of "avers" and has the following features:
- Liability is strict.
- Proof of damage must be shown by the plaintiff.
- Liability is that of the possessor.
- Plaintiff must show a possessory interest in the land.
- Trespass to land must be shown.

Liability under Dog Acts

[17.25] Statutory liability for the acts of one's dog (or cat) is imposed in all States except Queensland.[30] *Liability is strict and scienter does not have to be proved.* It is sometimes confined to the causing of personal injury, so that where the dog merely damages property, scienter liability or negligence will have to be established.

The relevant Acts divide into two groups: those imposing strict liability of a broad nature for injury caused by the dog, and those narrowing the liability to the case of injury or damage done in the course of an attack. Typical of the former type is the *Dog and Cat Management Act 1995* (SA), s 66(1) which holds the dog owner liable for "any injury caused by the dog". Section 66(2) provides that it is not necessary for the plaintiff to show negligence or "knowledge of dog's vicious, dangerous or mischievous propensity".[31] The section is limited to personal injury but otherwise the liability is in effect absolute. In particular it will cover the case where the dog causes a car accident and personal injury is sustained, or personal injury is caused by falling when trying to avoid an oncoming dog. Similar provisions to the South Australian legislation exist in the Northern Territory and Western Australia: *Law Reform (Miscellaneous Provisions) Act 1956* (NT), s 31; *Dog Act 1976* (WA), s 46.

An example of the narrower type of liability is s 25 of the *Companion Animals*

---

[29] In *Lade &Co Pty Ltd v Black* [2007] QSC 385 the defendants disputed the existence of the tort of cattle trespass; de Jersey CJ, however, proceeded on the basis that it did exist (at [46]).

[30] In Queensland, dogs (other than those caught by the restricted dog legislation) are treated the same way as other harmless animals: see *Jones v Linnett* [1984] 1 Qd R 570 where it was held that the owner of a dog was only liable if aware of the dog's vicious propensity. The *Local Government and Other Legislation Amendment Act (No 2) 2001* introduced a new Ch 17A (Regulation of restricted dogs) into the *Local Government Act 1933* giving power to local governments for dealing with restricted dogs, although it does not change existing law pertaining to liability for injury. A plaintiff would need to take an action in scienter, cattle trespass, negligence or nuisance.

[31] *Dog and Cat Management Act 1995* (SA), s 66(3)(c) sets out a number of defences available to a keeper including provocation.

Act 1998 (NSW). The owner is strictly liable for personal injury caused by the dog wounding the plaintiff[32] or for damaging the plaintiff's clothing in the course of an attack.[33] This sort of provision would not cover the case of the dog causing a road accident. Victorian and Australian Capital Territory Acts also limit recovery to the case of the dog making an attack: *Domestic (Feral and Nuisance) Animals Act 1994* (Vic), s 29; *Domestic Animals Act 2000* (ACT), s 55. The former statute applies to attacks on persons and livestock. The latter allows recovery for injury or damage in general.

Liability under all the provisions is placed on the owner of the dog, but the provisions of the various Acts generally include within "owner" a person in possession or control of the dog and an occupier of premises where the dog is kept or permitted to live.[34]

There are a number of defences available and they largely depend on statutory provisions:

- Contributory negligence
- Voluntary assumption of risk (volenti)
- Trespass

and although sourced in legislation, are similar in effect to the defences to negligence outlined in Chapter 12.[35]

Contributory negligence is either made a defence by the Act or assumed to be so by the courts.[36] Consent or volenti non fit injuria is not expressly provided for but certainly would operate as a defence. Provocation of the animal is expressly provided for as a defence in certain circumstances in the legislation in the Australian Capital Territory, New South Wales, South Australia, Tasmania and Victoria.[37] Perhaps the greatest difficulty surrounds the question whether it ought to be a defence that the plaintiff is a trespasser. For the defence to be successful there must be a substantial trespass. Resting an arm on the defendant's fence (*Simpson v Bannermann* (1932) 47 CLR 378), or waving an arm over the fence (*Rigg v Alietti* [1982] WAR 203) would not be sufficient to constitute a trespass. Legislation in the Australian Capital Territory, New South Wales, South Australia and Victoria expressly recognises as a defence the fact that the plaintiff was a trespasser;[38] while in New South Wales there is no liability

[32] Wounding does not require that the skin be broken and includes any hurt or injury: *Eadie v Groombridge* (1992) 16 MVR 263; *Zappia v Allsop* (unreported, NSWCA, 17 March 1994, 40192/1993). If the wounding by a dog leads to death, the *Companion Animals Act 1998* (NSW), s 26 permits the dependants of the deceased person to have a cause of action under the *Compensation to Relatives Act 1897* (NSW).

[33] It is not necessary for the dog to directly cause the wound to invoke the operation of s 25. A wounding that was an indirect result of an attack by a dog fell within the section: *Coleman v Barrat* [2004] NSWCA 27. See also *Crump v Sharah* [1999] NSWSC 884; *Eadie v Groomridge* (1992) 16 MVR 263; and *Zappia v Allsop* (unreported, NSWCA, 17 March 1994, 40192/1993), which were all decided on the basis of s 20 of the *Dog Act 1966* (NSW) which was the forerunner to s 25 of the *Companions Animal Act 1998*.

[34] See further on these statutory provisions, *The Laws of Australia* (Lawbook Co., subscription service) Torts, 33.6 at [26]. For a discussion as to the meaning of "owner" within the context of the *Domestic (Feral and Nuisance) Animals Act 1994* (Vic), see *Serbanescu v Herter* [2004] VSC 358. For the meaning of "keeper" within the context of the *Dog and Cat Management Act 1995* (SA), see *Pappas v Tran Thi-Foanh* [2005] SADC 43.

[35] Relevant legislation includes *Domestic Animals Act 1998* (ACT); *Companion Animals Act 1998* (NSW); *Civil Liability Act 1936* (SA); *Dog and Cat Management Act 1995* (SA); *Dog Control Act 1979* (SA); *Dog Control Act 2000* (Tas); *Dog Act 1976* (WA).

[36] See *Mary Aird v Grantham* [1998] WASCA 254 for a discussion on the applicability of contributory negligence as a partial defence to liability for animals.

[37] *Domestic Animals Act 2000* (ACT), ss 50(3)(a), 55(4)(c); *Companion Animals Act 1998* (NSW), s 16(2)(a); *Dog and Cat Management Act 1995* (SA), s 86(b); *Dog Control Act 2000* (Tas), s 19(5)(b); *Domestic (Feral and Nuisance) Animals Act 1994* (Vic), s 29(5)(a).

[38] *Domestic Animals Act 2000* (ACT), ss 50(3)(c)(i), 55(4)(a); *Companion Animals Act 1998* (NSW), ss 16(2)(b),

where the dog attack occurs on any land, premises or vehicle of which the defendant is an occupier, whether or not the plaintiff was trespassing there, unless the dog is one which has been declared to be dangerous under the Act: *Companion Animals Act 1998* (NSW), s 25(2)(a). The Tasmanian legislation expressly provides a defence if the injury is suffered while the dog was being used in the "reasonable defence of any person or property": *Dog Control Act 2000* (Tas), s 19(5)(a). The silence on this point in Queensland and the Northern Territory, together with the general relaxation of the legal attitude towards trespassers, may suggest that the former rule of the common law, under which the keeping of a dog on premises by way of a deterrent to trespass was regarded as being in a legitimate defence of property, has been superseded. However, this is still a "grey" area of liability.

Liability for negligence

[17.30] In *SGIC v Trigwell* (1979) 142 CLR 617 the High Court of Australia considered the question of whether to continue to apply the rule in *Searle v Wallbank* [1947] AC 341 under which an occupier of land or premises had no duty of care to prevent the occupier's domestic animals from straying onto the highway and causing damage there.[39] The High Court accepted that the rule had become anomalous with the steady increase in the use of highways by motorised traffic, but found that this was not a sufficient reason to change the rule, an obvious invitation to the various State legislatures which had not already done so to remove the rule. The rule now survives only in Queensland and the Northern Territory.[40] The majority of legislatures simply removed the rule, leaving the common law principles of negligence to operate in its place and it is suggested that the civil liability reforms that have been enacted to date will do little to change the common law position.[41] The the onus of establishing negligence will continue to rest on the party claiming damages, that is, they will have to establish a duty of care, a breach of that duty and damage must not be too remote. There will be no onus on a defendant to warn a plaintiff of an animal's propensity if it is an "obvious risk"[42] (for more detail on obvious and inherent risks, refer Chapter 10 at [10.30]ff).

The failure to abolish the rule in Queensland and the Northern Territory does not necessarily mean that the law there is markedly out of line with the other States

---

25(2)(1); *Dog and Cat Management Act 1995* (SA), s 66(3)(c); *Dog Control Act 2000* (Tas), s 19(5)(a); *Domestic (Feral and Nuisance) Animals Act 1994* (Vic), s 29(5)(b).

[39] See also *Smith v Williams* (2006) 47 MVR 169; [2006] QCA 439 where the Queensland Court of Appeal considered that the presence of the appellants' cattle on the bitumen surface of the highway was entirely consistent with a failure on the part of the appellants to prevent the egress of their animals onto the highway. That failure was held in *Trigwell* to be squarely within the immunity conferred by the *Searle v Wallbank* rule.

[40] *Civil Liability (Wrongs) Act 2002* (ACT), s 214; *Companion Animals Act 1998* (NSW); *Civil Liability Act 1936* (SA), s 18(4); *Law of Animals Act 1962* (Tas), s 19; *Wrongs Act 1958* (Vic), s 33.

[41] The *Civil Liability (Wrongs) Act 2002* (ACT), s 214; *Animals Act 1997* (NSW), s 7(2)(b); *Civil Liability Act 1936* (SA), s 18(1); *Law of Animals Act 1962* (Tas), s 19; *Wrongs Act 1958* (Vic), s 33(1); *Highways (Liability for Straying Animals) Act 1983* (WA), s 3(1) provide that liability for injury, damage or loss caused by animals generally shall be determined in accordance with the principles of the law of negligence and not only in the *Searle v Wallbank* situation.

[42] An "obvious risk" is a risk that would be obvious to a reasonable person in the position of the defendant and in New South Wales (*Civil Liability Act 2002*, ss 5F-5H); Queensland (*Civil Liability Act 2003*, ss 13-15); South Australia (*Civil Liability Act 1936*, ss 36-38); Tasmania (*Civil Liability Act 2002*, ss 15-17); and Victoria (*Wrongs Act 1958*, ss 53-54), while the provisions are not identical, the "obvious risk" provisions extend beyond "recreational activities". In Western Australia, the "obvious risk" sections are limited to "recreational activities" (*Civil Liability Act 2002*, ss 5E-5I). If it is established that the risk is "obvious", the common law defence of voluntary assumption of risk becomes easier to establish for a defendant as the provisions partially reverse the onus of proof. It will be assumed that the plaintiff was aware of the risk unless they can prove on the balance of probabilities that they were not aware of the risk.

and Territories. The rule in *Searle v Wallbank* did not apply where there were special circumstances of danger of which the occupier knew or should have been aware, relating for example to the particular animal, the locality in which it was kept or the circumstances of its keeping: *Ellis v Johnstone* [1963] 2 QB 8; *Bativala v West* [1970] 1 QB 716. It was also not applicable when the animal had been brought onto the highway.[43] A Queensland court found special circumstances to be present sufficient to displace the rule in *Searle v Wallbank* in *Graham v Royal National Agricultural & Industrial Assoc of Qld* [1989] 1 Qd R 624. In that case the occupiers of land which was being used for the purposes of a show of livestock were held liable for allowing the escape of a colt, which was in the course of being exercised along with other horses, through an unfastened gate onto the public highway, where it hit and damaged the plaintiff's vehicle. The defendants were not in the simple position of an occupier of land whose stock stray onto the highway. The court stated:

> It [the defendant] concentrates for a short period large numbers of livestock, many of them large animals, in a relatively small and congested area, all of them in the nature of things well fed and under exercised. The colt in question was not of a vicious propensity but shared ... a natural tendency, in these circumstances, to over-activity and to be unsettled in unfamiliar surroundings.

Even in those States that have abolished the rule in *Searle v Wallbank* the presence of special circumstances will be relevant towards establishing liability in negligence, even where the legislation in question expressly precludes the need to find such circumstances, as is the case in New South Wales. For example, in *Gregory's Properties Pty Ltd v Muir* [1993] Aust Torts Reports 62,284[44] the defendants owned a Santa Gertrudis cow which, after escaping from the defendants' premises onto the highway had collided with and caused damage to a truck leased by the plaintiffs. Santa Gertrudis cattle have a tendency which was known to the defendants to jump fences of ordinary height or to force their way through them and the court concluded that this explained the cow's presence on the highway. The defendants' argument denying negligence on the ground that they had maintained ordinary standard fencing in good repair around their premises, and that the cost of installing fencing sufficient to restrain the Santa Gertrudis variety was unreasonable, was dismissed by the court. Having elected to keep that variety of cattle and knowing of its special propensities the defendants had a duty of care to prevent its escape.[45] However, if the circumstances are such that it appears that the escape of the

---

[43] *Deen v Davies* [1935] 2 KB 282; *Cromberg v Smith* [1963] 1 QB 25. The harm must be foreseeable: see, for the outer limits of foreseeability, *Fardon v Harcourt-Rivington* [1932] All ER Rep 82 – dog left in car parked on highway jumped at car window smashing the glass and causing a splinter to enter the plaintiff's eye. But it is unnecessary to guard against acts of the animal contrary to the ordinary nature of the sort of animal in question, unless the owner has knowledge that these may occur: *Aldham v United Dairies* [1940] 1 KB 507.

[44] See also *Simpson v Blanch* [1998] Aust Torts Reports 81-458: the New South Wales Court of Appeal found that the owner of a property owed a non-delegable duty to the plaintiff to ensure that the fencing keeping in horses he was looking after was adequate under normal circumstances to prevent their escape. However, cf *Wayman v Davies* (unreported, NSWCA, 40047/96, 12 August 1998) where no liability was imposed on the owner of land onto which horses had strayed, as the court accepted that the measures taken by the respondents were all that could be reasonably done in the circumstances.

[45] *Gregory's Properties* was not so much concerned with the issue of non-delegable duty but rather with the standard of care required of an occupier erecting fences to keep stock contained within the property. See also *Le Poidevion Industries Pty Ltd v Triboli* (unreported, SASC, S3155, 5 December 1991) where the court, in trying to decide whether the conduct of the defendant was reasonable, considered the nature of the stock held on the property and whether the fencing conformed with accepted standards. In *A D & S M McLean Pty Ltd v Meech* (2005) 13 VR 241; [2005] VSCA 305, where a horse escaped from the appellant's property and collided with the respondent's car on the highway, the Victorian Court of Appeal in finding for the respondent considered

animals was beyond the control and knowledge of an owner (for example, because a stranger fails to close a gate or a freak accident causes damage to fencing) the owner will not be in breach of their duty of care: *Wayman v Davies* (unreported, NSWCA, 12 August 1998, 40047/96).

As regards liability in negligence in general, there is still a measure of doubt as to the circumstances in which an action for negligence arises where the animal is classed among the tame variety and there is no known propensity of the particular animal to cause harm in the way it has done. The South Australian legislation provides that in assessing this issue it is not necessary to establish prior knowledge of a vicious, dangerous or mischievous propensity of the animal: *Civil Liability Act 1936* (SA), s 18(3). On the other hand, there is authority for the point that it is not necessary to take precautions against the possibility that a tame animal will do something contrary to its ordinary nature: *Aldham v United Dairies* [1940] 1 KB 507. This was accepted to be the general position in *Galea v Gillingham* [1987] 2 Qd R 365, though in that case the defendant was found to be aware of his dog's propensity to attack. No doubt, however, the heightened aggressive tendency of animals such as bulls in general would be regarded as requiring a special degree of care in their keeping.[46] This draws support from *Draper v Hodder* [1972] QB 556. In that case the defendant was held liable for an attack on the plaintiff child by a pack of seven Jack Russell terriers, on the ground that he should have been aware of the propensity of this breed of terrier when allowed to form a pack to go on the attack. The propensities of a particular breed of dog are therefore relevant to liability in negligence, even though for the purpose of scienter liability all dogs are considered tame and knowledge of a propensity in a particular breed would not establish the scienter.

Trespass

[17.35] A person may be liable in actions for trespass to the person if animals are intentionally directed to attack by the defendant: *League Against Cruel Sports Ltd v Scott* [1986] QB 240. A cause of action may be founded in trespass to the land if animals are intentionally driven or encouraged onto the land of another by the defendant. For example, in *Dumont v Miller* (1873) 4 AJR 152, the defendant had ridden through the plaintiff's vineyard with a pack of hounds in pursuit of a hare, and even though no physical damage was done to the plaintiff's property, the court concluded that the defendant's actions still amounted to a trespass to land.

Nuisance

[17.40] A cause of action in private nuisance may arise out of the keeping of animals if they interefere with the enjoyment of another's land such that it can be said to be

---

"that the question in each case is whether the combined effect of the magnitude of the foreseeable risk of an accident occurring and the magnitude of the foreseeable potential injury or damage if an accident does occur, is such that an ordinary person acting reasonably would consider it necessary to exercise 'special care' or to take 'special precautions' in relation to it": at [23]. Thus the agistment of horses on land abutting a major highway must be considered to be dangerous for persons using the highway unless special care or special precautions are taken by the occupier to prevent the horses' escape on to the highway.

46   *Tippett v Fraser* [1999] SASR 522 – the defendants breached their duty of care to lawful entrants when they failed to erect a safe enclosure that would prevent a bull from escaping.

substantial and unreasonable; for example, because of smells[47] and noise.[48] The converse can also apply if a person is legally keeping animals on their property and an adjoining landowner maliciously sets out to scare or disturb the animals.[49]

Practice Questions

Revision Questions

17.1 Why does the law distinguish between animals ferae naturae and animals mansuetae naturae?

17.2 In order to establish a case of cattle trespass, what will a plaintiff need to establish?

17.3 Where there is statutory liability for the acts of one's dogs, is only the owner liable?

17.4 What is the rule in *Searle v Wallbank* [1947] AC 341? Does it still apply in Australia?

Problem Question

17.1 Sheena is a Cocker Spaniel dog. She is normally placid, but dislikes visiting the vet and getting injections. Whenever she goes to the vet to get an injection she tries to bite whoever is holding her with surprising ferocity. Her owner, Kym, knows about this. She decides to take Sheena to a new vet for her annual injections and asks a friend, Tony, to take her. At the vet Sheena appears to be quiet and placid. The nurse who is holding Sheena while the vet is inspecting her relaxes her hold. As the vet starts to give Sheena an injection, she suddenly manages to scratch and bite both the nurse and the vet sufficiently seriously for both of them to need to go to a doctor for stitches and antibiotics.

Advise Kym.

---

[47] In both *Aldred v Benton* (1610) 9 Co Rep 57 and *Bone v Seale* [1975] 1 WLR 797, the plaintiffs succeeded in a cause of action in private nuisance because of smells that emanated from the defendant's properties because of the keeping of pigs (the latter was a pig farm).

[48] In *Munro v Southern Dairies Ltd* [1955] VLR 332 the defendant company operated a dairy in the Melbourne suburb of Mentone. Delivery of milk was carried out by horse-drawn carts, with the horses stabled on the premises. The plaintiff-neighbour successfully sued the defendant in nuisance, claiming that the horses were noisy and that their manure and urine was smelly. In granting an injunction, Sholl J noted that the loss of a single night's sleep could amount to a substantial interference. A nuisance from stables was also successfully argued in *Painter v Reed* [1930] SASR 295; and *Rapier v London Tramways Company* [1893] 2 Ch 588.

[49] If a plaintiff carries on an abnormally sensitive activity on their property, they cannot complain of nuisance if the defendant's act would be considered reasonable by the reasonable person: *Rattray v Daniels* (1959) 17 DLR (2d) 134 (Can) (defendant clearing land with a bulldozer next to the plaintiff's mink farm at the same time minks were breeding, causing mother minks to kill their young because of their sensitivity to noise, but bulldozer only available then) but if there is an element of maliciousness in their actions, there may be an actionable nuisance: *Hollywood Silver Fox Farm v Emmett* [1936] 2 KB 468 (where the defendant maliciously created noise on his land to stop the foxes on the plaintiff's land from breeding during their breeding season).

Answers to Practice Questions

Revision Questions

17.1 In the case of wild animals, the sciener on the defendant's part is conclusively presumed, being based on the propensity of the species to attack human beings or other animals. In the case of domesticated animals, the plaintiff has to prove that the defendant has knowledge of the dangerous characteristics of the particular animal. Animals which can damage property or spread disease are not considered ferae naturae.

17.2 Cattle trespass requires proof of damage and liability will lie with the person who is the possessor of the cattle, not necessarily the owner. The plaintiff will have to show that he or she has a possessory interest in the land and that a trespass to land occurred.

17.3 Liability is placed on the owner under provisions in all States and Territories (except Queensland which does not have statutory liability). However, all States have generally included with "owner" a person in possession or control of the dog and an occupier of premises where the dog is kept or permitted to live.

17.4 The rule in *Searle v Wallbank* [1947] AC 341 provides that an occupier of land or premises had no duty of care to prevent the occupier's domestic animals from straying onto the highway and causing damage. It does not apply if the animal had been brought onto the highway or where there are special circumstances of danger of which the occupier knew or should have been aware (for example, the propensity of Santa Gertrudis cattle to jump fences, the locality in which the animal was kept or the circumstances of its keeping). In *SGIC v Trigwell* (1979) 142 CLR 617 the High Court accepted that the rule had become anomalous with the steady increase in the use of highways by motorists, but found that this was not a sufficient reason to change the rule. As a result, all States and Territories except Queensland and the Northern Territory passed legislation removing the rule, leaving the common rules of negligence to operate in its place.

Problem Question

17.1 Dogs are not a dangerous species, as they are commonly domesticated in Australia. However, Kym, as the keeper of the dog may face liability. In all jurisdictions in Australia except Queensland, legislation has been passed which dispenses with sciener and makes the owner strictly liable for any injury that the dog may cause. Reference should be made at this point to the relevant Act.[50] However, Kym may be able to successfully argue that in this case both the vet and the nurse consented or voluntarily assumed the risk of injury in treating animals, ie it is an occupational hazard and that they failed to take adequate precautions to ensure their safety: see, for example, *James v Wellington City* [1972] NZLR 978 and *Rand v McNeil* [1955] 1 QB 253.

---

[50] *Domestic Animals Act 2000* (ACT); *Companion Animals Act 1998* (NSW); *Law Reform (Miscellaneous Provisions) Act 1956* (NT); *Dog and Cat Management Act 1995* (SA); *Dog Control Act 2000* (Tas); *Domestic (Feral and Nuisance) Animals Act 1994* (Vic); *Dog Act 1976* (WA).

CHAPTER 17

Tony is unlikely to be liable as he does not appear to become a keeper simply by taking charge of the dog for the temporary purpose of taking it to the vet. He would appear to have no knowledge of the attributes of the dog.

Tutorial Questions

Discussion Questions

17.1 What arguments would have been put forward in Queensland and the Northern Territory for the retention of the rule in *Searle v Wallbank*?

17.2 Does contributory negligence constitute a defence to scienter liability? Discuss.

17.3 There are certain torts which are specifically associated with the acts of animals. These include scienter liability for the acts of a dangerous animal, cattle trespass and statutory liability that applies for the acts of dogs in all States (except Queensland) and Territories. Can scienter liability be reconciled with today's community needs?

Problem Question

17.1 Sam was riding his motorcyle along a road when Mike's German Shepherd jumped over the gate of Mike's property and ran parallel to Sam, before suddenly turning into him. Sam veered away from the dog in order to try to avoid hitting him but was unsuccessful. His bike collided with the dog, killing it and causing Sam to fall off and break his leg. Mike had spent a considerable sum of money increasing the height of the fence around his property because the dog had been able to jump over the fence but he had not increased the height of the gate to his yard because the dog had never attempted to jump over the gate.

Advise Sam and Mike.

CHAPTER 18

Defamation

Objectives

This chapter will explain:

- introduction of a new legislative regime;
- the nature of defamation generally;
- the concept of a statement that is defamatory or carries a defamatory imputation;
- the relationship between defamation and the implied constitutional right of freedom of speech;
- requisite elements of an action in defamation;
- defences to defamation;
- immunities from an action in defamation;
- remedies for defamation; and
- alternatives to litigation.

Principles

Preliminary considerations

A new regime

[18.05] The essence of the tort of defamation is the protection of reputation, that intangible something that we all hold dear and which can, especially for a public figure, be so much larger than the individual and exist in more than one location (and thus be damaged in more than one location). Thus it was somewhat incongruous that until recently, Australian defamation law was a complexity of inconsistencies across jurisdictions.[1] This was an issue that was on the law reform agenda for over 20 years until finally, January 2006 saw the implementation of a regime of uniform defamation legislation across all eight jurisdictions. This new legislative scheme is not a code, however, and maintains the general law unless it specifically, or by necessary implication, provides otherwise.[2] The objects of the uniform legislative scheme are clear:

Figure 18.1: Objects of uniform legislation

* promote uniform defamation laws
* ensure freedom of speech is not unreasonably limited
* provide effective and fair remedies
* promote speedy and non-litigious methods of dispute resolution
  (*Civil Law (Wrongs) Act 2002* (ACT), s 115; *Defamation Act 2005*
  (NSW), (Qld), (SA), (Tas), (Vic) and (WA), s 3; *Defamation Act
  2006* (NT), s 2)

At this stage there is yet to be significant judicial consideration of the uniform legislation. This chapter will address the law of defamation explaining both common law and legislative schemes and endeavour to clarify what impact the legislative regime will have. The discussion will initially focus on the identification of defamatory material and potential parties to an action. This will be followed by an explanation of the potential defences available and finally, the alternatives to litigation, as provided for in the legislation, will be addressed.

---

[1] The situation was a mix of common law and legislation (these provisions continue to be of residual relevance as defamatory publications made prior to January 2006 work their way through the court system). Defamation was fully encoded in two States, Queensland and Tasmania: *Defamation Act 1889* (Qld); *Defamation Act 1957* (Tas). The Western Australian *Criminal Code* had some sections relevant to civil defamation: *Criminal Code 1913*, Ch 35. New South Wales, originally a Code State, replaced the Code with its own comprehensive *Defamation Act 1974*. In other jurisdictions, the law was a mixture of common law and statute: *Defamation Act 1901* (ACT); *Defamation Act 1938* (NT); *Civil Liability Act 1936* (SA); *Wrongs Act 1958* (Vic).

[2] *Civil Law (Wrongs) Act 2002* (ACT), s 118; *Defamation Act 2005* (NSW), (Qld), (SA), (Tas), (Vic) and (WA), s 6; *Defamation Act 2006* (NT), s 5.

What is defamation?

[18.10] The essence of the tort of defamation is the protection of reputation. Defamation is the generic tort traditionally having two species: libel (written statements); and slander (limited to oral statements). Until recently there was legal relevance to the distinction based upon remedies and elements of proof (slander requiring proof of damage and libel being actionable per se). Prior to the introduction of the uniform legislation some jurisdictions had abolished the distinction between the two categories of defamation. This has now become consistent across all jurisdictions; thus the distinction between the two forms of action is no longer substantive and is merely of historical and linguistic interest.

Figure 18.2: Defamation

- Slander
  - a defamatory statement in oral or transient form actionable upon proof of damage; and
- Libel
  - a defamatory statement in written or other permanent form actionable per se.
- In all Australian jurisdictions, the distinction has been abolished: all defamation actions are actionable per se. (*Civil Law (Wrongs) Act 2002* (ACT), s 119; *Defamation Act 2005* (NSW), (Qld), (SA), (Tas), (Vic) and (WA), s 7; *Defamation Act 2006* (NT), s 6)

Must defame to third person

[18.15] A person's reputation exists in the minds of other persons. It is, therefore, not possible to defame someone to himself or herself. But it is possible to commit defamation by making a defamatory statement to one who does not believe it, even perhaps to one who knows it cannot be true: *Morgan v Odhams Press Newspaper* [1971] 1 WLR 1239 at 1246. This may be justified on the basis that even in these circumstances the statement has some capacity to do harm.

Protection of reputation versus free speech

[18.20] The tort of defamation clearly runs counter to what is sometimes regarded as a basic constitutional right in democratic countries, that of freedom of speech. That right is by no means absolute, being limited by crimes such as sedition or blasphemy, and other torts such as deceit and injurious falsehood. It is in any case not a right embodied as such, in either the Constitution of the United Kingdom or that of Australia,[3] and is better regarded as a privilege to speak freely in the absence of committing any legal wrong. But the tort of defamation is the most serious threat to that privilege, since, being actionable without proof of dishonest intent, it has the potential of restraining honest statements of fact or opinion that are critical of other persons. However, various

---

[3] Note, however, the defence of qualified privilege based on the constitutional provisions: see [18.240].

defences are allowed to actions in defamation, the effect of these defences being the most important recognition to some degree of a "constitutional" privilege of freedom of speech.

So at common law it is not defamatory to state the truth, a defence of justification being available. Previously, in some States, the defendant needed to not only prove the truth of the statement but also that it was made in the public interest (New South Wales) or for the public benefit (Queensland, Tasmania and the Australian Capital Territory). This additional requirement no longer exists in the uniform legislation. Defamatory statements are capable of being made without incurring liability on a number of occasions of absolute or qualified privilege. Also a comment is not defamatory where it is made on facts truly stated concerning a matter of public interest, provided the comment reflects an opinion which is honestly held by the commentator.

Defamation provides a direct challenge to free speech, but the defences to defamation attempt to strike a balance between free speech and protection of reputation.

Role of judge and jury in proceedings

[18.25] The role of a jury in defamation proceedings represents a point of departure between jurisdictions with a jury trial continuing to be a normal right of the parties to a defamation action in most jurisdictions,[4] no doubt because so much depends on the veracity of the parties and their witnesses, and the impression they make in the witness box, matters which historically have been thought the suitable province of a jury. The judge, however, retains an important controlling function over the trial. In particular, the judge decides:

- whether the statement is capable of bearing the meaning alleged by the plaintiff;
- whether it is capable in law and fact of being defamatory;
- whether it is capable of referring to the plaintiff; and
- whether the facts support the contention that it has been published by the defendant.

Failure on any of the requirements leads to the withdrawal of the case from the jury. The judge's controlling function is clearly one of law. Questions left to the jury are of fact, such as:

- whether the defendant has publised material about the plaintiff;
- whether the material is in fact defamatory of the plaintiff; and
- whether a defence has been established.

The jury's conclusions of fact are correctable only on appeal and only on the ground that they are wholly unreasonable and against the weight of the evidence. The calculation of damages is specifically reserved for the judge (see s 22(3), uniform legislation in the jury States).

---

[4]   See *Defamation Act 2006* (NSW), (Qld), (Tas), (Vic), (WA), ss 21 and 22.

Definition of defamatory statement

General principles

[18.30] The uniform legislation specifically preserves the common law; therefore, in the absence of a defintion of what constitutes defamatory material, we must turn to the common law for clarification. In determining whether or not a statement is defamatory the court will consider a number of different factors including the identification of the plaintiff, the surrounding circumstances and the context in which the statement is made. This can be a complicated process and involves the consideration of a number of broad, general principles:

- the statement need not be verbal;
- the statement must cause the plaintiff to be shunned among right-thinking persons;
- the statement may be true or false;
- the statement need not assign any immorality, wrongdoing or disparagement against the plaintiff in order to be defamatory;
- the statement may be expressed directly or by innuendo; and
- the meaning of the statement is determined from the natural and ordinary meaning of the words and the context within which it is placed.

Nature of statement

[18.35] It is well established that a statement need not be verbal. It may be conveyed by pictorial representation such as a cartoon (*Tolley v J S Fry & Sons* [1930] 1 KB 467), a film (*Youssoupoff v MGM Pictures* (1934) 50 TLR 581) or by conduct such as hanging the plaintiff in effigy: *Eyre v Garlick* (1878) 42 JP 68. The film *Youssoupoff* which featured a supposedly historical incident depicting the rape of the plaintiff, was found to be defamatory of the plaintiff by its combination of historical representation and spoken word. In *Monson v Tussaud's* [1894] 1 QB 671 the presentation of a waxwork effigy of the plaintiff in the Chamber of Horrors of the defendant's gallery close to other waxwork murderers was found capable of being defamatory. In both cases a statement was not difficult to find.

As to the content of the statement, it is now accepted that to limit the requirement to a statement which must expose the plaintiff to hatred, ridicule or contempt in the minds of right-thinking persons, is unduly restrictive. It may be enough to attribute to someone a misfortune that causes that person to be shunned, though not brought into disfavour among right-thinking persons. So, although it is not defamatory to say that someone has suffered a serious illness (*Grappelli v Block* [1981] 1 WLR 822), it is defamatory to attribute to him or her a "loathsome" disease. The original diseases encompassed were venereal disease and leprosy, but it seems clear that an attribution of AIDS to a person would nowadays qualify, as would a statement that the plaintiff was insane. Again, the cinematic representation of a film character in *Youssoupoff* that the plaintiff had been raped was found defamatory of her. In *Berkoff v Burchill* [1996] 4 All ER 1008 the statement that the plaintiff, an actor, was "hideously ugly" was found defamatory of him.

Social opinion and prevailing social climate

[18.40] The key to defamation is the impact (or potential impact) that a statement has on the mind of the audience; the question, therefore, is which members of the audience are to determine this? Is it the most conservative or those with the broadest minds? The courts have developed a test which is to consider the person who is deemed to be "right thinking": the "average" member of society. Or, as Kirby J summarised the test in *Chakravarti v Advertiser Newspapers* (1998) 193 CLR 519 at 573:

> *The recipient has been variously described as a "reasonable reader", a "right-thinking [member] of society", or an "ordinary man, not avid for scandal". Sometimes qualities of understanding have been attributed, such as the "reader of average intelligence". The point of these attempts to describe the notional recipient is to conjure up an idea of the kind of person who will receive the communication in question and in whose opinion the reputation of the person affected is said to be lowered. Special knowledge is excluded. So are extremes of suspicion and cynicism (on the one hand) or naivety and disbelief (on the other).*

The issue therefore is, when one considers the diverse range of opinions within society (with each group believing themselves to be those who are the "right thinkers"), the test of the right-thinking person becomes almost impossible to apply. The statement may make the plaintiff a hero in the eyes of some and a villain to others. So it has been found defamatory to call the plaintiff a "scab" (strike breaker): *Murphy v Plasterers Society* [1949] SASR 98. This decision reflects reality rather than the ideal attitudes of the right-thinking person. Other decisions are less satisfactory. For example, in *Byrne v Deane* [1937] 1 KB 818 the suggestion in a verse displayed in club premises that the plaintiff, a club member, was a police informant as to illegal activities within the club, was held to be not defamatory since it merely indicated that the plaintiff was carrying out his civic responsibilities. In *Bowes v Fehlberg* [1997] Aust Torts Reports 81-433 it was found that the plaintiff, a personal assistant to the Premier of Tasmania, was not defamed by a statement that he had engaged in surreptitious photographic surveillance of a member of Parliament in order to gain evidence of misconduct by that member, since this would have been a legitimate exercise of his duties towards the Premier. The difficulty with these cases is that a person can legitimately object to a false statement that lowers their reputation among a significant body of persons, even though those persons are not "right thinking". To allow the action is not to condone the response of those persons (nor to threaten "whistleblowing", since the genuine whistleblower is prepared to accept unpopularity).

Another problem is the relevance of the temporal climate to the issue of whether the statement is defamatory. Consider, for example, changing social attitudes to homosexuality, race and legitimacy. An early American case held the phrase "coloured gentlemen"[5] in an advertisement to be defamatory; would this still be the case? Again the difficulty may centre on the question of whether actual attitudes, as opposed to right-thinking attitudes, are taken as the test.

A final point is that statements relating to matters such as these may be made in the course of vulgar abuse and it is settled law that mere vulgar abuse cannot be defamatory. However, the line between satire and abuse can become difficult to tread. The appellants in *Australian Broadcasting Corporation v Hanson* [1998] QCA 306 argued that a satirical

---

5 *Upson v Times-Democrat* 104 La 141 (1900) – by mistake for "cultured gentlemen".

song about the well-known politician, Pauline Hanson, amounted to little more than vulgar abuse and was therefore not defamatory. The court, however, determined that the lyrics contained "grossly offensive imputations" amounting to a "mindless effort at cheap denigration" and held that there was "no room for debate" about the defamatory nature of the material: de Jersey CJ (McMurdo P and McPherson JA concurring).

The "right thinking" member of society is therefore open to interpretation and adjudication. The important concept to remember is that defamation is protecting reputation, and reputation exists in the minds of others.

Figure 18.3: What is reputation?

> • Reputation: views/opinions or impressions held by others in the community on the character of another regarding the person's personal or professional standing in matters of integrity, honour and honesty.
> • "[T]he law recognises in every man a right to have the estimation in which he stands in the opinion of others unaffected by false statements to his discredit": Cave J in *Scott v Sampson* (1882) 8 QBD 491.

Standing to sue

Personal action

[18.45] The very nature of defamation is personal and, because of this, the dead cannot be defamed. The cause of action for defamation is personal to the deceased, and does not descend to the estate. It makes no difference that the estate can prove temporal loss flowing from the statement. Nor is it possible to circumvent the bar by suing under the *Trade Practices Act 1974* (Cth) for deceptive or misleading conduct: *Krahe v Freeman* [1988] ATPR 40-871. There was considerable debate surrounding the ability (or not) of the deceased to bring an action in defamation and there was, for a short time, a possibility that the reform may introduce a limited right for protection of the reputation of a deceased person because, after all, the reputation is all that remains once someone dies. This position was eventually abandoned and the uniform legislation maintained the common law position: no cause of action for defamation of, or against, deceased persons (*Civil Law (Wrongs) Act 2002* (ACT), s 122; *Defamation Act 2005* (NSW), (Qld), (SA), (Vic) and (WA), s 10; *Defamation Act 2006* (NT), s 9. The Tasmanian legislation s 10 is left blank, thus the common law applies).

It is relevant to note that relatives and friends of a deceased person can, however, sue in defamation if the statement regarding the deceased also carries a negative imputation regarding their reputation. In *Krahe v TCN Channel Nine Pty Ltd* (1986) 4 NSWLR 536, for example, there were a number of articles upon the death of an ex-detective. The articles centred around allegations that he was corrupt. Along with these allegations there was some commentary regarding his funeral, including the clothing and jewellery of his widow and his children, and the fact that they arrived at the funeral in a Rolls

Royce car. His widow was unsuccessful in bringing an action regarding the broader allegations about her husband but was successful in her claim regarding the personal imputation that she profited from her husband's criminal activities.

Corporations, organisations and groups

[18.50] At common law a trading corporation was able to sue for defamation: *South Hetton Coal v NE News* [1894] 1 QB 133. It was held not to be defamatory to say of a corporation or other business entity that it had ceased business,[6] but it was deemed defamatory to say that it had "gone bust" (*Aspro Travel v Owners Abroad Group* [1996] 1 WLR 132) or that it is in liquidation (*Currabubula v State Bank of NSW* [1999] Aust Torts Reports 81-511). The justification for allowing the corporation to sue was mainly that its trading reputation is enjoyed independently of that of its directors or officers. However, it can only act through those officials and, were it to be accused of various types of misconduct, the action would probably be better brought by the company officials, claiming individual damage (indeed, this is the only avenue available under the uniform legislation). English cases have settled that a local government body has no capacity to sue for defamation, on the ground that it is against public policy to restrain criticism of such bodies, however ill-founded that criticism might be: *Derbyshire CC v Times Newspapers* [1993] AC 534.

Under the uniform legislation, however, a corporation cannot sue for defamation unless it has fewer than 10 employees or functions as a "not-for-profit" organisation (the objects for which it is formed do not include financial gain for its members or corporators) and is not a public body: *Civil Law (Wrongs) Act 2002* (ACT), s 121; *Defamation Act 2005* (NSW), (Qld), (SA), (Vic) and (WA), s 10; *Defamation Act 2006* (NT), s 9. The legislative definition of a public body is a local government body or other governmental or public authority, thus affirming the position established in *Derbyshire*.

Ingredients of tort

[18.55] The tort of defamation may be summed up in a single sentence: the defendant must make a defamatory statement about the plaintiff to persons other than the plaintiff. That sentence in fact contains four requirements that are the main ingredients of the tort. First, the statement must bear the defamatory meaning that the plaintiff alleges. This raises the important issue of the interpretation of the statement and the core question of what constitutes a defamatory statement. At this point it is merely useful to state that the defamatory meaning may not be apparent on the face of the statement but may exist by way of innuendo, that is, by a "reading between the lines". Thus it would be rare that a person would publish a statement that "Person A is a complete fool"; however, they may, in describing A's actions, leave the reader in no doubt that they are, in fact, a complete fool. This can be done through innuendo (either "true" or "false" innuendo: defined at [18.100] and [18.105]]). The view of Person A as a "complete fool" is the defamatory imputation carried by the description of their actions. Once the plaintiff is able to establish that the words bear the meaning alleged, the second, third and fourth requirements are that the words are in fact defamatory, that they refer to the plaintiff and that they have been published to persons other than the plaintiff.

---

6   *Ratcliffe v Evans* [1892] 2 QB 524.

Figure 18.4: Defamation – elements

> The plaintiff must prove that:
> * the subject matter relates to the plaintiff;
> * the subject matter has been published;
> * the subject matter contains a defamatory imputation or bears a defamatory meaning; and
> * there is no lawful excuse for making the defamatory statement.

Subject matter relates to plaintiff

[18.60] The subject matter must clearly identify the plaintiff. Where there is a jury trial the judge decides whether the publication is capable of referring to the plaintiff. If it is, it is then left to the jury to decide whether it does so in fact. This is not always a straightforward or clear issue; indeed, the defendant need not even know of the plaintiff's identity or intend to refer to that particular person, in order to be found to have referred to the plaintiff.[7] The defendant has been held liable where he intended to refer to the plaintiff without naming him, but supplied sufficient facts to enable a number of people to realise the plaintiff was the person referred to: *Bateman v Shepherd* [1997] Aust Torts Reports 81-417. The test is an objective one based upon considerations of whether the ordinary, reasonable recipient of the statement would take it as referring to the plaintiff.

Coincidence of name has proved a difficulty to those making public, especially press, statements. In *Hulton v Jones* [1910] AC 20, a fictitious piece appearing in the defendants' newspaper featured one Artemis Jones conducting an amorous liaison with a woman not his wife. The fictitious Jones was a church warden living at Peckham, but a genuine Artemis Jones, a barrister not living at Peckham, received £1750 damages on the ground that several persons testified that they thought the piece referred to him. That it was put forward as fiction did not excuse the defendant, which seems to mean that the usual formula in fictional works that all characters named are stated to be fictitious would be equally ineffective. In *Lee v Wilson* (1934) 51 CLR 276[8] a newspaper published a report of a police inquiry which it stated concerned allegations of bribery against a "Detective Lee". Two Detectives Lee brought successful libel actions, since the subject of the inquiry was a Constable Lee in the Motor Registration Branch.

Class of people not actionable

[18.65] With the essence of defamation lying in damage to personal reputation, it follows that if an individual cannot be specifically identified then he or she has not been personally defamed. To that end, a statement referring to members of a class is not actionable by individual members of that class. This rule yields its force if it can

---

[7]   Refer discussion at [18.105] regarding *Morgan v Odhams Press Newspaper* [1971] 1 WLR 1239 and *Cassidy v Daily Mirror Newspapers* [1929] 2 KB 331.

[8]   See also *Newstead v London Express Newspaper* [1940] 1 KB 377 – a newspaper report that Harold Newstead, a 30-year-old Camberwell man, had been convicted of bigamy was true of a Camberwell barman of that name, but untrue (and capable of being defamatory) of the plaintiff, a Camberwell baker of the same name and aged about 30.

be proved that the statement is capable of referring to all the individual members of the class. Thus, "all lawyers are thieves" is not actionable by any lawyer; however, a statement that "all lawyers working at Law Firm X" may indeed be actionable by all those employed at that firm. The group must be sufficiently confined that it is possible to identify individual members of that group: where 17 defendants had been indicted for murder, the defendant's statement that all took part in the murder was actionable by each defendant: *Foxcroft v Lacey* (1613) Hob 89. Each member of a group of seven Roman Catholic clergymen was entitled to sue in relation to a charge made against the group, since it implicated each one: *Browne v Thomson* [1912] SC 359. Sometimes what looks like a group charge is capable of being construed on a close reading to refer to a particular person. For instance in *Le Fanu v Malcolmson* (1848) 1 HLC 637; 9 ER 910, the court found that what looked like a general imputation of cruelty by Irish factory owners related specifically to factory owners in Waterford, including the plaintiff. Further, there is no difficulty in finding reference to the plaintiff where one unidentified member of a small group is defamed; nor where two persons are defamed in the alternative. A recent example of the latter point is *Random House Pty Ltd v Abbott* (1999) 94 FCR 296. The defendants had published a book which suggested that one of the wives (unidentified) of two politicians had, before marriage, slept with the two in order to change their political allegiance. This was held to be defamatory of both wives.

Publication

[18.70] The defamatory statement must be published to persons other than the plaintiff, and publication is not limited to the traditional meaning of the term (it can be oral, written, pictorial etc). There can be no publication to one who is incapable of understanding the statement because it is in a foreign language, or of reading it being blind, or of hearing it being deaf. Publishers and printers of defamatory material emanating from another person are equally liable along with the author; they are joint tortfeasors. It is not publication by either publisher or printer to deliver the printed material back into the hands of the author; it becomes so only on dissemination to other persons. Mechanical distributors of defamatory material are also liable for its publication, but have a special defence not available to the publisher or printer of the material: see [18.275] (defence of mechanical distribution now subsumed under innocent dissemination). Dictation to a typist is publication but may attract the defence of qualified privilege: see [18.235].

Where the defendant intends the statement to be read or overheard, there is, apart from the special cases above, no difficulty in finding publication. The law, however, may find publication proved even where that is not the case. For example, publication by postcard will be conclusively presumed since postcards are available to be read by anyone who sees them. There was publication where a business letter was opened by an employee in the ordinary course of business (*Pullman v Hill* [1891] 1 QB 524) and where a husband opened a letter addressed to his wife, which looked like a circular: *Thealler v Richardson* [1962] 1 WLR 151. But there was not publication where a letter was opened by an inquisitive butler, even though it was unsealed: *Huth v Huth* [1915] 3 KB 32. The test of publication here appears to turn on reasonable foreseeability. Again, where a third party overhears a slanderous statement about the plaintiff, the test of publication is whether the presence of the third party should have been foreseen: *White v Stone Lighting* [1939] 2 KB 827.

Foreseeability of publication

[18.75] The same test of reasonable foreseeability governs republication of defamatory material. In *Wild-Blundell v Stephens* [1920] AC 945 it was held that the showing of a confidential report made by the plaintiff, which was defamatory of two directors of a company, to those directors by the manager of the company into whose hands the report had mistakenly fallen, was not reasonably foreseeable. It therefore broke the chain of causation between the negligence of the accountant which had caused the mistake, and the ensuing damage to the plaintiff in having to pay damages to the directors. On the other hand, in *Slipper v BBC* [1991] 2 QB 283, where a defamatory film broadcast by the BBC had been subject to press review which repeated the defamatory sting of the libel, it was held that this was reasonably foreseeable and the reviews could be taken to account in assessing damages.

Liability can be incurred through "publication" by omission. In *Byrne v Deane* [1937] 1 KB 818[9] the failure by a club manager to take steps to remove an allegedly defamatory verse pinned to the notice-board of the club by a member was found to be a publication by the manager, though, as seen already, the action failed to establish the defamatory nature of the verse. The concept of publication by omission to act is no doubt a limited one. At the very least, the defendant would need to have control over the place of publication and knowledge of the defamatory nature of the material.

Place of publication

[18.80] As a general rule, publication is deemed to occur at the place at which the statement is made available. Therefore, if a pamphlet or newspaper is printed in New South Wales but sold in South Australia, publication occurs in both jurisdictions. This aspect of the law highlights the issues with respect to the differences in defamation laws throughout Australia and was one of the driving forces behind the calls for uniform defamation laws. One growing area in which the problems with this general rule are highlighted is publication on the internet, as demonstrated in *Dow Jones & Co Ltd v Gutnick* (2002) 210 CLR 575. In this case, information originating from the United States was published on the internet. This information cast aspersions on the character of Mr Joseph Gutnick, the imputations being that he was involved in money laundering and tax evasion. The publication drew a wide audience in the United States but only a limited number of subscription customers in Victoria. The action was brought in Victoria because, in the absence of a constitutional protection of free speech, it is easier to establish defamation in Victoria than in the United States.

The respondent argued the established principle that publication occurs where and when the information becomes available, while the appellant argued that in the case of the internet, publication should be deemed to occur where and when the information is uploaded. The court preferred the formulation of the respondent, as it was based on established legal principle, and declined to change the law for the convenience of internet publishers. The reality, therefore, is that at common law the rule regarding location of publication provided an opportunity for plaintiffs to "forum shop" for the most sympathetic jurisdiction, hence the need for a choice of law provision in the uniform legislation.

---

[9]   See also now *Godfrey v Demon Internet* [2000] 3 WLR 1020 – an item appearing on the internet is a publication by the internet service provider.

Choice of law

[18.85] Prior to the introduction of the uniform legislation there existed the unsatisfactory situation of different laws in each different jurisdiction; thus if defamatory material was published across different jurisdictions the law of each place of publication needed to be addressed and applied. On a practical level, along with the "forum shopping" outlined above, this meant that different laws (and in particular, different defences) had to be considered in the one action. This has been specifically addressed in the uniform legislation through the "choice of law" provision. Under the new regime, if there is a situation in which an item is published across different Australian jurisdictional areas, then the substantive law of the jurisdiction with the closest connection to the plaintiff is to be applied. The legislation sets out a number of relevant considerations in determining the area of "closest connection" and these include: ordinary place of residence of the plaintiff (at the time of publication), the extent of publication in each jurisdiction, extent of harm in each jurisdiction and, of course, any other matter deemed relevant.[10]

Interpretation of statement

[18.90] As indicated at [18.25], it is a matter for the court to determine whether the statement is capable of bearing a defamatory meaning. If the court decides that it is capable, the matter must go to the jury to decide whether it does bear that meaning. In jurisdictions without a jury, both of these steps are completed by the court. There is of course no difficulty with obvious defamatory statements, for example where the defendant has expressly accused the plaintiff of theft or murder. More difficulty surrounds the case of innuendo, where, in particular, the words are capable of being understood in a defamatory sense, but also capable of bearing a non-defamatory meaning. This is not a straightforward question that can be easily answered, indeed it has been noted that:

> the function the court exercises in determining whether a matter complained of has the capacity to convey a defamatory imputation is evaluative and one where judicial minds may differ.[11]

There are three ways in which defamatory imputation can arise:

* natural and ordinary meaning of the words; or
* false innuendo; or
* true innuendo.

Natural and ordinary meaning

[18.95] The simplest situation is that in which the plaintiff is clearly identified and the imputation is a straightforward statement which involves the court considering the statement on its face. The imputations are considered by reference to the "ordinary, reasonable, fair minded members of society": *Reader's Digest Services Pty Ltd v Lamb* (1982) 150 CLR 500 at 506. As noted by Kirby J in *Chakravarti v Advertiser Newspapers*

10   *Civil Law (Wrongs) Act 2002* (ACT), s 123; *Defamation Act 2005* (NSW), (Qld), (SA), (Tas), (Vic) and (WA), s 11; *Defamation Act 2006* (NT), s 10.
11   *Malcolm v Nationwide News Pty Ltd* [2007] Aust Torts Reports 81-915, per Beazley JA at [30].

(1998) 193 CLR 519 the ordinary members of society have been described as the "reasonable reader", "ordinary man, not avid for scandal" and the "reader of average intelligence".[12] In instances such as this, there is no reading between the lines or complex interpretation required; the meaning is clear.

False innuendo

[18.100] The situation of a false innuendo requires some interpretation of the statement, or a reading between the lines, and refers to an inferred or indirect meaning which the ordinary person would draw from the material: *Jones v Skelton* [1963] 1 WLR 1362 at 1370. The test to be applied in determining the matter is once again an objective one: how an ordinary, reasonable reader or recipient of the statement would understand it. Sometimes the matter is reasonably simple. For example, in *Random House Pty Ltd v Abbott* [1999] Aust Torts Reports 81-533 the defendants had published a statement indicating that two politicians had changed party immediately after having sex with an unnamed female, who later married one of the Ministers. The innuendo that each politician was prepared to abandon his political principles in exchange for sexual favours was readily enough drawn. Sometimes the question is more difficult.

In cases where there is reliance on a false innuendo, the court will generally require plaintiffs to specify the defamatory sense that they understand the words to contain. This expectation of specificity enables the defendant to justify the relevant part of the statement. The plaintiff is not, however, necessarily held to the strict content of its pleading if some defamatory nuance not very different from that alleged is capable of being established. In particular, if a similar though less serious defamatory allegation is proved, the plaintiff may be allowed to succeed. The plaintiff is entitled to select part of a given statement and sue in relation to that part, and it is immaterial that the rest of the statement contains allegations that the defendant is capable of justifying. Whilst this focused pleading is available, it is important to remember that the publication must be considered as a whole and the context of a statement is a relevant consideration: refer [18.110] below.

True innuendo

[18.105] A true innuendo exists where a statement, harmless in itself, becomes defamatory by reason of facts known to other persons and considered in combination with the statement. For example, in *Tolley v J S Fry & Sons* [1930] 1 KB 467, a leading amateur golfer of the day complained of the defendants' advertisement showing him, without any truth, to be in the course of consuming their chocolates while playing golf. His action for defamation succeeded on the ground that persons who knew him would assume, falsely, that he had forfeited his amateur status by accepting payment for the advertisement from the defendants. Of significance was the impact of the advertisement on those who had the extrinsic knowledge of his identity and his amateur status; to those without the knowledge it was a harmless picture depicting a golfer eating chocolate.

Cases of true innuendo are apt to demonstrate the strict nature of liability for defamation. *Cassidy v Daily Mirror Newspapers* [1929] 2 KB 331 is a leading example.

---

[12] His Honour was referring to *Jones v Skelton* (1963) 63 SR (NSW) 644 at 650-651; *Sim v Stretch* (1936) 52 TLR 669 at 671; and *Slatyer v Daily Telegraph Newspaper Co Ltd* (1908) 6 CLR 1.

The defendants published a photograph of Cassidy with a woman to whom it was said by the defendants he was about to be married. The defendants did not know that Cassidy was already married. The plaintiff, Cassidy's wife, brought a successful action for defamation against the newspaper on the ground that persons who knew her and read the newspaper would conceive her to have been "living in sin". An even more extreme example is *Morgan v Odhams Press* [1971] 1 WLR 1239. The defendants had published a story that a dog-doping gang had kidnapped a certain girl. The plaintiff sued for defamation and produced as witnesses six persons who deposed they knew the girl to be living with the plaintiff round about the time of the kidnapping and took the article to mean he was part of the gang. The House of Lords upheld the jury's verdict in favour of the plaintiff in this defamation action. The case goes one step further than *Cassidy*. The story about the kidnapping was true, unlike that about Cassidy's prospective marriage. The falsehood lay in its implication that the plaintiff was part of the gang, which created a false impression in the mind of certain persons.

It may seem just that if newspapers engage in this form of private sleuthing into criminal matters, they take the risk that someone may connect what is published with someone they know. Yet there must surely be limits to that. Suppose that a newspaper publishes a statement that the plaintiff had been in the presence of a person shortly before that person was murdered, though this fact was unknown to the newspaper at the time of publication. Is the newspaper liable to persons who know of the murder and the victim and consequently suspect the plaintiff of murder? *Grappelli v Block* [1981] 1 WLR 822 raises a related but distinct issue as to the extent of the doctrine of true innuendo. The defendants, the plaintiff's agents, had published an initially non-defamatory statement that the plaintiff, a violinist, was ill and unable to appear at certain concerts that had been arranged and advertised. Then press statements appeared giving accurate details of concerts to be held by the plaintiff that coincided with the dates of the cancelled concerts. The plaintiff sued in defamation on the basis that the later press information coupled with the earlier statement cast a slur on his integrity. His action failed, on the ground that other persons cannot convert an originally non-defamatory statement into a defamatory one through subsequent publication. No doubt this is generally true, but on the facts the defendants must have known of the likelihood of the appearance of the later publications. They must also have known that the plaintiff was not ill and had merely made the statement that he was ill to cover up the fact that the original bookings they, his agents, had made on his behalf were made without his authority.

Since a true innuendo depends upon knowledge by persons receiving the statement of facts not stated in it, it might be thought that the plaintiff would have to provide at least one such person as a witness. Clearly it is advisable to do so if it is possible, as *Morgan* shows, since in their absence it may be difficult to persuade a jury that such persons exist. But at the moment it is not clear that it is necessary. In *Hough v London Express Newspapers* [1940] 2 KB 507, a case where the nature of the plaintiff's complaint was the same as that in *Cassidy*, the plaintiff called two witnesses, both of whom testified that they did not believe the implication that she was not married to her husband. Nevertheless the court found in favour of the plaintiff. On the other hand, in *Cross v Denley* (1952) 52 SR(NSW) 112 the plaintiff failed in the absence of proof of publication to anyone who would connect him with the publication. The best explanation of *Hough* is that it seems to be the law that defamation is committed even by publication to a person who does not believe the statement. If so, it would seem to be in law insufficient for the plaintiff merely to prove the publication of the statement and the additional facts which make it defamatory.

Interpretation of statement as whole

[18.110] The publication must be considered in its entirety and the imputation may lie in the combined effect of different statements: in *Favell v Queensland Newspapers Pty Ltd* (2005) 221 ALR 186 the combined effect of discussion of a house fire alongside consideration of a controversial plan to redevelop the site was deemed sufficient to give rise to a defamatory imputation. Indeed, the innuendo lay in the linking of the two issues. When considering the context of a statement it is important to keep in mind the "*Polly Peck*" and contextual truth defence discussed at [18.140]. The combined effect of a publication may, however, alter the character of an otherwise defamatory statement and if a sufficient corrective to an earlier defamatory imputation appears in the statement itself, there will be no liability. The hypothetical, "Lord X, you are a thief, you have stolen my heart" is often used as an example. A real example is *Charleston v News Group* [1995] 2 AC 65. The plaintiffs (actors who played Harold and Madge in the popular television program, "Neighbours") complained about photographs of their heads and shoulders displayed above pictures of semi-naked models, the whole portraying various forms of sexual activity. The accompanying article below made it clear that the matter was lifted from another publication and criticised it as a form of pornography. The House of Lords held that the article removed any defamatory sense that the photographs might have borne. Bearing in mind that the lurid display above the article would make an immediate impression on the minds of numerous persons who would not bother to read the article, the decision is questionable. It was heavily criticised by Kirby J in *Chakravarti v The Advertiser Newspaper* (1998) 193 CLR 519 at 574 on the basis that it does not reflect the realities of the way in which people read (and are intended to read) newspapers. A further criticism was that it undermines the basis of defamation law which aims at repairing actual damage to reputation and therefore denies remedies to those whose reputations are damaged by the often superficial and casual approach to the reading of such publications.

A case going the other way is *Sergi v ABC* [1983] 2 NSWLR 240. The plaintiff had been defamed in a newspaper article and accompanying photograph which indicated that an inquiry had found him to be a member of a murderous Italian group of cannabis growers in the Griffith area of New South Wales. A week later the newspaper published a retraction and apology. The ABC then displayed on a television program that part of the newspaper containing the apology together with a not readily identifiable photograph of the plaintiff. It was found that even if this was enough to remove any impression that the plaintiff was one of this murderous group (which was doubtful), there had been no correction to a further allegation by the ABC that the plaintiff had been a party to the murder and disappearance of Donald Mackay, an anti-cannabis campaigner.

Repetition of libel or slander

[18.115] The basic rule is clear: it is defamatory to repeat a defamatory statement made by another person, even though the statement makes clear that the view stated is not that of the writer or speaker. Problems have arisen concerning the extent of the rule.

In *Cadam v Beaverbrook Newspapers* [1959] 1 QB 413, for example, the English Court of Appeal left open the question whether a newspaper item which correctly reported that a writ for conspiracy to defraud had been issued against the defendant could be interpreted as a statement that the defendant had actually committed that tort. On the other hand, *Lewis v Daily Telegraph* [1964] AC 234 contains the House of Lords' authority that a statement that the plaintiff is under suspicion of misconduct means no more than that and can be justified in that sense. The statement in the defendant newspaper in that case, that the fraud squad of the police was investigating the plaintiff's affairs, could therefore be justified merely by showing that this was the case. The House of Lords distinguished between allegations of suspicion on the one hand and repetition of rumour on the other. The latter could only be justified by proving the truth of the rumour.

Drawing a line of this sort may lead to complex problems. In *Stern v Piper* [1996] 3 WLR 713 the plaintiff complained of a newspaper article which contained extracts from a pleading in legal proceedings brought by another person, the gist of which was that the plaintiff was guilty of corporate malpractice or fraud. The Court of Appeal held that the defendant newspaper fell foul of the repetition rule here and could not justify the article merely by showing that these statements had in fact been made by the plaintiff in other proceedings. This was not, like *Cadam*, a mere statement that a writ in a stated matter had been issued which according to the Court of Appeal in *Stern* was not defamatory if true. The content of part of that writ had here also been revealed, and this went too far. The allegation in the pleading was therefore regarded as one of fact, whereas the fraud squad's investigation of the plaintiff in *Lewis* indicated only a reasonable suspicion of the plaintiff's guilt. The same distinction was drawn in *Shah v Standard Chartered Bank* [1998] 4 All ER 155, in which the defendants had repeated allegations by third parties throwing suspicion onto the plaintiffs of money-laundering activities. The Court of Appeal distinguished between third party allegations of reasonable suspicion against the plaintiff which could be justified by showing that the plaintiff's behaviour had given grounds for that suspicion, and repetitions of third party statements or rumours that the plaintiff was guilty of certain conduct which could be justified only by showing the plaintiff to be guilty of that conduct. The central allegation in *Shah* fell into the former category.

Single cause of action

[18.120] The very nature of defamation means that a single publication can contain multiple imputations and then be subject to multiple publications in multiple jurisdictions. This of course leaves open the possibility of a number of different actions based upon each imputation and each individual publication. The uniform legislation has addressed this issue limiting the availability of causes of action:

Figure 18.5: Single cause of action

> - Where there are multiple defamatory imputations contained in published material, only one cause of action is available:
>   - *Defamation Act 2005* (NSW, Qld, SA, Tas, Vic, WA), s 8
>   - *Civil Law (Wrongs) Act 2002* (ACT), s 120
>   - *Defamation Act 2006* (NT), s 7
> - Where an action for defamation has been brought in relation to published material, further proceedings cannot be brought, except with the permission of the court:
>   - *Defamation Act 2005* (NSW, Qld, Tas, Vic, WA), s 23
>   - *Civil Law (Wrongs) Act 2002* (ACT), s 133
>   - *Defamation Act 2006* (NT), s 20
>   - *Defamation Act 2005* (SA), s 21

Nature of liability

[18.125] Liability for the content of a defamatory statement is strict. The defendant may be liable for the statement even though there is no means of knowing that the statement is defamatory nor that it refers to the plaintiff (as *Morgan* and *Cassidy* considered at [18.105] particularly show). As regards publication of the statement, however, liability is not strict. The defendant must either intend to make the statement to other persons, or, if that is not the case, be negligent as to the way in which the statement is communicated to others. Strict liability for the content of the statement means that the defendant is liable for defamatory typographical errors occurring in the statement even if these occur without the defendant's own personal fault. Again there was liability where the defendant sent the statement to the wrong person mistakenly believing that publication to that person was privileged. The mistake was as to the content of the statement, not its publication: *Hebditch v McIlwaine* [1894] 2 QB 54.

The justification for strict liability for defamation is often said to be the importance the law attaches to reputation. There is something to this, though the elevation of reputation over an interest such as bodily safety may raise questions, and certainly the high level of damages awards for defamation by comparison with those awarded for personal injury has caused criticism and a degree of judicial response. Under the uniform legislation there are clear limits on the availability of damages and specific provisions relating to the mitigation of damage (refer [18.320]). It is also relevant to note that strict liability for defamation is not out of line with other torts such as trespass or conversion in which an intentional interference with the plaintiff or the plaintiff's property is tortious, even though the defendant has no reasonable means of knowing it is wrongful. A further consideration of relevance is the outcome of the publication of defamatory material, whether it is intentional or unintentional (or even unknowing), the effect is the same and a reputation is damaged. Intent is therefore irrelevant to the outcome.

Defences

[18.130] Whenever defamation becomes an issue there are two competing interests which must be balanced: the public interest in freedom of speech and the private interest in protection of reputation. The relevant balance is found through a comprehensive collection of defences. The availability of each defence turns on consideration of the nature of the information and purpose of communication. The greatest diversity between the jurisdictions was previously found in the area of defences but since the introduction of the uniform legislation this is no longer the case. It is relevant to note, however, that the common law defences are not automatically vitiated or limited by the legislative scheme:

Figure 18.6: Scope of defences

> *Defamation Act 2005* (NSW, Qld, Tas, Vic, WA), s 24
> *Civil Law (Wrongs) Act 2002* (ACT), s 134
> *Defamation Act 2006* (NT), s 21
> *Defamation Act 2005* (SA), s 22
> - A defence under the Act is additional to any other defence and does not of itself vitiate, limit or abrogate any other defence.
> - Malice is to be determined under the general law.

Truth and justification

[18.135] The defendant is entitled at common law to the defence that the defamatory statement is true: the defence of justification. The truth cannot be defamatory since whatever reputation is enjoyed by the plaintiff prior to the making of the statement, and is lowered thereby, is regarded as undeserved. This somewhat uncompromising attitude of the common law did not apply in certain Australian States in which the defendant pleading justification not only had to prove the truth of the statement but also that its making was for the public benefit ("public interest" in New South Wales).[13] As will be seen below, the uniform legislation has not adopted the public benefit/public interest approach and more closely resembles the common law position.

In establishing the defence, the defendant need only prove the substantial truth of the statement. The case most often quoted for this point is *Alexander v NE Rys* (1865) 122 ER 1221. A statement that the plaintiff had been sentenced to a fine or three weeks' imprisonment was justified by showing that he had been given the alternative of two weeks' imprisonment. Where the defendant is able to justify part but not all of the statement, the plaintiff is entitled to succeed, though what the defendant has proved may be sufficient to lower the plaintiff's reputation to such an extent that an award of damages might not seem appropriate. Thus in *Becker v Smith's Newspapers* [1929] SASR 469 the plaintiff, having been described as a blackmailer, liar, swindling

---

[13]   *Civil Law (Wrongs) Act 2002* (ACT), s 127; *Defamation Act 1974* (NSW), s 15; *Defamation Act 1889* (Qld), s 15; *Defamation Act 1957* (Tas), s 15 (all now repealed).

share pusher and illegal immigrant by the defendant was held to be entitled to UK£50 damages for defamation in relation to the last allegation, though the defendant could justify the remainder. The process of determining whether the defence is available involves a lengthy "fact finding" discussion, as demonstrated in *Habib v Nationwide News Pty Ltd* [2008] Aust Torts Reports 81-938 which saw McClellan CJ at CL carefully combing through transcripts of interviews and comparing what was said on separate occasions and finally reaching a conclusion as to what constituted the "truth" on the available evidence. The expectation of truth extends beyond the facts as stated to the imputation.

The common law requirement of substantial truth has been maintained by the uniform legislation:

Figure 18.7: Defence of justification

> *Defamation Act 2005* (NSW, Qld, Tas, Vic, WA), s 25
> *Civil Law (Wrongs) Act 2002* (ACT), s 135
> *Defamation Act 2006* (NT), s 23
> *Defamation Act 2005* (SA), s 23
> Imputations carried by the publication must be substantially true.

Partial justification: doctrine of common sting and contextual truth

[18.140] The focus of defamation is the actual harm done to the plaintiff's reputation. What then if there are multiple imputations within the one publication, some of which are true (and therefore covered by the defence of justification) and others which are not? This question becomes more complicated when the plaintiff chooses to plead the false imputations (which may be a minor component of the publication) and ignore the potentially more significant comments, which contained the true imputations. The approach to such a situation has been subject to some variation across jurisdictions but at the heart of each approach was the emphasis placed upon a consideration of the publication as a whole, the relevant question being: What was the impact of the publication, when read as a whole, upon the reputation of the plaintiff?

The common law approach was embodied in the English Court of Appeal decision in *Polly Peck (Holdings) v Trelford* [1986] QB 1000. The court held that where in the one publication there were two or more defamatory allegations, one of which the plaintiff complained of, the defendant could justify by proving the truth of one of the other allegations, provided it had a "common sting" with that chosen by the plaintiff. Significantly here, the defendant did not have to rely upon the imputations as pleaded by the plaintiff and could step outside the parameters of the pleading to point to the other, broader imputations contained within the publication. In short, if the imputations as pleaded by the plaintiff did no further damage to their reputation, then the defence of "partial justification" (later called the "*Polly Peck*" defence) was made out.

The doctrine of common sting has its own difficulties and was not met with enthusiasm in Australia. The doctrine was flatly rejected in the joint judgment of Brennan CJ and McHugh J in *Chakravarti v The Advertiser* (1998) 193 CLR 519 as being inconsistent with the fundamental principles of common law pleading (at [8]). Whilst these comments amounted to dicta and were not adopted by the rest of the court, other intermediate appellate courts have followed them and rejected the *Polly Peck* defence.[14] Ormiston JA of the Victorian Court of Appeal in *David Syme & Co Ltd v Hore-Lacy* (2000) 1 VR 667 referred specifically to the *Polly Peck* defence and the High Court's criticism of it and emphatically stated that "a defence which alleges a different meaning to that relied on by the plaintiff would merely be an argumentative plea" (at [10]). This is not to say that the overall context of the publication is irrelevant at common law. Under the principles outlined in *Hore-Lacy*, the court will consider other imputations so long as they are of the same type as those pleaded. The key question to ask is whether the additional, false imputations did any further harm or, as framed by Ormiston JA in *Hore-Lacey* (at [21]):

> the jury will have to be told that they cannot find for the plaintiff unless they agree with the meaning or one of the meanings put forward on behalf of the plaintiff, or unless the meaning they would give the publication was only a nuance or variant, not substantially different or more serious from that proposed by the plaintiff.

Prior to the uniform legislation there was some legislative consideration of the issues raised here and in New South Wales and Tasmania the relevant legislation provided that the defence of justification shall not fail if the untrue charges in the statement do not materially lower the plaintiff's reputation, having regard to the truth of the remaining charges. In New South Wales there was the additional requirement of public interest or qualified privilege (*Defamation Act 1974* (NSW) (repealed)). The uniform legislation has now clarified the position and introduced a straightforward contextual truth defence. It is worth noting that the effect of the provision is that it is a defence if the defendant can prove that if there are imputations in addition to those pleaded by the plaintiff that are "substantially true", and they do not further harm the reputation of the plaintiff, then the defence is established. This would appear to be a broader defence than that enunciated in *Hore-Lacy* as it allows the judge (and/or jury) to look beyond the actual pleadings of the plaintiff and consider the publication as a whole.

---

[14] *Fawcett v John Fairfax Publications Pty Ltd* [2008] NSWSC 139, referring to *David Syme & Co Ltd v Hore-Lacy* (2000) 1 VR 667.

Figure 18.8: Contextual truth

Defamation Act 2005 (NSW, Qld, Tas, Vic, WA), s 26
Civil Law (Wrongs) Act 2002 (ACT), s 136
Defamation Act 2006 (NT), s 23
Defamation Act 2005 (SA), s 24

Requirements:
• additional imputations are substantially true; and
• the additional imputations do not further harm the reputation
  of the plaintiff.

Fair comment (honest opinion)

[18.145] The delicate balance between free speech and protection of reputation is nowhere more apparent than in the defence of fair comment. This defence requires the apparently defamatory comment to clearly reflect an opinion on matters of public interest as opposed to a statement of fact. The essence of the defence is to provide an opportunity for the media and the general public to pass comment on matters affecting society, thus representing a clear protection to free expression in Australia. It does not matter if the opinion is one representing the common views of society. Indeed, as noted by Kirby J in *Channel Seven Adelaide Pty Ltd v Manock* (2007) 232 CLR 245 at [117]:

> It is by freedom of discussion, including the expression of unorthodox, heretical, unpopular and unsettling opinions, that progress is often made in political, economic, social and scientific thinking.

It is, of course, difficult to objectively test the truth of an opinion: it is enough that the opinion be one fairly and honestly held and stated by a defendant. But the word "fair" is misleading in this context since it implies a standard of reasonableness which is not in fact required. As explained by Gleeson CJ in *Manock* the "word 'fair' refers to limits to what any honest person, however opinionated or prejudiced, would express upon the basis of the relevant facts" (at [3]). The test is whether the opinion as stated is an honest one, which breaks down into two questions: whether it is actually held at all; and, if so, whether it is one which an honest person could have held. The effect of this is to allow comment of an extreme and arguably unreasonable nature to qualify for the defence.

The defence of fair comment has been preserved in the uniform legislation as honest opinion and in an endeavour to successfully balance the competing interests inherent in defamatory actions, there are specific requirements, each of which is discussed below.

Figure 18.9: Honest opinion

Defamation Act 2005 (NSW, Qld, Tas, Vic, WA), s 31
Civil Law (Wrongs) Act 2002 (ACT), s 139B
Defamation Act 2006 (NT), s 28
Defamation Act 2005 (SA), s 29

Requirements:
- expression of opinion rather than a statement of fact; and
- the opinion related to a matter of public interest; and
- the opinion was based on proper material; and
- the defence will be defeated if the opinion was not honestly held.

Fact and comment

[18.150] For the defence of honest opinion[15] to stand, there must be a clear delineation between fact and comment. The drawing of this distinction is not always easy and has been the basis of much judicial comment. It may be noted that this is a jury matter, though again the judge exercises the controlling function of deciding whether the matter should be left to the jury and if, as in the case of *Manock* it is determined that the distinction is not clear enough, then the defence will be struck out. It is clear that general expressions such as, "X is a liar (or a fraud)" will be regarded as conclusions of fact and must be justified, since there is no stated kernel of fact for them to be regarded as comment. If, however, the comment was "X has no formal financial qualifications but has been holding himself out as a CPA and obtaining financial gain, he is little more than a fraud", the defence would be made out as the comment is supported by the statement of fact. The factual basis is not always clearly spelt out but can be identified by inference or details known by others. The process of identifying the link between the comment made and the factual material relied on can appear in three ways:

(i) expressly stated in the same publication; or

(ii) referred to ("by a clear reference"); or

(iiii) the factual material can be "notorious".[16]

A clear example of a factual statement followed by a comment is provided by *Carleton v ABC* (2002) 172 FLR 398 at [220]. In this case allegations of plagiarism and "lazy journalism" were levelled at a reporter. These allegations were made after a clear comparison was made between his report and that of another journalist (which had been published first) and the similarities were identified and discussed. The conclusion was deemed to be clearly matters of opinion reached after consideration of the facts and the defence was made out.

---

15   With the common law defence of fair comment now enshrined in the uniform legislation as "honest opinion", ease of reference throughout this discussion calls for the use of one term: honest opinion.

16   *Channel Seven Adelaide Pty Ltd v Manock* (2007) 232 CLR 245, per Gummow, Hayne and Heydon JJ at [49] referring with approval to *Pervan v North Queensland Co Ltd* (1993) 178 CLR 309.

The appellant in *Manock* attempted to establish the defence based upon clear reference but failed (the defence being struck out by the High Court). The claim centred around promotional material for the "Today Tonight" television progam which referred to a well-known murder case with the presenter stating: "The new Keogh facts. The evidence they kept to themselves. The data and documents that don't add up. The evidence changed from one Court to the next."[17] Other statements were made and images of Dr Manock shown, giving rise to imputations of dishonesty and failure to carry out his professional role of supporting the court during criminal proceedings.[18] The defence was struck out (Kirby J dissenting) as there was no clear reference to external facts. Whilst the promotional material was designed to entice the public to view the program and ascertain the "truth" (through evaluation of the opinions expressed in the program) there was no clear delineation between fact and comment in the promotional material. Indeed, the statement itself was clearly framed as one of fact ("the new Keogh facts") of which the viewing public could not be aware. In this instance there was insufficient identification of the words as opinion, along with the admonishment that "the law of defamation distinguishes between comment and statements of fact, even if publishers and broadcasters do not" (Gleeson CJ at [12]). It is worth noting that Kirby J was reluctant to narrow the defence and argued that the facts were adequately identified and referred to with the promotion providing sufficient information to allow the recipients to "conveniently, promptly and without cost secure access to those facts" (Kirby J at [166]). His Honour's approach was guided by the imperative of freedom of expression and the significance of the striking out of the defence at an interlocutory stage (at [120]).

An example of the defence resting upon "notorious" facts is found in the decision of *Kemsley v Foot* [1952] AC 345. Foot, a journalist, had published a newspaper attack on the standards of the Beaverbrook Press, which he had headlined, "Lower than Kemsley". The question was whether the headline was fact or comment. The House of Lords held that a sufficient factual basis existed for it to be comment, in that Lord Kemsley was the proprietor of a number of newspapers, whose standards of journalism were being unfavourably commented on by the defendant. Kemsley's ownership of the newspapers and their content was public knowledge, a fact which goes some way towards explaining the case.

It is also of significance that Lord Oaksey, who gave the less frequently cited opinion in the House of Lords, thought that the statement indicating low standards could only be comment. It would have been different had Kemsley's newspapers been accused of fraud. The difference between fair comment and justification here is, however, to some extent more apparent than real. As Priestley JA pointed out in *New South Wales v Deren* [1999] Aust Torts Reports 81-502, in both defences the defendant may make use of facts not stated in order to prove the defence, and it is not to the point that not all the facts are proved. A statement that "X is a liar" can be justified by proof that X lied on four occasions, even though on a fifth occasion he was found to have told the truth. But justification requires that the main assertion be borne out; fair comment, only if it is a conclusion that can honestly be drawn.

---

17 Facts taken from the majority judgment of Gummow, Hayne and Heydon JJ at [16]ff.
18 Dr Manock is a forensic pathologist and was, at the time of the murder inquiry, the Senior Director of Forensic Pathology at the State Forensic Science Centre.

Public interest

[18.155] The comment must relate to a matter of public interest. The broad two-fold division of matters of public interest proposed by Fleming is adopted here.[19] First, there are matters of the national and local government of the country (including the behaviour of members of those governments) and the conduct of public institutions and services; second, there are matters submitted to the public for its attention, whether for its edification, instruction, entertainment or persuasion. Borderline cases will exist. The quality of education offered in a private school does not fall within the first category but might well qualify within the second. Public interest has, however, been given a broad interpretation and has been easily dealt with by the courts in other contexts. Consider *Habib v Nationwide News Pty Ltd* [2008] Aust Torts Reports 81-938 (discussed above at [18.135]) for example, where the fact that Mr Habib had been detained in various countries without charge and made well publicised claims about his treatment meant that discussions regarding his general credibility were deemed to be of "considerable public interest and public benefit" (at [154]).

Where the comment does not relate to a matter of public interest, it is defamatory even though it is based on true facts and is fair. Although the cause of action is for defamation, the gist of the plaintiff's complaint here is invasion of privacy. Thus a statement that a Member of Parliament was a wife-beater in relation to an incident that had occurred four years previously was found to have no relevance to the public interest and was therefore defamatory: *Mutch v Sleeman* (1928) 29 SR(NSW) 125. Further, artistic works cannot legitimately be criticised by reference to the morals of their authors: *Gardner v Fairfax* (1942) 42 SR(NSW) 171.

Truth (based upon proper material)

[18.160] The comment (or opinion) must be based upon proper material. Under the uniform legislation, to be proper the material must be substantially true, or publised on an occasion of absolute or qualified privilege (discussed below at [18.180]ff) or covered by the defence of a fair report of proceedings of public concern. This requirement is based upon a recognition of the nature of the material as once a matter is legitimately brought into the public domain, by publication of the report, comment should be free: *Mangena v Wright* [1909] 2 KB 958; *Brent Walker v Time Out* [1991] 2 QB 33; *Perran v North Queensland Newspaper* (1993) 178 CLR 309. The law allows a person commenting on a privileged report to comment fairly on the subject matter of the report without having to establish its truth.

Test of fairness

[18.165] There are various judicial statements to the effect that harsh or extreme expressions of opinion will not be judicially stifled. Most recently, Kirby J in *Manock* emphasised the importance of comment to a free society and reinforced earlier descriptions of the defence as the "bulwark" of free speech acknowledging the price to be paid, describing some comment as "intensely hurtful, unreasonable and unjust" (at [118]). Further examples can be found in the following decisions: In *Slim v Daily Telegraph* [1968] 1 All ER 497 at 503, Lord Denning MR said that the defence of fair comment is available to "an honest man expressing his honest opinion on a matter of public interest, no matter how wrong (that is, in the court's eyes), exaggerated or

---

[19]   Fleming, *Law of Torts* (9th ed, LBC Information Services, 1998), p 651.

prejudiced that opinion". In *Gardner v Fairfax Newspapers* (1942) SR(NSW) 171 at 174 Jordan CJ said: "A critic is entitled to dip his pen in gall for the purpose of legitimate criticism, and no one need be mealy-mouthed in denouncing what he regards as twaddle, daub or discord." A more recent example of this is *Grundmann v Georgeson* [1996] Aust Torts Reports 81-396. The defendant had accused the plaintiff, who ran a clinic at which legal abortions were performed, of being a murderer and of practising genocide. The Queensland Full Court held, by a majority, that these accusations could only be regarded as comment rather than fact; that being the case, the test of fairness was whether they represented the honest opinion of the defendant. The defence of fair comment under what was then s 377(8) of the *Queensland Code* succeeded. In order to protect free speech, the law accepts the existence of unpopular opinions and supports the right to express them.

Honest expression of opinion

[18.170] The honest expression of opinion requirement is assessed objectively; that is, the opinion is one which an honest person is capable of holding. If the plaintiff asserts actual dishonesty, the burden of proving that rests on the plaintiff. The same is true of malice, though that raises a further question as to how far proof of malice defeats the defence. A malicious state of mind existing in the defendant towards the plaintiff is not inconsistent with an honest belief in a comment made upon the plaintiff or the plaintiff's work. *Thomas v Bradbury Agnew* [1906] 2 KB 627 is often regarded as authority for the view that a malicious person is entirely precluded from the privilege of fair comment. But the judgment of Collins MR in that case is, to say the least, ambiguous. It envisages a jury finding that the comment has been distorted by malice, in which case "it is quite immaterial that someone else might without malice have written an equally damning criticism". Surely the test of distortion should be whether any but a malicious person could have made the comment. This would be in effect to apply the usual test for fair comment of whether the opinion stated is one that is capable of being honestly held. If it is, it is for the plaintiff to show that the opinion is not honestly held, whether for reasons of malice or otherwise. Under the uniform legislation, the defence of honest opinion will be defeated if the plaintiff proves that the opinion was not honestly held.[20]

Imputed dishonesty or malice

[18.175] Where there are several publishers of a statement which prima facie would attract a defence of fair comment, a question arises whether proof of dishonesty or malice on the part of one of the persons publishing the statement defeats the defence on the part of them all. The question arises also in the use of qualified privilege and is essentially the same question. It is therefore dealt with there: see [18.210]ff.

A different issue arises where the comment is found to be objectively one which no honest person could have made, but without any finding of dishonesty or malice against its author. Here none of the persons responsible for the publication is able to rely on fair comment: *Perran v North Queensland Newspaper* (1993) 178 CLR 309 at 329.

---

20   *Defamation Act 2005* (NSW), (Qld), (Tas), (Vic) and (WA), s 31(4); *Civil Law (Wrongs) Act 2002* (ACT), s 139B(4); *Defamation Act 2006* (NT), s 28(4) and *Defamation Act 2005* (SA), s 29(4).

Privilege

[18.180] The defence of privilege differs in principle from the two defences previously considered. Those defences (justification and honest opinion) depended on the defendant establishing a non-defamatory content to the statement. Privilege on the other hand accepts, at least in principle, the defamatory nature of the statement but defends it by reference to the occasion upon which it is made. Two types of privilege must be distinguished, absolute and qualified. Where the privilege is absolute, a defence exists whatever the purpose of making the statement, whether good or bad. In particular, the privilege is not lost by reason of the fact that the statement is made in bad faith, maliciously or for an improper purpose. Where the statement is subject to qualified privilege, proof of any of those three factors will defeat the privilege. The determination of the existence of a privileged occasion whether absolute or qualified is for the judge, not the jury.

Absolute privilege

Figure 18.10: Absolute privilege attaches to the occasion of the statement

> The three established occasions of absolute privilege are:
> * statements made in the course of parliamentary proceedings;
> * statements in the course of judicial proceedings; and
> * communications between high-ranking officers of state.

Parliamentary proceedings

[18.185] It is in the public interest that a national forum should exist for the ventilation of grievances without the fear of legal redress; to that end statements in Parliament are protected by absolute privilege. The privilege attaching to statements made in Parliament or during the course of parliamentary proceedings derived originally from Art 9 of the *Bill of Rights 1688* (specifically re-enacted at Commonwealth level *Parliamentary Privileges Act 1987* (Cth), s 16)[21] which provides: "the freedom of speech or debates or proceedings in Parliament ought not to be impeached or questioned in any court or place out of Parliament". The Article clearly goes beyond the protection of defamatory statements, but in relation to them it is clear that it serves both a public and a private purpose. Beyond facilitating open parliamentary discussion, privilege entails the giving of protection to Members of Parliament against legal proceedings being brought in regard to their parliamentary utterances. The public purpose underlying Art 9 (and similar provisions) means that an individual Member of Parliament cannot waive its protection. Indeed it is doubtful whether it can be waived by Parliament itself since the Article has statutory force and is in unqualified terms. However, its effect in Australia has come under recent doubt. In *Wright & The Advertiser v Lenin* (1990) 53 SASR 416 a South Australian court held that where a Member of Parliament brought

---

[21] This provision did have some State existence but these provisions are now repealed and absolute privilege dealt with under the uniform legislation as outlined in Figure 18.11.

proceedings for defamation in respect of criticism by the defendants of speeches he made in Parliament, the content of those speeches could be examined by the court, since otherwise it would be impossible for it to decide the questions raised by the Member's action.

This conclusion, however, was not accepted in a later Privy Council decision which held that it made no difference that the legal proceedings had been brought by, rather than against, a Member of Parliament: *Prebble v Television NZ* [1995] 1 AC 321. The three members of the Queensland Court of Appeal in *Laurance v Katter* (1996) 141 ALR 447 differed as to the effect upon *Parliamentary Privileges Act 1987* (Cth), s 16(3), of the High Court authority establishing a constitutional right to freedom of speech in relation to comment upon constitutional or political matters.[22] Fitzgerald P found that the constitutional right did not deviate from, nor was inconsistent with, the parliamentary privilege set out by s 16. Pierce J concluded that it was contradictory to and overrode that privilege. Davies J thought that it was unnecessary to resolve the matter for the purposes of the action since it was possible to examine the content of a parliamentary speech where its substance had been repeated outside Parliament. It is generally accepted as the law that statements made outside Parliament which repeat the content of parliamentary speeches are not subject to privilege.

Statute has extended absolute privilege to the broadcasting of parliamentary proceedings, and to the publication under the authority of either House of reports, papers, votes or proceedings by persons so authorised or their servants.[23] Fair and accurate reports of parliamentary and judicial proceedings are discussed under qualified privilege: see [18.210]ff.

Judicial proceedings

[18.190] The same public purpose inspires the absolute privilege of participants in the judicial process in respect of their statements in the course of the proceedings as exists for parliamentary privilege: the need to ensure that those participants speak what they consider to be the truth without the fear of legal consequences. The privilege attaches to the judge in the case, the parties, witnesses and legal counsel. Though there is undoubtedly absolute immunity from liability in defamation for these persons, this does not amount to an absolute immunity from suit. For example, a judge who makes an order without jurisdiction may be held liable in a trespass action such as false imprisonment: *Spautz v Butterworth* [1997] Aust Torts Reports 81-415. Counsel, while enjoying immunity from liability in negligence in relation to their conduct of litigation and of matters closely connected with litigation, may nevertheless be found liable in negligence in relation to their handling of matter not so closely connected: *Giannarelli v Wraith* (1988) 165 CLR 543.

The privilege here enjoyed has been extended to other decision-making bodies which function in the same manner as courts under authority of law, for instance in that they decide matters of dispute between parties, their procedure is modelled on that of a court, and their conclusions have legal effect. So, for example, it applies to a military court of inquiry: *Dawkins v Lord Rokeby* (1873) LR 8 QB 255. It applies to disciplinary proceedings before the Law Society: *Addis v Crocker* [1961] 1 QB 11. And it applies to

---

22 *Theophanous v Herald & Weekly Times* (1994) 182 CLR 104.
23 *Civil Law (Wrongs) Act 2002* (ACT), s 138; *Defamation Act 2005* (NSW), (Qld), (Tas), (Vic) and (WA), s 28; *Defamation Act 2006* (NT), s 25 and *Defamation Act 2005* (SA), s 26: Defence of publication of public documents.

appeals to the Public Service Board of New Zealand in a disciplinary matter: *Thompson v Turbott* [1962] NZLR 298.

The immunity extends not merely to statements made in court, but also to statements made preparatory to court proceedings as a necessary part of them; for example, matter put forward in witness statements prior to legal proceedings, even where the material was not in fact read by the court. This point and that made in the preceding paragraph are illustrated by *Hercules v Phease* [1994] 1 VR 411.[24] Complaints about a lawyer that had been addressed to the Victorian Law Society, the proper body for investigating and dealing with the matters raised, were found to enjoy immunity. But absolute immunity does not attach to statements that might conceivably in future form the subject of legal proceedings. In *Mann v O'Neill* (1997) 191 CLR 204 it was found that a complaint about a judge made by a litigant before that judge to the Attorney-General enjoyed qualified but not absolute privilege.

Absolute privilege under the uniform legislation

[18.195] Absolute privilege is enshrined in the uniform legislation without any material modification to the common law. The model provision provided the opportunity for legislative absolute privilege to extend beyond parliamentary and judicial proceedings through specific listing of occasions attracting privilege under Sch 1 to the Act. All jurisdictions besides the Australian Capital Territory and South Australia refer to "circumstances specified in Schedule 1" with only New South Wales opting to utilise Sch 1 (all other jurisdictions have left it empty, including it "for consistency with national model legislation"). In New South Wales, Sch 1 lists 32 specific occasions attracting privilege, ranging from matters relating to the Law Reform Commission to those arising under the *Greyhound and Harness Racing Administration Act 2004*. Possible diversity of privileged occasions under Sch 1 is provided for under the legislation with the effect that publications by the bodies and occasions as listed in New South Wales will be accorded protection even if they do attract the law of another jurisdiction.

Figure 18.11: Absolute privilege

Defamation Act 2005 (NSW, Qld, Tas, Vic, WA), s 27
Civil Law (Wrongs) Act 2002 (ACT), s 137
Defamation Act 2006 (NT), s 24
Defamation Act 2005 (SA), s 25

Occasions of absolute privilege:
- Proceedings of a parliamentary body including: publications of documents by parliamentary order, debates and proceedings of Parliament, evidence before Parliament and presentation or submission of a document to Parliament.
- Proceedings of an Australian court or tribunal including: any matter in any document filed or lodged or submitted to the court or tribunal, the giving of evidence and passing of judgment or order.

---

[24] As to the immunity of witness statements see also *Stanton v Callaghan* [1998] 4 All ER 961.

Solicitor and client

[18.200] Communications between client and solicitor receive privilege but the legal basis of this is not clear and there is a consequential doubt as to whether the privilege is absolute or qualified. *More v Weaver* [1928] 2 KB 520, an English Court of Appeal decision, took the former view but only on the basis that the statement was made in relation to future legal proceedings, and therefore was entitled to the immunity attaching to participants in those proceedings. The same is true of the case of *Waple v Surrey CC* [1997] 2 All ER 836, which also viewed the privilege as absolute. But the House of Lords in *Minter v Priest* [1930] AC 520 left this matter open as well as the precise basis of the privilege. There seems to be little reason for attaching absolute immunity to statements made between client and solicitor without reference to future legal proceedings. Qualified privilege should here be enough. And as Fleming points out, the statement must arise out of the solicitor-client relationship. A statement such as "Did you know that Mrs Smith had gone off with Mr Brown?", if mere gossip, would not qualify.

The privilege in question here protects either solicitor or client against liability for defamation by reason of subsequent disclosure of the statement. The client's privilege against such disclosure, however, is a quite distinct privilege, preventing repetition of the statement in the first place and capable of being waived by the client alone.

Communications between high-ranking officers of state

[18.205] This is an undoubted head of absolute privilege though one of ill-defined extent. Absolute privilege applies to communications between Ministers of the Crown, no doubt whatever level of post is held by the Ministers concerned. It was found to apply to a communication between the High Commissioner of Australia in the United Kingdom to the Prime Minister of Australia: *Isaacs v Cooke* [1925] 2 KB 391. But the High Court was equally divided as to the presentation of an annual report by the Commissioner of Taxation to the Federal Treasurer: *Jackson v Magrath* (1947) 75 CLR 293. Further, a report by a police inspector to the Metropolitan Superintendent was found to be not such as to attract absolute privilege: *Gibbons v Duffell* (1932) 47 CLR 520.

It is equally hard to determine what sort of subject matter attracts the privilege. The safety and well-being of the populace would clearly qualify, as doubtless would matters of general financial and economic information. But whether this element of generality is necessary or whether communications concerning individuals might also fall within this head of privilege is difficult to say on the present authorities.

Qualified privilege at common law

[18.210] Qualified privilege is a broad public interest defence and protects a statement that is "fairly warranted ... and honestly made for the common convenience and welfare of society": *Moit v Bristow* [2005] NSWCA 322 at [73] per McColl JA. Qualified privilege takes different forms: common law qualified privilege, statutory qualified privilege and fair reports or publication of public documents and proceedings. Each of these will be considered in turn.

Qualified privilege is a privilege which is defeated if the author of the statement is shown to have in some way exceeded or abused the privilege, most commonly where malice is found. At common law it requires a legally recognised duty or interest in the making of the statement on the part of its maker and a corresponding duty or interest in the receiving of the statement on the part of its recipient. Reciprocity between the parties to the statement is therefore an essential requirement of common law qualified privilege. The justification for qualified privilege of this sort is that the occasion excuses the making of what may turn out to be a false and defamatory statement, either because of the need to protect a legitimate private interest or because the interest of the public is being furthered.

Duty and interest

[18.215] The duty to convey information need not be a legal one; it may be professional, moral or social: see *Bashford v Information Australia (Newsletters) Pty Ltd* (2004) 218 CLR 366 at [71]. Members of the public have a moral duty to give information concerning the commission of crime to the police, who have both a professional interest and a duty in the receiving of such information. The police's duty to receive such information is a legal one arising out of the nature of the office, as is the duty of the Commonwealth Attorney-General in receiving complaints from a member of the public about the judicial behaviour of a Commonwealth magistrate: *Mann v O'Neill* (1997) 191 CLR 204. There is a moral duty to supply a reference to a prospective employer about a departed employee on the part of the former employer, either at the request of the prospective employer or employee.[25] Moral duty does not protect interfering busybodies. In *Watt v Longsdon* [1936] 1 KB 130 the defendant company director had received some defamatory allegations concerning the plaintiff, an overseas employee of the company. The accusations were of dishonesty and debauchery. These the defendant repeated to the chairman of the company and the plaintiff's wife. The former communication was held to be privileged because of the common interest between the defendant and the chairman in the plaintiff's conduct. The communication to the wife, however, was not privileged because, although the wife had an interest in the matter, the defendant had no duty of any sort (moral, social or legal) to make its communication, nor any interest of his own to protect.

Common interest between maker and recipient

[18.220] The interest may be that of the maker of the statement, or it may be a common interest with that of the recipient. Generally it must be a material interest such as protection of reputation or financial, professional or social well-being. It is established law that when one's reputation is attacked by another person, there is an interest in defending that reputation made to the persons who were the original recipients of the attack. So if attacked in the press, the victim of the attack may reply by publishing a press statement. *Watts v Times Newspapers* [1997] QB 650 is an example. *The Times* had published a photograph of one Nigel Watts, a property developer, in connection with its story about plagiarism by a well-known author (the plaintiff in the case, also called Nigel Watts). The story in question was defamatory of the author, but therefore also of the property developer. The newspaper published an apology to the property developer which at his insistence contained a further reference to the plagiarism of Watts, the author, and therefore a republication of that libel. In the author's action for libel against *The Times* and the property developer's solicitors (who stood in the developer's shoes) it was held that qualified privilege protected the apology in the case of the latter, whose client's reputation had been under attack and who was entitled to have it vindicated

---

[25] Cf *Spring v Guardian Assurance* [1995] 2 AC 296 – although qualified privilege protects the reference, there is liability for negligence in communicating false information in it.

even though this further injured the author's reputation. Qualified privilege did not, however, protect *The Times*, the reputation of which was not under attack, and which could have published a straightforward retraction of the imputation concerning the plaintiff without further reference to Nigel Watts, the author.

Common interest has mostly been limited to matters of a financial or professional nature, for example that existing between the shareholders in a company (*Telegraph Newspaper v Bedford* (1934) 50 CLR 632), the members of a trade union (*Duane v Granrott* [1982] VR 767), the members of a trade protection society (*Howes v Lees* (1910) 11 CLR 361), the landlord-tenant interest in the behaviour of other tenants (*Toogood v Spyring* (1834) 149 ER 1044) and occupational health and safety representatives and the publisher of an occupational health and safety bulletin (*Bashford v Information Australia (Newsletters) Pty Ltd* (2004) 218 CLR 366), but not the readers of a generalist financial publication: *Gutnick v Dow Jones & Co Inc (No 4)* [2004] Aust Torts Reports 81-748.[26]

There has been discussion whether the membership of a particular ethnic group may give rise to a sufficient common interest and in *Goyan v Motyka* [2008] Aust Torts Reports 81-939, which considered a series of letters circulated amongst the Ukrainian community and later reproduced in a book, Tobias JA suggested that it is not sufficient as the general Ukrainian community represented a class that was "far too wide" (at [84] and [89]). Handley JA, however, noted that he would like to reserve his judgment on whether statements regarding members of an ethnic community, especially if they hold an official position in one of its charitable, cultural or sporting organisations which conducts active fundraising within the community, would always be outside the scope of privilege (at [121]); thus there is some indication that the defence may apply if it relates to a position within a specific community group.

There is a clear emphasis on material interest and this makes it unlikely that the common interest of pressure groups, such as animal rights organisations, would be regarded as sufficient; still less that of persons who have a common hobby such as bird watching or wine tasting.

Reciprocity

[18.225] At common law it is necessary to communicate the statement to a person with whom the necessary reciprocity of relationship exists. This means that, in general, publication in the press or broadcasting media is not covered by qualified privilege. The idea that there is any common interest between a newspaper and its readers in relation to information supplied by the newspaper is fanciful. One clear exemption to the general rule arises where a newspaper statement is made in response to an attack appearing in that newspaper, as *Watts v Times Newspapers* [1997] QB 650 shows. No doubt this would cover other media. *Adam v Ward* [1917] AC 309[27] relies on a similar principle. In that case, an officer member of the armed forces had been subject to a parliamentary attack under privilege by the plaintiff. Having investigated the complaint, the Army Council exonerated the officer and published this exoneration in a press statement that also contained defamatory material aimed at the plaintiff. The statement was held to be subject to qualified privilege. The original attack had received wide publicity and it was, therefore, necessary to defend the officer before a similarly wide

---

26 These two decisions are discussed further below at [18.225].

27 Otherwise where the defendants issued a press release to defame the plaintiffs not in riposte to any press attack on them committed by the plaintiffs: *Heytesbury Holdings v City of Subiaco* [1998] Aust Torts Reports 81-488.

readership. On the other hand, excessive communication was the reason a claim of qualified privilege failed in *Guise v Kouvelis* (1947) 74 CLR 102. The defendant, a committee member of a club at which a card game was being played in the presence of some 50 or so members and non-members, accused the plaintiff in a loud voice of cheating in the game and of being a crook. This was held to be defamatory on the ground that, even on the assumption that a common interest existed among those present and the defendant in the integrity of the game, the proper procedure was to report the matter to the committee, which could conduct a proper investigation before pronouncing judgment.

It is illustrative to compare two recent cases: one in which the reciprocity requirement was found to exist, and another in which it was not. In the first case, *Gutnick v Dow Jones & Co (No 4)* [2004] Aust Torts Reports 81-748,[28] the audience of the journal in question was defined in wide terms as anyone who was interested in business or financial matters likely to access it. The court noted that to meet the requirement of reciprocity the publication must have a narrow focus with respect to both audience and subject matter. This can be contrasted with the publication in *Bashford v Information Australia (Newsletters) Pty Ltd* (2004) 218 CLR 366 which was an occupational health and safety bulletin purchased via subscription. The target audience was those who had responsibility for occupational health and safety within their organisation and the court found that, as this limited group had a specific and defined interest which furthered the common convenience and welfare of society, there was sufficient foundation for the defence of qualified privilege. It can be seen from both of these cases that the content of the communication was not under consideration; the defence operated (or not) purely on the basis of the purpose of the publication and the interests of its audience.

Publication during ordinary course of business

[18.230] One special problem concerning qualified privilege at common law is that of publication in the ordinary course of business to a typist or secretary for the purpose of having the statement relayed elsewhere. It is clear that where the eventual publication to the intended recipient of the message is subject to privilege, that extends to the typist also. This is sometimes explained on the basis of a privilege attaching to the publication to the typist which is derivative to, or ancillary on, that attaching to the main publication. This causes a problem where there is no main publication; in particular, where the message is sent to the plaintiff, or where it is not sent at all. In the former situation, the Court of Appeal in *Osborne v Thomas Boulter* [1930] 2 KB 226 adhered to the ancillary privilege explanation, despite its obvious illogicality. Diplock LJ did the same in his dissenting judgment in *Bryanston Finance v De Vries* [1975] QB 703, but Lord Denning in that case attempted to remove the difficulty by postulating a common interest between employer and typist in the sending of the message. This would remove the logical problem, but, although each party has an interest in the message being sent, it seems far-fetched to regard this as their common interest. A third view which appealed to Lawton LJ is that the statement to the plaintiff should be privileged even though it does not constitute a publication.[29]

---

[28] This case was one of the many surrounding the publication on the internet. It is discussed at [18.80] in the context of place of publication.

[29] This was the view expressed by Goodhart, "Defamatory Statements and Privileged Occasions" (1940) 56 LQR 262.

Statutory qualified privilege in absence of reciprocity

[18.235] Under the new uniform Acts, there exists a statutory qualified privilege which differs from the common law defence in two ways: the reciprocity requirement is not as stringent and there is an expectation that the publication was "reasonable in the circumstances".

Figure 18.12: Qualified privilege

> *Defamation Act 2005* (NSW, Qld, Tas, Vic, WA), s 30
> *Civil Law (Wrongs) Act 2002* (ACT), s 139A
> *Defamation Act 2006* (NT), s 27
> *Defamation Act 2005* (SA), s 28
>
> **Requirements:**
> • recipient has an interest or apparent interest in having information; and
> • matter is published; and
> • conduct of defendant in publishing is reasonable in the circumstances.

This uniform provision mirrors the old New South Wales *Defamation Act 1974* (NSW), s 22, so discussion regarding the earlier legislation can be illustrative. There is no definitive expectation of a reciprocal relationship between the maker of the statement and its recipient, instead there is a requirement that the recipient of the information should have an interest or apparent interest in receiving it and that the conduct of the publisher in publishing that matter is reasonable. The chief beneficiaries of a broad provision of this nature are of course the press or media, and the publishers and authors of books. In *Seary v Molomby* [1999] Aust Torts Reports 81-526, for example, it was found that allegations in a book written by the defendant about the plaintiff's behaviour in connection with the Hilton Hotel bombing incident in Sydney were protected by qualified privilege. The public had a sufficient interest in the matter to justify the publication of a book on the subject. The reasonableness of the defendant's action in publishing this matter was tested mainly by reference to the care he had taken to get his facts right. This will of course encourage responsible journalism or authorship but the absence of any requirement of an interest in making the statement or duty to make it in its publisher removes a guiding principle of the common law that privilege only attaches if there is a real necessity to make the statement.

As far as interest is concerned it must be a real interest that exists in fact and transcends mere curiosity.[30] This interest cannot diverge significantly from the common law requirement set out above and will often be grounded in a reciprocal relationship. There is of course the remaining question as to what constitutes "reasonable" publication.

---

[30] See, eg, *Moit v Bristow* [2005] NSWCA 322 at [75], referring to *Stephens v Western Australian Newspapers Ltd* (1984) 182 CLR 211: it is not sufficient that the readers of a newspaper may simply be interested in the subject matter.

The uniform provision sets out relevant considerations and these include: public interest, performance of public functions or activities, seriousness of defamatory imputation, distinguishing between suspicions, allegations and proven facts, nature of the sources of the information, attempts to publish a response of the plaintiff, steps taken to verify the information and other relevant considerations. Each of these requirements calls for a close examination of the circumstances of the publication and a factual determination of what constitutes a reasonable publication. It has been suggested that the uniform legislation reflects the position in the United Kingdom as expressed in *Reynolds v Times Newspapers Ltd* [1999] 3 WLR 1010 leaving open the question as to whether or not this statutory provision will provide an avenue of defence for media defendants who lack the common law reciprocal relationship.[31]

Freedom of speech under Constitution

[18.240] In *Theophanous v Herald and Weekly Times* (1994) 182 CLR 104 the High Court identified, in certain provisions of the Australian Constitution, an individual right of freedom of speech on constitutional and political matters within Australia sufficient to constitute a defence to an action for defamation. In *Lange v Australian Broadcasting Corporation* (1997) 189 CLR 520 the High Court felt itself able to reconsider the position accepted by the majority in *Theophanous* because of differences in the reasoning among that majority. The result of that reconsideration was that although the constitutional provisions were still seen as the foundation of freedom of speech on constitutional or political matters, they did not create by themselves a defence to actions for defamation based on the existence of a right of freedom of speech. The proper role of the constitutional provisions was to allow an extension to the defence of qualified privilege beyond its common law limits to remove the need for reciprocity between the maker of the statement and its recipient where the statement concerned constitutional or political matters. A further modification to that defence was, however, necessary, since if reciprocity was not required, the statement could legitimately be made to thousands of recipients and be very damaging. Accordingly, the defendant must prove as part of the defence that he or she acted reasonably, the same criteria as that in force under the uniform provision. At the same time, proof that the publication had been actuated by common law malice would defeat the defence to the extent that the elements of malice had not already been covered under the rubric of reasonableness.[32] A practical example of the operation of the defence in this context is *Roberts v Bass* (2002) 212 CLR 1 which involved a dispute regarding publications distributed during a State election. The High Court emphasised the context of the communication and the fact that it took place within the framework of an election meant that the accepted nature of communication at such a time was relevant. Kirby J explained that during an election campaign there is a reality of "passionate and sometimes irrational ... interchange" with an emphasis on "brevity, hyperbole, entertainment, image and vivid expression" (at [171]). In short, an election campaign is, by its very nature, about challenging the reputation of candidates, often with the assistance of colourful language. Thus, the freedom of political communication extends to a qualified privilege to protect those engaged in the "robust interchange" that is an election campaign.

---

[31] This discussion, and subsequent UK authority on *Reynolds* is set out in Mallam, Dawson and Moriarty, *Media and Internet Law and Practice* (Thomson/Lawbook Co.), [9.2300]ff.

[32] The impact of malice on the defence of qualified privilege is discussed in detail below at [18.265].

Fair and accurate reports

[18.245] In a number of situations, fair and accurate reports of public proceedings are subject to qualified privilege. The normal place for appearance of such reports would be in the press or other media (though that is not a limiting requirement for such reports) and clearly this publication represents a dispensation from the common law requirement of reciprocity between the parties to the statement. The two outstanding examples of this form of qualified privilege are reports of both parliamentary and judicial proceedings. The defence is not limited to parliamentary proceedings and can extend to other public events such as court proceedings and Royal Commissions. In South Australia fair and accurate reports of proceedings before a Royal Commissioner receive qualified privilege. In *Chakravarti v The Advertiser* (1998) 193 CLR 519 the newspaper failed to establish this defence, since it had inaccurately reported the Commissioner to have implicated Chakravarti in the taking of unauthorised loans from the subsidiary of the State Bank of South Australia, the subject of the inquiry. Thus the report must be accurate if the defence is to stand.

The essence of the defence lies in the nature of the report of proceedings. It must be a clear report without distortion of facts or comment or commentary. This was clearly stated by the court in *Waterhouse v Broadcasting Station 2GB Pty Ltd* (1985) 1 NSWLR 58 at 63:

> To be a fair report the matter complained of must with substantial accuracy express what took place in that part of the proceedings of which it purports to be a report ... the issue will be whether the report ... substantially altered the impression which the reader would have received if he had been in court; if there is in the report a substantial misrepresentation of the material facts prejudicial to the plaintiff's reputation, the matter complained of is not a fair and accurate report. A fair report is a substantially accurate summary of the proceedings, neither more nor less. The question is not whether it is fair or unfair to any particular person; the question is whether it substantially records what was said and done.

The question of what constitutes "fair" in the circumstances is of course, one of fact: *Chakravarti v Advertiser Newspapers Ltd* (1998) 193 CLR 519 at 540.

The original privilege of fair and accurate reports of parliamentary and judicial proceedings existed at common law and is now found in the uniform Act.

Figure 18.13: Fair report of proceedings of public concern

Defamation Act 2005 (NSW, Qld, Tas, Vic, WA), s 29
Civil Law (Wrongs) Act 2002 (ACT), s 139
Defamation Act 2006 (NT), s 26
Defamation Act 2005 (SA), s 27

Requirements:
- Must be a fair report of public concern (includes a report of information contained in an earlier published report, the earlier report must be fair *and the* defendant must have no knowledge that the earlier report was not fair).
- Material must have been published honestly and for the information of the public or advancement of education.
- Proceedings of public concern are broad and include parliamentary and judicial proceedings and public associations and committees (ie a "learned society" or sport or recreation association).

Contemporaneity

[18.250] There is no rule that the publication of the report must be contemporaneous with the proceedings reported. In *Tsikata v Newspaper Publishing plc* [1997] 1 All ER 655 the publication of a report of a public inquiry held ten years previously in the defendant newspaper was subject to qualified privilege. The matter was of public concern as required by the legislative provision affecting such reports, since Tsikata, the subject of the inquiry, remained in office. The issue of contemporaneity was more recently raised in *Goyan v Motyka* [2008] Aust Torts Reports 81-939 which saw Tobias JA specifically rejecting privilege as being available with respect to the reproduction of the original letters in a book on the basis of the lapse of time between their original and subsequent publication (at [79]). Of interest, however, is the equally emphatic statement by Handley JA that the time elapsed does not automatically take the publication outside the scope of qualified privilege (or afford evidence of malice) (at [120]). It is thus clearly a matter of examining the surrounding circumstances and it is relevant to note that later developments may affect the fairness of publication without reference to their closeness in time to the original report.

Excess or abuse of privilege (defeating the defence)

Excess of privilege

[18.255] Qualified privilege is not available as a defence where the defendant has exceeded or abused the privilege. Academic commentators tend to take the point that this occurs where there is excessive communication of the defamatory statement, but this is a dubious point. In a case such as *Guise v Kouvelis* (1947) 74 CLR 102 (see [18.225]) the question was regarded by the High Court as turning on whether any privilege existed to communicate the statement to the members and others present, not on whether such privilege had been exceeded. In *Adam v Ward* [1917] AC 309 the question turned on whether the defendants were privileged to make a press statement, not on whether such a privilege had been exceeded. A real excess of privilege case would exist where the defendant is privileged to make a defamatory statement to the person who actually receives the statement, but has gone beyond what is allowed by the privilege in the statement actually made. An example is the inclusion of irrelevant defamatory material in the statement. There is some support for the position that the inclusion of irrelevant material goes towards proving malice, but this should not be understood in the sense of spite or a mere desire to injure the plaintiff. The case of the inclusion of such material not germane to the privilege may legitimately be regarded as a case of excess of privilege or as one of abuse of privilege, malicious in the sense that the malice resides in the use of the privilege for an improper purpose. The old case of *Warren v Warren* (1834) 1 CM&R 250; 149 ER 1073 provides an example of a case where either interpretation is equally valid. The defendant's letter to the manager of a property in which he and the plaintiff had a joint interest was privileged insofar as it concerned the plaintiff's conduct in relation to that property but not in its assertions of misconduct by the plaintiff in his family relations. The general conclusion must be that it is doubtful whether the concept of excess of privilege serves any purpose.

Abuse of privilege

[18.260] The privilege is abused where the defendant has used it for an improper purpose. The concept of improper purpose is, as just pointed out, wider than malice. For instance, it covered a case where the defendant newspaper had given a sensational twist to a news item in order to increase the sales of the newspaper: *Broadway Approvals v Odhams Press* [1964] 2 QB 683. Actual malice in the form of a feeling of spite or ill-will towards the plaintiff must be proved by the plaintiff, and does not necessarily defeat the privilege. The High Court joint judgment in *Lange v Australian Broadcasting Corporation* (1997) 189 CLR 520 makes it clear that the defendant must be actuated by that malice when making the statement. Further, in *Roberts v Bass* (2002) 212 CLR 1, Gaudron, McHugh and Gummow JJ in their joint judgment explain that proof of express malice destroys qualified privilege as it is inconsistent with the duty or interest that gives rise to the privilege (at [75] and [79]). The plaintiff must establish that a desire to injure the plaintiff was the defendant's predominant purpose, not that of discharging the duty or protecting the interest embodied in the privilege. In *Howell v Haines* [1997] Aust Torts Reports 81-409 where the plaintiff had been accused by the defendant of corruption in his capacity as a member of Parramatta City Council, the defendant's attempt to defend this allegation by reference to the constitutional defence failed, because the plaintiff was able to establish a predominant intention on the part of the defendant to injure him politically. Proof of malice does not require that the plaintiff should establish dishonesty on the part of the defendant. But proof of such a state of mind in the form of absence of belief in the truth of the statement will invariably establish abuse, as will reckless indifference to the truth of the statement, though not a considerable degree of carelessness in making the statement.

Underlying discussions regarding qualified privilege is the further question of how much dishonesty or misstatement the law will tolerate. This issue was addressed in *Assaf v Skalkos* [2000] NSWSC 418 where Carruthers AJ acknowledged that qualified privilege is concerned with "defamatory and untrue imputations" (at [184]), thus there is a level of acceptance of falsehood or even individual dishonesty (his Honour adopted the words of Lord Hobhouse in *Reynolds v Times Newspapers Ltd* [1998] 3 All ER 961). The extent of the dishonesty becomes relevant when considering whether there was actual or inferred malice in the publication.

Malice

[18.265] Malice is also capable of being inferred by the court from the nature of the statement itself. This, however, is in general an unlikely occurrence as the courts tend to be sympathetic to the display of anger or the use of intemperate or pungent language where these arise out of the subject matter forming the provenance of the statement. In particular, a defendant who has been the subject of an attack is not expected in replying to that attack to observe the Queensberry rules. In *Horrocks v Lowe* [1975] AC 135 the defendant's attack on a town councillor, who had allegedly put his interests as a property developer above that of the Council, accused him of "brinkmanship, megalomania or childish petulance". The attack was found to be an honest, non-malicious expression of opinion on a privileged occasion. The style and choice of language can, on the other hand, provide clear evidence of malice. The language contained in the letters in *Goyan v Motyka* [2008] Aust Torts Reports 81-939 was described as vituperative, irrational, intemperate and splenetic (per Tobias JA at [79]) and this was sufficient to infer malice (Handley JA concurred finding that there was "ample evidence of malice" at [122]).

Imputed dishonesty, malice or improper purpose

[18.270] The question at issue here is in what circumstances the wrongful use of the privilege by one person who has made a defamatory statement should be imputed to other persons who are also participants in the making of the statement. The question arises in relation to both the defences of fair comment and qualified privilege and the present state of the authorities seems to indicate that the same principles apply to both. The law here is quite clear and can now be stated in relatively simple terms. The problem to be faced is whether, where there are several parties to the making of a statement which would on the face of it attract the defence of fair comment or qualified privilege, but one or more of those parties is dishonest or malicious, this makes the comment unfair or defeats the privilege in the case of all.

The common law originally accepted the logic of the position that the dishonesty or malice of one person should take away the protection of fair comment or qualified privilege for all the makers of the statement, since it vitiates the statement as a whole (see *Webb v Bloch* (1928) 41 CLR 331 in which the knowledge of two parties involved in the publication of a circular was attributed to all and defeated the privilege). The courts have now abandoned this position and have held that in the case of independent publishers of the statement, the malice of one person should not be imputed to those who are innocent publishers so as to make them liable for defamation. So where four trustees had presented a report on the plaintiff which would have been privileged apart from the malice of one of their number, only the latter person was held liable: *Longdon-Griffiths v Smith* [1951] 1 KB 295. Where the secretary of a club had written a letter containing a libel on the instruction of the committee of the club, the secretary was not liable for defamation, even though the qualified privilege attaching to the letter was defeated by the malice of certain members of the committee: *Egger v Viscount Chelmsford* [1965] 1 QB 248. Thus the publisher of a comment whose fairness is vitiated by the malice of its author is not "tarred with the author's brush" so as to be deemed malicious.

A decision of the Supreme Court of Canada (which has attracted some criticism) determined that in order to escape liability for himself and the newspaper, the editor had to show an honest belief in the substance of comments made in the newspaper: *Chernsky v Armadale* [1979] 1 SCR 1067. The central concern regarding such a decision is that it would lead to an excessive burden on editors and consequently of press freedom and the High Court declined to follow the Canadian lead: *Pervan v North Queensland Newspaper* (1993) 178 CLR 309. There is one well-established limitation to these principles: the malice of an employee or agent acting within the scope of his or her employment or agency is imputed to the employer or principal.

Innocent dissemination

[18.275] As outlined above, the tort of defamation is one of strict liability: see [18.125]. The reason for this was explained earlier, but the rule can undoubtedly work hardship against one who is innocent of fault as regards the defamatory content of the statement. At common law all parties involved in the publication of defamatory material can be liable for that material. This can extend to failing to remove or terminate publication: in *Urbanchich v Drummoyne Municipal Council* [1991] Aust Torts Reports 81-927 defamatory posters were on display and the plaintiff brought these to the notice of those in control of the area and there was a delay in the removal of the posters. Crucial to this decision was the control exercised over the area. The protection of those innocently involved in the publication of defamatory material was one of the areas of diversity across the jurisdictions; this has now been remedied through the uniform legislation with the clear provision of a defence of innocent dissemination.

Figure 18.14: Innocent dissemination

Defamation Act 2005 (NSW, Qld, Tas, Vic, WA), s 32
Civil Law (Wrongs) Act 2002 (ACT), s 139C
Defamation Act 2006 (NT), s 29
Defamation Act 2005 (SA), s 30

Under this provision it is a defence if the defendant can demonstrate that they published the matter as an employee or agent of a subordinate distributor and that the publication was innocent (absent any actual or imputed knowledge). The absence of knowledge cannot be the result of negligence on the part of the distributor. A subordinate distributor is defined as one who lacks editorial control and was not the first or primary distributor or author. The Act includes a list of potential "subordinate distributors" which includes, inter alia, booksellers, newsagents, librarians and broadcasters. This list is not exhaustive and thus is open to interpretation by the courts. The protection appears to extend to internet service providers (ISPs) (see subs (3)(f)(ii) "provider of services consisting of the operation of … system or service by means of which the matter is retrieved, copied or distributed or made available in electronic form"). ISPs are also afforded limited protection under the *Broadcasting Services Act 1992* (Cth). Schedule 5 of the Act provides that there is no requirement to actively monitor activities but stipulates that once a service provider receives a formal notification from the Australian Broadcasting Authority, they must remove any offending material.

The legislative defence of innocent dissemination thus provides protection for those previously covered under the "mechanical distribution" defence (for the common law defence refer *Vizetelly v Mudie's Library*[1900] 2 QB 170 and *McPherson v Hickle* [1995] Aust Torts Reports 81-348).

Defence of triviality

[18.280] Under the uniform legislation there is now a defence of triviality which requires that the defendant prove that the circumstances of the publication were such that the plaintiff was unlikely to sustain any harm:

Figure 18.15: Defence of triviality

Defamation Act 2005 (NSW, Qld, Tas, Vic, WA), s 33
Civil Law (Wrongs) Act 2002 (ACT), s 139D
Defamation Act 2006 (NT), s 30
Defamation Act 2005 (SA), s 31

This provision is similar to that of "unlikelihood of harm" which previously existed in New South Wales: *Defamation Act 1974* (NSW), s 13 (repealed). With the clear similarities between the "triviality" and "unlikelihood of harm defences" these interpretations will inform the application of the newer defence and are worthy of consideration in this context. In consideration of the earlier provision courts acknowledged that a pre-existing poor reputation may be relevant as a "characteristic" of the plaintiff and therefore to the circumstances of the publication (*Jones v Sutton* (2004) 61 NSWLR 614) although knowledge of the poor reputation will not be decisive: *King v McKenzie* (1991) 24 NSWLR 305 at 310. It has also been suggested that the defence usually applies to limited, probably oral, communication (*King* at 308) and whilst it was not necessary to establish that the plaintiff had not suffered any harm (likelihood of harm being the key, *Jones* at [44]-[50]) it has been described as a defence which places a significant burden on the defendant (*King* at 309).

Remedies

[18.285] Commentators and advocates for reform were vocal in their dissatisfaction with the approach to remedies for defamation. The main concern was the apparent disjoint between the remedy of damages and the nature of the loss (that is, harm to reputation). During the reform process the possibility of a closer match between remedy and harm was raised and alternative remedies were mooted; these included: court-ordered corrections, right of reply and apology (with substantially the same prominence as the original publication). The debate did not, however, bear fruit and the principal remedy for defamation continues to be an award of damages with the uniform legislation imposing limitations on the availability and size of the award. The existence of an apology can, however, serve to mitigate damages.

Damages

[18.290] The principles relating to damages for defamation are the same as for damages generally, but there are some special problems in their application in this context. In particular, the award is normally within the province of a jury, which has raised the problem of control by courts over jury awards. The second point is an aggravation of the first. The plaintiff is entitled in all cases where a cause of action in defamation has been established to general damages for injury to reputation. The assessment of such damages is of a particularly arbitrary and problematic nature especially when, as is usual, a jury performs it. The problem of arbitrary awards was addressed in the reform process and the uniform legislation now specifically provides that damages must bear a "rational relationship to the harm", places a limit on damages for non-economic loss and prohibits the awarding of exemplary or punitive damages.[33]

Compensatory and aggravated damages

[18.295] First, a distinction exists between general and special damages. The former damages reflect merely the injury to the plaintiff's reputation and are given as a means of vindicating it. There is no need for proof of any temporal loss for an award of general damages to be made. Special damages are awarded for actual loss flowing from the defamation that the plaintiff is able to prove. It is arguable, however, that there is a concealed element of compensation for the financial cost of loss of reputation in an award of general damages, even though the plaintiff is unable to establish any such loss. It is easy enough for a jury to imagine that the defamation will have had a serious effect on the plaintiff's career or financial opportunities without actual proof that that has been the case.

General damages may also include damages for injury to the plaintiff's feelings. Distress caused by the defamation itself is an obvious example, but this may be aggravated by the circumstances of the defamation, and, especially, the defendant's conduct. In that case, an award of aggravated damage is appropriate. These damages are at least in theory compensatory, representing the further injury to the plaintiff's feelings. For example, they were found appropriate in a case where the defendant's statement was made with reckless disregard of its truth, and for an improper purpose: *Howell v Haines* [1997] Aust Torts Reports 81-409. A number of Australian cases have found aggravated damages appropriate where the defendant has persisted in the imputation without retraction or apology long after it should have become apparent that the statement was false: for example, *Crampton v Nugewala* [1997] Aust Torts Reports 81-416. This situation may be altered under the limitations of the uniform legislation which are aimed at reducing excessive damages awards. Of note is the inclusion in the legislation of a provision that the state of mind of the defendant is generally not relevant in the awarding of damages. The provision specifically prohibits the court from giving any regard to the malice or other state of mind of the defendant at the time of the publication, except to the extent that the state of mind affects the harm sustained by the plaintiff. The practical import of this provision is, of course, as yet unknown.

---

[33] The discussion of damages will simply refer to the impact of the uniform legislation; for specific legislative references refer to Figure 18.16.

Exemplary damages

[18.300] Exemplary damages are not compensatory. They go towards punishing the defendant by reason of outrageous conduct on the latter's part. They are by their very nature anomalous since although they are intended only to punish the defendant, they form part of the damages payable to the plaintiff. They are no longer available in defamation actions in Australia.

Contemptuous damages

[18.305] These are damages which are intended to mark the court's (that is, usually the jury's) disapproval of the action having been brought. Their award is therefore in the smallest coin of the realm. In *Pamplin v Express Newspapers* [1988] 1 WLR 116 the plaintiff, who had devised a means of evading parking fees and the television licence fee by putting his car and television into the name of his infant son, had been described by the defendants as a "slippery, unscrupulous spiv". His action for defamation was directed to the final epithet alone, but evidence of his practice in relation to his car and television was admitted on the defendant's plea of justification. The jury found in his favour, awarding him a halfpenny in damages. The court followed the usual procedure in the case of an award of contemptuous damages of ordering the plaintiff to pay the costs of the action. The jury's verdict was upheld on appeal.

Judicial control over jury awards

[18.310] The actual mechanism by which courts control juries in their damages awards is weak. The controlling function of the trial judge is limited to the directions given to the jury at the conclusion of the evidence. An appellate court is entitled to interfere on the ground only that the award is manifestly excessive or, as is much less likely, unreasonably small. In Australia the appellate court is not entitled, if it finds that either of these circumstances is proved, to substitute its own award for that of the jury but must order a new trial. There has been concern in England and Australia about what are considered to be excessively high damages awards by juries in defamation actions, and, in particular, the way in which awards of general damages exceed by quite a margin those awarded for non-pecuniary loss for serious personal injury. The Court of Appeal in England has conducted an ongoing "battle" with juries over their awards of damages in defamation actions, and in a number of cases has reduced them: *Sutcliffe v Pressdram* [1991] 1 QB 153; *Rantzen v MGN* [1994] QB 670; *John v MGN* [1997] QB 586.

It is thought proper for the trial judge in England to draw the attention of the jury to the current amounts awarded for non-pecuniary loss (that is, for pain and suffering and loss of amenities) in serious personal injury cases as a suggested upper limit. In *Carson v John Fairfax* (1993) 178 CLR 44 a majority of the High Court also thought that this personal injury comparison was relevant, both at the appellate court level and in the trial judge's direction to the jury. So far this has borne no fruit by way of setting aside jury awards. Comparison with non-pecuniary loss damages for personal injury may be useful, but is not altogether comparing like with like. For example, a general damages award for defamation cases may contain a concealed amount reflecting the presumed financial cost of loss of reputation, whereas financial loss is always separately assessed in personal injury damages awards. Against this, success in a defamation action should bring restoration of reputation, whereas health and fitness are not restored where a plaintiff is compensated for serious personal injury. Control over and limitation of damages has been specifically addressed in the uniform legislation.

Character evidence as means of reducing damages

[18.315] A successful plaintiff is entitled to receive damages only in respect of the reputation he or she is generally known to possess. If that is already low, the damages awarded are correspondingly reduced. Evidence of general reputation is therefore admissible, though not of rumours surrounding the plaintiff, though Lord Radcliffe has protested that the two are barely distinguishable: *Plato Films v Speidel* [1961] AC 1090 at 1131. It is clear law that evidence of specific discreditable incidents from the plaintiff's past are not admissible, where these are not already known to affect the plaintiff's general reputation: *Plato Films*. On the other hand, evidence of specific incidents properly admitted on a plea of justification, which eventually fails, is admissible evidence as to the plaintiff's character for the purpose of assessing damages, as *Pamplin v Express Newspapers* [1988] 1 WLR 116 indicates: see [18.305]. There is still the problem that if the plaintiff selects one or more of several defamatory allegations in order to sue for defamation, evidence of those other allegations is not admissible as to the plaintiff's character, even if the defendant can justify them. There is the possibility that specific incidents from the past may be put to the plaintiff on a cross-examination as to the plaintiff's credit, but at this moment it is not clear that this can be done where it is the plaintiff's character that is the relevant issue, not the plaintiff's veracity as a witness on issues within the trial. Lord Denning in *Plato Films* (at 1143) would not have allowed a cross-examination of this sort. In any case the plaintiff may choose not to give evidence.

Mitigation of damages

[18.320] Under the uniform legislation there are a number of specific considerations which may be admitted as evidence in mitigation of damages. This is not an exclusive list with the section providing that the list does not act to limit matters that can be taken into account. The listed matters are: an apology, publication of a correction, recovery of damages in relation to any other publication of matter having the same meaning or effect, proceedings brought elsewhere and the receipt of compensation for defamation in relation to other publication of matter having the same meaning or effect. Clearly this is aimed at acknowledging the true harm done and reducing the chances of any "double dipping" for the same harm.

Figure 18.16: Damages under the uniform legislation

The court is to ensure an appropriate and rational relationship between the harm sustained and the amount of damages awarded:
>   *Defamation Act 2005* (NSW, Qld, Tas, Vic, WA), s 34
>   *Civil Law (Wrongs) Act 2002* (ACT), s 139E
>   *Defamation Act 2006* (NT), s 31
>   *Defamation Act 2005* (SA), s 32

Unless the court orders otherwise, maximum amount of damages for non-economic loss is $250,000 (or other amount adjusted in accordance with the section):
>   *Defamation Act 2005* (NSW, Qld, Tas, Vic, WA), s 35
>   *Civil Law (Wrongs) Act 2002* (ACT), s 139F
>   *Defamation Act 2006* (NT), s 32
>   *Defamation Act 2005* (SA), s 33

State of mind of the defendant is generally not relevant to awarding damages (see [18.295]):
>   *Defamation Act 2005* (NSW, Qld, Tas, Vic, WA), s 36
>   *Civil Law (Wrongs) Act 2002* (ACT), s 139G
>   *Defamation Act 2006* (NT), s 33
>   *Defamation Act 2005* (SA), s 34

Exemplary or punitive damages cannot be awarded:
>   *Defamation Act 2005* (NSW, Qld, Tas, Vic, WA), s 37
>   *Civil Law (Wrongs) Act 2002* (ACT), s 139H
>   *Defamation Act 2006* (NT), s 34
>   *Defamation Act 2005* (SA), s 35

Factors in mitigation of damages:
>   *Defamation Act 2005* (NSW, Qld, Tas, Vic, WA), s 38
>   *Civil Law (Wrongs) Act 2002* (ACT), s 139I
>   *Defamation Act 2006* (NT), s 35
>   *Defamation Act 2005 (SA), s 36*

Damages for multiple causes of action may be assessed as a single sum:
>   *Defamation Act 2005* (NSW, Qld, Tas, Vic, WA), s 39
>   *Civil Law (Wrongs) Act 2002* (ACT), s 139J
>   *Defamation Act 2006* (NT), s 36
>   *Defamation Act 2005* (SA), s 37

Injunction

[18.325] The remedy by way of final injunction is seldom sought in a defamation action; however if a defendant, after judgment, refuses to give an undertaking to the court not to repeat the libel, an injunction will be awarded. While the court has a discretion in the matter, there is a general reluctance to exercise that discretion by the award of an interlocutory injunction where the defendant intends to plead justification, fair comment or privilege.[34]

---

[34]   *Bonnard v Perryman* [1891] 2 Ch 269; *Herbage v Pressdram* [1984] 1 WLR 1160; *Khashoggi v IPC Magazines* [1986] 1 WLR 1412.

To restrain a defendant at the interlocutory level in these circumstances would infringe freedom of speech and (in those jurisdictions in which there is a jury trial), result in the judge usurping the function of the jury. This has been held to apply even where the plaintiff's main purpose in suing is to extract money from the defendant to which the plaintiff feels entitled: *Holley v Smyth* [1998] 1 All ER 85. But in the rare case where the defendant's case is sufficiently hopeless, the court will issue an injunction: *Chappell v TCN Channel 9* (1988) 14 NSWLR 153. Alternatively, an injunction will be awarded if the material is deemed to be particularly offensive and likely to amount to ongoing defamation, as with *Australian Broadcasting Corporation v Hanson* [1998] QCA 306.[35]

Resolution of civil disputes without litigation

[18.330] Consistent with the core object of promoting speedy and non-litigious methods of resolving disputes about the publication of defamatory material, the uniform legislation includes specific provisions relating to the resolution of civil disputes without litigation.[36] With the practical application of this aspect of the legislation not yet clear, the discussion in this section will merely provide an overview of the provisions. Division 1 applies where potentially defamatory material has been published and may be used instead of provisions of any rules of court or other law in relation to the payment into court or offers of compromise. The section specifically provides that this part of the Act does not prevent the reaching of a settlement agreement.[37] An offer to make amends may be made, without prejudice[38] but cannot be made if 28 days have passed since the giving of notice of concerns by the aggrieved person or a defence has been served in an action brought by the "aggrieved person".[39] The Act specifies the content of the offer to make amends[40] and that the offer to make amends can be withdrawn before it is accepted in writing (and a new offer can then be made if the publisher wishes).[41] Once an offer to make amends has been concluded (including the payment of compensation under the offer) the matter is at an end and the "aggrieved person" is prohibited from pursuing any further action on the matter.[42] If an offer to make amends has been made, but not accepted it can operate as a defence to an action in defamation if the offer was made as soon as practicable after becoming aware that the matter is (or may be) defamatory and the publisher was ready and willing to carry out the terms of the offer. To operate as a defence, the offer must be reasonable.[43] If there are later proceedings with respect to a matter which was subject to the making of an offer to make amends, there are limitations placed upon the use of evidence of any statement made in connection to either the making, or the refusal, of the offer.[44]

The role of an apology in the determination of liability is also considered by the

---

[35] Discussed at [18.40] with respect to relevance of social opinion. In this instance the lyrics of the song were deemed to be vulgar and abusive and if there was no injunction, would continue to be played and amount to ongoing defamation.

[36] Part 3, *Defamation Act 2005* (NSW, NT, Qld, SA, Tas, Vic, WA); Pt 9.3, *Civil Law (Wrongs) Act 2002* (ACT).

[37] *Defamation Act 2005* (NSW, NT, Qld, SA, Tas, Vic, WA), s 12; *Civil Law (Wrongs) Act 2002* (ACT), s 124.

[38] *Defamation Act 2005* (NSW, NT, Qld, SA, Tas, Vic, WA), s 13; *Civil Law (Wrongs) Act 2002* (ACT), s 125.

[39] *Defamation Act* (NSW, NT, Qld, SA, Tas, Vic, WA), s 14; *Civil Law (Wrongs) Act 2002* (ACT), s 126. A concerns notice is defined under subs (2).

[40] *Defamation Act* (NSW, NT, Qld, SA, Tas, Vic, WA), s 15; *Civil Law (Wrongs) Act 2002* (ACT), s 127.

[41] *Defamation Act* (NSW, NT, Qld, SA, Tas, Vic, WA), s 16; *Civil Law (Wrongs) Act 2002* (ACT), s 128.

[42] *Defamation Act* (NSW, NT, Qld, SA, Tas, Vic, WA), s 17; *Civil Law (Wrongs) Act 2002* (ACT), s 129.

[43] *Defamation Act* (NSW, NT, Qld, SA, Tas, Vic, WA), s 18; *Civil Law (Wrongs) Act 2002* (ACT), s 130. The section sets out factors that the court must consider in determining whether the offer was indeed reasonable.

[44] *Defamation Act* (NSW, NT, Qld, SA, Tas, Vic, WA), s 19; *Civil Law (Wrongs) Act 2002* (ACT), s 131.

legislation. Evidence of the making of an apology does not constitute an express or implied admission of fault nor is it relevant in the determination of fault. However, evidence of an apology continues to be relevant in the calculation of damages[45] (see above, [18.320]). The legislation is therefore aimed at encouraging discourse between the person aggrieved and the publisher with the overall aim of reducing litigation in this area.

Practice Questions

Revision Questions

18.1 Which two principles are in conflict in this area?

18.2 Does the truth of the statement always provide a defence to defamation?

Problem Questions

18.1 Bert Murphy was the Minister for Justice in Queensland for a considerable time: 12 years. During that time there were many rumours suggesting he was involved with many illegal activities. For instance, it was thought that he protected corrupt police and was negotiating in business dealings with members who were known to be involved in organised crime. These activities were said to benefit him financially through bribes. Although this view was widely held, nothing was published by the media until after his death. In fact two days after he died the *Country Wide Chronicle* ran a front-page story headed "Murphy, protector of the members of organised crime".

Is there an action for defamation?

18.2 An elderly lady had an argument with her family (her daughters and their husbands) the result of which was that she had to move out of the family home which was to be sold. The house was situated in the main street of a small country town. The lady discussed her family disagreement with a friend who agreed that he would paint a message formulated by the lady onto the brick wall of her home. The lady wrote out the message: "Buyer beware of plan to defraud widow by her daughters, John Smith and Fred Fuller." She gave the message to her friend and then went inside to ring the doctor. The friend painted the message on the wall, changing it slightly to: "Buyer beware of conspiracy to defraud widow by her daughters, John Smith and Fred Fuller."

Would the daughters' husbands, John Smith and Fred Fuller succeed in an action for defamation?

18.3 A local television station reported the demise of a local authority, stating: "The end of an era today for the City of Nowhere which has been dogged by controversy. The former Council of the City of Nowhere has today been sacked. This follows a lengthy period of scandal and controversy culminating in a Royal Commission that recommended the closure." George Phoney served as the Mayor of the City of Nowhere, along with 15 other councillors, and now claims that he has been defamed.

Advise him.

---

[45] *Defamation Act* (NSW, NT, Qld, SA, Tas, Vic, WA), s 20; *Civil Law (Wrongs) Act 2002* (ACT), s 132.

Answers to Practice Questions

Revision Questions

18.1 There is a conflict of interest in this area between:

- protection of an individual's reputation; and
- freedom of speech.

Defamation law tries to balance these interests, particularly in the area of defences, as public interest is often a consideration in whether or not a defence operates under the circumstances.

18.2 The common law holds that a truthful statement negatives an action for defamation. See [18.35]ff and Figure 18.7.

Problem Questions

18.1 If Murphy was alive when this statement was published then the words would be defamatory since they refer directly to him and they would certainly injure the reputation of Murphy in his professional life as he would more than likely lose his position. The paper may argue that it was justified in publishing the material since the public has a right to know about the illegal dealings of officials.

Since Murphy is dead, there is no action lying on his behalf. As the text states: "The cause of action for defamation is personal to the deceased, and does not descend to the estate." Also refer: *Civil Law (Wrongs) Act 2002* (ACT), s 122; *Defamation Act 2005* (NSW), (Qld), (SA), (Vic) and (WA), s 10; *Defamation Act 2006* (NT), s 9. If in Tasmania, the common law applies. If however, a member of Murphy's family can prove that they have been defamed by the statements then it may be possible for them to take an action for defamation on their own behalf. A case of relevance here is *Krahe v TCN Channel Nine Pty Ltd* (1986) 4 NSWLR 536.

18.2 While it can be seen that the words are defamatory since they allege that John Smith and Fred Fuller were involved in a crime, there are a couple of issues that are not so clearly evident. Can it be established that the words refer to the named men? Have the words been published? And if so, has the statement been published by the lady?

It could be argued by the lady that the names are quite common and that it is conceivable that there are a number of people with these names and anyone reading the message would not reasonably conclude that the message was directed to her sons-in-law. However, the facts state that this is a small town and so this argument is not strong.

The fact that the lady's house is situated on the main street of the town is sufficient to show that the message has been published.

The lady would contend that she did not paint the message and that the words were not as directed by her and so she did not publish the defamatory statement. But there are some old authorities that suggest that if the law did not consider the originator of the message liable because an agent did the actual publication, then this result would shield the real authors: *Parkes v Prescott* [1869]

LR 4 Ex 169 at 179. It would probably be considered irrelevant that there was a change of word from "plan" to "conspiracy".

Defamation is probable in these circumstances.

18.3 The television report has been careful not to name any particular individual and so the real issue here is whether George Phoney can establish that he has been identified. In most defamation actions the plaintiff is actually named. But to be actionable the statement must be of or concerning George Phoney. The question is not whether the television station intended to defame George Phoney but whether a sensible reader would reasonably identify him as a person defamed. When groups are involved identification becomes particularly problematic.

However, it has been held in a number of cases, for instance *Foxcroft v Lacey* (1614) Hobart 89, that the imputation is capable of being understood as being one directed at each member of the group. On these facts it seems probable it could be found that the words meant the whole Council was dismissed for very good reasons. Therefore the words were referring to each member of the Council. But even if George Phoney needed to be able to prove that he can be specifically identified out of the group, on our facts the group is quite small: some 16 people. It is also relevant that George Phoney is the Mayor.

A finding of defamation is probable.

Tutorial Questions

Discussion Questions

18.1 Can you formulate some practical rules that would help writers avoid defamation threats and actions?

18.2 Do you think the remedies available for defamation are effective? Include in your discussion a consideration of the legislative provisions limiting damages awards.

18.3 Consider the provisions relating to resolution of disputes without litigation. Are they practical and/or appropriate?

SECTION

Other Torts

This section of the book will deal with three categories of torts: economic torts, misuse of legal powers and injury to relational interests.

INTENTIONAL INTERFERENCE WITH ECONOMIC INTERESTS

The term "economic tort" is applied to a group of torts considered in Chapter 19 that protect mainly, but not exclusively, the economic interests of the plaintiff. Except for passing off, they all require an intentional invasion of the plaintiff's economic interests. Passing off does not allow the recovery of damages for inadvertent passing off.

The extent to which economic interests can be protected by the law of tort is still developing. Historically, negligent damage to a purely economic interest did not give rise to a cause of action. This position has changed in Australian jurisprudence, as this chapter will discuss.

The mere intentional infliction of economic loss cannot be proscribed by law, since this would disallow normal competitive behaviour. Accordingly the law requires either:

- that the defendant's intent goes beyond a mere desire to compete, because it is fraudulent (deceit) or malicious (injurious falsehood, conspiracy to inflict loss by lawful means); or
- that the intention to inflict loss is accompanied by unlawful conduct (intimidation, tortious use of unlawful means) or infringes a right of the plaintiff (inducement of a breach of contract).

The intention to cause loss to the plaintiff in the latter group of torts need not be malicious. But unsettled questions have arisen as to whether a desire to inflict loss on the plaintiff is necessary, or whether it is enough that such loss is substantially certain to follow from the defendant's conduct.

Liability under s 52(1) of the *Trade Practices Act 1974* (Cth), together with its various State and Territory equivalents, has to some extent reproduced, but in other ways considerably extended, the area of liability under the common law economic torts.

MISUSE OF LEGAL POWERS

There are five torts considered in Chapter 20 concerning the broad area of abuse of process. The first three, which are essentially the same tort, are:

- malicious prosecution;
- the institution of malicious civil proceedings; and
- malicious arrest or use of other legal process against the plaintiff.

These require malice on the defendant's part (absence of reasonable cause for instituting the proceedings). Termination of the proceedings in the plaintiff's favour is also required in relation to malicious prosecution and institution of malicious civil proceedings but is questionable in the case of malicious arrest.

The tort of abuse of legal process itself requires the institution of legal proceedings for a purpose other than that for which they are intended. There is no requirement of malice (absence of reasonable cause in the sense of the claim being groundless), nor of termination of the proceedings in the plaintiff's favour.

The tort of misfeasance in public office requires conduct on the part of the official which is either malicious or consciously in excess of the official's powers.

All the torts in this section are derived from the action on the case and therefore require the plaintiff to prove damage in order to establish the cause of action.

INJURY TO RELATIONAL INTERESTS

The general rule is that an economic dependency on another person is not protected by the law of tort. However, contractual rights are protected by the tort of inducement of a breach of contract. Damage to the dependency through causing the injury or death of that other person is pure economic loss, and at the moment at least, not the subject of a duty of care, nor covered by torts other than negligence, except within the special area of operation of those torts considered in Chapter 21.

Still surviving in Australia, though abolished in England, are:

- the husband's action for loss of his wife's consortium (companionship, including sexual companionship, and services);
- the employer's action for loss of an employee's services; and
- the parent's action for loss of the services of a child.

By far the most important exception to the general rule, however, is the claim for wrongful death on the part of family members who are dependants of the deceased.

The claims were abolished in England because they were thought to have an archaic or demeaning flavour since they were based on a proprietary right to the services. In response to this sort of criticism, some Australian States and Territories have extended the claim for loss of consortium to the wife; others have abolished the claim. Domestic services of the sort in question, which are gratuitously rendered, have a clear economic value to the recipient; for example, where a wife performs nursing services for her husband, or a child for the parent. But the question arises: why should recovery of damages for the cost of a substitute be limited to these relationships? It now seems possible for the victim of a tort to recover damages for his or her own inability to render services, and to this extent the consortium and parental claims may have become unnecessary. The matter is discussed further in Chapter 21.

CHAPTER 19

Intentional Interference with Economic Interests

Reading

Fleming, *The Law of Torts,* Chapters 28 (pp 695–704) and 30.

Objectives

This chapter will:

- examine those torts in which liability may be imposed for intentional interference with an economic interest including:
  — deceit;
  — injurious falsehood;
  — conspiracy by the use of lawful means;
  — intimidation;
  — causing loss by unlawful means;
  — conspiracy by the use of unlawful means;
  — inducement of breach of contract; and
  — passing-off;
- note the circumstances under which the Beaudesert principle no longer applies in Australia; and
- recognise the situations under which s 52 of the *Trade Practices Act 1974* (Cth), or the equivalent State and Territory fair trading legislation, operates.

Principles

Introduction

[19.05] In this chapter a number of torts are considered in which liability may be imposed for an intentional interference with an economic interest. The protection against economic loss is the main purpose of these torts, though a number of them, such as deceit or injurious falsehood, may give protection to other interests, such as the interest in security of person or property. The so-called economic torts reveal an area of the law in which proof of intentional rather than negligent injury is still important. As highlighted in Chapter 8, a duty of care regarding economic loss is much more difficult to establish than one in relation to personal injury or property damage, the tests are more rigorous and, in the context of intentional interference something more than mere intent is required.

Cut-throat competition is not a tort and the mere intentional infliction of economic loss on another person is not tortious. The cases in which the law has allowed an action in tort to lie include:

- cases where the defendant is dishonest or acting out of an improper motive: these are the torts of deceit, injurious falsehood, and conspiracy by the use of lawful means;

- cases where the defendant has inflicted loss through the use of unlawful means: these are the torts of intimidation, use of unlawful means and conspiracy to use unlawful means; and

- cases of the wilful violation of a right: the *Lumley v Gye* tort of inducement of a breach of contract, or the appropriation of an intellectual property right such as the tort of passing off, and other basically tortious appropriations such as infringement of copyright, patent or a registered trade mark.

Apart from the torts relating to appropriation of a right of intellectual property, these torts rest on intention. They all require some degree of "targeting" of the plaintiff as the object of the tort. Thus, it was found not to be tortious for the defendant to conspire to spread false rumours boosting the share price of a company and causing the plaintiff to lose money on a share option deal relating to those shares which the plaintiff had entered into with another person, in the absence of any knowledge of the plaintiff and the deal on the part of the defendants: *Vickery v Taylor* (1910) 11 SR(NSW) 119. Conduct of this sort might now attract liability under s 52(1) of the *Trade Practices Act 1974* (Cth) under which a corporation shall not, in trade or commerce, engage in conduct that is misleading or deceptive or is likely to mislead or deceive.[1] There is no need for targeting of the plaintiff under the *Trade Practices Act*: under s 82(1) the plaintiff need only show that they have suffered loss or damage by reason of the conduct. The trade practices liability is considered in more detail at [19.200]ff.

In adopting the approach of requiring something more than mere intent (that is, improper motive or unlawful means) the common law has placed an outer limit on how far intentional interference with economic interests should be actionable, and

---

[1] A claim may also be framed under the investor protection provisions of the *Corporations Act 2001* (Cth), ss 1041H, 1041I and 1325 or the *Australian Securities and Investments Commission Act 2001* (Cth), ss 12DA, 12GF and 12GM.

stopped short of imposing general liability for the malicious infliction of economic loss. Of course it would be possible to combine the two approaches, but that possibility was closed off by the House of Lords decision in *Allen v Flood* [1898] AC 1, in which a trade union official who had procured the plaintiff's dismissal from his job by issuing lawful though (as the jury found) malicious threats to his employer, was held not liable in tort. There is reason to believe that the decision was influenced by political considerations, in particular the fear that industrial strife which was prevalent at the time might be exacerbated by the willingness of juries to find malice established against trade union officials.[2] There is no doubt, however, that *Allen v Flood* represents the present state of the law, though with the curious qualification that malice becomes relevant when two or more persons have acted in combination to cause loss to the plaintiff. Here a malicious motive on their part establishes their liability for conspiracy, even though their conduct is otherwise lawful. The illogicality of this was pointed out by Lord Diplock in *Lonrho v Shell Petroleum Co Ltd (No 2)* [1982] AC 173 at 188: a multinational company, being a single person in law, is able to shelter behind *Allen v Flood*, while a combination of street grocers is caught by the conspiracy rule. American case law has not adopted *Allen v Flood*. In *Tuttle v Buck* (1909) 119 NW 946, for example, the court held liable in tort the wealthy defendant who had set up a barber's shop in a small village, not in order to compete with the plaintiff's existing barber's shop in the village, but in order to ruin him.

Dishonesty or improper behaviour

Deceit

[19.10] The tort of deceit "provides a legal remedy for harm suffered in consequence of dishonesty" (*Magill v Magill* (2006) 226 CLR 551 at [17]) and is generally limited in its application to situations of commercial fraud where damage is caused by reason of the plaintiff having relied on a fraudulent misrepresentation. Deceit is difficult to establish in a domestic context (such as deceit as to paternity of children: *Magill*).[3] However, while "there are problems involved in inappropriate intrusion by the law of deceit into the domestic context"[4] it may apply to situations such as the fraudulent procurement by husbands of the consent of their wives to guarantees, the consent of their wives to decisions affecting family companies or family trusts, and the consent of their wives, or their wives' relatives, to engage in particular proprietary dispositions or contractual steps: *Magill v Magill* (2006) 226 CLR 551. Deceit has four clear elements, as set out in Figure 19.1.

---

[2]   See Hoffmann (1965) 81 LQR 116 at 138.
[3]   Not all deceit cases involving loss have their origins in contractual dealings or with inducement to undertake financial obligations. For example, in *Richardson v Silvester* (1873) LR 9 QB 34, the defendant falsely advertised that a farm was available for letting and the plaintiff, at some expense to himself, inspected the property. It was held that the plaintiff was entitled to recover damages, ie, his wasted expenses in travelling to view the farm. In *Mafo v Adams* [1970] 1 QB 548 the plaintiff was awarded compensation for inconvenience and discomfort after being fraudulently induced to undertake an unpleasant trip.
[4]   *Magill v Magill* (2006) 226 CLR 551 at [34] per Gleeson CJ.

Figure 19.1: Deceit

> The tort of deceit requires:
> * the defendant to make a false statement of fact or to engage in conduct amounting to a statement;[5]
> * with knowledge of its falsity or being recklessly indifferent to its truth;
> * intending that the plaintiff or a class of persons including the plaintiff should act on it;
> * the plaintiff acts on the statement (reliance); and
> * the plaintiff suffers loss as a result (damage).

Because an allegation of fraud amounts to a serious allegation of deliberate misconduct the need to satisfy each element has always been strictly enforced. These requirements of the tort are examined in turn.

False statement

[19.15] Common law limitations on the notion of a "misrepresentation" do not affect the tort of deceit, where fraud is essential to the establishing of a cause of action. Thus fraudulent statements of intention, of opinion or of law are actionable as deceit. In relation to the first two categories Bowen LJ in *Edgington v Fitzmaurice* (1885) 29 Ch D 459 stated that a man's mind is as much a state of fact as the state of his digestion. If the intention or opinion is not honestly held, there can be liability for the statement. As to misrepresentations of law, a statement about the effect of a private Act of Parliament was held to be actionable as deceit in *West London Commercial Bank v Kitson* (1884) 13 QBD 360. There seems no good reason for thinking this would not also be the case as regards a fraudulent statement of the general law. There is liability for:

* positive action taken to conceal the truth;[6]

* stating half-truths (for example, the statement that a car being sold by the defendant was a demonstration model, which was true but concealed the fact that the car had also received extensive use as a rental model);[7] and

* for putting forward accounts of a company which were accurate in themselves but concealed the fact that they were based on dishonest trading: *Briess v Woolley* [1954] AC 333.

Where a statement which is true when made becomes false to the knowledge of its maker, there is liability where the maker of the statement continues to negotiate on its basis. In *Jones v Dumbrell* [1981] VR 199 the defendant had negotiated for the purchase of a company's shares on the basis that he and his family would be responsible

---

5   In certain circumstances silence may be sufficient to ground a cause of action in deceit where there is a legal or equitable duty to disclose something: *Krakowski v Eurolynx Properties Ltd* (1995) 183 CLR 563 where, during the course of negotiations, the defendant had failed to disclose to the plaintiffs that a collateral contract had been made with the lessee, and this was held by the majority to amount to a misrepresentation of fact.

6   *Schneider v Heath* (1813) 170 ER 1462 – transferring boat from dry-dock into water in order to conceal rotting timber at base.

7   *Thompson v J T Fossey* (1978) 20 ALR 496 – though the actual decision was based on s 53(a) of the *Trade Practices Act 1974* (Cth).

for running the company's business. Prior to purchase, the defendant changed his mind and decided to sell the shares. He was held liable for deceit on the sale of the shares. By the same reasoning, if an originally false statement was not known by the defendant to be false, there would be liability in deceit if the defendant having acquired knowledge failed to correct the statement before the plaintiff relied on it.

Knowledge of falsity

[19.20] The evidential burden of establishing knowledge rests on the plaintiff. Inferences as to knowledge may be drawn in the plaintiff's favour by the court from the circumstances surrounding the making of the statement. But proof of fraud is often difficult and the plaintiff may prefer the more prudent course of alleging negligence in the alternative. Reckless indifference to the truth of the statement is sufficient to establish fraud, but the fact that the statement was made without reasonable grounds establishes negligence rather than fraud since a person who has some ground for believing in the truth of the statement, however unreasonable, is not reckless: *Derry v Peek* (1889) 14 App 337.

An employer is vicariously liable for a fraudulent statement made by an employee where the statement is within the scope of the authority entrusted to that employee; so also is a principal for a fraudulent statement by an agent: *Briess v Woolley* [1954] AC 333. The principal is not, however, liable for a misstatement made innocently by an agent without the principal's knowledge, even though the principal would have known of its untruth: *Armstrong v Strain* [1952] 1 KB 232.

Intention that plaintiff act on statement

[19.25] The intention that a plaintiff act on the statement is illustrated by the case of *Peek v Gurney* (1873) LR 6 HL 377. Statements in a prospectus issued by the defendant were found to have been intended to be acted on only by persons acquiring shares in the company under the issue covered by the prospectus, not by those persons, including the plaintiff, who bought shares in the market on the strength of the prospectus. *Peek v Gurney* was followed in *T J Larkins v Chelmer Holdings Pty Ltd* [1965] Qd R 68. In that case the defendant architect had certified to building owners that building work on their properties was incomplete, thereby causing loss to the plaintiff builders. The plaintiffs' action for deceit failed, since it was a third party rather than the plaintiffs who had been intended to act, and who had acted, on the statement. The court left open the possibility of an action for injurious falsehood lying in this situation: see [19.40]. There is, however, no need for the statement to be made to the plaintiff personally, provided the plaintiff is a person intended to act on the statement. Various cases on negligence, to which the same principles apply, illustrate the point, including the decision in *Hedley Byrne v Heller* [1964] AC 465 (statement made to bank acting on plaintiffs' behalf was actionable in principle by the plaintiffs; for closer consideration of this decision see [8.65])). *Langridge v Levy* (1837) 2 M&W 519; 150 ER 863 illustrates the point in relation to deceit. A false statement about the safety of a gun made by the defendant to the plaintiff's father was held to be actionable by the plaintiff when the gun burst on firing and injured him. The defendant knew that the father intended his sons to use the gun so that the plaintiff was legitimately regarded as a person intended to act on the statement.

Plaintiff acts on statement and suffers loss

[19.30] Whether the plaintiff has acted on the statement raises the issue of reliance and this matter is dealt with in the same way as in the case of negligent misstatements: see

Chapter 8. A case where the plaintiff failed to prove reliance was *Smith v Chadwick* (1884) 20 Ch D 27.[8] The plaintiff had bought shares in a company on the faith of a prospectus which contained the false statement that a certain person was a director of the company. Since the plaintiff had never heard of this person, he could not show that he had relied on the statement in the prospectus and his action failed. On the other hand, as pointed out in relation to reliance on a negligent misstatement, the fact that there is a second factor such as another statement on which the plaintiff relies is not enough to preclude the plaintiff from establishing reliance on the defendant's statement, even if the second factor is equally influential. The test appears to be whether the defendant's statement is by itself a sufficient motivating factor for the plaintiff's action. In *Edgington v Fitzmaurice* (1885) 29 Ch D 459 the plaintiff was influenced to some extent by a mistaken belief in certain facts to which belief the defendant's statement had not contributed. Nevertheless the plaintiff was able to prove reliance on the defendant's statement.

The action for deceit is generally brought to seek recovery for financial loss incurred by the plaintiff but is not limited to that. Damages for personal injury are recoverable as *Langridge v Levy* (1837) 2 M&W 519; 150 ER 863 shows.[9] Damages were also obtainable for a false statement by the defendant inducing the plaintiff to engage in sexual intercourse with him in the belief that this was marital intercourse.[10] In *Magill v Magill* (2006) 226 CLR 551, Gleeson CJ saw no reason in principle why the tort should not include personal injury, or why personal injury should not include psychiatric injury, as long as the damage directly flowing from the alteration of the plaintiff's position occurred as a result of the inducement. In his view, damages could also be recovered for distress, disappointment, frustration and anger as they could be viewed as natural responses to the discovery of deception.

Damages

[19.35] The main remedy for deceit is compensatory damages. Injunctions may be available but are unlikely to be sought on the purely practical grounds that the damage is ordinarily suffered at the time of the original deceit, meaning that there is unlikely to be an ongoing behaviour which the plaintiff is seeking to stop. The measure of damages in deceit is the tortious measure: the plaintiff is entitled to be put back into the position he or she would have been in had the tort not been committed. Whilst this almost invariably means as if the plaintiff had not acted on the statement,[11] the compensatory principle has, on occasion been displaced. In *Smith Kline v Long* [1988] 3 All ER 887, for example, the defendant had obtained the plaintiffs' goods by fraud and the plaintiffs were held to be entitled to the full market value of the goods on the analogy of conversion, even though they were replaceable at no cost to the plaintiffs. A practical example of the more usual compensatory approach is found in *Doyle v Olby (Ironmongers) Ltd* [1969] 2 QB 158 the plaintiff bought a business from the defendants on the faith of certain fraudulent statements, including one to the effect that all the business was over the counter, whereas in reality the employment of a traveller was

---

[8]   Cf *Commercial Banking Co of Sydney Ltd v Brown* (1972) 126 CLR 337 – even though plaintiffs were contractually bound to act as they did, they relied on the defendant's statement since they were prepared to break their contract and would have done so but for the statement.

[9]   See also *Burrows v Rhodes* [1899] 1 QB 816; *Nicholls v Taylor* [1939] VLR 119.

[10] *Carnaut v Rouse* (1941) 43 WALR 29; *Graham v Saville* [1945] 2 DLR 489; but *Smythe v Reardon* [1949] QSR 74 required proof of other damage, and the action failed in the absence of that.

[11] *Clark v Urquhart* [1930] AC 28 at 67-68.

necessary. The plaintiff recovered damages for the difference between the amount he paid for the business and its actual value; for expenditure incurred in the course of running the business including rent and rates; and for further loss incurred in the course of running the business. The latter loss was increased by the fact that the plaintiff was unable to afford to employ a traveller, but the court found that the normal rule excluding damage caused by the plaintiff's impecuniosity did not apply in the case of deceit. Lord Denning expressed the view that in deceit the defendant was liable for all loss flowing directly from the fraud, whether foreseeable or not. This statement was quoted without disapproval by the High Court in *Gould v Vaggelas* (1983) 157 CLR 215, though it was left open whether damages should be awarded in relation to unforeseeable loss. Dawson J thought that the compensation awarded in relation to losses incurred in running the business in *Doyle* might be limited to the facts of that case, that is, that the business could not be sold without the landlord's consent. In the normal case, the plaintiff would be expected to mitigate damage by disposing of an obviously loss-making business,[12] though where there were difficulties in disposing of the business, it was held that it should be valued at the time of its disposition, not at the time the fraud was discovered: *Smith New Court v Scrimgeour Vickers* [1996] 4 All ER 769.

Aggravated and exemplary damages[13] may be awarded for deceit; also damages for disruption and inconvenience: *Saunders v Edwards* [1987] 1 WLR 1116.

Injurious falsehood

[19.40] Injurious falsehood (also known as malicious falsehood) is committed where the defendant maliciously publishes a false statement concerning the plaintiff or the plaintiff's goods, property or business to a third person, who acts on the statement to the plaintiff's loss. The tort is a generalisation of two earlier torts, slander of title to land and to goods. Those torts rendered actionable false statements about the plaintiff's title to land or goods causing the plaintiff loss. However, in *Ratcliffe v Evans* [1892] 2 QB 524 the Court of Appeal held that they formed part of a wider principle of liability for causing loss to the plaintiff by false statements made to third parties. In *Ratcliffe* the statement was to the effect that the plaintiff had ceased business. This was found to be an actionable misstatement. It will be noticed that the statement was not defamatory. While both torts are concerned with false statements concerning the plaintiff, and a defamatory statement may give rise to an action for injurious falsehood,[14] the tort of injurious falsehood does not require a defamatory statement. In fact, where the statement is defamatory in nature, the plaintiff is better advised to rely on defamation rather than injurious falsehood, since there is no need to prove malice in defamation (unless of course there is a defence which is defeated by malice (refer Chapter 18). Defamation is actionable without proof of damage, and the position as to the awarding of damages is more favourable.

The High Court of Australia recognised the existence of the tort of injurious falsehood in *Hall-Gibbs Mercantile Agency Ltd v Dun* (1910) 12 CLR 84 and reiterated it in *Sungravure Pty Ltd v Middle East Airlines* (1975) 134 CLR 1. In *Hall-Gibbs Mercantile Agency Ltd v Dun* (1910) 12 CLR 84 the statement was the same as that in *Ratcliffe*, that is, that the plaintiffs had ceased business, but the High Court found that statement

---

12   *Lucas (TN) Pty Ltd v Centrepoint Freeholds Pty Ltd* (1984) 52 ALR 467.

13   Aggravated: *Archer v Brown* [1984] 3 WLR 350; exemplary: *Musca v Astle Corp* (1988) 80 ALR 251; *Harris v Digital Pulse Pty Ltd* (2003) 56 NSWLR 298.

14   *Fielding v Variety Inc* [1967] 2 QB 841; *Joyce v Sengupta* [1993] 1 WLR 337.

not to be actionable in the common law tort on the ground that the plaintiff had not proved damage. Proof of actual damage is an essential requirement of the tort of injurious falsehood: *Swimsure (Laboratories) Pty Ltd v McDonald* [1979] 2 NSWLR 796.

Figure 19.2: Injurious falsehood

Injurious falsehood requires:
• a false statement of or concerning the plaintiff's property or business to a third person;
• a defendant to publish that statement to a third person;
• malice on the part of the defendant; and
• proof by the plaintiff of actual damage (which may include a general loss of business) suffered as a result of the statement.

False statement about plaintiff or plaintiff's property

[19.45] The tort of injurious falsehood is concerned with false statements; generally there must be a clear statement made to third parties about the plaintiff's property, business or profession. There have, however been occasions on which the plaintiff can rely on inference or imputation: *Palmer-Bruyn & Parker Pty Ltd v Parsons* (2001) 208 CLR 388. The plaintiff must identify each statement which it is alleged is false and such a statement must be identified in the pleading: *Gacic v John Fairfax Publications Pty Ltd* [2005] NSWSC 1210. An additional requirement is that the false statement must induce the third parties to take their business elsewhere, resulting in loss to the plaintiff. In *White v Mellin* [1895] AC 154 the defendant sold infant food produced by the plaintiff in his shop. He affixed to the bottles containing the food labels stating that the defendant's own baby food was better in several respects than any other baby food. This was held to be not actionable as an injurious falsehood by the plaintiff. The decision establishes that mere advertising "puffs" are not actionable, though the exact basis of this is not clear. It could be either that the falsity of the statement is not capable of being demonstrated, or that there is no sufficient likelihood of its causing damage. Statements which are readily capable of being objectively tested go beyond mere puffs and may be actionable; for example, a statement that the defendant's newspaper greatly exceeded the circulation of the plaintiff's (*Lyne v Nicholls* (1906) 23 TLR 86); and that the defendant's abrasive substance had been subjected to laboratory tests which showed its superiority to that of the plaintiffs: *De Beers Abrasive Products v International General Electric Co of New York* [1975] 1 WLR 972. These types of statements are also relevant to this chapter's consideration of s 52 of the *Trade Practices Act 1974* (Cth), and as a matter of practice, are likely to be prosecuted under the statutory scheme as opposed to the common law principles of injurious falsehood.

Malice

[19.50] In addition to proving that the statement was false, the plaintiff must also establish malice. It does not matter whether the defendant is aware or unaware of the falsity of the statement. If the defendant has acted entirely for the purpose of causing injury to the plaintiff rather than of advancing the defendant's own interest, malice may be established without reference to whether the defendant knew the statement was false: *Dunlop v Maison Talbot* (1904) 20 TLR 579.

The usual way of establishing malice is to establish knowledge by the defendant of the falsity of the statement.[15] Where this is the case, the defendant is liable even if motivated by the protection of the defendant's own business interests: *Joyce v Motor Surveys Ltd* [1948] Ch 252; *Swimsure (Laboratories) Pty Ltd v McDonald* [1979] 2 NSWLR 796. It is not yet clear whether the defendant could defeat an allegation of malice by showing that, although he or she knew the statement to be false, he or she was acting for the protection of the plaintiff's interests. Proof of this has been found to refute malice in the case of the tort of malicious prosecution,[16] but no authority exists as regards injurious falsehood. Where the plaintiff is able to establish malice on the defendant's part, there is no need for the plaintiff to show that the defendant intended to cause the damage that occurred. The latter need only be the natural and probable result of the falsehood: *Palmer-Bruyn v Parsons* (2001) 208 CLR 388.

Actual damage

[19.55] The plaintiff in injurious falsehood must prove damage in order to establish the cause of action, as the High Court's decision in *Hall-Gibbs Mercantile Agency Ltd v Dun* (1910) 12 CLR 84 shows.[17] Evidence of business loss must therefore be proved. This may be achieved by showing the loss of particular customers, though it has been held that proof of general business loss is sufficient: *George v Blow* (1899) 20 LR(NSW) 395. Damages can also be obtained in respect of the costs of correcting the falsehood, such as newspaper advertisements. Damages for injury to feelings are not recoverable: *Fielding v Variety Inc* [1967] 2 QB 841. The tort compares unfavourably in this respect with defamation, though in *Joyce v Sengupta* [1993] 1 WLR 337 the question was raised but left open whether damages for injury to feelings could be awarded in injurious falsehood where the plaintiff had proved the actual damage necessary to sustain the cause of action.[18]

Remedies

[19.60] As in the case of deceit, generally the only remedy a plaintiff will seek is compensatory damages. An injunction, though theoretically obtainable, is in the nature of things unlikely to be sought. However, where the injury is ongoing (such as information published on a website as was the position in *Kaplan v Go Daddy Group* [2005] NSWSC 636) an injunction becomes relevant. The defamation rule that the court will not issue an interlocutory injunction where the defendant intends to plead a defence of justification, fair comment or qualified privilege applies also to injurious falsehood: *Swimsure (Laboratories) Pty Ltd v McDonald* [1979] 2 NSWLR 796 at 801. The main effect is that the courts will not allow the plaintiff to sidestep the defamation rule by suing in injurious falsehood.

---

[15] See also *Roberts v Bass* (2002) 212 CLR 1 where, while the case was about qualified privilege in the context of defamation, the comments on malice apply equally to the tort of injurious falsehood.

[16] *Rapley v Rapley* (1930) 30 SR (NSW) 94 – son who took proceedings to have his mother declared an insane person was not malicious, since he acted out of a desire to protect her property, even though he had no reason to believe her to be insane.

[17] *Swimsure (Laboratories) Pty Ltd v McDonald* [1979] 2 NSWLR 796.

[18] See also the comments of Price J in *James v Faddoul* [2007] NSWSC 821 at [18] that "whilst in *Bride v KMG Hungerfords* (1991) 109 FLR 256 Murray J at 281 was of the opinion that no damages were available in respect of non-pecuniary harm or loss said to flow from an injurious falsehood, the issue was not determined in *Palmer Bruyn* and there is authority to the contrary in the United Kingdom: see *Joyce v Sengupta* (1993) 1 WLR at 347–348".

Conspiracy by use of lawful means

[19.65] The case of *Allen v Flood* [1898] AC 1, considered in Chapter 1 (at [1.50]), shows that a defendant who has acted lawfully but with the malicious intention of injuring or damaging the plaintiff does not by virtue of that malicious intent commit a tort, even though the intended injury or damage has resulted. The law is different where the defendant has conspired with another person to the same purpose and effect. Here the tort of conspiracy is committed by both parties. The illogicality of this position was pointed out at [19.05]. There are limitations on the extent to which a conspiracy will convert a lawful act into a tort. Thus a conspiracy to present false evidence in court is not an actionable conspiracy, because the public interest requires that persons giving evidence in court should be immune from civil action: *Cabassi v Vila* (1940) 64 CLR 130. It also seems clear that the rule in *Bradford Corp v Pickles* [1895] AC 587 allowing a landowner an absolute right of abstracting certain types of water flowing underneath his land would not be displaced if the landowner acted in combination with another person. Where the defendants have conspired to injure the plaintiff by the use of unlawful means, this is merely part of the general principle of liability for causing loss by unlawful means and will be considered under that heading: see [19.70]ff.

Figure 19.3: Conspiracy by lawful means – general principles

> To succeed in an action in conspiracy by lawful means the plaintiff must:
> - establish that there is an agreement between two or more persons;
> - prove malice on the part of the defendant; and
> - show injury or damage.

In order to succeed in conspiracy by the use of lawful means the plaintiff must prove a predominant intention on the part of the defendant to cause the plaintiff injury or damage, that is, malice. In *Crofter Hand Woven Harris Tweed Co Ltd v Veitch* [1942] AC 435 the defendant union officials had instructed dockers to refuse to handle yarn sent from the mainland of Scotland for delivery to the plaintiff's factory in the Outer Hebrides. The plaintiffs employed no union labour and the defendants' purpose was to frustrate the plaintiffs' competition with other mills on the island which employed union members, thus enabling the employers of those members to pay wage increases. This was found by the House of Lords not to be an actionable conspiracy since the defendants had not used unlawful means and were acting for the protection of their members' interests, not for the purpose of inflicting damage on the plaintiffs. The same result as in *Crofter* was arrived at in *Ansett (Operations) Pty Ltd v Australian Federation of Air Pilots* [1991] 1 VR 637. In that case the defendant union officials had induced pilots to resign their positions with the plaintiffs, which they were able to do without committing a breach of contract. This was not an actionable conspiracy since the predominant purpose was not to injure the plaintiffs but to avoid or limit the pilots' liability for committing other breaches of their contracts. The interests that may legitimately be furthered by the conspiracy need not be economic, nor need the action be taken in the selfish interest of the defendant or persons the defendant is seeking to protect. So a combination aimed against the plaintiff who operated a racist bar in his dance hall was held to be not actionable: *Scala Ballroom (Wolverhampton) v Ratcliffe* [1958] 1 WLR 1057. But a combination aimed against the plaintiff because of his religion, race or colour was thought to be actionable by Viscount Maugham in *Crofter* at 451.

The limits placed by *Crofter* on conspiracy have meant that success in this tort is unusual. Successful actions have been brought in matters arising out of industrial conflict where union officials have been shown to be acting vindictively rather than for the genuine protection of the interests of their members: *Quinn v Leathem* [1901] AC 495; *Huntley v Thornton* [1957] 1 WLR 321; *Latham v Singleton* [1981] 2 NSWLR 843. An example of a successful action is *Gulf Oil Ltd v Page* [1987] Ch 327. The defendant, having won a contractual battle with Gulf Oil, hired a plane to be flown over a racecourse towing the sign, "Gulf Oil exposed in fundamental breach". Although the words were true, this amounted to the tort of conspiracy since it was done for no other purpose than to damage Gulf Oil.

The final question is what persons may be held liable for a conspiracy. It is now accepted that husband and wife may be liable as conspirators, the old idea that they were one person in law having lapsed: *Midland Bank Trust Co v Green (No 3)* [1979] 2 All ER 193. A criminal case has held that a conspiracy may exist between a one-man company and the one man: *R v McDonnell* [1966] 1 QB 233. It has been held that a company may be a party to a fraudulent conspiracy on the part of directors of the company, even though it was to some extent a victim of the conspiracy, provided some benefit to the company was intended and the directors were acting within the scope of their apparent authority.[19] Employer and employee are still identified as one person for the purpose of conspiracy where the employee is acting in the course of the employment. But a trade union may be a party to a conspiracy with members of the union.[20] Where the requisite intent for a conspiracy is held by some but not all parties to it, only those with that wrongful intent will be held liable; their malice will not be imputed to other parties: *McKernan v Fraser* (1931) 46 CLR 343 at 408.

Causing loss by unlawful means

Intimidation

[19.70] The tort of intimidation by the threat of an unlawful act is clearly established in the so-called three-party situation, that is, where A makes a threat to B thereby causing B to act to the loss of C. The claimant must show that although the threats are directed at a third party they are really aimed at the claimant and that the intention is to cause harm to the claimant. In *Rookes v Barnard* [1964] AC 1129 the defendants were three union officials, two of whom were employed by BOAC. In order to maintain a closed shop at BOAC, they threatened the latter with breaches of their contracts of employment (or, in the case of the official not employed by BOAC that such breaches

---

[19] *Beach Petroleum NL v Johnson* (1993) 115 ALR 411. It is different where the company is solely the victim: *Belmont Finance v Williams Furniture* [1980] 1 All ER 393.

[20] *Martell v Victorian Coal Miners' Assoc* (1903) 29 VLR 475; *Brisbane Shipwrights v Heggie* (1906) 3 CLR 686; *Egan v Amalgamated Miners Assoc* (1917) 17 SR (NSW) 243; *Williams v Horsey* (1959) 103 CLR 30.

would be committed), unless the plaintiff, a non-union member employed by BOAC, was dismissed. BOAC thereupon lawfully dismissed the plaintiff. The plaintiff's action against the three defendants succeeded in the House of Lords on the ground that the individual unlawful threats constituted the tort of intimidation, and the threats uttered in combination constituted a conspiracy to intimidate, that is, a conspiracy to cause loss by unlawful means. The tort of intimidation in the three-party situation has received recognition in Australia. It has been held to be intimidation for a union to issue threats of unlawful picketing of the premises of club owners to those owners in order to induce them not to give their business to the plaintiffs which ran a booking agency for artists.[21] *Latham v Singleton* [1981] 2 NSWLR 843 was a repeat of the *Rookes* situation, that is, a case of conspiracy to intimidate by unionists threatening an employer with breaches of the contracts of employment of union members unless the plaintiff was dismissed, which he was. Again, this was found to be an actionable conspiracy to intimidate.

Figure 19.4: Intimidation

The essential features of intimidation are:
- an unlawful threat by the defendant (though need not be against the plaintiff);
- defendant intended the consequence of the threat (to harm the plaintiff); and
- that the person threatened complied with the demand, thereby causing loss to the plaintiff.

The essential features of intimidation are that the defendant should have intended the consequence of the threat resulting in the loss which the plaintiff suffers, and that the threat must be unlawful. On the former point, *Rookes* shows that an intention to cause the plaintiff harm is sufficient: it need not be the defendant's predominant intention. The fact that the defendants were not malicious and were acting in what they perceived to be the interests of their union was irrelevant. Absence of an intention to cause the plaintiff harm brought about the failure of the action in *Huljich v Hall* [1973] 2 NZLR 279 and *Australian Wool Innovation Ltd v Newkirk* [2005] ATPR 42-053; [2005] FCA 290. In the former case, although the defendant had issued a threat to the plaintiff and the plaintiff had then acted to his loss, that action was not intended by the defendant (the case in fact concerned a two-party intimidation, see below). Unlawful means include the commission of other torts[22] or a breach of contract: see *Rookes*. In *Latham* the threat was of the calling of a strike and English authority suggested that this was not a breach of contract where the threat was accompanied by proper strike notice: *Morgan v Fry* [1968] 2 QB 710. Thus, the threat to commmit a lawful act cannot form the basis of an action for intimidation: *Rookes v Barnard*; *Latham v Singleton* [1981] 2 NSWLR 843. In *Latham*, however, the proper notice was not given; the employees simply walked off the job without informing the employer.

---

[21] *Sid Ross Agency Pty Ltd v Actors Equity Assoc of Australia* [1971] 1 NSWLR 760; see also *Dollar Sweets Pty Ltd v Federated Confectioners Assoc of Australia* [1986] VR 383.

[22] *Tarleton v M'Gawley* (1794) 170 ER 153 – firing at customers to scare them off; *Keeble v Hickeringill* (1706) 103 ER 1127 – scaring off ducks.

The tort of intimidation has been thought to be less clearly applicable in the two-party situation, that is, where A makes an unlawful threat to B which B acts on to his loss. This may have been because A will generally possess remedies against B should the threat be carried out. But these remedies may only be available should B refuse to comply with the threat. This is hardly a good reason for denying a person a remedy who has suffered loss by acting in compliance with the threat. The matter now seems settled for Australian law by the approval given by the High Court in *Northern Territory v Mengel* (1995) 185 CLR 307 at 350 to a passage of Dixon J's judgment in *James v Commonwealth* (1930) 62 CLR 339. Dixon J (at 374) relied on a passage in *Salmond on Torts* which stated that it was an actionable wrong "intentionally to compel a person, by means of a threat of an illegal act, to do some act whereby loss accrues to him". In *James* the threat was made by officers of the Commonwealth to carry out a seizure of the plaintiff's goods if the plaintiff carried out his intention to ship them to another part of Australia. This threat was beyond the powers of the officers and would have constituted conversion if carried out. Dixon J found that the threat would have been actionable but for the fact that the plaintiff was influenced by the fear of prosecution rather than the threat of seizure; also that it was unlikely that he could have persuaded a shipper of the goods to carry them. Intimidation in the two-party situation might seem to raise a particular difficulty in the case of breach of contract. A threatened anticipatory breach of contract is in certain circumstances an immediate wrong, giving a right to the other party to treat the contract as repudiated and sue for damages in the law of contract. Even so, it is arguable that a right to sue for intimidation should exist. The plaintiff might have little choice but to comply with the threat rather than to sue for damages. In *Pao On v Lau Yiu Long* [1980] AC 614 the Privy Council, in determining whether a threat of the commission of a breach of contract with a company constituted improper duress against directors of the company who had in response to the threat agreed to guarantee the company's obligations under the contract, applied the test of whether the directors' action in response to the threat was truly voluntary, or was a submission to unfair pressure created by the threat. That test would appear to be satisfactory for intimidation.

Actual use of unlawful means

[19.75] It now seems established that the actual use of unlawful means to intentionally inflict loss on the plaintiff is a tort.[23] A number of English cases culminating in decisions of the House of Lords have pointed to this. However, since all these cases concerned actions for an interlocutory injunction, it is arguable that the existence of the tort was merely assumed rather than established.[24] Australian decisions also have recognised the existence of the tort.[25] The High Court in *Northern Territory v Mengel* (1995) 185 CLR 307 at 343 referred to the tort as "embryonic or emerging"; also as one which "does not extend to all unlawful acts and, at least in that regard is in need of further

---

[23] In *Deepcliffe v Gold Coast City Council* (2001) 118 LGERA 117; [2001] QCA 342 the Queensland Court of Appeal suggests that even if the tort were recognised then it would not extend to the conduct of public authorities of a public character.

[24] *Daily Mirror Newspapers Ltd v Gardner* [1968] 2 QB 762; *Acrow (Automation) Ltd v Rex Chainbelt Inc* [1971] 1 WLR 1676; *Breikes v Cattel* [1972] Ch 15; *Hadmor Productions Ltd v Hamilton* [1983] 1 AC 191; *Merkur Island Shipping Co v Laughton* [1983] AC 570; *Lonrho v Fayed* [1989] 3 WLR 631.

[25] *Copyright Agency v Haines* (1982) 40 ALR 264; *Ansett (Operations) Pty Ltd v Australian Federation of Air Pilots* [1991] 1 VR 637.

definition". In *Sanders v Snell* (1998) 196 CLR 329 the High Court thought it yet to be finally resolved whether the tort existed, finding that it did not apply on the facts before it.[26] The tort was applied in the earlier decision of *Ansett (Operations) Pty Ltd v Australian Federation of Air Pilots* [1991] 1 VR 637. In that case a union official acting on behalf of the defendant union gave a directive to air pilots to confine their working hours to those between 9.00am and 5.00pm. This directive was complied with in breach of the pilots' contracts of employment with Ansett, causing a loss to Ansett in the form of interference with the performance of its contracts with its customers. For this loss the union was held liable, since the procuring of breaches of the pilots' contracts of employment by the directive constituted the use of unlawful means to cause loss. The tort has also been applied in Canada (*Mintuck v Valley River Band No 63A* [1977] 2 WWR 309) and New Zealand: *Van Camp Chocolates Ltd v Aulsebrooks Ltd* [1984] 1 NZLR 354.

Figure 19.5: Establishing the tort of causing loss by unlawful means

Plaintiff must show that:
- defendant intended to cause loss to the plaintiff (though this need not be the defendant's predominant intention);
- unlawful means were used by the defendant (though they need not be against the plaintiff); and
- plaintiff suffered loss.

As in the case of intimidation, the defendant must intend to cause loss to the plaintiff, though again this need not be the defendant's predominant intention. Trinidade and Cane's suggestion to the contrary[27] arising from *Acrow Automation v Rex Chainbelt* [1971] 1 WLR 1676 confuses intention with motive or purpose. Acrow had obtained an injunction against SI to prevent the latter from acting in breach of contract with Acrow to impede Acrow's manufacture of machinery under licence from SI. SI had instructed Rex Chainbelt not to supply Acrow with components for use in Acrow's manufacturing process for that machinery and Rex Chainbelt had complied with this. Acrow succeeded in obtaining an injunction against Rex Chainbelt on the ground that they were causing them loss through the use of unlawful means, namely the contempt of court involved in assisting SI to breach the injunction. Clearly Rex Chainbelt were not motivated by a desire to injure Acrow as their correspondence with them indicated; they merely felt bound to comply with SI's instructions. It was equally clear that they intended to cause loss to Acrow since this was an inevitable result of their refusal to supply the components. The same distinction between intention and purpose appears in the House of Lords case *Hadmor Productions v Hamilton* [1983] 1 AC 191 in which trade union defendants ordered the blacking on television of a film produced by Hadmor on the ground that they wished to ensure all television films were produced by union labour. As Lord Diplock put it, "that purpose was not to injure Hadmor however inevitably injury to Hadmor might be one result of the blacking". The New Zealand case *Van Camp Chocolates* held

---

26 *Sanders v Snell (No 2)* (2003) 130 FCR 149.
27 F Trinidade and P Cane, *The Law of Torts in Australia* (3rd ed, OUP, 1999) p 239.

that the intention to injure the plaintiff in this tort must be at least a motivating factor though not the predominant one. In other words, but for that intention, the defendant would not have acted even though another factor might have been equally or more motivating. But this attempt to create a halfway-house position between the case of a predominant intent to injure the plaintiff and a mere intent to that effect creates a conceptual difficulty, and is not a solution to the problem.

As to what are unlawful means, the examples cited in the case of intimidation apply equally to the tort of unlawful means. As in the case of intimidation, it is generally clear that the means used need not be unlawful against the plaintiff itself. English cases have added the case of an agreement void under the *Restrictive Trade Practices Act 1956* (UK);[28] conduct which is in contempt of court;[29] and a fraudulent misrepresentation made to a Secretary of State even though the latter had not acted on the statement to his loss and therefore the statement was not by itself a tort, nor even, it seems, any other wrong.[30] New Zealand has added the case of breach of confidence,[31] and Canada the case of breach of the natural justice rule by a public body.[32] But the High Court in *Sanders v Snell* (1998) 196 CLR 329 rejected the latter as unlawful means. One reason for this was that if ultra vires conduct by public bodies were admitted to the category of unlawful means, it would be difficult to distinguish the tort from that of misfeasance in public office. In *Lonrho v Shell Petroleum Co Ltd (No 2)* [1982] AC 173 Lonrho failed in a claim against Shell for alleged "sanctions-busting" by the latter in breach of an Order-in-Council having statutory force, and causing loss to Lonrho which had complied with the Order. Lord Diplock's judgment in the House of Lords rejecting the claim depended on the fact that the breach of the Order gave rise to no independent tort liability to the plaintiff, and this has given rise to the view that this may be a requirement of the tort of unlawful means. But it is unlikely that the tort of unlawful means was being considered by the House of Lords in that case, since Shell clearly had no intention of injuring Lonrho. Nevertheless in a later case the judgment has been relied on to rule out a claim based on a director's breach of fiduciary duty to a company causing loss to the plaintiff creditor, on the ground that the breach was actionable only by the company.[33] It is surely mainly in the case where the unlawful means are not actionable as such by the plaintiff that the need for the tort exists. However, where the unlawful means themselves give rise to a cause of action in the plaintiff's favour, such as when they constitute a tort or breach of contract against the plaintiff, there may seem to be little purpose in regarding this conduct as giving rise to the tort of unlawful means. No cases suggest liability for using unlawful means in this situation, though to absolutely exclude the tort might go too far. For example, in the case of breach of contract, the plaintiff might be able to recover under the tort of unlawful means for loss which the defendant intended to inflict on him or her; whereas that loss might be irrecoverable in the action on the contract as not being within the contemplation of the parties at the time of contracting.[34]

---

[28]   *Daily Mirror Newspapers Ltd v Gardner* [1968] 2 QB 762; *Breikes v Cattel* [1972] Ch 15.

[29]   *Acrow (Automation) Ltd v Rex Chainbelt Inc* [1971] 1 WLR 1676; (not following) *Chaman v Honig* [1963] 2 QB 502.

[30]   *Lonrho Ltd v Fayed* [1989] 3 WLR 631; see also *National Phonograph Co Ltd v Edison-Bell* [1908] 1 Ch 535.

[31]   *Van Camp Chocolates Ltd v Aulsebrooks Ltd* [1984] 1 NZLR 354.

[32]   *Orchard v Tunney* (1957) 8 DLR (2d) 273.

[33]   *Yukong Line of Korea v Rendsburg Corp of Liberia* [1998] 4 All ER 82 – the action was brought for conspiracy to use unlawful means.

[34]   That is, because of the remoteness rule for contract in *Hadley v Baxendale* (1854) 9 Ex 1; 156 ER 145.

Interference with contract

[19.80] At one time it was necessary to attempt to bring a situation involving interference with a contract within the *Lumley v Gye* principle (see [19.95]), that is, to show that the use of the unlawful means had brought about breaches of contracts made with the plaintiff by third parties. In *JT Stratford & Co Ltd v Lindley* [1965] AC 269, the defendant union officials had given instructions to lightermen who were members of the union not to handle the plaintiffs' barges in breach of their employment contracts with the plaintiffs' customers. The result of this directive was that the barges became immobilised in the possession of the customers and the plaintiffs were prevented from entering into further agreements for the hiring of their barges. The House of Lords held that an interlocutory injunction should be issued against the defendants, on the ground that they had used unlawful means (that is, the tort of inducement of the lightermen's contracts) to bring about breaches by the barge hirers of their contracts to return the barges at the agreed time to the plaintiff. Two members of the House of Lords, Lords Reid and Upjohn, thought that the liability extended to the plaintiffs' inability to take on new business through the hiring out of the barges, that is, where no contract was yet in existence. Further, it is hard to see that the barge hirers were in fact in breach of contract in being unable to return the barges when it was impossible for them to do so. The reality of this was recognised by the House of Lords in *Merkur Island Shipping Co v Laughton* [1983] AC 570. In that case the House of Lords held that the tort of interference with contract does not require that the unlawful means used by the defendant should bring about an actionable breach of contract between the plaintiff and a third party, merely an interference with the performance of that contract causing loss to the plaintiff. If that is so, there appears to be no separate tort of interference with contract by unlawful means. The tort is that of the use of unlawful means causing loss to the plaintiff, interference with contract being merely one example of the type of loss covered by the tort. This is borne out by *Ansett (Operations) Pty Ltd v Australian Federation of Air Pilots* [1991] 1 VR 637 which, similarly to the *JT Stratford* case, involved a union directive to members to act in a manner inconsistent with their contracts (see [19.75] for more detail). In this instance, Brooking J took the view that the defendant's unlawful conduct, which caused interference with contractual relationships between the plaintiffs and third parties, was merely an example of the tort of unlawful interference with trade or business. If so, there is no need for the plaintiff to have to prove knowledge on the part of the defendant of the existence of the contract or its terms, provided it is an inevitable inference that some degree of interference with contractual business will be produced. In *Merkur*, Lord Diplock thought it to be an inevitable inference that a laden ship about to leave port would be carrying out a contract of carriage. In *Falconer v ASLEF* [1986] 1 RLR 331 it was held to be an inevitable inference that a rail strike would cause interference with previously booked journeys, so that the defendants were held liable to rail passengers affected, even though it was clearly not the purpose of ASLEF to injure those passengers. In *Ansett* the defendant's conduct "targeted" the plaintiffs, though there was no predominant intention to injure them. But in *Falconer* there was no targeting of the plaintiffs; they simply formed part of a class to whom loss was inevitable. Assuming the tort of unlawful means is part of Australian law, perhaps the most difficult question is how extensively the intention requirement should be framed.

Conspiracy by use of unlawful means

[19.85] The tort of conspiracy by use of unlawful means has been established for some time and, despite questionable utility, continues to be recognised by the courts. At the time when it was not clear whether there was a tort of using unlawful means as such, the action served an obvious purpose, particularly in view of the fact that it did not share with the tort of conspiracy by the use of lawful means the need to show a predominant intention to injure the plaintiff. An intention to injure the plaintiff is sufficient. This is clearly the law in Australia,[35] and has been reconfirmed as English law by the Court of Appeal.[36]

Figure 19.6: Establishing the tort of conspiracy by use of unlawful means

> Plaintiff must show:
> * an agreement or combination;
> * the commission (or threat) of an unlawful act;
> * an intention to injure the plaintiff; and
> * damage resulting from the threats or unlawful acts.

Now that the use of unlawful means by an individual to injure the plaintiff seems established as a tort, the need for this form of conspiracy has become questionable. There has been some judicial support for a doctrine of merger[37] (though the phrase is not particularly appropriate) under which a conspiracy to commit a tort is not actionable as a conspiracy once the tort is committed, since at that point it becomes merged in that tort. If we assume the existence in Australia of a tort of unlawful means, and that the test of unlawfulness is the same for the individual tort as it is for conspiracy, then conspiracy adds nothing to the liability of those conspiring to use those means, since each individual in using the means is a joint tortfeasor with the rest and is liable in respect of the total loss caused. Even if the ingredients of the individual tort are spread among those conspiring in such a way as to make it impossible to say of any one of them that that person has fulfilled the requirements of the individual tort, the individuals are still joint tortfeasors because they have taken concerted action in the furtherance of a common design[38] (and if the design has not yet been implemented, an injunction may

---

[35]   *McKernan v Fraser* (1931) 46 CLR 343; *Williams v Hursey* (1959) 103 CLR 30; *Galea v Cooper* [1982] 2 NSWLR 411; *Australian Wool Innovation Ltd v Newkirk* [2005] ATPR 42-053.

[36]   In *Metall & Rohstoff v Donaldson Lufkin & Jenrette Inc* [1989] 3 WLR 563 the Court of Appeal held that the unlawful means form of conspiracy required a predominant intention to injure the plaintiff, purporting to apply remarks made by Lord Diplock in *Lonrho Ltd v Shell Petroleum Ltd* [1982] AC 173 at 189. But the House of Lords held in *Lonrho Ltd v Fayed* [1991] 3 WLR 188 at 198 that this was a misinterpretation of those remarks and that there was no need for a predominant intention to injure the plaintiff in the tort of conspiracy by the use of unlawful means. This also represents New Zealand law: *SSC & B Lintas New Zealand Ltd v Murphy* [1986] 2 NZLR 436; and Canadian law: *Canada Cement Lafarge Ltd v British Columbia Lightweight Aggregate Ltd* (1983) 145 DLR (3d) 385.

[37]   *Galland v Mineral Underwriters Ltd* [1977] WAR 116; see also *Sorrell v Smith* [1925] AC 700 per Lord Dunedin at 716.

[38]   *Brooke v Bool* [1928] 2 KB 578.

be obtained against them on the same basis). In *Credit Lyonnais v ECGD* [1999] 1 All ER 929 an employee of ECGD and a rogue took part in a joint plan to defraud the Credit Lyonnais bank. The employee fraudulently obtained export guarantees from his employer, and the rogue used these to obtain credits from Credit Lyonnais. The two were held to be joint tortfeasors since they had used unlawful means in the furtherance of a common design to defraud the bank, but ECGD was not vicariously liable for its employee's participation, since only the fraudulent obtaining of the guarantee lay within the course of his employment, and there is no tort of aiding and abetting the tort of another person. Suing in conspiracy would have made no difference, since it would not have been complete until Credit Lyonnais was defrauded. However, at the moment conspiracy rather than unlawful means is the more established tort, and there is plentiful recent authority that a conspiracy to commit a tort is actionable as a conspiracy; for example, a conspiracy to intimidate (*Rookes v Barnard* [1964] AC 1129), to use unlawful means, or to use tortious physical violence to prevent the plaintiffs entering their workplace: *Latham v Singleton* [1981] 2 NSWLR 843.

Justification as defence

[19.90] In *Ansett (Operations) Pty Ltd v Australian Federation of Air Pilots* [1991] 1 VR 637 Brooking J was bound by authority to hold that justification was no defence to the trade union and its officials in relation to the torts of interference with the plaintiffs' trade or business by the use of unlawful means, nor to a conspiracy to the same effect, expressing the view that the authority seemed to him persuasive. The state of the law asserted in this judgment seems correct in principle. If these torts require no predominant intention to injure the plaintiff, it seems wrong to allow the defendant to plead that the action was taken to protect the defendant's own interests as a defence: *Williams v Hursey* (1959) 103 CLR 30. *Latham v Singleton* [1981] 2 NSWLR 843, which allowed the defence in relation to the tort of conspiracy to intimidate, is directly contrary to *Ansett* and is, it is submitted, wrong. (On the facts the defence failed in *Latham* on the ground that the actions of the defendants went well beyond what was needed to protect the interests of the members of the union.)

Wilful violation of rights

Lumley v Gye

[19.95] In *Lumley v Gye* (1853) 2 E&B 216; 118 ER 749 the plaintiff had contracted with Joanna Wagner, an operatic singer, to sing at his theatre. The defendant, knowing of the engagement of Miss Wagner by the plaintiff, persuaded her to break her contract with the plaintiff and to sing instead at the defendant's theatre. The defendant's conduct was held to be an actionable tort. Although the plaintiff had alleged a malicious intention to injure him on the part of the defendant, it is now clear that this is not a necessary ingredient of the tort and that it is enough if the defendant, knowing of the contract, deliberately brings about its breach: *James v Commonwealth* (1939) 62 CLR 339 at 370. The tort thus established is generally referred to as the tort of inducing (that is causing) a breach of contract. But the judgments in *Lumley v*

Gye speak in wider terms, basing the tort on a wilful violation of the plaintiff's right by the defendant. More recent authority in England has accepted the wider form of this liability, holding that it extends to a deliberate violation of an already accrued right to bring action for the inducement of a breach of contract, though dismissing the claim in the case itself on the ground that the particular enforcement of the right required by the plaintiff lay in the discretion of the court: *Law Debenture Trust Corp plc v Ural Caspian Oil Corp Ltd* [1995] 1 All ER 157. However, it is difficult to say at the moment how far the wilful violation of rights will be considered tortious outside the contractual sphere.

Distinguishing interference with contract by unlawful means

[19.100] The view was expressed at [19.80] that interference with contract by unlawful means is merely part of the generic tort of using unlawful means to deliberately inflict loss on the plaintiff, and that this view is supported by cases such as *Merkur Island Shipping Co v Laughton* [1983] AC 570 and *Ansett (Operations) Pty Ltd v Australian Federation of Air Pilots* [1991] 1 VR 637. Sometimes the distinction between the two forms of liability is drawn on the basis that *Lumley v Gye* lies for "direct" interference with contract, whereas interfering with contract by the use of unlawful means lies where there is indirect interference with contract. On this basis it has been held that where a person is prevented from performing a contract by a tort committed against that person (such as a trespass to goods[39] or the unlawful picketing of premises),[40] this is direct interference and is actionable under *Lumley v Gye* itself. This seems unsatisfactory. Cases of the latter sort should be excluded from the *Lumley v Gye* principle, since they depend upon the use of unlawful means by the defendant. The better distinction seems to be between persuading or otherwise bringing pressure to bear on a contracting party to break the contract, and conduct which renders it impossible for that party to perform the contract. In the latter case, the means used must be unlawful, but there is no longer a need to prove an actionable breach of contract. In the former case, it is essential that there should be a breach of contract but unlawful means are not required. However, there is no reason why, should the pressure brought on the contracting party to break the contract contain an illegal element, this should exclude the case from this category. The essential question is whether that party has a choice of whether or not to commit a breach. *Torquay Hotel Co v Cousins* [1969] 2 Ch 106 is an example of the confusion that exists in this area. The defendant unionists had "blacked" the plaintiffs' hotel by giving instructions to truck driver members of the union not to deliver oil to the plaintiffs. This was on its facts a case of prevention of the performance of contracts for the supply of oil to the plaintiffs. However, the court treated the case as one of direct interference because the plaintiffs were informed over the telephone of the fact that the truck drivers would not be allowed to deliver oil. This was an obvious error. The phone call was quite irrelevant to the infliction of loss on the plaintiffs.[41]

---

[39] *WK Co Ltd v Dunlop Rubber Co Ltd* (1926) 42 TLR 376.

[40] *Dollar Sweets Pty Ltd v Federated Confectioners Assoc Australia* [1986] VR 383.

[41] *Woolley v Dunford* (1972) 3 SASR 243, in which the defendant brought about a breach of a contract between the plaintiff and a third party by informing the third party that the plaintiff had been "blacked" by the union, was treated, debatably, by the court as a case of direct inducement by persuasion. The facts do not make it clear whether the third party could have performed if he had wished to.

General features of inducement of breach of contract

Figure 19.7: Tort of inducement of breach of contract – general principles

- Plaintiff must show that:
  - there is a valid contract in existence;
  - the defendant knew of the contractual relationship;
  - the defendant intended to interfere with the contractual relationship in order to harm or bring pressure to bear on the plaintiff;
  - the interference was occasioned, either directly by interference, or indirectly;
  - the interference is wrongful or unlawful (if the interference is indirect some independently unlawful means must be shown); and
  - the breach has resulted in damage to the plaintiff.
- Need not involve the contract breaker in acting unlawfully.
- Is not available to the contract breaker.

[19.105] Once *Lumley v Gye* is distinguished from the tort of unlawful interference with contract by unlawful means, its general features become clearer. There must be an intentional breach of contract induced by the defendant;[42] mere interference not bringing about a breach is actionable only under the tort of unlawful means. Equally, there is no cause of action under *Lumley v Gye* if a contracting party is persuaded to validly terminate the contract.[43] Liability in this situation would have to be sought under another tort such as conspiracy or injurious falsehood. So *Petree v Knox* (1917) 17 SR(NSW) 503[44] held there to be no liability under *Lumley v Gye* where the plaintiff's employer had lawfully terminated the plaintiff's contract on the persuasion of the defendant. However, if this had been as the result of a fraudulent misstatement, the action for injurious falsehood would have been available. The means used to persuade the contract breaker to commit the breach need not themselves be unlawful, though *Lumley v Gye* would lie also for unlawful persuasion. The action is not available to the contract breaker. Here again there is a difference between *Lumley v Gye* and the tort of unlawful means, since *Merkur Island Shipping Co v Laughton* [1983] AC 570 allows the action to either party where an interference with contract has been produced without there being a breach of that contract.

What amounts to inducement?

[19.110] Where the defendant's conduct takes the form of persuasion, the court must find that it has induced (that is caused) the contract breaker to break the contract. This may raise difficult questions of fact. Drawing a line between persuasion to break the contract

---

[42] *Northern Road Transport Motor and Horse Drivers and Their Assistants Industrial Union of Workers v Kawau Island Ferries Ltd* [1974] NZLR 617 (CA).

[43] See *Fightvision Pty Ltd v Onisforou* (1999) 47 NSWLR 473 where the New South Wales Court of Appeal reviewed the authorities and summarised the tort of interference with contractual relations.

[44] See also *Sanders v Snell* (1998) 196 CLR 329 – Minister's direction to terminate plaintiff's contract did not require that it should be terminated wrongfully.

and mere advice to do so is not helpful because it merely restates the issue as to causation. Where a contracting party has already decided to break the contract, it is not a wrongful inducement to accept a gift given in breach of the contract: *Batts Combe Quarry Ltd v Ford* [1943] Ch 51. Dealing with a party to the contract in the knowledge that if the deal goes through that party will commit a breach of contract is actionable; for example, a dealing with parties to contracts with the plaintiffs to buy cars from them, knowing this to be a breach of their contracts with the plaintiffs: *British Motor Trade Assoc v Salvadori* [1949] Ch 556.[45] On the other hand, in *Independent Oil Industries Ltd v Shell Co of Australia Ltd* (1937) 37 SR(NSW) 394 the court held there to have been no inducement where the defendants had merely indicated the terms on which they were willing to supply their petrol to retail petrol dealers, and that caused the dealers to break their contracts with the plaintiffs. In *James v Commonwealth* (1939) 62 CLR 339 it was held that a threat to prosecute common carriers of goods if they received the plaintiff's goods for carriage, the threat being made under an assertion as to the state of the law which was false but made in good faith, did not amount to conduct actionable under *Lumley v Gye*. The rationale of *James* is that it is against the public interest to find tortious liability on the part of a person who is threatening to prosecute another person on the strength of a genuinely held belief in the state of the law thought to justify prosecution. Dixon J assumed the *Lumley v Gye* principle would extend to inducing a breach on the part of the carrier of its normal public duty to carry goods brought to them for carriage.

Knowledge of contract on part of defendant

[19.115] As Dixon J observed in *James v Commonwealth* (1939) 62 CLR 339 at 370, malice is not an ingredient of *Lumley v Gye*. All that is necessary is "knowledge of the civil right or the facts from which it arises". The knowledge required of the defendant under the *Lumley v Gye* tort is greater than that required of the defendant under the tort of causing an interference with contract by unlawful means. Under the latter it is enough that the interference with contracts should be an inevitable inference on the facts known to the defendant. Neither the existence, nor the terms, of those contracts need be known. Under *Lumley v Gye* the defendant needs to intend to bring about a breach of contract, although it is clear that malicious intention is not required,[46] suggesting that both the existence and the terms of the contract need to be known.[47] As to the level of intention that a defendant must have, it seems that a "sufficient knowledge of the contract" will suffice even if the precise term breached is not known: *Allstate Life Insurance Co v Australia & New Zealand Banking Group Ltd* (1995) 58 FCR 26 at 43; *Film Financial Consultants Ltd v Becker Group Ltd* [2006] NSWSC 319. With respect to the motivation, the defendant may have been acting in good faith and still be liable. For example, where it is clear on the facts that the defendant intended to bring about a termination of the contract, the fact that the defendant thought it could be terminated lawfully does not operate as an excuse.[48] The same point emerges from *Greig v Insole*

[45] See also *National Foods Milk Ltd v McMahon Milk Pty Ltd* [2008] VSC 208 where Hargrave J accepted that the actions of McMahon Milk procured the breaches of non-competition provisions in their contract with National Foods and damaged the business interests of National Foods.

[46] *Zhu v Treasurer of NSW* (2004) 218 CLR 530 at 569-570; *Communications, Electrical, Electronic, Energy, Information, Postal, Plumbing and Allied Services Union of Australia v Corke Instrument Engineering Australia Pty Ltd* (2005) 223 ALR 480 at 485.

[47] See, for example, *British Industrial Plastics v Ferguson* [1940] 1 All ER 386; *Allstate Life Insurance Co v Australia & New Zealand Banking Group Ltd* (1995) 58 FCR 26.

[48] *Emerald Construction Co v Lowthian* [1966] 1 WLR 691.

[1978] 3 All ER 449 in which it was held that a general embargo on cricketers fulfilling their contractual obligations could not be excused on the basis that it was meant to apply only to those cricketers who could lawfully withdraw from their contractual engagements. On the other hand, in *Schindler Lifts Australia Pty Ltd v Debelak* (1989) 89 ALR 275 it was held that a supplier of lift maintenance services was not obliged to infer from the fact that a customer was already having its lifts serviced the continuing existence of a contract between the customer and the plaintiffs of which the supplier's dealing with the customer would bring about a breach. *H C Sleigh Ltd v Blight* [1969] VR 931 is a harder decision to defend. The defendant, at the time of entering into a contract for the purchase of a business, had no knowledge of the existence of a contract between the plaintiff and the vendor of the business for its sale to the plaintiff. He acquired such knowledge at the time when the contract was still voidable at his option. The defendant was held not liable for continuing with the contract.

Defence of justification

[19.120] The defence of justification is available in the case where the contract whose breach is induced by the defendant was inconsistent with and made in breach of an earlier contract made with the defendant. If A makes a contract with B to sell land for $100,000, and later contractually agrees with C to sell the same land for $120,000, B may lawfully induce a breach of A's contract with C.[49] The same applies where, even though there is no inconsistency with the earlier contract, that contract gives the defendant an equal or superior right to that of the plaintiff. In *Edwin Hill & Partners v First National Finance Corp* [1989] 1 WLR 225 the defendants had a mortgage on property of a developer who had contracted to employ the plaintiffs as architects. The development failed but the defendants, instead of exercising their power of sale under the mortgage (which would have validly terminated the plaintiffs' contract) joined as parties to the development but stipulated that the developer should employ a different architect. The defendants successfully pleaded justification to the plaintiffs' action based on *Lumley v Gye*: the power of sale gave them a right superior to that of the plaintiffs. It was found to make no difference that the defendants had adopted a proposal which did not require its exercise. In *Zhu v Treasurer of NSW* (2004) 218 CLR 530 the High Court confirmed that intentional interference with another's enjoyment of contractual rights generally results in liability for damages and will only be justifiable in cases where superiority is conferred by the proprietary nature of the right or found in statute.[50] The plaintiffs in *Zhu* had entered into a contract with the Olympic Club (TOC) to sell membership to Chinese nationals, the membership would be sold in conjunction with accommodation and transport services during the Sydney Olympic Games. Prior to the completion of the contract the Sydney Organising Committee for the Olympics (SOCOG) procured the termination of Zhu's contract. The main issue was whether SOCOG had just cause or excuse for its interference with Zhu's contractual relations with TOC. SOCOG had sought to justify its conduct on the basis that it had a "superior right" to the contractual rights of Zhu, alleging that its superior right was based in statute and in the fact that it had prior inconsistent contractual arrangements with TOC. The High Court held that not only did SOCOG not have the necessary statutory powers to justify its conduct, but that the prior arrangements between TOC and SOCOG did not amount to a legal

---

[49] On this point, see *Edwin Hill v First National Finance Corp* [1989] 1 WLR 225.
[50] For example, in *James v Commonwealth* (1939) 62 CLR 339, the superiority of right flowed from statute.

justification for the interference and that in the circumstances, SOCOG's conduct was not reasonably necessary in the circumstances.[51]

Cases like the above are clear enough in their principle, but the same cannot be said about *Brimelow v Casson* [1924] 1 Ch 302. This case held that justification was a defence to an action for breaches of contracts of employment of theatre actresses with the plaintiff, on the ground that he was paying such low wages that they were compelled to resort to prostitution. Of course if the main contract is void as being contrary to public policy there can be no successful action for inducing its breach, but that was not the case in *Brimelow*; the defence was of justification for terminating a valid contract. The case appears to rest on no secure basis.

Damage

[19.125] The tort requires proof of damage. Damage will not be presumed, but since the plaintiff must establish that through the breach he or she has suffered as a result of the loss of or interference with the contract, there will normally be little difficulty in proving damage.

Remedies

[19.130] The remedies are damages and/or an injunction, though the *Schindler Lifts* case suggested the further possibility of an account of profits made by the defendant. The plaintiff is entitled to damages for loss of profit that would have been made under the contract. This raises no theoretical difficulty over the award of an expectation measure of damages in tort. The plaintiff is entitled to be placed in the position as if the tort had not been committed. This necessarily involves compensation for the loss of profits arising from the contract. There seems no reason to doubt that aggravated or exemplary damages are capable of being awarded, the action being based on an intentional wrong.[52]

Appropriation of intellectual property rights: passing off

[19.135] Passing off is but one example of a number of torts by means of which the law recognises and protects a property in ideas or inventions, a so-called intellectual property right.[53] Other examples are rights of copyright, patent and rights in registered trade marks and designs. In all these cases, including passing off, the law provides a remedy against infringement by misappropriation through a tortious remedy by way of an action for damages and/or an injunction. An account of the various intellectual property rights other than passing off, however, is beyond the scope of this book, though

---

51   The High Court adopted the reasoning of Jordan CJ in *Independent Oil Industries Ltd v Shell Co of Australia Ltd* (1937) 37 SR(NSW) 394 at 415 where he had suggested that an act of interference may be justified "if shown to be no more than reasonably necessary for the protection of some actually existing superior legal right in the doer of the act". What is "reasonably necessary" can be answered by considering how a reasonable and prudent person or body in SOCOG's position would have behaved. In *Zhu's case* there was no reason why SOCOG could not have sought an injunction, corrective advertising or damages to enforce the rights that it relied on to justify its interference with the plaintiff's contractual rights.

52   *Whitfield v De Lauret & Co Ltd* (1920) 29 CLR 71 supports the availability of exemplary damages.

53   See generally McKeough, Stewart and Griffith, *Intellectual Property in Australia* (3rd ed, LexisNexis Butterworths, 2004).

an account appears at the end of this chapter of the statutory protection provided under s 52(1) of the *Trade Practices Act 1974* (Cth).

General features

[19.140] The tort of passing off recognises a right of property in matters such as the name, appearance or marketing get-up of the plaintiff's goods or services by protecting them against appropriation by another person.[54] The relevant date for determining whether a plaintiff has established the necessary goodwill or reputation of their product is the date of commencement of the conduct complained of: *Cadbury Schweppes Pty Ltd v Pub Squash Co Pty Ltd* [1981] 1 WLR 193 at 204, or when the passing off was first threatened: *Barnsley Brewery Co Ltd v RBNB* [1997] FSR 462, or whichever occurs first.

The classic case of passing off is where the defendant and plaintiff are in the same competitive field and the defendant in some way misrepresents its goods or services as those of the plaintiff. Passing off also protects against misappropriation by the defendant of the plaintiff's name or image where the defendant and plaintiff are not in the same competitive field. The second case of passing off exhibits differences of principle from the classic case and was once thought to be a merely analogous tort, rather than the tort of passing off itself. It now appears to be accepted that both situations fall within the one tort of passing off, a point brought out by the breadth of the definition of passing off provided by Lord Diplock in *Erven Warnink BV v J Townend & Son (Hull) Ltd* [1979] AC 731 at 742. In this case he identified the following as features of the tort of passing off (see Figure 19.8) (and these have been accepted in Australia: *Moorgate Tobacco Co Ltd v Philip Morris Ltd (No 2)* (1984) 156 CLR 414 per Deane J at 443-444; *ConAgra Inc v McCain Foods (Aust) Pty Ltd* (1992) 33 FCR 302 at 308-310 and *Betta Foods Australia Pty Ltd v Betta Fruit Bars Pty Ltd* [1998] ATPR 41-624 at 40,839 and 40,840):

Figure 19.8: General features of passing-off

- A misrepresentation:
  - made by a trader in the course of trade;
  - to prospective customers or ultimate customers of goods or services supplied by the trader;
  - which is calculated to injure the business or goodwill of another trader (in the sense that this is a reasonably foreseeable consequence); and
  - which causes actual damage to the business or goodwill of the trader by whom the action is brought or (in a quia timet action) will probably do so.[55]

---

[54] The tort of passing off is not limited to the name or trade mark of a product or business but encompasses other descriptive material such as slogans or visual images provided such descriptive material has become part of the goodwill of the product. "The test is whether the product has derived, from the advertising, a distinctive character which the market recognises": *Cadbury Schweppes Pty Ltd v Pub Squash Co Pty Ltd* [1981] 1 WLR 193 per Lord Scarman at 200.

[55] This statement has been accepted in this country: see *Moorgate Tobacco Co Ltd v Philip Morris Ltd (No 2)* (1984) 156 CLR 414 at 443-444; [1984] HCA 73 per Deane J; *Conagra Inc v McCain Foods (Aust) Pty Ltd* (1992) 33 FCR 302 at 308-310; and *Betta Foods Australia Pty Ltd v Betta Fruit Bars Pty Ltd* [1998] ATPR 41-624 at 40-839 and 40-840. However, there is some contradiction between the two last features. Clearly, the trader by whom the action is brought must be a person to whom damage is reasonably foreseeable under the second last feature (calculated to injure).

The definition clearly does not limit the tort to the case where the plaintiff and defendant are in the same competitive field. Notably, reference to misrepresentation does not mean that a verbal statement must be made by the defendant; in fact that would be an unusual type of passing off. The predominant method of committing the tort is by deceptive conduct: by imitating the plaintiff's goods or services in such a way as to misrepresent those of the defendant as being the plaintiff's, or to claim some connection with the plaintiff which does not exist. The range of conduct can, however, be broader than imitating the plaintiff's goods and, in *Campomar Sociedad, Limitada v Nike International Ltd* (2000) 202 CLR 45, the High Court recognised that the range of a defendant's conduct which could constitute passing off included inducing consumers to believe that the defendant's goods or services had an association, quality or endorsement which belonged, or would belong, to the goods or services of or associated with the plaintiff (at [88]-[89]).

There is no need for the plaintiff to establish that a substantial number of persons constituting a section of the public have suffered on account of the passing off: *ConAgra Inc v McCain Foods (Aust) Pty Ltd* (1992) 33 FCR 302; *Radio Corporation Pty Ltd v Henderson* [1960] NSWR 279 but it must be established that actual damage is caused to the trade of the plaintiff or that damage can be presumed to have occurred where there has been some misrepresentation or deception that falsely suggests some connection with another party's business.[56]

Passing off does not require fraud in the sense of a misrepresentation with knowledge of its falsity. Indeed the tort may operate as one of strict liability; that is, where there is a deceptive imitation of the plaintiff's goods or services, but the defendant neither knew nor ought to have known of it. However, knowledgeable imitation may be necessary in order to establish a right to substantial damages for the commission of the tort. The matter is not entirely clear on the authorities and is considered below. The matter is bound up with the question whether passing off is actionable only on proof of special damage (as Lord Diplock's definition above seems to require) or whether substantial damage may be presumed. This question is considered below.

Plaintiff and defendant in same field

Use of plaintiff's trade name

[19.145] Examples of this type of passing off are the successful actions brought to protect the trade name "Taco Bell" in New South Wales (*Taco Co of Australia Inc v Taco Bell Pty Ltd* (1982) 23 ALR 177) and "Yorkshire Relish" in England: *Birmingham Vinegar Brewing Co Ltd v Powell* [1897] AC 711. There is a general principle that names that are mere descriptions of the product are not protected. There is an exception to this principle where the description has become sufficiently and commonly identified with the plaintiff's goods. Thus in *Reddaway v Banham* [1896] AC 199 the plaintiffs were held to be entitled to succeed in an action for passing off as regards their description of their goods as "camel-hair belting". The courts are more willing to allow the plaintiff to succeed where the name, though descriptive, is formulated in a distinctive way. So in a number of decisions the plaintiffs have been found entitled to protect the trade name,

---

[56] The emphasis in a passing off action is usually upon damage to an interest in reputation rather than consumer protection. The latter is the focus of actions under ss 52 and 53(c) and (d) of the *Trade Practices Act 1974* (Cth).

"Budget Rent-a-Car": *BM Auto Sales Pty Ltd v Budget Rent a Car System Pty Ltd* (1977) 51 ALJR 254. On the other hand, the plaintiffs in *Hornsby Building Information Centre v Sydney Building Information Centre* (1978) 140 CLR 216 failed in an attempt to protect the phrase "Building Information Centre"; and in *New Zealand Natural Ice Cream Pty Ltd v Granny's Natural New Zealand Ice Cream Pty Ltd* (1990) 19 IPR 24 in their attempt to protect the name, "New Zealand Natural Ice Cream". As McKeough et al point out,[57] the defendants would arguably have been liable in *Hornsby* had they named their centre the "Sydney Building Information Centre" even if they were also operating in Sydney. This would be because, although they were entitled to describe their operation as a Building Operation Information Centre, they should do so to avoid confusion with another business using the same description, and which "got there first".

The converse case to that just considered is where a non-descriptive trade name for the product becomes common parlance for the type of product rather than the plaintiff's product. This is an unusual finding for a court to make. In the case on which the proposition rests, *Liebig's Extract of Meat v Anderson* (1886) 55 LT 206, the court found that the term "Liebig's extract" had become an accepted description of a particular process of meat extraction. It seems that the plaintiff had freely surrendered his rights to the term before it became generally adopted. On the other hand, the name "Laundromat" had not become associated in the minds of the public with any type of public laundering facility, at least at the time of the decision, so that the plaintiffs in *Westinghouse Electrical Corp v Thermoport Pty Ltd* [1968] WAR 39 were held not to be entitled to protect it.

Use of name specifically associated with product of particular region

[19.150] In *J Bollinger v Costa Brava Wine Co (No 2)* (1961) 1 WLR 277 the plaintiffs, who were producers of French champagne, were held to be entitled to protect the name "champagne" against the defendants who were producing a drink which they marketed as "Spanish Champagne". The ratio of the case was that the name "champagne" was associated exclusively with champagne produced in the Champagne region of France. That being so, any of the producers of champagne were entitled to protect the name against its use by producers outside that region which supports the view that a passing off action can be based upon a shared reputation. Also, the use of "Spanish" as a prefix was found to be insufficient to distinguish the defendants' own product and to prevent the public from being misled. Since *Bollinger* the passing off action has been used to protect the trade names in sherry (*Vine Products Ltd v MacKenzie* [1969] RPC 1) and Scotch Whisky (*John Walker & Sons v Henry List & Co Ltd* [1970] RPC 489), though the successful plaintiffs in *Bollinger* failed in an attempt to protect the name against the producers of Babycham, a drink described as "champagne perry" or "champagne cider", on the ground that there was sufficient differentiation of product to prevent the public being deceived: *HP Bulmer Ltd v J Bollinger SA* [1978] RPC 79.[58]

Use of name specifically associated with product of particular composition

[19.155] *J Bollinger v Costa Brava Wine Co (No 2)* [1961] 1 WLR 277 was approved and extended by the House of Lords in *Erven Warnink VB v J Townend & Sons (Hull) Ltd*

57 McKeough, above, n 53.
58 But see *Taittinger v Allbey Ltd* [1995] 4 All ER – defendants injuncted against selling "Elderflower Champagne", a non-alcoholic drink having no connection with the Champagne region.

[1979] AC 731. A producer of the drink, Advocaat, made from a mixture of eggs and spirits, was held to be able to protect that name against a person who sold under the same name a drink which they marketed as "Old English Advocaat" and which was made up from dried eggs and Cyprus sherry. The defendants would have been quite entitled to produce and sell Advocaat made in the traditional way. The gist of the complaint was that by introducing different ingredients they were able to undercut the plaintiff product; for example, sherry carried a lower tax rating than other spirits. *Warnink* was anticipated many years earlier by *Sales Affiliates Ltd v Le Jean Ltd* [1947] Ch 295, which must now be regarded as being approved. In that case, the plaintiffs marketed materials which were used in a permanent wave process known as "Jamal", and there was evidence in the trade that this was exclusively associated with the use of the plaintiffs' materials. They succeeded in passing off against the defendant hairdresser who had been describing a hair treatment as Jamal but was using other than the plaintiffs' materials.

Use of defendant's own name

[19.160] There appears to be an unqualified right for a person to trade in his or her own name as the description of the business being run, even though the effect of this is to create confusion with a business of the same name run by the plaintiff: *Joseph Rodgers & Sons Ltd v W N Rodgers & Co* (1924) 41 RPC 277. This is limited to the extent that where the name is capable of being expressed in such a way as to avoid confusion with that of the plaintiff, the defendant should do so: *Baume & Co Ltd v A H Moore* [1958] Ch 907. The liberty to trade in the defendant's own name does not extend to affixing that name to the defendant's product. Here it is clear that passing off is committed against a person who has acquired a prior right to describe the product under that name: *Parker v Knoll International* [1962] RPC 243; *Jenyns v Jenyns* [1927] St R Qd 313.

Imitation of appearance or get-up of plaintiff's goods

[19.165] The decision of the House of Lords in *Reckitt & Colman Products v Borden* [1990] 1 All ER 873 shows that imitation of the appearance of the plaintiff's product may be passing off where that appearance is sufficiently distinct and the plaintiff is able to show it has become specially associated with the plaintiff's product. In *Reckitt* the plaintiffs sold their lemon juice in lemon-shaped containers. There was evidence to show that the plaintiffs had originated this practice and that the appearance of the container had become associated in the minds of the public with the plaintiffs' lemon juice. The defendants were liable for selling their lemon juice in a similar container, even though they had taken other steps to distinguish their product from that of the plaintiffs.

Whether there can be an exclusive reputation in the use of a colour is open to question. In a dispute going back more than five years, Cadbury had objected to Darrell Lea's use of various shades of purple in its store signage, uniforms and products. In *Cadbury Schweppes Pty Ltd v Darrell Lea Chocolate Shops Pty Ltd* (2007) 159 FCR 397 at 418-419, an appeal from the decision of Heerey J in *Cadbury Schweppes Pty Ltd v Darrell Lea Chocolate Shops Pty Ltd (No 4)* (2006) 69 IPR 23, Black CJ, Emmett and Middleton JJ observed that the principles relating to passing off do not necessarily require a plaintiff to establish an exclusive reputation in relation to the use of a particular colour, in that case, purple. In their view the question was whether the plaintiff could establish facts that demonstrate that a particular use by the defendant of the colour was likely to mislead or deceive consumers into believing that there was relevant connection between the defendant and the plaintiff or their respective products. The matter was remitted back to Heerey J where he dismissed Cadbury's claims that Darrell Lea, in using the colour purple, had passed off it business or products as those of Cadbury: *Cadbury Schweppes Pty Ltd v Darrell Lea Chocolate Shops Pty Ltd (No 8) (2008)* 75 IPR 557; [2008] FCA 470. Conduct which resulted in mere confusion, or consumers being "caused to wonder", did not amount to conduct which could be considered as actionable passing off. See also *Woolworths Ltd v BP plc (No 2) (2006)* 154 FCR 97; [2006] FCAFC 132.

The *Reckitt* reasoning does not apply where the appearance of the product is inevitably dictated by the nature of the product itself. The High Court of Australia has gone further by holding that the plaintiff is unable to protect matters of the appearance or design of the product which are relevant to its functional efficiency even though the plaintiff is the first person to design the product in that way: *Puxu Pty Ltd v Parkdale Custom Built Furniture Pty Ltd (1980)* 43 FLR 405. So the maker of a more efficient cricket bat cannot protect it against imitators. This seems defensible: to hold otherwise would create an undesirable monopoly right and work against the interests of consumers. But it is necessary, as in *Parkdale* itself, that the defendant use other means to distinguish its product, for example by properly labelling it under its own name.

In *Cadbury Schweppes Pty Ltd v Pub Squash Pty Ltd* [1981] 1 WLR 193 the Privy Council held that in principle the plaintiff was able to protect the advertising and marketing features of the product against imitation by the defendant, while finding on the facts there was no likelihood of deception and so the action failed. The plaintiffs had marketed a drink called "Solo" which they sold in a yellow can with a medallion design, accompanied by an advertising campaign under which the drink was for "real men" and referred to a former drink which had been sold in pubs as pub squash. The defendants produced a similar lemon drink in a can of similar design, called it "Pub Squash" and advertised it under a similar campaign emphasising the virility of those to whom it would appeal. The Privy Council held that the action failed on the ground that there was no likelihood of confusion of members of the public as between the two products. The imitation practised here was quite blatant, and the question arises whether the defendant should be held liable, even in the absence of public deception, on the basis that making use of the plaintiffs' good idea is engaging in unfair competition, namely "reaping without sowing". The question is difficult but it is suggested that the answer should be "no". Although there may be support for the view that the defendant ought to pay a royalty to the plaintiff for use of the plaintiff's name or image where defendant and plaintiff are not in the same field of competition and there is no likelihood of any deception of the public, it hardly seems that the same treatment should be accorded to a mere marketing operation. Although American case law supports the idea of compensation on the basis of reaping without sowing,[59] the Australian High Court ruled against any general tort of unfair competition in *Moorgate Tobacco Co Ltd v Philip Morris Ltd (1984)* 156 CLR 414.

Extensions to normal passing off situation

[19.170] Some extensions to passing off in its classic form have been recognised. For example, it is passing off to sell the plaintiffs' footballs in such a way as to indicate

---

[59]   *International News Service v Associated Press* 248 US 215 (1918).

they were another type of football produced by the plaintiffs: *AG Spalding Bros v AW Gamage Ltd* (1915) 32 RPC 273. And also to sell champagne produced by the plaintiffs under forged labels suggesting the product was another type of champagne produced by the plaintiffs: *Champagne Heidsieck et Cie v Scotto* (1926) 43 RPC 101. The gist of the complaint here is not that business is being taken away from the plaintiff but that the plaintiff's business reputation and goodwill are likely to suffer (rendering dubious the decision in *Ingram v India Rubber Gutta Percha & Telegraph Co Ltd* (1903) 29 VLR 172 where the two products of the plaintiffs were to all intents and purposes equal in merit). Another extension is where the defendant sells the plaintiff's product in such a way as to imply that it is the defendant's, the case of so-called reverse passing off: *Testro Bros v Pennant* (1984) 2 IPR 469; *British Conservation Ltd v Conservatories Custom Built Ltd* [1989] RPC 455. There is also the case where the defendant claims for its goods and services a quality exclusively belonging to those of the plaintiff. An example is a representation that tests had been carried out on the defendant's goods which had only been carried out on the plaintiffs' goods: *Fuel Economiser Co Ltd v National School of Salesmanship Ltd* (1943) 60 RPC 290. Another is that the defendants' goods were "as shown on television", where only the plaintiffs' goods had been shown on television: *Copydex Ltd v Noso Products Ltd* (1952) 69 RPC 38. Under this line of authority, the earlier case of *Cambridge University Press v University Tutorial Press* (1928) 45 RPC 335 cannot be now supported in the context of passing off. It is not passing off to represent that the defendants' book had been prescribed for examination in the University of London, whereas only the plaintiffs' book had been prescribed.

Likelihood of deception

[19.175] In relation to the classic form of passing off, there must be a reasonable likelihood that members of the public will be deceived or confused by the misrepresentation. It is enough for the plaintiff to show that a significant section of the public is likely to be deceived, and in deciding this the court may advert to the particular characteristics of that section. So in *William Edge & Sons Ltd v William Nicholls Sons Ltd* [1911] AC 693 the packaging of laundry blue was found to be likely to confuse "washerwomen, cottagers and other persons in a humble station of life", even though the defendants' name was clearly marked on the package. In *Reckitt & Colman Products Ltd v Borden Inc* [1990] 1 All ER 873 the average member of the public was found to be capable of being deceived by the lemon shape of the container into thinking it was the plaintiffs' product, and it did not matter that there could have been no deception were that member "more careful, more literate or more perspicacious". *J Bollinger v Costa Brava Wine Co (No 2)* (1961) 1 WLR 277 also illustrates the point. No regular drinker of champagne would have been misled into thinking that Spanish Champagne was a product from the Champagne region of France, but the court found there to be a sufficient likelihood of deception of some members of the public to hold the defendants liable. A perhaps surprising decision is that in *Clark v Associated Newspapers* [1998] 1 All ER 959. The plaintiff was a politician and author of some notorious and scandalous diaries. The defendants parodied the diaries in their newspaper, presenting them under titles such as "Alan Clark's secret election diary" with an accompanying photograph of the plaintiff at the top. The overall effect was obviously enough a humorous spoof, particularly as the name of the parodist appeared in block capitals at the top of the diary. Nevertheless the defendants were held liable for substantial damages for passing off, on the ground that a substantial number of readers would have been deceived into thinking the plaintiff was the author. On the other hand, where the only sale by the plaintiff is to a specialist public, the plaintiff must establish the likelihood of confusion of that public. In *The Cricketer Ltd v Newspress Pty Ltd* [1974] VR 471 the English publishers of a magazine called *The Cricketer* were unable to succeed against the Australian publishers of a cricket magazine which they brought out in Australia under the same name. The English magazine sold only a small number of copies in Australia and it was unlikely that any of those persons would have been misled into buying the Australian magazine thinking it to be the English magazine.

Plaintiff and defendant not in same field

[19.180] The basis of this form of passing off differs from the ordinary case of passing off. The gist of the complaint is not that the defendant is taking business away from the plaintiff, but is causing the plaintiff loss by other means. The other means may take one of two forms:

- the implied association with the plaintiff or its product causes damage to the plaintiff's business reputation and goodwill; and
- the plaintiff is denied a fee for the defendant's making use of the plaintiff's name and reputation.

As regards the first form it is plain there must be the same element of deception in the tort as exists in the ordinary case of passing off. English decisions have refused to take passing off in this situation beyond this case, that is the deceptive claim of association with the plaintiff must cause or be calculated to cause harm to the plaintiff's goodwill. In *Associated Newspapers v Insert Media Ltd* [1990] 1 WLR 900 the defendants had inserted, without the permission of the plaintiffs, advertising material in newspapers published by the plaintiffs, the material being inserted at the retail level. The court granted the plaintiffs an injunction on the ground that this was calculated to harm the plaintiffs' business reputation since they strictly controlled the quality of advertisements placed in their newspapers, and did not wish to be seen by members of the public as approving the advertisements inserted by the defendants. Sometimes, however, courts have gone to great lengths to find damage to reputation, for example, finding in *Hilton Press v White Eagle Youth Holiday Camps* (1951) 68 RPC 126 that "Eagle" comics might be damaged by accidents at training camps. Where the plaintiff is unable to demonstrate this detrimental effect on reputation the action fails: *McCullough v May* [1947] 2 All ER 845.[60] In this case a well-known broadcaster was unable to restrain the use of his broadcasting name, "Uncle Mac", by the defendants who manufactured a cereal described as "Uncle Mac's Puffed Wheat".

Australian cases on the other hand have recognised the force of the argument that the plaintiff, if it is unable to charge a licensing or sponsorship fee for the defendant's use of its name etc is suffering a form of damage which the law should recognise and give compensation for. The case law follows the decision of the High Court in *Henderson v Radio Corp Pty Ltd* (1960) 60 SR(NSW) 576 where the use of a dancing group's pictures on records produced by the defendants was restrained by injunction, on the ground that to allow it to continue would deprive the group of an ability to

---

[60]   To similar effect: *Lyngstad v Anatas Products* [1977] FSR 62 (pop group); *Wombles Ltd v Womble Skips Ltd* [1977] RPC 99 ("Wombles of Wimbledon").

make profitable endorsements. *Henderson* has been followed in a number of decisions, for example *Nicholas v Borg* (1987) 1 PR 1 (defendant liable for using the term "Melbourne Cup" to describe a drink) and *LSK Microwave Advance Technology Pty Ltd v Rylead Pty Ltd* (1989) 16 IPR 107 (held to be passing off for a food manufacturer to use language in its promotional literature suggesting endorsement by the plaintiff, which conducted a school for cooking classes and produced recipe books). *Wickham v Associated Pool Builders Pty Ltd* (1988) 12 IPR 567 contradicts this line of authority, finding the defendants in that case not liable for calling their product "Tracy Wickham Swimming Pools".

Sometimes the action based on damage caused through deprivation of a licensing fee fails on the ground that the defendant's conduct is not calculated to deceive the public into thinking there is a connection between the plaintiff and the defendant's product (in the form of licensing or approving it): *Honey v Australian Airlines Ltd* (1990) 18 IPR 185. However, the position taken by Pincus J in *Hogan v Koala Dundee* (1988) 20 FCR 314 at 325; 83 ALR 187 at 198 rejecting this restriction seems the better one. The defendants had taken advantage of the publicity surrounding the film "Crocodile Dundee" to use various images taken from the film as a means of selling items of Australian souvenirs in their shops. Clearly the plaintiff, the leading actor in the film and the defendants were not in a common field of competition. Granting an injunction, Pincus J observed:

> The essence of the wrong done ... is not ... a misrepresentation that there is a licensing or sponsoring agreement between the applicant and the respondent. It is ... the wrongful appropriation of a reputation or, more widely, wrongful association of goods with an image properly belonging to the applicant.

Passing off in the *Henderson* situation has therefore moved away from being a truly tortious claim to becoming a proprietary one, its basis here not being the infliction of damage but the need to pay a fee for the unauthorised use of property.

In the case of passing off where plaintiff and defendant are not in the same field of competition, there is no requirement that the misrepresentation should be on a matter of trade or business. So a religious body is entitled to protect its name against an imitator: *Holy Apostolic & Catholic Church v Attorney-General* (1989) 18 NSWLR 291. Further, a society of accountants was held to be entitled to the protection of the action: *Australian Society of Accountants v Federation of Australian Accountants* [1987] ATPR 40-796. In cases like these the plaintiff must show that the misrepresentation is in some way calculated to cause it harm (in the absence of any possibility of showing economic detriment arising from the misrepresentation).

Establishing business reputation for purpose of suing

[19.185] There is a conflict of authority as to whether the plaintiff in a passing off case must show some actual trading on its part in the relevant jurisdiction, or whether it is enough that it possesses an established business reputation there at the time of the misrepresentation. One English first instance decision supports the former position (*Athlete's Foot Marketing Assoc Inc v Cobra Sports Ltd* [1980] RPC 343); another the latter: *Maxims Ltd v Dye* [1978] 2 All ER 55. The decision of the Full Federal Court in *Taco Co of Australia Inc v Taco Bell Pty Ltd* (1982) 43 ALR 177 required evidence of trading within the jurisdiction. Deane and Fitzgerald JJ ascribed this requirement to the need to prove damage, ignoring the fact that by refusing a remedy the plaintiff is rendered incapable of charging a licensing fee. The preferable view is that it should be enough for the plaintiff to prove it enjoys an established business reputation in the relevant jurisdiction without the need to show that it actually trades there: *ConAgra Inc v McCain Foods (Aust) Pty Ltd* (1992) 33 FCR 302.[61] This view is supported by cases that have allowed an injunctive remedy to companies which have been formed recently where they have been able to establish a sufficient reputation to establish a likelihood of damage. In *Fletcher Challenge v Fletcher Challenge Pty Ltd* [1981] 1 NSWLR 196 the plaintiff company, whose formation from three previous companies had been announced amid widespread press and television publicity, was held to be entitled to an interlocutory injunction against the defendant company which adopted the same name within hours of the announcement. In *Turner v General Motors (Aust) Pty Ltd* (1929) 42 CLR 352 the plaintiff was held to be entitled to injunctive relief where it had widely advertised its intention to operate under the name, "General Motors", and the defendant began to operate under that name, even though at the time of his doing so the plaintiffs had not commenced business in the relevant area. However, in *Hansen Beverage Company v Bickford's (Australia) Pty Ltd* [2008] FCA 406 relief was denied to both parties as neither was able to establish to the satisfaction of the court the required reputation to satisfy their claims. The court found that both Hansen and Bickford's had only just commenced the development of a reputation in Australia and it cannot be assumed in a market where the product has not previously been sold or directly advertised that either party had established a sufficient reputation in the relevant market that warranted protection. The court affirmed the decision in *ConAgra Inc v McCain Foods (Aust) Pty Ltd* (1992) 33 FCR 302 that it was sufficient if the applicant establishes a reputation in a jurisdiction. The evidence necessary or sufficient to found a case for passing off includes factors such as high volume of sales, extensive advertising and product promotion. Given that the court must be satisfied, on the balance of probabilities, as to existing reputation, the lack of appropriate evidence concerning the reputation of either Hansen or Bickford's products in Australia did not provide a proper basis for Middleton J to find that Hansen had established sufficient reputation in Australia at the relevant date.

Damage and remedies

[19.190] As to whether there is a need to prove damage in order to be able to claim substantial damages for passing off, there is a degree of conflict in the authorities on two issues. The first is whether substantial damages may ever be awarded against an innocent passer off. The view that fraud is necessary, in the sense of "persistence after notice", is supported by Australian authority (*Hogan v Koala Dundee Pty Ltd* (1988) 83 ALR 187 at 201) but runs contrary to opinions expressed by the Court of Appeal in the English decision of *Draper v Trist* [1939] 3 All ER 513. But that case has been explained in Australia on the basis that the defendant had consented to an inquiry to be made as to damages: see *Petersville Sleigh Ltd v Sugarman* [1988] VR 426 per Phillips J. The second question is whether, assuming the case to be one in which substantial damages may be awarded, damage may be presumed or needs actual proof. The need for proof of damage is supported by the definition of passing off given by Lord Diplock in *Erven*

---

61   For support, see *Dominion Rent A Car Ltd v Budget Rent A Car System Ltd* (1987) 9 IPR 367.

Warnink BV v J Townend & Son (Hull) Ltd [1979] AC 731. But damages were not an issue in that case, so the authority provides weak support for the need to prove damage, though it was used by O'Brian J to support his view in *Petersville* that the plaintiff must prove actual damage in order to be awarded damages. The ratio of *Petersville*, common to all three judges, is that damage will not be presumed in a case where the plaintiff and defendant are not in competition with each other. *Draper* provides clear support for the view that damage may be presumed by the court in the classic passing off situation. In that case, Lord Greene MR referred to the difficulties that having to prove actual damage would present to a plaintiff. A loss of business generally or a loss of particular customers might be accounted for by alternative explanations. In the case itself substantial damages of UK£2,000 were awarded on the basis of a presumption of damage.

The other remedies in the case of passing off are the injunction and the claim for an account of profits. The injunction is by far the most common form of relief sought in passing off actions. However, an account of profits is seldom sought by plaintiffs, no doubt on account of the difficulties of proof it would present. A defendant has to account for, and is then stripped of, profits which have dishonestly been made by the infringement and which it would be unconscionable to retain. Its purpose is not to punish but to prevent unjust enrichment.

Removal of Beaudesert tort

[19.195] In *Beaudesert SC v Smith* (1966) 120 CLR 145 at 156 the High Court held that a person who suffered harm or loss as the "inevitable consequence of the unlawful, intentional and positive act of another" was entitled to claim damages for a tort. The case was considered in a number of later Australian cases, in all of which it was distinguished from the factual situation in those cases. It was held to form no part of English[62] or New Zealand law[63] by decisions in those jurisdictions. The High Court in *Northern Territory v Mengel* (1995) 185 CLR 307 at 344 overruled its earlier decision in *Beaudesert* and found that the principle on which it was based forms no part of Australian law. One of the tort's chief functions might well have been the protection of the interest in economic welfare or security. But with its removal that protection must be sought within the other torts considered in this chapter.

Trade Practices Act s 52

Figure 19.9: Section 52(1) TPA

- A person (ie principally a corporation);
- shall not in trade or commerce engage in conduct;
- that is misleading or deceptive.

---

62   *Lonrho Ltd v Shell Petroleum Ltd (No 2)* [1982] AC 173 at 187-188.
63   *Takaro Properties Ltd v Rowling* [1978] 2 NZLR 314 at 339; *Van Camp Chocolates Ltd v Aulsebrooks Ltd* [1984] 1 NZLR 354 at 359.

[19.200] Section 52(1) of the *Trade Practices Act 1974* (Cth) provides that a person shall not in trade or commerce engage in conduct that is misleading or deceptive. The relevant test of whether conduct is misleading or deceptive is an objective test and involves a question of a finding of fact to be determined in light of the evidence of the impugned conduct. The original Commonwealth legislation was limited to corporations, but State legislation has extended its scope to persons generally.[64] Taken together with s 82(1) of the Act which allows a person to sue for loss or damage caused by conduct falling within s 52(1), the effect is the creation of a statutory tort which either extends or reproduces the common law liability under torts considered in this chapter. There are two exclusions from liability under s 52(1). Section 65A excludes from the ambit of s 52(1) and the other provisions of Div 5 of the Act prescribed information providers such as newspapers and other media, except insofar as such a provider is attempting to market its own product or property. Section 51AF excludes the operation of s 52(1) in relation to the provision of financial services, which is covered by different legislation. Although s 52(1) appears within a Division of the Act entitled "Consumer Protection", its availability is not limited to consumers. Indeed one of the most fertile grounds for its enlistment has been actions between rival traders.

Trade or commerce

[19.205] This remains a limiting factor after the States' extension of the Commonwealth provision to persons other than corporations. The literal interpretation of this limitation could lead to the position that the extent of s 52(1) and its State equivalents was vast, applying whenever the defendant or its servants or agents was engaging in some commercial activity. However, in *Concrete Constructions v Nelson* (1990) 169 CLR 594 the majority of the High Court held that the section must be read down to cover *only* dealings in trade or commerce, not activities in the *course* of trade or commerce. In that case, a supposedly negligent instruction given to a workman on a building site was not given in trade or commerce. The giving of a speech by a Minister in which he sought to allay fears that the price of wool would fall was not given in trade or commerce: *Unilan v Kerin* (1993) 44 FCR 481.[65] Private house sales are not made in trade or commerce: *Franich v Swannell* [1993] 10 WAR 459.[66] But the sale of a business is: *Bevanere v Lubidineuse* (1985) 7 FCR 325.

Misleading or deceptive

[19.210] *Taco Co of Australia Inc v Taco Bell* (1982) 42 ALR 177 and *McDonald's v McWilliams Wines* (1979) 41 FLR 476 have shown that the nature of the conduct falling within s 52(1) must be such that it constitutes a misrepresentation inducing a mistaken belief in the mind of the public or the relevant section of it (whether or not this includes the plaintiff). The end result may be described as causing confusion, but merely to cause confusion is not enough. The confusion must result from misleading or deceptive

---

[64]   The State and Territory statutes are universally termed *Fair Trading Act*, except in the Northern Territory where the statute is the *Consumer Affairs and Fair Trading Act 1990*.

[65]   See also *Tobacco Institute of Australia v Woodward* (1993) 32 NSWLR 559 – public statement on behalf of lobby group opposed to the sale of cigarettes not made in trade or commerce.

[66]   But sale of a unit by a vendor/builder was in trade or commerce: *Demagogue Pty v Ramensky* (1992) 39 FCR 31.

conduct. Thus in *McDonalds* the appellation "Big Mac" applied to one of McWilliams' wines was not conduct within s 52(1) since, although it might have caused confusion in the minds of consumers who jumped to the conclusion that there was some connection with the product of McDonalds, there was no deceptive conduct sufficient to induce the consumer into that belief. In *Cadbury Schweppes Pty Ltd v Darrell Lea Chocolate Shops Pty Ltd (No 8)* (2008) 75 IPR 557; [2008] FCA 470 Heerey J was not convinced that a hypothetical ordinary and reasonable member of the class constituted by prospective purchasers of chocolate would be misled or deceived by the colour of a chocolate wrapper. Again, in *Parkdale Furniture v Puxu* (1982) 149 CLR 191 the High Court held that the defendants who had produced and marketed furniture which was strikingly similar to that produced by the plaintiffs (though only in its functional characteristics) were not responsible for misleading the consumer. Their product was properly labelled, and they could not be held responsible for retailers' displaying of the furniture without the labels clearly showing.

Relevant public and member of public

[19.215] Where the plaintiff alleges that the defendant's product is misleadingly creating confusion in the minds of the public with the plaintiff's product, the plaintiff must establish its presence in the area of operation of the defendant's product. The plaintiffs failed on this issue in *Dairy Vale Metro v Browne's Dairy* (1981) 54 FLR 243 in that, although they were able to prove similarity between the defendants' yoghurt containers and their own and the use by the defendants of similar advertising campaigns, they were unable to show any presence of their product in Western Australia where the defendants' product was sold (the applicant was too late into the market by 48 hours). In *Taco Co of Australia v Taco Bell* (1982) 42 ALR 177 a Sydney company of the name "Taco Bell", which had established a local reputation in Sydney for the sale in its Bondi restaurant of Mexican food, was held to be entitled to succeed against an American multinational which sought to use the same name for its sale of Mexican food in Sydney and elsewhere in Australia. The overseas reputation of the American company was not sufficient to defeat the claims of the Sydney company in the Sydney market.

The nature of the target audience is relevant to a determination of whether information is deceptive or likely to mislead. Some types of consumer may be expected to be knowledgeable and discerning, with the result that where the product is aimed specifically at that sort of consumer there is no misleading or deceptive conduct. In *Crago v Multiquip* [1998] Aust Torts Reports 41-620 the court found that the purchaser of incubators for ostriches would be expected to have some degree of sophistication and awareness of what successful breeding required; similarly in *Parkview (Keppel) v Mytarc* [1984] Aust Torts Reports 40-486 — relevant section of public among which brochure would be distributed was travel agents, who would not be misled by its contents. This may be the situation even where there is a broader audience, as was the case in *Cadbury Schweppes Pty Ltd v Darrell Lea Chocolate Shops Pty Ltd (No 8)* [2008] FCA 470 where it was found that the hypothetical ordinary and reasonable member of the class constituted by prospective purchasers of chocolate would not be misled or deceived by the colour of a chocolate wrapper. On the other hand, it may be necessary to protect the "ignorant, the unthinking, the credulous", as demonstrated by *Finucane v NSW Egg Corp* (1988) 80 ALR 486. (In this case the plaintiff misled into buying a contract carrier "run" was able to rely on s 52(1) even though the court regarded him as impetuous and gullible.) Gibbs CJ in *Parkdale Furniture v Puxu* (1982) 149 CLR 191 attempted to objectify the relevant standard as one pertaining to the reasonable member of the relevant class. There is some conflict here which awaits an authoritative resolution.

Nature of liability

[19.220] The common law notion of misrepresentation covered only positive misstatement as to present fact. Failure to state some fact could not be a misrepresentation unless it was coupled with other misleading conduct or statements. Misstatements of the general law, statements as to future conduct, and statements of opinion were excluded from the category of common law misrepresentation, unless there was fraud. Conduct within s 52(1) is wider than the common law notion of misrepresentation. Misstatements as to the general law are certainly included. But there is an unresolved issue as to whether mere silence can constitute misleading or deceptive conduct, and there are special rules concerning statements of future intent and of opinion.

There is, however, no doubt that where the conduct falls within the s 52(1) definition, liability for it is strict. Neither the proof of knowledgeable intent nor negligence is necessary to establish liability: *Parkdale Furniture v Puxu* (1982) 149 CLR 191 per Gibbs CJ at 197; *Hornsby Building Information Centre v Sydney Building Information Centre* (1978) 140 CLR 216 per Stephen J at 223.

Silence

[19.225] A mere failure to state some fact, even a material fact, does not necessarily constitute conduct falling within s 52(1). There must be more in the circumstances of the case, making the failure misleading or deceptive. Attempts to rationalise the law as to whether silence is misleading or deceptive in terms of whether the plaintiff has a reasonable expectation that a statement will be made or that the defendant has a duty of disclosure, seem merely to restate the problem.[67] Further, although omission to do something is within the definition section of conduct in s 4(2)(c) of the Act, provided it is not inadvertent, this is a mere definition section and does not tell us in what circumstances silence is misleading or deceptive. In most of the cases in which failure to state something has been held to be actionable, there has been something more than mere silence on the part of the defendant. In *Henjo Investments v Collins Marrickville* (1988) 79 ALR 83 a statement that a restaurant could seat 128 people was misleading and deceptive in that the restaurant licence allowed only 84 to be served. It is not necessary that the person misled should have made his or her own inquiries and that had they done so, it would have revealed the true position. In this case the restaurant was also displayed to the purchaser with the larger number of places, an additional reason for finding deceptive conduct. In *Demagogue Pty v Ramensky* (1992) 39 FCR 31 a vendor of land was held liable for failing to reveal that the land had no vehicular access to it. But in this case there was also a misleading statement on the matter by the vendor's agent, and the plan in the agent's office showed there to be a driveway leading to the land. In *Finucane v NSW Egg Corp* (1988) 80 ALR 486 the plaintiff who had purchased "a run" to become a contract carrier for the defendants' products had been told that there were reorganisations to be made in relation to contract carriers, but not

---

[67] This was the ground relied on in *Henjo Investments v Collins Marrickville* (1988) 79 ALR 83.

that this was likely to affect him on the "last in, first out" principle. This was held to be misleading and deceptive conduct. The court in *Franich v Swannell* [1993] 10 WAR 459 held that in principle a failure by a vendor to disclose defects in the house prior to sale was misleading and deceptive, but the vendor escaped liability on the ground that the sale was not in trade or commerce. Here, again, there seems to have been something more than mere silence. A report on the condition of the property had been made available at a previous auction sale, at which the property was passed in, but was not made available to the plaintiff. *Henjo* may be contrasted with *Rhone-Poulenc Agrichimie SA v UIN Chemical Services* (1986) 12 FCR 477, in which it was held that a failure to disclose by the seller of a fungicide that it was not registered under State law and that sale of it would therefore be illegal was not misleading or deceptive. *Crisp v ANZ Bank* [1994] Aust Torts Reports 41-294 stands out as a case where mere silence qualified as misleading or deceptive conduct. A failure by a bank manager, who had obtained guarantees of a person's indebtedness, to disclose that he had previously dishonoured cheques drawn by that person on the bank was conduct falling within s 52(1).

The defendant's failure to speak must be inadvertent. In *Costa Vasca Pty Ltd v Berrigan Weed & Pest Control Pty Ltd* (1998) 155 ALR 714; [1998] FCA 693 an answer to a question about what chemicals a crop spraying machine had been exposed to, which failed to mention the use of a particular chemical, was in principle misleading or deceptive, but no liability existed for it since the omission was inadvertent.

Statements of future intent and predictions

[19.230] At common law, statements of future intent were not actionable as misrepresentations, but only as contractual promises. However, where the intention was not held by the representor at the time of speaking, this was a misrepresentation of fact which was actionable as deceit. This matter is now governed by s 51A(1) of the *Trade Practices Act*. Where a person makes a representation with respect to any future matter (including doing or refusing to do any act) and that person does not have reasonable grounds for making the representation, it shall be taken to be misleading. Under s 51A(2) the defendant has the burden of showing that there were reasonable grounds for the making of the representation. There is therefore a statutory negligence liability. The subsection is not limited to statements of intent. It also covers representations as to future matters in general, including contractual promises: *Futuretronics v Gadzhis* [1990] ASC 56-009.

Reasonable grounds are tested at the time of making the representation. In *Lyndel Nominees v Mobil Oil* (1997) 37 IPR 599 a Mobil executive made a speech at a company conference in which he stated that franchisees who reached a certain level of performance would have their franchises automatically extended. A change of policy caused the company to change its mind on this point, but there was no liability under s 52(1) since the executive had reasonable grounds for the statement at the time it was made.[68] Conversely, in *McPhillips v Ampol Petroleum* [1990] Aust Torts Reports 41-014 the plaintiff had been induced to buy a franchise by virtue of a statement that it would be subject to automatic renewal. This was actionable on the basis that it had been made without reasonable grounds.

---

[68] See also *Cream v Bushcolt Pty Ltd* [2002] ATPR 41-888; [2002] WASC 100 – where the statement at the time it was made was honestly held and based upon reasonable grounds, the statement is neither misleading nor deceptive.

Statements of opinion

[19.235] Again, these were generally excluded from common law misrepresentation unless the opinion was not genuinely held. This was due both to the fact that the truth of matters of opinion was difficult to test, and that a mere expression of opinion was not reasonably relied on. Opinions are not as such excluded from s 52(1), but the fact that an expression of opinion turns out to be wrong does not mean that it is misleading or deceptive. In *Saints Gallery Pty Ltd v Plummer* (1988) 80 ALR 525 the defendants' art gallery proprietor had sold four paintings on the defendants' behalf to the plaintiff. The proprietor expressed the belief that, by virtue of what he had been told by the person from whom he acquired the paintings, they were by well-known Australian artists. The proprietor was known by the respondent to have no professional skill in identifying paintings, whereas the respondent was a professional valuer and art dealer. The paintings were forgeries. The proprietor was found not to have been guilty of misleading or deceptive conduct as there was no express or implied acceptance of responsibility. The proprietors stood in the position of an intermediary or conduit between the owner and the respondent, who, like the appellant, did not check the owner's assertions and assumed them to be true. The outcome would have been different if the proprietors could be shown to have done, or purported to have done, anything other than explain what the owner had claimed to be the facts. For example, the particular representations relied on about the paintings were specifically representations as to their authenticity.

On the other hand, an honest expression of opinion may be actionable not on the basis that it proves to be untrue but that it was made without due care. This was the basis of liability imposed on a valuer at first instance in *MGICA v Kenny & Good* (1996) 70 FCR 236. Hodgson J found liability to exist under s 52(1) on the part of the valuer on the basis that the valuation carried with it an implied representation that it was made on reasonable grounds and was the product of due care and skill. This matter was not contested in the later appeals. Liability for opinions is therefore based on negligence, and seems likely to be limited to expert opinions.

Disclaimers and exclusion clauses

[19.240] Section 52(1) imposes a mandatory liability for misleading and deceptive conduct and its operation cannot be defeated by any form of disclaimer, contractual or otherwise: *Henjo Investments v Collins Marrickville* (1988) 79 ALR 83. The effect of a disclaimer may be to render conduct not misleading or deceptive. In *Sony Music Australia v Tansing* [1993] Aust Torts Reports 41-271 the release of unauthorised recordings of Michael Jackson's songs was marked "Unauthorised" in several places and was found not to fall within s 52(1).

Remedies

[19.245] There are three remedies available to the person complaining of misleading or deceptive conduct under s 52(1) or the making of a representation without reasonable grounds under s 51A(1). Section 80 of the *Trade Practices Act* provides the remedy of an injunction against the conduct. As always in the case of an injunction the remedy is discretionary. Section 82(1) provides the remedy of a claim for damages where a person has suffered loss or damage "by" the misleading or deceptive conduct. Section 87 allows the making of various discretionary orders, including an order for rescission of a contract and one for the payment of compensation for loss or damage resulting from the conduct.

The plaintiff under s 82(1) needs to establish only a causal connection between the conduct and the loss or damage suffered. There is no need to show that it was reasonably foreseeable. In a number of cases the plaintiff, in order to establish causation, will need to show reliance on the conduct in question. There is no need to show that the reliance is reasonable or reasonably foreseeable: these issues are embraced in the determination whether the conduct is misleading or deceptive: *Sykes v Reserve Bank of Australia* [1999] ATPR 41-699. Damages will generally be based on the tort measure already considered in relation to negligent misstatement. The plaintiff is put into the position it would have been in had the defendant's conduct been other than misleading or deceptive; not the position it would be in if statements made to the plaintiff were true (the so-called contractual expectation measure). In *Gates v City Mutual Life* (1986) 160 CLR 1 the plaintiff had been induced to buy an insurance policy by virtue of a statement that it covered him against certain injury, that statement being untrue. When that injury occurred he was therefore without cover against it. Nevertheless his damages claim against the insurance company, based on the loss of the amount of cover that would have been available had the statement been correct, failed. An award of that sort of damages would have been to apply the expectation measure. Since the insurance policy was worth what he paid for it, no loss or damage had been proved for which damages were available. *Gates* assumes that had the plaintiff been told the truth he would simply have kept his money. Had he attempted to convince the court that he would instead have sought insurance cover against the injury which occurred, then damages based on that forgone opportunity could have been awarded, as the success of the plaintiff in a later decision demonstrates: *Warnock v ANZ Banking Group Ltd* [1989] ATPR 40-928. However, in the absence of an alternative available transaction meeting the plaintiff's demands, the plaintiff (as in *Gates*) will be unable to establish any loss, given that an expectation measure of damages is not available. This was the position in *Marks v GIO Australia Holdings Ltd* (1998) 196 CLR 494 in which borrowers had been told by the lender that the interest rate was fixed, whereas the terms of the borrowing allowed for some variation. Since better borrowing terms were not available elsewhere, the borrowers' claim for damages failed. The issue of recovery of damages for consequential losses caused by market falls is dealt with in Chapter 12.

Exemplary damages may not be awarded under s 82(1) since they are not intended to compensate for damage caused: *Musca v Astle Corp* (1988) 80 ALR 251. But damages for injury to feelings have been awarded for conduct within s 52(1), and one of the cases seems to go beyond the availability of such damages for breach of contract.[69] The damages sought under s 52(1) are usually for financial loss, but "damage" in s 82(1) is clearly wide enough to cover physical injury or damage.

Comparison of s 52(1) with other torts

[19.250] The overall limitation on s 52(1) that it applies only to conduct in trade or commerce obviously does not affect the common law torts. Apart from that, the

---

[69]   *ACCC v Top Snack Foods* [1999] FCA 752 – in awarding damages to misled franchisees for anxiety and distress the case goes beyond contractual principles; *Holloway v Witham* (1990) 21 NSWLR 70 complies with contractual limitations in awarding damages for distress, since there was a factor of physical inconvenience caused by the misleading conduct.

statutory liability has the clear advantage over deceit and injurious falsehood that it does not require proof of a wrongful intent. It has the advantage over negligence that it may operate as a tort of strict liability, though we saw that for liability to arise in the case of statements as to future matters and statements of opinion, negligence is required, and liability for silence cannot apply where the silence is inadvertent. Substantively it appears there is very little difference between the common law tort of passing off, now extended to cover cases where plaintiff and defendant are not competitors (the "character appropriation" situation) and the statutory liability under s 52(1). The common law tort has some advantages over the statutory liability. In the classic passing off situation where plaintiff and defendant are in competition, the court will presume damage, whereas under s 52(1) it must be proved. The statutory remedies available do not include an account of profits, which is a useful remedy for passing off. Damages for passing off will not, however, be awarded against an innocent defendant; whereas there is no reason why such a claim should not succeed under s 52(1), where the plaintiff can prove damage.

Practice Questions

Revision Questions

19.1 List and discuss the requirements that must be established in the tort of deceit.

19.2 How does the tort of injurious falsehood differ from that of defamation and what are the consequences for a plaintiff of the distinction? Discuss.

19.3 Can a person incorporate an effective disclaimer clause into a contract with another person and avoid the operation of the *Trade Practices Act 1974* (Cth)?

Answers to Practice Questions

Revision Questions

20.1 Discussion should centre around the elements necessary to establish the tort of deceit including:

- the defendant makes a false statement or engages in conduct amounting to a statement (what is a false statement? fraudulent statements of intention, of opinion or of law are actionable as deceit);

- with knowledge of its falsity or being recklessly indifferent to its truth (note the difficulty in the plaintiff establishing a fraudulent intention on the part of the defendant, leading to the plaintiff alleging negligence in the alternative);

- intending that the plaintiff or a class of persons including the plaintiff should act on it; and

- the plaintiff acts on the statement and suffers loss as a result (although there is no need for the statement to be made to the plaintiff personally, provided the plaintiff is a person intended to act on the statement).

19.2 Injurious falsehood resembles the tort of defamation in that each involves a false and harmful imputation concerning the plaintiff and is made to a third party. They differ in that the law of defamation protects an interest in the plaintiff's personal reputation while injurious falsehood protects an interest in the disposability of the plaintiff's products, property or business.

For a plaintiff the consequences of the differences between the two actions are significant. A defamation action is generally actionable per se, falsehood is presumed and liability is strict. In the case of injurious falsehood, the onus is on the plaintiff to establish that he or she sustained actual economic loss, that the offensive statement was false and that it was made by the defendant with the intention of causing injury to the plaintiff without lawful justification.

19.3 Section 52(1) of the *Trade Practices Act 1974* (Cth) imposes a mandatory liability for misleading and deceptive conduct. Its operation cannot be defeated by any form of disclaimer (contractual or otherwise) although it is possible to render conduct not misleading or deceptive: see, for example, *Sony Music Australia v Tansing* [1993] Aust Torts Reports 41-271.

Tutorial Questions

Discussion Questions

19.1 Compare and contrast the statutory liability with other torts.

19.2 Discuss the remedies available to the person complaining of misleading or deceptive conduct under s 52(1) or the making of a representation without reasonable grounds under s 51A(1) of the *Trade Practices Act 1974* (Cth).

19.3 The tort of passing off can be considered an effective instrument of economic regulation as well as a consumer protection weapon. Discuss.

CHAPTER 20

Misuse of Legal Powers

Reading

Fleming, *The Law of Torts,* Chapter 27.

Objectives

This chapter will explain:

- tort of malicious prosecution;
- tort of malicious institution of civil proceedings;
- tort of malicious use of legal process;
- the factors that go to establishing the torts; and
- the defences and remedies available.

Principles

Introduction

[20.05] A number of torts protect against an abuse of legal process that inflicts damage on the plaintiff. These are the torts of malicious prosecution, malicious institution of civil proceedings, malicious use of legal process (such as malicious arrest), and the tort generally identified as abuse of legal process. This chapter contains an account of each of these torts. It also considers the extent to which judges may be held liable in tort for erroneous decisions, and the tort of misfeasance in public office. Two concepts relevant to this area are the torts of maintenance and champerty. Maintenance means the provision of support for the plaintiff or defendant in a civil action, usually by financing it. Champerty constitutes an agreement to share the proceeds of a successful action; thus they both involve support of a legal action in which the supporter has no interest. These torts are of declining importance as both are subject to numerous exceptions[1] and have been abolished in Victoria, the Australian Capital Territory, New South Wales and South Australia: see *Wrongs Act 1958* (Vic), s 32; *Civil Liability (Wrongs) Act 2002* (ACT), s 221; *Maintenance, Champerty and Barratry Abolition Act 1993* (NSW); *Criminal Law Consolidation Act 1935* (SA), Sch 11. In the context of the funding of a legal action the practice of contingency fee arrangments (under which the solicitor charges a fee only in the event of success in the action) is of residual relevance only as the recent model legal profession Acts have prohibited such arrangements unless the costs agreement adopts an applicable costs determination.[2]

Figure 20.1: Torts protecting against misuse of legal powers

- Malicious prosecution.
- Malicious institution of civil proceedings.
- Malicious use of legal process.
- Abuse of legal process.

Malicious prosecution

[20.10] It is a tort to maliciously cause a prosecution to be brought against another person. A prosecution is deemed to be actuated by malice where there is no reasonable cause for bringing the prosecution, where the prosecution has terminated in the plaintiff's favour, and where the plaintiff has suffered damage as a consequence. The High Court clearly enunciated the elements of malicious prosecution in *A v State*

---

[1] For example, funding of action by an insurance company or a trade union; cases of common interest, for example, the members of a particular trade or profession, or a group of manufacturers of a product funding an action by one member. Legal aid is a statutory form of maintenance.

[2] *Legal Profession Act 2006* (ACT), s 285; *Legal Profession Act 2004* (NSW), s 325; *Legal Profession Act* (NT), s 320; *Legal Profession Act 2007* (Qld), s 325; *Legal Profession Act 2007* (Tas), s 309; *Legal Profession Act 2004* (Vic), s 3.4.29; *Legal Profession Act 2008* (WA), s 285. As at September 2008, the *Legal Practitioners Bill* (SA) was still before Parliament.

of New South Wales (2007) 230 CLR 500 (per Gleeson CJ, Gummow, Kirby, Hayne, Heydon and Crennan JJ at [1]):

> *For a plaintiff to succeed in an action for damages for malicious prosecution the plaintiff must establish: (1) that proceedings of the kind to which the tort applies (generally, as in this case, criminal proceedings) were initiated against the plaintiff by the defendant; (2) that the proceedings terminated in favour of the plaintiff; (3) that the defendant, in initiating or maintaining the proceedings acted maliciously; and (4) that the defendant acted without reasonable and probable cause.*

There has been significant judicial discussion concerning the nature of malice and this has involved a consideration of the distinct, but closely aligned, concept of reasonable and probable cause along with the nature of the belief a prosecutor should entertain in order to justify the laying of a charge. This discussion has given rise to some conflicting authorities. According to Jordan CJ in *Mitchell v John Heine & Son Ltd* (1938) 38 SR (NSW) 466, the question is whether a prosecutor believes that the accused is probably guilty, while Dixon J in *Sharp v Biggs* (1932) 48 CLR 81 and *Commonwealth Life Assurance Society Ltd v Brain* (1935) 53 CLR 343 suggested it was enough to defeat a claim of absence of reasonable and probable cause if a prosecutor believed that the probability of the guilt of the accused was such that, upon general grounds of justice, a charge was warranted. The High Court in *A v New South Wales* (2007) 230 CLR 500 at [40] confirmed that each of the elements serves a different purpose and remains separate, yet did little to reconcile these earlier conflicting authorities. The majority did, however, acknowledge that the absence of reasonable and probable cause may, in a given case, be evidence of malice (but this will not always be the case).

The formidable series of obstacles the plaintiff must surmount in order to succeed in this tort are accounted for by reason of the public interest in ensuring that prosecutors should not be readily deterred from bringing a case to court (though the same requirements apply to the malicious institution of civil proceedings where it might be thought that the public interest against the action being brought was less paramount).[3] The plaintiff, who has the burden of proof on all these issues, must show both a wrongful state of mind on the part of the defendant *and* also an objective lack of strength in the prosecution case. However, the plaintiff's burden on both issues is generally discharged by showing an absence of honest belief on the part of the prosecutor in the plaintiff's probable guilt of the charge for which the prosecution was brought or that the prosecutor did not honestly form the opinion that there was a proper case for prosecution (*A v New South Wales* (2007) 230 CLR 500 at [118]): see [20.25].

Figure 20.2: Malicious prosecution – general principles

To succeed in a tort for malicious prosecution, the plaintiff must show:
- a prosecution was initiated against the plaintiff by the defendant;
- termination of the prosecution in the plaintiff's favour;
- absence of reasonable and probable cause;
- evidence of malice on the defendant's part; and
- actual damage suffered.

---

[3] *Commonwealth Life Assurance Society Ltd v Brain* (1935) 53 CLR 343 at 379.

Prosecutor and prosecution

[20.15] The action in malicious prosecution is brought against the prosecutor, that is the person who "instituted or continued" the proceedings (*Wan v Sweetman* (1998) 19 WAR 94 at 101), otherwise referred to as any person who is "actively instrumental" in instituting legal proceedings: *Danby v Beardsley* (1880) 43 LT 603 per Lopes J. "Who was the prosecutor?" is a question of fact and depends on the circumstances of the case. Of course, the person who actually conducts a case is termed the prosecutor, but it can just as easily be a person who counsels or persuades the prosecutor to prosecute or procures a prosecution by dishonest means or false information. An example of the latter can be found in *Noye v Crimmins* [2002] WASC 106 which was based upon a claim that the defendant had "induced" the complaints via "wilfully false representations" to a police officer (at [5]). Thus it is possible for a lay informant to be regarded as a prosecutor where it can be established that he or she wanted and intended the prosecution, that the facts were so peculiarly within their knowledge that it was virtually impossible for the professional prosecutor to exercise any independent discretion or judgment and that proceedings were commenced by the professional prosecutor through either furnishing information which was known to be false or by withholding information which was known to be true (or both): *Mahon v Rahn (No 2)* [2000] 1 WLR 2150. A person who has merely given information about a crime to the police as a result of which the police later decide to prosecute is not regarded as a prosecutor: *Evans v London Hospital and Medical College* [1981] 1 All ER 715 (in this instance the employees in a hospital's forensic medicine department gave results of a postmortem to police, who charged the plaintiff with murder, but the malicious prosecution failed because the police had decided independently of those results to charge the plaintiff with murder). The position was held to be different where such a person had sworn an information of felony against the plaintiff: *Avery v Wood* (1872) 2 QSCR 4.[4] Even where the information given to the police may be construed as an instruction to arrest the plaintiff, this will not be interpreted to mean that a person is a prosecutor in a prosecution launched by the police, in the absence of an authority given to prosecute: *Maine v Townsend* (1882) 4 ALT 122. And a person who actually prosecuted was found not to be the prosecutor where he had been directed to prosecute by the Attorney-General: *Zeplin v North German Insurance Co* (1880) 1 LR(NSW) 321.

The question of what is a prosecution is sometimes concerned with how far the proceedings need to have gone in order to constitute a prosecution. The answer in general appears to be that once the court or magistrate has begun to inquire into the merits of the case, then a prosecution has commenced, because at that point the possibility of damage to the plaintiff's reputation is established: *Mohamed v Banerjee* [1947] AC 322.[5] It is different if the court has dismissed the prosecution for the absence of its jurisdiction in the matter: *Mohamed* at 331. On the other hand, where the court has, in excess of its jurisdiction, begun to inquire into the merits of the case, this has been held to be sufficient to constitute a prosecution: *Arnold v Johnson* (1876) 14

---

[4] Compare, however, the decision of the House of Lords in *Martin v Watson* [1995] 3 WLR 318 in which false information given by the defendant to the police leading to the plaintiff's prosecution rendered the defendant a prosecutor. On the facts, the police could not have tested the information and therefore exercised no independent discretion in prosecuting the plaintiff.

[5] This will be so even where the prosecutor himself withdrew the charge, though only after the magistrate had begun to hear the matter: *Casey v Automobiles Renault* [1965] SCR 607; see also *Martin v Watson* [1995] 3 WLR 318 – sufficient prosecution even though the prosecution offered no evidence.

SCR(NSW) 429. Whilst it has been recognised that internal disciplinary hearings can do serious harm to the reputation of an individual, the courts have declined to extend the definition of prosecution to include administrative proceedings: *Noye v Robbins* [2007] WASC 98 (internal police disciplinary hearings not prosecution) and *Gregory v Portsmouth City Council* [2000] 1 AC 419 (House of Lords unanimously held that malicious prosecution is limited to criminal proceedings and certain civil actions and does not extend to internal disciplinary proceedings – in this instance investigation of the activities of a councillor).

Termination of prosecution in plaintiff's favour

[20.20] The obvious case is an acquittal of the plaintiff on the merits of the case, but the law goes well beyond this in its decisions on the point. For example, there is termination in the plaintiff's favour where a conviction is quashed for technical reasons, such as a misdirection to the jury by the trial judge, or for a defect in the indictment: *Wicks v Fentham* (1791) 4 TR 247. A refusal by a magistrate to commit the plaintiff for trial also counts as a favourable termination as does discontinuance of the prosecution by the prosecutor before verdict: *Balbhaddar Singh v Badri Sah* (unreported, PC 66/1924); *Commonwealth Life Assurance Society Ltd v Smith* (1938) 59 CLR 527 at 535-536 (obiter); *Martin v Watson* [1995] 3 WLR 318.

There is, however, some doubt regarding the effect of the filing of a nolle prosequi (decision not to proceed with the prosecution). The High Court decision in *Davis v Gell* (1924) 35 CLR 275 that the Attorney-General's entering of a nolle prosequi stopping the prosecution did not constitute favourable termination is flatly contradictory to the later High Court case of *Commonwealth Life Assurance Society* which held that the Attorney-General's refusal to file an indictment amounted to such termination, and with earlier and later Australian authority: *Gilchrist v Gardiner* (1891) 12 LR (NSW) 184; *Mann v Jacombe* (1960) 78 WN (NSW) 635; *Taylor v Shire of Eltham* [1922] VLR 1. *Davis* seems contrary to principle. This contradiction was addressed by Heenan J in *Noye v Robbins* [2007] WASC 98. His Honour acknowledged that the filing of the nolle prosequi places the accused person in a powerless position as they are unable to achieve a "more favourable outcome" (at [238]). He concluded that such a result "constitutes as much of a favourable termination" as was possible in the circumstances (at [242]) but noted that the conclusion was equivocal of innocence. The question then became one of whether or not the filing of the nolle prosequi was sufficient, on its own, to amount to a termination in the plaintiff's favour. In this instance his Honour was able to look to extrinsic evidence such as the statements of the plaintiff, the pleadings against the plaintiff and, most significantly, the demeanour of Ms Crimmins, the main source of evidence against the plaintiff (she was described as contrived, manipulative and greatly prejudiced, at [249]).

On the other hand, there was held to be no favourable termination where the magistrate held that the offence had been proved against the plaintiff but then dismissed the information under the rule concerning first offenders: *Cameron v James* [1945] VLR 113. Though the plaintiff has been acquitted in the trial, the prosecutor/defendant is allowed to present evidence of the plaintiff's guilt in the civil proceedings for malicious prosecution, on the ground of the relevance of this evidence to whether there was reasonable cause for the prosecution: *Earnshaw v Loy* [1959] VLR 248.

Absence of reasonable and probable cause

[20.25] The phrase, "reasonable cause", is sometimes referred to as reasonable and probable cause, but the word "probable" is archaic and adds little to the meaning. Reasonable cause embraces two questions. First, whether the prosecutor had an honest belief in the plaintiff's liability on the strength of the facts known to the prosecutor. Secondly, if so, whether the facts on which the prosecution case was based constituted reasonable cause for bringing the prosecution: *Hicks v Faulkner* (1878) 8 QBD 167 per Hawkins J at 171; *Herniman v Smith* [1938] AC 305 per Lord Atkin at 316. There is, therefore, both a subjective and an objective aspect to the question. It is settled law that to establish an absence of honest belief in liability on the prosecutor's part is enough to establish absence of reasonable cause, since it would be "outrageous" to hold that a defendant who was both malicious and had no honest belief in the plaintiff's liability should escape liability, even if the facts viewed objectively might raise a reasonable suspicion of that liability: *Haddrick v Heslop* (1848) 12 QB 268 per Lord Denman CJ at 274. As we shall see, the absence of an honest belief as to liability on the defendant's part is normally also sufficient for the courts to infer malice on the part of the defendant. Further, the matter of honest belief is a question for the jury; whereas the general question of whether there was reasonable cause for the prosecution is for the judge, not the jury[6] (on the ground that juries through sympathy for the plaintiff would be very reluctant to find there was reasonable cause in a case in which the plaintiff was acquitted): *Leibo v Buckman* [1952] 2 All ER 1057 at 1062-1063. However, the judge controls the issue as to whether there is sufficient evidence of absence of honest belief for the matter to be put to the jury.[7] And the prosecutor need only be found to have had an honest belief in the fact that there was a sufficient case to launch a prosecution against the plaintiff, not a belief that a conviction would be secured: *Tempest v Snowden* [1952] 1 KB 130 at 137; *Glinski v McIver* [1962] AC 726 at 760-761, 767-768.

An early case ruled that the defendant did not have reasonable cause for bringing the prosecution where the plaintiff had given him an explanation consistent with the plaintiff's innocence and the defendant had failed to test the truth of this: *Jenner v Harbison* (1879) 5 VLR (L) 111. In the case itself, the plaintiff had explained that he had come into possession of the defendant's property by acquisition from a third party. The court found that since this story was easily proved by questioning the third party, there was no reasonable cause for the prosecution where the defendant had not done this. In a later case (*Turner v Wright* (1880) 6 VLR (L) 273) the court found there to have been no need for the defendant to have tested the plaintiff's information before prosecuting in order to establish reasonable cause, and a requirement such as this seems out of line with modern society in which inquiries of this sort are best left to the police (though this is not to deny a possible need to refer the matter to the police before prosecuting).

That leads to the next question, which is the relevance of the defendant having obtained advice before prosecuting. Logically, this seems relevant only to the issue of the prosecutor's belief in the plaintiff's liability, rather than to the question of whether the facts viewed

---

6   *Panton v Williams* (1841) 2 QB 169; *Lister v Perryman* (1870) LR 4 HL 521; *Herniman v Smith* [1938] AC 305 at 316-317; *Mitchell v J Heine* (1938) 38 SR (NSW) 466 at 470-471.

7   There is a right to jury trial in actions for malicious prosecution in all States, except South Australia: *Juries Act 1927* (SA), s 5. The Australian Capital Territory also excludes jury trial: *Supreme Court Act 1933* (ACT), s 14. In Western Australia the *Supreme Court Act 1935*, s 42 provides that a court or judge may order a trial without a jury where documents or accounts or any scientific or local examination cannot conveniently be made with a jury.

objectively constitute reasonable cause for the prosecution (even on the issue of honest belief the evidence would not be conclusive). English cases have tended to regard this evidence as sufficient to determine the issue in the defendant's favour on both questions; for example, where the defendant obtained counsel's opinion before prosecuting (*Abbott v Refuge Assurance Co Ltd* [1962] 1 QB 432), or that of his superiors in the legal department of Scotland Yard (*Glinski v McIver* [1962] AC 726 per Viscount Simonds at 745), or even the advice of a police officer: *Malz v Rosen* [1966] 1 WLR 1008. Recent Australian authority on this question is lacking, though in *Cheney v Bardwell* (1899) 20 LR (NSW) 401 the court found that the taking of advice of a barrister or solicitor constituted evidence of reasonable cause; whereas in *McCaffrey v Hill* (1903) 3 SR (NSW) 303 Simpson GB thought this to be relevant only to the issue of malice rather than to that of reasonable cause. In *McCaffrey* the court also took the view that the taking of the advice of a police officer prior to prosecution is relevant to neither issue, a position supported by *Assheton v Merrett* [1928] SASR 11. The decision in *Mackenzie v Hyam* (1908) 8 SR (NSW) 587, that the advice of a solicitor to prosecute for an offence not known to the law could not be used to establish reasonable cause, seems open to question.

The issue of reasonable and probable cause was most recently considered by the High Court in *A v State of New South Wales* (2007) 230 CLR 500, in the leading judgment of Gleeson CJ, Gummow, Kirby, Hayne and Crennan JJ. Their Honours emphasised the forensic difficulty of proving a negative (that is, the *absence* of reasonable and probable cause) (at [60]) and reiterated the subjective and objective elements of the question: what the prosecutor made of the material and what the prosecutor *ought* to have made of the material (at [70]). The judgment distilled the discussion down to three "critical points" (at [77]): these are set out at Figure 20.3.

Figure 20.3: Absence of reasonable and probable cause – three critical points

- It is a negative proposition that must be established;
- That proposition may be established in either or both of two ways:
  - the defendant prosecutor did not "honestly believe" the case that was instituted or maintained; and/or
  - the defendant prosecutor had no sufficient basis for such an honest belief.
- The critical question is: what does the plaintiff demonstrate about what the defendant prosecutor made of the material that he or she had available when deciding whether to prosecute or maintain the prosecution?

Malice

[20.30] Proof that the prosecutor acted without reasonable and probable cause is not enough on its own to establish the tort of malicious prosecution; the plaintiff must also demonstrate the presence of malice. The line between lack of reasonable and probable cause and malice is sometimes blurred with the existence (or lack) of the former evidencing the presence of malice: *A v State of New South Wales* (2007) 230 CLR 500. In this instance the majority of the High Court cautioned that "no little difficulty" arises if what constitutes malice is related to what will suffice to demonstrate absence of reasonable and probable cause (at [90]). But in recognising that there are common elements to establishing the presence of malice and the absence of reasonable and probable cause, the High Court explained (at [90]) that "no universal rule relating to proof of the separate elements can or should be stated".

Malice in general means a wrongful or improper purpose in bringing the prosecution, that is the "dominant purpose of the prosecutor must be a purpose *other* than the proper invocation of the ... law": *A v State of New South Wales* (2007) 230 CLR 500 at [91]. This may be established by showing spite or vindictiveness on the part of the prosecutor towards the plaintiff, but cases turning on this form of malice are unusual, since feelings of anger or a spirit of vengeance arising out of the commission of the crime itself are not sufficient to constitute malice but are the very feelings "on which the law relies to secure the prosecution of offenders".[8] One leading means of establishing malice is to show an improper, collateral purpose for the bringing of the prosecution. But the purpose must be one of which the law disapproves. Thus, there was no malice where the prosecutor prosecuted without reasonable cause a person he found to be in possession of his property, thinking this to be necessary to establish title to the property (*Assheton v Merrett* [1928] SASR 11); nor where the prosecution was brought in order to establish the right to bring civil proceedings, because of the rule that in the case of felony the criminal proceedings must precede the civil: *Abbott v Refuge Assurance Co Ltd* [1962] 1 QB 432. Improper purpose has been found in cases where the prosecution was brought in order to silence the plaintiff in other legal proceedings (*Haddrick v Heslop* (1848) 12 QB 267; 116 ER 869), or to punish him for having given evidence against the police in earlier proceedings (*Glinski v McIver* [1962] AC 726 per Viscount Simonds at 745), or to prevent the holding of a meeting of shareholders: *Commonwealth Life Assurance Society Ltd v Brain* (1935) 53 CLR 343 at 387, or in response to pressure from an external agency: *A v State of New South Wales* (2007) 230 CLR 500. In cases of improper purpose of this sort, the tort may be difficult to distinguish from the tort of abuse of process (see [20.50]) under which it is a tort to use a legal process for a purpose other than that for which the process is designed in order to gain an advantage from the plaintiff. If the case fits within the requirements of the latter tort, there is no need to show malice on the defendant's part nor absence of reasonable cause for the use of the process.

An inference of malice may be drawn where the defendant is shown to have no honest belief in the plaintiff's guilt: *Mitchell v J Heine* (1938) 38 SR(NSW) 466; *Haddrick*. That this justifies an inference of malice rather than providing conclusive evidence of it is shown by *Rapley v Rapley* (1930) 30 SR(NSW) 94. A son had his mother committed to an asylum as an insane person wandering at large. The son had no honest belief in the facts on which the committal was based, but escaped liability on the ground that he had considered his action necessary for the protection of the mother's property, and therefore was not malicious.

In general, however, malice is an almost conclusive inference from the prosecutor's absence of honest belief in the plaintiff's guilt. Malice may also be inferred when the facts, viewed objectively, do not show any reasonable cause for the bringing of the prosecution. In such a case the court may impute feelings of spite or ill-will towards the plaintiff: *Trobridge v Hardy* (1955) 94 CLR 147 at 163-165, 174.[9] Although in

---

[8] Fleming, *Law of Torts* (3rd ed, LBC Information Services, 1998) p 685.
[9] See also *Lutich v Walton* [1960] WAR 109 – malice inferred where arrest was procured for a non-existent offence.

these situations malice may be inferred from the absence of reasonable cause for the prosecution, the reverse process is not possible. Where actual malice on the defendant's part towards the plaintiff is found, the court may not infer from this absence of reasonable cause: *Glinski*; *Mitchell* at 474 (containing a lucid statement as to when malice may be inferred).

In a jury trial, malice is a question of fact, answered by a jury; whereas the issue of whether a particular purpose is improper is a question of law, to be answered by a judge. The question of whether there is sufficient evidence of malice to be left to the jury is also a question of law.

Damage

[20.35] The plaintiff in malicious prosecution must prove actual damage in order to establish the cause of action. The plaintiff may do this under one of three heads. These are injury to reputation, injury to the plaintiff's person or property, and injury to the plaintiff's pecuniary interests: *Saville v Roberts* (1698) 1 Ld Raym 374; *Berry v British Transport Commission* [1961] 1 QB 149. With respect to reputation, the charge brought against the plaintiff must be necessarily defamatory of the plaintiff. The fact that it could have defamatory overtones (that is, is capable of being understood in a defamatory sense) is not enough. Malicious prosecution is narrower than defamation itself. So in *Berry* a prosecution for having pulled a train's emergency cord was found not to be defamatory of the plaintiff in the necessary sense. This differed in the case of a prosecution for having travelled by train without paying the fare: *Rayson v South London Tramways Co* [1893] 2 QB 304.[10] The only form of injury to the plaintiff's person normally relevant in cases of malicious prosecution is that arising from imprisonment should the charge be proved. The mere existence of imprisonment as a possible penalty for the offence seems to be sufficient: *Houghton v Oakley* (1900) 21 LR(NSW) 26; *Wiffen v Bailey & Romford VDC* [1915] 1 KB 600. The pecuniary loss recoverable by the plaintiff in an action for malicious prosecution is generally the legal costs incurred in defending the charge, though pecuniary loss emanating from the defamatory imputation of the charge brought is also recoverable. In relation to legal costs, the plaintiff is entitled to full reimbursement, in the absence of any power to award costs residing in the court in the criminal proceedings (and semble to any excess of costs over any amount awarded to the plaintiff out of public funds).[11]

Once the plaintiff has succeeded in proving harm, damages in malicious prosecution are at large in the sense that aggravated damages may be awarded for feelings of distress arising from the prosecution. The awarding of damages has been described as subject only to the condition that the damages must not be "grossly disproportionate to the losses or injury sustained": *Noye v Robbins* [2007] WASC 98 at [755]. This matter is clearly settled for the closely analogous tort of malicious institution of civil proceedings: *Coleman v Buckingham's Ltd* [1964] NSWR 363 at 373. There is no reason to doubt that malicious prosecution is governed by the same rule. There is a doubt whether damages are at large where the plaintiff is able to establish damage only under the third head, that is, for pecuniary loss.[12]

---

10   Compare *Wiffen v Bailey & Romford VDC* [1915] 1 KB 600 – notice requiring landlady to clean rooms not necessarily defamatory.

11   *Berry v British Transport Commission* [1961] 1 QB 149. Apparently it makes no difference that the court may have awarded the accused part of the defence costs out of public funds. The reader may note that the accused in a criminal trial will virtually always be able to establish damage under the third head.

12   Left open in *Coleman v Buckingham's Ltd* [1964] NSWR 363 at 373.

Malicious institution of civil proceedings

Figure 20.4: Malicious institution of civil proceedings – general principles

> To succeed in a tort for malicious institution of civil proceedings,
> the plaintiff must show:
> - absence of reasonable cause;
> - evidence of malice on the defendant's part;
> - termination of the proceedings in the plaintiff's favour; and
> - actual damage.

[20.40] The action for malicious institution of civil proceedings is now recognised as a tort in Australia.[13] As in malicious prosecution the plaintiff must show malice, absence of reasonable cause, termination of the proceedings in the plaintiff's favour and damage. There was at one time doubt as to the scope of this form of liability, confining it to the malicious institution of bankruptcy proceedings and the bringing of a petition for the winding up of a company.[14] However, the majority decision of the Victorian Full Court in *Little v Law Institute of Victoria* [1990] VR 257 showed that this doubt related not to the availability of the action but as to whether the plaintiff could ever establish damage as the result of civil proceedings being wrongfully instituted against him. It is true that civil proceedings differ from criminal in that there is never any possibility of the plaintiff being imprisoned as a result of them and the defendant, if successful, is entitled to be awarded the costs of defending them through an order made by the court. However, the court exposed as fallacious the former attempt to distinguish the two sets of proceedings on the basis that civil as opposed to criminal proceedings could never affect the plaintiff's reputation, on the ground that in the case of civil proceedings "the poison and the antidote are presented simultaneously": *Little v Law Institute of Victoria* [1990] VR 257 at 281, adopting the words of Buckley LJ in *Wiffen v Bailey & Romford VDC* [1915] 1 KB 600 at 607. That is, the defendant's reputation will be cleared, if it deserves to be, by the trial of the action. The idea that civil proceedings will not attract publicity undesirable to the defendant prior to trial and resolution of the action was found to be out of touch with modern reality. In particular, the case of a solicitor, who had an injunction issued against him to stop him practising and then was committed for contempt of court for disobeying the injunction, would be likely to attract considerable publicity before the action was tried. Also, the period of three weeks' detention in prison for contempt of court would damage his pecuniary interests arising from his inability to conduct his professional practice.

The position of the plaintiff as to claiming damages for the costs of the defence is less satisfactory than in the case of malicious prosecution. It appears that where the trial

---

[13] *Houghton v Oakley* (1990) LR(NSW) 26; *Coleman v Buckingham's Ltd* [1964] NSWR 363; *Jervois Sulphates (NT) Ltd v Petrocarb Explorations NL* (1974) 5 ALR 1; *Little v Law Institute of Victoria* [1990] VR 257. However the tort is not yet clearly established in England: *Metall & Rohstoff AG v Donaldson Lovkin Inc* [1989] 3 All ER 14 at 51 – "we have great doubt whether any general tort of maliciously instituting civil proceedings exists", and in *Gregory v Portsmouth City Council* [2000] 1 AC 419 the House of Lords stated that in English law "the tort of malicious proceedings is not at present generally available in respect of civil proceedings. It has only been admitted in a civil context in a few special cases of abuse of legal process."

[14] *Johnson v Emerson & Sparrow* (1871) LR 6 Exch 329 – bankruptcy proceedings; *Quartz Hill Gold Mining Co v Eyre* (1883) 11 QBD 674 – winding up petition.

judge has power to make an order for costs in the defendant's favour, the liability for costs is not recognised as a head of damage in the action for the malicious institution of civil proceedings: *Houghton v Oakley* (1900) LR(NSW) 26. This ignores the fact that the costs awarded will be taxed costs not full costs, and thereby deprive the plaintiff of a right to full reimbursement of costs in defending an action found to have been brought against the plaintiff maliciously and without reasonable cause. The matter is different where the trial judge has no power to award costs. Here, as in the case of malicious prosecution, the full costs of defending the action may be awarded as damages: *Coleman v Buckingham's Ltd* [1964] NSWR 363. This was extended in *Jervois Sulphates (NT) Ltd v Petrocarb NL Explorations* (1974) 5 ALR 1 – the legal costs of bringing certiorari proceedings were recognised as damage, on the ground that the trial judge had not considered the matter of costs and had made no order in respect of it.

Malicious process and malicious arrest

Figure 20.5: Malicious process and malicious arrest – general principles

It is a tort to use legal process (other than legal proceedings in court) against the plaintiff:
- maliciously;
- without reasonable cause; and
- thereby causing the plaintiff damage.

[20.45] The action in malicious use of process and malicious arrest is a close relation to the two actions just considered; it manifests their features as *applied to legal process* rather than legal proceedings in court. The process usually complained of is one under which the defendant has obtained an order for the plaintiff's arrest. Where such an order has been obtained through the use of legal process, an action for false imprisonment is not available as it is based upon a lawful justification and lacks the requisite directness. The interposition of legal process makes it indirect, and the person arrested must therefore show that the order has been obtained maliciously and without reasonable cause.[15] The High Court in *Varawa v Howard Smith Co Ltd* (1911) 13 CLR 35 pointed out a difference between the action for malicious prosecution or institution of civil proceedings, and malicious arrest. In the case of the latter, there is no requirement that the process should terminate in a manner favourable to the plaintiff if it is incapable of so terminating. The court differed, however, as to the application of this principle to an arrest on mesne (intermediate) process. Griffith CJ and O'Connor J held that the mesne process being in the nature of an ex parte procedure could not terminate favourably to the plaintiff: Griffith CJ (at 55-56) and O'Connor J (at 69-71). Isaacs J thought (at 91-92) that it could, since the plaintiff could take proceedings to have it set aside. The majority view received support in *Smith v Cotton* (1927) 27 SR(NSW) 41.

---

[15]   For the differences between false imprisonment and malicious prosecution see Chapter 5.

It is not a tort to swear false evidence in court causing the plaintiff damage: *Hargreaves v Bretherton* [1959] 1 QB 45. The fact that this was done maliciously and without reasonable cause makes no difference. Equally, a conspiracy to present perjured evidence is not actionable in tort: *Cabassi v Lila* (1940) 64 CLR 130. It is in the public interest that witnesses should be free of the pressure of a threat of further legal action when giving evidence. In a proper case a prosecution for perjury may be brought. Where the defendant has committed a tort of malicious use of legal process, and the use of that process was obtained by false evidence, there is no exemption from liability. So, in *Coleman v Buckingham's Ltd* [1964] NSWR 363 at 373, where an action for the malicious institution of civil proceedings contained an allegation that evidence of the malicious purpose was provided in part by the swearing of a false affidavit, the plaintiff was not thereby precluded from success in the action. Similarly, in *Roy v Prior* [1970] 1 QB 283 the plaintiff was allowed to proceed in an action for malicious arrest in circumstances in which he claimed that a warrant for his arrest was obtained by the defendant's swearing of false evidence.

Abuse of legal process

Figure 20.6: Abuse of legal process – general principles

In an action for abuse of legal process, the plaintiff must show:
• the use of process to gain some collateral advantage; and
• that he or she suffered damage as a result.

[20.50] The torts previously considered in this chapter all require the abuse of a legal process. The tort specifically referred to as abuse of legal process, though it has affinities with those torts, differs from them in a number of important respects. The tort was established and applied in the ancient case of *Grainger v Hill* (1838) 132 ER 769 and its existence has been confirmed in a number of Australian decisions.[16]

In *Grainger* the defendant obtained a writ of "capias ad respondendum" for the plaintiff shipmaster's arrest for non-payment of a mortgage debt owed to the defendant by the plaintiff. The purpose of the defendant was found to be not to obtain payment of the debt but to compel the plaintiff to surrender the ship's register to the defendant. The plaintiff, succumbing to the pressure exerted by the capias, surrendered the register with the consequence that, being unable to put to sea without the register, he suffered financial loss. The court held that the plaintiff was entitled to recover damages for this loss by suing in tort. It found that the basis of the tort was the use of a legal process to achieve a purpose for which it was not designed in order to inflict damage on the plaintiff. The action did not require proof of absence of reasonable cause or termination

---

[16]   The High Court first recognised the tort's existence in *Varawa v Howard Smith & Co* (1911) 13 CLR 35; see now *Hanrahan v Ainsworth* (1990) 22 NSWLR 73; *QIW Retailers v Felview* [1989] 2 Qd R 245; *Williams v Spautz* (1992) 107 ALR 635. English law continues to recognise the tort: *Speed Seal v Paddington* [1985] I WLR 1327; *Metall & Rohstoff v Donaldson Lufkin Inc* [1989] 3 All ER 14.

of the process in the plaintiff's favour, distinguishing the torts of malicious prosecution and malicious civil proceedings on these grounds. The plaintiff had claimed that the mortgage debt was not due for repayment at the time it was claimed, but the ground on which the decision is based makes this fact irrelevant. Indeed, the making of a knowingly false legal claim or defence is not enough to establish the cause of action if the purpose designed to be achieved is that for which the claim or defence exists: *Metall & Rohstoff v Donaldson Lufkin Inc* [1989] 3 All ER 14. However, an absence of belief in the claim or defence must clearly be relevant to whether it is made for an improper purpose.

In order to succeed in the action for abuse of process the plaintiff must therefore show the use of the process to gain some collateral advantage (that is, other than that of winning the action) and that damage has been sustained by the plaintiff in consequence. Examples of this apart from *Grainger* are the use of defamation proceedings against a Royal Commissioner to stifle the Commissioner's public inquiry (*Packer v Meagher* [1984] 3 NSWLR 486); the bringing of criminal defamation proceedings against another member of the university in order to secure an academic's reinstatement (*Williams v Spautz* (1992) 107 ALR 635); and the bringing of an action for conspiracy against a person in order to pursue a private vendetta against that person and to vilify him (*Lonrho v Fayed (No 5)* [1991] 1 WLR 1489). The claim that proceedings are abusive may be raised as a defence, as in *Packer* and *Williams*. In such a case, if the defence succeeds, the claim is simply struck out and there is no need for the defendant to show any damage to itself as a result of the proceedings: see also *Goldsmith v Sperrings* [1977] 1 WLR 478. However, there is no rule that the defendant must raise the claim as a defence rather than bring a separate tort action in respect of it: *Hanrahan v Ainsworth* (1990) 22 NSWLR 73. Nor is there any requirement that the allegedly abusive proceedings should have terminated before the tort claim is brought: *Hanrahan*. An abusive defence is as capable as an abusive claim of giving rise to an action in tort if it inflicts damage on the plaintiff: *Hamer-Matthew v Gulabrai* [1994] 35 NSWLR 92.

The law relating to the award of damages for abuse of process, like those regarding many of the torts that protect against an abuse of legal process, is at an early stage. It appears that damages are at large, and, like defamation, include general damages for injury to reputation. These were awarded in *Hamer-Matthew* as well as damages for injury to feelings and exemplary damages (in a case where a defence had been abusively raised). The question of the availability of damages for costs incurred in the abusive proceedings is not clearly settled. A Queensland court applied the rule for malicious civil proceedings, and refused damages for costs on the ground that they could be awarded in the allegedly abusive civil proceedings themselves: *QIW Retailers v Felview* [1989] 2 Qd R 245. In earlier proceedings in *Hanrahan*, however, the court regarded the malicious proceedings rule as inapplicable on the ground that there was no requirement that the abusive proceedings should terminate in favour of a person who was suing for abuse of process, and was in favour of awarding full legal costs. The difference may be accounted for by the fact that in the Queensland decision the plaintiff had already succeeded in having the civil proceedings struck out as an abuse of process, whereas in *Hanrahan* the allegedly abusive proceedings were still continuing.

Misuse of legal powers and misfeasance in public office

[20.55] The question here under consideration is not the abuse of legal process but the misuse of legal powers by those in whom they are vested: on the one hand, by judges and other persons enjoying judicial status; on the other, by persons enjoying the status of a public officer or public body, for which group consideration of the tort of misfeasance in public office is involved.

Misuse of legal powers

[20.60] In relation to judges, it is not a tort to inflict damage through the giving of an erroneous judgment. It is generally accepted that all judges enjoy immunity from the possibility of an action in negligence being brought in relation to such an error. As far as judges of Supreme Court and superior status are concerned, they are immune from an action in tort in relation to an exercise of their judicial power which is in excess of their jurisdiction or is malicious: *Anderson v Gorrie* [1985] 1 QB 668, though an action in tort is available against them where they have acted in actual bad faith: *McC v Mullan* [1984] 3 All ER 908 per Lord Bridge at 916. In the cases of judges of inferior courts, an action in tort is possible where they have acted maliciously or where the judgment given is outside their jurisdiction. In the former case, the action is brought on the case and is similar to (if not the same as) the action brought for misfeasance in public office. In the case of excess of jurisdiction the action generally brought is for false imprisonment where the judge makes an order for the plaintiff's imprisonment.

In *McC* the House of Lords held that the liability of inferior court judges for decisions beyond their jurisdiction was extant. Jurisdictional excess was to be construed narrowly and to be limited to cases where there was no power to make the order in question. In particular, defects in the decisions of administrators (such as failure to afford natural justice, error of law and abuse of discretionary power) which would have the effect of making the decision void on judicial review, would not have this effect in a tort action requiring proof of absence of jurisdiction on the part of the judge. In *McC* itself liability in tort was established on the ground that the justices in that case had made an order for the plaintiff juvenile offender's detention without first informing him of his right to apply for legal aid, and it was found that non-compliance with that requirement meant that the justices had no power to make that order. Similarly in *Spautz v Butterworth* [1999] Aust Torts Reports 81-415 the plaintiff was committed to prison under a warrant of committal issued by the defendant magistrate for non-payment of court costs. Since there was no power to issue the warrant in these circumstances the defendant was held liable for false imprisonment. On the other hand, in *Sirros v Moore* [1974] 3 All ER 776 a judge of the Crown Court (acting in this situation as an inferior court) was held not liable to a person whose detention he had ordered on the ground that the making of an order of detention lay within the court's jurisdiction, even though the way in which the order was made was entirely irregular.[17]

---

[17]   The ground of distinction is not very satisfactory. The only way the judge could have imposed a detention order in *Sirros v Moore* [1974] 3 All ER 776 was to go through a legal process of hearing an appeal against a recommendation for deportation. Why the failure to do this should constitute a mere irregularity, whereas the failure to inform the offender in *McC v Mullan* [1984] 3 All ER 908 of his rights should be a matter going to jurisdiction, is not readily apparent.

Lord Bridge in *McC* expressed the opinion obiter (at 916) that the liability of justices of the peace for malicious judgments was obsolete and no longer existed. It is difficult to see why lay justices should be regarded as being incapable of reproach in this way, particularly bearing in mind the now established liability of public officers for malicious misfeasance in office.

Misfeasance in public office

Figure 20.7: Misfeasance in public office

In an action for misfeasance in public office, the plaintiff must be able to show:
• that the defendant is a public officer;
• that there is an invalid or unauthorised act;
• that the act or omission was done maliciously;
• that the act or omission was done in the purported discharge of their public duties; and
• that the act or omission caused loss or harm.

[20.65] The tort of misfeasance in public office is now an established, albeit still evolving, tort in Australia following the decision of the High Court in *Northern Territory v Mengel* (1995) 129 ALR 1,[18] though finding it to be inapplicable on the facts of the case. It is difficult to establish because it depends on the impugned act being committed by the public officer with the requisite state of mind both in committing the act and in holding the requisite intention to cause the loss or damage that is alleged to flow from the impugned act. It is a serious allegation to be made against a person who holds public office. As such, it requires particularity in setting out the facts that can, if proven, establish the cause of action: *Leinenga v Logan City Council* [2006] QSC 294.[19]

The tort began as a means of imposing liability on public officers, more particularly justices of the peace, for malice in the exercise of their public powers. In the case of justices, this operated as an extension of their liability for malicious or extra-jurisdictional judgments to acts which were not an exercise of their judicial powers: *Cave v Mountain* (1840) 1 Man & G 257; 113 ER 330; *Taylor v Nesfield* (1854) 3 El & Bl

---

[18] The majority of the High Court in *Sanders v Snell* (1998) 196 CLR 329 at 347 endorsed what the majority said in *Mengel* on what constitutes misfeasance in public office. In *Sanders'* case it was sent back for a new trial on the question of the officer's knowledge that he was acting in excess of power. When the case was retried at first instance, the defendant was found liable. However, on appeal the Full Court of the Federal Court upheld Sanders' appeal: *Sanders v Snell* (2003) 130 FCR 149, emphasising that the essence of the tort is the dishonest abuse of power.

[19] This includes identifying what damage is said to flow from each alleged act of misfeasance. Because a claim for misfeasance in public office is not actionable without proof of injury and proof of the requisite knowledge, the plaintiff must establish that the impugned conduct would cause or be likely to cause the particular loss or damage attributed to the misfeasance. The damages that are claimed must be linked to the relevant act of misfeasance in public office that is said to have caused those damages: *Leinenga v Logan City Council* [2006] QSC 294 at [100].

724; 118 ER 1312. An analogous extension to the malicious acts of other public officers was then made: *Harman v Tappenden* (1801) 1 East 555; 102 ER 214; *Whitelegg v Richards* (1823) 2 B&C 45; *Henley v Mayor of Lyme* (1828) 5 Ring 91. Whether the presence of malice as regards non-judicial acts was regarded as taking the official outside his or her powers was never clearly decided,[20] though that is clearly its effect under modern administrative law. However, the 20th century brought recognition that an excess of power by an official, though non-malicious, might be equally damaging. So the tort has been extended to cases where the official consciously exceeded his or her powers but was not malicious: *Farrington v Thomson & Bridgland* [1959] VR 286; *Bourgoin v Minister of Agriculture* [1986] QB 740. This aspect of the tort was confirmed by the High Court in *Mengel*.

However, recent English authority retains the distinction between malice and excess of power in terms of providing alternative methods for the tort's commission. According to *Three Rivers DC v Bank of England* [2000] 3 All ER 1 these are:

* where a public officer performs or omits to perform an act with the object of injuring the plaintiff or a class of which the plaintiff is a member (that is, where there was targeted malice and intention is established by evidence); or

* where the officer performs an act which he knew he had no power to perform and which he knew would injure the plaintiff (here, intention is established by inference).

The test of knowledge under the second method requires either actual knowledge of the consequences of the act or reckless indifference as to those consequences. The High Court in *Mengel* also took the view that the excess of power must be conscious on the officer's part, but left open the question of the knowledge required of the public officer as to its effect on the plaintiff. As in *Three Rivers*, it was accepted that reasonable foreseeability provided too wide a test, departing in this from the English decision in *Bourgoin*. Without conclusively deciding the point, the majority favoured a test that the act should be calculated in the ordinary course to cause harm, as in *Wilkinson v Downton* [1897] 2 QB 57, or should be done with reckless indifference to the harm that is likely to ensue. But "calculated to cause harm" in connection with *Wilkinson* seems to mean no more than "reasonably foreseeable", according to the High Court decision in *Bunyan v Jordan* (1937) 57 CLR 1, so that there may still be a need to define the knowledge requirement more narrowly.[21] "Public officer" and "public power" are terms incapable of exact definition. The decision in Tasmania that a Director-General of Education was not a public officer is surprising: *Pemberton v Attorney-General (Tas)* [1978] Tas SR 1. The House of Lords in *Jones v Swansea CC* [1990] 1 WLR 54 held that the tort of misfeasance extended to a misuse of the contractual powers of the defendant

---

[20] In the notorious Canadian decision in *Roncarefli v Duplessis* (1959) 16 DLR (2d) 689 the Prime Minister of Quebec, in pressuring the Liquor Commission to revoke the plaintiff's restaurant licence, was both malicious and acting outside any powers vesting in him as Prime Minister.

[21] In *Neilson v City of Swan* (2006) 147 LGERA 136; [2006] WASCA 94 Buss JA, with whom the other members of the court agreed, concluded at [75] that the majority in *Mengel* did not approve "a foreseeability test", because it was sufficient for the purposes of the proceedings for the majority to proceed on the basis that liability for misfeasance in public office requires an act which involves a foreseeable risk of harm; see also *Leinenga v Logan City Council* [2006] QSC 294.

council.[22] Nor can an office be characterised as a public office for the purpose of the tort if no relevant power is attached to it: *Cannon v Tahche* (2002) 5 VR 317; *Noori v Leerdam* [2008] NSWSC 515.

There is a also a judicial difference of opinion about the "member of the public" element of the tort. In *Tampion v Anderson* [1973] VR 715 at 720, the court said that to be able to sustain an action in the tort of misfeasance, a plaintiff must not only show damage from the abuse but also show that he or she was a member of the public, or one of the members of the public, to whom the holder of the office owed a duty not to commit the particular abuse complained of.[23] In *Mengel,* only Brennan J, in a single judgment concurring as to the outcome, raised the "member of the public" issue and expressed a view about it.

Practice Questions

Revision Questions

20.1 What factors distinguish a malicious prosecution from a malicious institution of civil proceedings?

20.2 In an action for malicious prosecution, what does the plaintiff need to establish in order to succeed? Discuss.

20.3 In what way does an action for malicious prosecution or institution of civil proceedings differ from malicious process or arrest?

20.4 In what ways does the tort of abuse of legal process differ from the tort of malicious arrest?

Answers to Practice Questions

Revision Questions

20.1 Both actions share a number of common factors including:

- the need to show malice;
- absence of reasonable cause; and
- termination of proceedings in the plaintiff's favour.

---

[22] See, for example, Buss JA in *Neilson v City of Swan* (2006) 147 LGERA 136; [2006] WASCA 94 at [37]. A "public officer" not only includes those appointed to discharge a public office and receive compensation (*Henley v Mayor of Lyne* (1828) 5 Bing 91) but a local authority exercising private-law functions as a landlord (*Jones v Swansea City Council* [1990] 1 WLR 54), a government ministry (*Dunlop v Woollahra Municipal Council* [1982] AC 158; *Bourgoin SA v Ministry of Agriculture, Fisheries and Food* [1986] QB 716). According to *Three Rivers,* a corporate body (such as the Bank of England) could be named as a defendant without having to give particulars of the individual officials whose decisions and actions combine to bring about the alleged misfeasance but where the acts are attributable to the actions of natural persons through whom the body corporate acts the individual officials must be identified: *Leinenga v Logan City Council* [2006] QSC 294.

[23] See also *Pemberton v Attorney-General (Tas)* [1978] Tas SR 1.

However, in civil proceedings the plaintiff is never going to face imprisonment and the defendant may be awarded costs in defending the action if successful.

20.2 The plaintiff must prove:

- termination of the prosecution in the plaintiff's favour;
- absence of reasonable cause;
- evidence of malice on the part of the defendant; and
- that he or she suffered actual damage.

The plaintiff must show both a wrongful state of mind on the part of the defendant *and* an objective lack of strength in the defendant's case.

20.3 Malicious process or arrest is concerned with legal process, whereas malicious prosecution and malicious institution of civil proceedings are concerned with legal proceedings in court.

20.4 The tort of abuse of legal process does not require proof of absence of reasonable cause on termination of the process in the plaintiff's favour. However, the plaintiff must show the use of the process to gain some collateral damage and that he or she has suffered this damage as a consequence. The claim that proceedings are abusive may be raised as a defence or brought as a separate tort action.

Tutorial Questions

20.1 How do the actions of misuse of legal powers and misfeasance in public office differ?

20.2 In order to establish the tort of malicious prosecution, the plaintiff has to show absence of reasonable cause on the part of the defendant. What amounts to "reasonable cause"? Discuss.

CHAPTER 21

Injury to Relational Interests

Objectives

This chapter will examine:

- the circumstances under which a person may claim damages for the infliction of injury or death to another human being.

Principles

Introduction

[21.05] This chapter is concerned with the circumstances under which a person may claim damages for "pure" economic loss in tort for an injury suffered by him or her through the actions of a third party. Initially it should be noticed that there are two types of cases. First, a tort may be committed even though there is no tortious injury to the third party as such, for example, the husband's action for enticement of his wife. Torts of this sort are now effectively dead because of their archaic nature. No account of them appears in this book, even though, unlike England, Australia has not entirely removed them from the law. The second type of case is that in which the plaintiff is suing for damage arising from the tortious infliction of injury or death to another human being. Generally there is no cause of action based upon the injury of a third party but the law has modified this general position in the following, limited circumstances:

- A dependant may sue for loss suffered by death wrongfully caused to the person upon whom he or she is dependent.

- A husband may sue for the wrongful deprivation of his wife's consortium. This right, which is also now regarded as having an archaic flavour, being based on a proprietary right to the wife's services and society, has been removed by statute in four Australian States.[1]

- A parent may sue for the wrongful deprivation of a child's services.

- An employer may sue for the wrongful deprivation of the employee's services.[2]

Following the High Court decision in *Griffiths v Kerkemeyer* (1977) 139 CLR 161, the plaintiff is entitled to recover damages for gratuitous services rendered to the plaintiff by a third party. This remedy, unlike those considered in this chapter, belongs to the tort victim, not the third party. It will, therefore be considered in Chapter 22 on remedies. The same is true of the now recognised right of the victim to recover damages for his or her inability to render services to other persons within the family. This is the victim's own right and will be considered in Chapter 22.

It was not until *Van Gervan v Fenton* (1992) 175 CLR 327, and emphasised in

---

[1]   All the torts of causing loss of consortium or services (whether through the infliction of personal injury or through enticement, harbouring and the like) were abolished in England by s 2 of the *Administration of Justice Act 1982* (UK). In Australia, the husband's action for the loss of his wife's consortium has been abolished in the Australian Capital Territory, New South Wales, Tasmania and Western Australia: *Civil Liability (Wrongs) Act 2002* (ACT), s 218; *Law Reform (Marital Consortium) Act 1984* (NSW); *Common Law (Miscellaneous Actions) Act 1986* (Tas), s 3; *Law Reform Miscellaneous Provisions) Act 1941* (WA), s 3. It is limited in Queensland: *Civil Liability Act 2003* (Qld), s 58 (to the death of the injured person or where general damages are assessed at $30,000 or more before allowing for contributory negligence) but still allowed in South Australia: *Civil Liability Act 1936* (SA), s 65 with both States choosing to modify the right by extending the right to wives as well as husbands. In the Northern Territory: *Compensation (Fatal Injuries) Act 1974* (NT), s 10 has gone even further than either Queensland or South Australia by extending the right to husbands, wives, de facto spouses of either sex and to spouses of either sex recognised as such by Aboriginal tribal law. The original action still exists in Victoria but statutory compensation schemes exist to prevent the action from applying in most cases. The actions for enticement and harbouring of a wife and for damages for adultery were abolished in Australia by the *Family Law Act 1975* (Cth), s 120.

[2]   *Commissioner of Railways v Scott* [1973] 2 NZLR 238; *Marinovski v Zutti* [1984] 2 NSWLR 571.

Grincelis v House (2000) 201 CLR 321, that the High Court made it clear that an award of *Griffiths v Kerkemeyer* damages compensates a plaintiff for a pecuniary loss. The civil liability reforms of 2002-2003, the Australian Capital Territory aside, codified the position by restricting the awarding of *Griffiths v Kerkemeyer* damages: *Civil Liability Act 2002* (NSW), ss 15, 18(1)(b) (see also *Kendrick v Bluescope Steel (AIS) Pty Ltd* [2007] NSWSC 1288); *Personal Injuries (Liabilities and Damages) Act 2003* (NT), ss 23, 29(b); *Civil Liability Act 2003* (Qld), s 59; *Civil Liabiity Act 1936* (SA), s 58; *Civil Liability Act 2003* (Tas), s 28B; *Wrongs Act 1958* (Vic), ss 281A, 281B; *Civil Liability Act 2002* (WA), s 12. Relying in part on the decision in *Griffiths v Kerkemeyer*, the NSW Court of Appeal held in *Sullivan v Gordon* (1999) 47 NSWLR 319 that a plaintiff who had a claim for personal injury may have been able to recover damages to compensate them for their loss of capacity to provide domestic assistance to a dependant. Damages of the kind awarded in *Sullivan* differ from those awarded in *Griffiths v Kerkemeyer* because they were awarded for the loss of the plaintiff's capacity to provide services to another person rather than for the cost of services that the plaintiff had required or would require in the future. In *CSR Ltd v Eddy* (2005) 226 CLR 1; [2005] HCA 64, the High Court overruled a line of cases of which *Sullivan v Gordon* formed part. As a result, at common law in Australia a plaintiff in a personal injury claim cannot recover special damages to compensate the plaintiff for the loss of the plaintiff's capacity to provide domestic services to his or her dependants. At least in New South Wales, in an attempt to award damages of the kind recognised by the Court of Appeal in *Sullivan*, s 15B of the *Civil Liability Act 2002* (NSW) now provides that a court may award damages for any loss of the claimant's capacity to provide gratuitous domestic services to the claimant's dependants: see, for example *Kendrick v Bluescope Steel (AIS) Pty Ltd* [2007] NSWSC 1288. The Australian Capital Territory also permits recovery of *Sullivan v Gordon* damages: *Civil Law (Wrongs) Act 2002* (ACT), s 100.

Figure 21.1: Who has a cause of action?

A cause of action may arise in the following cases:
- Dependant – may sue for loss suffered by death wrongfully caused to person upon whom they are dependent.
- Husband – may sue for wrongful deprivation of wife's consortium (no longer available in three Australian States and the ACT). South Australia, Queensland and the Northern Territory have reduced the discriminatory features of the action with only Victoria retaining the original action.
- Parent – may sue for wrongful deprivation of child's services.
- Employer – may sue for wrongful deprivation of the employee's services.

Death as cause of action

Figure 21.2: General principles

> To establish a claim of wrongful death, a claimant (usually the executor or administrator) needs to establish:
> * the defendant wrongfully caused the death through the commission of a tort (or breach of contract or statutory right);
> * the deceased, had they not died, could have successfully maintained an action against the defendant;
> * on whose behalf the action is brought;
> * they fall within the statutory list of "relatives"; and
> * that they suffered a foreseeable loss (a pecuniary loss except in South Australia and the Northern Territory which still have provisions for solatium) by the death of the victim upon whom they were dependent in a familial sense.

[21.10] Whilst the original common law rule was that no action lay for causing the death of another person this is no longer the case. All State and Territory jurisdictions have made statutory provision to allow a dependant to claim damages for loss of the value of their dependency where the defendant has, by the commission of a wrong, caused the death of the person upon whom the dependant was dependent.[3] Outside the statutory cause of action, the original common law rule continues to apply: *Swan v Williams Demolition Pty Ltd* (1987) 9 NSWLR 172 (plaintiff company held not entitled to recover damages for the loss of the services of its dead employee).[4]

The statutory cause of action arising out of the relationship of dependence (between the plaintiff[5] and the deceased) is often referred to in the same terms as the original English Act, *Lord Campbell's Act*. It is in effect a cause of action, generally speaking in tort,[6] for pure economic loss.[7] As such it has been described as "new in its species, new in its quality, new in its principle, in every way new": *The Hera Cruz* (1884) 10 App

---

[3]   *Civil Law (Wrongs) 2002* (ACT), s 149; *Compensation to Relatives Act 1897* (NSW); *Compensation (Fatal Injuries) Act 1974* (NT); *Succession Act 1981* (Qld), s 66; *Civil Liability Act 1936* (SA), Pt 5, Pt 9 Div 5; *Fatal Accidents Act 1934* (Tas); *Wrongs Act 1958* (Vic), Pt 3; *Fatal Accidents Act 1959* (WA). Limitation provisions for bringing of actions for wrongful death vary between jurisdictions: *Limitation Act 1985* (ACT), ss 16, 39; *Limitation Act 1969* (NSW), ss 50A, 50C; *Limitation Act 1981* (NT), s 17; *Limitation of Actions Act 1974* (Qld), s 11; *Civil Liability Act 1936* (SA), s 25; *Limitations Act 1974* (Tas), s 5A; *Wrongs Act 1958* (Vic), s 20; *Limitation Act 2005* (WA), s 5.

[4]   *Swan v Williams (Demolition) Pty Ltd* was followed by Cox J in the Tasmanian Supreme Court in *Whayman v Motor Accidents Insurance Board* [2003] TASSC 149.

[5]   Examples of those who could be a plaintiff include the deceased's personal representative, dependants or family.

[6]   For example, a tort such as negligence, trespass to the person (assault, battery), breach of statutory duty of nuisance but it may, alternatively, be a breach of contract: *Woolworths v Crotty* (1942) 66 CLR 603 (where it was alleged that Woolworths was in breach of an implied condition that the goods were reasonably fit for purpose) or a breach of fiduciary duty.

[7]   In *Woolcock Street Investments Pty Ltd v CDG Pty Ltd* (2004) 216 CLR 515; [2004] HCA 16 McHugh J observed at [47] that in limited cases the common law and the Australian equivalents of *Lord Campbell's Act* "allowed a person to recover 'pure' economic loss in a derivative action based on a breach of a duty owed to a physically injured person".

Cas 59 per Lord Blackburn at 70. Nevertheless it is clear that the defendant must have committed an actionable wrong towards the deceased person, described in the Acts as a "wrongful act, neglect or default". The usual defences, such as volenti non fit injuria (voluntary assumption of risk), will apply against the dependants, if they could have been established against the deceased. On the other hand, contributory negligence is generally only a partial defence against the deceased, which does not rule out an actionable wrong by the defendant. However, in the Australian Capital Territory, New South Wales, Queensland, Tasmania and Victoria contributory negligence can defeat a claim altogether if it is determined that the victim was 100% to blame for the injury that resulted in death: see the discussion at [21.130].

The distinctness of the dependants' action from that of the deceased is shown by the fact that a contractual limitation on damages binding the deceased has no effect on the action of the dependants: *Nunan v Southern Railway* [1924] 1 KB 223.[8] The law is not yet settled as to whether a settlement of the action or judgment against the defendant obtained by the deceased in his or her own lifetime bars an action brought on behalf of the dependants. There is an obiter dictum of Evatt J in the High Court denying this position (*Harding v Lithgow Corp* (1937) 57 CLR 186 at 196) and one by Lord Salmon in an English case supporting it: *Pickett v British Rail Engineering Ltd* [1980] AC 136 at 152. In principle, Lord Salmon's view that the dependants have no cause of action here seems correct, but it leaves a difficulty in cases where the dependants have been disinherited under the deceased's will. In such a case, the dependants' remedy is to contest the deceased's will.[9]

The "wrongful act, neglect or default" of the defendant must have "caused" the death according to the basic statutory provision. Normal principles of causation and remoteness of damage will apply to determine this, although in *Haber v Walker* [1963] VR 339[10] the majority of the court thought that in the case of suicide following depression brought on by the injury, the "but for" test of factual causation alone was relevant and that of reasonable foreseeability was excluded. This approach appears to deny the force of the word "wrongful", since the act must be wrongful in respect of the death; other cases have found it necessary to determine also the reasonable foreseeability of the death.[11]

---

[8]   Nor does a statutory limitation – *Union SS Co of NZ v Robin* [1920] AC 654; but cf *Unsworth v Commissioner for Railways* (1958) 101 CLR 73.

[9]   The *Compensation (Fatal Injuries) Act 1974* (NT), s 7(2) provides that a settlement, release or judgment made, given or obtained by the deceased does not bar the dependants' action.

[10] *Pigney v Pointers Transport* [1957] 1 WLR 1121.

[11] *Richters v Motor Services Ltd* [1972] Qd R 9; *Versic v Conners* [1968] 3 NSWR 770; but in *Zavitsanos v Chippendale* [1970] 2 NSWR 495; *Cuckow v Polyester Products Pty Ltd* (1970) 19 FLR 122, the court thought foreseeability to be unnecessary. The High Court in *Chapman v Hearse* (1961) 106 CLR 112 applied a test of foreseeability without discussing the issue.

Dependency

Figure 21.3: Definition

A "dependant" is someone who:
- falls within statutory list of relatives created by relevant Act in each jurisdiction; and
- has a reasonable expectation of future benefit from continuance of deceased's life.

[21.15] The persons who may recover damages under the statutory provisions are generally described as the dependants of the deceased. They must be able to establish that they fall within the statutory list of relatives created by the relevant Act in each jurisdiction and that they have a reasonable expectation of future benefit from the continuance of the deceased's life.

To determine whether a claimant meets the first requirement, individual legislative instruments must be consulted as there are minor jurisdictional differences in the definition of relatives. However, the term "relatives" generally comprises spouses, parents, children and siblings of the deceased. Under the *Compensation to Relatives Act 1897* (NSW), "spouse" includes a person in a de facto relationship (s 7); "parent" includes father, mother, grandfather, grandmother, step-father and step-mother; "brother" includes half-brother and step-brother; likewise with sister; and "child" includes son, daughter, grandson, granddaughter, step-son and step-daughter. The relationships indicated here are limited to legitimate relationships and the only non-familial relationship recognised is that between putative spouses. But in other jurisdictions there is recognition of the claims based on illegitimate familial relationships and on those between co-habitees, Victoria having gone furthest in this regard.[12]

The legislation generally provides that not more than one action can be brought on behalf of all claimants in respect of the same subject matter. This provision mirrors the common law as demonstrated in *Palmer v Riverstone Meats* [1988] Aust Torts Reports 80-223, where the claim of certain dependants but not others was statute-barred by the expiry of a limitation period; those dependants whose claim was not statute-barred could bring the action on behalf of themselves and the dependants whose claim was statute-barred. Thus, there was a single action for all identified dependants.

It is not necessary to show an existing dependency at the time of death in order to meet the second requirement of economic dependency. A reasonable expectation of future financial benefit is sufficient: *Taff Vale Rail v Jenkins* [1913] AC 1.[13] Also, that expectation need not be demonstrated on the balance of probabilities. In common with the rule for damages generally, that the courts will compensate for the loss of

---

12   The Victorian provision merely requires establishment of a dependency: *Wrongs Act 1958* (Vic), s 17(2).
13   Nor need there be any legal right to the benefit: *Franklin v SE Railway* (1858) 3 H & N 211; 157 ER 448.

a speculative chance, the court will attempt to assess that chance and to reduce the amount of the benefit accordingly, for example to 15% of its actual amount (though this may appear to contravene the usual rule that the plaintiff must prove loss necessary to establish the cause of action on the balance of probabilities).[14]

Nature of benefit claimable

[21.20] The assessment of the benefit turns on identifiable financial loss suffered by the dependant as a result of premature death. It is not possible to award damages for grief, fear and/or distress as these are considered normal emotions to a distressing experience[15] (unless it can be established that it is the starting point of a recognised psychiatric illness).[16] That is the province of the action for a solatium payment which is only available in South Australia and the Northern Territory: *Civil Liability Act 1936* (SA), s 28(1); *Compensation (Fatal Injuries) Act 1974* (NT), s 10(3)(f). The courts take a broad view of what is financial loss. In particular, it has been held that children can show a specific loss in losing a father or mother going beyond that of the amount that that parent would have spent on their support and the financial value of actual services rendered by that parent in the home: *Mehmet v Perry* [1977] 2 All ER 529; *Regan v Williamson* [1976] 2 All ER 241; *Fisher v Smithson* (1978) 17 SASR 223. The amount awarded for this will, however, be a relatively small conventional sum. The benefit must be one expected from a familial relationship rather than a professional or economic one. Thus, the claim of a father for the loss of a son was denied in *Sykes v North Eastern Railway Co* [1880] All ER 1892 on the ground that the son was the father's employee and was being paid the standard rate in terms of wages. The benefit must therefore be somewhat in the nature of a gratuity. For example, where the payment of wages by the deceased to the plaintiff is greater than the services would warrant, the excess will be ascribed to the existence of the "family" relationship rather than to the business relationship: *Malyon v Plummer* [1964] 1 QB 330.

Assessment of damages

[21.25] Only the general principles of what is often a very complicated matter can be indicated in the text here as compensation in this area is, by its very nature, speculative.[17] Specialist works should be consulted for the details. The loss of each dependant must be assessed individually, even though only one action under the relevant legislation can be brought on the behalf of the class of dependants. In *Pym v Great Northern*

---

[14] *Davies v Taylor* [1974] AC 207. The courts will reject a benefit that is too speculative: *Edwards v Breeze* [1964] NSWR 736; see also *Lamb v Tablelands CC* [1988] Aust Torts Reports 80-220 – compensation awarded for loss of an inheritance expectation assessed at 25%.

[15] *Hinz v Berry* [1970] 2 QB 40; *Mount Isa Mines Ltd v Pusey* (1970) 125 CLR 383; *Whayman v Motor Accidents Insurance Board* [2003] TASSC 149.

[16] In exceptional circumstances, severe emotional distress may trigger a resulting recognised psychiatric illness for which damages may be recovered if it is the result of a recognised tort. See, for example, the comments of Windeyer J in *Mount Isa Mines Ltd v Pusey* (1970) 125 CLR 383 at 394 (although he did not use the expression "recognised psychiatric illness") and Gleeson J in *Tame v New South Wales; Annetts v Australian Stations Pty Ltd* (2002) 191 ALR 449 at 453. In *Swan v Williams (Demolition) Pty Ltd* (1987) 9 NSWLR 173, a majority of the Court of Appeal upheld an appeal by a husband who was still grieving more than 18 months after his wife's death; in *Whayman v Motor Accidents Insurance Board* [2003] TASSC 149 Cox J considered the reaction of the parents to the death of their son to be so abnormal that it could be described as a psychiatric illness.

[17] The speculative nature of the assessment was explicitly recognised by Gleeson CJ in *De Sales v Ingrilli* (2002) 212 CLR 338 at 351; see also 363–364, 372–375, 388–389.

Railway (1863) 4 B&S 396; 122 ER 508, the deceased derived his income entirely from estates which passed on his death to the eldest of his nine children. It was argued that the family as a whole had suffered no loss but this argument was rejected on the ground that the widow and the other eight children had suffered a loss of dependency. Nevertheless, it has been common practice, especially in the case of jury trial to record one lump sum and then to apportion that sum among the dependants concerned.[18] The alternative method of evaluating each dependant's claim separately and then of adding up the separate amounts is greatly superior in that it produces a more accurate result. This method tends to be adopted by judges sitting alone in the absence of a jury.

The method of assessment is essentially one of assessing past and future economic loss arising from the injury and subsequent death. Calculation of loss of past earnings up to the date of trial of the deceased cannot be precisely defined. In relation to loss of future earnings after trial, a formula needs to be applied to it which is in effect the same as that applied to the loss of future earnings of a living accident victim. That formula is considered in Chapter 22 (a prior reading of [22.10]ff dealing with the principles upon which damages for personal injury are based will be helpful towards an understanding of the basis of the damages award in claims for wrongful death). The whole of the deceased's loss of earnings will not be awarded; only that amount which the deceased would have been expected to expend on his dependants. Assessment of dependency in the case of both spouses working and pooling a part of their incomes in a joint fund or for joint expenses causes a difficulty in determining the amount of the dependency. In *Halvorsen Boats v Robinson* [1993] Aust Torts Reports 81-221 the New South Wales Court of Appeal adopted a general rule that the parties would each have spent a third of their incomes "selfishly" and pooled the rest. This did not produce the result that the wife's dependency on the deceased was two-thirds of his income but that the wife was entitled to two-thirds of his unselfishly spent income, giving a dependency of some 40% on the husband. This seems justifiable, given that the husband's share in the pooled assets would no longer arise, though the court emphasised that whatever method was chosen could produce only a rough estimate rather than a precise calculation.

The court must also be careful not to duplicate awards. Where there are shared benefits, such as mortgage payments and home and maintenance payments (such as heating and food), adequate compensation will normally be made by compensating the wife for her loss of dependency with no further award to the children since it is presumed that they will draw the same benefit from the shared benefit as before: *Gullifer v Pohto* [1978] 2 NSWLR 352. Nevertheless, there has been a more recent tendency to allocate some greater amount of the total award to the children, on the basis of the risk to them of improvidence by the wife, of imprudent investments, or the wife's remarriage: *Gillespie v Alperstein* [1964] VR 740.[19]

The personal expenditure of the deceased must be excluded from the "dependency". Nevertheless, a husband might apply some of his income for the acquisition of income-producing or capital gain-producing assets which the wife would expect to inherit on his death; this will be taken into account: *Gillett v Callagher* [1963] ALR 392. On the

---

18   Now subject in all Australian jurisdictions except South Australia to the making of consent orders for periodic payments under: *Civil Law (Wrongs) Act 2002* (ACT), s 106; *Civil Liability Act 2002* (NSW), Pt 2, Div 7; *Personal Injuries (Liabilities and Damages) Act 2003* (NT), Pt 4, Div 6; *Civil Liability Act 2003* (Qld), Ch 3, Pt 4; *Civil Liability Act 2002* (Tas), Pt 5; *Wrongs Act 1958* (Vic), Pt VC; *Civil Liability Act 2002* (WA), Pt 2, Div 4.

19   In *Goodburn v Thomas Cotton* [1968] 1 QB 845 the Court of Appeal thought that the children might be actually worse off in the likely event of the wife's remarriage, and so their share of the damages was increased though the wife's was reduced to reflect the contingency.

other hand, the wife's immediate inheritance of whatever assets the deceased presently possessed may be seen to be a gain, at least to the extent of acceleration of the benefit and of the certainty of its inheritance. Considerations of this sort indicate the almost impossibly speculative nature of the courts' task in performing their assessments. The indications are that some small deduction may be made representing acceleration of the benefit in relation to investments generally: *Public Trustee v Nickisson* (1964) 111 CLR 500; *Lamb v Tablelands CC* [1988] Aust Torts Reports 80-220. In relation to the matrimonial home, however, the wife (since she still needs a residence and since no real benefit accrues to her through its inheritance) will not have her damages reduced,[20] even though at the time of the trial the matrimonial home has been sold and a cheaper one purchased.[21]

Loss of services provided in the home, for example by husband or wife, is a compensable loss. The High Court in *Nguyen v Nguyen* (1990) 169 CLR 245 held that gratuitous services performed by a spouse for the benefit of her husband and children had a monetary value and should be compensated even where those services were not to be replaced by the hiring of commercial services. A claim for lost services of this kind was not based on *Griffiths v Kerkemeyer* (1977) 139 CLR 161 because in *Nguyen*, the giver of the services was dead. Following dicta of the High Court in *Nguyen*, Derrington J in a similar action,[22] awarded a husband, who was unemployed and who was providing replacement services for those of the wife, an amount representing the commercial cost of replacement services. The sum was scaled down because the services were being rendered in the comfort and convenience of home, the services were performed to some extent at the husband's convenience, and pleasure was to be derived from performing the services. That figure, also, should not exceed the figure representing the notional loss of wages given up by the husband (notional since the husband was in fact unemployed). Although *Nguyen* concerned a claim made on a different basis than *Griffiths v Kerkemeyer*, its choice of a rate of compensation based on the lost earnings of the service provider seems to be out of line with the principles established by the High Court for a claim based on *Griffiths v Kerkemeyer* in *Van Gervan v Fenton* (1992) 66 ALJR 828. In that case, the majority of the High Court thought the lost earnings of the provider generally irrelevant to the determination of the award which was to be based upon the market value of those services. The fact that the wife's services to the dependant have been replaced gratuitously by another person will not prevent the claim under *Nguyen* arising: *Hay v Hughes* [1975] QB 790.

A particularly difficult problem is that of the effect of the remarriage of a widow or widower (or of the prospects of such a remarriage), on the damages recoverable as a dependent spouse. As a matter of strict logic, both are relevant considerations granted that financial loss is being compensated in the award. The usual case confronting the courts is that of the widow, but *Nguyen* shows that the factors operate also in the case of widowers.

In Australia, both the actual remarriage of the widow or widower and the prospects of such remarriage are of limited relevance in the assessment of damages: *Carroll v Purcell* (1961) 107 CLR 73; *Parker v Commonwealth* (1965) 112 CLR 295;

[20] *Bishop v Cunard White Star* [1950] P 240; *Heatley v Steel Co of Wales* [1953] 1 WLR 405; *Zordan v Metropolitan (Perth) Passenger Transport Trust* [1963] ALR 513.
[21] *McCullagh v Lawrence* [1988] Aust Torts Reports 80-193 – no deduction was made in that case in respect of the accelerated vesting of partnership assets since these would be likely to have increased had the husband lived. See also *Lamb v Tablelands CC* [1988] Aust Torts Reports 80-220.
[22] *Mehmet v Perry* [1977] 2 All ER 529.

De Sales v Ingrilli (2002) 212 CLR 338.[23] Where remarriage of a widow has taken place at the time of the trial it is relevant only to the extent that it goes to replace the lost dependency.[24] Where no marriage has taken place, and in the absence of legislative intervention, the court has the invidious task of assessing the contingency of remarriage.[25] The assessment is made in relation to the individual plaintiff, the court rejecting statistical evidence as to the likelihood of remarriage of persons of a certain age. This tends to work in the plaintiff's favour since the contingency chosen is always less than the statistical probability of remarriage. In some cases the court accepts the plaintiff's assurance that there is no question of future remarriage (as in *McCullagh v Lawrence* [1988] Aust Torts Reports 80-193); in other cases a deduction is made despite such an assurance, as in *Parker*.[26] A further criticism of the common law on this point is that it tends to have a distorting effect on the social pattern of people's lives. A desirable marriage may be postponed for an indefinite period awaiting the outcome of the legal action. But change in the law would now seem to require further legislative intervention. Actual remarriage on the part of a widow or widower may go towards reduction of damages for other dependants, especially children. There is some English authority that this applies to the contingency of remarriage, though this is not easy to defend: *Mead v Clarke Chapman & Co Ltd* [1956] 1 All ER 44; cf *Goodburn v Thomas Cotton* [1968] 1 QB 845.

The legal attitude towards remarriage of the plaintiff may be compared with that towards the earnings of a surviving spouse where that spouse, who was previously dependant upon the deceased, has taken a job after the death. These earnings are to be ignored for the purpose of making the assessment: *Carroll*; *Gillett v Callagher* [1963] ALR 392; *Public Trustee v Nickisson* (1964) 111 CLR 500, the rationale for not taking them into account being that the earnings are in return for the plaintiff's labour and therefore do not replace a former dependency.

Deductibility of benefits arising from death

[21.30] As a matter of legislative provision in all States and Territories, certain payments made to the estate resulting from the death are not to be taken into account in assessing the damages of the dependants. This mirrors the original *Fatal Accidents Act 1976* (UK). Section 5(2) of the *Fatal Accidents Act 1959* (WA) is a typical example.[27] It excludes consideration by the court of the following payments:

---

23 The *Compensation (Fatal Injuries) Act 1974* (NT), s 10(4)(h) also provides that neither remarriage nor its prospect are to be taken into account. The High Court in *De Sales v Ingrilli* (2002) 212 CLR 338 confirmed that solatium was not available under the Western Australian *Fatal Accidents Act 1959*, effectively abolishing the "remarriage" discount. See also *McKenna v Avior Pty Ltd* [1981] WAR 255 where Smith J was required to consider whether solatium was available under the *Civil Aviation (Carriers' Liability) Act 1959* (Cth), where damages were to be assessed on the same principles as the Western Australian *Fatal Accidents Act*, and came to the conclusion that it wasn't.

24 *Hollebone v Greemwood* (1968) 71 SR (NSW) 424 where divorce proceedings were in progress in the second marriage.

25 In response to *De Sales v Ingrilli* (2002) 212 CLR 338, the Victorian Parliament amended s 19 of the *Wrongs Act 1958* by passing the *Wrongs (Remarriage Discount) Act 2004*. This had the effect of precluding courts, when assessing damages, from taking into account as a separate discount both a claimant's actual remarriage or formation of a new domestic partnership, or prospects of remarriage or formation of a domestic partnership (s 19(2)). See also *Supreme Court Act 1995* (Qld), s 23A.

26 See also *Knight v Anderson* [1997] Aust Torts Reports 81-430 – pregnancy of plaintiff wife not to be taken as establishing a certainty of remarriage.

27 *Civil Law (Wrongs) Act 2002* (ACT), s 26; *Compensation to Relatives Act 1897* (NSW), s 3(3); *Compensation (Fatal Injuries) Act 1974* (NT), s 10(4); *Supreme Court Act 1995* (Qld), s 23; *Civil Liability Act 1936* (SA), s 36; *Fatal Accidents Act 1934* (Tas), s 10(1); *Wrongs Act 1958* (Vic), s 19(1); *Fatal Accidents Act 1959* (WA), s 5(1)(c).

* any sum paid or payable on the death of the deceased under any contract of insurance;

* any sum paid or payable out of or under any superannuation, provident or like fund or scheme, or by way of benefit from a friendly society, benefit society or trade union; and

* any sum paid or payable by way of pension (under the provisions of various enactments).

Where the sum paid or payable does not fall within any of these categories, the sum will not be automatically deducted. This depends upon general principles relating to collateral benefits (considered in Chapter 22).

Transmission of causes of action on death

[21.35] The common law rule concerning the survival of causes of action in tort was expressed in the Latin phrase "actio personalis moritur cum persona" (a personal action dies with death).[28] The effect was that the cause of action survived neither to the estate of a deceased victim nor against the estate of a deceased tortfeasor.

Survival of causes of action in tort for benefit of deceased's estate

[21.40] While legislative changes now permit claims by the estate of the deceased the scope for claims is very limited.[29] Actions for defamation, and for the seduction and enticement of a spouse are expressly excluded, as are claims in any tort for exemplary damages.[30] The estate is not able to claim damages in the case of personal injury for the deceased's non-economic loss, for example the deceased's pain and suffering prior to death. A claim cannot be made for the deceased's lost future earnings, that is, the earnings the deceased would have made in the post-trial period.[31] This involves no hardship, since the deceased's dependants have an independent cause of action which includes compensation related to the deceased's assumed loss of earnings after trial. The general effect of the legislation is that the estate receives compensation only in respect of actual economic loss incurred by the deceased until the moment of death. Should death be instantaneous there will be no such loss.

Survival of causes of action in tort against deceased's estate

[21.45] The legislative reversal of the common law position with respect to allowing actions against the estates of deceased tortfeasors is a far more significant change. No

---

28   *Kirk v Todd* (1882) 21 Ch D 484 at 488-489; *Quirk v Thomas* [1916] 1 KB 516 at 530.

29   *Civil Law (Wrongs) Act 2002* (ACT), s 16; *Law Reform (Miscellaneous Provisions) Act 1944* (NSW), s 2; *Law Reform (Miscellaneous Provisions) Act 1992* (NT), s 6; *Succession Act 1981* (Qld), s 66; *Survival of Causes of Action Act 1940* (SA), s 3; *Administration and Probate Act 1935* (Tas), s 27; *Administration and Probate Act 1958* (Vic), s 29; *Law Reform (Miscellaneous Provisions) Act 1941* (WA), s 4.

30   *Civil Law (Wrongs) Act 2002* (ACT), s 16(2); *Law Reform (Miscellaneous Provisions) Act 1944* (NSW), s 2(a)(i); *Law Reform (Miscellaneous Provisions) Act 1992* (NT), s 6(a); *Succession Act 1981* (Qld), s 66(2)(b); *Survival of Causes of Action Act 1940* (SA), s 3(1)(b); *Administration and Probate Act 1935* (Tas), s 27(3)(a); *Administration and Probate Act 1958* (Vic), s 29(2)(a); *Law Reform (Miscellaneous Provisions) Act 1941* (WA), s 4(2)(a). With respect to defamation refer to the uniform Defamation Acts and discussion at [18.45].

31   *Civil Law (Wrongs) Act 2002* (ACT), s 16(3)(b)(ii); *Law Reform (Miscellaneous Provisions) Act 1944* (NSW), s 2(2)(a)(ii); *Law Reform (Miscellaneous Provisions) Act 1992* (NT), s 6(1)(c)(iii); *Succession Act 1981* (Qld), s 151(d)(ii); *Survival of Causes of Action Act 1940* (SA), s 3(1)(a)(iv); *Administration and Probate Act 1935* (Tas), s 27(3)(c)(iii); *Administration and Probate Act 1958* (Vic), s 29(2)(c)(iii); *Law Reform (Miscellaneous Provisions) Act 1941* (WA), s 4(2)(e).

system of law could tolerate a position where the chance of death deprived an injured person of a right to compensation. The statutory right extends to claims for contribution against deceased tortfeasors.

One difficulty requiring specific legislative removal is that where a wrongdoer has died before the damage necessary to complete a cause of action in tort against that wrongdoer has occurred. In that instance, the cause of action is deemed by the statutory provision to have subsisted against the wrongdoer at the time of death. This settles the difficulty in the case where a tortfeasor has caused the death of another person but has predeceased the victim. At the time of the tortfeasor's death, no cause of action is vested in the dependants of the victim since that does not occur until the victim's death. But under the legislative provision, the cause of action of the dependants is deemed to be subsisting at the time of the tortfeasor's death.[32]

Funeral expenses

[21.50] Funeral expenses have a curiously indeterminate status. Their recovery from the tortfeasor has been regulated by statute. The survival legislation in all States and Territories allows recovery of such expenses on the part of the estate. The legislation allowing recovery of damages by dependants for wrongful death also, in general, allows recovery of funeral expenses by dependants.[33]

Solatium

[21.55] This phrase refers to a compensatory payment made for wrongful death to a person for grief and distress arising from the death. As such it is distinguishable from the other claims for wrongful death. There is no need to establish dependency or pecuniary loss. Nor is the claim one which was available to the deceased in the deceased's own lifetime. The claim is entirely one created by statute and is limited to South Australia and the Northern Territory. The South Australian legislation limits the claim to the parents of an infant and to the spouse of an adult, and is subject to a maximum financial limit: *Civil Liability Act 1936* (SA), s 28(1). The court has a discretion whether to order a specified payment of a solatium (s 30(2)) and it is awarded in addition to, and not in derogation of, any other rights conferred on the parent, husband or wife (s 30(1)). The Northern Territory claim is available to anyone who can establish a claim as a dependant under the death legislation; there is no upper financial limit: *Compensation (Fatal Injuries) Act 1974* (NT), s 10(1). In both cases, the award of the solatium payment does not operate to reduce the award of damages under the award to dependants or to the estate under the relevant legislation.

Action for loss of consortium

[21.60] At common law, the husband had an action for the loss of his wife's consortium

---

[32]   *Civil Law (Wrongs) Act 2002* (ACT), s 25(4)(a); *Compensation to Relatives Act 1897* (NSW), s 3(2); *Law Reform (Miscellaneous Provisions) Act 1992* (NT), s 6(1)(c); *Succession Act 1981* (Qld), s 66(3); *Survival of Causes of Action Act 1940* (SA), s 3(1)(d); *Administration and Probate Act 1935* (Tas), s 27(4); *Administration and Probate Act 1958* (Vic), s 29(3); *Law Reform (Miscellaneous Provisions) Act 1941* (WA), s 4(4).

[33]   *Civil Law (Wrongs) Act 2002* (ACT), s 15(1); *Compensation to Relatives Act 1897* (NSW), s 6C; *Law Reform (Miscellaneous Provisions) Act 1992* (NT), s 5(1); *Succession Act 1981* (Qld), s 66(2)(d)(i); *Survival of Causes of Action Act 1940* (SA), s 5; *Administration and Probate Act 1935* (Tas), s 27(3)(c)(i); *Administration and Probate Act 1958* (Vic), s 29(2)(c)(i); *Law Reform (Miscellaneous Provisions) Act 1941* (WA), s 4(1)(c).

arising from injury to her wrongfully caused by the defendant.[34] Consortium may be translated as the society and services of the wife. The wife herself had no such claim at common law. In *Best v Samuel Fox* [1952] AC 716 the House of Lords considered this rule and admitted that the wife's lack of claim had no logical basis, concluding that legislative implementation of a claim by the wife for loss of consortium was needed. This has occurred in two Australian jurisdictions, where moderate awards have been made for loss of consortium.[35] In the Australian Capital Territory, Northern Territory and Victoria only the husband may claim while in New South Wales, Tasmania and Western Australia the right to consortium has been abolished.[36]

Claims under the action for loss of consortium fall under three heads (see Figure 21.4).

Figure 21.4: Consortium – heads of damage

Claims under the action for loss of consortium can be made for:
- loss of society of wife as such, including sexual companionship;
- loss of wife's domestic services; and
- medical and other expenses incurred by the husband arising from the injury.

The matter was summarised by the High Court in *Toohey v Hollier* (1955) 92 CLR 618 in relation to the first two heads. The damage must be of a "material and practical kind because of greatly reduced capacity of his wife to perform the domestic duties, to manage the household affairs and give him her support and assistance" (at 627).

The action for loss of consortium does not protect the husband for mere loss of happiness, although as will be seen some of the cases are very much on the borderline. *Toohey* also resolved, rightly it is submitted, a question that troubled the House of Lords in *Best* and on which it was evenly divided. The High Court held that the action protects the husband against impairment of the consortium as well as its total loss. So, the action is available if the wife's society is less amenable than previously, or if services are less perfectly rendered.

The action requires proof of injury to the wife causing the loss of consortium. Where it is the husband who is injured and the wife leaves him in consequence, that is not claimable by the husband as damages for loss of consortium, although it might sound in damages in the husband's own action: *Cameron v Nottingham Insurance Co* [1958] SASR 174.[37] It is generally accepted that a claim for loss of consortium does not

---

[34] See, for example, the comments of McPherson JA and Mullins J in *Karanfilov v Inghams Enterprises Pty Ltd* [2001] 2 Qd R 273; [2000] QCA 348.

[35] *Law Reform Act 1995* (Qld), s 13 (see, for example, *Lebon v Lake Placid Resort Pty Ltd* [2000] QSC 49; *Daly v D A Manufacturing Co Pty Ltd* [2002] QSC 308); *Civil Liability Act 2003* (Qld), s 58; *Civil Liability Act 1936* (SA), s 65; cf *Civil Liability (Wrongs) Act 2002* (ACT), s 100 – claim for loss of either spouse's ability to do housework available and the *Civil Liability Act 2002* (NSW), s 15B allows a dependant to claim damages for loss of capacity to provide domestic services (see, for example, *Kendrick v Bluescope Steel (AIS) Pty Ltd* [2007] NSWSC 1288). The Northern Territory has adopted the position that a wife may claim damages for her husband's loss of consortium as a dependant suing for his wrongful death: *Compensation (Fatal Injuries) Act 1974*, s 10(3)(c)).

[36] *Law Reform (Marital Consortium) Act 1984* (NSW), s 3; *Common Law (Miscellaneous Actions) Act 1986* (Tas), s 3.

[37] For the possibility of parasitic damages being awarded for this loss, see *Lampert v Eastern National Omnibus* [1954] 1 WLR 1047.

survive the death of the wife, though there is no compelling logic about this where the death results from the injury. Of course, the husband may have claims under the death legislation but these do not cover all the losses covered by a consortium claim. It has also been held that the consortium claim fails insofar as it relates to the period after divorce which those injuries have brought about: *Sloan v Kirby* (1979) 20 SASR 263 (death of partner); *Parker v Dzandra* [1979] Qd R 55 (divorce).

Loss of wife's society

[21.65] Here the courts tread a rather thin line between refusing to compensate the husband for mental disturbance and distress arising from the wife's condition and yet compensating him for the reduced benefit of the companionship he previously enjoyed. No compensation was therefore awarded to a husband who experienced no loss of companionship but only grief arising through his helpless wife's condition: *Meadows v Maloney* [1972] 4 SASR 567. On the other hand, compensation will be awarded where the wife is no longer able to participate with the husband in sporting or recreational activities which previously they enjoyed together: *Facer v Brewarine* (1962) 1 DCR (NSW) 1.

The cases on the loss of enjoyment of the wife's sexual society have moved from an original position of compensating only where the effect of the injury was to preclude the procreation of children (*Birch v Taubmans* [1957] SR (NSW) 93) to one of awarding damages where sexual enjoyment is precluded or impaired per se: *Curator of Estates v Fernandez* (1977) 16 ALR 445; *Shim v Extract Wool* (1969) 113 Sol Journal 672.[38]

Loss of wife's services

[21.70] This claim has a more obviously pecuniary basis than that for loss of society. Whatever services the wife is unable to render in the home need to be replaced by the husband at cost to himself. In *Cutts v Chumley* [1967] 1 WLR 742 where the injuries to the wife left her totally incapable of rendering services within the home, the husband was awarded UK£5,000 representing the future cost of employing a housekeeper to look after the three young children of the marriage. Where the wife is still able to render services although with greater difficulty than before, there is apparently no compensation.[39] Here, there is no substantial impairment of consortium. In England, where the action for loss of consortium was abolished some years ago, the wife is allowed to claim damages for her inability to render services to members of her family under an analogous principle to that in *Griffiths v Kerkemeyer* (1977) 139 CLR 161 and a similar approach has been adopted in some Australian decisions (to be considered in Chapter 22): *Daly v General Steam Navigation Co* [1980] 3 All ER 696.

Husband's out-of-pocket expenses

[21.75] Medical expenses actually incurred by the husband at the time of the action are recoverable by him; so it seems are future medical expenses. This claim is made in

---

[38]   See also *Talbot v Lusby* [1995] QSC 143 where Fryberg J suggested compensation can include damages for the loss in diminution in quantity or quality of sexual intercourse.

[39]   At least where there is no impairment in the quality of the services. "Whether she renders them with a scowl or a smile is immaterial": *Kealley v Jones* [1979] 1 NSWLR 723 per Hutley JA.

the husband's action for loss of consortium, though it is available in the absence of and substantial loss of society or even of services. It may therefore have an independent basis, that of the husband's legal obligation to maintain his wife: *Toohey v Hollier* (1955) 92 CLR 618.

The husband may also be able to claim for other out-of-pocket expenses, in particular the expense of hospital visits and even loss of earnings where, for example, the husband has given up his job in order to be able to visit his wife in hospital. The basis of the husband's claim here is sometimes said to be that he is mitigating damages by taking action to reduce the loss of consortium between himself and his wife: *McNeill v Johnstone* [1958] 1 WLR 888. This rather artificial explanation lies behind the decision in *Kirkham v Boughey* [1958] QB 338 at 342. In that case the husband had employment in Africa while his wife was resident in England. In consequence of his wife's injuries, the husband gave up his African employment in order to be near his wife in England and therefore sustained loss of earnings. This loss was held to be not recoverable by the husband since it could not be regarded as a means of sustaining consortium; nor did it make any difference that the action taken by the husband was reasonable. The principle of this case is in some doubt at the present time. If the husband's action could be seen as a reasonable one helping to alleviate his wife's condition, he might be able to establish a claim qua third party rather than qua husband, even though full consortium did not exist between himself and his wife.[40]

Conclusion

[21.80] The husband's action for loss of his wife's consortium is both archaic and anomalous. Its limitation to husbands reflects the common law thinking that the wife was the husband's property, or at least that he had a property right in her services and society. The assessment of damages involves the distasteful process of putting a monetary value on the wife's general and sexual companionship, this being necessary despite judicial assertions that the husband is not allowed to claim for loss of happiness. The deserving parts of the husband's claim (those relating to loss of services and recoverability of medical expenses) are capable of being covered by an extension of the *Griffiths v Kerkemeyer* principle, a development which has to some extent already taken place and one which creates no invidious gender distinction.

Parent's claim for injury to child

[21.85] Again, there must be a wrongful act by the defendant. Any tort causing injury to the child is sufficient.

Nature of parent's loss

[21.90] The loss for which this tort provides compensation is narrower than that of the husband's action for loss of consortium. The focus is on the loss of the services of the child, there is no compensation for loss of companionship. Nevertheless, the courts

---

[40] There is some support for this in *Hunter v Scott* [1963] Qd R 77. The husband was there allowed travel expenses and immediate loss of wages in transporting his wife to hospital, even though he had been awarded full damages for loss of consortium.

574 TORT IN PRINCIPLE

have not placed too stringent a test upon the proof of service. Thus trivial services, such as the making of a cup of tea (*Carr v Clarke* (1818) 2 Chit 260) or the milking of cows (*Bennett v Allcott* (1787) TR 166; 100 ER 90), engender a right to compensation. Indeed the presence of a child under the age of majority in the parent's household is normally enough to establish the fact of service: *Jones v Brown* (1794) 1 Esp 216; 170 ER 334. The child must, however, be of a sufficient age to render service; so damages were denied in the case of a two-year-old child: *Hall v Hollander* (1825) 4 B&C 660; 107 ER 1206. The fact that the child has attained majority does not exclude proof of service.

The damages claimable in this action, as in the case of the husband's action for loss of his wife's consortium, may not include anything to compensate for distress or grief arising from the injury to the child: *Flemington v Smithers* (1826) 2 C&P 292; 172 ER 131. Again, there is no claim for loss of services after the child's death. The parent may claim in this action the cost of medical bills that he or she has had to discharge as a result of the injury. This has been explained on the ground of the legal obligation of the father to pay expenses of this sort. However, although the parent may be made the subject of a maintenance order under statutory provisions for failing to provide the child with adequate means of support, it is unlikely that in the absence of express statutory provision or the applicability of the rules of contract there is any legal liability on the parent to meet the child's medical costs. Recoverability may therefore simply be an incident of the parent's claim for loss of services, and this means that the claim for medical expenses fails unless the parent is able to establish he or she was in receipt of the child's services. As in the case of the husband's action for loss of consortium, the difficulty would be solved if the child were able to claim in its own action for medical expenses incurred on its behalf under an extension to the *Griffiths v Kerkemeyer* principle.

In South Australia, where the death of an infant is caused by a wrongful act, neglect or default such that if death had not occurred the infant would have been able to maintain an action to recover damages against the defendant, the surviving parent or parents may be able to claim to a maximum financial amount as the court thinks just, by way of solatium for suffering caused to the parents by the death of their child: *Civil Liability Act 1936* (SA), s 28(1).

Who may claim

[21.95] Most of the cases on this are old; they confer a right of action on the father of the child. The rule is sometimes stated only in terms of recovery of damages by the father. However, the earlier cases were decided at a time when the father was regarded as having legal custody of his children to the exclusion of the mother. This has been abandoned in favour of the notion of joint custody vested in both parents where the marriage is subsisting; after divorce it might be in one or the other. In these circumstances, there is clearly no reason why the mother should not also be able to bring the action.

In South Australia, the surviving parent or parents may be able to claim to a maximum financial amount and the proceeds shall be divided between them in such shares as the court sees fit: *Civil Liability Act 1936* (SA), s 28(2). If only one parent brings an action, that parent is only entitled to such amount as he or she claims to be due to them (s 28(3)).

Conclusion

[21.100] The parent's action for loss of services of the child is even more anachronistic than the husband's claim for loss of his wife's consortium. The notion of services rendered by child to parent is out of keeping with modern society. But the action subsists throughout Australia. In cases where there is a genuine rendering of services by the child, for example in looking after a disabled parent, their loss through injury to the child should be recoverable under the child's own action under the suggested extension of *Griffiths v Kerkemeyer* (covered in Chapter 22).

Actio per quod servitium amisit

[21.105] At common law, the employer of an employee has an action against a third party who has, by the tortious infliction of injury on the employee, deprived the employer of the services of the employee, or by enticing or harbouring the employee, a liability which at least in theory continues to form part of Australian law.

The employer's action is in effect an action in tort for purely economic loss. That loss must be established as the basis of the action. The action, like the husband's action for loss of consortium and that of the parent for loss of the services of the child, has in recent years been regarded as anomalous. In England, prior to its total abrogation by statute, the Court of Appeal held that it was restricted to menial service, that is, to the loss of services of domestic servants living within the household: *Inland Revenue Commissioners v Hambrook* [1956] 2 QB 641. In effect this meant the almost entire abolition of the action in view of the rarity of that type of service. In Australia, however, this restriction has not been followed: *Commissioner for Railways (NSW) v Scott* (1959) 102 CLR 392. The action does not, however, apply in the case of "public officers" as opposed to "employees"; examples of the former category include members of the armed services (*Commonwealth v Quince* (1944) 68 CLR 227) and of the police force: *Attorney-General (NSW) v Perpetual Trustee Co Ltd* (1952) 85 CLR 237.

Figure 21.5: Deprivation of employee's services – general principles

- Employer must show economic loss.
- Economic loss may arise from:
  - loss of profits;
  - payment to employee of sick pay or pension; and/or
  - out-of-pocket expenses (eg medical expenses).

Loss of profits

[21.110] If the employer can show an actual loss of profit arising from the injury to the employee, damages may be recovered for it. However, it will be difficult to show such loss arising from the absence of a particular employee: in most cases the hiring of a substitute will avoid it, though in such a case any additional expense through hiring the substitute is recoverable. It will, therefore, be necessary to establish that the employee in question is not easily replaceable either because the employee has some special talent (*H E Round v Abbott* (1972) 1 ALJ 23) or is a member of a unique team: *Hanks v Scala Theodrome* [1947] KB 257.

Sick pay or pension

[21.115] Sick pay presents some difficulties. Two initial points should be noted. Where the employer has paid wages during the period of injury, the injured employee cannot recover the amount of those wages from the tortfeasor unless there is an express stipulation by the employer that anything recovered from the tortfeasor representing those wages must be repaid. The employer, will, in general, suffer an economic loss through the payment of wages to the employee during the period of injury. Second, the courts make no distinction in this question according to whether the payment of wages is voluntary or contractual: *Graham v Baker* (1961) 106 CLR 340; *Lind v Johnson* [1937] 4 All ER 201; *Dennis v LPTB* [1948] 1 All ER 779.[41]

On the question of the recovery of wages paid to the employee from the tortfeasor, three differing viewpoints have been espoused by the courts. A minority of judges have rejected the amount of wages paid as an indication of the value of the services lost.[42] A majority of judges have accepted it as evidence of that value and have awarded it as damages.[43] An in-between view is that the employer does not succeed merely by showing the payment of wages to an employee not at work; the employer must also show that a substitute has been engaged, or that the existing workforce has been paid extra money in order to cover the absence of the relevant employee.[44]

The case law is against the recovery of a pension paid by the employer to the injured employees: *Admiralty Commissioners v SS Amerika* [1917] AC 38.[45]

Out-of-pocket expenses

[21.120] There is little authority on this question. The statutory indemnity against the payment of workers' compensation payments given to the employer against the tortfeasor will, in general, preclude recovery of this loss in the action for loss of services. It has been suggested, though not decided, that medical expenses incurred by the employer are only recoverable where there is a legal obligation to pay them: *Attorney-General (NSW) v Perpetual Trustee Co Ltd* (1952) 85 CLR 237 per Fullagar J. The point remains undecided.

---

[41] South Australian courts have refused to deduct where the payment is voluntary: *Francis v Blackstone* [1955] SASR 270; *Volpato v Zachary* [1971] SASR 166.

[42] For example, McTiernan J in *Commonwealth v Quince* (1944) 68 CLR 227; Fullagar J in *Attorney-General (NSW) v Perpetual Trustee Co Ltd* (1952) 85 CLR 237.

[43] For example, the majority of judges in *Commonwealth v Quince* (1944) 68 CLR 227; the New South Wales Court of Appeal in *Sydney CC v Bosnich* [1968] 3 NSWR 725; *Bradford Corp v Webster* [1920] 2 KB 135; *Attorney-General v Valle-Jones* [1935] 2 KB 135.

[44] This point was accepted by Fullagar J in *Attorney-General (NSW) v Perpetual Trustee Co Ltd* (1952) 85 CLR 237.

[45] The basis is that the pension is deferred remuneration for past services and therefore cannot be used as a basis for evaluating the loss of future services. The point has some validity, but the pension is surely economic loss that the employer has suffered through losing his employee.

Conclusion

[21.125] The employer's action for loss of services is different in principle from the parent's action for loss of services of a child. The services in question are now almost exclusively commercial in nature, and the nature of the action is one for pure economic loss. It would normally be possible for employers to take out insurance against financial loss caused through injury to their employees, and it is suggested that additional protection through the actio per quod servitium amisit no longer serves a useful purpose. If the main purpose of the action were to be the protection of the "good employer" who continues to pay wages after sickness or injury of the employee, the same could be achieved by not deducting the amount of those wages from damages in the employee's own action. But the courts appear unwilling to adopt this position. The action has been abolished in England.

Defences

[21.130] In all the torts protecting against loss of consortium or services through infliction of injury, a wrongful act on the part of the defendant is required. This means that any defence which would have existed against the victim of the tort, for example volenti non fit injuria, will also prevail against the plaintiff. Traditionally the common law excluded the defence of contributory negligence from such claims. The independent nature of the claim of the husband, the parent or the employer thus attracted no reduction of damages for contributory negligence of the victim.[46] Statute now permits the defence in all cases where the defendant could have pleaded the defence against the victim, in most Australian jurisdictions. The *Civil Liability Act 1936* (SA), s 45, for instance provides that "[i]n a claim for damages brought on behalf of the dependants of a deceased person, the court is to have regard to any contributory negligence on the part of the deceased person". It is to be noted that the *Civil Liability Act 2002* (NSW), s 5S, takes the defence of contributory negligence to its logical (albeit extreme) conclusion by providing:

> In determining the extent of a reduction in damages by reason of contributory negligence, a court may determine a reduction of 100% if the court thinks it just and equitable to do so, with the result that the claim for damages is defeated.

Similar provisions can be found in the civil liability legislation of the Australian Capital Territory, Queensland, Tasmania and Victoria. In these jurisdictions, it is therefore possible for a claim to be defeated altogether where it is determined that the victim contributed "100%" to his or her own injury which resulted in death.[47]

---

[46] *Mallet v Dunn* [1949] 2 KB 180 establishes this in relation to negligence of the wife where a husband is claiming for loss of consortium; this was followed by the High Court in *Curran v Young* (1965) 112 CLR 99.

[47] See also *Civil Law (Wrongs) Act 2002* (ACT), s 47; *Civil Liability Act 2003* (Qld), s 24; *Wrongs Act 1954* (Tas), s 4; *Wrongs Act 1958* (Vic), s 63.

Practice Questions

Revision Questions

21.1 Under what circumstances may a person claim death as a tortious cause of action? Discuss.

21.2 In an action involving loss of consortium, what sort of damages are claimable by a plaintiff?

21.3 Under what circumstances, if any, can an employer recover damages for an injury to an employee?

21.4 Can a parent recover damages for injury to a child? Discuss.

Answers to Practice Questions

Revision Questions

21.1 A dependant may claim damages for loss of the value of the dependency by reason of the death of the person upon whom he or she was dependent as a result of the wrong committed by the defendant. The common law rule was that no action lay; but a statutory cause of action now exists in all jurisdictions. The persons who may be able to recover damages under the statutory provisions are those who satisfy the two conditions that establish dependency: that is, they fall within the statutory list of relatives; and they have a reasonable expectation of future benefit from the continuance of the deceased's life.

21.2 In an action for loss of consortium, which originally was restricted to a right only belonging to the husband and which has now been abolished in New South Wales, Tasmania and Western Australia, a husband could claim for:

- loss of society of the wife, that is, reduced companionship including sexual companionship;
- loss of her domestic services; and
- medical and other expenses incurred or to be incurred by the husband arising from the injury.

21.3 The employer must be able to show that the tortious infliction of injury on the employee has deprived the employer of the services of the employee and that as a consequence has resulted in economic loss arising from:

- loss of profits, for example arising from some special talent that is not easily replaced;
- payment of sick pay or pension entitlements; and/or
- other out-of-pocket expenses, such as medical costs.

21.4 Provided there is a wrongful act by a defendant causing injury to the child, the answer is yes. The loss that is recoverable is only for the loss of the services of the child. There is no compensation for loss of companionship from the injury as such. Note, however, that in some jurisdictions, such as South Australia where the injury leads to death, the parent will be entitled to claim a limited amount as solatium: *Civil Liability Act 1936* (SA), s 28(1).

Tutorial Questions

Discussion Questions

21.1 In the assessment of damages in the case of death as a cause of action, discuss some of the matters you think a court should consider in arriving at a just figure for the dependants.

21.2 Where death is the cause of action, why should it be difficult for the courts to assess damages? Discuss.

SECTION

6

Remedies

The character of the different areas of tort law is found in the nature of the wrong committed. The majority of this book has focused on the identification of an actionable wrong and thus of the categorisation of individual torts. We now turn to the question of how these legal wrongs are redressed. In tort, the legal redress for wrongs is found under the general heading of "remedies" and may, for example, consist in enforcing a right, preventing a potential wrong or seeking compensation for, or "correcting", a wrong that may have been committed. The domain of remedies then underpins the very essence of the practice of the law of torts. In this section of the book we consider the various forms of redress or "remedies" that are available to a person who has experienced a breach of right in tort law. With the essence of each individual tort lying in the specific nature of the wrong (and thus loss or harm incurred) a wide range of remedies have developed; thus it could be said that there are as many remedies as there are torts (because for every tort, there is a remedy). The most common form of remedy is "self-help". This generally consists in the offended person "taking the law into their own hands" to correct a perceived wrong or tort. Another type of remedy is a "declaration". In this type of remedy, the offended party usually seeks a "declaration" from the court as to his or her legal rights. The essence of the remedy is that it clarifies and vindicates a legal position and thus provides satisfaction to the parties who seek it. In addition to these forms of remedies there are more substantive remedies in the form of compensatory damages and injunctions. The focus of this section of the book will be on these two latter remedies.

CHAPTER 22

Remedies for a Tort

Reading

Sappideen, Vines, Grant and Watson, *Torts: Commentary and Materials*, pp 68-81, 99-110, 142-154 and Chapter 15.

Objectives

This chapter will:

* examine the two main remedies for a tort: damages and an injunction;
* consider the role and function of damages in tort;
* consider the different classification of damages;
* examine the different categories of damages available for personal injury;
* explain deductibility of collateral benefits from damages;
* explain the duty to mitigate damages;
* consider the liability of a third party to the plaintiff;
* explain under what circumstances property damage is valued for the purpose of awarding damages; and
* examine the principles under which an injunction may be granted by a court.

Principles

Introduction

[22.05] There are two principal remedies in tort. The first is the action for damages, the second the action for an injunction.

A plaintiff who proves that he or she has suffered personal injury and establishes that it was the defendant who was responsible must be awarded damages, unless there are statutory restrictions on recovery.[1] Damages are assessed in terms of "the purchasing power of the currency at the date of assessment of the damages": *O'Brien v McKean* (1968) 118 CLR 540 per Barwick CJ at 544. Failure to award them can result in an appealable error and the ordering of a new trial limited to damages: *Wilton v Commonwealth* (1990) 12 MVR 243.

Figure 22.1

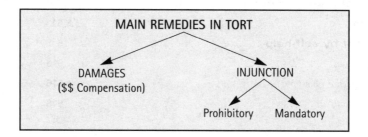

Injunctions are of two kinds:

- the prohibitory injunction, ordering the defendant to desist from some tortious activity; and

- the mandatory injunction, ordering the defendant to perform an act necessary to stop a tort being committed by the defendant.

A third remedy, self-help, is considered in Chapter 7. Other remedies may be available, such as the action for a declaration that a tort is being committed, but they lie outside the scope of this book.

Damages

[22.10] Damages in tort, apart from exemplary damages, have a *compensatory function*. In the tort of negligence usually only compensatory damages are awarded to an injured party while in the case of the intentional torts, nominal, compensatory, aggravated and

---

1   New South Wales and Victoria have capped damages for non-pecuniary loss: *Civil Liability Act 2002* (NSW), s 16; *Wrongs Act 1958* (Vic), ss 28G, 28H. Western Australia sets a threshold amount that must be reached before damages for non-pecuniary loss will be awarded: *Civil Liability Act 2002* (WA), ss 9, 10. South Australia requires that an injured party suffers significant impairment of normal life for at least seven days or medical expenses of a statutory prescribed minimum: *Civil Liability Act 1936* (SA), s 52. For further detail regarding the legislative scheme with respect to non-pecuniary loss, refer Figure 22.4.

exemplary damages can be awarded. Their general aim, to the extent that monetary compensation can provide it, is to restore the plaintiff to the position he or she was in before the tort was committed.[2] The limitations of monetary compensation in cases of personal injury are obvious. A lost leg cannot be truly compensated for by an award of damages but the aim is to restore, as far as possible, the pre-tort standard of living. The function of tort damages in attempting to restore the plaintiff to the former position he or she enjoyed to some extent differentiates tort damages from contract damages, although contract damages may fulfil the same function.

An alternative basis of the award of contract damages is to put the plaintiff into the position he or she would have been in had the contract been properly performed, allowing a claim in relation to the expected profit under the contract which has been lost by its breach. Expectation damages of this sort are unusual in tort, although the line of decisions compensating persons for lost expectations under a will shows that damages of this sort may be awarded in a tort case: see [8.110]. Furthermore, tort damages will allow a claim for loss of profits where a profit-earning chattel has been destroyed, or for loss of future earnings in cases of personal injury.

Damages of this sort are not quite the same as damages for lost expectations in contract. In the first place, they are awarded for the future developments of a loss which is not itself an expectation loss. Second, they are based on the court making reasonable assumptions as to what the future loss is likely to be, whereas expectation damages in contract compensate for a specific loss defined by the contract.

In assessing damages in the case of negligence, a defendant is liable to the full extent of any injuries the defendant causes to the plaintiff, even if the injuries were more extensive than would normally be expected because of the plaintiff's unusual susceptibility: *Australian Capital Territory Schools Authority v El-Sheik* [2000] Aust Torts Reports 81-577. This principle applies not only where the damage sustained by the plaintiff is personal injury, but also where it is damage to property: *McColl v Dionisatos* [2002] Aust Torts Reports 81-652 at [27]-[33]. The wrongful act or omission of the defendant *must* cause the injury or damage to the plaintiff. The causative link between the defendant's conduct and the harm suffered by the plaintiff is thus crucial in any claim for remedies. It is thus the case that a defendant is not responsible for harm to the plaintiff which would have occurred independently of the defendant's conduct in any case.[3] The onus is on the defendant to establish that the plaintiff's condition was traceable to causes other than the defendant's actions: *Purkess v Crittenden* (1965) 114 CLR 164.

Classification of damages

[22.13] Whilst damages are primarily compensatory, there are four different classes of damage which can be awarded to meet specific needs identified by the court.

---

2 *Haines v Bendall* (1991) 172 CLR 60 at 63.
3 For example, in *Watts v Rake* (1960) 108 CLR 158 where the plaintiff, prior to the accident, was suffering from a disease which would have crippled him within 10 to 13 years, the court only awarded damages assessed on his incapacity caused by the accident for the 13 years following the accident.

Figure 22.2: Types of damages

- Contemptuous (the plaintiff has a cause of action but the court feels it should not have been brought) OR nominal (the plaintiff has a right but suffered no loss).
- Special (awarded in relation to pre-trial losses arising from injury) OR general (awarded for future loss).
- Aggravated (awarded to compensate the plaintiff for injured feelings) OR exemplary (punitive damages intended to punish the defendant).
- Parasitic (awarded for infringement of an interest which is not protected by the relevant tort).

Contemptuous and nominal damages

[22.15] Contemptuous and nominal damages are the same in that they award a token sum to the plaintiff equivalent to no damages at all although neither would be available in either negligence or nuisance as damage is central to both actions.[4] They differ in purpose. Nominal damages are awarded to the plaintiff to vindicate the right that has been violated where the plaintiff has not suffered a loss for which substantial damages might be awarded. In *Constantine v Imperial Hotels* [1944] KB 693 the plaintiff was unjustifiably refused accommodation in the defendants' hotel, in breach of their common law duty as an innkeeper. This was a tort. The plaintiff could show no actual loss arising from the tort, but nevertheless recovered UK£5 damages which were in effect nominal. Contemptuous damages are damages limited to the smallest coin of the realm,[5] and indicate the opinion of the court that although the plaintiff has established his or her case, *the action should not have been brought*. The invariable result is that the plaintiff will be penalised in the costs of the action.

Special and general damages

[22.20] Special damages are those which arise prior to the plaintiff coming to court and require precise pleading and proof; general damages are those which may be presumed to arise from the fact that the tort has been committed, and require a certain amount of speculation as they are awarded in anticipation of future loss, thus they do not require precise pleading and proof. An award of general damages is particularly appropriate in the case of torts actionable per se, where damages are said to be "at large". A particularly clear example of this process is the tort of defamation, where large general damages are routinely awarded for presumed injury to reputation without proof of any actual loss. The term, "special damages", must be distinguished from the term, "special damage". Special damage is used to denote the damage necessary to establish a cause of action for a tort actionable only upon proof of damage. For example, in the case of negligence causing personal injury, the special damage is the injury. Special damages are awarded

---

4   Nor are nominal damages available under s 82(1) of the *Trade Practices Act* (Cth) for the same reason.

5   For example, the award of a farthing (quarter of a penny) damages to the plaintiff in *Newstead v London Express Newspapers* [1940] 1 KB 377, for defamation; see also *Dering v Uris* [1964] 2 QB 669; *Pamplin v Express Newspapers (No 2)* [1988] 1 WLR 116.

in relation to the *pre-trial loss* arising from such an injury. General damages are awarded for *future loss*, which is presumed by the law to occur in the case of a permanent injury. The plaintiff must precisely plead and prove damages for loss of earnings or medical expenses incurred prior to the trial of the case. On the other hand, general damages for future loss of earnings and medical expenses do not need precise proof, though the plaintiff is generally expected to provide evidence upon which such an award can be based.

Aggravated and exemplary damages

[22.25] These two forms of damages differ in function. Aggravated damages are awarded to *compensate the plaintiff for injured feelings or outrage* arising from the commission of the tort, ie they compensate the injured person for mental harm which falls short of psychiatric illness.[6] Exemplary damages, sometimes also called punitive damages, are awarded to *indicate the law's disapproval of the defendant's conduct* and are concerned with the nature of the tortious conduct rather than its effect on the plaintiff. Aggravated damages are in their basis compensatory; exemplary damages are not, although the actual award of exemplary damages goes to swell the damages award of the plaintiff. Despite this difference in function, the two sets of damages have much in common. First, both were originally thought to be limited to torts actionable per se, though it is now clear that this limitation no longer exists. For example, aggravated damages have been awarded in the tort of deceit (*Archer v Brown* [1984] 3 WLR 350),[7] a tort requiring proof of damage. However, there are questions of law about whether aggravated damages can be awarded for nuisance: *Willoughby Municipal Council v Halstead* (1916) 22 CLR 352 or negligence: *Hunter Area Health Service v Marchlewski* (2000) 51 NSWLR 268 at 284-288. Second, both types of damages generally presuppose the existence of a morally delinquent defendant. For this reason, some courts have taken the view that where the same conduct would justify an award of both aggravated and exemplary damages, a single award should be made to cover both. For example, in *Johnstone v Stewart* [1968] SASR 142, Bray CJ made a single award to cover both sets of damages where a private inquiry agent had committed trespass to land and battery against the plaintiff ($700 for the trespass to land and $2,400 for the battery). On the other hand, where police officers had combined in an attack on a person in police custody and one of them had urinated on him, the court awarded $10,000 under each head of damages against the defendant.[8] The court in this case emphasised the difference in function between the two sets of damages, expressing disagreement with the approach taken in *Johnstone*. But the evidence in *Henry v Thompson* [1989] Aust Torts Reports 80-265 revealed that the defendants in that case would have had their aggravated but not exemplary damages paid by the police force, and this may be thought to have been an influential factor in the making of separate awards.

---

[6]   Aggravated damages are not available in cases of pure mental harm unless it can be established that the mental harm amounts to psychiatric illness: *Hunter Area Health Service v Marchlewski* (2000) 51 NSWLR 268.

[7]   They may also be awarded for injurious falsehood: *Joyce v Sengupta* [1993] 1 WLR 337.

[8]   In *Schmidt v Argent* [2003] QCA 507, Schmidt succeeded in an action against both police officers and the police force for false imprisonment, battery and assault and successfully recovered both aggravated and exemplary damages against the police officers, aggravated damages against the State of Queensland (exemplary damages are not recoverable for torts committed by police officers), as well as recovering special damages. See also *De Reus v Gray* (2003) 9 VR 432; [2003] VSCA 84 where Gray was the subject of an unnecessary and unauthorised police strip search at a police station and was awarded punitive and compensatory damages (which included aggravated damages).

It was a matter of some conjecture whether an award of substantial damages could be made in torts such as trespass where the defendant's conduct had caused the plaintiff no injury, unless there was an aggravated element in the conduct of the defendant (though it has always been clear that substantial damages may be awarded as general damages for defamation, whatever the nature of the defendant's conduct). This matter has been clarified by recent decisions holding that a plaintiff is entitled to an award of substantial general damages for the trespass by reason of its effect on the plaintiff in the form of humiliation or injury to feelings, independent of the nature of the defendant's conduct in committing the trespass: *Spautz v Butterworth* (1996) 41 NSWLR 1; *Vignoli v Sydney Harbour Casino* [2000] Aust Torts Reports 81-541; *Thompson v Commissioner of Police* [1997] 3 WLR 403. If that conduct is outrageous or insulting, the plaintiff is entitled to an additional award of aggravated damages.[9] The case law has confirmed the tort of false imprisonment, but the principle established is not limited to that tort.

Exemplary damages are by their very nature anomalous. Though intended as punishment of the defendant, their effect is to increase the plaintiff's compensation. In Australia, the law appears to be that in an appropriate case any tort may attract an award of exemplary damages,[10] although some jurisdictions have placed statutory restrictions on the awarding of exemplary damages.[11] The High Court in *Lamb v Cotogno* (1987) 164 CLR 1 at 8 approved a statement in *Mayne and MacGregor on Damages* to the effect that their award is appropriate where the defendant's conduct discloses "fraud, malice, violence, cruelty, insolence or the like, or (the defendant) acts in contumelious disregard of the plaintiff's rights".[12] In *Coloca v BP Australia* [1992] 2 VR 441 it was held that the cause of action did not determine whether exemplary damages could be awarded, and that they might therefore be awarded in an action for negligence (actions brought by workers against employers alleging prolonged exposure, in the one case to benzol fumes causing leukemia and in the other to asbestos dust causing asbestosis).

In *Lamb* the High Court approved an award of $5,000 exemplary damages made against the defendant motorist who drove in such a way as to throw the plaintiff off the bonnet of his car, and then drove off leaving the plaintiff injured. The small size of the award reflected the fact that the plaintiff had been engaged in serious provocative conduct.[13] It emerged at the trial that exemplary damages awarded by the court would be paid by the defendant's compulsory insurer. Nevertheless the court approved their award. This seems unsatisfactory, and no convincing explanation for making the award in these circumstances appears in the judgment, except that a token disapproval is better than none at all, and conceivably may have deterrent force. On the other hand, in *Canterbury*

---

[9] As in *Vignoli v Sydney Harbour Casino* [2000] Aust Torts Reports 81-541 in which the plaintiff also received exemplary damages.

[10] *AB v South West Water Services Ltd* [1993] QB 507; cf *Commonwealth v Murray* [1988] Aust Torts Reports 80-207 in which exemplary damages were awarded in nuisance.

[11] New South Wales in *Civil Liability Act 2002*, s 21, the *Motor Accidents Act 1988*, s 81A, the *Motor Accidents Compensation Act 1999*, s 144 and the *Workers Compensation Act 1987*, s 151R; Queensland in the *Civil Liability Act 2003*, s 52, the *Motor Accident Insurance Act 1994*, s 55 and the *Workers Compensation and Rehabilitation Act 2003*, s 309(2); Northern Territory in the *Personal Injuries (Liabilities and Damages) Act 2003*, s 19; South Australia in the *Motor Vehicles Act 1959*, s 113A; Western Australia in a surviving cause of action under the *Law Reform (Miscellaneous Provisions) Act 1941*, s 4(2), *Workers Compensation and Rehabilitation Act 1981*, s 93B(3); Tasmania in a surviving cause of action under the *Administration and Probate Act 1935*, s 27(3); Australian Capital Territory in a surviving cause of action under the *Civil Law (Wrongs) Act 2002*, s 16(2).

[12] See also *Midialco Pty Ltd v Rabenalt* [1989] VR 461. But exemplary damages are unavailable as a matter of law in an action by dependants under Lord Campbell's Act: *Reindel v James Hardie* [1994] 1 VR 619.

[13] For a similar factual situation to *Lamb*, see *Andary v Burford* [1994] Aust Torts Reports 81-203 – exemplary damages reduced to $3,750 because of plaintiff's provocation.

Bankstown Rugby League Football Club Ltd v Rogers [1993] Aust Torts Reports 81-246, where the plaintiff received injury from the foul tackle of an opponent (which was nevertheless regarded by the court as being merely an unauthorised mode of performing the player's duties and not outside the course of his employment), the court ordered the club to pay aggravated but not exemplary damages to the plaintiff. The aggravated damages award was based on the fact that the club had the same liability vicariously as that of the player who committed the tackle, but there was no ground to award exemplary damages, by way of punishment, against a defendant who was not at fault. An English decision in *Archer v Brown* [1984] 3 WLR 350, refusing to make an award of exemplary damages where the defendant had been convicted and sentenced before a criminal court for the conduct producing the tort, was followed by the High Court in *Gray v Motor Accident Commission* (1998) 196 CLR 1, though the court indicated that this conclusion was not inevitable. Provocative conduct on the part of the plaintiff may justify a reduction in the amount of either aggravated or exemplary damages awarded. But the High Court held in *Fontin v Katapodis* (1962) 108 CLR 177 that such conduct cannot be a reason for reducing damages awarded as compensation for actual injury or damage. So, where UK£2,800 had been awarded to a plaintiff for an injury caused by having a pane of glass thrown at him, while he had to some extent provoked the attack, these damages should not have been reduced to UK£2,000 for that provocation because they contained no aggravated or exemplary element.

To the extent that exemplary damages are punitive in character, the place of such damages in the law of torts (which primarily seeks to compensate) has always been problematic. As noted by the majority in the American case *State Farm Mutual Automobile Insurance Co v Campbell* 123 S Ct 1513 (2002): "defendants subjected to punitive damages in civil cases have not been accorded the protections applicable in a criminal proceedings". Not surprisingly, exemplary damages became an issue in the tort reform initiatives in 2000. Exemplary damages are now excluded in personal injury claims in New South Wales under the *Civil Liability Act 2002*, s 21.[14] Similarly s 19 of the Northern Territory's *Personal Injuries (Liabilities and Claims) Act 2003* provides that "a court must not award aggravated damages or exemplary damages in respect of a personal injury". The *Civil Liability Act 2003* (Qld), on the other hand, restricts the award of such damages in personal injuries to only instances where the act that caused the injury was either an unlawful intentional act done with intent to cause personal injury, or an unlawful sexual assault (or other unlawful sexual misconduct): see s 52 (there is clear rejection of this type of damage in most other jurisdictions as well: refer detail in n 11). The uniform defamation laws also specifically exclude the awarding of exemplary damages: *Civil Law (Wrongs) Act 2002* (ACT), s 139H; *Defamation Act 2005* (NSW), (Qld), (Tas), (Vic) and (WA), s 37; *Defamation Act 2006* (NT), s 34; *Defamation Act 2005* (SA), s 35. Nor are exemplary and aggravated damages available under the *Trade Practices Act 1974* (Cth).

Parasitic damages

[22.30] This term refers to damages awarded for the infringement of an interest which is not protected by the tort concerned. While the term "parasitic damages" was not favoured in a number of cases (*Spartan Steel & Alloys Ltd v Martin & Co (Contractors) Ltd* [1973] QB 27 at 35 and in *Caltex Oil (Australia) Pty Ltd v The Dredge Willemstad* (1970) 136 CLR 529 at 598), it is used here because it reflects the fact that the damages

---

[14] Exemplary damages are still recoverable in intentional tort cases: *New South Wales v Ibbett* (2005) 65 NSWLR 168.

awarded are "secondary" in nature and derive from "primary" direct conduct of the defendant which is unlawful. Where that tort can be established without reference to the infringement of that interest, parasitic damages may be awarded. So, damages for loss of reputation have been awarded in the torts of conversion (*Thurston v Charles* (1905) 21 TLR 659) and false imprisonment: *Childs v Lewis* (1924) 40 TLR 870; *Walter v Alltools Ltd* (1944) 61 TLR 39.[15] In *Lampert v Eastern National Omnibus* [1954] 1 WLR 1047, a woman who suffered severe facial disfigurement in a car accident received damages for the resulting loss of her husband's consortium, even though she could not have claimed for this separately. Parasitic damages are sometimes also referred to as "secondary" damages.

Measure of damages

Figure 22.3: Measure of damages

> Measure of damages concerns VALUATION of the foreseeable loss, not foreseeability.

[22.35] It is clear law that *foreseeability is not relevant* to the measure of damages in tort. Foreseeability is of course generally necessary in order to establish the initial tortious liability but once this is done, the financial consequences do not themselves have to be foreseeable. So, it costs far more to inflict personal injury on a person with high earnings (assuming there is some loss of those earnings) than on an unemployed person. The explanation for this is that it is part of the same rule considered in Chapter 11 under which the extent of foreseeable injury or damage need not be reasonably foreseeable. The rule concerning measure of damages is therefore one concerning the *valuation* of the foreseeable loss. Some financial consequences of the tort may not be foreseeable, and are therefore too remote. There is also a rule at present of uncertain status enunciated in *Liesbosch Dredger v SS Edison* [1933] AC 449 to the effect that, where the victim of the tort is impecunious, any damages flowing from that impecuniosity are not recoverable from the tortfeasor: see [22.100] and [22.130]. It is also important to note the clear provision under the uniform defamation laws that the damages awarded must "bear a rational relationship to the harm": *Civil Law (Wrongs) Act 2002* (ACT), s 139E; *Defamation Act 2005* (NSW), (Qld), (Tas), (Vic) and (WA), s 34; *Defamation Act 2006* (NT), s 31; *Defamation Act 2005* (SA), s 32.

Damages for personal injury

[22.40] Damages are potentially complicated, thus only an extremely broad account can be offered here.[16] The broad categories of damages are pecuniary (economic) and non-pecuniary; these can be subdivided as set out in Figure 22.4:

---

[15] But *Lonrho v Fayed (No 5)* [1991] 1 WLR 1489 held that damages for injury to reputation cannot be awarded in conspiracy.

[16] For an extremely detailed account, see Luntz, *Assessment of Damages for Personal Injury and Death* (4th ed, Butterworths, 2002).

Figure 22.4: Categories

> Damages for personal injury may be divided into:
> • Pain and suffering ⎫
> • Loss of amenity ⎬ Non-pecuniary losses
> • Loss of expectation of life ⎭
> • Loss of expected benefits (for example earnings)
> • Out-of-pocket expenses, in particular, medical expenses

The first three points are often referred to as damages for non-pecuniary loss. Courts awarding damages now invariably itemise the award in the above manner. It should be noted that the awards of damages for non-pecuniary loss are adjusted from time to time to take account of inflation. There are, however, problems in making this adjustment in relation to awards for future pecuniary loss which are considered below.

Pain and suffering

[22.45] Three points may be noted. First, there is no scientific means of measuring damages for pain and suffering. Generally, as a matter of practice the award was made on a "tariff" basis, though the standard differed from State to State and the use of a tariff system was to some extent discouraged by the High Court in *Planet Fisheries Pty Ltd v La Rosa* (1968) 119 CLR 118. Second, the phrase "pain and suffering" was not restricted to physical pain but extended to worry, anxiety, frustration, inconvenience and discomfort that may follow from an injury and its subsequent treatment: *Sharman v Evans* (1977) 138 CLR 563; *Wickham v Treloar* [1960] NSWR 86. Finally, the predominant purpose of these damages was to compensate for the *subjective* fact of the injury on the plaintiff. Thus an unconscious plaintiff could not claim this head because the pain and suffering of an unconscious plaintiff would be less than that of a conscious plaintiff. In other words, the plaintiff who suffers less, receives less. In the case of *Skelton v Collins* (1966) 115 CLR 94, the plaintiff was not awarded any damages for pain and suffering because he was unconscious, which meant he could not experience pain and therefore could not suffer. Similarly, a plaintiff who is prepared to "put up" with the pain and suffering compared with a plaintiff who is not will receive less under this head although the former may recover more than the latter under the head of loss of amenity: *Burke v Batchelor* (1980) 24 SASR 33. Where actual mental illness supervened on the injury, additional compensation was awarded for this: *Admiralski v Stehbens* [1960] Qd R 510.[17]

How does one ascribe monetary value to "pain and suffering"? The assessment of damages for pain and suffering was and remains a complex exercise. In common law it is a matter of discretion based on what is fair and just in the particular circumstances, but having regard to similar awards.[18] In the case of a jury assessment for pain and suffering, it is not unusual for a defendant to appeal against quantum on the grounds that it is

---

[17]   But see *Overland Sydney Pty Ltd v Piatti* [1992] Aust Torts Reports 81-191 – pre-existing vulnerable personality led to a reduction of damages for the neurosis by 7.5%.

[18]   *Miller v Jennings* (1954) 92 CLR 190 sets out the circumstances under which an appellate court may interfere with a trial judge's assessment for pain and suffering.

manifestly excessive. In such cases, the onus is on the defendant to show either that no properly instructed jury could arrive at that figure (*Australian Iron and Steel Pty Ltd v Greenwood* (1962) 107 CLR 308) or that the verdict was not one that reasonable jurors could make based on the totality of the evidence: *Calin v Greater Union Organisation Pty Ltd* (1991) 173 CLR 33.

The award of damages *in negligence* for non-economic loss (which includes pain and suffering) is now regulated by statute in all Australian jurisdictions. Under the *Civil Liability Act 2002* (NSW) for instance, "no damages may be awarded for non-economic loss unless the severity of the non-economic loss is at least 15% of a most extreme case". Section 16(2) also provides that "the maximum amount of damages that may be awarded for non-economic loss is $350,000, but the maximum amount is to be awarded only in a most extreme case". There are similar limits under the *Personal Injuries (Liabilities and Claims) Act 2003* (NT), s 24 (for more detail, refer Figure 22.5).

Loss of amenity

[22.50] Damages under this head differ from pain and suffering in that they are said to be established upon an "objective" basis. In Queensland, for example, in assessing where non-pecuniary loss lies for loss of amenity, the court is required to adopt an entirely objective approach when assessing the gravity of the plaintiff's injury by adopting an "injury scale value" of 0 to 100 where 100 is an "injury of the gravest conceivable kind": *Civil Liability Act 2003*, (Qld), s 61(1). New South Wales (*Civil Liability Act 2002*, s 16), South Australia (*Civil Liability Act 1936*, s 52) and the Commonwealth (*Trade Practices Act 1974*, s 87P(2)) have also adopted statutory scale systems but refer to the gravity of the plaintiff's non-pecuniary loss. Determining the severity of a plaintiff's non-economic loss under a statutory scale system involves an evaluative process and an exercise of discretion: *Woolworths Ltd v Lawlor* [2004] NSWCA 209. The loss is that particular function that the relevant limb or organ conferred upon the plaintiff, whatever the plaintiff's own subjective feelings about it. The difference is a questionable one. The claim for loss of amenity (or loss of enjoyment of life) is an almost invariable associate of a damages claim for personal injury. Loss of amenity includes difficulty in going about everyday affairs, such as dressing oneself, scarring as the result of an accident,[19] and in participation in sporting and recreational activities (probably increased in the case of professional players, though actual authority is not conclusive on this). It extends to the inability to participate in or obtain enjoyment from sexual activity: *Linsell v Robertson* [1976] 1 NSWLR 249. As in the case of pain and suffering, there is no possibility of money replacing the loss suffered. Again, therefore, the sum awarded will tend to be fixed upon a "tariff" basis.

The problem whether these damages are subjective or objective is particularly emphasised where the loss of amenity is that of an unconscious plaintiff. As seen in [22.45] damages for pain and suffering may not be awarded to such a plaintiff. Nevertheless, in *West v Sheppard* [1964] AC 326 the House of Lords made a very substantial award of damages for loss of amenity, even though the plaintiff was either unconscious, or only dimly conscious, of her condition. The dissentient minority was

---

[19]   The subjective element in the assessment of damages under this head does not extend to permitting the court to assume that women suffer a greater degree of loss as a result of scarring than men because they attach greater importance to their appearance: *Ralevski v Dimovski* (1987) 7 NSWLR 485. However, the court is entitled to assume (without evidence to the contrary) that appearance is subjectively important to a woman: *Ponte v Del Ponte* (1987) 11 NSWLR 498.

willing to award the plaintiff some, but much less, damages for loss of amenity on the ground that she had some very limited perception of her condition. However, the High Court in *Skelton v Collins* (1966) 115 CLR 94 held that in cases of loss of amenity where the plaintiff was totally unconscious, only a small, conventional sum should be awarded (in that case $3,000 for loss of amenity and loss of expectation of life: it is worth noting that Windeyer J would, on these facts, have made a nil award under the head of loss of amenity). A considerably higher award will be made where the plaintiff has some awareness of his or her condition. In *Dundas v Harbour Motors Pty Ltd* [1988] Aust Torts Reports 80-161 the plaintiff had received brain damage which placed him mentally in the bottom 1% of the population. He was fully conscious but had little awareness of his condition. An award of $15,000 was approved.

Loss of expectation of life

[22.55] It should be remembered that Australian legislation precludes this head of damages surviving to the estate: see [21.40]. Nevertheless, the deceased may claim for it in his or her own lifetime. The sum awarded is a small, conventional sum variable within the factors stated by the House of Lords in *Benham v Gambling* [1941] AC 157: the sum would vary not according to the length of the life that was lost but to the loss of future happiness that the death caused. The character and habits of the deceased, his or her personal circumstances and state of health were identified as relevant considerations to the award. The original sum suggested by *Benham* has had to be revised by reason of inflation: *Yorkshire Electricity Board v Naylor* [1968] AC 529; *Sharman v Evans* (1977) 138 CLR 563.[20] Where the plaintiff is aware of his or her reduced life expectancy, additional damages beyond that of the conventional sum may be awarded for pain and suffering, though sometimes these damages are regarded as part of those for loss of expectation of life.[21] It is important to note, however, that as a form of non-pecuniary loss, any damages awarded in negligence under this head of damage is subject to the general limits under relevant State and Territory legislation on civil liability claims. In the context of personal injury claims, the civil liability legislation across all jurisdictions has provided some clear guidelines to be followed.

[20]   In *Hannell v Amaca Pty Ltd* [2006] WASC 310 (Le Miere J's decision was later reversed in *Amaca Pty Ltd v Hannell* (2007) 34 WAR 109 but not on the grounds of the proper assessment of damages), Le Miere J awarded $15,000 for lost expectation of life calculated calculated at 21.78 years.
[21]   Where this is the case, the High Court in *Sharman v Evans* (1977) 138 CLR 563 thought that the damages should be awarded under the head of pain and suffering.

Figure 22.5: Damages for non-pecuniary loss (personal injury)

Juris	Legislation	Sec	Provision
ACT	*Civil Law (Wrongs) Act 2002*	s 99	Tariffs for damages for non-economic loss
NSW	*Civil Liability Act 2002*	Div 3	Fixing Damages for non-economic loss (general damages)
		s 16	Determination of damages for non-economic loss.
		s 17	Indexation of maximum amount relating to non-economic loss
		s 17A	Tariffs for damages for non-economic loss
NT	*Personal Injuries (Liabilities and Damages Act) 2003*	Pt 4 Div 4	Non-pecuniary Loss
		s 24	Purpose of Division
		s 25	Damages other than for pecuniary loss
		s 26	Assessment of degree of impairment
		s 27	Damages for non-pecuniary loss
		s 28	Declaration of maximum amount of damages for non-pecuniary loss
Qld		No mention	
SA	*Civil Liability Act 1936*	s 52	Damages for non-economic loss
		s 56	Exclusion of interest on damages compensating non-economic loss or future loss
Tas	*Civil Liability Act 2002*	s 27	Restrictions on damages for non-economic loss (general damages) Enables recovery for pure mental or nervous shock.
		s 28	Tariffs for damages for non-economic loss (general damages)
Vic	*Wrongs Act 1958*	s 28G	Fixing damages for non-economic loss
		s 28H	Indexation of maximum amount for non-economic loss
		s 28HA	Tariffs for damages for non-economic loss
WA	*Civil Liability Act 2003*	Pt 2 Div 2	Damages for non-pecuniary loss (general damages)
		s 9	Restrictions on damages for non-pecuniary loss (general damages)
		s 10	Amount A and Amount C (sets out limitations)
		s 10A	Tariffs for damages for non-pecuniary loss

Loss of earnings

[22.60] Loss of earnings may be taken as the most typical case of future loss through injury. In *Arthur Robinson (Grafton) Pty Ltd v Carter* (1968) 122 CLR 649 Barwick CJ expressed opposition to the idea that there was any difference between damages for loss of earnings pre- and post-trial. Damages were awarded for loss of earning capacity which commenced as soon as the injury was sustained. This emphasis on loss of earning capacity is necessary to provide a means of compensating those persons who have no earnings at the time of injury but have the capacity to produce earnings in the future and this capacity has been destroyed or affected. Injured children are the most obvious example of this problem. It is clear that the court must make an award of damages in these cases, but no entirely satisfactory basis for determining the basis of the award has yet emerged. In *Burford v Allen* (1993) 60 SASR 428 where the plaintiff had been rendered a quadriplegic at the age of seven, the court assessed her future earning capacity on the basis of school reports, assumed a normal working life from the age of 16, but made a larger than usual reduction (20%) in damages to reflect contingencies. A similar problem exists where the plaintiff was not utilising his or her earning capacity either at all or in full at the time of the injury. Here the court must assess the chance of an increased use of the earning capacity at some future date in deciding on the award, and award damages for the loss of this chance together with damages for the loss of the earning capacity that was actually being used. In accordance with the principles governing damages claims in general, the chance need not be a probable one: *Mann v Ellbourn* (1974) 8 SASR 298. The contingency of a later increase in earning capacity on the part of a plaintiff who was fully employed at the time of the injury must also be taken into account, even though less than probable. Where the plaintiff, an Australian film actor, was able to demonstrate a less than probable contingency of very high earnings in the future, in the form of the possibility of Hollywood stardom, the court indicated that it must first attempt to establish the probable loss and then add an additional amount to compensate for the loss of that contingency: *Norris v Blake* (1997) 41 NSWLR 49.[22]

Another problem is that of the worker who has retained his or her job, but whose earning capacity has been diminished. In *Moeliker v Reyrolle & Co Ltd* [1977] 1 All ER 9 a small award for lost earning capacity was made to such a worker. This may seem not entirely satisfactory, since the suspicion exists in such cases that the employer is continuing to employ the worker only until the damages award in cases where the employer's liability is in question. In *Wright v Albany SC* [1993] Aust Torts Reports 81-239 an injured worker who had been retained in employment by the employer was held to be entitled to damages based on a 50% loss of earning capacity, together with additional compensation for the chance estimated at 75% of losing his present position at an early stage in the future.

Damages for loss of earning capacity are awarded on the basis of the destruction of capacity of the person producing the earnings. Where a husband had entered into a partnership with his wife under which the partners split his earnings equally, thereby saving tax, the damages awarded to the husband for his injury were based on 100% of his earnings. The court was entitled to look at the reality of the situation. The husband was the sole earner, and could have terminated the partnership at any time: *Husher v Husher* [1999] Aust Torts Reports 81-519.

In 2000, a report by Trowbridge Consulting recommended to the Australian Heads of Treasuries that loss of earnings should be capped with a limit of $2,000 per week after tax. The report also recommended that awards for pain and suffering (general damages) should be limited. The consultants justified their position on the basis that "reform to general damages will have the greatest impact among the range of reasonable options". But the 2002 Ipp Report commissioned by the Commonwealth Government recommended more stringent limits. The Report recommended that general damages should be capped nationally at $250,000. It further proposed that damages for loss of earning capacity should be capped at twice the average full-time adult ordinary time earnings. It was also recommended that compensation for gratuitous services should be limited.

---

22   The trial judge had incorrectly taken a weighted average of a number of less than probable contingencies.

In the tort reform initiatives that followed the reports, nearly all jurisdictions imposed caps on loss of earnings in civil liability schemes at three times average weekly earnings: see, for example, *Civil Liability Act 2003* (Qld), s 54. New South Wales, Victoria, South Australia and Northern Territory have caps on general damages running from $240,000 in South Australia to $271,380 in Victoria (indexed from 2002). Except for South Australia, the States have lower caps on general damages from motor vehicle accidents. For example, New South Wales capped loss of earnings due to motor accidents to $2,712 per week (indexed from 2002) while Western Australia capped general damages from motor vehicle accidents at $200,000 (indexed from 2002).

Lump sum award

[22.65] Damages for personal injury may be awarded in the form of a lump sum, or in the form of periodical payments through a structured settlement. This once-and-for-all assessment precludes the possibility of later actions being brought by the plaintiff: the cause of action having merged in the judgment becomes extinct.[23] There is therefore no possibility of changing the award in the light of later developments, such as a worsening of the plaintiff's injury or a significant increase in inflation having the effect of diminishing the size of the award. Developments such as these can only be reflected by making contingent provision for them in the award itself; but this is an imperfect solution. The court may, for example, award damages reflecting a 20% chance that the injury will worsen. If it does, the plaintiff is under-compensated; if it does not, the defendant has had to pay too much.

One of the early initiatives of the civil liability reforms in 2002 and 2003 in all jurisdictions was the enacting of legislation to allow the courts to award damages in the form of periodical payments.[24] Lump sums are popular among plaintiffs for obvious reasons (though their reasoning is short-sighted) and among insurance companies (which welcome the opportunity to close their books on the case).

A structured settlement is one where payment of an award for personal injury damages is made in the form of periodic payments rather than a lump sum settlement. It only applies where there is a written agreement for compensation for personal injury against a defendant, and not in the capacity of an employer or under workers' compensation law. Some or all of the compensation must be used to purchase an annuity.

Annuity basis of computation for damages for loss of future earnings

[22.70] The court uses as the basis of its calculation the post-tax earnings of the plaintiff, where information on this is available, and the amount of probable working life left to

---

[23] But only as regards that cause of action, not as regards a different cause of action arising in the same incident: *Brunsden v Humphrey* (1884) 14 QBD 141 – plaintiff having received damages for damage to vehicle could bring later action for personal injury through the same act of negligence.

[24] The *Taxation Laws Amendment (Structured Settlements and Structural Orders) Act 2002* (Cth) amended the *Income Tax Assessment Act 1997* by removing tax disincentives for agreeing to or awarding structured settlements: *Civil Liability Act 2002* (NSW), ss 22-26; *Civil Liability Act 2003* (Qld), ss 64-68; *Statutes Amendment (Structured Settlements) Act 2002* (SA) added to the *Magistrates Court Act 1991* (SA), s 33A, *District Court Act 1991* (SA), s 38A and the *Supreme Court Act 1991* (SA), s 30BA; *Civil Liability Act 2002* (Tas), s 8; *Wrongs Act 1958* (Vic), ss 28M-28N; *Civil Liability Act 2002* (WA), ss 14-15; *Civil Law (Wrongs) Act 2002* (ACT), s 45; *Personal Injuries (Liabilities and Damages) Act 2003* (NT), ss 29, 31-32.

the plaintiff. After some judicial divergence in the High Court, it is now settled that *earnings must be calculated net of tax*: *Cullen v Trappell* (1980) 29 ALR 1.[25] The plaintiff must not receive a benefit from the award, damages not being taxable, though the approach of the courts on this matter may be compared with their approach to the deductibility from damages of so-called collateral benefits, in the case of which the desire to ensure the plaintiff does not profit from the award is less apparent: see [22.95].

The method used for computing the lump sum is the annuity method. The calculation is based on what capital sum invested at a certain rate of interest will provide the plaintiff with an annual sum representing post-tax earnings for the period of working life determined to be still available to the plaintiff and which will be exhausted at the end of that period. The annuity method of calculation of course does not mean the plaintiff receives an annuity: the damages awarded may be freely disposed of by the plaintiff as soon as they are received.

The chosen rate of interest is the rate of "discount". The capital sum representing the total loss of future earnings must be discounted to reflect the benefit to the plaintiff from receiving a present capital sum ready for immediate investment rather than a future flow of income. The discount rate chosen must be based to some extent on prevailing interest rates. However, to discount at the whole of prevailing interest rates would penalise the plaintiff, since that interest rate partly reflects the loss in value of money due to inflation and the plaintiff does not receive a benefit through receiving this component of the interest rate. On the other hand, the plaintiff does obtain a benefit through present receipt of a capital sum in being able to invest at the real interest rate, which may be described as the element of the prevailing interest rate not representing the hedge against inflation, and to the extent of that rate the capital sum ought to be discounted. This expresses the theory behind the computation: in practice, the courts have no reliable evidence upon which to base estimates of future interest rates or future inflation. Further, the courts have excluded the use of actuarial evidence to assist them in their calculations, except on the issue of determination of life span left to the plaintiff, since even actuaries are unable to foretell the future and their calculations merely reflect what the actuary regards as probable.

A further complication regarding the computation of damages for future loss of earnings is the question of tax. At the early point starting after receipt of the lump sum and assumed investment in an interest bearing investment, the interest on the investment is very high, far exceeding the annual earnings loss the sum is intended to replace. There will also be interest on interest. Interest is taxable, so that the basis of the computation under which the plaintiff is assumed to be able to draw out his or her pre-tax earnings for the duration of working life is invalidated.

The High Court of Australia faced both the problem of how to allow for the element of future inflation and that of the incidence of taxation on the capital sum in *Todorovic v Waller* (1981) 37 ALR 481. Clearly, once the High Court had accepted that actuarial evidence should be excluded, its options were limited. No acceptable formula could, it seems, be devised for increasing the capital sum awarded beyond the actual total of assumed earnings lost. The court was therefore reduced to the one solution lying under its control: manipulation of the discount rate. The majority of the High Court adopted a discount rate of 3%, intended to cover both the elements of inflation and tax. The dissenting minority favoured making no discount at all to the capital

---

[25]   Not following its own previous decision in *Atlas Tiles v Briers* (1978) 21 ALR 129, but following the earlier decision of the House of Lords in *British Transport Commission v Gourley* [1956] AC 185.

sum, since otherwise the award would be swallowed up by, in particular, inflation. The clear indications are that the minority was right on this viewpoint. If we compare the figures arrived at for the allowable cost of home nursing in *Sharman v Evans* (1977) 138 CLR 563 and *Burford v Allen* (1993) 60 SASR 428, two cases where the injuries were similar but separated in time by 16 years, the cost in *Sharman* was some $400,000 and in *Burford* some $4.4 million. Even had the original sum been invested at 10% with no withdrawals for the whole period, the total at the end would not have approached the amount awarded in *Burford*.

The precise status of the rule in *Todorovic* was a matter of doubt. However, it was expressed by the High Court as a rule of practice; it was thus left open to a lower court whether to adopt it: *Commonwealth v Blackwell* (1987) 163 CLR 428. But the case was invariably followed by lower courts, and in *Rosniak v GIO* [1997] Aust Torts Reports 81-440 the court stated that a challenge to *Todorovic* must be made in the High Court. Whatever the status of the rule in *Todorovic* may have been, it has been superseded by legislation in most Australian jurisdictions.[26]

Lost years

[22.75] It is now clear law that in the case of a living plaintiff whose life expectancy has been reduced by injury, the plaintiff is entitled to be compensated for the loss of future earnings during the whole period of working life which the court concludes would have been left to the plaintiff but for the injury, no deduction being made in respect of those years commencing with the plaintiff's assumed death: *Sharman v Evans* (1977) 138 CLR 563. The reason for allowing this form of compensation loss is not to compensate the plaintiff. Rather, it is to prevent the anomaly that if the plaintiff had died from the injuries and the claim been brought by dependants, the latter would be compensated on the basis of the whole of the presumed working life left to the plaintiff, but for the injury. If compensation for the lost years were not allowed to a living plaintiff, the dependants would be deprived of that amount. However, the amount awarded must be reduced to take into account the savings on personal expenditure during the period commencing with the plaintiff's presumed death: *Sharman*. The plaintiff also will receive no damages representing future medical expenses for the period of the lost years.

Contingencies

[22.80] The court invariably adjusts the award to reflect contingencies such as disabling illness, accident or unemployment within the period chosen by the court as representing the plaintiff's future working life. These contingencies of course reflect what would have happened to the plaintiff had he or she remained uninjured. They need not be proved as probabilities; the court in its award merely assesses the chance of their occurrence because they relate to the future and cannot be predicted with any great degree of certainty. A usual reduction is 15% and this is made in relation to damages for both

---

[26]   Some jurisdictions have legislated a higher discount rate of 5%: *Civil Liability Act 2002* (NSW), s 14; *Civil Liability Act 2003* (Qld), s 8; *Wrongs Act 1958* (Vic), s 28I; *Common Law (Miscellaneous Actions) Act 1986* (Tas), s 4(1); *Personal Injuries (Liabilities and Damages) Act 2003* (NT), s 22 while in Western Australia it is 6%: *Law Reform (Miscellaneous Provisions) Act 1941* (WA), s 5. However, each jurisdiction except Queensland allows the rate to be changed by regulation. Others have maintained the 5%: *Civil Liability Act 1936* (SA), s 55 (cross-reference with s 3).

pecuniary and non-pecuniary loss: *Koeck v Persic* [1996] Aust Torts Reports 81-386. Therefore, these contingencies are thought to work in general adversely to the plaintiff. But *Wynn v NSW Insurance Ministerial Corporation* (1995) 184 CLR 485 indicated a change of approach. In that case the High Court approved a reduction of only 5% in the case of a plaintiff who was in secure employment largely free from the risk of accident and had good promotion prospects at the time of her injury. The matter is therefore variable according to the plaintiff's circumstances. The actual reduction made in *Wynn* was 12.5% to reflect the further fact that a previous injury might have affected her earning capacity.

One highly unpopular contingency which Australian courts continue to allow for is that of the prospect of remarriage of a plaintiff dependant in a fatal accident claim: see Chapter 21 n 19. The question of the desirability of making this assessment and how it is achieved was discussed in Chapter 21 at [21.25]ff.

In the case of a living plaintiff, on the other hand, the prospects of marriage and of consequent loss of earnings through retirement from the workforce are regarded as too uncertain and will therefore be ignored (as in the case of the female plaintiff aged 20 at the time of her injury in *Sharman v Evans* (1977) 138 CLR 563). The distinction that exists between this case and that of the widow (or widower) dependant is defensible on the ground that a future dependency through marriage does not replace the plaintiff's own loss of earning capacity. As a matter of reality, a severely injured plaintiff may have little or no chance of marriage, so that any reduction would have to be balanced against the possible destruction of the plaintiff's chance of obtaining a valuable dependency. On the other hand, the possibility of a married woman's retirement from the workforce during two intended pregnancies was regarded as a contingency justifying a small reduction in *Wynn*.

Medical and other expenses

[22.85] Expenses already incurred are special damages and must be pleaded and proved. The court must decide whether future medical expenses are reasonably necessary for treatment or alleviation of the plaintiff's condition. Medical treatment for conditions such as quadriplegia where the victim is conscious are very costly, and particularly subject to inflationary price rises. Again, there is no judicial method of providing for this inflation apart from adjusting the discount rate. It has been decided that there is no difference in principle between the award of damages for future medical expenses and future loss of earnings and that accordingly the discount rate fixed in *Todorovic v Waller* (1981) 37 ALR 481 applies. As regards future medical expenses, no award is made for the lost years period.

One frequently troublesome question for courts in cases of serious injury is whether to assess medical expenses on the basis of home or institutional nursing assistance. The latter is very much more costly, being estimated in *Sharman v Evans* (1977) 138 CLR 563 as about four times that of home care. The question of which should be allowed is not a matter of the plaintiff's preference, or which would be the more conducive to happiness, but whether the additional cost of home nursing is justified on the basis that being at home is more conducive to the plaintiff's health. *Sharman* reached a "clear" conclusion that the expense of medical and nursing assistance required for a quadriplegic with numerous attendant complications was excessively high if provided in the home and consequently that it should be provided by a hospital although in that case Evans went home from hospital to live with her mother as soon as she was able. The plaintiff was entitled to an additional award for the pain and suffering produced through having to be institutionalised. On the other hand, the court in *Burford v Allen* (1993) 60 SASR 428 approved an award of medical expenses based on home nursing in the case of the plaintiff who had been rendered a quadriplegic at the age of seven. This was because of the plaintiff's particular and special needs which a hospital was unable to provide. In *Grimsey v Southern Regional Health Board* (1997) 7 Tas R 67 the court approved an award to the plaintiff of the cost of building a specially designed home so that her needs could be catered for. These past judgments must, however, now be considered in the changing health care climate which favours (and encourages) home care over institutional.

The High Court of Australia held in *Nominal Defendant v Gardikiotis* (1996) 186 CLR 49 that the cost of employing a fund manager to invest the damages lump sum award was not claimable from the defendant, since on commonsense principles of causation under *March v E&MH Stramare Pty Ltd* (1991) 171 CLR 506 that cost was not caused by the injury but by the verdict in the case. This reasoning appears questionable and in any case does not apply where the plaintiff is mentally disabled from investing the sum personally, whether this is caused by the injury itself or by some previous condition.

Duplication of damages

[22.90] Since the practice of itemising damages awards has become universal, it has become easier to determine whether the award contains an element of duplication. Merely adding up the sums awarded under the individual heads is likely to produce over-compensation. In *Sharman v Evans* (1977) 138 CLR 563 the High Court held that the court's decision that the plaintiff needed hospital care meant that a reduction of damages for lost future earnings should be made to reflect savings on food and accommodation. An allowance should be made also for savings on other outgoings such as transport costs and clothing for employment, though the saving on child care costs by parents is not an allowable deduction, since that cost is not inevitably incurred in order to go out to work: *Wynn v NSW Insurance Ministerial Corporation* (1995) 184 CLR 485. The court in *Sharman* disapproved of the approach taken by the Court of Appeal in *Fletcher v Autocar Transporters* [1968] 2 QB 322 to the effect that allowance should be made for the fact that the plaintiff is no longer able to indulge in his or her previous expensive pastimes. The plaintiff may wish to indulge in equally expensive substitutes.

Deductibility of collateral benefits from damages

[22.95] A collateral benefit may be defined as a payment made to the plaintiff by a third party in consequence of the plaintiff's injury and they accrue from sources such as social security payments, sick pay, insurance policies, and gratuitous payments or services. The question at issue here is whether that payment is deductible from the damages claimed from the tortfeasor. In *National Insurance Co of New Zealand v Espagne* (1961) 105 CLR 569 the test for determining whether the benefit was deductible from damages was said by the High Court to be the nature and purpose of the benefit and, in particular, whether the intention behind its conferment was that it should be enjoyed by the plaintiff in addition to his common law damages.

The test laid down by the High Court is a vague one and its application has caused difficulty. The actual intention of the donor of the benefit is usually difficult or impossible to determine, so that the court in general looks at the nature of benefit and whatever statutory provisions govern its conferment. Social security benefits, which seem to have the character of state charity, have caused considerable problems for courts in the past, but most of these problems are now solved by provisions in the *Social Security Act 1991* (Cth) providing for repayment of the benefit to the Commonwealth on receipt of compensation from the tortfeasor.[27] Benefits covered by the provision will therefore not be deducted from damages.

One general principle that has largely been adhered to by the courts is that deduction should be made of those payments which are designed to compensate the plaintiff for a measurable actual loss. So, it is established that sick pay from an employer, whether paid as of right or ex gratia, is deductible[28] (unless the contract stipulates for repayment in the event of recovery of damages). Similarly, English cases have deducted unemployment benefit and redundancy pay.[29] Charitable payments and the payment of fixed sums under accident insurance policies are, however, not taken into account in assessing damages. This dates back to the rule in *Bradburn v Great Western Railway Co* (1874) LR 10 Exch 1 in which it was argued that to deduct insurance payments from damages awarded to the plaintiff would cause the plaintiff to lose the value of the insurance or the plaintiff's thrift in saving to pay the insurance premiums.

A disability pension which was contributory and earnings related was found to be not deductible from a damages award in *Parry v Cleaver* [1970] AC 1.[30] Some members of the House of Lords in that case supported the decision on the basis that the pension was contributed to by the plaintiff but in the later House of Lords decision in *Hussain v New Taplow Paper Mills* [1988] 2 WLR 266 it was explained on the basis that the pension continued to be payable after employment ceased without reference to whether the plaintiff was earning money in outside employment. It was therefore intended to be enjoyed in addition to earnings, not as a replacement for them (distinguishing the facts in *Hussain* itself, where sick pay provided under the contract was held to be deductible even though the plaintiff had contributed towards an insurance policy to provide the payment). The principle in *Parry* and *Hussain* has been applied in Australia in holding a superannuation insured benefit on injury to be not deductible from damages: *Jongen v CSR Ltd* [1992] Aust Torts Reports 81-192. The court in *Jongen* went a stage further in the generally benevolent attitude shown by courts to plaintiffs in these matters. The plaintiff was held to be entitled to compensation in respect of lost future superannuation contributions to be made by the employer, and refused to examine the question whether the maturity value of the policy would have been any greater than the amount already received as insured benefit.

---

[27]   *Social Security Act 1991* (Cth), ss 1165 and 1178-1181 – though it appears that the blind pension is still not one of the relevant benefits and will therefore continue to be governed by *National Insurance Co of New Zealand v Espagne* (1961) 105 CLR 569.

[28]   *Graham v Baker* (1961) 106 CLR 340; *Hobbelen v Nunn* [1965] Qd R 105; *Lind v Johnson* [1937] 4 All ER 201; *Dennis v London Passenger Transport Board* [1948] 1 All ER 779. South Australian cases, however, refused to make a deduction in the case of wages paid voluntarily: *Francis v Brackstone* [1955] SASR 270; *Volpato v Zachary* [1971] SASR 166.

[29]   *Evans v Muller* (1981) 47 ALR 241; *Nabi v British Leyland* [1980] 1 WLR 529 (unemployment benefit); *Colledge v Bass* [1988] 1 All ER 536 (redundancy pay). Also deductible are medical expenses paid by a third party on the victim's behalf: *Blundell v Musgrave* (1956) 96 CLR 73 (though in that case there was an express stipulation for repayment if damages were recovered, so the High Court refused to make a deduction).

[30]   Though see *Paff v Speed* (1961) 105 CLR 549.

The present law regarding collateral benefits requires the drawing of difficult distinctions as to the nature of the benefit provided, and has the result that in a number of cases plaintiffs are compensated beyond their actual loss. This, however, became inevitable once the courts decided not to disturb the early decisions concerning charitable and insurance benefits, but to apply them to the more complicated types of benefit payable under modern conditions.

Duty to mitigate damages

Figure 22.6: Where there is an ability to mitigate

- Defendant has *evidential burden* of showing that plaintiff should have taken reasonable steps to mitigate.
- Plaintiff has *legal burden* of proof and on balance of probabilities must show that reasonable steps were taken to mitigate damage.

[22.100] It is accepted law that a person injured as a result of a tort has a duty to take *reasonable* measures to mitigate the damage which may arise from the tort: *British Westinghouse Electric & Manufacturing Co Ltd v Underground Electric Railways Co of London Ltd* [1912] AC 673.[31] The following rules apply:

- The test of what is reasonable is an objective one, subject to what is said below.

- There is no enforceable duty in the strict sense of that word: the plaintiff's failure to take reasonable steps to mitigate loss operates as a new cause of any succeeding damage or injury.

- The defendant has the evidential burden of showing that the plaintiff could have taken reasonable steps to mitigate the damages. The plaintiff, having the legal burden of proof, must therefore convince the court on the balance of probabilities that he or she could not have taken those steps or that it would have been unreasonable to have been expected to do so.

Many of the cases concern the issue of whether the plaintiff should have mitigated damages by having an operation. English decisions have applied an objective standard to this question. If having the operation would have been reasonable, the plaintiff is in breach of his or her duty to mitigate, independently of the plaintiff's own personal characteristics: *Marcroft v Scruttons Ltd* [1954] 1 Lloyd's Rep 395; *McAuley v London Transport Executive* [1957] 2 Lloyd's Rep 500. Australian cases lean more towards taking the plaintiff's personal characteristics into account. For example, where a neurosis had supervened upon the injury, this might be a relevant factor in assessing reasonableness:

---

[31] In Queensland, the consequences on damages payments of a failure to mitigate has been included in the *Civil Liability Act 2003*, s 53. If a defendant is not satisfied with the action taken by a plaintiff to mitigate damages, the defendant may give the plaintiff written notice suggesting specified action the plaintiff should take to mitigate damages (s 53(1)), while the court must consider whether the plaintiff has taken reasonable steps to mitigate damages: s 53(4).

Glavonjic v Foster [1979] VR 536. So too may the plaintiff's language difficulties (*Polidon v Staker* (1973) 6 SASR 273) or the plaintiff's previous medical history including unhappy experiences with doctors: *Karabotsos v Plastics Industries Pty Ltd* [1981] VR 675; see also *Lorca v Holts Pty Ltd* [1981] Qd R 261. Nevertheless the duty is a stringent one. In *Hisgrove v Hoffman* (1982) 29 SASR 1 the court found that the plaintiff should mitigate the loss of earning power resulting from an ankle injury by having a below the knee amputation and having a prosthesis fitted. Damages were to be assessed on the basis that this should be done (though the plaintiff was to be given a year to make the decision).

Where the plaintiff has taken reasonable steps to mitigate damage which have failed (for example, by having an operation which has failed to improve the condition) the defendant is liable for the additional cost of those steps: *Tuncel v Renown Plate* [1979] VR 501.

Since the question of *mitigation turns on a question of causation*, rather than the existence of a duty, it is not essentially different from the question which arises as to whether a deliberate act of the plaintiff interrupts causation. This matter was considered in Chapter 11.

The cases concerning the duty to mitigate apply only where there is an *ability* to mitigate. In *Liesbosch Dredger v SS Edison* [1933] AC 449, however, it was held by the House of Lords that where the plaintiffs' dredger had been sunk through the negligence of the defendants, damages were limited to the purchase of a replacement dredger and consequential loss until the time of replacement. Because of the plaintiffs' lack of means, they were unable to purchase the replacement dredger and therefore had to hire a replacement which was both expensive to hire and costly to operate. However, they could not claim these amounts as damages because their lack of means operated as a new cause insulating the defendants from any further financial loss arising from that condition.

A number of points may be noted. The decision is not concerned with the duty to mitigate, since ex hypothesi the plaintiffs were unable to mitigate their loss. The "new cause" theory is suspect: the impecuniosity of the plaintiffs was a pre-existent condition. Why therefore should not the defendants have taken the victim as the victim was found? Lord Wright attempted to supply an answer in terms of policy and in particular of the extensive financial detriment that might arise to the victim of the tort from the victim's own lack of means and the inequity of transferring this loss to the tortfeasor. There are recent signs that the principle of the decision may be confined to the commercial sphere in which it operated. No doubt it is reasonable to expect a participant in that sphere to arrange proper capital backing against accidents, whether by way of insurance or otherwise. The same avenue may not be open to the impoverished private person. Thus in *Fox v Wood* (1981) 35 ALR 607 there were statements by the High Court to the effect that an injured plaintiff who has been impoverished by loss of earnings caused through the tort-inflicted injury is not affected by the rule. A majority of the Court of Appeal in *Perry v Phillips* [1982] 3 All ER 705[32] thought that the plaintiff could recover damages in tort for a neurosis arising from his inability to repair his house (arising from the defendant's tort) even though that inability arose from his own impecuniosity. Finally, in *Dodd Properties v Canterbury CC* [1980] 1 WLR 433, the Court of Appeal drew a distinction between the case where the plaintiff has the ability to mitigate, though the mitigation increases his "financial stringency", and the case where through impecuniosity there is no ability to mitigate. The former case turns

---

[32] See also *Egan v STA* (1982) 31 SASR 481 – defendant converted plaintiff's machinery and was held liable for consequential loss, even though it occurred through the plaintiff's inability to purchase replacement machinery.

upon the rules concerning the duty to mitigate rather than on the *Liesbosch* decision. Where, as in the case itself, the plaintiff had postponed the doing of repairs to his building caused by the defendant's negligence until after he had recovered damages (on the ground that to effect the repairs would have meant increasing his bank overdraft and in consequence the "financial stringency" on his business), this was found to be a reasonable commercial decision and was not therefore a breach of his duty to mitigate his loss. The plaintiff recovered damages, therefore, for the higher cost of repairs existing at the date of the trial.

Another ground for questioning the extent of the *Liesbosch* rule is the decision of the High Court in *Hungerfords v Walker* (1989) 171 CLR 125. In that case, the court, while maintaining the existence of the common law rule that interest cannot be awarded by a court for late payment of damages, held that that rule had no application where the defendant by means of the tort had caused the plaintiff the loss of use of money which otherwise the plaintiff would have enjoyed. In that case the plaintiff was entitled to damages based on the opportunity cost of being deprived of the money, for example through not being able to pay off high interest debts or otherwise put the money to profitable use. The *Liesbosch* decision was mentioned in the joint judgment of Mason and Wilson JJ in the High Court without disapproval. At least with respect to the clearing-off of existing high interest debt the High Court decision seems inconsistent with it, since in this case it was the plaintiff's impecuniosity which prevented them from avoiding a loss.

In the context of defamation, the uniform defamation law has specifically listed factors relevant in the mitigation of damages. These include apology, correction, previous recovery of damages, similar actions and compensation for other publications with the same meaning or effect: *Civil Law (Wrongs) Act 2002* (ACT), s 139J; *Defamation Act 2005* (NSW), (Qld), (Tas), (Vic) and (WA), s 39; *Defamation Act 2006* (NT), s 37; *Defamation Act 2005* (SA), s 37.

Third parties

[22.105] The first point to note is that no third party is entitled to establish any damages claim arising out of a tortious injury to another person, apart from the special cases of relational claims considered in Chapter 21. The second is that in certain circumstances, the victim may claim in his or her own action damages for gratuitous services rendered by a third party. There are two main instances of the second point:

- the rendering of gratuitous services by the third party to the victim; and
- the visiting of the victim in hospital by the third party at cost to the latter.

Gratuitous services

[22.110] The High Court in *Griffiths v Kerkemeyer* (1977) 139 CLR 161[33] held that the plaintiff may recover in his or her own action damages representing the value of services provided gratuitously by third parties under the following conditions:

---

33 See also *Veivers v Connolly* [1995] 2 Qd R 326 – although the third party who has rendered gratuitous services to a tort victim generally has no claim in respect of these services against the tortfeasor, such a claim is possible where a duty of care to the person rendering services can be independently established. In *Veivers* the defendant medical practitioner, in failing to test for rubella in the plaintiff mother and thereby failing to allow her to terminate pregnancy, was liable to the plaintiff in respect of the gratuitous services she rendered to the child born disabled as the result of the rubella.

- The damages are awarded to the victim of the accident because the need that the services fulfil is the victim's own. The victim does not sue as representative of the third party.
- The value of the services is taken to be their market cost, not their opportunity cost; that is, the value is not measured by the loss of earnings of the third party. This was confirmed by the decision of the High Court in *Van Gervan v Fenton* (1992) 175 CLR 327.[34] The reasoning of the majority was based:
  - on the fact that there was unlikely to be a correlation between the nature and duration of the services rendered and the nature and duration of the employment forfeited;
  - on the need to provide fairness to the provider of the services (though it is clear that the principle in *Griffiths v Kerkemeyer* does not impose any legal obligation on the plaintiff to recompense the service provider);
  - as regards future services, on the fact that it was impossible for a court to determine how long such services would continue to be provided.
- The majority in *Van Gervan* drew no distinction between past and future services for the purposes of determining compensation. The former also should be compensated at the market rate for those services. The dissenting judgments of Deane and Dawson JJ stated that where, as in *Van Gervan*, the services were supplied by a spouse who would normally in any case be rendering gratuitous services as part of the mutual give and take of marriage, the plaintiff should receive compensation representing only the additional nursing services provided. In *Van Gervan* itself, though the additional services were considerable, it was thought that an appropriate valuation of them was based on the spouse's loss of earnings under the employment relinquished.
- The principle in *Griffiths v Kerkemeyer* applies in the absence of any legal obligation to recompense the third party. Where such an obligation exists, the cost of the services is recoverable simply as part of the expense to which the plaintiff has been subjected by the tort.
- The principles in *Griffiths v Kerkemeyer* do not avail hospitals or other institutions providing gratuitous medical or nursing services to tort victims. These institutions may have a claim against the tortfeasor under the provision of the health and other services (compensation) legislation.

A problem that to some extent has divided courts in Australia arises over whether a tort victim is able to recover for loss of the ability to provide services to other persons. In principle this seems to be distinguishable from the *Griffiths v Kerkemeyer* situation, since the need in question is not that of the plaintiff but that of the person denied the plaintiff's services. However, there is no doubt that a carer may suffer an actual financial loss in having to purchase substitute services for the carer's own services previously rendered without cost. The prevailing trend of authority is now to recognise the claim in respect of services rendered to household family members, an obvious example of which, the services provided by a mother to her infant children, was the factual situation in both the cases in which the claim was recognised. In *Sturch v Wilmott* (1997)

---

[34] South Australia limits the carer's claim to services rendered by a parent, spouse or child, and places limits on the amount recoverable: *Civil Liability Act 1936* (SA), s 58.

2 Qd R 310 the Queensland Court of Appeal held that the mother's claim was based on an analogous principle to that in *Griffiths v Kerkemeyer*, and that the claim survived into the years of lost service. In *Sullivan v Gordon* (1999) 47 NSWLR 319 the majority in the New South Wales Court of Appeal, in recognising once again a mother's claim, found that the claim was based on the *Griffiths v Kerkemeyer* principle. However, both cases were subsequently overruled by the High Court in *CSR Limited v Eddy* (2005) 226 CLR 1.

The head of damages for loss of capacity to provide gratuitous personal or domestic services for another person, which had become known as the rule in *Sullivan v Gordon*, was challenged in *CSR Ltd v Eddy*. In *Eddy*, due to the defendant's admitted negligence, Thompson (the deceased) contracted mesothelioma as a result of exposure to asbestos and died in 2003. In its award of damages, the Dust Diseases Tribunal of New South Wales included an amount of $165,480 for his loss of capacity to care for his disabled wife, including care that she would need after his death (*Sullivan v Gordon* damages). Gleeson CJ, Gummow and Heydon JJ (Callinan J specifically agreeing on this point) distinguished *Griffiths v Kerkemeyer* and specifically rejected the rule in *Sullivan v Gordon* (overruling at the same time *Sturch v Wilmott*).

The position at common law is that the *Sullivan v Gordon* head of damages no longer exists and, instead, damages for loss of capacity to care for others are to be awarded under the heads of loss of amenity and pain and suffering. In other words, the loss is non-pecuniary rather than pecuniary and compensation should be assessed accordingly. However, *Sullivan v Gordon* damages are recoverable by statute in the Australian Capital Territory and New South Wales.[35] In Queensland, the *Civil Liability Act 2003* (Qld), s 59(3), while confirming the rule in *Eddy*, permits recovery of damages for gratuitous services provided by the injured person to others outside the injured person's household. In Victoria, the *Wrongs Act 1958* (Vic), s 28ID limits any award of damages that might be recoverable for the loss of the capacity to provide care for others.

The High Court in *Kars v Kars* (1996) 187 CLR 354 has now settled the difficulty that arose over the situation where the defendant is the service provider. The House of Lords refused to allow a claim by the plaintiff here on the ground that it leads to the absurd result that the defendant is paying itself for its own services: *Hunt v Severs* [1994] 2 AC 350. The High Court in *Kars* refused to follow this for a number of reasons, including:

- the need for the services is the plaintiff's own and the amount awarded is not intended as compensation for the service provider;
- the reality should be recognised that the services are being paid for not by the defendant but normally by a compulsory insurer; and
- to hold otherwise might cause an interference with reasonable arrangements by operating as an inducement to plaintiffs in this situation to hire professional carers.

Where a claim for loss of consortium is available to a spouse as well as a claim under *Griffiths v Kerkemeyer* to the other spouse, the court must take care to avoid double compensation. Thus in *Thorne v Strohfeld* [1997] 1 Qd R 540 the parties to the marriage shared household tasks on an equal basis, but after the husband was injured he was no longer able to perform these services. The husband received compensation for the need

---

[35] *Civil Law (Wrongs) Act 2002* (ACT), s 100; *Civil Liability Act 2002* (NSW), s 15B.

for services to be provided for him under *Griffiths v Kerkemeyer*. The court held that in the circumstances of this case, to allow the wife's claim for loss of consortium in respect of loss of her husband's services would amount to double compensation and it was therefore refused. Whether there is this element of duplication would depend on the domestic arrangements of the parties to the marriage.

Hospital visits

[22.115] Generally, the only possibility of recovery for the expense of hospital visits is through the victim's own action. The basic test is whether the cost of the hospital visit is reasonable, balanced against the end to be achieved. In *Schneider v Eisovitch* [1960] 2 QB 430 the plaintiff and her husband were involved in a serious car accident in France in which the husband was killed and the plaintiff injured and rendered unconscious. Her brother-in-law and his wife travelled from England to France in order to help the plaintiff bring her husband's body back to England and to assist the plaintiff to return to England. These expenses were held to be reasonable and to be recoverable in the plaintiff's action against the tortfeasor. In circumstances where the plaintiff is not placed in the same acute difficulty, the plaintiff is still entitled to recover damages based upon the expense of hospital visits of third parties where these are regarded as reasonably necessary for the alleviation of the plaintiff's condition and/or the improvement of the plaintiff's mental state. So in *Wilson v McLeay* (1961) 106 CLR 523 a successful claim was made in relation to the cost of air-fares and hotel accommodation incurred on three visits by a mother to her injured daughter.[36] Similarly, a successful claim for costs of moving home to be nearer their injured child was made by the parents in *Timmins v Webb* [1964] SASR 250. The decision can be rationalised on the basis that the visits have the effect of alleviating the plaintiff's condition and thus of reducing damages. Where, however, the plaintiff's condition was a desperate one, the expense of bringing his brother out from Italy to Australia for the purpose of arranging his return to Italy was not reasonably incurred − there could be no question of the visit alleviating the plaintiff's condition: *Taccone v Electric Power Transmission Pty Ltd* [1962] Qd R 545.[37]

Torrent v Lancaster [1991] Aust Torts Reports 81-089 held that the recoverability of such expenses in the victim's own action finds a theoretical justification in the *Griffiths v Kerkemeyer* principle, and this seems correct since the visits are serving a need of the victim.

Damages for damage/destruction of property

[22.120] This section contains an account of the basic principles upon which property damage is valued for the purpose of awarding damages. The measure of damages in conversion and detinue has already been considered, though the principles applicable to those torts also to some extent apply in the situation now under consideration. Aggravated or exemplary damages may be awarded for torts protecting property under the usual principles associated with the award of those damages. They are particularly likely to be awarded in cases of intentional trespass to chattels or land: *Healing Sales v Inglis Electrix* (1968) 121 CLR 584 (chattels); *Pollock v Volpato* [1973] 1 NSWLR 653 (land).

CHAPTER 22

---

[36]   The court approved an award of general rather than special damages. The effect of this was that the whole of the costs were not awarded.

[37]   See also *Richardson v Schulz* (1980) 25 SASR 1 − condition of unconscious plaintiff could not be alleviated by parental visits.

Damage to chattels

[22.125] The main torts associated with this form of damage are trespass to chattels and negligence, though of course other torts may be involved. Once again, the underlying principle is restoration to the pre-tort condition thus the main heads of damages for partial damage to a chattel are repair costs or loss in value of the chattel, and consequential losses such as loss of profits. Whether to award the plaintiff the cost of repair or merely the loss in value of the chattel is often a troublesome question. The basic question is one of reasonableness on which the plaintiff has the burden of proof. Where the cost of repair is high compared with the loss in value of the chattel, the plaintiff must in some way satisfy the court that the particular chattel is of special value to the plaintiff. For example, it may have scarcity value (*O'Grady v Westminster Scaffolding* [1962] 2 Lloyd s Rep 238) or be hard to find a substitute for at that moment: *Anthoness v Bland SC* [1960] SR(NSW) 659. Mere sentimental attachment to the chattel is not enough: *Darbyshire v Warren* [1963] 1 WLR 1067.

Consequential financial loss may arise either during the period of repair or the period of finding a replacement. In keeping with the normal rule for measure of damages the loss need not be foreseeable, but the plaintiff, in both cases, is under a duty to mitigate damages and so must proceed with reasonable expedition to get the repairs done or to find a replacement. With respect to profit-earning chattels, if no specific profit-earning venture can be pointed to by the plaintiff the court may award a reasonable profit; however, identifiable loss of profits for the relevant period are claimable, as is loss of a profit that would have been made in a future period but has been lost as a result of the damage, though subject to the duty to mitigate damage: *The Argentino* (1889) 14 App Cas 519. The plaintiff is entitled to the cost of hiring a replacement: *Giles v Thompson* [1993] 3 WLR 908. The principles on which damages are awarded for the loss of use of a non-profit-earning chattel were considered in Chapter 5.

Destruction of chattels

[22.130] The chattel is valued at the time of its destruction. Its value is normally assessed by reference to the cost to the plaintiff of purchasing a comparable chattel; though where no such chattel is obtainable, the plaintiff is entitled to the cost of a new chattel.[38] The same principles apply to consequential loss as to damage to chattels. Where the plaintiff is legally bound to complete an existing contract, the only compensable loss may arise in relation to the performance of that contract.

In *Liesbosch Dredger v SS Edison* [1933] AC 449 the plaintiffs had suffered the total loss of a dredger which was required to carry out a contract with the harbour authority in Patras. They were held to be entitled to:

- the market price of a comparable dredger; and
- the costs associated with making such a dredger available to perform the contract, for example adaptation of the dredger, transport and insurance; and
- compensation for disturbance and loss in the performance of the contract until the time at which a replacement dredger could reasonably have been made available for use at Patras.

---

[38]   For example, see *Dominion Mosaic Tiles v Trafalgar Trucking* [1990] 2 All ER 246 – no second-hand market in the particular chattels existed.

The plaintiffs were not entitled to compensation for hiring a repl…
at very high cost since this loss stemmed from their impecuniosity (alth
earlier in this chapter at [22.35], this part of the *Liesbosch* decision is 1.
Where the destroyed chattel would otherwise have been available to
the plaintiff is entitled to compensation for these, subject to the duty to
loss. However, it is sometimes argued that since the value of a profit-earn…   … is
based on its capacity to make future profits, the plaintiff is adequately compensated by
being awarded the capital value of the chattel at the time of its destruction, and there is
authority in support of this: *The Llanover* [1947] P 80. However, the contrary argument
that an award of capital value does not adequately compensate for actual loss of profits
during the replacement period is supported by some (albeit old) authority: *The Kate*
[1899] P 165; *The Philadelphia* [1917] P 101; *The Fortunity* [1961] 1 WLR 351.

Damage to land and damage/destruction of buildings

[22.135] The main torts are trespass to land, the action for mesne profits, negligence and
nuisance. Land is indestructible and the total value of the land will hardly ever represent
the measure of the loss, though if the plaintiff, having been ousted from the land by
the defendant, chose to accept its loss and sued in trespass rather than ejectment, the
total value of the land would be the appropriate measure. Buildings on the other hand
are capable of being totally destroyed, in which case the appropriate measure would be
either the present value of the building or the cost of either rebuilding on the land or
of a suitable substitute.

Where repairable damage to land or buildings has occurred, a similar question arises
to that relating to damage to chattels: namely, whether to allow reinstatement cost or
merely the loss in value. Again, the question is one of reasonableness on which the
plaintiff bears the burden, but the courts are generally far more willing to entertain the
claim for reinstatement than they are in the case of damage to chattels. This is certainly
the position in regard to buildings which are used by the plaintiff as residences. The
fact that reinstatement cost is high compared to the loss in value of the land as a
whole is an irrelevant factor as regards residences, since the plaintiff whose dwelling
has been damaged or destroyed still has to find somewhere to live: see, for example,
Evans v Balog [1976] 1 NSWLR 36 and *Parramatta CC v Lutz* (1988) 12 NSWLR
293 where the buildings on the land added very little to its value. Where on the other
hand, the building is held purely as an investment, courts will generally be unwilling
to award reinstatement cost where this markedly exceeds the loss in value.[39] In *Hansen
v Gloucester Developments* [1992] Aust Torts Reports 81-067 the plaintiffs owned a
vacant block of land on which they eventually planned to build a holiday home. The
land, which was worth $37,000, was damaged as the result of the defendants' trespass.
The loss in value as a result was $17,000. Reinstatement of the land to its former
condition would have cost $60,000 whereas a more "basic" repair, under which the
land as altered by the trespass was consolidated and made safe for building, would cost
$17,000. The court held that in these circumstances and especially bearing in mind
the high cost of reinstatement compared to the fall in value of land, the plaintiffs were
entitled to $17,000.[40]

---

[39]   *Hole v Harrisons of Thurscoe* [1973] 1 WLR 345; *CR Taylor v Hepworths* [1977] 1 WLR 659; a fortiori, where the
       plaintiff had sold it at the time of the action: *Murphy v Brentwood DC* [1991] 1 AC 398.

[40]   See also *Jones v Shire of Perth* [1971] WAR 56.

Where the land or buildings are being used as a business, the plaintiff is entitled to compensation for disturbance in that business, including loss of profits. In a case of this sort, the court may find the plaintiff under a duty to mitigate the loss to the business by finding a substitute site, in which case an additional award will be made for the cost of obtaining that site. This was the position in *Dominion Mosaics Co Ltd v Trafalgar Trucking* [1990] 2 All ER 246 in which the plaintiffs were held to be entitled to the cost of leasing new premises in order to run their business. The plaintiff is also entitled under the so-called wayleave cases to compensation for chattels originally forming part of the land but which have been extracted or severed by the defendant and taken for its use. The main question here is the valuation of the severed chattel. The law seems to be reasonably settled that in the case of a wholly innocent defendant, the plaintiff is entitled to the market value of the chattel (that is, what the plaintiff could sell it for) less the defendant's reasonable costs of severance: *Bilambil-Terranova Pty Ltd v Tweed SC* [1980] 1 NSWLR 465. The latter deduction is, however, not allowed to a non-innocent defendant, and this includes not only the defendant who is in bad faith but also one who is merely negligent: *Livingstone v Rawyards Coal Co* (1880) 5 App Cas 25 at 39-40 per Lord Blackburn. *Minter v Eacot* (1952) 69 WN(NSW) 93 seems to run counter to the general trend of authority in allowing the plaintiff damages based on the value of extracted sand at the site rather than its market value, thus rendering the plaintiff liable for the costs of transportation to a suitable market, even though the defendant was found to have acted in contumelious disregard of the plaintiff's rights.

Restitutionary claim

[22.140] Where the defendant in trespass to land or the action for mesne profits has enjoyed the use of the land for the defendant's purposes, the plaintiff is entitled to compensation for this on a restitutionary basis. This means that the plaintiff need not show that it would have put the land to a profitable use but for the trespass.

The case is comparable to the claim which may be made against a person for withholding the use of a chattel. The approved compensation appears to be a reasonable rental for the period of use: *Swordheath Properties v Tabet* [1979] 1 WLR 285; *Whitwham v Westminster Brymbo Coal & Coke Co* [1896] 2 Ch 538. The modern case law has not held the plaintiff entitled to claim the actual profits made by the defendant by use of the land; though that claim might be justified on a restitutionary basis and this sort of claim may have been possible under the action for mesne profits itself (though it is not clear what were profits for the purposes of that action). A claim will lie for damage inflicted on the land together with a restitutionary claim for its use: *Whitwham* (claim in trespass lay for damaging the land by tipping of refuse on it, and for rental for use of the land for this purpose).

Betterment

[22.145] The issue of betterment is related to mitigation. The problem arises in all cases where the court approves a measure of damages based on the cost of repair, reinstatement or finding a substitute. The issue is whether a deduction should be made from damages for the fact that by the adoption of this measure of damages the plaintiff is better off than it was before the tort. Repairs to an item of property may increase its value beyond the original. A replacement item may be more valuable than the item replaced.

Despite the House of Lords decision in *British Westinghouse Electric Co v Underground Electric Railways* [1912] AC 673 which suggests that, in principle, betterment ought to be taken into account in fixing damages, the English courts decisions are against making deductions for betterment, the view being taken that a plaintiff should not be compelled to repair, or invest in new property to some extent at its own expense, in situations where it has no real choice in the matter. So, in *Harbutt's Plasticine Ltd v Wayne Tank* [1970] 1 QB 447,[41] where the plaintiffs' factory premises were destroyed by fire, and they had been compelled to construct new premises, no deduction was made from damages for the improved quality of the new premises. The Australian case law has tended to accept the *British Westinghouse* position, emphasising the compensatory function of damages. In *Hoad v Scone Motors Pty Ltd* [1977] 1 NSWLR 88 the plaintiffs' tractor had been destroyed in a fire through the defendants' negligence. The tractor at the time of the fire was worth some $1,500 but the plaintiffs being unable to find a comparable replacement in the local area purchased a new tractor costing some $5,000 in order to be able to go on farming. The evidence showed that, although the plaintiffs were accustomed to having to replace their tractor every five years, they had no such intention with regard to the present one since the lease on their farm was due to expire in 18 months' time and it was presumed they would then give up farming and sell their equipment. The Court of Appeal followed the *British Westinghouse* decision in holding that the plaintiffs' damages must be reduced to reflect the betterment conferred by having a new tractor, and that this was without reference to whether the plaintiffs acted reasonably in purchasing the replacement. The court did not attempt to fix the deduction to be made (ordering a new trial on the matter) but it is suggested that in these circumstances it would have been small, granted the rapid depreciation on farm vehicles after their purchase. It is suggested that there is no necessary difference of principle between this case and *Harbutt's Plasticine*. In *Hoad* the facts indicated a clear likelihood of sale in the fairly near future. In *Harbutt's Plasticine* there was no indication of an intention on the plaintiffs' part to dispose of the new factory premises; rather an intention to continue to use them indefinitely as a factory. This distinction draws support from the judgment of Moffit P in *Hoad*, though Hutley JA in the same case held that *Harbutt's Plasticine* was inconsistent with *British Westinghouse* and ought not to be followed.

Measure of damages in tort and contract

[22.150] The tort measure of damages is based on the core principle of putting the plaintiff back into the position he or she was in before the commission of the tort. In the case of contract, it is to place the innocent party into the position he or she would have been in had the contract been performed. This leads to the difference that the tort measure compensates for out-of-pocket loss, whereas that in contract (though it does allow in certain cases for a reliance or indemnity measure giving out-of-pocket losses) allows the plaintiff so-called expectation losses, that is profits

---

[41]   See also *Dominion Mosaics Ltd v Trafalgar Trading Co* [1990] 2 All ER 246 – plaintiffs who had bought leasehold premises when their original premises were destroyed by the defendants did not have to bring into account a windfall capital gain on the premises.

to be expected out of full performance of the contract.[42] The difference between the two in tort cases of injury or damage caused by wrongful acts is clear enough. But some difficulties arise in distinguishing them in tort cases concerning wrongful words; that is, in cases of deceit, negligent misstatement, statutory liability for misrepresentation and for misleading or deceptive conduct under the trade practices legislation.

The tort position is clear in principle. The plaintiff is to be put into the position they would be in had there been no wrong; not into the position they would be in had the words been true. The latter position is available to the plaintiff in contract, where the defendant has warranted the truth of the words. Surveyors and valuers of property, for example, generally give no warranty as to the truth of their valuation, but merely undertake to use care to provide an accurate valuation. Whether sued in contract or tort they are liable only for the difference between the amount lent or paid by the plaintiff on the strength of the valuation and its actual value, not the difference between the amount paid and the amount of the valuation.[43] The assumption is generally made that the lender or buyer, rather than advancing or paying less, would not have entered the transaction at all had it known the truth.

Some qualification needs to be made to this, in that it is now settled that the plaintiff may be entitled to the opportunity cost of relying on the advice; that is, for loss of the alternative advantage they would have gained had the defendant given careful advice and the plaintiff had therefore known of the true position. This is in addition to the actual loss sustained. Thus, although in *Gates v City Mutual Life* (1986) 160 CLR 1 the plaintiff was denied damages for a misleading statement by the defendant that his insurance policy covered a certain risk, on the ground that the policy was worth what he paid for it, a different result was reached in *Warnock v ANZ Banking Corp* [1989] ATPR 40-928 on the ground that the plaintiff proved in evidence that she would have taken out additional insurance against that risk had she known the truth. *Gates* is now, therefore, explicable only on the ground that the plaintiff had failed to provide evidence of this sort. Again, in *Kyogle SC v Francis* (1988) 13 NSWLR 396 the plaintiff's claim that he had lost an opportunity for acquiring land for subdivision purposes by reason of the defendants' certificate that the land he was acquiring was capable of subdivision, failed on this point because he had failed to prove that he could have bought at that time land capable of subdivision. Damages for lost opportunities of this kind are similar to expectation losses, but differ in that they cover a hypothetical loss rather than a specific loss covered by the contract.[44]

---

[42] *Commonwealth v Amann Aviation* (1991) 174 CLR 64 – where the contract is shown to be profitable the plaintiff is entitled to recover profit plus actual reliance expenditure; where it is loss-making, the recovery of actual reliance expenditure is reduced by the loss; in cases of difficulty in determining the profitability of the contract, the plaintiff is aided by a presumption that the contractual return will equal total reliance expenditure, so that actual reliance expenditure may be recovered in full.

[43] So that where as is usual the valuation exceeds the amount lent, the loss is assessed in relation to the latter. The principle stated in the text also has been found to mean that the cost of repairing property is not available to buyers of houses against negligent surveyors, since the surveyor gives no warranty that the house is sound. The buyer is therefore limited by way of damages to the difference in value stated in the text: *Phillips v Ward* [1956] 1 WLR 471; *Watts v Morrow* [1991] 1 WLR 1421. But in many cases the buyer will be under circumstantial constraints which make selling difficult, and the rule in such cases may yield where the cost of repair is not disproportionate to the difference in value. The question of the recovery of damages for a fall in the market value of property after a negligent over-valuation was dealt with in Chapter 11.

[44] An expectation measure of damages was allowed in *Rentokil v Channon* [1990] 19 NSWLR 417, but this appears to be explained by the fact that the defendant did not contest this part of the award.

The difference may be illustrated by *Swingcastle v Gibson* [1991] 2 AC 223. The plaintiffs had been induced to lend money on a mortgage of property at a very high rate of interest by a negligent over-valuation of the property given by the defendants. By way of compensation they were held to be entitled, among other things, not to damages based on loss of the high rate of interest under the mortgage (since that would have amounted to putting them into the position as if the defendants had warranted the mortgagors' performance of the contract), but to compensation for the loss of use on their money, based on market rates available at the time of the loan, it being assumed that had they known of the over-valuation they would not have made the loan. On the other hand, the opportunity cost assessment may be identical to the contractual measure. For example, were the plaintiff to seek advice concerning the purchase of a particular share and the defendant negligently advised against purchase, the opportunity cost to the plaintiff would be the loss of profit on that particular share. The courts have applied what is basically an expectation measure in one particular situation where there is no question of opportunity cost; that is, in the case of the disappointed would-be beneficiary under a will who has been deprived of a legacy through the negligence of the testator's solicitor.

Injunction

[22.155] The other important remedy in tort is the injunction. The principles governing its award may be stated quite briefly. Final injunctions, also known as perpetual injunctions, are of two types. They may be prohibitory: an order to the defendant to stop doing the activity of which the plaintiff complains. They may be mandatory: an order to the defendant to take positive steps to remove the tort of which the plaintiff complains and they must be capable of performance: *Attorney-General v Colney Hatch Lunatic Asylum* (1868) LR 4 Ch App 146 per Lord Hatherley LC at 154. Or finally, the plaintiff may claim an interlocutory injunction, that is an interim injunction (almost invariably of a prohibitory nature) pending the final determination of the action. The plaintiff may claim a quia timet injunction to prevent the future commission of a tort only if the act to be prohibited is sufficiently clearly established to justify the court's intervention and damages are not ascertainable or would not suffice.[45]

Figure 22.7: Types of injunction

Final or perpetual AND either:
- prohibitory (stopping the defendant from doing something); OR
- mandatory (ordering the defendant to remove a tort).
- Interlocutory or interim (pending final determination of the action).
- Quia timet (for future apprehension of a tort).

---

[45]   *Bankstown City Council v Alamdo Holdings Pty Ltd* (2005) 223 CLR 660. In quia timet proceedings, the court will have regard to the degree of probability of the apprehended injury, the degree of the seriousness of the injury, and the requirements of justice between the parties: see, for example, *Owners Strata Plan 4085 v Mallone* (2006) 12 BPR 23,691; [2006] NSWSC 1381 where Young CJ took into account that the defendant, a widowed pensioner in old age, only had limited financial resources compared with the plaintiff.

Nature of remedy by way of injunction

[22.160] An injunction may issue against the commission of any tort, but in general injunctions tend to be issued for torts of a continuing nature, of which trespass and nuisance are obvious examples. But an injunction may issue against an assault or battery which has taken place and is complete, where there is a justified fear of its being repeated.[46] The injunction is also available for the tort of defamation to cease, or halt, publication of defamatory material. It is a power that is exercised with some caution because of the potential limitation on free speech. It is, however, awarded where the potential for defamation can be ongoing (such as repeated playing of a song with defamatory lyrics: *Australian Broadcasting Corporation v Hanson* [1998] QCA 306). The injunction is a peremptory remedy. Its breach by the defendant is a contempt of court and may justify an order by the court for the imprisonment of the defendant.

Conditions under which court may issue injunction

[22.165] *The injunction is a remedy the issue of which lies within the court's discretion.* A plaintiff does not have a right to this, or any other equitable remedy, in the same way that the plaintiff may have a right to the common law remedy of compensatory damages. The principles underlying the exercise of that discretion in relation to the tort of private nuisance are set out in Chapter 16. The court in exercising its discretion is far less ready to issue a mandatory injunction than a prohibitory one. In *Redland Bricks v Morris* [1970] AC 652 the defendants had, by their excavations on their own land, caused subsidence on the plaintiff's land. The House of Lords refused to issue a mandatory injunction against the defendants to restore the loss of support, on the ground that doing this involved great cost, actually exceeding the value of the plaintiff's land. A mandatory injunction is more likely to be issued where the defendant's conduct is other than bona fide: *Break Fast Investments Pty Ltd v PCH Melbourne Pty Ltd* [2007] Aust Torts Reports 81-930.

Where an interlocutory injunction is sought by the plaintiff, certain principles govern the discretion of the court in deciding whether to grant the injunction. It must be established by the plaintiff that there is a serious question to be tried,[47] and it will only be granted if the evidence establishes a clear case in favour of the applicant.[48] Since the decision of the House of Lords in *American Cyanamid v Ethicon* [1975] AC 396 it is no longer necessary for the plaintiff to establish a prima facie case that the tort is being committed. Granted that the plaintiff can establish that there is a serious question to be tried, the court must then consider the balance of convenience in deciding whether an injunction should issue. This means considering which party will be the more disadvantaged by the grant, or the refusal to grant, an injunction pending trial. The plaintiff may show, for example, that it will suffer serious and possibly irreparable damage if the tort is allowed to continue. This argument is also available to the defendant as regards, for example, business activity stayed by the granting of an injunction. In such

---

[46]   For case law, see Chapter 4.

[47]   For example, *Daily Telegraph Co Ltd v Stuart* (1928) 28 SR(NSW) 291 – where the court was satisfied that it was not reasonable for a builder to make so much noise that it made it impossible for his neighbours to carry on their business.

[48]   Young CJ suggested a "strongly arguable case" and not just an arguable case where the interlocutory injunction would for all practical intents and purposes solve the dispute between the parties: *West Harbour Rugby Football Club Ltd v NSW Rugby Union Ltd* [2001] NSWSC 757 at [13].

a case, the court may refuse to issue the interlocutory injunction. Alternatively, it may require the plaintiff to give an undertaking in damages, that is, an undertaking to pay damages to the defendant for loss arising from the stoppage of the business should the tort not be proved at the trial. An interlocutory injunction will not be granted if the interference is regarded as trivial or temporary as in such cases a court will consider damages will be an appropriate award.

Injunction and damages

[22.170] Damages may be awarded by the court either in addition to the issue of an injunction or in substitution for it. The original courts of equity had no power to award damages and this had to be conferred by statute, the *Chancery Amendment Act 1858* (UK) (commonly referred to as Lord Cairns' Act). The Act has its equivalent in all Australian States.[49] Any court with power to issue an injunction may award damages together with the issue of the injunction or in substitution for it. The principles upon which the court will in its discretion refuse an injunction and award damages instead were considered in Chapter 16. It may be observed that damages may even be awarded in lieu of a quia timet injunction, leading to the somewhat extraordinary position that the plaintiff receives damages though it has not proved a tort: *Leeds Industrial Co-operative Society Ltd v Slack* [1924] AC 851.

Abatement by self-help

[22.175] A person who is entitled to exclusive possession of land can take reasonable steps to protect their use or enjoyment of that land by removing the offending interference by a right of abatement by self-help. It applies to situations which would not justify the expense of legal proceedings such as overhanging branches and tree roots, or the unauthorised entry of a person on to the plaintiff's land. In the case of the latter, if the defendant has entered forcibly, they can be removed forcibly but if the defendant has entered peacefully, they must be asked to leave and have a reasonable time to do so before they can be forcibly ejected. In both cases, no more force than is reasonable can be used: *Housing Commission of New South Wales v Allen* (1967) 69 SR (NSW) 190.

A right of abatement by self-help is an alternative remedy to legal proceedings and results in the plaintiff losing their right to institute proceedings except in respect of damages that occurred before the abatement: *Young v Wheeler* [1987] Aust Torts Reports 80-126. The onus of justifying the abatement rests on the person attempting to put an end to the trespass or nuisance and if that involves entering the land of another, notice of entry is generally required: *Trojan v Ware* [1957] VR 200. Notice may not be required where it can be established that there is an immediate danger to the life or health of the plaintiff: *Jones v Williams* [1895] AC 1.

---

[49] *Supreme Court Act 1970* (NSW), s 68; *Supreme Court Act 1995* (Qld), s 180; *Supreme Court Act 1935* (SA), s 30; *Supreme Court Civil Procedure Act 1932* (Tas), s 11(13); *Supreme Court Act 1986* (Vic), s 38; *Supreme Court Act 1935* (WA), s 25(10).

Practice Questions

Revision Questions

22.1 Is the function of tort damages the same as that for contract damages?

22.2 Losses recoverable in tort encompass pecuniary and non-pecuniary losses. Explain the difference between each and provide examples.

22.3 Damages have traditionally been divided into special and general damages. What is the difference between the two types of damages, if any? Discuss.

22.4 Under what circumstances will a court be prepared to award "aggravated damages"?

22.5 When calculating damages for personal injury, three principal categories of non-pecuniary loss can be identified. Identify and briefly describe each.

22.6 Is there any duty on the plaintiff injured as a result of a tort to take any measures to mitigate the damage which may arise from the tort?

22.7 Under what circumstances will a court be prepared to grant a party an injunction for a tort?

Answers to Practice Questions

22.1 While damages are available to a plaintiff for both a tort and a breach of contract, the function of damages is different in each case. The function of tort damages is *usually* compensatory to try and restore the plaintiff to the position the plaintiff enjoyed before the tort was committed. There are obvious problems in doing this where the plaintiff has lost a limb, for example. The function of contract damages *is* compensatory, that is to compensate the innocent party for the loss it suffered rather than to penalise the defaulter and put the innocent party into the position it would have occupied had the contract been properly performed.

22.2 "Pecuniary losses" are equated with the remedy for money damages and include lost profits, lost earnings and losses incurred in restoring or replacing damaged property, as well as expenses incurred in mitigating the loss.

"Non-pecuniary losses" are those losses which have no real monetary equivalent and extend to personal loss of a non-financial nature including pain and suffering, nervous shock, loss of amenities and interference with enjoyment of property.

In many tort actions the plaintiff will combine the two types of loss.

22.3 "Special damages" are those requiring precise pleading and proof and are awarded in relation to pre-trial loss arising from an injury. They must be capable of arithmetical calculation and include quantifiable items such as medical expenses and loss of earnings.

"General damages" include past and future losses sustained by the plaintiff presumed to arise from the fact that the tort has been committed. Unlike special damages, they are not susceptible to precise calculation. Examples are pain and suffering and loss of enjoyment of life.

22.4 Aggravated damages are awarded to compensate the plaintiff for injured feelings or outrage arising from the commission of the tort. They are usually restricted to torts which are actionable as of right, without proof of damage, such as trespass, conspiracy, defamation, intimidation and deceit.

22.5 The three areas of non-pecuniary loss are:

- pain and suffering, which denotes actual physical or mental pain. It is generally calculated on a tariff basis, although the standard varies from State to State. They are predominantly intended to compensate for the subjective fact of the injury to the plaintiff;

- loss of amenity, which is established upon an objective basis and, like pain and suffering, tends to be fixed upon a tariff basis. It is a head of damages that can encompass a very broad range of loss, and allows the court some scope for recognising new kinds of non-pecuniary loss; and

- loss of expectation of life, which is awarded for the life which is lost.

22.6 The duty to minimise the loss is the same in tort and contract. It requires the plaintiff to take *reasonable measures* to mitigate the damage which may arise from the tort. What constitutes reasonable measures is determined through an objective test. If the court is satisfied that the plaintiff has acted reasonably in taking remedial steps, the plaintiff will be entitled to recover the cost of such measures even if he or she fails or it subsequently turns out that less costly measures could have been taken.

22.7 If common law damages are inadequate, injunctive relief may be granted. However, injunctions are discretionary and tend to be limited to torts of a continuing nature such as trespass and nuisance. The court in exercising its discretion is far less ready to issue a mandatory injunction than a prohibitory one. A mandatory injunction may be granted to compel the performance of some positive act to remove the tort, but because of its potential to result in greater cost to the defendant than the actual loss incurred by the plaintiff, the courts are reluctant to issue such relief unless the defendant's conduct has been less than bona fide or the consequences for the plaintiff would be grave.

Where an interlocutory injunction is sought, it must be established by the plaintiff that there is a serious question to be tried. If the court can be satisfied on this point, the court must then consider the balance of convenience in deciding whether an injunction should be issued.

Tutorial Questions

Discussion Questions

22.1 Under what circumstances will a court award contemptuous or nominal damages?

22.2 In what tort actions can a court award exemplary damages? How do they differ from aggravated damages?

22.3 Under what circumstances can a plaintiff claim in his or her own action damages for gratuitous services rendered by a third party?

22.4 Once it has been determined that a plaintiff is entitled to recover a particular head of loss, the court must quantify that loss in dollar terms. That is, the plaintiff should as far as possible be placed in the same position he or she was in before the tort was committed. What factors does the court take into account in determining quantification?

22.5 In their report to the Commonwealth Government, the Ipp Committee noted at [13.49] that:

> *[a] strong argument can be made that levels of compensation for pain and suffering and loss of the amenities of life should be more or less uniform throughout the country. "Pain is pain whether it is endured in Darwin, Townsville, Burnie or Sydney."*

Do you agree with this view?

Index

[References are to paragraph numbers]